OLE CONTROLS
INSIDE OUT

ADAM DENNING

Foreword by Roger Heinen,
Senior Vice President, Microsoft Corporation

Microsoft Press

PUBLISHED BY
Microsoft Press
A Division of Microsoft Corporation
One Microsoft Way
Redmond, Washington 98052-6399

Library of Congress Cataloging-in-Publication Data
Denning, Adam, 1960
    OLE controls inside out : the programmer's guide to building
componentware with OLE and the Component Object Model / Adam
Denning.
       p.   cm.
   Includes index.
   ISBN 1-55615-824-6
    1. Object-oriented programming (Computer science)   2. OLE
(Computer file)   I. Title.
QA76.64.D46 1995
005.7--dc20   95-24704
                                              CIP

Printed and bound in the United States of America.

1 2 3 4 5 6 7 8 9 MLML 0 9 8 7 6 5

Distributed to the book trade in Canada by Macmillan of Canada, a division of Canada Publishing
Corporation.

A CIP catalogue record for this book is available from the British Library.

Microsoft Press books are available through booksellers and distributors worldwide. For further information
about international editions, contact your local Microsoft Corporation office. Or contact Microsoft Press
International directly at fax (206) 936-7329.

Acquisitions Editor: Eric Stroo
Project Editor: Jack Litewka
Technical Editor: Marc Young

To my daughters, Asphodel, Phoebe, and Xanthe, and to my wife, Melissa.
Now we can begin to remember each other again....

Chapters at a Glance

Contents

Contents

Contents

Contents

Contents

Contents

Foreword

OLE controls present software developers with three enormous opportunities.

OLE controls are a unique architectural opportunity that offers a single, widely available mechanism for developers to expose applications to enhancement by others and to customize the applications of others. Developers who build applications that can contain OLE controls are saying, "Look here, add insanely great features to my app that I haven't thought of yet!" Developers who create OLE controls are saying, "Hey, this is great! I don't have to write the whole app to make a business out of my Widget control."

OLE controls offer developers an opportunity to increase their productivity. OLE compound-document capabilities pioneered this concept by making it easy to allow one document to embed and edit the content of another. By using OLE controls, developers can capture their unique function in a control once and then have confidence that the control can be used widely within many applications. Likewise, by including OLE control containment, developers gain access to the wealth of other developer efforts that can improve their app.

OLE controls are a unique business opportunity. Sure, many of us have had business success using control mechanisms in the past—for instance, VBX controls available in Microsoft's Visual Basic—but we've had only a limited number of tools that support them. OLE controls, on the other hand, are supported by many container applications, by many developers, and on several system architectures. This spells "big potential market" for those of us with a unique idea.

If you are the type of developer who assembles things you buy without reading the directions, you likely don't need this book. After all, you learn by experience! However, if you want to get off to a fast start and be successful the first time out, this is a "must have" book. Why? Because writing great OLE controls will be a challenge for the unprepared. Sure, there are many great tools on the market—such as Microsoft's Visual C++—that can aid you in the task. But there is no substitute for the tutoring, thinking, notes, and archives of one of the key developers of the technology, Adam Denning. This book provides the inside knowledge you'll need to transform your idea, not merely into an OLE control but into an exceptional OLE control.

Foreword

Finally, two *-ances* are important to remember as you write your control. Tack these on your monitor: Perform*ance* and Conform*ance*. Pay attention to the performance of your control—make it efficient and snappy. Also pay attention to conformance with the OLE Controls specification by adhering to the guidelines in this book about how to write a control that can work within a large variety of containers.

Happy OLE controls development!

Roger Heinen
Senior Vice President
Microsoft Corporation

Acknowledgments

Many people helped me in the creation of this book. I fastidiously maintained a list of those involved (he lied), so anyone I have neglected to mention can write me for a free latte coupon. I am eternally grateful to a whole group of people for their contributions, and there are a few who have helped me along the way without necessarily realizing it.

So, I need to thank a host of people for their contributions to this book, as well as five for whom the opposite is true: my daughters Asphodel and Phoebe, who are past masters at keeping me from working and sleeping; my wife, Melissa, who for some reason expects me to speak to her at least once a week; and two friends and colleagues at Microsoft Limited in the United Kingdom (now both at Microsoft Corporation in Redmond, Washington), Mark Daymond and Bill Champion, who have contributed precisely nothing to this book (indeed, some may say less than nothing, but I couldn't possibly comment) but insist on their names being mentioned at pain of death.

Many people at Microsoft, both in the UK and in Redmond, have helped me greatly in writing this book. In particular, I would like to thank Solveig Whittle for not only acting as a superb guide into the labyrinths of Microsoft but also for doggedly pursuing my cause and getting so many people to back the concept of this book. Numerous people at Microsoft Press have moved this thing along, most notably Jack Litewka, the project editor; Marc Young, the technical editor and guardian of the program code that is on the companion CD-ROM; and Eric Stroo, the big boss man. Quite how Jack put up with an author as unreliable as I, I shall never know. Also, Dean Holmes, formerly acquisitions director at Microsoft Press, was instrumental in getting the project started.

For their technical review of early drafts of chapters, I'd like to thank Kraig Brockschmidt, John Elsbree (who actually wrote most of the OLE CDK), Eric Lang (who now has the lucky job of being my boss), and David Stutz. I'd also like to thank Dan Jinguji and John Thorson, who persuaded me that the first few chapters of this book needed to be altered in major ways.

For working with me on getting OLE controls to be successful, my thanks to Blair Howland, Rob Copeland, Dave Massy, Dean McCrory, Kim Hightower, Matt Pohle, and Chris Zimmerman. For writing the OLE CDK documentation from which I

Acknowledgments

so liberally stole, Frank Crockett. For agreeing to write the foreword to this book, Roger Heinen. For being the best project manager I know and a good friend when needed, Nick Mundy. For letting me do this while still being gainfully employed, Adam Warby and Pieter Knook. Finally, for general mentorship and getting me over to Redmond in the first place, Jim McCarthy.

Oh, and for getting me into computers in the first place, Khan Busby.

Without you all, I would have had a life over the past year.

Adam Denning

Introduction

This book has a trace of Windows 95-itis about it. I started writing it in earnest in July 1994, with the expectation of having it written by January 1995. It is now August 1995, and I'm just putting on the finishing touches. It seems the lack of rules that can be successfully applied to the software development process also apply to the book-writing process!

When I set out on this task, I was a senior consultant for Microsoft Consulting Services (MCS) in the United Kingdom. As I end it, I am the program manager for MFC (which includes the main topic of this book, the OLE CDK) and the C runtimes inside the Visual C++ group here at Microsoft in Redmond, Washington, USA. I also have a new daughter to add to my already extensive collection. So if you think this book is late in the coming, at least I have some reasonable excuses.

ABOUT THIS BOOK

Most developers for Microsoft Windows will be aware of Visual Basic custom controls, or so-called VBXs, no matter what programming tool(s) they use. VBXs are add-ons to Visual Basic that enhance its functionality in some way. (I discuss this subject in detail in the first chapter.) When Visual Basic was first released in 1991, there was no such thing as a VBX. Now there are hundreds of commercially available VBXs and thousands more developed for in-house use by corporations worldwide. They're not even limited to Visual Basic anymore. Microsoft's Visual C++ was amongst the first to add a degree of support for these controls, and a variety of programming languages and development tools followed suit. So the market gets bigger, more VBXs are produced, the market gets bigger again...and so on.

But there's a problem. The underlying architecture of Visual Basic custom controls (VBXs) is not portable to 32 bits or to non-Intel platforms. So what do you do? If you're a VBX vendor and you can see the rushing tide of 32-bit operating systems, this question is particularly relevant because your livelihood depends on an answer. If you're an in-house developer, the question is still important because no doubt at some point your company will upgrade to a 32-bit operating system and will ultimately want all its applications altered, too. Well, there's no answer, so you may as well give up now and start selling used cars.

But then this book wouldn't exist either—which can't be true, otherwise my children would remember who I am. (Don't ask how I managed to generate another child during this process—I still don't remember.) So we must have an answer. *OLE controls* address the need by being capable of performing all the same tasks as traditional VBXs while being portable between platforms and between bit sizes (that is, 16-bit and 32-bit). They also happen to have greater functionality.

This book is all about writing OLE controls. It first sets out to explain how they work from a conceptual standpoint. Clearly, this needs at least some knowledge of OLE itself, so the first few chapters explore some of the basic OLE concepts. If you want to study further, read the excellent *Inside OLE 2,* by Kraig Brockschmidt.

Chapter 1 discusses the concept of "componentware," a new category of software characterized by chunks of reusable functionality conveniently packaged and useful in many different environments. It also contains the first compilable and usable OLE control in this book. Chapter 2 begins the discussion of OLE itself—what it is, its purpose in life, and how it works. Chapter 3 takes a much more in-depth look at this and also discusses the additions made to OLE and the Component Object Model (COM), its plumbing, for OLE controls. (If you already know all there is to know about OLE or if you just want to get about creating OLE controls without knowing how they work, you can skip Chapters 2 and 3.)

Chapter 4 starts the practical section, as it were, by introducing Microsoft's tools for OLE control creation, all contained within the OLE Control Developer's Kit (OLE CDK). The next few chapters look at attributes of controls themselves, starting with properties in Chapter 5. Chapter 6 briefly covers the topic of property persistence, or the ability of a container (an application in which controls are used) to store a control's state between sessions, with help from the control. Chapter 7 looks at control methods, one of the areas in which OLE controls offer greater functionality than do VBXs. Chapter 8 then looks at events, or notifications from the control to its container. Chapter 9 shows ways in which errors and exceptions can be robustly handled in controls. Chapter 10 brings all these topics together and introduces a few new ones. As you progress through Chapters 5 through 10, you'll be creating and modifying a control that reaches its functional conclusion in Chapter 10.

Chapter 11 examines another feature new to OLE controls: property pages. Chapter 12 looks at the new Microsoft Foundation Class Library used to create OLE controls and their property pages, and Chapter 13 shows you how to make use of font-based properties in your controls. Chapter 14 skims through the subject of data binding, in which properties of a control are connected to a database. (As you'll see, the scheme is open-ended, so the container can in fact connect a bound property to anything it chooses.) Chapter 15 shows ways in which you can regulate the use of your control through the licensing additions to COM, and Chapter 16 covers the idea of one control visually containing other controls (for example, radio buttons inside a standard Windows group box). Chapter 17 looks at two subjects that are often connected by circumstance: how to convert an existing VBX to an OLE control and how to create OLE controls that are subclasses of standard Windows controls. Chapter 18 looks at the issues involved in creating controls for 16-bit and 32-bit environments, as well as cross-platform issues. Finally, Chapter 19 addresses the topic of control and container guidelines, which if used will ensure that a given control will work inside any container that complies with the guidelines and will likewise ensure that a given container can make use of any controls that are written to comply with the guidelines.

There are two appendixes to this book. Appendix A is an introduction to Microsoft's Visual C++ compiler and its accompanying MFC library. Read this appendix if you use other manufacturers' compilers or if you have not yet used a class library. Appendix B shows just how long it took to write this book—it's a write-up of the major differences between the Visual C++ version 2.x line of compilers used in this book and the release of Visual C++ version 4.0, which is due to be released at about the same time this book hits the streets. Read this appendix if you're using Visual C++ version 4.0 or later.

WHO CAN USE THIS BOOK?

OLE controls *can* be easy to develop, and if you're already *au fait* with OLE technology, they can also be easy to understand. This book is for people who want to know more about them and more about how to write them.

The book aims to get you to the point where you will understand how OLE controls work and how to develop them in C++ using the OLE CDK. You'll also learn a bit about how they're used in host containers, such as Visual Basic, and a fair amount about the issues involved in porting OLE controls to other platforms. You need to be at least competent at Windows programming and C++ programming. You don't need to be a current user of Visual C++ or of the MFC library, but it helps. All the examples in this book are written using the OLE CDK, which is centered around MFC, so you'll need the product to build the OLE controls. You also don't need to know OLE in any great detail; the relevant bits will, as I said earlier, be explained up front.

I'll feel that I've succeeded with this book if, as a result of reading it, putative OLE control writers feel confident enough to start work in earnest on their own controls and if this in turn leads to an even more healthy component market.

I'm a major believer in the "componentware" concept realized by OLE controls, and I've made every attempt not only to help simplify the creation of OLE controls but also to demonstrate their real value to software developers. This attempt applies as much to in-house developments by large companies as it does to software houses creating off-the-shelf packages. To further this aim, I have made every endeavor to ensure that the sample controls used in this book are both useful in and applicable to the real world.

PREREQUISITES

To be able to use the example controls in this book and to develop controls of your own, you'll need some skills at the start of the process. You'll need to be able to write Microsoft Windows programs either at the SDK level in C or C++ or by using the MFC library version 2.0 or later. (MFC version 2.0 was shipped with Visual C++ 1.0.) If you already have MFC experience, you're off to a better start. You don't need to have written OLE programs before using either the OLE SDK or the MFC version 2.5 or later (shipped with Visual C++ version 1.5), but again, all prior experience helps.

You'll need some programming tools. The controls I develop in this book can in the main be compiled without change both for 16 bits and for 32 bits. The controls have been tested on Windows 95 and Windows NT version 3.51 for Intel. They've all been created using the Microsoft Visual C++ version 2.2 package. Visual C++ 2.2 itself is a 32-bit compiler that produces only 32-bit executables; however, the CD-ROM on which it is shipped also includes an updated version of 16-bit Visual C++ version 1.52a. This contains some amendments for OLE control support and a few bug fixes for 1.5. The CD-ROM also contains the OLE CDK in both 16-bit and 32-bit incarnations. You'll need to use Visual C++ version 2.1 or later for 32-bit development (version 2.0 will compile all the controls here except those that use ODBC) and Visual C++ version 1.52 or later for 16-bit development (again, version 1.51 will work for all controls except those using ODBC).

The controls have been tested using the Test Container application that comes with the OLE CDK as well as with Visual Basic version 4.0 and Visual C++ version 4.0.

All my development (as well as the writing of this book) was performed under Windows NT Workstation 3.51 on a Compaq 486c/66, followed by Windows 95 running on a Toshiba T4800CT laptop when I moved to Redmond, Washington. The book's text was mostly written using Microsoft Word version 6.0 for Windows, but I took advantage of the new version of Word (7.0) inside Microsoft Office for Windows 95.

When it comes to choosing development systems, there's a lot to be said for using a 32-bit operating system even if you're targeting 16 bits. Two things spring to mind: speed (because disk I/O is faster, particularly under Windows NT) and robustness (you can create a control that crashes but won't bring down the system). As always with tools such as C++ compilers and linkers, the more memory you have, the better; my system has 32 MB of RAM.

USING THE COMPANION CD-ROM

The companion CD-ROM included with this book contains all the source files and make files for building 16-bit and 32-bit versions of the sample controls. None of the OCX or DLL files is included on the companion CD-ROM; you can compile the sample projects that interest you.

To install the companion CD-ROM's files on your hard disk, first insert the CD-ROM into your CD-ROM drive. If you're installing from Windows 95, select Run from the Start menu, and then type *d:\setup.exe* in the Run dialog box. If you're installing from Windows NT, select Run from Program Manager's File menu, and then type *d:\setup.exe* in the Run dialog box. In either case, after the setup program executes, follow the on-screen instructions.

CODING STYLE

I have my own coding style, which is used throughout this book. This can get to be a religious issue, so substitute your own format as you please. My style is to be fairly liberal with white space and to use braces even where the language expressly allows one to be lax, because I believe this results in fewer programmer errors later. I also indent my braces according to the "vertical" style:

```
void CMyClass::MemberFunction ( LPCSTR lpszTitle,
    short nLength )
{
    if ( nLength == 0 )
    {
        return;
    }

    for ( int i = 0; i < nLength; ++i )
    {
        if ( lpszTitle [ I ] == 'A' )
        {
            MsgBox ( "This string contains an 'A'!" );
            break;
        }
    }
}
```

I attempt wherever possible to use Microsoft-wide naming conventions, so-called Hungarian notation. I also use the MFC extensions to this convention, such as the use of *C* at the start of a class name to designate it as a class name. (Some people really hate this.)

SOME GENERAL NOTES

When I refer to the Visual C++ compiler, I refer either to a specific version, such as version 2.0, or to a series based on the same version, such as 2.x. If I'm specific, I mean to be; and if I'm general, I mean to be. For example, OLE controls can make use of the MFC ODBC classes only in Visual C++ versions 2.1 and later; the OLE control in Chapter 1 can be compiled with Visual C++ version 1.5x for 16 bits and Visual C++ version 2.x for 32 bits.

Likewise, when I refer to Windows, version 3.x refers to 16-bit Windows such as versions 3.1 and 3.11. Win32, unless expressly mentioned otherwise, refers to Windows 95, Windows NT, and Win32s.

One of the most intriguing things for me as I wrote this book is the way in which my natural humor and grammatical excellence were compromised during its conversion to American. I was shocked and stunned when I discovered that the world will now think that I use the word "gotten," when of course I would rather sit on an ant's nest. Please therefore bear in mind that any jokes that aren't funny are entirely the result of bad editing, or your lack of a sense of humor.

Two things the main text of this book does not cover: OLE controls performance and determining when it's appropriate to use a control rather than another solution. I won't cover either of these in much detail here, either. Performance: a control that uses OLE must be fat and slow, right? Well, not necessarily. First, consider that most Windows controls use Windows messages to set attributes, whereas OLE controls use OLE Automation. In the in-process case, which applies to almost all OLE controls, an OLE Automation call uses considerably fewer processor instructions than does a traditional *PostMessage* or *SendMessage* call. An orders-of-magnitude difference.

On the other hand, getting a control onto a form and having it display itself is definitely more expensive in the OLE control case at present. The overhead of control-to-container negotiation, and in-place activation, cause initial creation of controls to be generally slower than in the native Windows control case. Expect this to improve dramatically in the future.

Finally, it's easy to take the componentware concept too far and expect to be able to use OLE controls in any situation, almost as if they were library functions or system functionality. No doubt you can get these things to work, but is it really appropriate? As an example, you'll notice that in the discussion of Visual C++ version 4.0 in Appendix B, I mention that a number of OLE controls are shipped with the product. Some OLE controls, though, we decided *not* to ship. In particular, the OLE controls used by Visual Basic to provide access to the new Windows 95 common controls, such as tree views and list views, are not supplied with Visual C++. Why not? The MFC library provides wrapper classes for the base Windows 95 controls themselves, and therefore the typical C++ programmer is going to be more inclined to use the more efficient MFC wrappers to the real objects than an OLE control wrapper to those same objects.

Is there a rule for when it is appropriate to use an OLE control and when it is not? Probably not, but it's one of those areas where common sense can be successfully applied.

Part I

Setting the Scene

Chapter 1

Componentware

This chapter sets the scene for the rest of the book by looking at some of the concepts and problems that have caused software developers to move gradually but inexorably toward object-oriented techniques. It then shows how in many respects the benefits of object-oriented programming are not being realized in quite the way anticipated, but that the concept has been taken one step further with greater success. This one step is the creation of objects that are "binary reusable," which means that they are for all intents and purposes analogous to adapter cards in personal computers or to car stereo systems; because such objects all follow the same standard, they can be interchanged at will. This is the basis for what is fast becoming widely known as "componentware."

The first true manifestation of this component phenomenon is the Microsoft Visual Basic custom control, or VBX. The OLE Controls specification addresses the issues presented by VBXs, such as portability and the close association with Visual Basic.

Oh, and in case you're wondering, this chapter also describes how to create an OLE control!

THE PHILOSOPHY OF THE DEVELOPMENT PROCESS

Software development processes have not really changed much over the years. People still write code in arcane languages that only those with specialized training can understand. Programmers, and even project managers, always underestimate the length of time or the resources needed to build a specific project. Intriguingly, despite many years of development by many thousands of programmers the world over, the amount of code shared between projects even within the same company is very small indeed. Microsoft Corporation itself was guilty of this not so long ago, with the individual Microsoft Office products (for example, Microsoft Word and Microsoft Excel) having different code to create standard features (such as toolbars and status bars).

Software Reuse

The constant reinvention of code and algorithms is a phenomenal waste of software developer resources and causes us all to tax our brains for solutions that someone somewhere has already thought of. Okay, I'm talking about reusability here: has anyone <u>really</u> achieved it? Early attempts involved source code sharing, which meant that someone borrowed a given routine from a colleague or friend. It's likely, however, that over time both copies of the routine were changed in different ways, so after a while they are manifestly <u>not</u> reusable. Then there were precompiled libraries of routines (functions), such as those supplied with your favorite C-language compiler. These come in a couple of flavors: those that are "standard" and should be shipped with a compiler (for example, the classic *stdio* functions in C) and those that are custom (for example, a given compiler vendor's graphics library). The difference here is that, in theory at least, everyone's implementation of standard library functions (*printf*, for example) should take the same parameters, perform the same actions, and return the same results. Those functions from custom libraries, on the other hand, are governed by no such laws and can almost be guaranteed to be different.

Nevertheless, libraries clearly provide a set of routines that <u>are</u> reusable. Only thing is, we have a problem if we want to alter the behavior of a specific routine. Taking *printf* again, if we wanted to make it perform some task in addition to its defined task, we must either write our own routine or, if we've paid a source license to our compiler vendor, we can probably take the *printf* source and make our changes. By recompiling the source, we have a new function. But what happens if we don't change its name from *printf*? All hell is let loose. Worse, we're lowering our reusability quotient again, because our customized routine is not shipped with the compiler.

Object Orientation

"Object orientation" (or, as it's commonly referred to, OO) is the holy grail that has offered to solve the reuse problem once and for all. I'm a believer, but it's got to be said that it's taken an awfully long time to deliver on this promise. The concept of object orientation is a collection of ideas that individually give benefit to the developer (and the user of the programs, as you shall see) and that collectively define a paradigm. It's about time we had one of those!

OO is of course a deeply religious subject about which many views exist. Therefore, the following description must be considered as my opinion rather than as hard and fast fact. (Luckily, my opinion is shared by many others.) The three key benefits of OO are:

- Encapsulation — the hiding of an object's implementation details

- Inheritance — the ability to take what already exists and create new objects from it

- Polymorphism — the ability to exhibit many behaviors (as discussed below)

"Polymorphism" is often a consequence of inheritance, although it doesn't need to be. Imagine a hierarchy in which you have an insect and, in addition, a series of specific types of insect each derived from insect: *wasp, fly, ant,* and *bee.* (See Figure 1-1.) The insect thing has a way of causing pain, which we'll call the *HurtHuman* method, where a "method" is a specific request to a thing to cause it to do something. The derived types automatically inherit this *HurtHuman* method. However, each insect type defines its own *HurtHuman* method that does something specific to that type — the wasp stings, for example, and the bee stings and then dies. Each of the four derivations <u>overrides</u> the insect's definition. "Overriding" means that the derived object's method is used rather than the method from any objects from which it is derived.

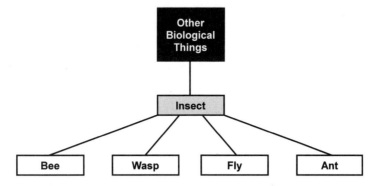

Figure 1-1. *An insect inheritance tree.*

Now imagine that you have a process (not necessarily in the computing sense) that manipulates insects; you want it to deal with any type of insect that comes along, not only those you know about at the moment. You know that each insect type will have a *HurtHuman* method (or will use the generic insect's *HurtHuman* method if it happens to be the way in which this insect type hurts humans). The process knows how to speak to the generic insect type but would like to keep itself nonspecific; it wants to know nothing detailed about any derived insect types. Nevertheless, when the process invokes the *HurtHuman* method, it wants to do so using the specific insect type's method. How does it do this? Through polymorphism, which means "the ability to have many shapes." It speaks to the basic insect but might in fact be speaking to something derived from it. So long as the insect has been implemented appropriately, it will polymorphically call the correct method.

So, the benefit of polymorphism is that you can remain (relatively) general and yet ensure the specific case is dealt with. Clearly a benefit.

Object-Oriented Programming

To see the benefits of OO techniques from a programming point of view, we need to convert the concepts to those embodied in "object-oriented programming," or OOP. The "programming" part is important here, as OO techniques can be applied elsewhere in a development cycle, with or without the use of OOP. Likewise, OOP can be used whether or not other object-oriented techniques have been used elsewhere in the development's life cycle. I happen to believe that maximum benefit is accrued from OO techniques if they are used at all applicable stages of development.

In programming terms, then, we need a language that can implement encapsulation, inheritance, and polymorphism on behalf of a programmer. Many languages can do this: some do it better (that is, more purely, whatever that means) than others, while some are more pragmatic (that is, they cause programs to be created that execute at reasonable speed) than others. By far the most popular OOP language, and one that has a slightly more pragmatic than pure bent, is C++. That's the language of choice for this book.

Hence, in C++:

```
class Insect
{
public:
    virtual void HurtHuman ( void );
};
class Wasp : public Insect
{
public:
    void HurtHuman ( void );
};
Wasp *aWasp = new Wasp;
Insect *anInsect = aWasp;
anInsect -> HurtHuman ( );
```

This code defines two classes, *Insect* and *Wasp*, where *Wasp* is derived from *Insect* and both contain the *HurtHuman* method. The last three lines of code first create an instance of the *Wasp* class and save a pointer to it in *aWasp* and then create a pointer to an *Insect* and store the address of the *Wasp* object in that *Insect* pointer. This means that C++ thinks *anInsect* points at the generic *Insect,* but we know that it really points at *Wasp. Insect::HurtHuman* is declared virtual, so when the *HurtHuman* method is invoked through this pointer, C++ causes *Wasp::HurtHuman* to be called rather than *Insect's* implementation. This is polymorphic behavior.

So, we know that an object is something that implements a certain set of behaviors and that provides an interface or set of interfaces through which this behavior can be accessed or invoked. This interface is typically in the form of methods, but in some object implementations (for example, those in C++) it's also possible to make object data visible.

Now we can get back to software reuse and how OO helps this.

Software Reuse and Object Orientation

The software-reuse benefits of object orientation (OO) are not something that comes by default: you still need to plan for them. In C++, classes can obviously be reused by inheriting from them. The class, however, needs to be worth inheriting from in the first place. If a given class provides functionality that is not general enough, few people will need to use it; similarly, a class that is too general will be of little use.

The problem with reuse of this kind is that it's really still at the source code level and subject to breaking if any of the derived-from classes in a hierarchy tree changes its interface (the so-called "fragile base classes" problem). I say that it's still at the source code level because almost every set of C++ classes (a "class library") worth its salt comes equipped with source code so that its users can debug their own applications as well as make use of the source code of a base class member function to customize the behavior of their own implementation. For example, you might want the way in which files are opened by a Microsoft Foundation Class (MFC) Library program to be subtly different in your application from that provided by default, so you take the source code for the relevant file opening member function, alter it, and use it as the implementation for your override. There's also the rather acute problem that a C++ class library can only be used by C++ programs, unless you go to a lot of trouble. This is worsened by compiler-specific details, meaning that it's often the case that a class library can only be used by the manufacturer's C++ compiler, unless it's recompiled.

So, although you often get more software reuse by using OO than you would if you didn't use it, there are still some constraints. The software-reuse benefits of OO are best realized if you defer work on the implementation — coding — and work instead at the analysis level. If you begin to imagine a system as a series of objects, you can fairly quickly work out which of these elements are reusable by the system or by future enhancements to the system and which of these elements are general-purpose enough to perhaps, maybe, hopefully, have been written by someone else before in a form you can use.

NOTE Remember, the series of objects are black boxes — you only care what they do, not how they do it. You also care that the interfaces these black boxes present remain constant.

Binary Reuse

The breakdown of a system into its logical components is the essence of "object-oriented analysis" (OOA). I'd argue that it's also the basis for "componentware," a nonword that to me means "reusable black boxes, logically distinct pieces of a system that have uses in more than one process." These reusable black boxes are in fact nothing more than software components — plug-in units that present a standard set of functionality through a set of interfaces. These components can fall into a number of categories: truly generic ones such as printing components and spelling checkers, dialog controls such as radio buttons, or task-oriented ones that fit given business requirements. The key point about them, though, is that they can be reused as they stand; they don't need to be recompiled, you don't need the source code, and you don't need to stick to one language. The common term for this kind of reuse is "binary reuse."

Let's imagine you're designing a new system for a life insurance company. Perhaps you've already modeled your corporate data and processes to arrive at a logical object-oriented analysis. If you have, you might have found that a number of your business processes deal with this thing called a "customer" and that others deal with "quotations," "policies," and "proposals." A quotation application might make use of all four of these things; a customer management system might use only the customer and policy things. You find that in fact some of these are used by more than one business process, so they are inherently reusable as long as you can create them in such a way that this logical reuse can be realized. If they were software components, you probably could.

Take the customer object, for example. Careful analysis will have allowed you to define all the interfaces a customer object would need to present to its known users, allowing that new interfaces might be required of it in the future by some unknown, unforeseen new user. The same analysis might well have brought you down to a knowledge of exactly what this object must do in business terms, and the data modeling will tell you what persistent data (database tables and records) it should be manipulating. By providing this object as a "business service" to each of the business processes which need to use it, you've achieved at least two things: you have reuse, as the object is used by more than one process, and you have centralization of business policy, as all users of customer data now go through this customer object to get there. Therefore, you can implement your business rules in this object and be assured that they are always observed, as long as you ensure that all business processes that need to use customer data actually do make use of the customer object, of course!

Imagine: you give your data users freedom to get the information they desire and the ability to manipulate it in any which way, and they will always use it in a way consistent with the business — because you've enforced those rules in the thing that gives them access to the data in the first place. Information systems heaven!

Other Instances of Binary Reuse

A case of binary reuse that seems wholly different at first glance from those discussed earlier but that is actually another facet of the same idea, is that of a dialog box containing numerous controls, such as a grid, a series of radio buttons, and a couple of pushbuttons. Some of these might be provided centrally by Microsoft Windows itself (therefore itself a profoundly important source of components), while the grid might be provided as a component from someone else's spreadsheet application. Each of these controls provides a known set of interfaces, acts in a known way, and are general enough to be useful in this arbitrary dialog box as well as in any other application that needs similar controls.

CREATING REUSABLE OBJECTS

I've discussed how systems can be separated conceptually into a series of components, but I haven't yet shown how this can be done. What mechanisms exist for integrating components into a system? The mechanisms used are often referred to as the "glue" that ties components together, and glues come from a variety of sources. Some are good glues, others give off harmful fumes, and still others are limited in the types of materials they can glue together. Let's look at some of these glues.

Windows SDK Custom Controls

The "custom control" specification is one of the first glues available for Microsoft Windows programmers who want to make use of special, custom-built dialog controls. This specification dictates how a visual control interacts with the Dialog Editor, the tool used to create dialogs in programs developed using the Microsoft Windows Software Development Kit (SDK), making it easier to add custom controls to a standard Windows dialog box. This variety of custom control, however, is severely limited in scope: it can only be used by programs that speak the language, generally ruling out development tools other than C and C++, and that rely on a glue that is not very feature-rich. Custom controls are essentially limited to sending notification messages of events (for example, "I've been clicked on") to the parent <u>window</u> containing them. Although many custom controls exist, such as the MUSCROLL sample in the Windows SDK, very few developers these days create them and even fewer third parties sell them.

Microsoft Visual Basic and VBXs

Microsoft Visual Basic is one of the most popular glues and is also a programming language in its own right. When this language system was designed, its creators determined that the idea of a "custom control" was a powerful one. They decided to allow Visual Basic to be extended through a new kind of custom control, called the "Visual Basic custom control," or, more commonly, "VBX," after the standard file extension given to these custom controls. VBXs are ordinary Windows DLLs (dynamic link libraries) that follow a few conventions. (DLLs are pieces of code that are loadable at runtime and can be shared amongst processes.) The Professional versions of Visual Basic version 3.0 and earlier came with the Control Development Kit (CDK), which allow custom VBXs to be written, typically in C.

The Visual Basic programmer can use a VBX by adding the VBX file to a project. A single VBX file can in fact contain many custom controls. Adding the file to a project causes each control's icon to be added to the Visual Basic toolbox, making them available for use by clicking on the relevant icon and drawing the control on the form. The control's properties can then be set, and code can be written to handle the events it generates. A "property" is an attribute of a control, such as its background color or shape; an "event" is a control-generated message, which notifies its container that something has happened. This message might be as mundane as "someone has clicked me" to something as complex as "a mail message has arrived for you." VBXs don't support user-written methods, so a standard technique has evolved: methods are simulated by writing so-called "action properties," which cause the control to perform an action when a property value is set. This is somewhat out of the object-oriented mold.

As each version of Visual Basic was released, the functionality of VBXs was increased, culminating in the version 3.0 VBX, which also supports the notion of data binding. "Data binding" is the establishment of a connection between the control and a column in a table in a database — for example, tying an edit field to the "Surname" column of a table. After the edit field is changed by the user, the changes can be communicated to the database, and vice versa.

VBXs were originally conceived as custom controls with much the same scope as the old SDK-style custom controls — typically, visual elements that supplemented the standard set of controls provided by Microsoft Windows. A number of VBXs are shipped with the Visual Basic system; some of these provide three-dimensional controls, others provide control of multimedia devices, others provide graphing capabilities, and so forth. Some of these VBXs are written for Microsoft Corporation by third parties, who in many cases also sell enhanced versions of these controls. It is now possible to buy VBXs, from a vast number of sources, to provide all sorts of added functionality — from customized list boxes to full-featured word processors and spreadsheets to complex business-oriented tasks. Further, numerous companies who use Visual Basic for in-house development have created a number of customized VBXs for internal use. (For example, one large retail bank in the United Kingdom has over 75 custom-built VBXs.)

An excellent reason for the rapid rise in popularity of the VBX is the fact that a single unifying development environment, Visual Basic, is provided in which VBXs could be used. Once the enormous popularity of VBXs was understood, people began to want to use them in development tools other than Visual Basic. Microsoft Visual C++, for example, supports VBXs in its 16-bit incarnation, as do many other programming languages. In general, the level of support offered by these tools is actually less functional than that offered by Visual Basic, because some of the more advanced VBX features require extensive support in the runtime system.

VBXs seem to have gotten us pretty close to the true component model: plug-in black boxes, available from a variety of sources, which perform a wide range of services. An article in *Byte* magazine in early 1994 actually declared that object-oriented programming had failed in this respect but that Visual Basic, with its VBXs, had succeeded. Certainly, the third-party market is much larger than anyone could have anticipated.

The VBX model, however, is not perfect. First, VBXs are supposed to be extensions to Visual Basic, and therefore support from other languages is not as good as Visual Basic's support. Second, the format is proprietary, meaning that it could change (and indeed has, through Visual Basic versions 1.0 to 3.0, although the changes have been mostly compatible). Third, the VBX architecture is very much tied to Intel Corporation's 80x86 processors running in 16-bit mode. The future is widely predicted as being both 32-bit (not a difficult prediction to make) and not necessarily Intel-dependent, so VBXs have no long-term future unless they can be easily ported to all new platforms.

Enter OLE!

Microsoft Corporation examined the option of porting VBX technology to other platforms and to the 32-bit world — and determined that it wasn't going to be easy. At the same time, a technology known as OLE had become prevalent in Microsoft operating systems. OLE is many things, as I'll show in Chapters 2 and 3; its prime purpose is to act as a glue between objects. Seems ideal! However, at the time the portability problem came to a head, OLE did not support a standard mechanism for an object to talk to its container asynchronously — all communication was from container to object. Events require asynchronous communication in the opposite direction.

NOTE Let's be very certain about my meaning here: by "asynchronous" I mean that the object can send notifications to its container whenever it chooses rather than only at the request of the container. I specifically do not mean that the notification is itself asynchronous, which would allow the object to continue processing immediately after calling a function to notify its container, which would happen "some time later."

Consequently, Microsoft decided that OLE should be used as the basis for the new breed of control because OLE forms the ideal glue, it's portable across platforms, and it works on both 16-bit and 32-bit operating systems. The new control specification, OLE Controls, was drawn up and distributed to VBX vendors in late 1993 and early 1994. Microsoft was relieved to discover that the majority of VBX vendors actually liked it. One obvious reason for them liking it is that it substantially increases their market, because Visual Basic is no longer the only thing capable of supporting the new OLE controls. Microsoft's other development tools, as well as its business applications, would be enhanced to support OLE controls, and the expectation was that major third parties would follow suit. The first major application to support OLE controls was Microsoft Access version 2.0, released in April 1994. At that point, the specification was not complete, so Access's control support was not as functional as that of Visual Basic version 4.0 or Visual FoxPro version 3.0, both released in 1995.

Interfaces and Containment

OLE is going to be covered in much greater detail in the next few chapters. One important point to make now is that OLE is basically a specification for interfaces between objects. Rather than using "inheritance," which demands that interfaces between elements in each level of a hierarchy remain the same, OLE uses "containment," which is a technique allowing one object to embody another and to expose any number of the contained object's interfaces as its own. Also, when new functionality is to be added to an object, it can be implemented simply as a new interface rather than having to alter or extend an existing one.

OLE provides the object-oriented virtue of polymorphism by allowing any object to support a given interface.

OLE Automation

OLE controls need to be at least as functional as existing VBXs, so support for properties and events is essential. One of the cornerstones of OLE controls is an OLE technology called "OLE Automation," which provides a mechanism for one program to control another by setting and reading properties on objects and by invoking methods on them. Use of this technology means that OLE controls also support custom, or user-defined, methods. Further, they must support data binding, the ability to be invisible at runtime if necessary (some controls don't need a visual representation at runtime), and a host of other esoteric features that you'll discover as you progress through this book.

For OLE controls to be successful, a number of factors needed to be taken into consideration. First, of course, OLE controls had to be able to do all that VBXs can do. Second, they needed to be as easy to use in programs as VBXs. They also needed to be fairly easy to write in the first place, and it would help if a simple conversion method existed to transform a VBX control into an OLE control. The more development tools and applications that support them the better, too, as this increases the size of the market. Most of this was delivered as the OLE Custom Control Developer's Kit (OLE CDK), which shipped with Visual C++ versions 2.0 and later.

OLE controls would therefore seem to be the state of the art in componentware: it is a mechanism for creating reusable objects that can be made use of by many different kinds of application development tools, that can perform many jobs, and that can be extended by the provision of new interfaces rather than by having to rely on inheritance.

No doubt the future holds even more promise for component software. Imagine, for example, when the functionality of Microsoft Office is provided as a series of OLE controls, each usable in its own right by any number of applications. This would bring a whole new modus operandi to your software development process, particularly if you develop software for sale. Licensing is always a key issue here, as the creators of such components are likely to want to get paid for the fruits of their labors; Chapter 3 contains details of how OLE controls help developers in this respect. Componentware also makes it easier for solution providers — those who take a set of components and build custom solutions from them.

CREATING AN OLE CONTROL

Now you're going to create the "Smile" control. I'm going to walk you through the steps, but I won't spend any time explaining them in detail because that's the purpose of the next few chapters in this book. My sole aim here is to show you how easy it is to create an OLE control and to use it in an application.

System Requirements

I'm going to make the assumption that you're running Microsoft Windows 95 on a personal computer with suitable hardware to run Visual C++. I'm also going to assume that you've installed Visual C++ version 2.1 and the 32-bit OLE CDK (Visual

C++ version 2.0 will also be fine). If you happen to be running a 16-bit version of Visual C++, it needs to be version 1.52, and the 16-bit OLE CDK needs to be installed. Barring one minor part of the build process and opening the project file itself, the steps to create and test the control are the same for the 32-bit and 16-bit worlds. If you're running Windows NT or a version of Windows earlier than Windows 95, the steps are the same although the look and feel of the control will be different.

Creating the "Smile" Control Example

I'm actually going to use an OLE control example that my boss Eric Lang wrote and that was published previously in the *Microsoft Systems Journal*. (This may mean a promotion, particularly when I say that the code is of such a high quality that I was simply awestruck!) The code for the sample is on the companion CD-ROM in the OLECTRLS\CHAP01\SMILE directory. You should copy the contents of that directory below it to your hard disk, and then follow the steps below:

1. For Visual C++ versions 2.0 and later, choose File Open and open the SMILE32.MAK make file. For Visual C++ version 1.52, choose Project Open and open SMILE.MAK. If you're using Visual C++ version 1.52, choose Make TypeLib from the Tools menu and wait for the command to complete successfully. You might notice a command window appearing: don't worry — it's supposed to!

2. Choose Project Rebuild All and wait until all compiling and linking has finished.

3. Register the control by choosing Register Control from the Tools menu.

4. Run the Test Container application by choosing it from the Tools menu.

5. In Test Container, choose Insert OLE Control from the Edit menu, and choose Smile Control from the list presented.

6. Notice that a Smile control is inserted in Test Container's window. Click on the control to ensure that it's selected.

7. Open up Test Container's event log by choosing Event Log from the View menu. Now watch for events by clicking on various parts of the control and by pressing keys while the control is selected.

8. View the control's properties by choosing Properties from the View menu. Play around with changing a few of the values to see what happens.

9. View and change the control's properties through the control's property pages by choosing Smile Control Object Properties from the Edit menu. (If that option doesn't appear, the control isn't selected. Click on it to select it.)

10. Be awestruck by the change in the control's appearance when you change the value of the Sad property through Test Container's View Properties dialog. (Use *0* for false and *-1* for true. Through the control's property pages, just check or uncheck the appropriate check box.)

The end! All will be explained as you progress through this book.

WHERE TO GO FROM HERE

You've now created your first OLE control and tried it out in the Test Container application. Even though the steps to build this control are simple, an awful lot is going on behind the scenes to make this control work. Chapter 2 is an overview of COM and OLE, skimming the surface of most of the pertinent areas. Chapter 3 then goes into some depth on those parts of OLE important to controls, including those parts specific to controls. So, what's the best way to proceed? Here are some guidelines:

■ If you want to know in detail how controls work, read Chapters 2 and 3.

■ If you're primarily interested in writing controls and aren't particularly interested in the low-level mechanics, you can skip Chapters 2 and 3.

■ If you want an overview of OLE without jumping into the depths, read Chapter 2 but skip Chapter 3.

■ If you need to know more about the Microsoft Foundation Class (MFC) Library, read Appendix A, which contains a fairly detailed fly-past.

OLE
Backgrounder:
Important Concepts

Chapter 1 introduced OLE as the glue between objects. Now I want to expand on that a great deal. This chapter is not supposed to be — and will not suffice as — an OLE tutorial. If that's what you need, *Inside OLE 2* by Kraig Brockschmidt (Microsoft Press) is the best introduction to OLE. My aim here is to cover the ground in pretty basic terms so that we share the same concepts and meanings, with a clear understanding of those bits that are really important to OLE controls. I will discuss some parts of OLE in much greater detail than others because they are of extreme significance to OLE controls and might not be fully understood by all readers. I skim through other areas, alighting briefly on those aspects that are directly relevant.

The areas that need to be covered in greater detail, such as OLE Automation and additions to OLE and COM for controls, are covered in the same depth in this chapter as the other areas but are examined in far greater detail in Chapter Three.

NOTE If you don't want to know what OLE is all about and how it works, you may skip this chapter and the next chapter and still be perfectly able to create powerful and useful OLE controls. On the other hand, if you want to know the nitty gritty details, you'll find a lot of valuable information in Chapters 2 and 3.

COM

The best place to start is at the fundamental concept of OLE: the OLE "Component Object Model," or COM. COM is all about the basic protocols for object communication. It defines the truly basic things, such as what constitutes a "COM object" and how one is instantiated. OLE is just one of the services logically placed above COM and that uses its facilities. COM, and therefore OLE, is centered around the idea of an "interface," where an interface represents a contract between an object and its user. (See Figure 2-1.) OLE itself provides many interfaces; developers can add others as they see fit. Interfaces, in programmatic terms, are arrays of pointers to functions, which is C-speak for a list of entry points to defined routines. A COM object never exposes <u>itself</u> or any of its data to the outside world; there is no concept of a pointer to a COM object. Instead, COM objects provide pointers to interfaces that they expose. I'll demonstrate what that means as the chapter progresses.

Figure 2-1. *An OLE interface on an object. This is the standard, OLE-approved way in which an interface is drawn.*

In its role as the glue between objects, OLE <u>implements</u> a wide variety of interfaces and defines a whole lot more. Implementation of an interface means that OLE supplies code that performs the actions expected of each of the member functions in the interface. You might be familiar with the use of OLE to help Microsoft Excel embed its charts inside Microsoft Word documents. In fact, this is one of the common descriptions of what OLE is about. This is a view that Chapters 2 and 3 will go some way towards changing, as OLE offers much more than merely the ability to embed objects. If I list some of the more important technologies of OLE, you'll see just how much more functional it is than its common description.

Technology	Description
OLE Automation	The ability of an application to control another application's objects programmatically. An integral part of OLE Automation is the ability of an object to describe its capabilities through type descriptions. This feature is absolutely key to OLE controls.
OLE Documents	All the document-centric features of OLE, such as linking and embedding, drag-and-drop, and visual editing.
OLE Controls	OLE objects that support the in-place activation features of OLE Documents in a way known as "inside out." (Does this ring a bell?) These objects make use of OLE Automation to expose properties and methods and to provide event support.
OLE Messaging	A uniform interface for messaging (actually using OLE Automation).
OLE Schedule+	An automation interface for group scheduling.

OLE is becoming the standard for system interfaces as well as for user-specific ones, so more technologies of the form "OLE something" will come along over time. The important thing is that it is an evolving technology that can be compatibly extended by any developer without affecting the way in which earlier users of OLE services operate.

As Figure 2-2 on the next page shows, OLE has many components and many interfaces. At first this might look daunting; in reality, however, a number of things work in your favor:

■ A number of these interfaces are implemented by OLE itself or by tools you can use to develop your applications and therefore only need to be used by your applications.

■ You can create perfectly serviceable OLE objects using very few of these interfaces.

■ C++ class libraries such as the Microsoft Foundation Class Library (the MFC library, for short) do almost all the grunge work for you, often making OLE appear merely as another facet of Windows C++ programming.

■ Some high-level languages such as Microsoft Visual Basic allow the creation of OLE objects without any C++ or C coding at all. This trend will continue, so that OLE objects will be creatable through a wide variety of tools.

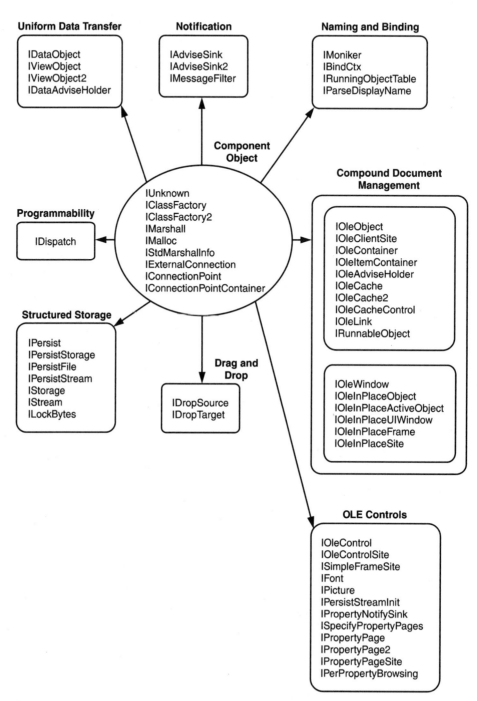

Figure 2-2. *The building blocks of OLE and the most important interfaces.*

IUNKNOWN

The most fundamental of interfaces is called *IUnknown*. (The naming convention here, common to all COM interfaces, is to start an interface name with capital *I*, followed by the word-capitalized interface name itself. As an example, an interface you might want to call *MyInterface* would actually be presented as *IMyInterface*.) *IUnknown* contains three pointers to functions: *AddRef, Release,* and *QueryInterface*. Every other COM interface must contain the *IUnknown* methods. It is convenient now to move straight into C++ terms; if an interface were represented as an abstract base class (which is what it amounts to), then all interfaces are derived from *IUnknown*. *IUnknown* could be represented as

```
class IUnknown
{
public:
    virtual ULONG AddRef ( void ) = 0;
    virtual ULONG Release ( void ) = 0;
    virtual HRESULT QueryInterface ( REFIID riid,
        LPVOID FAR *ppv ) = 0;
};
```

There are some things in here that I won't explain at this point. The important detail is that *IUnknown* contains <u>declarations</u> of these three methods. Every interface is an abstract base class — that is, it contains nothing but pure virtual functions — because an interface is no more than a table of pointers to functions. The actual implementation is something the programmer needs to create or, in many cases, the programmer needs to make use of someone else's implementation. C++ usefully creates a "virtual function table" (or "vtable") for any class containing one or more virtual functions. The vtable is actually an array of pointers to functions, which is exactly the realization of an interface. The vtable contains the addresses of the various functions derived from the abstract base class. If you're doing this in C or some other low-level language, you need to create the vtables yourself; worse, you also need to fill them with the function addresses. This isn't actually that difficult, but it's work that a C++ compiler would do for you. (This is a none too subtle plug to remind those who still insist on programming in C that it's a dead language and has been superseded by C++!)

The three *IUnknown* methods are absolutely key to COM. *AddRef* and *Release* implement reference-counting, which determines the lifetime of the related COM object. *QueryInterface* is the mechanism by which a user of a COM object determines what else that object can do. The job of *QueryInterface* is to get a new interface pointer on an object. If you have an *IUnknown* pointer and want to get the object's *IMyInterface* interface, you ask *IUnknown::QueryInterface* to provide a pointer to it. Likewise, you can call *IMyInterface::QueryInterface* to get the object's *IUnknown* interface or any other interface the object supports.

WHEN *QUERYINTERFACE* DOESN'T WORK

There are times when an object implementor might choose not to return a pointer to a specific interface through *QueryInterface*. Applications that can contain OLE controls might often choose to do this, as you'll see in the next chapter. In these instances, the object will typically provide its own mechanism for allowing access to the "hidden" interface or will deliberately not expose it for external use.

Here are two important points to get from *QueryInterface*:

■ Querying for *IUnknown* by calling *QueryInterface* on <u>any</u> interface the object supports must return the same *IUnknown*. (See Figure 2-3.) This allows a programmer to determine whether two interface pointers relate to the same object by comparing the result of *QueryInterface* for *IUnknown* on each pointer. So, although all other interfaces contain the *IUnknown* methods and can therefore be treated as *IUnknown*, it is important that one of these is chosen as what I'll call for the moment the "main *IUnknown*."

■ If you ask *QueryInterface* for an interface that the object doesn't support, an error is returned. Therefore, an object's capabilities can be determined at runtime on an interface-by-interface basis.

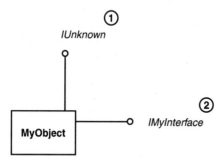

IMyInterface::QueryInterface (IID_IUnknown, ppv)
returns a pointer to interface ①.

IUnknown::QueryInterface (IID_IUnknown, ppv) also
returns a pointer to interface ①.

Figure 2-3. *Interface relationships and QueryInterface.*

Importantly, an interface is a <u>contract</u> between its implementor and its user. This means that if an object implements a given interface and provides access to it, the user of that object can assume that all methods within the interface are supported and retain their defined semantics. This also means that once an interface is defined, it <u>can't</u> be changed. Changing the interface would break the contract and therefore any application or object that used or implemented that interface. If changes to an interface are needed or desired, a new interface must be created. (I'll show a few of these new interfaces and explain why they were created as this chapter and the next progress.)

QueryInterface takes two parameters, which I've ignored so far. The first is a REFIID, an OLE type definition with which you'll become a lot more familiar. This REFIID specifies the particular interface you want. The second parameter is a place in which to store the newly allocated pointer to the requested interface. I'm first going to examine reference-counting in greater detail, and then I'll take a closer look at REFIIDs and what they mean.

Reference-Counting

When you retrieve an interface pointer from an object, the mechanism that passes the pointer to you will generally call *AddRef* on that interface so that the interface knows that it has a "user." As more pointers to that interface are created, the reference count goes up. Whenever an interface pointer is no longer required, the user of that pointer must call *Release* on it. This decrements the count. An object is not supposed to die in normal circumstances until all reference counts on all interfaces on it are at zero. As I've said, an OLE interface will often be implemented as a C++ class; a simple implementation can create a new instance of this class each time a new pointer to that interface is requested. Therefore, each object needs to keep its own reference count so that it can destroy itself when it is no longer required. This means that each interface implementation is responsible for its own reference count.

Another approach, however, is possible. If each interface is implemented in such a way that a new object is <u>not</u> created each time a new interface pointer is handed out (for example, by using C++ nested classes), then there is usually little benefit to be gained (unless you're debugging) by having each interface maintain its own count of its users. The general rule in this case is to delegate all *AddRef* and *Release* calls to the object's main *IUnknown*. The MFC library takes this approach, as do most of the sample programs in this book. In this way, the object as a whole knows how many users it has and can determine when to die simply by checking this value for zero each time *Release* is called. The object can then cause itself to die; if it is contained within an executable file, for example, it can at this time choose to close the window it's using to keep itself alive and therefore quit. If the object is implemented as a DLL (dynamic link library), the DLL can't unload itself. Instead, it remembers its state so that OLE can free it up if need be.

REFERENCE-COUNTING LORE

Some rules for reference-counting and optimization are specified in the *OLE 2 Programmer's Reference, Volume One* (Microsoft Press). The basic idea is that interface pointers must always be reference-counted, especially when local copies are taken, except when the user of a given interface knows that it's safe not to call *AddRef*. One example is when the pointer to a given interface is held and used <u>entirely</u> <u>within</u> <u>the</u> <u>lifetime</u> of a pointer to another interface on the same object. If in doubt, reference-count!

Reference-counting is usually straightforward, but some situations should be avoided. In particular, it is possible to get circular references when, either directly or via another object, one object holds a reference on another object that also holds a reference on it. If the situation is such that neither object calls *Release* on the other object's interface until its reference-count reaches zero, we have a deadlock. One way out of this is of course to avoid the situation in the first place, but that isn't always practical! Another way out is to be aware of the symbiosis and "cheat" by making one object not reference-count the other.

IUnknown::QueryInterface is by far the most common way in which new interface pointers are allocated. If *QueryInterface* successfully returns an interface pointer, it must have obeyed the OLE reference-counting rules and has also executed an *AddRef* on that interface pointer. Therefore, after you've finished with the interface pointer, you must call *Release* on it.

Class IDs, GUIDs, IIDs, and REFIIDs

One of the questions that usually comes up about now is "How do I get a pointer to an interface on an object?" I'm not actually going to address this until the section titled "My First Interface Pointer," beginning on page 26; however, one thing of significance from the discussion of *IUnknown* is the concept of a REFIID (reference to an Interface ID), and it's also rather important for creation of that first pointer. A REFIID is a C++ reference (a pointer in C) to an IID, or "interface identifier." Each and every interface exposed by an object must have an ID. COM defines the format for these IIDs, and they're one of the things for which GUIDs are used. "GUID" stands for "*globally unique ID*," where <u>globally</u> means just that. The idea is that a GUID generated by anyone, anywhere, will not conflict with another generated by someone else. The easiest way to deal with GUIDs is to treat them as big numbers that uniquely identify something, such as an interface. (See the "GUIDS and UUIDS" sidebar.)

GUIDs AND UUIDs — THE INSIDE STORY

Those familiar with OSF DCE RPC (which stands for "Open Systems Foundation distributed computing environment remote procedure call"!) might know GUIDs (see the preceding paragraph) as UUIDs, or "universally unique IDs." They are the same. A GUID is a structure with the following format:

```
struct GUID
      {

          DWORD Data1;
          WORD  Data2;
          WORD  Data3;
          BYTE  Data4 [ 8 ];
      }
```

By adding up the bytes, you'll find that a GUID is a 16-byte quantity. You can get GUIDs in two ways: you can either write to or phone Microsoft Corporation, which will allocate to you a set of 256, or you can use the *CoCreateGuid* function that COM provides. Various tools exist that call *CoCreateGuid* on your behalf, such as the *GuidGen* utility (which comes with the OLE SDK and with Microsoft Visual C++ version 2.0 or later) or Visual C++'s AppWizard. But don't worry: the algorithm used for GUID creation ensures that you can't run out! The chief architect of OLE, Tony Williams, explained the GUID creation algorithm in an internal Microsoft e-mail message as follows:

> CoCreateGuid *(used by AppWizard) uses the machine ID (uniqueness in space) and current time with high resolution (uniqueness in time) and some additional bits to deal with clocks turning backwards, etc. This is the OSF DCE generation algorithm.*
>
> *The machine ID is the network address, unless there is no network on the machine, in which case another algorithm is used to generate a set of bits unique to the machine with high probability, and guaranteed not to be a network address.*

On closer inspection, a GUID is a 16-byte number, usually expressed as a series of 32 hex digits in the so-called "portable format," such as *{37D341A5-6B82-101B-A4E3-08002B291EED}*. The individual "fields" within this notation, just as those in the GUID structure itself, have no pertinent meaning alone, and the number should always be considered in its entirety.

As I said earlier, every COM interface has an IID. A "class ID," or "CLSID" for short, is a GUID that identifies a type of OLE object. If you go back to the insect taxonomy of Chapter 1, then insect, wasp, fly, ant, and bee would all have CLSIDs. I'll show you where CLSIDs fit into the whole equation a little later.

REMOTING, MARSHALING, AND THE DISTRIBUTION OF INTERFACES

One of the most notable things about OLE is the relative ease with which the implementation of an interface can be "remoted." This means that the interface implementation lives and executes on a different machine from its user. Distributed COM, or "OLE Network," is the realization of this mechanism.

Microsoft Corporation has always promised that objects and object users written now will require no change to become remotable. This is a fairly easy promise to keep, because COM and OLE were designed that way. There are, of course, a whole host of problems involved in getting an interface exposed on one machine and implemented on another. As OLE Network is not useful for OLE controls, this sidebar does little more than introduce the concepts and explain the basic workings.

An interface method call is nothing more than a function call. So, by making each interface method call into an RPC (remote procedure call) client proxy (if you like, a "fake" interface implementation), the parameters can be put onto the network in standard DCE (distributed computing environment) RPC format and transmitted to the server. The server then has an RPC stub, which calls the real interface on the real object. Any return values are returned to the stub, which moves them onto the network and returns them to the client via its proxy.

This process means that the user of an interface has no notion that the interface implementation is remote, except that it typically takes rather longer to execute a given method call. Likewise, the implementation of the interface has no knowledge of the fact that its caller actually lives on a different machine. Clearly, there's nothing stopping the interface user and interface implementation from executing on different processor architectures, or even on entirely different operating systems.

(continued)

(continued)

This is a radically simple explanation of how the process works. The point is that COM supports the concept and, with OLE Network, the reality of remote interface implementations. This facility is not limited to Microsoft-defined interfaces, either. The tools exist to allow new, programmer-defined interfaces to be remoted. It isn't a difficult job: the only real step is to define the interface in a way that is meaningful to the remoting code. This "interface description file" is created using an extension of the "object description language (ODL)," which I describe later in this chapter and which is used throughout the book.

Note that Microsoft makes no attempt to remote the Windows interface itself. Therefore, it is not possible to embed an Excel chart in a Word document if Excel is not executing on the same machine on which Word is running. (There are rumors that third parties will offer such support.)

One of the fundamentals of remotable interfaces, which is highly pertinent to OLE even without remoting, is something known as "marshaling." This is getting data between processes (and therefore potentially onto the network) in a standard format so that it can be "unmarshaled" and understood at the other end. Marshaling is required for all interfaces (barring a few minor exceptions), whether remoted or not, because the mechanism OLE uses to communicate between local processes is a form of RPC called "LRPC" (for "lightweight remote procedure call"). Most of the time, marshaling is handled by the system automatically.

You can elect to take over responsibility for marshaling, if you so choose, in which case you are implementing "custom marshaling." You also need to provide marshaling for any interfaces you define. Tools exist for 32-bit OLE that take the interface description file mentioned above and derive proxies and stubs from it; these proxies and stubs also contain standard marshaling and unmarshaling code. The 16-bit version of OLE requires that you code any custom marshaling yourself. We don't do any custom marshaling in this book.

HRESULTs AND SCODEs

I've mentioned in passing that interface methods, and indeed COM and OLE APIs themselves, can return status values. By convention, interface methods have a return type of "HRESULT" (with a few exceptions, such as *IUnknown::AddRef* and *IUnknown::Release*). HRESULT is a "handle to a result" whose actual value should not be interpreted in any way other than that zero indicates success. Actual error and status values are held as SCODEs (status codes). An "SCODE" is a 32-bit value with three fields: the status code itself (16 bits), the facility (that is, the component in which the error occurred), and the severity (success or failure). Each of the system-defined SCODEs is defined in the WINERROR.H header file.

NOTE   Unlike its 32-bit relation, 16-bit OLE is not part of the operating system. Therefore, 16-bit OLE defines standard codes and facilities in the SCODE.H header file that comes with the 16-bit OLE version 2.0x SDK and with 16-bit Microsoft Visual C++. It also defines each set of SCODEs in a header file relevant to the specific OLE technology. For example, OLE Automation SCODEs are defined in the DISPATCH.H header file.

Components that are not (yet) part of the system and that define SCODEs typically provide a header file with the appropriate definitions.

OLE provides a number of functions and macros to deal with SCODEs and HRESULTs. *GetScode* takes an HRESULT and returns the SCODE it references. *ResultFromScode* does the opposite. *SUCCEEDED* and *FAILED* are macros that test an SCODE to see whether it represents a successful or failed operation. *MAKE_SCODE* is used to create custom SCODEs.

Although HRESULTs are described as result handles, implying at least an opacity and potentially a level of indirection, current OLE implementations actually store the SCODE directly in the HRESULT itself, which is also a 32-bit value. The 32-bit OLE version has taken this further, in that SCODE and HRESULT are now regarded as synonyms and the macros described above do absolutely nothing. For compatibility with 16-bit code, stick with the macros, but bear in mind that SCODE means HRESULT means SCODE—that is, SCODE is the dominant synonym!

Most of the SCODEs you'll use are those defined for OLE Controls; these are in the OLECTL.H header file.

MY FIRST INTERFACE POINTER

Now I get to answering the crucial question: "How do you get hold one of these interface pointers?" The answer depends on where you're coming from. If you're writing in Visual Basic, for example, you might execute code such as

```
Dim MyIP As Object
Set MyIP = CreateObject("MyApp.MyClass.1" )
```

These two lines of code hide a fair number of steps, and they will only retrieve a pointer to a specific interface, *IDispatch*, from the object. (Actually, *IDispatch* is the object's "default programmability interface," but I haven't been through these niceties yet.) *IDispatch* is an interface used for OLE Automation, which is highly significant for OLE controls. Let's walk through the steps that Visual Basic, the OLE system, and the object will take when together they execute these lines of code. Handily, these are the same steps you might take if you were trying to obtain the interface pointer through C or C++:

1. (Visual Basic) Create a variable of type *Object* called *MyIP*.

2. (Visual Basic) Look up *MyApp.MyClass.1* in the registry under *HKEY_CLASSES_ROOT*. If not found, this fails now; otherwise, extract the value of the CLSID key for this entry from the registry.

3. (Visual Basic) Call *CoCreateInstance* with the CLSID retrieved above and the IID for *IDispatch* ({00020420-0000-0000-C000-000000000046}, just in case you care!).

4. (OLE) Call *CoGetClassObject* with the given CLSID and the IID for *IClassFactory*. If this succeeds, the executable or DLL holding the object is now loaded and running.

5. (Object) Call *CoRegisterClassObject* to tell OLE that its class factory is now available.

6. (OLE) Call *IClassFactory::CreateInstance* with the IID passed to *CoCreate-Instance*. If this succeeds, a pointer to the object's *IDispatch* interface has been created.

7. (OLE) Call *IClassFactory::Release* to release the pointer to object's *IClass-Factory* interface.

8. (Visual Basic) Store the returned *IDispatch* interface pointer in *MyIP*.

CoCreateInstance and *CoGetClassObject* are functions within the COM libraries (as the prepended *Co* signifies). I've left out some peripheral information, some of which I'll fill in later. I will, however, first explain what I mean by the registry and *IClassFactory*.

The Registry

The "registry" (or the "registration database" in Windows version 3.x is the systemwide database of information. This information is held under a number of keys; one of these, *HKEY_CLASSES_ROOT*, holds all the OLE-related information in which we're interested. The Windows 3.x registration database has only one root key, *HKEY_CLASSES_ROOT*; in Windows NT and in Windows 95, this key is actually a shortcut to *HKEY_LOCAL_MA-CHINE\SOFTWARE\Classes*.

For an OLE object to be used, it must first be registered in this systemwide database. Most applications, such as Microsoft Excel, do this during their installation and also ensure that the information is still there and accurate each time they're run.

When the OLE object lives in a DLL, as OLE controls do, the story's slightly different, as I'll show.

Each registered class has a key under *HKEY_CLASSES_ROOT* that holds, among other things, the CLSID and the name of the executable and/or DLL holding the object. (See Figure 2-4.) There is also a *CLSID* key under *HKEY_CLASSES_ROOT*, which contains all the CLSIDs in the system. There's also an *Interface* key, which holds the IIDs of all the interfaces known about (both those provided by OLE itself and those from applications). Paths to entries in the registry are generally expressed as if they were directories, so the CLSID for an object would be expressed as *HKEY_CLASSES_ROOT\CLSID\{...}*. As you discover more about OLE generally and OLE controls in particular, you'll be looking more closely at what's held in the registry.

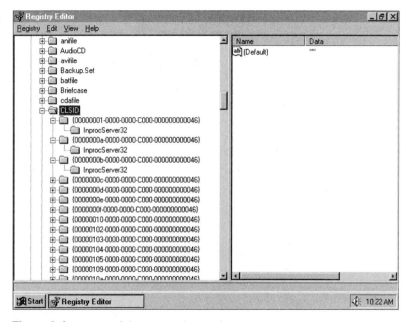

Figure 2-4.   *Some of the registry hierarchy.*

In my scenario above, Visual Basic has examined the registry and found my object there. It has extracted the CLSID and passed this onto the COM API function *CoCreateInstance* along with the IID of the interface to which it wants a pointer — *IDispatch*. *CoCreateInstance* then calls *CoGetClassObject*, whose function is to find the object and load it and to ask for a pointer to the passed-in IID. In almost all cases, the looked-for IID will be that of *IClassFactory*, the OLE interface for object creation. When determining where the object's executable or DLL lives, the OLE libraries look for the keys *LocalServer, LocalServer32, InProcServer* and *InProcSer-ver32* in the registration database under *HKEY_CLASSES_ROOT\CLSID\{my class ID}*. The *LocalServer* keys refer to the object as an executable file while the *InProcServer* keys refer to it as a DLL. There will be values in each respective key if the object exists in that form. For example, if the object comes only as a 32-bit DLL, only the *InProcServer32* key will have a value. The other keys might not even be present. (In fact, they generally won't be.)

Because a DLL is in the same process as the program using it, communication between an "inproc server" (in-process server — the OLE colloquialism for objects implemented as DLLs) and its client will be much faster than that between a local server and its client, which would have to instigate a "context-switch" for each communication. A context switch is what happens when the operating system switches from one executing task to another, and it's generally an expensive (time-consuming) operation. Consequently, OLE always tries to resolve an object to its DLL version first; if this fails, it then tries the executable. In a 32-bit environment such as Windows 95, a 16-bit object client can talk to either a 16-bit or 32-bit object server, and a 32-bit client can speak to either a 32-bit or a 16-bit object. Neither side of a conversation cares about the type of the other side, so all this is invisible. Note that some combinations are not possible: for example, Win32 won't load a 16-bit DLL into a 32-bit executable's process space, so a 16-bit in-process server cannot be used by a 32-bit client. However, 16-bit processes can communicate successfully with 32-bit in-process servers, except through the *IDispatch* interface.

IClassFactory

IClassFactory is the secondmost fundamental of COM interfaces. It serves as a gateway to any interface on a given class. When you call *CoGetClassObject* to retrieve a pointer to a given object's *IClassFactory* interface, you're not really getting the object itself. Even though the code for the object is now (probably) in memory, all you actually have is a pointer to an interface whose sole job is to create an instance of the thing that implements the interface you really want. In many cases, this thing is a C++ class.

In addition to the *IUnknown* methods, *IClassFactory* introduces another two methods, *CreateInstance* and *LockServer*:

```
class IClassFactory : public IUnknown
{
public:
    HRESULT CreateInstance ( LPUNKNOWN pUnkOuter, REFIID iid,
        LPVOID *ppvObj );
    HRESULT LockServer ( BOOL fLock );
};
```

CreateInstance is the COM equivalent of the C++ *new* operator; it creates a new object and returns a pointer to the requested interface on that object. I'll ignore the first parameter to *CreateInstance* for now. The second parameter is a reference to the

IID you want; in my Visual Basic scenario, it's the IID for *IDispatch*. The third parameter is a pointer to a location in which to store the newly allocated interface pointer.

CreateInstance can of course fail, for a variety of reasons. Either something went wrong when the new object was created (for example, because of a lack of memory), or the requested interface is not supported by the object. The status of the call is returned as its result.

LockServer is an optimization routine that enables faster dynamic creation of objects of a particular class. It is used to hold the application providing the object in memory, even if instances of the object might not exist at the time. This saves the system having to load the executable or DLL each time a new object of that class is created. Earlier in this chapter, I said that provision of an interface is a guarantee that the interface as a whole is implemented. *LockServer* is often implemented so as to perform no operation at all. In this rare case, this does <u>not</u> mean that the contract is broken. First, the method exists. Second, it exhibits the correct semantics in that it allows, from a conceptual standpoint, the object server to be locked. It doesn't matter that it doesn't actually perform any physical operation. No caller of *LockServer* is in a position to determine, or care, whether it causes the server to be locked in memory or not. Therefore, the only side effect of not providing true *LockServer* functionality is that each creation of a given object can take a little longer than if *LockServer* were "correctly" implemented.

IClassFactory2

The OLE Controls specification introduces a new variant to the *IClassFactory* interface, *IClassFactory2*. The two interfaces are the same except that *IClassFactory2* supports licensing. This is discussed in Chapter 16, and it's a fine example of the contractual nature of interfaces. The OLE Controls team determined that they required extra functionality from the class factory object to support licensing. As *IClassFactory* is defined already, it can't be changed, so they had to create the new interface, *IClassFactory2*.

USING OTHER OBJECTS — CONTAINMENT

In Chapter 1, I discussed the virtues of object-oriented programming, and of <u>inheritance</u>, which is one of its main beneficial features. Inheritance, as discussed there, is the ability to be given the features of a given class by deriving a new class from it. This is clearly a development benefit rather than a user benefit — the user doesn't care how something is done, so long as it works. Well, COM and OLE don't provide inheritance. Inheriting from a runtime object has a number of inherent (pun not intended!) problems that the designers of OLE decided to avoid. One of the problems oft quoted is that of "fragile base classes." If you inherit, you rely upon the interfaces from which you inherit remaining the same, or at least compatibly different. This is not easy to do, as the future can never be predicted. (An example of such unpredictability is the addition of the *IClassFactory2* interface to the OLE Controls specification.)

COM comes with its own solution to the problem: containment through aggregation. "Aggregation" has occurred when an existing object is taken and incorporated into a new object. The outside world sees only one object, with whatever interfaces it decides to support. Some of those interfaces could be ones supported by the aggregated object; others will be those supported by the aggregating object. Still others may be composite. There is an example of this with OLE controls in the next chapter.

An object can aggregate any number of other objects; likewise, an aggregated object might itself be an aggregate. Now, if one object contains another in this way, what happens when a *QueryInterface* call is made on one of the object's interfaces? Clearly, without further work, if the exposed interface is one of the containing object's interfaces, you'll end up with a pointer to an interface on the containing object; if the interface is one on the contained object, you'll receive a pointer to an interface on the contained object. This becomes particularly undesirable when both the contained and containing objects are able to provide the same interface type (for example, they both support *IDispatch*).

Aggregation solves this problem with a simple rule: all external interfaces on the contained object, excluding *IUnknown*, must delegate all three *IUnknown* methods to the containing object. This containing object is known as the "control object," and its *IUnknown* implementation for the aggregate is known as the "controlling unknown." The controlling unknown is the only implementation of *IUnknown* exposed outside the object. When the control object instantiates the controlled object, it passes a pointer to its controlling unknown interface to the controlled object. This is the purpose of the first parameter to *IClassFactory::CreateInstance*. If this parameter is not *NULL*, the object being created is being created as part of an aggregate. If it does not support aggregation, it should fail the *CreateInstance*; otherwise, it should hold this pointer to the controlling unknown internally and use it to delegate each interface's *IUnknown* methods except those on its own *IUnknown* implementation.

The controlled object typically stores the pointer to the controlling unknown in a local variable, putting a pointer to its own *IUnknown* there if it is not being aggregated. By dereferencing this local pointer, it can use the same code whether or not it is being aggregated.

The control object decides which of the controlled object's interfaces are exposed to the outside world. It can also combine its interfaces with those of the controlled object's in order to present a composite interface to the outside world.

This discussion has focused on the control of one object by another. This is not a limit: objects can aggregate any number of other objects, and these objects can themselves be aggregated. An object can decide, however, whether or not it wants to be aggregated.

OLE AUTOMATION AND *IDISPATCH*

I've mentioned OLE Automation before; it's the ability to program an object externally through OLE facilities. It's designed primarily for use by high-level languages such as Visual Basic and application macro languages (which, for Microsoft, means Visual Basic and variants on the theme thereon!), although it can equally be used by C and C++ programs. The clients of automation are described as "OLE Automation controllers." OLE Automation is a cornerstone of OLE controls, so we need to study it in depth. This chapter covers it in much the same depth as the rest of OLE and COM, while the next chapter takes it a great deal further and actually includes coding examples. You don't need to read Chapter 3 if you merely want to know what automation is about, but it is educational if you would like to know how it works.

Object Exposure Through Properties, Methods, and Events

The first premise of OLE Automation is that an object exposes itself through automation as a series of properties, methods, and events. Here are some working definitions:

■ A "property" means an attribute, such as a color, the zip-code section or the postal-code section of an address, or another object.

■ A "method" in automation terms means the same as it does elsewhere; it is a request to an object to perform an action.

■ An "event" is a notification from an object that something has happened; it is very similar to a method call except that it occurs from the object to its user. (I won't cover events again in this chapter, as the mechanism that supports them is described in the next chapter. However, it is important to note the way events fit into the automation family, because they are described to a user of an object through type libraries and are generally invoked through an automation mechanism.)

Properties clearly have types; the postal-code section of an address can be a string, for example, or a long integer, depending on the country in which you're living. Properties can also be parameterized, which can be useful if you have an array of one type representing a collection of properties (for example, the lines of an address). A parameter would then be defined for that property; this parameter represents the index into the array of the individual property value being read or written. Methods can also take parameters and can return results.

OLE Automation allows for hierarchies of automation objects by allowing methods and properties to return pointers to other objects. So, for example, you might envisage a customer object that has as one of its attributes the customer's address. Rather than exposing each element of the address as properties, the customer object exposes the address itself as a programmable object through OLE Automation. This object in turn then provides properties for each address line, for the postal code, the county/state, and so forth. Further, as the address is an object in its own right, it can be asked through one of its methods to perform address-specific actions such as postal-code validation. The address object then becomes reusable elsewhere.

OLE Automation is really best defined as the standard mechanism through which OLE allows an object to define its properties, methods, and types and to provide access to them. The standard interface that can be used for automation is *IDispatch*. This is used by most existing OLE Automation controllers, as it is the first mechanism that was provided and is eminently suited to high-level languages such as Visual Basic. OLE Automation, however, also supports the concept of a "dual interface," which has *IDispatch* methods and normal interface methods. Both of these are described in the following sections of this chapter.

Fundamental to OLE Automation is the way in which an object publishes information about itself — via so-called "type libraries." Type libraries are vital to the operation of OLE Controls and are also examined in much greater detail in the next section.

OLE Automation Through *IDispatch*

As I said, an object's properties and methods can be exposed to the outside world through *IDispatch*, the OLE Automation interface. *IDispatch* does <u>not</u> expose each object method as one of its own methods; instead it provides access to object methods and properties through its *Invoke* method.

In addition to the *IUnknown* methods, *IDispatch* has four methods: *GetIDsOf-Names*, *GetTypeInfo*, *GetTypeInfoCount*, and *Invoke*. If you take the Visual Basic code sample from the beginning of the chapter, which extracted an *IDispatch* interface from an object, you can read an automation property's value from the object as follows:

```
MsgBox (MyIP.SomeProperty)
```

This will ask the object whose *IDispatch* pointer is stored in *MyIP* to return the value of its property named *SomeProperty*. Visual Basic will then display it. Here are the steps:

1. (Visual Basic) Call *MyIP::GetIDsOfNames* to find the dispid (dispatch identifier) for *SomeProperty*. If this fails, the object doesn't have a property called *SomeProperty*, so Visual Basic throws a runtime error.

2. (Visual Basic) Call *MyIP::Invoke* with the dispid for *SomeProperty*.

3. (Visual Basic) If this succeeds, display the value; otherwise, Visual Basic throws an error based on the exception returned by the *Invoke* call.

IDispatch::GetIDsOfNames is the function that allows automation through *IDispatch* to support late binding. Later you'll see that type libraries provide early binding information. Here, "late binding" means that an automation controller determines whether a property or method exists at runtime, while "early binding" means that the invocation's correctness is checked at compile-time. Both have their benefits: early binding is safer, as property and method names, parameters, and so forth are checked prior to the code being executed, while late binding will result in runtime errors if an unrecognized property or method is used or if incorrect parameters are passed. Late binding, however, allows a program to determine the capabilities of objects dynamically, so a program can be written for a given set of objects but will in fact be able to use additional objects of which it previously had no knowledge. Visual Basic version 3.0 supported only late binding, while subsequent versions understand type libraries and therefore support early binding as well.

Dispatch IDs (dispids)

Although to the high-level-language programmer it seems as if OLE Automation objects allow reference to their methods and properties by name, the objects are in fact called by numeric identifier. This numeric identifier is known as the "dispatch ID," or "dispid" of the property or method. Likewise, parameters can be named; however, the automation controller passing the parameters must first convert the names into parameter dispids. *GetIDsOfNames* is the *IDispatch* method that converts between a human-readable name and the internal dispid assigned to that name by the OLE Automation object's creator. Each call to *GetIDsOfNames* can convert one property or method name and any number of parameter names (to the given property or method) to their dispids. *GetIDsOfNames* fills an array passed by the caller by reference with the dispids of all the names passed. If any of the names are not recognized by the automation object, the method returns *DISP_E_UNKNOWNNAME* and each unknown-name slot in the array is filled with *DISPID_UNKNOWN* (-1) rather than a dispid.

Why would parameters be named? Well, there is no need to name parameters to a method or property if all parameters are required — it's just a convenience. However, some automation objects allow themselves to accept an arbitrary number of a given set of parameters, in any order, and either ignore the missing parameters or give them default values. OLE Automation supports this through the concept of "named parameters," in which an automation controller allows the parameters to be specified by name rather than by the traditional "by position" method. This method invocation uses the standard method, where all the parameters to *MyMethod* are mandatory,

```
If MyIP.MyMethod (1, "Hello") = False Then...
```

The automation controller knows that the first parameter is the first in the list (*1* in this example) and that the second is second in the list (*"Hello"* in this example). It therefore doesn't need to get the parameters' dispids because it will pass them to *IDispatch::Invoke* by position. On the other hand, look at this code:

```
If MyIP.MyOtherMethod (String := "Hello") = False Then...
```

This no longer makes the assumption that *MyOtherMethod* has only one parameter, and the automation controller doesn't know where *MyOtherMethod* expects to find the parameter called *String* in its parameter list. Therefore, it needs to get the dispid for *String* and pass this to *Invoke*.

After a property or method and its named parameters, if any, are converted to dispids, the *IDispatch::Invoke* method is used actually to call the OLE Automation object. Notice that properties are implemented as function calls, as are methods. The implementation functions are marked internally as property functions rather than as methods — typically, two per property (one to get the property value and one to set it). Some automation controllers are in fact unable to distinguish between properties and methods.

IDispatch::Invoke calls an automation object's property and method functions. Among the parameters it takes, the important ones are

■ The dispid of the method or property being called

■ A pointer to the array of arguments to the method or property

■ A pointer to the location in which to store the result, if any

■ A pointer to an *EXCEPINFO* structure

The last one raises an interesting point. If *Invoke* returns *DISP_E_EXCEPTION*, it means that the called routine, or OLE, has raised an exception. In the OLE Automation context, an "exception" is a message from the called routine or OLE that says something is wrong. This could be as basic as one of the arguments being of the wrong type or out of range or it could be as complex as a network error notification. The *EXCEPINFO* structure contains a wealth of information about the exception for use by the caller. This includes a meaningful string describing the situation (note that the error string for object exceptions is provided <u>by the object</u>, the only logical place from which it can come); a Help filename and Help file context ID, so help on the error can be displayed by the calling application; and of course the error number or SCODE, which allows Basic-style *On Error Goto* statements. OLE Automation is targetted at scripting-type languages such as Visual Basic, so the information in the *EXCEPINFO* structure is vital. This is particularly true with late-bound objects, as late binding relies on the object or OLE throwing runtime errors.

The array of parameters passed to *Invoke* is actually an array of structures called *VARIANT*s. *VARIANT*s contain unions, which can take any type of data recognized by *IDispatch* (and therefore marshaled by it). The structure also contains a type field, which allows the type of data held in the union to be determined. Apart from giving *Invoke* a standard set of array elements to parse, *VARIANT*s also allow methods and properties to be written to accept varying types of parameters.

OLE Automation Through Dual Interfaces

IDispatch provides a highly flexible, easy-to-use interface to an object's properties and methods, which makes it ideal for use by high-level languages such as Visual Basic, but the cost of this flexibility and ease of use is speed. A call to an object's methods through *IDispatch::Invoke* is clearly going to be slower than a call to the method directly. Why? For a start, there's the extra function call, followed by the inefficiency of passing parameters and return values in *VARIANT*s when you might only want to pass an integer.

A higher-bandwidth interface to OLE Automation is therefore much in demand, which has led to the creation of the dual interface concept, where an object can present an interface that acts like a regular *IDispatch* interface to those OLE Automation controllers which expect that sort of behavior and as a custom interface to an automation controller that can deal with them. A custom interface in this context is simply an interface that happens to be derived from *IDispatch* and that has a set of functions over and above the *IDispatch* methods which the controller can call directly. These extra methods represent the property and method access functions of the object. The same type-library information describes both interface mechanisms, so it's still perfectly possible to use early binding or late binding with dual interfaces, whether using *IDispatch* or not.

As methods and properties invoked through a dual interface do not need to use *IDispatch*'s *Invoke* mechanism, a new error interface is exposed, which provides the same information as *Invoke*'s *EXCEPINFO* but must be called by the automation controller when a method call or property call reports that exception information is available.

Type Libraries

Earlier I briefly touched on the subject of type libraries and type information. A "type library" is a way of telling the outside world which properties and methods (and events) you support, which return types and parameter types they have, which dispids they use, and even which Help file and Help topic should be used to display information about the object and its properties and methods.

Type libraries are created by writing an "object description language" (ODL) text file and compiling it with the *MkTypLib* utility. Type libraries are used by OLE Automation controllers that want to support early binding and by tools that provide object-browsing capabilities (such as the object browser in Microsoft Excel). A good example of the early binding usage of a type library is the facility within Microsoft Visual C++'s ClassWizard that lets you take a type library and use it to create class definitions for "proxy objects" that represent the automation interfaces described. For example, if I created a type library for an automation object and read it in using ClassWizard, I'd get a Visual C++ source file defining a class for each automation object in the type library, with class member functions to access the methods and properties. Manipulation of this class in a Visual C++ program would (after the appropriate steps have been taken to connect the class instance to an instance of the real running object) result in manipulation of the object in the real object server. Hence the term proxy object.

Type libraries are the key part to OLE Automation, as they describe the interface(s) exposed by the object(s) in an application. The actual mechanisms for accessing those interfaces, such as *IDispatch* or through dual interfaces, are almost secondary in importance.

Type libraries are generally registered, as are OLE objects. There is a key under *HKEY_CLASSES_ROOT*, called *TypeLib*, subkeys of which are the GUIDs allocated to each type library. An object that implements a type library is likely to register that library and also to include a reference to it in its own registry entry. For example, the next chapter's *AutoProg* sample's *CLSID* entry might refer to its type library thus:

```
HKEY_CLASSES_ROOT\CLSID\{AEE97356-B614-11CD-92B4-
08002B291EED}\TypeLib = {4D9FFA38-B732-11CD-92B4-08002B291EED}
```

Type libraries can contain a great deal more information than this. Some of it you'll come across as you develop OLE controls throughout this book. Other aspects are not directly relevant to OLE controls; to find out more about them, read Chapter 7 onwards of the *OLE 2 Programmer's Reference, Volume Two* (Microsoft Press).

Type libraries have a number of OLE interfaces implemented to support them and their users. In particular, *ITypeLib* and *ITypeInfo* are used to query type libraries, and *ICreateTypeLib* and *ICreateTypeInfo* are used to create them. The *MkTypLib* utility uses the last two interfaces during its conversion of an ODL file to a type library.

GetTypeInfo and *GetTypeInfoCount*

If you remember that far back, you'll recall that I deferred the discussion of two *IDispatch* methods until I could discuss type libraries. Well, now that I have discussed type libraries, it seems we'll have to talk about these methods. The methods are *GetTypeInfo* and *GetTypeInfoCount*. *GetTypeInfoCount* returns the number of type descriptions in the *IDispatch*, and *GetTypeInfo* returns an *ITypeInfo* pointer for a given type description index.

With the addition of dual interfaces as a mechanism to use OLE Automation, ODL has been enhanced to support a few extra keywords. You can find out more about these by reading the OLE Automation section of the online help for the Win32 SDK released with Windows NT 3.51 and Windows 95.

OLE STRUCTURED STORAGE

There is a time in the lives of all computer users when they decide to stop what they're doing, close down their systems, and go home. Furthermore, it's quite likely that the next day, they'll come in, turn on their computers, and expect to be able to continue from where they left off the night before. Not an unreasonable expectation. Now, if the task being performed involves the use of components, as it increasingly will, how can these components save themselves?

The concept here is "object persistence," or the ability for an object to live while the computer is switched off. It has become common to describe an object as capable of "persisting itself," which, in addition to being a fine example of the crimes against the English language perpetrated by the computing fraternity, also means that the object can make itself persistent and therefore be used successfully from session to session. It is not actually accurate to describe the object as persistent, because code is clearly unable to execute while the computer is switched off. However, if the object is able to "persist" enough of its "state" (data) such that an object with exactly the same characteristics can be created at a later date, we have in effect a persistent object.

The ability to copy state from object to storage medium is often called "serialization," as it's taking whatever the object's internal structure happens to be and copying it out as a series of bytes to persistent storage. The fact that it has to be this way is a consequence of trying to save structured data in a flat (unstructured) file. Without application intelligence to interpret it, every Win32 or MS-DOS file is actually a flat file. This makes it very difficult for anything that is not aware of an application's file format to make any sense of one of its files, so browsers (and competitors' products!) traditionally have a fairly tough job. This can make the application writer's job pretty difficult, as inserting or removing blocks of data from flat files requires work. It also makes the concept of querying the data a little hard to implement.

The best solution is an object-oriented file system. This comes in the next major version of Windows NT, code-named "Cairo." Right now, though, we need a solution that works for existing file systems. OLE's answer to this is known as "structured storage." The OLE model provides the capability to treat a standard file as a file system in its own right, with the analogs of directories and files. OLE refers to the directories in a structured storage as "storages" and the files as "streams." Storages and streams are named, just like directories and files, and even have individual access rights, a feature missing for directories in MS-DOS (but present in Win32). The corresponding interfaces through which these storages and streams are manipulated are *IStorage* and *IStream*, and objects that want to be persistent will implement *IPersistStorage* or will make use of the OLE-implemented *IPersistSteam* interface if they have truly basic requirements. By implementing one of the interfaces underlying structured storage, *ILockBytes*, it is also possible to have the data stored and retrieved from places other than a file.

Most of the responsibility for opening, maintaining, and closing storages and streams rests with the applications that use objects (rather than with the objects themselves). Think of it this way: if a Microsoft Word document has a Microsoft Excel chart embedded within it, then when it saves its data file it needs to ensure that the Excel chart is also saved into the same file. It does this by opening the file through structured storage, writing its data to the file in whatever combination of storages and streams it deems appropriate, and then passing an *IStorage* to Excel and asking it to save its object onto that storage. All Excel needs to do is create any substorages it requires and then save its data into streams within these storages.

Because scenarios like this are so common, OLE provides a few functions to automate most of the process. *OleSave*, for example, can be called by an application to save each of the objects embedded within it. *OleSave* takes a pointer to the object's *IPersistStream* interface, a pointer to the *IStorage* onto which the object is to store itself, and a flag saying whether this *IStorage* is the same as the one from which it was originally loaded. The use of structured storage for this sort of operation, where what is being saved is conceptually a document comprised of different parts, has led to the use of the term "compound file."

There's more to structured storage than merely the mechanism to treat files as file systems in their own right. *IStorage* and *IStream* interface pointers can be passed from process to process, thereby providing a means of sharing data between applications. But there's even more....

Structured Storage and Transactions

One of the key benefits of OLE's structured storage model is that it allows operations to be "transacted." This means that changes can be made to a storage or stream but not actually committed to physical storage, so the changes can be undone if required. Each individual storage can be transacted, which means that changes can be done and undone at will. To make the change permanent, *IStorage::Commit* needs to be called; to throw away the changes, *IStorage::Revert*. Transactions in nested storages raise interesting issues: if an inner storage commits, nothing is written to a physical disk until the outermost storage also commits. If the outermost storage doesn't commit, even committed substorages are lost. It is perfectly possible to have some storages in a given hierarchy open in transacted mode and some open in direct mode. Direct mode means that the changes made are the changes made, with no option for reversal! By the way, although the *IStream* interface also has *Commit* and *Revert* methods, current OLE implementations don't support transacted streams.

Structured Storage and OLE Controls

The requirements placed on structured storage by OLE controls are normally pretty light. Mostly, a control wants only to make its properties persistent, and even then it will probably select only those few that make sense to keep around between sessions. Controls can therefore implement *IPersistStorage* so that applications making use of a control can ask that control to save its property values. As OLE controls use structured storage merely for property persistence, they do not need to use the extra functionality offered by storages and can usually save quite happily to a stream. The *IPersistStream* interface offered by OLE, however, is not always quite good enough for a control's needs. Controls can therefore implement a new interface, *IPersistSteamInit*, which the application containing the control should use if it's present. It isn't sensible to explain why now, so I'll wait until Chapter 3 to discuss what *IPersistStreamInit* is and why OLE controls need this new interface.

OLE DOCUMENTS

To most users of desktop applications, the main benefit of OLE is the ability to put objects created by one application into documents created by another. The example I used in the structured-storage section is a classic example of this — a Microsoft Word document containing a Microsoft Excel chart. Why is this important to the user? Because it allows the user to create complex documents using information in a variety of formats and from a range of sources. If the applications that create these different data types could also allow them to be edited in a uniform way, the user sees the benefit of closer integration, even between products from different vendors. Eventually, we'll get to the point where the user is effectively unaware of what applications are being used to create different parts of a document. OLE helps to achieve this.

Visual Editing

The part of OLE that deals with embedding, linking, and editing objects is generically called "OLE Documents," and it contains a few subcategories that deal with specific document-centric functionality. For example, after an Excel chart is embedded in a Word document, it can be edited from within Word by double-clicking on it. Unlike the first version of OLE, this doesn't launch a copy of Excel and copy the chart into it, making the user painfully aware of using two different applications. OLE provides the ability for the two applications to work together so that the user can edit the chart in place. The toolbars and menu choices required by the object-providing application (Excel) are merged with those of the object-containing application (Word), so the user can make use of the tools relevant to the thing being edited rather than the application that happens to contain this object. The two applications actually negotiate about what goes where, so it's possible for almost all the menus and toolbars to change to reflect the object-providing application. Likewise, it's possible for only a couple of new menu options to be added. This ability to edit a contained object in situ is called "OLE Documents Visual Editing."

Currently, OLE Documents is without doubt the most complex part of OLE, yet it is only one relatively small part of the OLE picture. It is the part of OLE that confused programmers in the past, giving them the impression that all of OLE programming is difficult. As I show in the next chapter, it's perfectly possible to write an OLE-enabled application that knows nothing of OLE Documents and that, as a result, is extremely simple. However, I do need to look at OLE Documents because many of the features it provides are used by OLE Controls. First, let's sort out some terminology:

Term	*Meaning*
Container	An application that allows objects to be embedded within it (for example, Microsoft Word).
Object Application	An application that provides objects that can be embedded within containers; sometimes called "object servers."
Embedding	A container "embeds" an object when it provides the persistent storage for the entire object (therefore, for its data); there is no separate file owned by the object application. (In my example, the Microsoft Excel chart is embedded within the Word document if that document contains the only instance of the chart.)
Linking	A container "links" an object when it holds only a reference to the object; generally, this reference will be to a filename that holds the object. Linking allows many different containers to use information from one object and also allows updates to the object to be reflected in all containers using the object.
Compound Documents	Documents containing linked and/or embedded objects from a variety of sources, not only from the application that owns the document. Document is a metaphor: it applies just as well to a spreadsheet, source file, card file, and so forth.

Compound Documents

Now let's get to the heart of the matter. Suppose my user who has embedded the Excel chart into the Word document now saves that document and goes home. What's saved? As you've probably guessed from the structured-storage section, Word uses storages and streams to save its documents as compound files. One of these storages will have been given to Excel by Word when the document was saved, and Excel would then have created its own set of storages and streams within this outer storage and saved its information.

Something else is also saved, though, because when my user comes back to work the next day and reloads the document in Word, he can still see the Excel object even though he knows Excel hasn't been loaded. (He's a very perceptive user.) As it would clearly consume memory and time to load every object application to which embeddings or links exist in a given compound document each time that document were opened, OLE Documents-aware applications typically don't. Instead, they keep a graphical rendition of the object, referred to as "presentation data," so that it can always be displayed. This rendition is typically a Windows metafile (at least), so the image can be displayed consistently on different screen resolutions and can also be printed. (Many embedded and linked objects provide other formats simultaneously.) The code that draws the object for the container when the object server is not active is called an "object handler." This is a DLL that is living in the same process as the container application and that is responsible for acting as the object server in certain areas when the real object server is not running.

MORE ABOUT OBJECT HANDLERS

OLE implements a default object handler, which most object servers will use. There are some cases, though, where an object server needs to use a custom object handler. The object server signifies this to OLE and to the container by including an *InProcHandler* and/or *InProcHandler32* key under the appropriate *HKEY_CLASSES_ROOT\CLSID\{...}* key. Object handlers are purely an optimization, as the container is calling a function in the same process space, and they are never needed by object servers that are themselves implemented as DLLs (in-process servers), because such servers themselves give the performance benefits of being in-process. However, in-process servers (and indeed, custom handlers) can make use of the default handler to simplify their own implementations.

So now the document is open and the user can see the Excel chart. The chart is said to be in the "loaded" state and, through the auspices of the object handler, the container can get pointers to various interfaces to draw and otherwise manipulate that chart. When the user wants to change the chart, he double-clicks on it. Now Word, via OLE, does try to invoke Excel. In the case of failure, he gets an error message and then returns to where he was. In the case of success, Excel is invoked and told that it's being executed for editing an embedded object. The container does this by putting the *Embedding* flag on Excel's command line. (Actually, whichever command-line flags Excel has put in the registry for this kind of invocation will get passed.) It then retrieves the data for its embedded object from the container and displays it. Exactly in what the object displays it can be quite a complex problem. Depending on the type of container and the type of object server, the display might be in an area of the container's document window, it might be in a window created by the container for the object, or it might be a window provided by the object. In this latter case, it's a window created by Excel. Excel then negotiates with Word to determine which toolbars and other graphic items it can place and where, and which menus and menu items it would like to be displayed by Word on its behalf.

At this point, Word is running and Excel is running; the object is said to be in the "running" state. If the user were to click on a part of Word's document window away from the embedded Excel object, Excel would relinquish control back to Word, and the toolbars and menus would return to Word's normal ones. Otherwise, all keypresses and mouse activity get sent to Excel by the container if they're not ones with which the container wants to deal. Excel is said to be "UI Active," where "UI" stands for "user interface." This is distinct from "Active," when the server is running but doesn't own the toolbars and menus. (As I'll discuss in the next chapter, the distinction between these two states is important for OLE controls.)

I've shown that it is possible to view an embedded object whether or not the server for that object is running. The object can be edited only by executing the object server, logically enough. To get from the displayed state to the editable state, the user needs to double-click the object or select it and then choose an appropriate menu option (usually on the Edit menu) that UI-activates the object. This means that the object server is loaded only on user demand — when he wants to change the object's content. In OLE parlance, this is known as "outside-in" activation. To date, most object-container interactions have been outside-in, the rationale being that object servers are relatively slow to load and it would be cumbersome to load all object servers as soon as a document is opened.

The OLE designers knew that time would bring with it OLE objects that are a great deal more lightweight than Excel or Word. They also knew that there would be circumstances in which an object should be "alive" as soon as its rendition is visible. To cater to these needs, OLE also supports "inside-out" activation. OLE controls depend on inside-out activation. A control needs to be active as soon as it is displayed because it needs to react to user actions immediately and because it might want to send "events" to its container asynchronously of any user action. Further, a control needs to be able to respond to key and mouse presses immediately, rather than having to wait to be double-clicked first. (It would be a pretty useless button that needed to be double-clicked before it could react to itself being clicked!)

FYI   OLE controls written in this book are all OLE in-process servers (DLLs), which support inside-out activation. (This allows me to derive the awful pun used in the title of the book.) Although an object might want to be activated inside-out, not all containers support it. Therefore, it might be possible to embed an OLE control into an older OLE container application, but it might not prove very useful. Containers written prior to the release of the OLE Controls specification will also of course be unaware of the other features of OLE controls, such as events, so they'll also be unable to take advantage of them.

Linked Objects

The discussion of how objects and containers cooperatively deal with embedded objects applies, almost unchanged, to linked objects as well. From the user's perspective, a linked object behaves very much like an embedded object. However, whereas an embedding contains all the information about the object, a link maintains only the presentation data and a reference to the data source. When the server application needs to be activated, OLE uses this data source information to determine which server application to run and where to find the file to be loaded into it.

An interesting difference between embedded and linked data is that embedded data gets changed only by the user of the document containing it — it's the only data store — whereas a linked object can be altered by anyone who has access to the linked file. This means that the presentation data stored with the link information might well be out of date when the link is activated.

Drag and Drop

Another facet of OLE Documents is the ability to "drag and drop" something from one place to another, such as from an Excel chart to a Word document. I hear you ask, "What's this got to do with OLE?" Well, it's true, drag and drop can certainly be implemented without the help of OLE, as it has been in the File Manager of Microsoft Windows 3.1. This allows files to be dragged from File Manager and dropped on any window that has registered itself as a drop target. That window then receives a WM_DROPFILES message. Therein lies the key: this sort of drag and drop is very file-oriented and is difficult to use for more generic purposes. It's also pretty easy to implement drag and drop yourself, but this means that every application which wants to be able to have things dragged from it or dropped onto it has to support drag and drop in the manner in which you have defined it. Consequently, it makes sense to have a systemwide defined mechanism, and because OLE offers certain other features that prove useful to drag and drop, OLE is the mechanism through which Microsoft has provided drag-and-drop facilities.

"OLE Documents Drag and Drop," to give it its full title, allows dragging and dropping within an application's window, between windows in an application, and between applications. OLE drag and drop is basically the same as cut and paste but is more intuitive than the menu options and keypresses required by cut-and-paste actions. Because the clipboard can contain data in a wide variety of formats, including user-defined, OLE drag and drop is far more useful than that provided by File Manager. As drag and drop is very document-centric, it's considered to be part of the OLE Documents group.

Drag and drop is easy to implement. If you're wanting to be a drag-and-drop source, from which users can drag items to drop elsewhere, you need to implement the *IDropSource* interface. You also need to support *IDataObject*, which we'll look at a little later. To accept items dragged on to you, you need to implement *IDropTarget*, and you need to understand how to use an *IDataObject* pointer.

IDropSource has two methods over and above the *IUnknown* ones: *QueryContinueDrag* and *GiveFeedback*. *QueryContinueDrag* is called when the user drops the data or takes actions that might cancel the drag, and *GiveFeedback* is called to allow the source application to specify which cursors to draw as the item is dragged. If that's all *IDropSource* does, how does the receiving application know what's being dropped? Well, when a drop source initiates a drag and drop, it calls the OLE API function *DoDragDrop*. This API function takes a pointer to the source's *IDataObject* interface, a pointer to its *IDropSource* interface, and a set of flags saying what sort of operations it allows.

Applications that wish to receive drops will have registered themselves with calls to *RegisterDragDrop* for each window that is to be a target. This OLE API function takes a window handle and a pointer to the *IDropTarget* interface. The *IDropTarget* methods will then get called when a drag-and-drop operation occurs. Certain of these calls — *DragEnter*, *DragOver*, and *DragLeave* — are called as the mouse pointer is moved over the target window. If a drop actually occurs over one of these windows, the *IDropTarget::Drop* method is called for the window in question. This method is called with a pointer to the *IDataObject* implementation of the dragged object.

OLE Document Interfaces

OLE Document interfaces are composed almost entirely of those whose names begin with "IOle." The available set includes *IOleAdviseHolder, IOleCache, IOleCache2, IOleCacheControl, IOleClientSite, IOleContainer, IOleInPlaceActiveObject, IOleInPlaceFrame, IOleInPlaceObject, IOleInPlaceSite, IOleInPlaceUIWindow,*

IOleItemContainer, *IOleLink*, *IOleObject*, and *IOleWindow*! In addition to these, I need to consider *IDataObject* (again!), and there's a whole host of others I could choose to look at.

I'm <u>not</u> going to examine all these interfaces in detail. However, when you're examining OLE Documents, there are two sides to consider: the objects that allow themselves to be embedded and/or linked and the containers that allow things to be embedded within them. Both sides of the divide need to do a lot of work and need to communicate with each other a great deal to get visual editing to work.

Let's take it from the container side first. One way or another, the user is going to want to embed an object into a container document. (Bear in mind that "document" here is definitely a metaphor and, for the purposes of controls, might be more accurately referred to as "forms.") There are many ways to do this: ones that come to mind are dragging from another window (perhaps in another application), pasting from the clipboard, reading from existing file on disk, and selection through a dialog box. In the end, these all amount to much the same process, and I'm going to focus on the last — a selection dialog box that allows the user to pick and choose which object to insert.

The selection dialog box would typically be the standard OLE Insert Object dialog box that can be seen in numerous container applications (such as in any Microsoft Office product — Word, Excel, Access, and so forth). How is this dialog box populated? As you've probably guessed, OLE uses the font of all knowledge about objects, the registry, to determine which objects are known by the system. Just because a class is registered, however, does not mean that it appears in this dialog box. So how does OLE know? It certainly doesn't go around instantiating all object classes in the system merely to ask them whether they support OLE Document interfaces. Instead, OLE defines a registry key, *Insertable*, which, if present under the *HKEY_CLASSES_ROOT\CLSID\{...}* key for a particular object server, means that the object server supports creation of its objects through the OLE Documents interfaces — and thus it can appear legitimately in the Insert Objects dialog box.

When an object is chosen from this list, the container can attempt to instantiate it in the normal way via a call to *CoCreateInstance*. Alternatively, OLE provides an API function, *OleCreate*, which does this and a lot more besides. Generally, containers will choose to use *OleCreate*. This takes some parameters similar to *CoCreateInstance*, such as the CLSID being requested (retrieved from the Insert Object dialog box) and the REFIID of the required interface (generally, containers will ask for *IOleObject*). There's no place for a controlling unknown, though, because containers aren't expected to aggregate the objects they want to embed. Extra parameters tell OLE and the object how the container wants to render the object, and an *IStorage* interface pointer that is the storage to be used for the object. Finally, *OleCreate* takes a pointer to an *IOleClientSite* interface, which is used in a call to *IOleObject::SetClientSite* on the object being created. So what's a client site?

Basically, a "client site" is the means by which an embedded or linked object communicates with its container. The client site provides the object with context information, such as where the object is physically placed on the container's document, as well as any other container-related information it needs. The container must implement a client site for every object embedded or linked within it. I get to a subtle distinction here, because although I might naturally say something like "the container has a pointer to my object's *IOleObject* interface," that's actually wrong. The <u>client</u> <u>site</u> has the interface pointer. Why is this important? Because each client site is different and responsible for its object only. The container merely has responsibility for the sites.

You can define a basic container, capable of supporting embedded objects, as one that understands what sites mean in its context and implements the *IOleClientSite* interface. Containers must also implement at least *IAdviseSink*, which the object uses to tell it of changes to the data. Likewise, simple embeddable objects can be defined as those which implement <u>or provide</u> the *IOleObject*, *IDataObject*, *IOleCache*, *IPersistStorage*, and *IViewObject* interfaces. Why did I emphasize "or provide?" Because an object can delegate various of these interfaces to parts of OLE. *IViewObject*, for example, is often (that is, almost always) implemented by OLE's default handler located in OLE32.DLL (OLE2.DLL in Win16).

The basic responsibilities of each object-side interface are as follows:

Interface	*Purpose in Life*
IOleObject	The life and soul of the object. It forms a deep and meaningful relationship with the client site.
IDataObject	A way to get the data from the object in a format you want and that it provides.
IViewObject	Somewhat similar to *IDataObject*, but used to get drawings of the object rather than its data. Some methods of *IDataObject* are passed a Windows HDC (handle to a device context), which cannot be passed between processes. Therefore, *IViewObject* is unusual in that it cannot be marshaled and so cannot execute anywhere but in a DLL — another good reason why most servers delegate this interface to OLE's default handler!
IPersistStorage	The object side of structured storage. A container calls an object's *IPersistStorage* to get it to perform serialization operations on the *IStorage* passed.
IOleCache	*IOleCache* is implemented by OLE and used by objects to control which data is cached (kept around) in an embedded object and which data is available to the container when the server is not running.

OLE Documents containers and objects can use other interfaces to provide extra functionality. None of the interfaces in the above table, for example, has any dealings with visual editing or even in-place activation; the *IOleInPlace<thing>* set of interfaces are the ones that containers and object servers must implement to get this capability. And one interesting method, *IOleInPlaceActiveObject::Translate-Accelerator*, which is called on each in-place active object for each keypress received to give the embedded object(s) the chance to react to their accelerators. The first active object to accept the keypress stops the search. I single out this interface method because OLE Controls needs improvements on the *IOleInPlaceActiveObject* implementation.

OTHER OLE INTERFACES OF NOTE

To bring this chapter to a logical conclusion, I want to examine the remaining few OLE interfaces of note. I don't go into great detail here, as the information is interesting rather than vital. Some of these interfaces are used by or implemented by OLE Controls, but they are not as fundamental to it as they are, for example, to OLE Automation. The most important one is *IDataObject*, which I've mentioned many times before; however, I've deferred a description of it until now.

IDataObject

IDataObject is the key to an OLE facility called "uniform data transfer," or UDT. The premise here is that no matter how data is transferred, the mechanism should be the same. So, if data is dragged and dropped, copied via the clipboard, copied programatically by some other means or in any other way imaginable, the recipient of the data receives a pointer to an *IDataObject* implementation on the object providing the data. It then uses methods from this interface to retrieve the data.

IDataObject provides more functionality than the clipboard because it allows a richer set of data types to be transferred and it allows a wide variety of "transfer media" to be used. Two data structures are the key to *IDataObject*'s flexibility: *FORMATETC* and *STGMEDIUM*. The first, *FORMATETC* (pronounced "format et cetera"), defines the format in which the data can be retrieved from the *IDataObject*. Just as applications that write data to the clipboard can provide a number of formats simultaneously, so can an *IDataObject* provide a range of *FORMATETC*s at a time. Unlike clipboard data formats, however, *FORMATETC*s allow extra information to be provided, most notably, the target device for the format, if any, and the "aspect" of the data, where currently defined aspects are content (that is, everything), thumbnail (small representation), iconic, and printed document. The third piece of interesting information is the medium through which transfer should occur. This can be shared memory (through a global memory handle), a file, an *IStorage*, an *IStream*, a bitmap, or a metafile.

The second data structure of interest is *STGMEDIUM*, which is used to pass information about a transfer medium. This is a structure containing a flag saying what the medium actually is (as in the *FORMATETC* field discussed above), a union that can hold the relevant medium (say, a global handle, a bitmap handle, and an *IStream* pointer), and a pointer to an *IUnknown* that, if not *NULL*, should be called to release the storage (by calling *IUnknown::Release*).

IDataObject has the following methods of note:

Method	*Description*
GetData	The key to the interface. This method retrieves the object's data in a given format to a given medium.
GetDataHere	Similar to *GetData* except that it retrieves the data and puts the data into a medium supplied by the caller.
QueryGetData	Checks whether a call to *GetData* would succeed with a given *FORMATETC*.
EnumFormatEtc	Returns an enumerator to iterate over the formats in which a given *IDataObject* is prepared to send its data. The enumerator is a pointer to the *IEnumFORMATETC* interface.
DAdvise	Creates an advise link between the data object and something that wants to know when the data changes. The interested party passes to this method a pointer to its *IAdviseSink* interface. Data objects can accept more than one advise request at a time, so it is common to hold all the advises in a group through the *IDataAdviseHolder* interface.

IMoniker

Tony Williams, the chief architect of OLE, is English. (A personality trait I can personally recommend!) That's why Microsoft had to explain what "moniker" meant to a mostly American crowd at the OLE developers' conference in Seattle in May 1993. I'm also English, so to me a moniker is just what it is to Tony — a name for something. A handle, if you like.

OLE uses the term "moniker" to refer to an item that implements the *IMoniker* interface and that conceptually refers to a linked item. It is possible to use monikers for things other than links, such as for the call to *RegisterActiveObject* discussed in the OLE Automation section of this chapter, although this is really still a link because it's providing a mechanism for other OLE Automation controllers to get access to an existing running object.

Monikers are the mechanism through which link-tracking takes place. Rather than holding the name of the linked file in the container's storage, OLE holds one or more monikers. This set of monikers defines where the referred-to item lives. Links are often stored in terms of relative path and absolute path, so that in most circumstances the link source can still be found when moved.

Monikers come in a variety of flavors. These are the currently supported monikers:

- "Composite monikers" are a sequenced collection of other monikers.

- "File monikers" represent pathnames and always occur as the leftmost moniker in a composite.

- "Item monikers" refer to a specific item such as a spreadsheet range.

- "Anti-monikers" neutralize the effect of the moniker immediately to the left of them.

- "Pointer monikers" wrap real pointers.

The most common operation on a moniker, through its *IMoniker* interface, is to "bind" to it. This means getting hold of the thing to which it refers. *IMoniker::BindToObject*, for example, takes a moniker, runs the object to which it refers, and returns a pointer to the requested interface. *IMoniker::BindToStorage* does much the same except that it retrieves access to the object's storage.

As OLE control writers, monikers are not terribly important to us. They do, however, form an interesting aspect of OLE.

IRunningObjectTable

The "running object table," or ROT, is designed primarily to hold references to running objects so that moniker bindings to existing objects are resolved quickly. It can also be used as a general-purpose list of running OLE objects, bearing in mind that the only ones that appear there are those which so choose. The API function *GetRunningObjectTable* returns a pointer to an *IRunningObjectTable* interface, which can be used to add entries to and remove them from the ROT, as well as to check whether an object with a given moniker is running and to retrieve an "enumerator" (an *IEnumMoniker* interface pointer). This interface allows you to step through the entries in the ROT. There is of course also a method to retrieve an *IUnknown* pointer from an entry in the ROT.

Microsoft Visual C++ and the OLE SDK come with a tool called *IRotView*, which shows the content of the ROT dynamically.

IF YOU REALLY WANT TO KNOW MORE ABOUT OLE

This chapter has taken a fairly rapid journey through OLE-land, making many stops — but few stopovers. There is no requirement to know anything more about OLE: you can go off and write controls right now, if you want to, by skipping Chapter 3 and going straight to Chapter 4. On the other hand, if you're still itching for "the how," you'll want to read Chapter 3.

OLE Extensions for Controls

This chapter continues the theme of the previous one and takes it a step further by going into greater depth on those aspects of OLE and COM that specifically affect controls. It begins by diving into the implementation of a small OLE Automation sample program — <u>not</u> an OLE control — and then shows some structured storage features by adding to this program. The chapter then examines the OLE Controls architecture and looks at how OLE and COM have been extended to support the new features required. The word "extended" does not imply a new release of COM and OLE, or even a change to the standard COM and OLE DLLs. As I demonstrated in the previous chapter, extending OLE is a case of defining more interfaces and perhaps of providing extra DLLs for support of these new interfaces.

NOTE The Microsoft OLE Control Developer's Kit (OLE CDK), which will be discussed in Chapter 4, successfully hides a large number of the details of the OLE Controls architecture from us developers. Some of the things I'll cover in this book, however, will not make sense unless you understand the basic mechanics underlying them. If you're not interested in the underlying mechanics, skip now to Chapter 4. Otherwise, read this chapter because it walks through those mechanics, covering the salient points. A full description of the OLE Controls architecture can be found in the OLE CDK documentation.

THIS UNICODE THING

Most personal computer operating systems to date have been based on an 8-bit character set, usually the IBM PC character set or the ANSI character set. This is great if you're from any English-speaking country and not too bad if you're from a country that at least uses the same alphabet as the English language, with perhaps some additional weird characters like ÿ, Å, and É. If you're from a place that uses an entirely different character set, you need to wait for special versions of these operating systems to be built for you (such as the Far Eastern versions of Microsoft Windows) or you have to put up with using the English-language (US) version. These special versions use variable length characters called "MBCS" (multi-byte character sets).

For some time now, the Unicode consortium has been interested in developing a better multi-lingual solution. "Unicode" is the name of the character set that it came up with. Unicode characters are all 16-bit, making them on average faster to interpret than MBCS characters (because Unicode characters are fixed length) and giving space for up to 65,536 different characters to be represented.

Certain areas of the Unicode map are already reserved. For example, the characters with values 32 to 127 are equal to their ASCII equivalents. Others fulfill the needs of various Far Eastern languages, Cyrillic text, and so forth. The problem is, if nothing understands Unicode, how can it be used? Microsoft Corporation decided to support Unicode some time ago and decided that Windows NT would be implemented in its entirety as a Unicode-based system. This means that internally all characters and strings it deals with are Unicode and that all ASCII or ANSI strings passed to it are first converted to Unicode prior to being otherwise processed. All error messages, system-information messages, and so forth are also held as Unicode.

32-bit OLE is also Unicode-based. This is particularly intriguing when you consider that some variants of the Win32 API remain ANSI-based, such as that supplied with current versions of Windows 95. Nevertheless, OLE remains Unicode on these platforms. However, the OLE Automation sample program listings beginning on page 60 deliberately make no mention of Unicode and yet can be compiled for 16 bits and 32 bits and will run on all Win32 implementations. If I made a few slight changes to this program and recompiled it for Unicode, the program would then run only in 32-bit mode on Windows NT and would fail elsewhere. What is going on?

(continued)

(continued)

Well, 32-bit OLE provides an invisible wrapper to convert between ANSI and Unicode magically on the fly. Win32 platforms that don't support Unicode use this layer, and the application knows nothing of it. Such "wrapped" applications also run on Windows NT, again with the wrapping layer in place. Clearly, native Unicode OLE programs will run (slightly) faster on Windows NT than will wrapped programs, but they won't run anywhere else. The rule of thumb is to compile specifically for Unicode if your OLE application, whether container or object, is to run on Windows NT only. Otherwise, build for ANSI and think about supporting a Unicode build for Windows NT.

To build a Microsoft Visual C++ application for Unicode, follow these steps:

1. Be sure that any variables that would otherwise be *char* or *char ** or some variant thereof now use the type macros from WCHAR.H, such as *TCHAR* and *LPTSTR*. The MFC library's *CString* class is Unicode-enabled from MFC version 3.0 onwards, so there is no need to change *CString* variable declarations. These macros ensure that the right type of variable is allocated, depending on whether ANSI or Unicode is the chosen implementation.

2. Be sure that all string literals in your code are contained within macros to compile them as ANSI or Unicode as specified. For example, a string literal should be specified as follows:

```
_T ( "String" )
```

3. Remove any definitions of *_MBCS* or *_DBCS* from the build tools command lines, and add *_UNICODE*.

4. Change the program entry point to *wWinMainCRTStartup*.

5. Rebuild the entire project.

Each of the macros and types used for Unicode programming is also defined for 16-bit Visual C++ versions 1.51 and later, which means that the programs can still be recompiled for 16 bits. 16-bit Windows and 16-bit Windows applications and even 16-bit Windows applications running under Windows NT do not support Unicode.

I will follow the above steps in all the programs and samples throughout the rest of this book — except for the first program, an OLE Automation sample that is deliberately kept as simple as possible.

AN OLE AUTOMATION OBJECT EXAMPLE

I am a believer in the maxim that something is absorbed more completely if it is introduced through active participation rather than passive reading. So, what I need to do now is to write the most basic of C++ programs to implement a very simple OLE Automation object in C++. The object will expose one property, *Salary*, and one method, *Payraise*. *Salary* is a long integer value that can be read and written; *Payraise* takes a long integer value and adds it to the current value of the *Salary* property. It would be hard to define a simpler automation object!

I'll be testing the object with the following Microsoft Visual Basic code (which also works in any application supporting Visual Basic for Applications):

```
Sub TestObj()
    Dim x As Object
    Set x = CreateObject("AutoProg.CAuto.1")
    x.Salary = 1234
    MsgBox (x.Salary)
    x.Payraise (1)
    MsgBox (x.Salary)
    Set x = Nothing
End Sub
```

This creates the object, sets the Salary property to 1234, retrieves and displays the value (to ensure that it worked), invokes the Payraise method with an increment of 1 (well, times are tough!), and once again retrieves and displays the value of the Salary property (to ensure that it has been updated). Finally, the line

```
Set x = Nothing
```

causes Visual Basic to call *Release* on the pointer it holds to the object's *IDispatch* interface in correspondence to the implicit *AddRef* performed when the object was created through *CreateObject*. This causes the interface's reference count to go to *0*.

A Walk Through the Object's Implementation

The OLE Automation object I create in this section uses the Microsoft Foundation Class Library (the MFC library, for short) to make the Microsoft Windows side of it easier, but it makes <u>no</u> use of any of the significant OLE support provided by the MFC library. Also, although the object exposes two interfaces, I write the code for only one of them (*IClassFactory*). As you'll see, OLE provides

API functions to make the creation of *IDispatch* automatic and therefore simpler than if you had to implement the interface yourself.

NOTE This approach cannot support dual interfaces and has other limitations, which I outline at the end of the example. Although this program is undeniably simple, it's rewritten in Appendix A ("Visual C++ and MFC — Writing OLE Objects") to make use of the MFC library's OLE support and the wizards that come with Visual C++. It then becomes <u>literally</u> trivial.

This chapter is not the young person's guide to the MFC library (that's Appendix A), so I won't go into too much detail about the Windows side of things. Suffice it to say that *CWinApp* is the MFC class that contains the application's message pump (the loop which retrieves messages for the application from Windows and dispatches them to the relevant window) and that *CFrameWnd* is the generic frame window class. The *InitInstance* and *ExitInstance* members of the *CWinApp*-derived class (*CAutoProg*) are called at program start and program termination, respectively, so they're good places for program initialization and clean-up.

In my *InitInstance*, I create a window and show it in minimized form. This window is created purely to keep the application alive until someone closes it or until it terminates itself (which it will do when there are no more pointers to any of its interfaces). *ExitInstance* deletes the C++ window object.

This application can be compiled for 16-bit or 32-bit Windows without change. As with all the (non-control) applications in this book, it has been created using Visual C++ version 2.x — and then I've manually created a compatible 16-bit make file. (The OLE CDK produces 16-bit and 32-bit make files automatically.) One of the consequences of making each of these programs portable between both platforms is that I can't take advantage of certain advanced and useful features that exist on Win32, such as proper C++ exception-handling (described in more detail in Appendix A). The class header file for this automation object, named *AutoProg*, is shown in Listing 3-1, beginning on the next page. The implementation file for *AutoProg* is shown in Listing 3-2, beginning on page 61.

NOTE The source code and make files for the *AutoProg* sample program are in the \OLECTRLS\CHAP03\AUTOPROG directory on the companion CD-ROM.

AUTOPROG.H

```
class FAR CAuto
{
public:
    STDMETHOD ( QueryInterface ) ( REFIID riid,
        void FAR * FAR *ppv );
    STDMETHOD_ ( ULONG, AddRef ) ( void );
    STDMETHOD_ ( ULONG, Release ) ( void );

    class FAR CAutoDisp
    {
    public:
        STDMETHOD_ ( void, PutSalary ) ( long lSalary );
        STDMETHOD_ ( long, GetSalary ) ( void );
        STDMETHOD_ ( void, Payraise ) ( long lSalaryIncrement );
        CAutoDisp ( CAuto FAR *pAuto )
        {
            m_pAuto = pAuto;
        }
    private:
        CAuto FAR *m_pAuto;
    };
    friend CAutoDisp;
    CAutoDisp m_AutoDisp;
    CAuto ( );
private:
    ULONG m_ulRefs;
    IUnknown FAR *m_punkStdDisp;
    long m_lSalary;
};

class FAR CAutoCF : public IClassFactory
{
public:
    STDMETHOD ( QueryInterface ) ( REFIID riid,
        void FAR * FAR *ppv );
    STDMETHOD_ ( ULONG, AddRef ) ( void );
    STDMETHOD_ ( ULONG, Release ) ( void );
    STDMETHOD ( CreateInstance ) ( IUnknown FAR *punkOuter,
        REFIID riid, void FAR * FAR  *ppv );
    STDMETHOD ( LockServer ) ( BOOL fLock );
    CAutoCF ( ) { m_ulRefs = 1; m_pAuto = 0; }
    ~CAutoCF ( );
```

Listing 3.1. *The AutoProg class header file, AUTOPROG.H.*　　　(continued)

```
private:
    ULONG m_ulRefs;
    CAuto FAR  m_pAuto;
};
class CAutoProg : public CWinApp
{
public:
    DWORD m_dwAutoCF;
protected:
    virtual BOOL InitInstance ( void );
    virtual int ExitInstance ( void );

    BOOL CreateClassFactory ( void );
private:
    BOOL m_fOleInitSuccess;
    CAutoCF FAR  m_pAutoCF;
};

enum
{
    IMETH_PUTSALARY = 0,
    IMETH_GETSALARY,
    IMETH_PAYRAISE,
};

enum
{
    IDMEMBER_SALARY = DISPID_VALUE,
    IDMEMBER_PAYRAISE,
};
```

AUTOPROG.CPP

```
//AEE97356-B614-11CD-92B4-08002B291EED
#include <afxwin.h>
#include <afxole.h>
#if ! defined ( WIN32 )
    #include <olenls.h>
#endif
#include <initguid.h>
#include "autoprog.h"
```

Listing 3-2. *The* AutoProg *implementation file, AUTOPROG.CPP.*   *(continued)*

(continued)

```
CAutoProg theProg;
DEFINE_GUID(CLSID_CAuto, 0xAEE97356L, 0xB614, 0x11CD, 0x92,
    0xB4, 0x08, 0x00, 0x2B, 0x29, 0x1E, 0xED);
BOOL CAutoProg::InitInstance ( void )
{
      // Initialize OLE.
    m_fOleInitSuccess = TRUE;
    HRESULT hRes = OleInitialize ( NULL );
    if ( FAILED ( hRes ) )
    {
        m_fOleInitSuccess = FALSE;
        return FALSE;
    }
        // Now go and create the class factory object and expose
            it!
    if ( CreateClassFactory ( ) == FALSE )
    {
        return FALSE;
    }
        // Create a window and show it.
    m_pMainWnd = new CFrameWnd;
    ( ( CFrameWnd    ) m_pMainWnd ) ->
        Create ( NULL, _T ( "AutoProg Server" ) );
    m_pMainWnd -> ShowWindow ( SW_SHOWMINNOACTIVE );
    m_pMainWnd -> UpdateWindow ( );
    return TRUE;
}

int CAutoProg::ExitInstance ( void )
{
    delete m_pMainWnd;

    if ( m_fOleInitSuccess )
    {
        OleUninitialize ( );
    }
    return 0;
}

BOOL CAutoProg::CreateClassFactory ( void )
{
    m_pAutoCF = 0;
    BOOL bResult = TRUE;
```

(continued)

```
    TRY
    {
        m_pAutoCF = new FAR CAutoCF;
    }
    CATCH ( CMemoryException, e )
    {
        bResult = FALSE;
    }
    END_CATCH

    if ( FAILED ( CoRegisterClassObject ( CLSID_CAuto, m_pAutoCF,
                                           CLSCTX_LOCAL_SERVER,
                                           REGCLS_SINGLEUSE,
                                           &m_dwAutoCF ) ) )
    {
        bResult = FALSE;
    }
    m_pAutoCF -> Release ( );
    return bResult;
}

/////////////////////////////////////
// Class factory implementation
CAutoCF::~CAutoCF ( void )
{
    CoRevokeClassObject ( theProg.m_dwAutoCF );
}

STDMETHODIMP_ ( ULONG ) CAutoCF::AddRef ( void )
{
    return ++m_ulRefs;
}

STDMETHODIMP_ ( ULONG ) CAutoCF::Release ( void )
{
    if ( —m_ulRefs == 0L )
    {
        delete this;
    }
    return m_ulRefs;
}

STDMETHODIMP CAutoCF::QueryInterface ( REFIID riid,
    void FAR * FAR *ppv )
```

(continued)

(continued)

```
    {
        if ( riid == IID_IUnknown || riid == IID_IClassFactory )
        {
            AddRef ( );
            *ppv = this;
            return S_OK;
        }
        return ResultFromScode ( E_NOINTERFACE );
    }

    STDMETHODIMP CAutoCF::CreateInstance ( IUnknown FAR *,
        REFIID riid, void FAR * FAR *ppv )
    {
        // Do we have an object? If not, create one.
        if ( m_pAuto == 0 )
        {
            TRY
            {
                m_pAuto = new FAR CAuto;
            }
            CATCH ( CMemoryException, e )
            {
                return ResultFromScode ( E_OUTOFMEMORY );
            }
            END_CATCH
        }
        return m_pAuto -> QueryInterface ( riid, ppv );
    }

    STDMETHODIMP CAutoCF::LockServer ( BOOL )
    {
        return S_OK;
    }


    //////////////////
    // IDispatch class implementation

        // Parameters to properties and methods
    static PARAMDATA pdataSalary = { "Amount", VT_I4 };
    static PARAMDATA pdataPayraise = { "Increment", VT_I4 };

        // Description of interface
```

(continued)

```
#if defined (WIN32)
    #define    CALLCONV    CC_STDCALL
#else
    #define    CALLCONV    CC_PASCAL
#endif

static METHODDATA rgmdataCAuto [ ] =
{
    { "Salary",  &pdataSalary,  IDMEMBER_SALARY,
        IMETH_PUTSALARY, CALLCONV, 1, DISPATCH_PROPERTYPUT,
        VT_EMPTY },
    { "Salary",  0,              IDMEMBER_SALARY,  IMETH_GETSALARY,
        CALLCONV, 0, DISPATCH_PROPERTYGET, VT_I4 },
    { "Payraise", &pdataPayraise,    IDMEMBER_PAYRAISE,
        IMETH_PAYRAISE,    CALLCONV, 1, DISPATCH_METHOD,
        VT_EMPTY }
};

#define DIM(x) (sizeof(x)/sizeof(x[0]))

static INTERFACEDATA g_idataCAuto =
{
    rgmdataCAuto, DIM(rgmdataCAuto)
};

CAuto::CAuto ( void ) : m_AutoDisp ( this )
{
    m_ulRefs = 0L;
    m_punkStdDisp = 0;
    ITypeInfo FAR *pTypeInfo;
    HRESULT hres = CreateDispTypeInfo ( &g_idataCAuto,
        LOCALE_SYSTEM_DEFAULT, &pTypeInfo );
    if ( FAILED ( hres ) )
    {
        Release ( );
    }
    else
    {
        IUnknown FAR *punkStdDisp;
        hres = CreateStdDispatch ( ( IUnknown FAR * ) this,
            &m_AutoDisp, pTypeInfo, &punkStdDisp );
        pTypeInfo -> Release ( );
        if ( FAILED ( hres ) )
```

(continued)

(continued)

```
            {
                Release ( );
            }
            else
            {
                m_punkStdDisp = punkStdDisp;
            }
        }
    }

STDMETHODIMP CAuto::QueryInterface ( REFIID riid,
    void FAR * FAR *ppv )
{
    if ( riid == IID_IUnknown )
    {
        *ppv = this;
        AddRef ( );
        return S_OK;
    }
    else if ( riid == IID_IDispatch )
    {
        return m_punkStdDisp -> QueryInterface ( riid, ppv );
    }
    else
    {
        return ResultFromScode ( E_NOINTERFACE );
    }
}

STDMETHODIMP_ ( ULONG ) CAuto::AddRef ( void )
{
    return ++m_ulRefs;
}

STDMETHODIMP_ ( ULONG ) CAuto::Release ( void )
{
    if ( --m_ulRefs == 0 )
    {
        if ( m_punkStdDisp )
        {
            m_punkStdDisp -> Release ( );
        }
        theProg.m_pMainWnd -> PostMessage ( WM_CLOSE );
```

(continued)

```
        delete this;
    }
    return m_ulRefs;
}

STDMETHODIMP_ ( void ) CAuto::CAutoDisp::PutSalary ( long
    lSalary )
{
    m_pAuto -> m_lSalary = lSalary;
}

STDMETHODIMP_ ( long ) CAuto::CAutoDisp::GetSalary ( void )
{
    return m_pAuto -> m_lSalary;
}

STDMETHODIMP_ ( void ) CAuto::CAutoDisp::PayRaise
    ( long lSalaryIncrement )
{
    m_pAuto -> m_lSalary += lSalaryIncrement;
}
```

Most of the rest of the code is implementation of the OLE Automation object. That's the part I'm interested in here. Looking at the header file first, essentially three classes are defined here: *CAuto*, *CAutoCF*, and *CAutoProg*. *CAutoProg*, as I've already discussed, is the application class derived from *CWinApp*. You can see that in addition to the initialization and termination functions, *CAutoProg* also contains a member function called *CreateClassFactory*. (This function will be discussed in the section "Creating the Class Factory Object," beginning on page 70.) *CAutoCF* is the class that implements the *IClassFactory* interface for this automation object, so it's derived from *IClassFactory*. Notice its five member functions corresponding to the *IClassFactory* methods. Each of these functions is declared with a macro from the OLE header files: *STDMETHOD* or *STDMETHOD_*. Both declare the appropriate calling conventions (currently *pascal* for Win16 and *stdcall* for Win32), but the former declares a member function that returns an *HRESULT*, as most OLE interface APIs do, while the latter declares a member function that returns whichever type is given as its first parameter. Therefore,

```
STDMETHOD ( QueryInterface ) ( REFIID riid, void FAR * FAR *ppv );
```

declares *QueryInterface* as returning an *HRESULT* and taking two parameters, a *REFIID* and a *void FAR * FAR *, while

```
STDMETHOD_ ( ULONG, AddRef ) ( void );
```

declares *AddRef* as a function returning a *ULONG* (declared elsewhere as an unsigned long integer) and taking no parameters. Use of these macros makes your code considerably easier to port between the different platforms supporting COM and OLE.

CAutoCF also declares itself a constructor that does no more than initialize two private variables, *m_ulRefs* and *m_pAuto*. The former is used as the reference-count of the class factory interface (note that it's initialized to one), and the latter holds a pointer to the object that this class factory is used to create.

Implementing the Dispatch Interface with a C++ Nested Class

Rather more interesting is the *CAuto* class definition. This class exposes the object's properties and methods through *IDispatch*, yet it is not derived from *IDispatch*. Also, below the three *IUnknown* interface methods is another class definition, for *CAutoDisp*. The nested class definition is an easy way of implementing OLE interfaces in C++. Notice that I declare the inner *CAutoDisp* class as a friend of the outer *CAuto* class so that it can access the outer class's private data.

FRIEND?

If you're a C programmer or not aware of some of the esoterics of C++ programming, the *friend* keyword is used to signify that a class is allowing a function or another class special access privileges to its private and protected members. It's basically a convenience, showing once again the virtues of C++ being a pragmatic language.

The outer class holds an embedded instance of the nested class in *m_Auto-Disp*, which is initialized during the construction of a *CAuto* by having a pointer to the *CAuto* under construction passed to the *CAutoDisp* constructor. (This actually causes a compiler warning at level 4, because it is usually erroneous to pass a pointer to an under-construction object; in this case it is benign because all I do is save the pointer.) The *CAutoDisp* constructor saves this pointer in its private member *m_pAuto*.

The *CAuto* class contains the variable that is used to hold the *Salary* property's value; it also contains a pointer to an *IUnknown*. This is all to do with the way in which I've chosen to implement *IDispatch* (discussed a few paragraphs below). The *CAutoDisp* class contains the three functions used to implement the *Salary* property and *Payraise* method. *Salary*, as a property to which I allow both reads and writes, has two member functions to implement it, one to "put" (or set) the property value and one to "get" it. Although I've named the three implementation functions to reflect their use, bear in mind that there is <u>no</u> relationship between the names you choose internally as the implementation of a given property or method and the name exposed externally. Clearly, it aids readability somewhat if you can maintain a meaningful relationship.

Each of the classes in this program are defined as *FAR*; in Win32, this equates to nothing, but in Win16 it becomes the *__far* keyword, which causes all the member functions in the class to be *__far* functions. The reason for doing this is to ensure that the vtables created by the C++ compiler for the various interfaces contain far (long) function pointers, because they'll be called from external programs. The 16-bit version of OLE defines all interfaces in terms of far pointers.

Two enumerations are also defined in the header file; the first contains symbolic names representing the position within the vtable of the individual method and property functions. This set of values must <u>exactly</u> correspond with the order of the functions as declared in the implementation. Here, I have declared the put function for the *Salary* property, the get function, and the *Payraise* method implementation. The enumeration reflects this order exactly. Again, the choice of names in this type is arbitrary. (The second enumeration is discussed in the following paragraph.)

Dispatch IDs and the "Value" Property

The second enumeration is composed of the dispids for each of the properties and methods in the object. These can be any values you choose, so long as they're all different. I've decided to set the *Salary* property's dispid to an OLE-defined value, *DISPID_VALUE*, which causes the property so marked to be considered the "value" property. This becomes the default property, so that code such as

```
MsgBox (x)
```

has, in our case, the same effect as

```
MsgBox (x.Salary)
```

Setting a value property also makes it possible to "convert" a pointer to an object's *IDispatch* interface into the "value" of that object, where the value is defined as the property that the object chooses to mark that way. Only one property can be given this dispid.

Looking at the main body of code, you'll notice the *DEFINE_GUID* macro with a series of numbers as parameters. This is the preferred way to define and declare GUIDs in programs. *DEFINE_GUID* either declares a variable, or, if INITGUID.H has been included, defines it (that is, it actually allocates space for the variable and initializes it to the value given). In this case, I'm defining a variable called *CLSID_CAuto* as having the GUID value *{AEE97356-B614-11CD-92B4-08002B291EED}*. I generated this GUID by running the *GuidGen* utility; it places the GUID on the clipboard as both the form shown as a comment at the very top of the listing and also as a *DEFINE_GUID* call. Remember that GUIDs are guaranteed to be unique; consequently, you can safely use this same GUID (that is, the one I've generated) for this program in the knowledge that you won't cause a conflict with any other program (unless someone chooses to take this GUID and use it for her or his own, different, OLE object — which is not recommended).

The *CAutoProg::InitInstance* function is called at program startup. Its first job is to initialize OLE by calling *OleInitialize*. This function takes one parameter, a pointer to an *IMalloc* implementation. *IMalloc* is the interface used for memory allocation in OLE, and you can (if you want to) provide your own implementation. By passing *NULL*, I'm saying "No thanks, let's have OLE do the work."

FYI With the release of 32-bit OLE in Windows NT 3.5, it was decided that *OleInitialize* and its COM counterpart *CoInitialize* would accept only *NULL* as the allocator parameter. This means that OLE's *IMalloc* implementation is always used. The prime reason for doing this is to ensure that the allocator is capable of working properly in a multi-threaded environment. Extra hooks have been added to allow programs to catch allocator debug events so that they can check for memory leaks.

If the OLE initialization fails, I quit the program. Notice that I set a member variable *m_fOleInitSuccess* to *TRUE* or *FALSE*, depending on whether OLE initialization succeeded; this is to allow me to balance a successful call to *OleInitialize* with one to *OleUninitialize*, which must be done. (I do it in *ExitInstance*.) *InitInstance* then calls *CreateClassFactory*, which returns *TRUE* if it successfully creates a class factory object. Assuming it does, the code then creates a window and displays it as an icon.

Creating the Class Factory Object

CAutoProg::CreateClassFactory first of all uses the *new* keyword to create an instance of the *CAutoCF* class. It then uses the MFC library's *TRY* and *CATCH* mechanism to catch memory errors so that it can return *FALSE* if there isn't enough memory to create one. (These macros and the rest of MFC's exception-handling mechanisms are described in more detail in Appendix A.) If an instance of *CAutoCF* is successfully created, a pointer to it is stored in the member variable *m_pAutoCF*, and *CoRegisterClassObject* is called to tell OLE that a class factory for the *CLSID_CAuto* class now exists. Notice the flags I pass into *CoRegisterClassObject*: *CLSCTX_LOCAL_SERVER* tells it that I've implemented the factory in a local executable, and *REGCLS_SINGLEUSE* tells it that the class factory supports only one connection to it. In this simple case, I could quite successfully have used the alternative, *REGCLS_MULTIPLEUSE*.

Now I release my pointer to the class factory interface and return success (*TRUE*) or failure (*FALSE*) as appropriate. The *CAutoCF* destructor follows, and that just calls *CoRevokeClassObject* to balance the earlier call to *CoRegisterClassObject*. I really should check that the class object was successfully registered before I call *CoRevokeClassObject*, but I don't — for simplicity's sake. (There's always room for shortcuts when you can put things down to "simplicity.")

CAutoCF::AddRef, CAutoCF::Release, and CAutoCF::QueryInterface calls are classic implementations. *Release* deletes the class factory object when the reference count reaches zero, and *QueryInterface* calls *Addref* and returns a pointer to the class factory object if it's being asked for *IUnknown* or *IClassFactory*. Any other interface request gets *E_NOINTERFACE* in response. *CAutoCF::CreateInstance* has to create an object that exposes the requested interface; it does this by creating a new *CAuto*. Again, exceptions are handled using the MFC library's *TRY* and *CATCH* mechanism; the only exception I expect here is a lack of memory. The object's implementation of *QueryInterface* is then called to get the interface pointer requested. Notice that the *CreateInstance* function first checks to see whether I already have an object; other implementations might choose to create a new object each time *CreateInstance* is called. The point is that you have the choice. Also, this function should check that its first parameter, a pointer to an outer unknown, is *NULL*, as it does not support aggregation. For simplicity, I haven't put this code in — again!

FYI   This first parameter is not explicitly named in the function's definition, unlike the rest of the parameters, because it is not used by the function. This is a seemingly little-known C++ trick: if a function you're writing takes some parameters it doesn't use, you can avoid compiler warnings about unused parameters by leaving the parameter name out. Naturally, you still need to define the type of the parameter.

The final class factory implementation routine is *LockServer*. Because my object is so simple, I ignore the functionality required of this routine and simply get it to return success (*S_OK*). No other action is taken. This course of action is <u>not</u> recommended — and is actually wrong! I should return *E_NOTIMPL*, which indicates that I don't implement the functionality. Please take this only as my third aid to simplicity. Real applications should implement *LockServer* properly.

That's it for the class factory implementation — there's really not much to it. Most of the esoteric work is done when the *CAuto* object is created. Its constructor takes on the task of creating the *IDispatch* interface.

The Programmable Object Itself

I first declare two static *PARAMDATA* arrays. *PARAMDATA* is a structure defined in OLE Automation that contains information about each parameter that a method or property call expects. The first element of the structure is the name of the parameter; apart from being displayed by tools that are capable of interrogating automation objects, they also serve to allow the named parameters discussed in the previous chapter. One of my variables declares the parameter list for the *Salary* property, which is a single-entry list containing the 4-byte integer (notified by *VT_I4*), *Amount*. The second variable declares the parameters for the *Payraise* method. Again, there is only one — another 4-byte integer called *Increment*.

NOTE The *PARAMDATA*, *METHODDATA*, and *INTERFACEDATA* structures I use in *AutoProg* are provided with OLE because at the time that OLE was first released (April 1993), the type library definition wasn't complete. These structures, and the function that creates a type information record from them, *CreateDispTypeInfo*, are now regarded as obsolete and will probably not be supported in some future version of OLE. I use them here because it allows me to provide a small, self-contained sample without too many supporting files — but it would <u>not</u> be a good idea to rely on this mechanism.

I now have a conditional define for the calling convention of the method and property functions. A "calling convention" defines how parameters are passed to a function, whose job it is to clean up the stack after the call, and some information on how the function name should be altered. OLE Automation cares only about the first two (how parameters are passed and who cleans up the stack after the call), as it calls the functions by indirection though the vtable, without reference to the function's name. By default, 16-bit OLE uses the *pascal* calling convention, whereas the 32-bit version uses the *stdcall* convention. Both these conventions define the called function as the one responsible for cleaning up the stack (that is, removing the parameters that were pushed onto the stack during the function call). Note, however, *pascal* passes its arguments on the stack from left to right, whereas *stdcall* passes them from right to left. OLE needs to know which convention is used so that it can make the correct call during an *IDispatch::Invoke* execution.

I then define an array of *METHODDATA* structures. Again, this type is defined in the OLE Automation headers. Each structure in this array holds information about one function. The first element is the method or property name that this function represents. The second is a pointer to its parameter list; notice that the *Salary* put function has a parameter while the get function doesn't. The third element is the dispid for the function; again, notice that the two property functions for *Salary* share the same dispid. The fourth element is the function's position in the vtable. The fifth is the calling convention used. The sixth is the number of parameters to the function, which needs to be the same as the number of elements in the *PARAMDATA* structure referenced by the second parameter. The seventh element is a flag saying what kind of function this is; *DISPATCH_PROPERTYPUT* means that it's a property's put function, *DISPATCH_PROPERTYGET* means that it's a get function, and *DISPATCH_METHOD* means that it's a method. The eighth and final element of the array is the return type of the function; *VT_EMPTY* means that nothing is returned (it's a *void* function).

Finally, I have an *INTERFACEDATA* structure. This contains two elements: a pointer to an array of *METHODDATA* structures followed by the number of elements in that array. I define a simple macro, *DIM*, to calculate this last element for me.

Now I'm into the *CAuto* constructor. It passes a pointer to the *CAuto* under construction to the constructor of the embedded instance of its nested *CAutoDisp* class, *m_pAutoDisp*. It sets its reference-count variable (*m_ulRefs*) and the pointer to an *IDispatch* interface (*m_punkStdDisp*) to zero. It then calls *CreateDispType-Info* passing it the address of the *INTERFACEDATA* structure created above, the locale — basically, the spoken language — in which this is to be considered, and a pointer to a variable in which to store the *ITypeInfo* interface pointer that this function returns. (There is, of course, much more to locale than simply the spoken language, but it's beyond the scope of this book — which is a useful excuse.) *CreateDispTypeInfo* is a quick way of creating an OLE type information record "typeinfo" from an *INTERFACEDATA* structure. The typeinfo returned by this function is a simple form of a standard type library, and is created dynamically. If this succeeds, I then call *CreateStdDispatch*, a function provided by OLE Automation's creators to make it considerably easier to implement an *IDispatch* interface. Rather than implementing it myself, I use a built-in *IDispatch* implementation that uses the object pointer and type information pointer I pass in to allow it to satisfy *GetIDsOfNames*, *Invoke*, and the other *IDispatch* interface calls. I also pass into the *CreateStdDispatch* function a pointer to an *IUnknown* interface (the *CAuto* object). Assuming success, I then store the newly allocated *IDispatch* pointer in the *m_punkStdDisp* member variable and return. It really is that easy.

CreateStdDispatch creates for me an object that I aggregate: my *IUnknown* is the controlling unknown, and its *QueryInterface* delegates requests for *IDispatch* to the aggregated object. *CreateStdDispatch* is an easy way of implementing *IDispatch*, but it has a couple of limitations. First, the created *IDispatch* supports only one national language; if you create your own *IDispatch* implementation, you can support as many languages as you choose. Second, its *Invoke* implementation only allows dispatch-defined exceptions to be returned. This means that your methods and properties can't raise user-defined exceptions. These limitations are generally not significant for small examples such as this one, but they become considerably more important in larger systems. In particular, the exception limitation becomes difficult to live with.

The next three functions are *CAuto*'s implementation of *IUnknown*. As for the class factory, these functions are pretty straightforward. *QueryInterface* returns a pointer to this object if *IUnknown* is being requested. If *IDispatch* is requested, it gets a new *IDispatch* pointer by calling *QueryInterface* on the stored *IDispatch* interface pointer. *CAuto::Release* also calls *Release* on the stored *IDispatch* interface pointer and then posts a close message to the application's window prior to deleting itself if the reference count has reached zero.

The final three functions are the implementation of the property and method. Notice the *CAuto::CAutoDisp::PutSalary* notation: this is the necessary C++ syntax when defining member functions of a nested class.

That's it. This program can be compiled with either 16-bit or 32-bit Visual C++. In both cases, create a new project and choose as the base project type an application with MFC support. (Do not choose an *AppWizard* application.) Then add AUTOPROG.CPP to the project list. For the 16-bit compiler, you'll also need to add the OLE libraries to the linker options. The libraries used by this program are COMPOBJ.LIB, OLE2DISP.LIB, and OLE2.LIB. The 16-bit compiler will also complain about the lack of a DEF file and offer to create one for you: accept the offer.

Registering and Running the Automation Sample

After the program is built, it needs to be registered. These are the keys and values you need to add to the registry:

```
HKEY_CLASSES_ROOT\AutoProg.CAuto.1 = AutoProg Server
HKEY_CLASSES_ROOT\AutoProg.CAuto.1\CLSID =
    {AEE97356-B614-11CD-92B4-08002B291EED}
HKEY_CLASSES_ROOT\CLSID\{AEE97356-B614-11CD-
    92B4-08002B291EED} = AutoProg Server
HKEY_CLASSES_ROOT\CLSID\{AEE97356-B614-11CD-92B4-
    08002B291EED}\ProgID = AutoProg.CAuto.1
HKEY_CLASSES_ROOT\CLSID\{AEE97356-B614-11CD-92B4-08002B291EED}-
    \LocalServer32 = C:\OLECTRLS\CHAP03\AutoProg\WinDebug\Auto-
    Prog.Exe /Automation
HKEY_CLASSES_ROOT\CLSID\{AEE97356-B614-11CD-92B4-08002B291EED}-
    \LocalServer = C:\OLECTRLS\CHAP03\AutoProg\AutoPr16.Exe /Auto-
    mation
```

The first line tells the system that the ProgID *AutoProg.CAuto.1* is known in human-readable form as *AutoProg Server*. The second line adds a subkey to this entry to tell the system which CLSID this object exposes. The rest of the lines create entries under the *HKEY_CLASSES_ROOT\CLSID* key. The first creates the key for the object's CLSID and again, for documentation purposes only, shows the human-readable form. The second creates the *ProgID* key, which cross-refers back to the object's entry. The last two lines describe the path to the 32-bit executable (*LocalServer32*) and the 16-bit executable (*LocalServer*). Provide the entry for whichever version you build, and be sure that the path entered corresponds to the location of the executable on your machine. Notice that in these two entries I pass a command-line switch, */Automation*, to the object server. This is to allow the server to know that it's being invoked as a result of an automation call. (I'm supposed to check for this situation, but don't — for simplicity, of course.) The server might then choose to take a different startup action than if it were being run normally; for example, it might choose to make its window initially invisible.

Normally, registry entries like these would be added through a registration (REG) file. For two reasons, however, I haven't provided one here. The first reason is that the formats differ between 16-bit and 32-bit Windows. The second reason is that as more and more objects become self-registering on startup, registration files are becoming recognized as a somewhat untidy means of updating the registry.

FYI   None of the OLE controls in this book uses a registration file.

Now that the object server exists and is registered, you can test it by running the Visual Basic sample given earlier. This will display a message box saying *1234* followed by a message box with *1235*. Following the execution of the

```
Set x = Nothing
```

statement, the object should be removed from memory. (Use a tool such as the task list or the *Windows Process Status (WPS)* utility that comes with the *OLE SDK* to verify that this is the case.)

I've now demonstrated how to implement an OLE Automation object in C++ using the second most difficult method there is. The most difficult is to implement the whole *IDispatch* interface yourself. To enhance your understanding of automation, you might find it useful to play around with this program, adding methods and properties and using Visual Basic to test it. (In Appendix A, I'll use this program and re-implement it using MFC's OLE support.)

There is one more thing I could have done in this program — and friendly automation objects are supposed to do it. This is to register the "active" object so that applications can get an interface pointer on it using the equivalent of Visual Basic's *GetObject* statement. I would do this by calling *RegisterActiveObject* after my *IDispatch* interface is in place. I'd need to undo it when the program goes away, by calling *RevokeActiveObject*. The active object function places an entry for this object into the running object table, an OLE-maintained list of all objects registered in this way.

TYPE LIBRARIES IN DEPTH

To best understand a type library and its associated ODL, let's begin from this position of knowledge: *AutoProg*. The ODL for this program could look like this:

```
[ uuid(4D9FFA38-B732-11CD-92B4-08002B291EED), version(1.0),
    helpstring("AutoProg OLE Automation Server") ]
library AutoProg
{
    importlib("stdole32.tlb");

    //  Dispatch interface for AutoProg

    [ uuid(4D9FFA39-B732-11CD-92B4-08002B291EED),
        helpstring("Dispatch interface for AutoProg Server") ]
    dispinterface _DCAuto
    {
        properties:
            [id(0)] long Salary;
        methods:
            [id(1)] void Payraise(long Increment);
    };

    //  Class information for CAuto

    [ uuid(AEE97356-B614-11CD-92B4-08002B291EED),
        helpstring("AutoProg Server") ]
    coclass CAuto
    {
        [default] dispinterface _DCAuto;
    };
};
```

The first three lines together form one statement declaring the type library. The library is called *AutoProg*, is version 1.0, and has the helpstring specified. This helpstring serves as a comment for display by type browsers. Notice also that the library has a GUID (referred to as a UUID in ODL) of its own, different from the one for the object itself. A type library must have a GUID of its own because it will usually be registered as an entity in its own right. Inside the braces, the first statement is a command to include the contents of another type library, STDOLE32.TLB (or STDOLE.TLB for 16-bit Windows). This type library, the standard one supplied as part of OLE, describes all the system-defined interfaces, such as *IUnknown* and *IDispatch*. The next few lines define the *dispinterface* for our object. The term *dispinterface* is shorthand for *IDispatch* implementation. Notice again that *dispinterface* has its own GUID and a helpstring. I've chosen to name the interface *_DCAuto*, which follows the convention used by the OLE CDK. Although this interface has its own GUID (because ODL defines the *dispinterface* keyword as one of the few for which a GUID is mandatory), this GUID is not used by the program.

The braces following the interface declaration contain the interface definition. This is split into two sections: *properties* and *methods*. ODL provides another way to define dispatch interfaces as well, but I'll stick to this way because it's fairly straightforward and is used by the OLE CDK in the files it creates for us. Each property is listed, followed by each method. The order of the sections, and the entries within them, is not important. The *[id(nnn)]* part of each description defines the property or method dispid. I defined the *Salary* property as being the object's value property by giving it the dispid *DISPID_VALUE*. This is defined as zero in the OLE header files, so I know that the dispid for the *Salary* property is zero. It would have been safer to include the relevant header file in the ODL (using the standard C *#include* syntax), because I could have used the symbolic name instead. The dispid for the *Payraise* method is *1*, because the symbolic value used for it in *AutoProg* comes from the enumeration in which the first member, *IMETH_SALARY*, is defined as *DISPID_VALUE* (that is, zero). In C and C++, by definition the value of enumeration elements without specified values follow on from the value of the preceding element. *Salary* is declared as being of type *long*, and *Payraise* is defined as taking a long parameter called *Increment* and returning nothing.

The next part of the type library defines the COM object itself; this is referred to in ODL as the *coclass*. Again, this has a GUID, but this time it's the same GUID as the one I created as the object's CLSID. It also has a helpstring in this case. I've decided to call the object *CAuto* — similar to *_DCAuto* for the dispinterface. (It's really rather arbitrary what we use.) I define the class as consisting of the *_DCAuto* interface, which is also marked as the default interface.

That's the end of my type library source code. If you compile this with *MkTypLib*, the resulting type library can be examined by utilities such as *OLE2View*, which comes with Microsoft Visual C++ versions 2.0 and later. (See Figure 3.1 on the next page.)

When a type library source file is compiled into a type library, it can then be used as a source of information about an object's interfaces, properties, and methods. Typically, the type library itself is included as a binary resource in the object application's resources and then registered in the Windows registry. Applications that want to use the object can then use functions to get hold of pointers to type library interfaces such as *ITypeInfo*, and use member functions on these interface pointers to walk through the information.

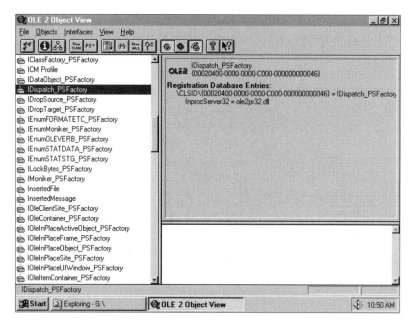

Figure 3-1.   *The contents of a type library, seen by using the* OLE2View *tool of Microsoft Visual C++ versions 2.0 and later.*

STRUCTURED STORAGE REVISITED

I'm going to demonstrate some of the structured storage mechanics discussed in the previous chapter by modifying the *AutoProg* sample I created earlier. I'm not going to create a true object-side implementation of structured storage (for example, *IPersistStorage*) because doing so would make *AutoProg* too complicated. (Simplicity, simplicity.) Instead, I'm going to add another automation method, *Store*, to *AutoProg*, which will create a structured storage file called TEST.AUT in the root directory. In this storage, it will create a stream called *MyStream*, into which it will store the current value of the Salary property, as a text string in the form "Salary = value."

NOTE   The source code and make files for the updated *AutoProg* sample are in \OLECTRLS\CHAP03\AUTOPRO2 on the companion CD-ROM.

The additions to the earlier version of the program are as follows: in AUTO-PROG.H, immediately after the declaration of the *Payraise* member function, I add

```
STDMETHOD_ ( void, Store ) ( void );
```

This declares the new *Store* member function. Then I add the entry *IMETH_STORE* to the first of the two enumerations at the bottom of the file and the entry *IDMEM-BER_STORE* to the second. The changes to the main file, AUTOPROG.CPP, are equally straightforward. I add the details for the new *Store* property to the *rgmdataCAuto* array:

```
{ "Store", 0, IDMEMBER253_STORE, IMETH_STORE, CALLCONV, 0,
    DISPATCH_METHOD, VT_EMPTY }
```

Then I add the member function itself to the end of the file:

```
STDMETHODIMP_ ( void ) CAuto::CAutoDisp::Store ( void )
{
    LPSTORAGE lpStg;
    HRESULT hres = StgCreateDocfile ( "C:\\TEST.AUT",
        STGM_CREATE | STGM_SHARE_EXCLUSIVE | STGM_READWRITE,
        0, &lpStg );
    if ( FAILED ( hres ) )
    {
        MessageBeep ( UINT ( -1 ) );
    }
    else
    {
        LPSTREAM lpStrm;
        hres = lpStg -> CreateStream ( "MyStream",
            STGM_CREATE | STGM_SHARE_EXCLUSIVE |
            STGM_READWRITE, 0, 0, &lpStrm );
        if ( FAILED ( hres ) )
        {
            MessageBeep ( UINT ( -1 ) );
        }
        else
        {
            char szBuf [ 32 ];
            ::wsprintf ( szBuf, "Salary = %ld",
                m_pAuto -> m_lSalary );
            hres = lpStrm ->
                Write ( szBuf, ::lstrlen ( szBuf ), 0 );
            if ( FAILED ( hres ) )
            {
                MessageBeep ( UINT ( -1 ) );
            }
            lpStrm -> Commit ( STGC_DEFAULT );
            lpStrm -> Release ( );
        }
        lpStg -> Commit ( STGC_DEFAULT );
        lpStg -> Release ( );
    }
}
```

This code uses the *StgCreateDocFile* OLE API function to create the structured storage. ("DocFile" was the old name used internally at Microsoft Corporation for structured storage files, which made its way into the outside world and began to be used by other OLE developers. Its use is now frowned upon.) The flags passed to the function are *STGM_CREATE*, which tells it to overwrite any existing file of the same name; *STGM_SHARE_EXCLUSIVE*, which tells it that I want to open this file for exclusive access; and *STGM_READWRITE*, which tells it that I want to read and write this file. The lack of a flag indicating transaction mode means that I'm using direct mode.

FYI   The OLE documentation isn't clear in telling you that you need a share mode flag, such as *STGM_SHARE_EXCLUSIVE*, in every storage-creation and stream-creation routine. This caught me out for a while!

Having opened the storage, *IStorage::CreateStream* is called to create a stream called *MyStream* inside the storage returned by *StgCreateDocFile*. Assuming success here, an appropriate string is built up using *wsprintf*, and it's written to the stream using *IStream::Write*. The function closes up by committing and releasing first the *IStream* pointer and then the *IStorage* pointer before returning. Remember that even though *IStream::Commit* does nothing in the current releases of OLE, it might in the future, so it's always good manners to call it in this way.

The Visual Basic program I used to test *AutoProg* can be extended to test the new *Store* method by adding one line, before the object is released:

```
x.Store
```

NOTE   Be sure that *AutoProg*'s *LocalServer32* (or *LocalServer*) registry entry points to the updated executable file.

I can now examine and verify the content of the created structured storage using the *DfView* utility that comes with the OLE SDK.

OLE CONTROLS ARCHITECTURE

An OLE control is not radically different from other OLE objects: it implements a number of interfaces, and it uses others. At a minimum, an OLE control is capable of being in-place activated as an inside-out object, and it supports OLE Automation by allowing its properties to be set and read and its methods to be called. Although it's perfectly possible to implement OLE controls as EXEs (that is, as local servers), it is anticipated that the vast majority will be DLLs (that is, in-process servers); certainly, all the ones created in this book fall into that category.

OLE controls need to be able to do a few things that standard OLE interfaces don't support, such as "firing" events, binding to data sources, and supporting licensing. Consequently, the OLE Controls architecture adds a few more bits and pieces to the standards already set.

Logic impels me to introduce some OLE control-specific terminology now, but not all of it can be fully defined at this point, so please bear in mind that the "definitions" in the following table will be expanded in future chapters.

Term	*Meaning*
Event	When a control needs to tell its container that something (anything) has happened, it "fires" an "event." Thus, an event is an asynchronous notification from control to container, and its semantics are defined by the control. Some events are pre-defined events; I introduce these in Chapter 8, "Events."
Ambient property	Containers can provide a set of environmental values that controls should take note of when they are loaded. For example, a container can set a default background color or a default font. Controls that use properties of these types have the choice of whether to read and use the ambient properties. (Strictly, it's the client site rather than the container that exposes the ambient properties. This is discussed in later pages.)
Extended property	Some properties that a control user might associate with a given control, such as its position and size, are actually properties managed by the container rather than the control. The control doesn't normally position itself within a form, but it lets the form designer put it wherever it is required. Properties that are not exposed by the control but that are logically associated with it are called "extended properties." They are exposed to the container (as if they were control properties) through something called the "extended control." It is also possible for a container to implement extended methods and events.

The following sections of the chapter examine the basic principles of each of these concepts; they do not necessarily go into great detail, because many of the subjects mentioned have whole chapters dedicated to them later in the book. The first area of interest that I discuss is the way in which controls are programmed by the user of the container in which they are embedded. I then go on to look at ambient properties, events, and other control-to-container notifications, standard types defined by or for OLE controls, persistence of properties, licensing, versioning, and other (sometimes arcane) aspects of the technology!

NOTE As stated in the note on the first page of this chapter, it is by no means essential that you read and understand everything here to be able to create useful controls, although the knowledge might come in handy when you want to perform more complex or esoteric actions with a control or its container. So, depending on your needs, you can either continue through to the end of this chapter . . . or skip to Chapter 4.

Language Integration

OLE controls are inherently programmable entities, which is one of the things that differentiates them from standard embedded objects. This programmability is exposed through OLE Automation, and the container in which controls are embedded must therefore provide a programming language to manipulate these controls. Microsoft applications, for example, include a variant of Visual Basic; Microsoft Visual C++ provides a mechanism to program the controls from C++. The way in which the programming language is integrated with the container does not impact on the use of OLE controls at all: that is, they don't care how the user programs them, as long as it ends up being through OLE Automation. The language, however, must support setting and getting control properties, invoking control methods, and reacting to control events. Visual Basic does this. The following table shows Visual Basic's language integration with OLE Controls, assuming that *MyControl* is a Visual Basic variable of type *Object* that has been initialized to point at a running control on a form and that the running control is called *TheControl1*:

Property put	`MyControl.TheProperty = 12`
Property get	`x% = MyControl.TheProperty`
Method invocation	`If MyControl.TheMethod = True Then...`
Event handler	`Sub TheControl1_TheEvent ( params )...`

The section on OLE Documents in the previous chapter mentioned the concept of a "client site," an object implemented by a container that is responsible for acting as the embedded object's gateway to the container. OLE controls make use of the client site, as they are also embedded objects. In addition, containers sometimes implement a parallel object called the "extended control." This object is created by aggregating with the control itself. Controls should therefore allow themselves to be aggregated. All controls created with Microsoft's OLE CDK are aggregatable, although the programmer can write code that specifically is not. In this latter case, the programmer should also cause the control to fail when it is being created if the container creating it is also attempting to aggregate it.

The aggregated object is seen by the container's programming language as if it were the control: it exposes the properties and methods of the control as well as the extended properties (and methods, if there are any) through a single *IDispatch* interface. This is one case in which aggregation is used to merge two objects' interfaces together; what happens internally is that the extended control's *IDispatch* immediately passes on to the control's IDispatch any property or method invocations it doesn't recognize.

FYI   Many times throughout this book I refer to *IDispatch*. As I discussed in Chapter 2, OLE Automation now supports the concept of dual interfaces, so in many cases it might not actually be *IDispatch* that is used to access a specific set of properties, methods, or events; it might instead be a dual interface. However, the OLE CDK in versions 1.0 and 1.1 provide only *IDispatch* support.

Applications that want to allow OLE controls to be embedded within them and that want to take advantage of some of the advanced features offered by controls (such as events and data binding) need to do more than "standard" OLE embedding containers. Older-style containers such as Excel version 5.0, for example, can still generally embed controls and even allow them to be programmed through OLE Automation, but they are unable to react to some of the more useful things controls can do. Also, some old-style containers, of course, don't allow objects to be inside-out and so force them to be outside-in. The interfaces exposed by an OLE control are shown in Figure 3-2 (on the next page), together with those that need to be implemented by a container if it is to be entirely OLE Controls-compliant. These interfaces, together with other aspects of OLE Controls architecture, are described in the remainder of this chapter.

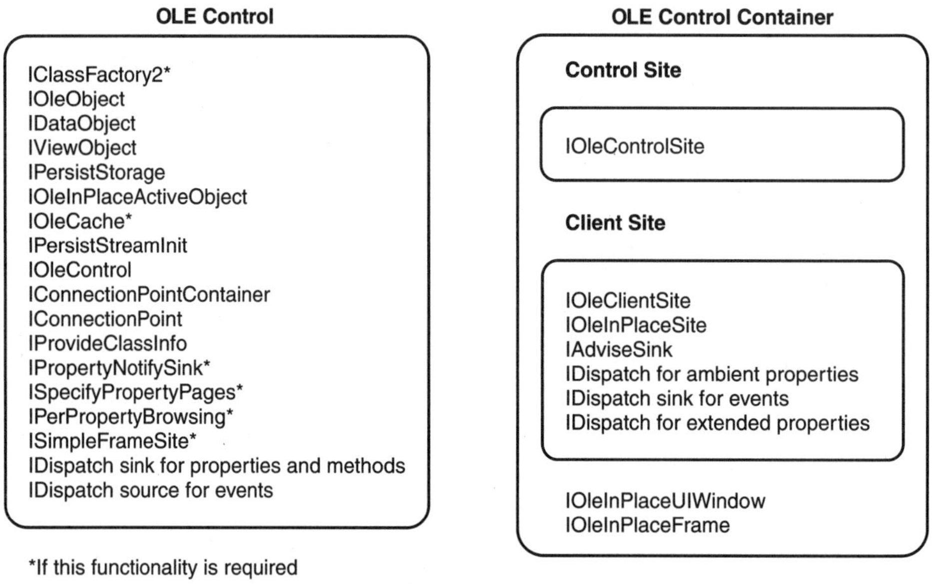

OLE Control

IClassFactory2*
IOleObject
IDataObject
IViewObject
IPersistStorage
IOleInPlaceActiveObject
IOleCache*
IPersistStreamInit
IOleControl
IConnectionPointContainer
IConnectionPoint
IProvideClassInfo
IPropertyNotifySink*
ISpecifyPropertyPages*
IPerPropertyBrowsing*
ISimpleFrameSite*
IDispatch sink for properties and methods
IDispatch source for events

OLE Control Container

Control Site

IOleControlSite

Client Site

IOleClientSite
IOleInPlaceSite
IAdviseSink
IDispatch for ambient properties
IDispatch sink for events
IDispatch for extended properties

IOleInPlaceUIWindow
IOleInPlaceFrame

*If this functionality is required

Figure 3-2. *The interfaces exposed by OLE controls and their containers.*

Ambient Properties

"Ambient properties" are properties that the container manages as environmental values for any embedded control to read and use. A control is unable to set the values of ambient properties, so they are effectively read-only. Generally, the container providing the properties also supplies mechanisms through which they can be changed by the user. A container that doesn't provide this functionality is certainly less useful than one that does! Common ambient properties include background and foreground colors, fonts, and page size.

STANDARD AMBIENT PROPERTIES

The OLE Controls specification provides a list of standard ambient properties, and I'll be looking at these in more detail and seeing how to access and use them in Chapter 6, "Properties." For now, all you need to know is that ambient properties aren't limited to the specification's list and that a control must have prior knowledge of an ambient property to make sensible use of it. This means that you, the control writer, need to be aware of the ambient properties you want to use.

(continued)

(continued)

Each of the standard ambient properties is assigned a specific dispid in addition to its name. Importantly, it's the dispid that is guaranteed, <u>not</u> the property name. Therefore, don't rely on *BackColor* being the name of the background color ambient property; use its defined dispid instead: –701 (yes, a negative number).

Property names are susceptible to localization, so what I write and use in English might be completely different in French or German. Of course, I should use the manifest constant *DISPID_AMBIENT_BACKCOLOR* from OLECTL.H rather than the dangerously specific –701. Ambient properties in addition to the standard list should be given positive dispids. If a container supports a given standard ambient property, it should implement it in the defined way and not use the property to mean something else.

It is possible for a control to be designed for use inside a particular container and therefore make use of ambient properties supplied by that container alone. Such a control should code for the situation in which access to these properties fails, because it might be embedded within a different container. If the control really does work with that one container only, it should disallow itself from being embedded elsewhere.

Two standard ambient properties can be used by controls to determine specific action to take. *UserMode* (*DISPID_AMBIENT_USERMODE*) is used by containers that support two modes of operation, such as Microsoft Visual Basic's design mode and run mode. The control might want to take specific action in one of these modes when it becomes active, or it might want to display itself in different ways. The property is Boolean, so its value is either *TRUE* (in run mode) or *FALSE* (in design mode). *UIDead* (*DISPID_AMBIENT_UIDEAD*) is also Boolean, and it allows the control to determine whether the container wants it to react to user interface operations now. For example, if the container includes a debugger, it might be that the container would set the value of *UIDead* to *TRUE* when the program hits a breakpoint to tell all controls that they should not respond to user input at this time. A well-behaved control will respect this.

Related to this container modality are two other standard ambient properties: *ShowGrabHandles* and *ShowHatching*. When an embedded object is UI-active, it is supposed to provide grab handles around it so that it can be changed in size. (The container does this for it when the embedding is only in-place active.) In containers such as Visual Basic, however, showing grab handles is fine in design mode but is not what is wanted in run mode. Therefore, a control should examine the *ShowGrabHandles* (*DISPID_AMBIENT_SHOWGRABHANDLES*)

(continued)

(continued)

> ambient property when it goes UI-active to determine whether to show grab
> handles. Similarly, an embedded object should display a hatched border around
> it when it is UI-active (again, the container does it for the embedding when it
> is in-place active) as feedback to say that the embedding is active. In run
> mode, this might not be appropriate for controls, so the control should
> check the value of the *ShowHatching* (*DISPID_AMBIENT_SHOWHATCH-*
> *ING*) ambient property before it draws any hatching.

How does the control access the ambient properties? As you'd expect by now,
OLE Automation is the answer. The client site exposes the properties through its
automation interface — note that I said client site, not container. This means that
different sites on the same container could potentially expose different sets of ambient
properties, which would, for example, happen in a spreadsheet, where each cell might
want to reflect its font and color selections as its ambient properties. To get at the
automation interface for ambient properties, the control calls *QueryInterface* on any
of the site's interfaces, asking for *IID_DISPATCH*. It then calls *IDispatch::Invoke*
with the relevant dispid to retrieve the value. If the client site does not support that
ambient property, it will return the *SCODE DISP_E_MEMBERNOTFOUND*.

Events

Events provide an interesting addition to the standard OLE architecture because
they require that the container provide the implementation. That is, the events a
control can generate are described by the control, but it requires that the container
provide an interface that implements the event functions.

Events are notifications from the control to its container that something has
happened. The exact nature of the "happening" is up to the control. Events are fired
by the control asynchronously, which means that a container must be capable of
receiving and dealing with them at any time after the control has been embedded.

Events are implemented as standard OLE Automation methods, with the catch
being that the automation interface that exposes these methods is in the container,
not in the control. When the control wants to fire an event, it calls the relevant
container method through its *IDispatch::Invoke* implementation. The control requires
the container to provide the *IDispatch* implementation, so the control is known as
the event "source" while the container's *IDispatch* is known as the event "sink."
The control's type library describes the event methods that the control wants
implemented, exactly as if the implementation were provided by the control.
However, the interface is described in the *CoClass* section of the ODL file as being
a source, which means that the control does not in fact implement it.

As an example, if *_DHexocxEvents* is the events dispatch interface in a control and *_DHexocx* is the control's standard properties and methods dispatch interface, then the coclass description would be something like this:

```
[ uuid(37D341A5-6B82-101B-A4E3-08002B291EED),
    helpstring("Hexocx Control") ]
coclass Hexocx
{
        [default] dispinterface _DHexocx;
        [default, source] dispinterface _DHexocxEvents;
};
```

Here, the coclass *Hexocx* is defined as having two dispatch interfaces, *_DHexocx* and *_DHexocxEvents*, where *_DHexocx* is implemented by the control but *_DHexocxEvents* is not. The *default* attribute signifies that an interface is the one that should be used for programmability when requested unless told otherwise. Thus, *_DHexocx* is the coclass' "primary dispatch interface" and *_DHexocxEvents* is its "primary event set." It would be possible for this control to expose a greater set of functionality to so-called power users (that's us, right?!?) through another dispinterface (for example, *_DHexocxPowerUser*). This new dispinterface wouldn't be marked as the default, so nothing would make use of it unless told to (by asking for its IID directly).

The question this raises is "How does the control connect to the container's automation interface for its events?" It can't call *QueryInterface* on the client site because it is defined to return the ambient properties *IDispatch* interface. The OLE Controls specification solves the problem by defining for COM a generic mechanism by which an object can say that it is a consumer of a given interface rather than the provider of that interface: that is, it is expressing a willingness to communicate with an implementation of that interface. The mechanism is known as the "connection point."

Connection Points

Connection points are a generic COM mechanism exploited by OLE controls to support events. A "connection point" is an interface exposed by an object that is used to hook up to implementations of an interface with which the object wants to communicate. In the case of control events, a control describes the event interface in terms of an OLE Automation interface in its type library, marking the interface as "source." This means that the control does not implement the interface. The control then provides a connection point through which the container can connect its implementation of the event's automation methods.

NOTE   It is very important to understand that connection points are an extension to COM and are not specific to OLE controls. Therefore, any mechanism (including events) that uses connection points can be implemented by any COM object. Chapter 4 includes a version of *AutoProg* that does precisely that.

A connection point is easily defined as an implementation of the *IConnectionPoint* interface. The container gets to the connection point through another interface, *IConnectionPointContainer*, which allows an external object to iterate through the list of connection points maintained by the control or to get at a specific one by asking for it by "name." (A connection point's name is usually defined as the IID of the interface to which it is designed to connect.)

A CLOSER LOOK AT CONNECTION POINTS

The connection-point mechanism works by allowing an object to present a list of "points" to which it would like implementations of certain interfaces to connect. The list is managed by the *IConnectionPointContainer* interface, which contains the following methods:

```
HRESULT EnumConnectionPoints (
    IEnumConnectionPoints FAR * FAR *ppEnum );
HRESULT FindConnectionPoint ( REFIID iid,
    IConnectionPoint FAR * FAR *ppCP );
```

EnumConnectionPoints returns a pointer to an *IEnumConnectionPoints* interface. *IEnumXXX*, where *XXX* refers to a kind of item, is the standard OLE way of enumerating collections of items. All *IEnumXXX* interfaces have the same methods: *Next*, *Skip*, *Reset*, and *Clone*. These interfaces are known as "enumerators," as they allow you to iterate over a collection. OLE Automation provides a generic (to automation) enumerator object, *IEnumVariant*, to iterate over collections exposed by a dispatch interface. The actual type of the collection is whatever is held in the *VARIANT* collection's elements: for example, it can be used by an object to expose the list of documents it currently has open. The *VARIANT* data type contains a union that can hold a wide variety of data types, from simple integers through *IDispatch* pointers. Collections exposed through the help of *IEnumVariant* are iterated over in Microsoft Visual Basic programs by the *For Each...Next* statement. In the connection-point

---

(continued)

(continued)

case, the returned enumerator object allows you to iterate over collections of connection points.

FindConnectionPoint returns a specific connection point based on the interface ID to which that connection point wants to connect. So, to find the connection point an object exposes that wants to talk to an *IMyInterface* implementation, pass in *IID_MYINTERFACE*. The interface ID requested by a connection point can be viewed as that connection point's "name." It is actually possible for an object to have more than one connection point requesting a given interface. In this case, however, *FindConnectionPoint* will fail and other techniques such as iterating through the list of connection points would need to be used to connect.

When a connection point is designed to connect to an *IDispatch* implementation rather than to a general COM interface, its *FindConnectionPoint* method shouldn't be passed *IID_DISPATCH* but should instead be passed the IID given to the specific methods and properties interface that will be exposed through *IDispatch*. Therefore, a connection point designed to allow a container to implement the events associated with the coclass *Hexocx* from earlier in this chapter would respond to the IID for *_DHexocxEvents*, not to *IID_DISPATCH*. Hopefully, the reason for this is clear: *IDispatch* is generic and does not itself provide a contract stating which properties and methods it supports. A specific implementation, on the other hand, is exactly that.

IConnectionPoint itself contains these methods:

```
HRESULT GetConnectionInterface ( IID FAR *pIID );
HRESULT GetConnectionPointContainer ( IConnectionPointContainer
    FAR * FAR *ppCPC );
HRESULT Advise ( IUnknown FAR *pUnkSink, DWORD FAR *pdwCookie );
HRESULT Unadvise ( DWORD dwCookie );
HRESULT EnumConnections ( IEnumConnections FAR * FAR *ppEnum );
```

GetConnectionInterface returns the IID of the interface to which this particular connection point wants to connect. *GetConnectionPointContainer* is a back-pointer to allow code to traverse back up to the *IConnectionPointContainer* implementation holding this connection point. *Advise* is called by the interface implementor (the sink) to connect the interface implementation to the connection point. Note that no matter what interface pointer is passed into this method by the caller, *QueryInterface* is always called to retrieve the desired interface pointer. *Advise* returns a special value in *dwCookie* that acts as a handle for this connection.

(continued)

(continued)

This value is defined to be zero if *Advise* failed. *Unadvise* breaks a connection, taking the connection's handle value as its parameter.

EnumConnections is interesting: it allows you to iterate through the list of connections to a given connection point. Yes, that's right, a connection point can actually be connected to more than one implementation of its desired interface. This allows "multi-casting," when a connection point can, for example, send events to more than one interface implementation at a time. It is the responsibility of the code calling through the connection point to ensure that any method calls to the connected interface go to <u>all</u> connections on that interface.

There's one final interface that helps with connection points: *IProvide-ClassInfo*. It has only one method,

```
HRESULT GetClassInfo ( ITypeInfo FAR * FAR *ppTI );
```

which returns a pointer to an *ITypeInfo* interface that describes the object's connection points. The *ITypeInfo* interface actually describes the coclass object in the object's type library, so in my *Hexocx* example, it would describe both *_DHexocx* and *_DHexocxEvents*. The latter, however, would be marked to say that it is a source interface, which tells the reader of this information that it should implement this interface if it wants to connect to the appropriate connection point.

Connection points are not specific to OLE controls and can be used by any other object type that wants to connect to one or more container-provided interfaces. Figure 3-3 shows the way in which connection points and connection-point containers connect to a provider of an interface, together with the option of multi-casting.

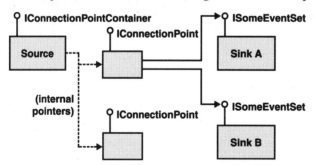

Figure 3-3. *Connection points and connection-point containers.*

Returning again to events, a container must read the event type information from the control and dynamically create from it an IDispatch implementation. It then passes this through to the relevant connection point's Advise method on the control. Henceforth, any events fired by the control will come through to this implementation. Generally, containers that support OLE controls will want to pass these events through to the container programmer, so that the programmer can write code that deals with the event. This is another aspect of a container's language integration discussed earlier, beginning on page 82. Visual Basic, for example, allows the programmer to write a Sub procedure that is called whenever the event is fired. This Sub procedure is passed the event parameters defined by the control.

Some events are predefined by the OLE Controls specification, such as the Error event. This is used to pass up to the control container a notification that something has gone wrong, but it is only used asynchronously: that is, if the error occurs during a method or property call, the error is synchronous to the call so it is reported to the container using the standard OLE Automation exception mechanism. If the error occurs at some other time, the control must fire the Error event. As with OLE Automation exceptions, the OLE Controls Error event allows the control to pass useful information up to the container, such as the Help file and Help context ID for this error. In addition to allowing Basic-like languages to catch the error with On Error statements, this mechanism also allows the user program to display the relevant help information.

Property Change Notifications

One of the aspects of Microsoft Visual Basic custom controls that OLE controls also needs to support is "data binding," which is when a property is closely tied to a data source, such as a column in a database, so that the property reflects the value of the column in a specific record, and changes to it are sent back to the database. Likewise, the bound property can be used to add new values to the database. Typically, data binding is used for controls that are naturally parts of forms because this allows data source values to be easily displayed. For example, an edit control can be data bound so that it shows a column value and allows user edits. However, there is nothing that prevents a property from being data bound even if it is not visible.

NOTE I have used the generic term "data source" here because data binding should not specifically imply a relational database. As computing evolves, more and more entities become capable of being viewed as a source of data, including of course relational databases and ISAM-type databases, and also including diverse things such as file systems, mainframe transactions, word processor files, and so forth.

OLE Controls support data binding. In fact, the OLE Controls designers have implemented it in such a way that it is a good deal more flexible than data binding. OLE controls can be written to allow any of their properties to be bound, including multiple properties. Further, it is entirely up to the container in which the control is embedded to determine what action is taken when a property value changes or the thing to which a property is bound changes. Consequently, the binding does not have to be to a database column; it can be to any data source, including real-time data feeds, another control, and so forth. The second of these — another control — is actually very common in Visual Basic programs because one of the chief suppliers of data to a program is the data source control.

Property binding is implemented very simply in an OLE control. A property that is defined as bindable sends its container a notification when its value changes; the container is free to do what it chooses with this notification. Further, a property can request from its container the ability to be changed prior to actually being changed.

As this process involves notification to the container, it's natural that the mechanism used to supply this notification is the same as with events — connection points. A control that supports property binding will implement a connection point that wants to be a consumer of the *IPropertyNotifySink* interface. The container then implements this interface, connects it to the control's connection point, and is subsequently notified of all changes to properties that are declared to be bound. Likewise, the same interface is used when a control wants to ask its container whether a particular property's value can be changed.

Properties are marked as bindable in the type library. Some new attributes have been added to standard ODL to support data binding. A property in toto is regarded as having the attribute, so when a property occurs more than once in the ODL (for example, because it has get and put functions), the flags must be applied to both occurrences. The first new attribute is *Bindable*, which indicates that a property will send notifications when it is changed. *RequestEdit* indicates that a property will attempt to call the container's *IPropertyNotifySink::OnRequestEdit* before its value is changed. Because properties that support edit requests must also be bindable, the *Bindable* attribute must be specified in addition to the *RequestEdit* attribute. Whenever these mandatory dependencies occur, the type library compiler (*MkTypLib*) enforces the rules.

The *DisplayBind* attribute, which can only be used on properties that also have the *Bindable* attribute, tells the container that if it has a mechanism for displaying which properties in a control are bindable, then this property should be thus displayed. If a bindable property does not want its end users to know that it is bindable, it shouldn't set this flag. The *DefaultBind* attribute, which can also only be used on properties that also have the *Bindable* attribute, tells the container that this property most completely represents the control and is therefore the logical thing to which to bind. For example, the text in an edit box would be a classic case for being the default binding. Only one property per control can be given this attribute.

IPROPERTYNOTIFYSINK INTERFACE DETAILS

The *IPropertyNotifySink* interface contains two methods:

```
HRESULT OnChanged ( DISPID dispid );
HRESULT OnRequestEdit ( DISPID dispid );
```

OnChanged is called by the control when a bound property's value is changed. The dispid parameter to the method identifies the property that has been changed. Note that this method is called <u>after</u> the change has taken place. *OnRequestEdit* is called by the control when a property marked with the "request edit" flag is about to be changed. If the container returns *S_OK*, the property can be changed; if *S_FALSE* is returned, the property cannot be changed. Also, the container can perform other actions during the *OnRequest-Edit* call, such as retrieving and saving the current property value. A control that supports edit requests for its properties must be able to react to the container saying "no," allowing the action that would change the property value to be canceled and ensuring that the method call is always made before the property actually changes value.

Bound properties must call *OnChanged* no matter how the property value is altered — whether it is by user code, by user interaction, or through some other means, including through the property page. The only times it should not call the notification method are when it is being deserialized (that is, read in from disk or memory) or being created. Properties are assumed to have changed when a control is created, so no notification is necessary.

If a number of properties are changed in one operation, the control does not need to call *OnChanged* for each property. Instead, it can call *OnChanged* with a dispid of *DISPID_UNKNOWN* (-1), which tells the container that more than one property has changed and it should retrieve the values of any in which it is interested.

Control and Container Communication

In addition to defining the event mechanism, the OLE Controls specification defines a set of interfaces to allow more specific control and container communication. These interfaces are used to pass information such as ambient property changes and are not directly related to the programmable interface of the controls. One interface, *IOleControl*, is implemented by the control, and the other, *IOleControlSite*, by the container.

IOleControl has four methods:

```
HRESULT GetControlInfo ( CONTROLINFO FAR *pCI );
HRESULT OnMnemonic ( MSG FAR *pMsg );
HRESULT OnAmbientPropertyChange ( DISPID dispid );
HRESULT FreezeEvents ( BOOL bFreeze );
```

GetControlInfo returns a *CONTROLINFO* structure, which tells the container about keyboard-handling. This is discussed in greater detail in the next section ("Keyboard-Handling"), together with *OnMnemonic,* which is called by the container when a key in the control's accelerator table is pressed. *OnAmbientPropertyChange* is called when the value of one or more of the container's ambient properties is changed. If one property is changed, the parameter passed to the method is the dispid of the changed property. If more than one are changed, the parameter is *DISPID_UNKNOWN*(-1), and the control must interrogate the client site for the new value of every ambient property it uses. *FreezeEvents* allows the container to tell the control not to fire events. *FreezeEvents* implements a count of the times it is called: calls with a parameter of *TRUE* increment the count, and those with a parameter of *FALSE* decrement it. When the control is first loaded, the value of the count is zero, so events are fired. The control can decide that it queues up events when they're frozen, so that they can all be fired after the freeze is removed; the alternative is to discard all events that would otherwise have been fired. This is a control-specific decision.

IOleControlSite has seven methods:

```
HRESULT OnControlInfoChanged ( void );
HRESULT LockInPlaceActive ( BOOL fLock );
HRESULT GetExtendedControl ( IDispatch FAR * FAR *ppDisp );
HRESULT TransformCoords ( POINTL FAR *lpptlHimetric,
    POINTF FAR *lpptfContainer, DWORD flags );
HRESULT TranslateAccelerator ( MSG FAR *lpMsg,
    DWORD grfModifiers );
HRESULT OnFocus ( BOOL fGotFocus );
HRESULT ShowPropertyFrame ( void );
```

OnControlInfoChanged and *TranslateAccelerator* are the client side of special keyboard-handling and are discussed in "Keyboard-Handling." *LockInPlaceActive* is called by a control to tell its container to stop it from being taken out of the in-place active state. It is usually used around event firings if a demotion from in-place active might cause a problem. It is also used during the handling of certain messages to stop a bug in Microsoft Windows 3.1 from crashing the system. When a control is locked in-place, the container itself cannot enter the loaded or running states, as this would in turn demote the control. *GetExtendedControl* returns a pointer to the automation interface implemented by the client site when the control is aggregated. This allows the control to determine the current values of its extended properties (those managed by the site) and is therefore fairly container-specific. *TransformCoords* is discussed on page 101. *OnFocus* is used by the control to tell its container that it is grabbing the focus. This might be necessary in order to perform certain actions immediately before the control becomes UI active, when it normally grabs the focus anyway. The final method, *ShowPropertyFrame*, brings me to the subject of property pages, which I discuss in the "Property Pages" section beginning on page 105.

Keyboard-Handling

Embedded OLE objects are already able to react to most keypresses as they choose. Some keys, however, are designated as "special" and typically are not seen by embedded objects. Also, as OLE controls will be used to implement many aspects of the componentware marketplace, you'll see things such as label controls that perform no action other than reacting to a given keypress and passing the focus to another control. Labels in conventional Microsoft Windows dialog boxes are implemented as static text, with one letter typically designated as a mnemonic. When this key is pressed, the Windows dialog manager passes activation to the next control capable of receiving focus. OLE controls need to do this themselves, or at least need to provide a mechanism by which it can be done. The only outstanding question, then, is "How?"

A control tells its container which accelerators it is interested in by passing it a handle to its accelerator table (among other things) when the container calls *IOleControl::GetControlInfo*. The container builds up this information for every control embedded within it. If a control dynamically changes this information, which is certainly possible, it calls *IOleControlSite::OnControlInfoChanged*. This is a signal to the container that it should call *IOleControl::GetControlInfo* again on that control.

The information passed to the container in the structure returned by *GetControlInfo* includes a set of flags indicating whether the control makes use of either the Return or Escape keys when it is UI-active. This allows the container to deal with UI issues such as whether the default button should be highlighted (which indicates to the user that pressing Return will trigger this button).

A container can decide which key combinations it allows as accelerator-key combinations to be passed to the embedded controls. For example, a control might decide that it wants to see Ctrl+Enter, but if the container decides that Ctrl-key combinations are for its own uses, then the control will not see it. When a keypress is received that is recognized as a control's mnemonic, the container calls *IOleControl::OnMnemonic*. The control can then do whatever it chooses.

Controls that are to be treated as buttons need further special handling by containers. They must first communicate to their container their requirement to be treated as a button by setting the *OLEMISC_ACTSLIKEBUTTON* status bit (as described in the "*MiscStatus* Bits" section beginning on page 103).

When a container that supports the concept detects that a control is a button, the container should do a number of things. A button can read the *DisplayAsDefaultButton* ambient property to see if it should display itself in a way that the user understands as meaning the default button. This means that if the Return key is pressed, the button should be activated. This can only happen for controls that don't themselves use the Return key. The container sets this ambient property to the appropriate value for each buttonlike control embedded within it. If the Return key is pressed while a control button is highlighted, the container calls the button's *IOleControl::OnMnemonic* method.

A button can also be designated as a Cancel button, although the button itself knows nothing of this: it's purely a container concept. In this case, the container looks for the Escape key being pressed and in response activates the button designated as the Cancel button.

Finally, there's the problem of radio buttons, or any button type, that acts like a radio button. A "radio button" is a control that acts in concert with a set of like controls; only one of the buttons can be selected at a given time, and clicking on one deselects all the others in the group. The issue here is that there is no way for a control to work with other controls as a group. If you've caught the theme so far, you'll have guessed that it's the container's responsibility to do this, but the buttons have to say that they are capable of being radio-button-like, and they also need to provide the container with a means for setting and unsetting them.

In addition to being marked with *OLEMISC_ACTSLIKEBUTTON*, controls say they can act like radio buttons and provide the mechanism at the same time by having a *Value* property (which must also be the default property) of type *ExclusiveBool*. Only the *Value* property can have this type, which is defined in the OLE Controls standard type library. This property must also be marked as bindable.

Some controls, in particular check boxes, have three states: on, off, and grey (that is, indeterminate). OLE Controls again defines a standard type for this, *OLE_TRISTATE*, which is an enumeration containing values for each state. Check boxes and other controls that want to be of this type must expose their *Value* properties as being of this type.

Types and Coordinates

Having just introduced the concept of standard types, it seems a good point at which to examine all the standard types that OLE Controls supports and provides. Standard types are useful when information needs to be expressed in a container-independent way or when specific information is being communicated, such as whether a button can act as a radio button.

OLE_COLOR is used to hold color information for use by controls and their containers. For example, the standard ambient property *BackColor* is of type *OLE_COLOR*. There's also a helper API function, *OleTranslateColor*, that converts an *OLE_COLOR* value to a *COLORREF* value. (*COLORREF* is the standard Microsoft Windows color type.) A few other standard types of this nature are defined by the OLE Controls specification. More interestingly, two particular types make a control writer's life much easier: one is a standard way to use and define fonts, and the other is a way to use and define "picture" objects.

The Standard Font Object

The standard OLE Controls font object provides a uniform mechanism for creating and using fonts in OLE controls. The object supports a dispatch interface to get and put its properties and also supports a creation and manipulation interface called *IFont*. The *IFont* interface contains the methods shown in the following table:

IFont *Method*	*Description*
IsEqual	Determines whether two OLE Controls font objects are equal — that is whether they represent fonts with the same characteristics. (This does not necessarily mean they share the same underlying Microsoft Windows font object.)
Clone	Creates a new OLE Controls font object with the same characteristics as an existing one.
SetRatio	Sets the aspect ratio of the font.
AddRefHFont	Increments the use count on the Windows font handle (*HFONT*) represented by this object. (See the main text for the reason why.)
ReleaseHFont	Decrements the use count on the *HFONT* represented by this object. (See the main text for the reason why.)
QueryTextMetrics	Fills a standard Windows *TEXTMETRIC* structure with details of this font in the current device context (DC).

The font object's properties available through OLE Automation are shown in the table on the next page. Most of these properties can be set as well as read (with *HFont* being an exception).

Font Object Property	Description
Name	The typeface of the font, such as Times New Roman. This property has the type *BSTR*.
Size	The size of the font, in points. This property has the type *VT_CURRENCY*, a fixed-point format used primarily for currency values. It's used here as a convenience because it's a great deal faster than the floating-point format.
Bold	Determines whether the font is bold. This property, which is Boolean, is allied to the *Weight* property and follows normal Microsoft Windows font conventions. If the weight is over 550, the font is considered bold. Setting this property to *TRUE* sets the weight to 700, and setting it to *FALSE* sets it to 400. See the *Weight* property, below.
Italic	Determines whether the font is italic.
Underline	Determines whether the font is underlined.
Strikethrough	Determines whether the font is struck through.
Weight	Legal *Weight* values are between 0 and 1000, although the most common values are 400 (normal) and 700 (bold). See the *Bold* property, above.
Charset	Specifies the desired character set, such as ANSI, Unicode, or OEM.
HFont	The handle to the underlying Windows font object.

The problem with font objects implemented elsewhere is that they often re-create the underlying Windows font object each time a property is changed. If you're changing both the font size and font weight, the process is going to be a great deal slower than it needs to be if each change causes a new Windows font object to be created. The OLE Controls font object is more intelligent than this. It doesn't create a Windows font object for itself until it really needs to, so setting multiple properties in one go is not inefficient. The object also caches Windows *HFONT* handles, so two identical font objects in the same process might well get the same underlying *HFONT*. Again, this is just an optimization. It has the side-effect, however, of making any *HFONTs* returned by the object transient; any alteration to the font or even to another font can render the handle invalid. Consequently, *IFont's* *AddRefHFont* and *ReleaseHFont* methods can be used to up the reference count on an *HFONT* so that it is kept around and valid for as long as you need it. This clearly detracts from the optimizations possible by caching fonts, so use these methods sparingly.

The font object supports *IPersistStream* and *IDataObject*, so it is capable of saving itself to disk in both binary (*IPersistStream*) and human-readable text (*IDataObject*) format. Normally, a control asks any font objects it contains to save themselves during its own persistence process.

OLE provides an API function, *OleCreateFontIndirect*, for creating font objects. It takes a pointer to a new structure, *FONTDESC*, and returns a pointer to the new object's *IFont* interface. OLE controls should use font objects for any font-based properties they use.

Finally, the font object has a problem: it gets changed by user code. How does it communicate these changes back to the control that owns it? Once again, the flexibility of the connection-point idea is demonstrated here. The font object provides a connection point for *IPropertyNotifySink*, and the control provides the implementation. The control then connects to the font object's connection point and gets called whenever one of the font's attributes is changed.

The Standard Picture Object

The standard picture object is very similar in concept to the font object. It's a standard way that you can use to express and display a picture, where a "picture" is defined as a bitmap, a metafile, or an icon, as it is in a Visual Basic version 3 picture control. Like the font object, the picture object has a dispatch interface, *IPictureDisp*, and an *IPicture* interface. The methods in *IPicture* are shown in the following table:

IPicture *Methods*	*Description*
Render	Causes the picture object to draw itself into the given device context.
PictureChanged	Should be called by a control if it has taken a picture object, extracted the underlying Microsoft Windows object handle, and altered the picture in any way.
SaveAsFile	Asks the picture object to save itself to a file.
get_KeepOriginalFormat	Gets the current value of a flag internal to the object that says whether the object should always keep around the format in which it was originally created. In some instances, the object might determine that it can be more efficient if it converts the object to another type and discards the original format. If this internal flag is set, it won't discard the original.
set_KeepOriginalFormat	Sets the internal flag described above.
get_CurDC	Along with *SelectPicture*, below, is present to circumvent the Windows limitation that an object can be selected into only one device context at a time. As it is possible to have a picture object rendered more than once, the object provides these methods to save device contexts between paints.
SelectPicture	Selects a picture into a given device context, returning the device context in which the picture was previously selected, together with the picture's GDI object handle. See *get_CurDC*, above.

The properties exposed through the dispatch interface are shown in the following table:

Property	Description
Handle	The Microsoft Windows handle of the underlying GDI object.
hPal	The handle of the palette with which the picture is to be realized.
Type	A flag saying whether the picture object is actually a bitmap, a metafile, or an icon.
Width	The width of the object, in units of type OLE_XSIZE_HI-METRIC. (See the "Coordinates" section, below.)
Height	The height of the object, in units of type OLE_YSIZE_HI-METRIC. (See the "Coordinates" section, below.)

Sharing once more the same concepts as the font object, the picture object notifies its owning control of any changes in property values through a connection point for *IPropertyNotifySink*.

Two OLE API functions are provided to create these objects. *OleCreatePicture-Indirect* creates a picture object from an existing bitmap, metafile, or icon or creates a new empty one. *OleLoadPicture* creates a picture object from the standard Windows file formats for bitmaps, metafiles, or icons.

Coordinates

The *Width* and *Height* properties of the standard picture object are shown in the previous table as being of type *OLE_?SIZE_HIMETRIC*, where *?* is either *X* or *Y*. So far, this is unlikely to mean much as I haven't explained these things. The OLE Controls specification defines special types for size and position coordinates, primarily because different containers show and use coordinates in different ways. Furthermore, the container owns the coordinate model, not the control.

This has ramifications beyond just a set of type definitions. A container needs to know which control event parameters are coordinates so that it can convert them into its own coordinate space. For example, if a control fires a MouseDown event, the control will naturally state the position at which the event occurred in, say, pixels. The container, on the other hand, might want the user to see this position in inches, so it has to convert pixels to inches. It can determine which of the event parameters need such conversion by examining the control's type library, so long as each such parameter is given one of the standard types defined by OLE.

This mostly doesn't work for control properties and methods, though, because a container generally doesn't do much between the control's properties and the user code or user interface accessing those properties. This means that if a control has a property whose value is 1234, then user code in an arbitrary application will typically see the value of the property as 1234, rather than a magically converted value that might be more meaningful to the container. Worse, though, is the fact that OLE controls provide a mechanism for property examination and change which is at first glance <u>totally</u> <u>independent</u> of the container in which they're placed — property pages. How can a control display its coordinate-based properties in container-specified units?

The control maintains responsibility for its property values but is able to ask the container, via the client site, to convert. The *IOleControlSite* interface contains a method, *TransformCoords*, which the control calls to perform the conversion. In addition, the control can indicate to its container which of its properties are in container units, by using one of another set of OLE-defined standard types for coordinates. The container also exposes the name of the units it uses as a string-based ambient property, *ScaleUnits*.

Persistence

An object that needs to save its persistent state when asked to do so by its container generally implements the *IPersistStorage* interface. The container invokes methods on this interface using an *IStorage* interface pointer it has implemented. Because controls generally save little more than the values of some of their properties, *IPersistStorage* is somewhat over the top. Therefore, the OLE Controls specification allows an OLE control to save its state to an *IStream*. This would imply that the OLE-supplied and OLE-implemented *IPersistStream* interface would suffice. This is not actually the case, however, because *IPersistStream* has no equivalent of *IPersistStorage*'s *InitNew* method. When a control is loaded, it might want to read the values of some of the ambient properties before its persistent state is loaded. Without an *InitNew* method, it cannot do this, which means that the following are true:

■   The control cannot read ambient property values until its persistent state is loaded.

■   When it has loaded, the control might be provided with ambient property values that override its persistent state, causing it to read these values twice.

The new interface *IPersistStreamInit* gets around these problems and allows a control to be created in such a way that it can read and use ambient properties before it loads its persistent state. It can then choose to ignore parts of its persistent state or to not even save them next time around. For this to work, the container must give the control its client site object before the container asks the control to load its persistent state. The control tells a container that it can support this by setting the *OLEMISC_SETCLIENTSITEFIRST* miscellaneous status bit. (Miscellaneous status bits are examined in the "*MiscStatus* Bits" section, beginning on the facing page.) Containers written prior to the OLE Controls specification will not know of this bit and will not know of *IPersistStreamInit*. Therefore, controls that want to be compatible with older containers should also support *IPersistStorage*.

A container should determine the presence of the *OLEMISC_SETCLIENTSITE-FIRST* bit and ensure that it does call *SetClientSite* before loading the control's persistent state. Of course, only new containers written to be control-aware can do this, so the control itself can determine whether its container supports this concept by checking whether its *SetClientSite* method is called before its *InitNew* or *Load* methods.

The only difference between *IPersistStream* and *IPersistStreamInit* is the addition of the *InitNew* method. *IPersistStreamInit*, however, cannot be derived from *IPersistStream* because that would imply that a container could use the standard *IPersistStream* interface, causing *InitNew* not to be called and therefore rendering the new contract meaningless.

Property Sets

Users of Microsoft Visual Basic will be aware that it is possible to save Visual Basic programs in textual format so that they are (mostly) readable by humans. This text includes the persistent properties of any controls in the program. In those instances in which data cannot meaningfully or easily be converted to text, Visual Basic uses binary files (such as its FRX format) in which to save the information. In the new world of OLE controls, how does a container such as Visual Basic maintain this capability?

You'll have noticed from the way in which OLE controls support property notification (data binding) that they're quite happy to delegate as much hard work as possible to the container. This continues with textual representations! Basically, the OLE control supplies just enough information to the container to allow it to save its persistent properties as text. The information passed is an OLE data structure known as a "property set." The property set specification at the back of the *OLE 2 Programmer's Reference, Volume One* is pretty vague, so the OLE Controls people have kindly tidied it up and been rather more definitive. I won't go into the property set specification here, except to say that a property set essentially is a table of IDs and values, where the ID defines something having a value and the value is that something's value.

The IDs used by OLE Controls property sets map to property names, and the values are typed according to the types of the properties. In addition to the standard type values that can be accommodated by OLE Automation's *VARIANT* data type, the property set representation also allows BLOBs of various kinds to be stored. (A "BLOB" is a "binary large object" — another phrase for some arbitrary chunk of otherwise pretty opaque binary data.)

The container's job is to read this property set and convert it, where possible, to text. Anything that can't be saved as text must remain as binary, but the idea of the "save as text" mechanism is to allow as much of the object's state as possible to be represented in human-readable format. The container's saved representation should be semantically equivalent to that saved by the *Save* method in *IPersistStream* or *IPersistStorage*, which means it should save the same information. Likewise, the property set passed back from the container to the control when the textual format is reread should be semantically equivalent to the Load method of *IPersistStream* or *IPersistStorage*. This means that the control's state as it was saved should be entirely restorable from its property set representation.

Property sets are communicated from and to the control via the *IDataObject* interface, implemented by the control.

MiscStatus Bits

A container might want to know various things about a given OLE server before creating any instances of the objects provided by that server, because it's considerably cheaper than creating an instance and therefore loading the server. OLE provides this capability through a registry entry under the *CLSID* entry for the class called *MiscStatus*. This entry doesn't have to exist, but if it does, it contains a set of binary "flags" (that is, bits) for which OLE defines specific meanings. An object can also have different bits for different aspects (renderings) of the object, and these can be found as separate keys under the *MiscStatus* key. If a subkey is present for a given aspect, it will be named by the integer value of the aspect. (For example, the *MiscStatus* value for *DVASPECT_ICON* appears under the subkey 4.) These aspect-specific values override the default given for all aspects under the *MiscStatus* key itself.

A container reads the bits by calling *IOleObject::GetMiscStatus* or by reading the registry directly. The default handler's implementation of this method does not load the object if it is not currently running. OLE defines the meanings of the bits, and the OLE Controls specification adds a few more to the list. Ones pertinent to controls from the original OLE list include *OLEMISC_INSIDEOUT*, which tells a container that this object would like to be activated inside-out (that is, is capable of being in-place active as well as UI-active), and *OLEMISC_ACTIVATEWHENVISIBLE*, which tells the container that the object would like to be activated whenever it becomes visible, even if it isn't UI-active.

Some of the additions to these flags provided by the OLE Controls specification are shown in the table beginning on the next page.

Flag	Description
OLEMISC_INVISIBLEATRUNTIME	Controls that don't intend being visible at runtime, such as a timer control, should set this bit. If the container has a concept of runtime, it should respect this bit and hide the control when in the running mode.
OLEMISC_ALWAYSRUN	This bit tells a container that the object always wants to be in the running state and that the default handler should <u>not</u> delay the loading of the object until the last possible moment. Because most OLE controls are themselves in-process, there is usually no need to specify this bit.
OLEMISC_ACTSLIKEBUTTON	This bit tells the container that this control has buttonlike behavior. In particular, this allows the container to tell the control to draw itself as the default button or as a normal button.
OLEMISC_ACTSLIKELABEL	Standard Microsoft Windows dialog boxes use labels (items of window class "static") to label a control and to specify the mnemonic for that control. If an OLE control is being implemented to have the same behavior as a label, this bit should be set. This allows the container to handle the control properly when it passes focus on to the control that it's labeling.
OLEMISC_NOUIACTIVATE	This bit tells the container that the control has no user interface that it wants activated, as it will be dealt with solely through OLE Automation and the events mechanism. Note that controls can already indicate that they don't support a separate in-place active state by not including the OLEMISC_INSIDE-OUT bit.
OLEMISC_ALIGNABLE	This bit is used by a container that supports aligned controls. This bit is set by a control that is most useful when aligned on some side of its container. Containers that support such aligned controls can use this bit to decide whether the user should be allowed to align a particular control.
OLEMISC_IMEMODE	International versions of Windows using double-byte character sets (DBCS), such as Japanese, support "input method editors" (IMEs) to create extended characters. This bit signifies that a control supports such things. Typically, a container that also supports IME will provide the control with an extended IMEMode property.

(continued)

(continued)

Flag	Description
OLEMISC_SIMPLEFRAME	Imagine the situation where you have written an OLE control that you intend to be little more than a holder for other controls. (An example would be a group box control, into which you would typically place radio buttons, check boxes, and so forth.) As the area inside the control is owned by the control, any controls placed inside of it need to be treated specially. A control marked with this bit is saying that it supports calling the *ISimpleFrameSite* interface, allowing it to be a control container but delegating most of the work up to the real container.
OLEMISC_SETCLIENTSITEFIRST	Normal OLE embeddings have their client site set when the container has loaded their persistent state from disk using *OleLoad* or when a new instance has been initialized using *IPersistStorage::InitNew*. However, OLE controls might need to be able to access the client site very early on in their creation (for example, to get the current values of ambient properties) and before their persistent state has been loaded. This flag allows a control to mark itself thus.

OLE containers that are not aware of OLE controls or of these new *MiscStatus* status bits will ignore these bits, which means that controls must be prepared to live with a container's failure to support them fully. Likewise, existing non-control OLE objects do not specify these bits, but new containers that are intended as control containers should respect them and deal with them appropriately.

Property Pages

Prior to the advent of the OLE Controls specification, all custom control models supported a means by which a control's container could interrogate a control's properties and display them for view and alteration. Visual Basic, for example, uses its Properties window for this task. However, there are cases of containers where such an interface is not sensible, such as an operating system shell into which the capability to embed OLE controls has been added. Coupled with the fact that, more and more, the user interface paradigms in use are becoming "object-centric" (where an object is selected and then actions performed on it), there needs to be a container-independent way to display and alter a control's properties.

The OLE Controls specification's answer to this is the property page. A "property page" is a piece of user interface implemented by the control that allows control properties to be viewed and set. (See also Chapter 11). Given that controls can have large numbers of properties, each control can have as many property pages as it chooses. Also, standard system-provided property pages are provided for font objects, picture objects, and colors.

The mechanism is this: something implements a "property frame" in which the property pages will be displayed in whatever is the prevailing UI mechanism of the day. Right now, it's tabbed dialog boxes. A classic tabbed dialog box is shown in Figure 3-4.

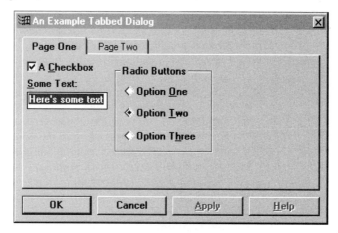

Figure 3-4.   *A set of property pages in a tabbed dialog box, the current user-interface favorite.*

The control sees property pages as a set of dialog box templates. These templates contain fields for each of the properties that a control wants to expose through the property pages, and code behind the dialogs manages the content.

Property pages are all OLE objects, with their own CLSIDs and interfaces. This allows property pages to be shared among controls, if they happen to share the same set of properties. This is the mechanism through which the standard property-page implementations are provided for general use. The OLE interface exposed by a property page is *IPropertyPage*, which contains methods to set the property-page site within the frame, activate and deactivate the page, and so forth. The property frame implements sites for each of the property pages supplied by a control through the *IPropertyPageSite* interface. A property frame can determine the set of property pages exposed by a control through the *ISpecifyPropertyPages* interface, which has only one method, *GetPages*. This returns an array of property page CLSIDs, allowing each of them to be created through, for example, *CoCreateInstance*.

The OLE Controls runtime system provides a standard implementation of the property frame and can be accessed using *OleCreatePropertyFrame*. Microsoft Windows 95 and other versions of Windows also have standard property-page implementations, and these will ultimately become the standard frames. Property frames can be invoked on more than one object at a time, which means that it is possible for a specific property page to be asked to show the properties for a set of controls at a time.

Differences might exist between properties displayed in a container's property browser, such as Visual Basic's Properties window, and each control's property page(s). Property browsers will typically also show a control's extended properties, such as its position and size, although this might not be sensible for a property page. Also, each individual browser is likely to provide different user interface mechanisms for changing the values of certain property types. For example, the *BackColor* and *ForeColor* properties shown by Visual Basic in its Properties window can be changed by selecting a color from a dialog box that Visual Basic provides or by typing in a not-quite-so-user-friendly hexadecimal number. Property pages will also have their own mechanisms, perhaps combining the setting of many property values into one user-interface mechanism. As is usual with these things, standards will eventually emerge that the whole world chooses to use, making life easier for users as well as for us programmers.

Per-Property Browsing

One more thing needs to be addressed here: the concept of "per-property browsing." The property-page mechanism allows groups of properties to be viewed and edited at one time, but some containers require the ability to examine individual properties. Most of the time, this can be performed through the type library proferred by a control, except that this doesn't allow for validation of values entered into properties and doesn't cater to types that can't be exposed through OLE Automation directly.

If an object has a property or set of properties for which it wants to support more specific per-property browsing by containers, it must implement the *IPerPropertyBrowsing* interface, which contains methods to return the property's displayable name, a set of predefined string or numeric values for it, and the ability to jump to the control's property page for this property. To aid this last one, property pages can also implement *IPropertyPage2*, which is the same as *IPropertyPage* except for the addition of the *EditProperty* method, which sets the focus within the page to a specific property field. If the control doesn't support this interface, the focus is left with the first control on the page.

Property pages are remarkably easy to implement with the OLE CDK, so there's no excuse for not providing property pages for your controls. For those containers that don't know of property pages, a new OLE verb has been added (Properties), which will normally be displayed by a container when a control with property pages is selected. Execution of the verb causes the standard property frame to be displayed, populated with the selected control's property pages.

Licensing

I devote a chapter to the subject of licensing later in the book (see "Chapter 15"), but here I must look at the extensions provided to COM by the OLE Controls specification. The defining problem with a piece of componentware is that it can get used in all sorts of places, which is good, as that is what it is designed to do. For users of these components, this is hardly a problem. For vendors of them, it can be a major problem! If vendors distribute an application containing one of your controls, they presumably paid for the right to do so. But if users of that application are then able to take the control and use it in new applications all of their own, the vendor is potentially out of pocket. What you need, then, is a mechanism that allows an OLE control to be used in some circumstances but not in others, depending on the state of the license.

You need to be aware of a number of control-use situations:

- Design-time use of a control

- Application-specific runtime use of a control

- Generic runtime use of a control

The differentiation here between design-time and runtime refers to the ability to create new applications (design-time) versus the ability to use a control in a ready-built application (runtime). Matters get a little complicated with containers that don't differentiate, but we'll ignore that level of sophistication. The two runtime cases allow for a license to use a control in a single application and a license to use it in any set of applications.

The OLE Controls licensing model is designed to be relatively simple and yet deal with all the needs discussed above. Also, it can easily be extended to provide more complex licensing schemes or mechanisms. For example, it is fairly easy for a control to support different levels of licensing, so you get access to more or less functionality depending on the license you have.

The COM extensions for licensing are manifested through the *IClassFactory2* interface. This is a variant of *IClassFactory* (and is in fact derived from it), with three extra methods that allow containers to get license information from the control (*GetLicInfo*), to request the control to provide a key for use at runtime (*RequestLicKey*), and to create an instance of the control based on a license key passed in by the container (*CreateInstanceLic*). The license information returned by *GetLicInfo* is returned in an instance of the newly defined *LICINFO* structure, which contains three fields:

- The length of the structure

- A flag saying whether this object can supply a runtime key

- A flag saying whether the object has already verified the machine or user license

The examination of licensing in this chapter is restricted to a discussion of the capabilities of the system rather than looking at ways in which it can be implemented. The first thing to notice is that containers which use *IClassFactory2* are implicitly aware of licensing and therefore can make use of all its functionality. Programs that aren't aware of this interface will carry on using *IClassFactory*. Importantly, any application that uses the OLE wrapper functions (such as *CoCreateInstance* or *OleCreate*) implictly use *IClassFactory* and cannot be made aware of *IClassFactory2*. Therefore, such applications will be limited in their abilities to support a control's licensing scheme.

Be aware that *IClassFactory2* contains a method, *RequestLicKey*, which allows a control's container to request a key that can be used at runtime. What does this mean? Well, imagine a situation in which you're writing an application using some third-party OLE control. If that control wants to limit you to using it only in that application unless you (or, more specifically, your users) are otherwise licensed, it can supply a key to the container that will allow that container to create instances of your control. As this key is saved with your application and is used invisibly by it, it can create instances of the control for its own use even if the user of the application is otherwise unable so to do.

The nature of all licensing keys and the semantics of the licensing scheme are entirely up to the control. The OLE CDK implements a simple scheme that can be overridden by a control as it sees fit.

Registration

All OLE objects need to be entered in the system registry before any other application can use them, as this is where OLE looks to identify the executable or DLL required to instantiate a given object. Executable programs typically register themselves automatically when they're run. DLL-based OLE controls, however, in common with other in-process servers, are unable to do this as they cannot run outside the context of a client application. Consequently, they must be registered either by an installation program or by containers that provide browsing facilities to their users. Such facilities allow a user to identify an OLE control that has not yet been registered and get the container to call a function within the DLL containing the control that causes it to register itself. It can then be used by the container, and other containers, as an OLE object.

For this to work, DLLs that support this registration functionality must implement the OLE self-registering protocol. This means that they export a routine called *DllRegisterServer*. They also export a routine called *DllUnregisterServer*, to remove information about them from the system registry. Containers and browsers need to be able to determine if a given DLL supports these entry points without needing to load the DLL, as loading can have undesirable side effects and is of course relatively time-consuming. OLE Controls specifies an addition to the standard Windows version information that lets self-registration support be determined. The addition is very simple: a new entry is required in the *StringFileInfo* block, *OLESelfRegister*. If this string is present (it doesn't need a value — its presence is all that is checked for), then the DLL is considered to be self-registering. DLLs must additionally support existing OLE requirements and export a function called *DllGetClassObject*, which is functionally equivalent to calling *CoCreateInstance* and asking for *IID_CLASSFACTORY*.

As a point of interest, executable files can also be marked as self-registering by the same technique. Rather than exporting functions that might be called, a self-registering executable file accepts */REGISTER* and */UNREGISTER* as command-line arguments.

Although not a requirement, OLE controls conventionally have the file extension OCX. This makes it easier for users to identify files and also simplifies file selection in browsers and containers.

Some Registry Keys

Like all OLE objects, OLE controls make use of keys within the registry to convey more information about them to their users. Some of the keys used by controls are standard ones provided by older-style OLE servers. Others are new to controls. The pertinent ones are *Insertable*, *Control*, *DefaultIcon*, and *ToolboxBitmap*. Each of these keys appears under *HKEY_CLASSES_ROOT\CLSID\{...}*.

The *Insertable* and *Control* keys have no value associated with them — that is, they are empty keys. If either key exists for a given control, the control has that attribute. *Insertable* means that the control will appear in Insert Object dialog boxes presented by containers. The standard OLE Insert Object dialog, as well as specific ones used by applications, trawl through the registry looking for all objects that have the *Insertable* key defined. These servers are then displayed in the dialog box. If an object does not have this key, it does not imply that it is not insertable; rather, it simply causes the object not to appear in Insert Object dialog boxes. It might be useful to remove this key if an object is designed to be inserted only in containers that know about its existence or if the object designer doesn't want this object to be randomly embedded in any container. Controls are often not marked insertable because in many cases controls are useful only in containers that are control-aware.

Control is a new key; it tells the container that this object is an OLE control. Again, this is used primarily for filling dialog boxes. The new generation of containers that recognize OLE controls typically distinguish between them and standard insertable objects, allowing the user to select the display of any mixture of insertable objects and controls. Dialog boxes that are designed to show only OLE controls will use this key to determine whether a specific object is displayed.

Typically, OLE controls are <u>not</u> marked as insertable but <u>are</u> marked as controls. This means that they can't be "seen" by users of containers that were written prior to OLE controls being released, although they can still in some cases be successfully inserted. (The presence or otherwise of the *Insertable* key does <u>not</u> imply that the control cannot be embedded!) Some controls, however, are either private to a given container or have no use unless the container is capable of dealing with the control's events. In the first case, neither key would be present; in the second case, the *Control* key would be present but the *Insertable* key would not.

The *DefaultIcon* key is another standard OLE key. When an object is to be displayed as an icon, the container uses this key to determine which icon to display. *DefaultIcon* contains two pieces of information: the name of the executable or DLL containing the icon and the resource ID of the icon. These pieces of information can then be used in a call to the Windows *ExtractIcon* API function.

The final key of interest is one new to OLE controls: *ToolboxBitmap* (and *ToolboxBitmap32*). When controls are registered with certain containers, such as Visual Basic, the control's icon appears in the container's control toolbox. Standard icons, however, are far too big for this, so controls should include a bitmap to be used. Currently, these bitmaps are defined to be 15 pixels by 16 pixels. The information held in this key resembles that for *DefaultIcon* — the executable or DLL holding the bitmap and the resource ID of the bitmap.

Versioning

Prior to the advent of the OLE Controls specification, OLE defined a mechanism designed to allow objects to be seamlessly upgraded without affecting their consumers. For example, an object could be embedded in a container and saved. Later, when the object comes to be reactivated, the user has installed a later version of the object server on her system. So long as it follows the OLE-defined rules, the new object server can manage the old object happily.

In fact, two modes of management are supported: emulation and conversion. "Emulation" means that the new version of the server decides to act as if it were the old version; the new version can read the old object's storage format and will also write any changes to that object back in the old format. "Conversion," on the other hand, means that the object decides to update the old object to the new version; therefore, it accepts the object's old storage format but replaces it with the new format.

The choice between emulation and conversion, in most cases, is made when the object is saved. OLE uses its own storage within the object's storage to hold a flag saying which operation should take place when this object is loaded by a newer version of the server. However, some containers and/or objects also allow the user to make this choice at runtime.

If an object server decides to support versioning, which of course it should, then it registers itself with a new CLSID but adds special forwarding references to the registry using the OLE API functions *CoSetTreatAsClass* and *OleSetAutoConvert*. This causes attempts to invoke an object using the old CLSID to invoke the new one, invisibly to the user.

This all works successfully because OLE embeddings rely on the fact that interfaces are contracts that don't change and because they don't rely on interfaces specific to a given object. It also depends on the object storing its persistent state using *IStorage* because that's where OLE holds the information about whether to emulate or convert.

The bad news is that OLE controls break these conditions. OLE controls expose interfaces to which the container binds. For example, when a control is loaded into a container, the container will read the control's type library and extract the specific automation interface for properties and methods and the event set interface description. These interfaces too are contracts, but they are very specific to a given control: they are not polymorphic. Cast your mind back to the section earlier in this chapter on events (beginning on page 86), and you'll remember the discussion about a control whose coclass exposes two interfaces: *_DHexocx* and *_DHexocxEvents*. The control implements the first as its standard automation interface for properties and methods. The container implements the second interface, so that the control can fire its events. These two interfaces are specific to the *Hexocx* coclass.

Also, most OLE controls don't use only *IStorage* for persistence; many support the other various persistence interfaces such as *IStreamInit* and OLE property sets through *IDataObject*.

Now, when someone provides a new version of a control, it is likely that the new control has more than just bug fixes — it is very likely to have new functionality, and this might mean changes and additions to existing interfaces. Bang goes our contract! Fortunately, various scenarios are defined in which this seemingly nasty problem can in general be satisfactorily resolved. These scenarios are binary compatibility, source compatibility, and the two combined.

A control is said to be "binary compatible" with an earlier version if it can be plugged in to an existing application that was designed and built with the old version in such a way that the application continues to work exactly as before. A control is said to be "source compatible" if the new version of a control continues to work without modification to the user code in a container application, but because of changes to IDs, names, and so forth, the user program must be rebuilt.

Consider a Visual Basic program that has been written to work with a control's version 1.0. Version 1.1 of the control has just been released and the user buys it and installs it. If the new version is binary-compatible, the program continues to run. If it is only source-compatible, the program must be recompiled first but will then run without further change. Controls should typically strive to be both binary- and source-compatible with previous versions.

For a control to achieve binary compatibility, it must appear to a container as if it were the old version; it must support the old CLSID and all the interfaces exactly as they were (that is, the same IIDs, names, dispids, parameters, and so forth), and it must also provide all the same connection points to accept the original sink IIDs. This is not to say that the control can't also support a new CLSID, if required. It can also support completely new interfaces in addition to the old ones, of course. More subtly, interfaces can be added to without harming the application's view of those interfaces. For example, automation interfaces can have new methods and properties added, as long as they use dispids that weren't present in the old version. Likewise, non-dispatch interfaces can have new methods added, as long as the old methods appear in the vtable in the order and position in which they were present in the old version.

A control might also decide to accept *QueryInterface* calls with the IIDs of old interfaces and actually return pointers to new interfaces, as long as the new interfaces can absolutely fulfill the old interfaces' contracts.

Connection-point compatibility can be slightly harder to achieve, as a given connection point is designed to *QueryInterface* its sink for the chosen IID during the call to its *Advise* method. If the new control version asks for a new IID, the container will be unable to supply it because it was written to expect to be asked for the old IID. Therefore, the control should call *QueryInterface* for the old IID if it fails for the newer one.

A control achieves source compatibility by supporting all the old interfaces with the same properties, methods, and parameters as before. Interfaces can be altered in other ways, and the control might well have a new CLSID (really, it should if it isn't also binary compatible), but the original code won't need to be changed to support the new version.

Nonetheless, instances will exist in which a new version of a control simply can't achieve one or other of these levels of compatibility, in which case the new version should be regarded for all intents and purposes as a new control.

NOTE   Some of the practical issues concerning versioning, particularly as they relate to persistent properties, are examined in Chapter 10.

APPENDIX A

That's really the end of my in-depth look at OLE and COM and the specifics of importance to OLE controls. The next chapter introduces Microsoft's toolset for creating OLE controls — the OLE CDK. The CDK relies heavily on the Microsoft Foundation Class (MFC) Library, so you really should be at least aware of MFC. If you're not, or if you'd like a refresher of more details, Appendix A provides a quick run-through of MFC concepts and the major classes it contains. Appendix A also looks at the wizards and other tools that come with Microsoft Visual C++, which make development using the MFC library even easier. If you're already an MFC expert or content to let the details be someone else's problem, you don't need to read Appendix A.

Chapter 4

Creating a Control

If you've read through the previous chapters and perhaps taken a glance at Appendix A, you'll know all about "componentware," OLE's role in this, and how it works. You'll also understand the specifics of OLE and COM and how they relate to OLE controls. What I want to do now is find a way of tying this all together so that you can actually get and create some real OLE controls.

To do this, I first start with a hypothetical extension to *AutoProg*, which adds some of the new interfaces used by controls. You can skip this bit if you want to, although reading this section will help with the understanding of a later section, where I rewrite the control using the Microsoft OLE Control Developer's Kit (OLE CDK, for short). You'll see that although writing the basic connection-point interfaces is in itself not too difficult, it becomes a great deal easier when you let the OLE CDK do it for you.

IMPLEMENTING SOME OF THE NEW INTERFACES

This chapter is all about creating OLE controls using the OLE CDK. If you made it through Chapters 2 and 3 (and perhaps Appendix A), you might just be crazy enough to want to know how to write OLE controls <u>without</u> using the OLE CDK. This book doesn't attempt to fully address this topic, but in this section I do show how to implement some of the new COM interfaces required by controls. The example I look at is the addition of connection-point interfaces to an existing program.

NOTE To repeat, you do not need to know <u>any</u> of this to create excellent
OLE controls.

The *AutoProg* program is a good place to start, because *AutoProg* is a basic
OLE Automation server. It can't be <u>that</u> difficult to add an events connection point
to it followed by all the requisite visual editing support, can it? Well, I'll start by
adding support for connection points to *AutoProg*. I'm going to start from the
AutoPro2 version of the program (which you can find on the companion CD-ROM),
completed at the end of Chapter 3. (See also Appendix A, which introduces
AutoPro3, an MFC version.) I'm now going to add lazy connection-point support—
"lazy," because it has the following limitations:

- *IEnumConnectionPoints* is not implemented.

- *IEnumConnections* is not implemented.

- Multi-casting is not supported.

- Only one connection point is supported, and that's for a very simple
  events interface.

- Connection points are separate COM objects, akin to client sites, but this
  implementation actually includes the *IConnectionPoint* interface implementation as part of the same, big object as the rest of the program.

The entire source code to this application can be found on the companion
CD-ROM in the \OLECTRLS\CHAP04\AUTOPRO4 directory. Here is what you need
to add for connection-point support:

- An implementation of the *IProvideClassInfo* interface

- An implementation of the *IConnectionPointContainer* interface

- An implementation of the *IConnectionPoint* interface

- An events interface

- A type library

Taking the interface implementations first, you can add nested classes to the
CAuto class for each of these interfaces, together with appropriate member variables
in the *CAuto* class itself and back pointers to the containing *CAuto* object in each
of the interface nested classes. You also need to define each nested class as a *friend*

of *CAuto*, so that each nested class can access *CAuto*'s private member variables if necessary. And you also need to change the *CAuto* constructor to pass its *this* pointer to each nested class constructor, so that each constructor can create its back pointer to the containing *CAuto* object. Listing 4-1 shows the new *CAuto* class.

CAuto

```
class FAR CAuto
{
public:
    STDMETHOD ( QueryInterface ) ( REFIID riid,
        void FAR * FAR *ppv );
    STDMETHOD_ ( ULONG, AddRef ) ( void );
    STDMETHOD_ ( ULONG, Release ) ( void );

    class FAR CAutoDisp
    {
    public:
        STDMETHOD_ ( void, PutSalary ) ( long lSalary );
        STDMETHOD_ ( long, GetSalary ) ( void );
        STDMETHOD_ ( void, Payraise ) ( long lSalaryIncrement );
        STDMETHOD_ ( void, Store ) ( void );

        CAutoDisp ( CAuto FAR *pAuto )
        {
            m_pAuto = pAuto;
        }
    private:
        CAuto FAR *m_pAuto;
    };
    friend CAutoDisp;
    CAutoDisp m_AutoDisp;

    class FAR CAutoPCI : public IProvideClassInfo
    {
    public:
        STDMETHOD ( QueryInterface ) ( REFIID riid,
            void FAR * FAR *ppv );
        STDMETHOD_ ( ULONG, AddRef ) ( void );
```

Listing 4-1. *The* CAuto *class definition with the three connection-point interfaces added.* *(continued)*

(continued)

```
        STDMETHOD_ ( ULONG, Release ) ( void );

        STDMETHOD ( GetClassInfo ) ( LPTYPEINFO FAR *ppTI );
        CAutoPCI ( CAuto FAR *pAuto )
        {
            m_pAuto = pAuto;
        }
    private:
        CAuto FAR *m_pAuto;
    };
    friend CAutoPCI;
    CAutoPCI m_AutoPCI;

    class FAR CAutoCPC : public IConnectionPointContainer
    {
    public:
        STDMETHOD ( QueryInterface ) ( REFIID riid,
            void FAR * FAR *ppv );
        STDMETHOD_ ( ULONG, AddRef ) ( void );
        STDMETHOD_ ( ULONG, Release ) ( void );

        STDMETHOD ( EnumConnectionPoints ) (
            LPENUMCONNECTIONPOINTS FAR *ppEnum );
        STDMETHOD ( FindConnectionPoint )( REFIID iid,
            LPCONNECTIONPOINT FAR *ppCP );

        CAutoCPC ( CAuto FAR *pAuto )
        {
            m_pAuto = pAuto;
        }
    private:
        CAuto FAR *m_pAuto;
    };
    friend CAutoCPC;
    CAutoCPC m_AutoCPC;

    class FAR CAutoCP : public IConnectionPoint
    {
    public:
        STDMETHOD ( QueryInterface ) ( REFIID riid,
            void FAR * FAR *ppv );
        STDMETHOD_ ( ULONG, AddRef ) ( void );
```

(continued)

```
        STDMETHOD_ ( ULONG, Release ) ( void );

        STDMETHOD ( GetConnectionInterface ) ( IID FAR *pIID );
        STDMETHOD ( GetConnectionPointContainer ) (
            IConnectionPointContainer FAR * FAR *ppCPC );
        STDMETHOD ( Advise ) ( LPUNKNOWN pUnkSink,
            DWORD FAR *pdwCookie );
        STDMETHOD ( Unadvise ) ( DWORD dwCookie );
        STDMETHOD ( EnumConnections ) (
            LPENUMCONNECTIONS FAR *ppEnum );

        CAutoCP ( CAuto FAR *pAuto )
        {
            m_pAuto = pAuto;
            m_dwCookie = 0;
        }
    private:
        CAuto FAR *m_pAuto;
        DWORD m_dwCookie;
    };
    friend CAutoCP;
    CAutoCP m_AutoCP;

    CAuto ( );
private:
    ULONG m_ulRefs;
    IUnknown FAR *m_punkStdDisp;
    long m_lSalary;
};
```

This is pretty much standard stuff now, following on from the dispatch interface nested class. Basically, I'm declaring a (nested) class for each connection-point–related interface and declaring the methods for each. In every case, the connection-point–related interfaces themselves are derived from *IUnknown*, so the three *IUnknown* methods are present in each.

The only slight change from this norm is the initialization of the *m_dwCookie* variable in the *CAutoCP* class. This "connection cookie" variable, whose name I derived from the parameter name to *IConnectionPoint::Advise* in the OLE Controls specification, is used to hold the connection ID (a magic number meaningful only to the connection point).

Now I can get to the interface implementation. The first interface, *IProvide-ClassInfo*, presents the first problem. This interface has only one non-*IUnknown* method, *GetClassInfo*. This method sets up a pointer to an *ITypeInfo* implementation, which reflects the type info of the coclass object represented by this application. Does this mean you need to implement *ITypeInfo* as well? Thankfully no, but it does mean that you need to define a type library now and register it with the system. You can then use that type library later to provide the requisite *ITypeInfo* pointer.

Bearing in mind that the main reason for exposing *IProvideClassInfo* in the first place is to allow the connection-point interface requirements to be queried, I'd better define the events interface and add type-library information for it. I'm going to have one event, as follows:

```
void OurEvent ( void )
```

The complete *AutoPro4* ODL file appears in Listing 4-2.

AUTOPROG.ODL

```
[ uuid(4D9FFA38-B732-11CD-92B4-08002B291EED), version(1.0),
    helpstring("AutoProg OLE Automation Server") ]
library AutoProg
{
    importlib("stdole32.tlb");

    //  Dispatch interface for AutoProg
    [ uuid(4D9FFA39-B732-11CD-92B4-08002B291EED),
        helpstring("Dispatch interface for AutoProg Server") ]
    dispinterface _DCAuto
    {
        properties:
            [id(0)] long Salary;
        methods:
            [id(1)] void Payraise ( long Increment );
            [id(2)] void Store ( void );
    };

    [ uuid(808CD080-D12D-11CD-92B4-08002B291EED),
        helpstring("AutoProg Server Events Interface") ]
    dispinterface _DCAutoEvents
    {
        properties:
        methods:
            [id(1)] void OurEvent ( void );
    };

    //  Class information for CAuto
```

Listing 4-2.   *The* AutoPro4 *ODL file.*   *(continued)*

```
[ uuid(AEE97356-B614-11CD-92B4-08002B291EED),
    helpstring("AutoProg Server") ]
coclass CAuto
{
    [default] dispinterface _DCAuto;
    [default, source] dispinterface _DCAutoEvents;
};
};
```

Notice that the coclass type info marks the (one and only) dispatch interface as the object's default (primary) dispatch interface and marks the events interface, *_DCAutoEvents*, as the default (primary) events interface. For convenience, I'll include the compiled type library in the program's resources, so it's always available, and I'll make it self-register so that the registry always reflects the correct location of the type library.

FYI Including a compiled type library in a program's resources is a recognized and recommended technique, used by OLE controls themselves as well as by OLE servers to provide type information.

To add the library to the resource file, you'll need to open the program's resource file in text mode. In Microsoft Visual C++ version 2.0, this means choosing the File Open dialog, selecting the RC file, and setting the Open As combo box to Text, and clicking OK. Then add this line to the file:

```
1 TYPELIB MOVEABLE PURE "WinDebug\\AutoProg.Tlb"
```

This defines a resource identified as *1* to be a type library, held in the file *WinDebug\AutoProg.Tlb*. Set the filename as appropriate.

NOTE I always keep a copy of the type library in one directory, *WinDebug*, so that it can always be found. If you do this, you've got to ensure that the copy is kept in step with the ODL file.

The next trick is to write some code to register this type libary with the system whenever the program is run. A good location for this code would be during the program's call to *InitInstance*, so I'll add a new function to the *CAutoProg* class to perform this action. For reasons that will become apparent, I'll also keep an *ITypeLib* pointer around for the duration of the program, so you need to add a member variable to the class as well as a public function to access it. Listing 4-3, beginning on the next page, contains the complete new class definition for *CAutoProg*.

CAutoProg

```
class CAutoProg : public CWinApp
{
public:
    DWORD m_dwAutoCF;

    LPTYPELIB GetTypeLib ( void ) const { return m_pTlib; }
protected:
    virtual BOOL InitInstance ( void );
    virtual int ExitInstance ( void );
    BOOL CreateClassFactory ( void );
    BOOL RegisterTypeLibrary ( void );
private:
    BOOL m_fOleInitSuccess;
    CAutoCF FAR *m_pAutoCF;
    LPTYPELIB m_pTlib;
};
```

Listing 4-3. *The declaration of* CAutoProg *with the new type-library registration function.*

Here you see a new member function called *RegisterTypeLibrary*, a private member variable called *m_pTlib*, which holds the *ITypeLib* pointer; and an inline public member function *GetTypeLib*, which returns the current value of *m_pTlib*. The three interfaces I'll be implementing are currently defined only in the OLE Controls header file, so you need to include this in the AUTOPROG.CPP file as well. Let's look at the code from *RegisterTypeLibrary*, which is shown in Listing 4-4 (and is available on the companion CD-ROM).

RegisterTypeLibrary

```
BOOL CAutoProg::RegisterTypeLibrary ( void )
{
    BOOL bSuccess = FALSE;

        // The type library is contained within the EXE file,
        //   so get the filename.
    CString strPathName;
    ::GetModuleFileName ( m_hInstance,
        strPathName.GetBuffer ( _MAX_PATH ), _MAX_PATH );
    strPathName.ReleaseBuffer ( );

    LPTYPELIB ptlib = NULL;
```

Listing 4-4. *The* RegisterTypeLibrary *member function.*   *(continued)*

```
    if ( SUCCEEDED ( LoadTypeLib (
        ( LPTSTR ) ( LPCTSTR ) strPathName, &ptlib ) ) )
    {
        ASSERT_POINTER ( ptlib, ITypeLib );
            // Register the type library
        if ( SUCCEEDED ( RegisterTypeLib ( ptlib,
            ( LPTSTR ) ( LPCTSTR ) strPathName, NULL ) ) )
        {
            bSuccess = TRUE;
        }
        m_pTlib = ptlib;
                                    // Save the ITypeLib pointer
                                    //   away for use during any
                                    //   calls to IProvideClassInfo.
    }
    return bSuccess;
}
```

The *RegisterTypeLibrary* member function uses *GetModuleFileName* and a couple of relatively esoteric *CString* methods to get the full pathname of the executable itself, because you know that the executable contains its own type library. It then calls *LoadTypeLib* to load the type library, returning a pointer to an *ITypeLib* if successful. The *ASSERT_POINTER* macro is defined at the top of the file; it checks that the returned pointer is valid. The type library is registered through a call to *RegisterTypeLib*, and the *ITypeLib* pointer is saved away in the class variable *m_pTlib* before the function ends, returning its success or failure as appropriate.

FYI The *ASSERT_POINTER* macro, as well as some other macros, and most of the *RegisterTypeLibrary* function itself are actually stolen from the OLE CDK!

Notice that I call *RegisterTypeLibrary* from *InitInstance*, checking the return value but only throwing out a message to the debugger if it fails. The *ITypeLib* interface pointer must be freed at the end of the program, so you also need to change *ExitInstance* to release it if it's set. This is done using another macro, *RELEASE*, which is also defined in the file and which calls *Release* on an interface pointer if that pointer is not zero. Now I can implement the *IProvideClassInfo* interface, as shown in Listing 4-5 on the next page.

IProvideClassInfo Implementation

```
//////////////////////////////
// IProvideClassInfo Implementation
STDMETHODIMP_ ( ULONG ) CAuto::CAutoPCI::AddRef ( void )
{
    return m_pAuto -> AddRef ( );
}


STDMETHODIMP_ ( ULONG ) CAuto::CAutoPCI::Release ( void )
{
    return m_pAuto -> Release ( );
}


STDMETHODIMP CAuto::CAutoPCI::QueryInterface ( REFIID riid,
    void FAR * FAR *ppv )
{
    if ( riid == IID_IProvideClassInfo )
    {
        AddRef ( );
        *ppv = this;
        return S_OK;
    }
    else
    {
        return m_pAuto -> QueryInterface ( riid, ppv );
    }
}


STDMETHODIMP CAuto::CAutoPCI::GetClassInfo ( LPTYPEINFO FAR
    *ppTI )
{
    LPTYPELIB ptlib = theProg.GetTypeLib ( );
    if ( ptlib )
    {       // Return coclass typeinfo
        return ptlib -> GetTypeInfoOfGuid ( CLSID_CAuto, ppTI );
    }
    else
    {
        return ResultFromScode ( TYPE_E_CANTLOADLIBRARY );
    }
}
```

Listing 4-5. *The implementation of the* IProvideClassInfo *interface,
from AUTOPROG.CPP.*

The implementation of *AddRef* and *Release* both delegate instantly to the outer *CAuto* implementations. This means that *CAuto*'s reference count no longer applies only to it. However, because all the interfaces are implemented as nested classes of *CAuto*, one cannot exist without the others, so it is perfectly safe to do this. *QueryInterface* also pretty much delegates to *CAuto*, unless the requested interface is *IProvideClassInfo*, in which case it returns a pointer to the *CAutoPCI* object within *CAuto*.

GetClassInfo is a very straightforward implementation. It retrieves the *ITypeLib* pointer from the application object and then calls *ITypeLib::GetTypeInfoOfGuid*, which returns an *ITypeInfo* pointer for the requested item in the type library. The item is referred to by its GUID, and I'm asking for the coclass object by passing in the GUID I've allocated as its CLSID. Assuming this works, I return the *ITypeInfo* pointer to the caller; otherwise I return an appropriate error code.

Okay, so that interface was pretty easy. Now I'll do *IConnectionPointContainer*, shown in Listing 4-6, which is also straightforward. Its implementation of the *IUnknown* methods are identical except that *QueryInterface* checks for *IID_IConnectionPointContainer* rather than *IProvideClassInfo*. I don't implement the enumerator interface for connection points within the connection point container, so the *EnumConnectionPoints* method returns the standard *E_NOTIMPL SCODE*, which tells the caller that the method isn't implemented. It actually wouldn't be a gross amount of work to write the *EnumConnectionPoints* method, because it's just like any standard OLE enumerator. (Code for these beasts can be found in *Inside OLE* by Kraig Brockschmidt.)

IConnectionPointContainer Implementation

```
STDMETHODIMP CAuto::CAutoCPC::EnumConnectionPoints (
    LPENUMCONNECTIONPOINTS FAR * )
{
    return ResultFromScode ( E_NOTIMPL );
}


STDMETHODIMP CAuto::CAutoCPC::FindConnectionPoint ( REFIID iid,
    LPCONNECTIONPOINT FAR *ppCP )
{
    if ( IsEqualGUID ( iid, GUID_Events ) )
    {
        return m_pAuto -> m_AutoCP.QueryInterface (
            IID_IConnectionPoint, ( LPVOID FAR * ) ppCP );
    }
    return ResultFromScode ( CONNECT_E_NOCONNECTION );
}
```

Listing 4-6. *The implementation of the* IConnectionPointContainer *interface.*

FindConnectionPoint is easy because I support only one connection — to your events interface. If the IID passed into the method is the same as the events IID, I return a pointer to the connection point by calling the *QueryInterface* method with the IID of *IConnectionPoint*. Notice that I'm not cheating here: each *IConnection-Point* implementation is supposed to be a different object, so the object that implements *IConnectionPointContainer* isn't the same as the one that implements *IConnectionPoint*. That's why I call through *CAuto's CAutoCP* member variable (*m_AutoCP*) to get to *IConnectionPoint's QueryInterface*.

That leaves me with the implementation of *IConnectionPoint* itself, shown in Listing 4-7. This listing shows all the non-*IUnknown* methods.

IConnectionPoint Implementation

```
STDMETHODIMP CAuto::CAutoCP::GetConnectionInterface (
    IID FAR *pIID )
{
    *pIID = GUID_Events;
    return S_OK;
}


STDMETHODIMP CAuto::CAutoCP::GetConnectionPointContainer (
    IConnectionPointContainer FAR * FAR *ppCPC )
{
    return m_pAuto -> QueryInterface (
        IID_IConnectionPointContainer, ( LPVOID FAR * ) ppCPC );
}


STDMETHODIMP CAuto::CAutoCP::Advise ( LPUNKNOWN pUnkSink,
    DWORD FAR *pdwCookie )
{
    if ( m_dwCookie )          // We only allow one connection.
    {
        return ResultFromScode ( CONNECT_E_ADVISELIMIT );
    }
    LPVOID ptr;
    if ( FAILED ( pUnkSink -> QueryInterface ( GUID_Events,
        &ptr ) ) )
    {
        return ResultFromScode ( CONNECT_E_CANNOTCONNECT );
    }
    m_dwCookie = 1;
    *pdwCookie = m_dwCookie;
```

Listing 4-7. *The implementation of* IConnectionPoint *from AUTOPROG.CPP*   *(continued)*
      in AutoPro4.

```
    m_pEvents = ( LPUNKNOWN ) ptr;    // Store the pointer.
    return S_OK;
}

STDMETHODIMP CAuto::CAutoCP::Unadvise ( DWORD dwCookie )
{
    if ( dwCookie != m_dwCookie )
    {
        return ResultFromScode ( CONNECT_E_NOCONNECTION );
    }
    else
    {
        m_pEvents -> Release ( );
        m_dwCookie = 0;
        return S_OK;
    }
}

STDMETHODIMP CAuto::CAutoCP::EnumConnections (
    LPENUMCONNECTIONS FAR * )
{
    return ResultFromScode ( E_NOTIMPL );
}
```

The *GetConnectionInterface* method is easy: I just put the events IID into the location I'm given. *GetConnectionPointContainer* is also not dramatically difficult to write; I simply call *QueryInterface* on the *CAuto* pointer I'm storing, asking for *IID_IConnectionPointContainer*. The *Advise* method is slightly more complicated. I've written the code to support only one connection, and I can tell if that connection has already been established by checking the member variable *m_dwCookie*. If this variable isn't zero, it's already connected, so I return the standard SCODE *CONNECT_E_ADVISELIMIT*. On the other hand, if it doesn't have a connection, I call *QueryInterface* on the passed-in interface pointer, asking it for a pointer to its implementation of <u>my</u> events interface. If this fails, another standard SCODE, *CONNECT_E_CANNOTCONNECT*, is returned.

Assuming success, I set *m_dwCookie* to *1* and return it to the caller. I also store away the pointer I got back from *QueryInterface,* in a member variable of type *LPUNKNOWN* called *m_pEvents*, which I'll use later to fire the event. You need to add *m_pEvents* to the class, as well as a public function, *GetEventIP*, which returns the events interface pointer. To add the variable, add this declaration immediately after the declaration of *m_dwCookie*:

```
    LPUNKNOWN m_pEvents;
```

To add the access function, add this line immediately after *CAutoCP*'s constructor:

```
LPDISPATCH GetEventIP ( void ) { return LPDISPATCH (
    m_dwCookie ? m_pEvents : 0 ); }
```

This inline function examines *m_dwCookie* to check whether you have a connection. If this is non-zero, implying that *m_pEvents* is valid, it returns *m_pEvents*; otherwise, it returns 0. In both cases, I know that the events interface is a dispatch interface, meaning that I'm going to be calling *Invoke* on it at some point, so I cast the return value to *LPDISPATCH*.

Unadvise basically reverses the actions of *Advise*, as you'd expect. It first checks to ensure that there is a connection and that the connection cookie passed in is the one given out earlier. (The caller doesn't know, or rather shouldn't know, that this class returns only zero or one!) If the connection isn't the same, you return *CONNECT_E_NOCONNECTION*. Otherwise, I release the interface pointer in *m_pEvents* and reset *m_dwCookie* to zero. Finally, I don't implement the connection enumerator, so I return *E_NOTIMPL* for the *EnumConnections* method.

As I said, there is a slight cheat in this implementation: my *IConnectionPoint* object happens to be the same as my *IConnectionPointContainer* object. The only place this could make a difference in this case is if my implementation of *IConnectionPoint::QueryInterface* delegated to *CAuto*'s implementation, which would allow it to return pointers to interfaces that it doesn't actually implement itself. So I ensure it doesn't, as shown in Listing 4-8.

IConnectionPoint::QueryInterface Implementation

```
STDMETHODIMP CAuto::CAutoCP::QueryInterface ( REFIID riid,
    void FAR * FAR *ppv )
{
    if ( ( riid == IID_IConnectionPoint ) ||
         ( riid == IID_IUnknown ) )
    {
        AddRef ( );
        *ppv = this;
        return S_OK;
    }
    else
    {
        return ResultFromScode ( E_NOINTERFACE );
    }
```

Listing 4-8. *The implementation of the* IConnectionPoint::QueryInterface *method.*

Now all that remains is to use the events interface that's connected to the object. If I say that I'm going to fire the event whenever the *Payraise* method is used to set the salary to a multiple of 100, I can amend the *Payraise* method to that shown in Listing 4-9.

Payraise

```
STDMETHODIMP_ ( void ) CAuto::CAutoDisp::Payraise (
    long lSalaryIncrement )
{
    m_pAuto -> m_lSalary += lSalaryIncrement;
        // Fire the event if the new salary is a multiple of 100.
    if ( m_pAuto -> m_lSalary % 100L )
    {
        m_pAuto -> FireYourEvent ( );
    }
}
```

Listing 4-9. *The amended* Payraise *method.*

I now need to write *CAuto::FireYourEvent*. What I do here is to call the connection-point access function, *GetEventIP*, to get the dispatch interface pointer. If this isn't zero, meaning I have a valid connection, I call *Invoke* on that pointer. Once again, I've taken the easy way out and made the *Invoke* call as simple as possible — first, by having no arguments and no return value from the method I'm calling, and second, by not checking the *Invoke* return value or the exception structure on return. I just assume it worked. The first parameter to *Invoke*, by the way, is the dispid of the routine you're calling "on the other side." Because I've defined the interface, I don't need to ask the value of this dispid. It's *1*. Listing 4-10 shows the code in full.

FireYourEvent

```
void CAuto::FireYourEvent ( void )
{
    LPDISPATCH lpEvents;
    if ( lpEvents = m_AutoCP.GetEventIP ( ) )
    {
        EXCEPINFO ex;
        unsigned int uTmp;
        DISPPARAMS dp = { 0, 0, 0, 0 };
        lpEvents -> Invoke ( 1, IID_NULL, LOCALE_SYSTEM_DEFAULT,
            DISPATCH_METHOD, &dp, 0, &ex, &uTmp );
    }
}
```

Listing 4-10. *The* FireYourEvent *code.*

What I've actually done here is to prove that connection points, and events specifically, are not only for controls: any COM object can create and use events. What I've created with *AutoPro4* is not an OLE control, yet it most certainly is a COM object with a connection point for events. This fact actually makes it rather difficult to test the program, because a container that doesn't support OLE Controls won't know about connection points, and one that does also expects some of the other OLE control interfaces to be there, and will refuse to embed the object. So, if you <u>really</u> want to test it, you'll have to write a simple container yourself, one that can talk to this object's dispatch interface but that can also interrogate the object and create the events dispatch interface.

NOTE Oh, and one other little point that might stop you. At the time of this writing — and this is likely to be true through most of 1995 — Microsoft does not provide remoting code for the *IConnectionPoint* family of interfaces. This means that the interfaces are supported only in in-process situations — local servers simply won't work. Microsoft Corporation is well aware of this and will be shipping the remoting code in one way or another as soon as it can find a suitable shipping vehicle.

CREATING A CONTROL THE EASY WAY . . . WITH THE OLE CDK

If you read the section "Implementing Some of the New Interfaces" (beginning on the first page of this chapter), you might be wondering why we've gone through the pain of creating something that is not particularly useful. The point was to demonstrate that the interfaces required of controls are not of themselves necessarily difficult to implement, but that there's more to a control than connection points and events interfaces. So let's write a real control. But I don't want to go through all that again, so I'll take the easy (and smart) way out: I'll use the Microsoft OLE Control Developer's Kit (OLE CDK).

What's in the CDK?

The OLE CDK was first distributed to the public with the release of Microsoft Visual C++ version 2.0 in September 1994. The Visual C++ CD-ROM contains the 32-bit compiler, a slightly updated version of the 16-bit system, Visual C++ version 1.51, and the OLE CDK for both 16-bit and 32-bit implementations. With both versions, the OLE CDK is an add-on that is installed on top of the compiler(s). This was updated slightly in January 1995 with Visual C++ version 2.1, which also includes version 1.1 of the CDK. The CDK improvements over the first release are support for Win32s, support for some of the MFC ODBC classes, and performance enhancements.

So what's in the OLE CDK? In brief, everything you need to develop 16-bit and 32-bit OLE controls for Intel platforms using Microsoft's Visual C++ compilers. There might be other OLE CDKs coming along from other compiler vendors, but I'm sticking with this one.

When you install the OLE CDK, this is what you get:

■ The OLE Controls runtime DLL

■ New MFC classes, libraries, and header files

■ A "test container" application for verifying your control

■ A skeleton control generator, ControlWizard

■ In the case of the 16-bit compiler, an updated ClassWizard

■ Lots of online Help

■ Samples showing all the different features of OLE Controls

Installation

The OLE CDK is installed over an installation of the relevant C++ compiler. The OLE CDK setup program detects the operating system under which it is running and which Visual C++ compilers are installed, and it allows you to install only the relevant CDKs. In other words, if you have Visual C++ version 1.51 running under any flavor of Windows, you'll be able to set up the 16-bit OLE CDK; if you have Visual C++ version 2.0 <u>and</u> you're running a 32-bit version of Windows, you can install the 32-bit version. If you have both compilers installed and you're running 32-bit Windows, you can install both versions of the OLE CDK. (Be aware, however, that you need to run the setup program twice to do this!)

The noticeable effects of installation are the creation of a new program group (or folder, if you're running Microsoft Windows 95), the addition of some items to the Visual C++ Tools menu, and the consumption of yet more disk space. The program group contains the OLE CDK Books Online program, the Test Container application, and the readme file for the CDK. Books Online is the documentation system used in Microsoft's Visual C++ compilers and tools; it provides all the documentation on line (hence, the name), with complete indexing for full-text searches, so it's very fast to find things in comparision with the manual, paper-based way.

CREATING AN OLE CONTROL WITH THE OLE CDK

The first step in creating a control using the OLE CDK is to invoke the control equivalent of AppWizard, known as ControlWizard. You'll find the ControlWizard on the Visual C++ Tools menu after you've installed the CDK. When ControlWizard is invoked, it presents an AppWizard-like dialog box in which you can select the directory in which your control will be built and the name of the control DLL itself. For the purposes of this chapter, select any working directory you like and call the project *First.* Click the Project Options button, and the dialog box shown in Figure 4-1 appears.

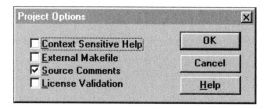

Figure 4-1. *The ControlWizard Project Options dialog box.*

Notice here that you can choose to have context-sensitive help in your control, which means that some basic Help files and the hooks for Help invocation will be included in your project. Leave this off for now. You can also choose to create an external make file, which is an option I'll ignore throughout this book. The third option is one that you should select in all control projects you create: it puts sensible comments in the code it generates to tell you what steps you need to take and to explain the meaning of some lines. The fourth option, license validation, is also one I'll ignore for a while.

The next dialog box that you can invoke is the Control Options dialog box, as shown in Figure 4-2. This dialog box contains a wealth of options:

- The name of the control class within the project to be manipulated

- Whether the control should be activated when visible

- Whether the control's registry entry should include the *Insertable* key, to allow it to be displayed in a standard OLE Insert Object dialog box

- Whether the control should be invisible at runtime (like Microsoft Visual Basic's timer control)

- Whether the control should support calling the *ISimpleFrameSite* protocol, allowing it to contain other OLE controls

- Whether the control should be equipped with the standard *AboutBox* method and a standard, but customizable, implementation

- Whether the control should be a derivative of a standard Windows control and, if so, which one

- Whether the control should derive its properties, methods, and events from an existing Visual Basic custom control (VBX)

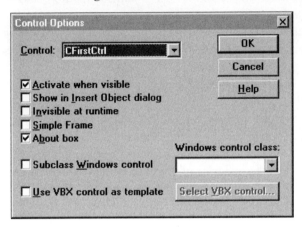

Figure 4-2. *The ControlWizard Control Options dialog box.*

As you'll see in the next ControlWizard dialog, a single project can contain multiple controls, resulting in a single OCX file. The Control Options dialog allows you to select the behavior of each of the controls based on the name of the MFC class that it generates for that control. Most controls will be activated when they become visible, if the container will support it. The ControlWizard option sets the *OLEMISC_ACTIVATEWHENVISIBLE* status bit within the OLE control's registry entry if this option is chosen. Some controls might be listed not only in control-specific dialogs but also in standard Insert Object dialogs. For this to be the case, the control must have the *Insertable* key in its registry entry, as discussed in Chapters 2 and 3. The ControlWizard option named Show In Insert Object Dialog ensures this if it is selected.

Although the vast majority of OLE controls will have a visible representation at runtime, some will show no user interface. Such controls, however, should still display something at design time so that the user can recognize and manipulate the control. An obvious example of this is Visual Basic's timer control, which can be seen at runtime and can be placed on a form. Once there, though, it makes no visual appearance when the form is executed. If you want this behavior in your control, select the Invisible At Runtime option.

If the control you're creating is likely to contain other OLE controls (such as a group box or a 3-D panel), you'll want it to support the *ISimpleFrameSite* protocol. This is easy: simply select the Simple Frame option in the ControlWizard Options dialog box. (I look at this in greater detail in Chapter 16.)

It's always nice for users to be able to tell who wrote a control and when. (Well, let's be honest: it's great for the egos of the people who wrote the control.) OLE Controls defines a specific dispid for the *AboutBox* method, and by choosing the appropriate Control Options option, your control is automatically equipped with this method and with a simple implementation. The dialog box presented by this standard code can easily be changed if necessary, and you can of course increase the sophistication of the method itself.

A few of the controls shipped with versions of Visual Basic over the years, as well as quite a number of old-style SDK custom controls, are versions of standard Microsoft Windows controls with expanded functionality. For example, you might want a list box that has special drag-and-drop behavior. The Control Options dialog allows you to say that a given control is a subclass version of a standard Windows control, making it have all the behavior of that Windows control but letting you have control over any aspect to which you can get access. If you select the Subclass Windows Control option, the combo box to its side is populated with the names of the controls it is possible to subclass.

The last option in this dialog, Use VBX Control As Template, is useful if you've created a VBX in the past and you now want to convert it to an OLE control. While there is no mechanism to convert the implementation of a generic VBX to an OLE control, this option does read a VBX file and create from it a skeleton OLE control with the same properties and events as the VBX. I cover this subject in greater detail in Chapter 17.

For the purposes of this chapter, leave all the Controls Options dialog box selections as shown in Figure 4-2 (on page 133).

Finally, let's look at the Controls dialog box, shown in Figure 4-3. This dialog box allows you to add more controls to the project (and thus to the OCX file) or to remove some. You also get the option to change the names of the C++ classes that ControlWizard generates, the name of the control as it appears in the registry, and the names of the files in which the control's implementation is held. The Class drop-down list allows the class being manipulated to be switched between the control implementation class (shown in Figure 4-3) and the property page class.

Each OLE control generated by ControlWizard has an empty property page, which is wrapped by a C++ class separate from the control. Also, as every OLE control property page is an OLE object in its own right, with its own class factory, it too has a ProgID.

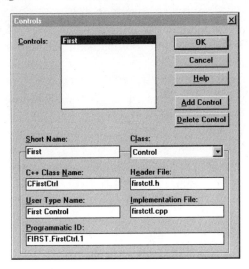

Figure 4-3. *The ControlWizard Controls dialog box.*

Once again, for this chapter's example, don't change any of the default names. After you've dismissed the Controls dialog box and returned to ControlWizard proper, click the OK button. As with AppWizard, this action displays a text box containing some really interesting information that very few people read after they've read it the first time, so go ahead and click the Create button. This will create the project files and open the project inside Visual C++. The rest of this chapter assumes the use of 32-bit Visual C++ version 2.0 under Windows 95 and later or Windows NT versions 3.5 and later; however, almost all of the discussion applies to 16-bit Visual C++ version 1.52 as well. I'll point out any differences as I go along.

What Did ControlWizard Give You?

Having created your control, let's look at the files that ControlWizard generated for you and what each of them contains. Three make files have been created for you: FIRST.MAK is for 16-bit Visual C++ version 1.52, FIRST32.MAK is for 32-bit Visual C++ version 2.0, and MAKEFILE is for command-line builds of either type. Unless you're into command-line builds, you can delete this last file. Each make file has both retail and debug builds included in them, and the 32-bit make file also has the option to build a Unicode control or an ANSI control.

NOTE As Chapter 3 explains, Unicode controls are limited to working on Windows NT, whereas 32-bit ANSI controls will work on all Win32 platforms. Build the Unicode control if you're specifically targeting Windows NT or if you're building all versions of a control so that your installation program can install the best ones for the target system.

Two DEF files are also produced, one for 16-bit and one for 32-bit builds. A readme file, README.TXT, is generated; it briefly describes the files that have been produced. The 32-bit DEF file contains less information than the 16-bit version because DEF files have a slightly less-elevated role in the 32-bit Windows world. FIRST.CLW and FIRST.VCW are compiler support files. (The CLW file is the ClassWizard database, which tracks where the classes are contained.) FIRST.RC, FIRST.RC2, and RESOURCE.H are the project's resource files: FIRST.RC includes the other two files, and RESOURCE.H is also used by the C++ files that want to access resources. The control has an icon, which is displayed on the default About box and is contained in FIRST.ICO. Likewise, it has a bitmap, which is used as the toolbox bitmap when the control is embedded in a container such as Visual Basic; this bitmap is held in FIRSTCTL.BMP. If there were more controls in the project, each would have separate bitmap files to allow them each to have different graphics in the toolbox.

As with any other MFC DLL, each control file has a *CWinApp*-derived object. With OLE Controls, the application class is actually derived from a new control class, *COleControlModule*, which is itself derived from *CWinApp*. The class that Control-Wizard has derived from *COleControlModule* for you is *CFirstApp*, and it's contained in the FIRST.CPP and FIRST.H files. The class for the OLE control itself is derived from *CWnd*, via the *COleControl* class. Your class is called *CFirstCtrl*, and it's contained in the files FIRSTCTL.CPP and FIRSTCTL.H. Your property page class, *CFirstPropPage*, is derived from *COlePropertyPage* and is held in FIRSTPPG.CPP and FIRSTPPG.H. *COlePropertyPage* is derived from *CDialog*. STDAFX.CPP and STDAFX.H are the standard MFC files for efficient use of precompiled headers.

The only remaining file is FIRST.ODL, which is the automatically generated object description language source file for the control(s) within the project. Right now, the file is essentially empty. It defines the type library itself as *FirstLib*, as well as the control's as-yet-empty primary dispatch interface, called *_DFirst*, and its primary events interface, also empty, called *_DFirstEvents*. Finally, the coclass *First* itself is defined. As you add properties, events, and methods with ClassWizard, this ODL file is updated appropriately. When compiled, the type library is included within the project's resources.

Let's now take a look at the three classes that ControlWizard generated for you and the nature of the code therein. You need to look at these things in fairly close detail to understand not only what has been generated but also what it actually does.

NOTE   Again, this is one of those areas in which you don't need all the detail to write controls; however, background information on what an automated tool is generating for you gives you a far better chance of understanding any strange behavior that your control might be exhibiting.

The Control Module Class: *CFirstApp*

If you look more closely at the implementation of *CFirstApp*, you'll notice that ControlWizard has created code only for the *InitInstance* and *ExitInstance* member functions. It's also put two global (non-class) functions in the same file: *DllRegisterServer* and *DllUnregisterServer*. These functions are exported by the DLL containing the control and are used for entry and removal of the control's details from the registry.

Listing 4-11 shows the FIRST.H header file for the class, and Listing 4-12 shows the main body of code that implements the First control.

FIRST.H

```
// first.h : main header file for FIRST.DLL

#if !defined( __AFXCTL_H__ )
    #error include 'afxctl.h' before including this file
#endif

#include "resource.h"        // main symbols

/////////////////////////////////////////////////////////////////////
// CFirstApp : See first.cpp for implementation.

class CFirstApp : public COleControlModule
{
public:
    BOOL InitInstance();
    int ExitInstance();
};

extern const GUID CDECL _tlid;
extern const WORD _wVerMajor;
extern const WORD _wVerMinor;
```

Listing 4-11.   *FIRST.H header file.*

The header file includes RESOURCE.H, which gets definitions for each of the resource IDs used in the program. It then declares *CFirstApp* as a derivative of *COleControlModule* and defines *InitInstance* and *ExitInstance* as the only two public member functions of this class. (You can add more if you like.) It then declares three global variables (as externs, because although they're defined in FIRST.CPP, they're used elsewhere and this header file is included elsewhere). The variables are *_tlid*, which holds the control's type library GUID, *_wVerMajor* and *_wVerMinor*, which together hold the control's version number.

The code in Listing 4-12 first creates a global instance of the *CFirstApp* class, called *theApp*, and defines the three global variables, one of which is initialized to the type library GUID and two of which are initialized to a version number of 1.0. It then defines *CFirstApp::InitInstance*, which calls the base class *InitInstance* to set up the control module and then allows user code to be inserted. *ExitInstance* is similar; you can add your own code to the termination routine before it calls its base class implementation. Then come the two global registration functions: *DllRegisterServer* and *DllUnregisterServer*. *DllRegisterServer* first calls a peculiar macro, *AFX_MANAGE_STATE*, which sets up a class of type *AFX_MAINTAIN_STATE*, which holds the module context. It then attempts to register the control's type library using a more functional variant of the way I did it in *AutoPro4*. If this fails, it returns *SELFREG_E_TYPELIB*. If it succeeds, it attempts to register the control itself in the system registry, returning *SELFREG_E_CLASS* if this fails; otherwise, it returns with no error. *DllUnregisterServer* is almost identical except that it unregisters the type library and removes the control information from the registry.

FIRST.CPP

```
// first.cpp : Implementation of CFirstApp and DLL registration.

#include "stdafx.h"
#include "first.h"
#ifdef _DEBUG
#undef THIS_FILE
static char BASED_CODE THIS_FILE[] = __FILE__;
#endif


CFirstApp NEAR theApp;

const GUID CDECL BASED_CODE _tlid =
        { 0x14bc5f83, 0xdbd2, 0x11cd, { 0x92, 0xb4, 0x8, 0x0, 0x2b,
```

Listing 4-12. *The implementation of the First control.*   *(continued)*

```
        0x29, 0x1e, 0xed } };
const WORD _wVerMajor = 1;
const WORD _wVerMinor = 0;


/////////////////////////////////////////////////////////////////
// CFirstApp::InitInstance - DLL initialization

BOOL CFirstApp::InitInstance()
{
    BOOL bInit = COleControlModule::InitInstance();

    if (bInit)
    {
        // TODO: Add your own module initialization code here.
    }

    return bInit;
}


/////////////////////////////////////////////////////////////////
// CFirstApp::ExitInstance - DLL termination

int CFirstApp::ExitInstance()
{
    // TODO: Add your own module termination code here.

    return COleControlModule::ExitInstance();
}


/////////////////////////////////////////////////////////////////
// DllRegisterServer - Adds entries to the system registry

STDAPI DllRegisterServer(void)
{
    AFX_MANAGE_STATE(_afxModuleAddrThis);

    if (!AfxOleRegisterTypeLib(AfxGetInstanceHandle(), _tlid))
        return ResultFromScode(SELFREG_E_TYPELIB);

    if (!COleObjectFactoryEx::UpdateRegistryAll(TRUE))
        return ResultFromScode(SELFREG_E_CLASS);
```

(continued)

139

(continued)

```
    return NOERROR;
}


/////////////////////////////////////////////////////////////
// DllUnregisterServer - Removes entries from the system registry

STDAPI DllUnregisterServer(void)
{
    AFX_MANAGE_STATE(_afxModuleAddrThis);

    if (!AfxOleUnregisterTypeLib(_tlid))
        return ResultFromScode(SELFREG_E_TYPELIB);

    if (!COleObjectFactoryEx::UpdateRegistryAll(FALSE))
        return ResultFromScode(SELFREG_E_CLASS);

    return NOERROR;
}
```

The Control Class: *CFirstCtrl*

The *CFirstCtrl* control class is the main class you'll be manipulating as you add to the control. This is always the case with OLE controls created with the OLE CDK: the *COleControl*-derived class is the one into which the majority of the control's functionality will be put. The FIRSTCTL.H header file is shown in Listing 4-13.

FIRSTCTL.H

```
// firstctl.h : Declaration of the CFirstCtrl OLE control class.

/////////////////////////////////////////////////////////////
// CFirstCtrl : See firstctl.cpp for implementation.

class CFirstCtrl : public COleControl
{
    DECLARE_DYNCREATE(CFirstCtrl)

// Constructor
public:
```

Listing 4-13. *FIRSTCTL.H header file.*

(continued)

```
    CFirstCtrl();
// Overrides

    // Drawing function
    virtual void OnDraw(
                CDC* pdc, const CRect& rcBounds,
                const CRect& rcInvalid);

    // Persistence
    virtual void DoPropExchange(CPropExchange* pPX);

    // Reset control state
    virtual void OnResetState();

// Implementation
protected:
    ~CFirstCtrl();

    DECLARE_OLECREATE_EX(CFirstCtrl)    // Class factory and guid
    DECLARE_OLETYPELIB(CFirstCtrl)      // GetTypeInfo
    DECLARE_PROPPAGEIDS(CFirstCtrl)     // Property page IDs
    DECLARE_OLECTLTYPE(CFirstCtrl)      // Type name and misc status

// Message maps
    //{{AFX_MSG(CFirstCtrl)
        // NOTE - ClassWizard will add and remove member functions
        //   here.
        //    DO NOT EDIT what you see in these blocks of generated
        //      code !
    //}}AFX_MSG
    DECLARE_MESSAGE_MAP()
// Dispatch maps
    //{{AFX_DISPATCH(CFirstCtrl)
        // NOTE - ClassWizard will add and remove member functions
        //   here.
        //    DO NOT EDIT what you see in these blocks of generated
        //      code !
    //}}AFX_DISPATCH
    DECLARE_DISPATCH_MAP()

    afx_msg void AboutBox();

// Event maps
```

(continued)

(continued)

```
    //{{AFX_EVENT(CFirstCtrl)
        // NOTE - ClassWizard will add and remove member functions
        //   here.
        //    DO NOT EDIT what you see in these blocks of generated
        //      code !
    //}}AFX_EVENT
    DECLARE_EVENT_MAP()

// Dispatch and event IDs
public:
    enum {
    //{{AFX_DISP_ID(CFirstCtrl)
        // NOTE: ClassWizard will add and remove enumeration
        //   elements here.
        //    DO NOT EDIT what you see in these blocks of
        //      generated code !
    //}}AFX_DISP_ID
    };
};
```

The class definition comes first. The *DECLARE_DYNCREATE* macro sets up the class for dynamic creation, as per normal MFC standards. This will be matched by a call to *IMPLEMENT_DYNCREATE* in the implementation file. Then follows the constructor, the virtual drawing function (*OnDraw*), the property persistence function (*DoPropExchange*), and *OnResetState*. This last function is called when the control is asked by the container to reset itself; in general, this will cause it to reset its property values to their default states. The destructor is then declared, followed by four innocuous-looking macros. These macros, as is characteristic of some MFC macros, hide a great deal of detail. *DECLARE_OLECREATE_EX* declares functions to set up the object's class factory; *DECLARE_OLETYPELIB* declares functions to get an *ITypeLib* pointer for this control's type library and to implement type library caching (an optimization performed by the OLE CDK); *DECLARE_PROPPAGEIDS* declares a member function to retrieve the control's property page CLSIDs; and *DECLARE_OLECTLTYPE* declares member functions to retrieve the control's ProgID and misc status bit values.

Next there are empty message map and dispatch map declarations and a declaration of the function that will be called when the *AboutBox* method is invoked. These are followed by an empty event map declaration and an empty enumeration, which will hold the dispids of the control's properties, methods, and events as they are added.

This leads us on to the FIRSTCTL.CPP implementation file, shown in Listing 4-14.

FIRSTCTL.CPP

```
// firstctl.cpp : Implementation of the CFirstCtrl OLE control class.

#include "stdafx.h"
#include "first.h"
#include "firstctl.h"
#include "firstppg.h"


#ifdef _DEBUG
#undef THIS_FILE
static char BASED_CODE THIS_FILE[] = __FILE__;
#endif


IMPLEMENT_DYNCREATE(CFirstCtrl, COleControl)


/////////////////////////////////////////////////////////////////
// Message map

BEGIN_MESSAGE_MAP(CFirstCtrl, COleControl)
    //{{AFX_MSG_MAP(CFirstCtrl)
    // NOTE - ClassWizard will add and remove message map entries
    //     DO NOT EDIT what you see in these blocks of generated
    //       code !
    //}}AFX_MSG_MAP
    ON_OLEVERB(AFX_IDS_VERB_PROPERTIES, OnProperties)
END_MESSAGE_MAP()


/////////////////////////////////////////////////////////////////
// Dispatch map

BEGIN_DISPATCH_MAP(CFirstCtrl, COleControl)
    //{{AFX_DISPATCH_MAP(CFirstCtrl)
    // NOTE - ClassWizard will add and remove dispatch map entries
    //     DO NOT EDIT what you see in these blocks of generated
    //       code !
    //}}AFX_DISPATCH_MAP
    DISP_FUNCTION_ID(CFirstCtrl, "AboutBox", DISPID_ABOUTBOX,
        AboutBox, VT_EMPTY, VTS_NONE)
```

Listing 4-14. *The FIRSTCTL.CPP implementation file.* (continued)

(continued)

```
END_DISPATCH_MAP()


/////////////////////////////////////////////////////////////
// Event map

BEGIN_EVENT_MAP(CFirstCtrl, COleControl)
    //{{AFX_EVENT_MAP(CFirstCtrl)
    // NOTE - ClassWizard will add and remove event map entries
    //     DO NOT EDIT what you see in these blocks of generated
    //        code !
    //}}AFX_EVENT_MAP
END_EVENT_MAP()


/////////////////////////////////////////////////////////////
// Property pages

// TODO: Add more property pages as needed.  Remember to increase
//    the count!
BEGIN_PROPPAGEIDS(CFirstCtrl, 1)
    PROPPAGEID(CFirstPropPage::guid)
END_PROPPAGEIDS(CFirstCtrl)


/////////////////////////////////////////////////////////////
// Initialize class factory and guid

IMPLEMENT_OLECREATE_EX(CFirstCtrl, "FIRST.FirstCtrl.1",
    0x14bc5f80, 0xdbd2, 0x11cd, 0x92, 0xb4, 0x8, 0x0, 0x2b, 0x29,
    0x1e, 0xed)


/////////////////////////////////////////////////////////////
// Type library ID and version
IMPLEMENT_OLETYPELIB(CFirstCtrl, _tlid, _wVerMajor, _wVerMinor)


/////////////////////////////////////////////////////////////
// Interface IDs
const IID BASED_CODE IID_DFirst =
```

(continued)

```
        { 0x14bc5f81, 0xdbd2, 0x11cd, { 0x92, 0xb4, 0x8, 0x0,
        0x2b,0x29, 0x1e, 0xed } };

const IID BASED_CODE IID_DFirstEvents =
        { 0x14bc5f82, 0xdbd2, 0x11cd, { 0x92, 0xb4, 0x8, 0x0,
        0x2b,0x29, 0x1e, 0xed } };


/////////////////////////////////////////////////////////////////////
// Control type information

static const DWORD BASED_CODE _dwFirstOleMisc =
    OLEMISC_ACTIVATEWHENVISIBLE |
    OLEMISC_SETCLIENTSITEFIRST |
    OLEMISC_INSIDEOUT |
    OLEMISC_CANTLINKINSIDE |
    OLEMISC_RECOMPOSEONRESIZE;

IMPLEMENT_OLECTLTYPE(CFirstCtrl, IDS_FIRST, _dwFirstOleMisc)


/////////////////////////////////////////////////////////////////////
// CFirstCtrl::CFirstCtrlFactory::UpdateRegistry -
// Adds or removes system registry entries for CFirstCtrl

BOOL CFirstCtrl::CFirstCtrlFactory::UpdateRegistry(BOOL
    bRegister)
{
    if (bRegister)
        return AfxOleRegisterControlClass(
                AfxGetInstanceHandle(),
                m_clsid,
                m_lpszProgID,
                IDS_FIRST,
                IDB_FIRST,
                FALSE,                          //  Not insertable
                _dwFirstOleMisc,
                _tlid,
```

(continued)

(continued)

```
            _wVerMajor,
            _wVerMinor);
    else
        return AfxOleUnregisterClass(m_clsid, m_lpszProgID);
}


/////////////////////////////////////////////////////////////////
// CFirstCtrl::CFirstCtrl - Constructor

CFirstCtrl::CFirstCtrl()
{
    InitializeIIDs(&IID_DFirst, &IID_DFirstEvents);

    // TODO: Initialize your control's instance data here.
}


/////////////////////////////////////////////////////////////////
// CFirstCtrl::~CFirstCtrl - Destructor

CFirstCtrl::~CFirstCtrl()
{
    // TODO: Clean up your control's instance data here.
}


/////////////////////////////////////////////////////////////////
// CFirstCtrl::OnDraw - Drawing function

void CFirstCtrl::OnDraw(
        CDC* pdc, const CRect& rcBounds, const CRect& rcInvalid)
{
    // TODO: Replace the following code with your own drawing
    //    code.
    pdc->FillRect(rcBounds,
        CBrush::FromHandle((HBRUSH)GetStockObject(WHITE_BRUSH)));
    pdc->Ellipse(rcBounds);
}


/////////////////////////////////////////////////////////////////
// CFirstCtrl::DoPropExchange - Persistence support
```

(continued)

```
void CFirstCtrl::DoPropExchange(CPropExchange* pPX)

{
    ExchangeVersion(pPX, MAKELONG(_wVerMinor, _wVerMajor));
    COleControl::DoPropExchange(pPX);

    // TODO: Call PX_ functions for each persistent custom
    //    property.

}


//////////////////////////////////////////////////////////////////
// CFirstCtrl::OnResetState - Reset control to default state

void CFirstCtrl::OnResetState()
{
    COleControl::OnResetState();   // Resets defaults found
                                   //    in DoPropExchange

    // TODO: Reset any other control state here.
}


//////////////////////////////////////////////////////////////////
// CFirstCtrl::AboutBox - Display an "About" box to the user

void CFirstCtrl::AboutBox()
{
    CDialog dlgAbout(IDD_ABOUTBOX_FIRST);
    dlgAbout.DoModal();
}


//////////////////////////////////////////////////////////////////
// CFirstCtrl message handlers
```

The first thing of note in the implementation is the empty message map, excepting the *ON_OLEVERB* entry that was added by ControlWizard. This allows the control to react to an invocation of one of its "verbs," or OLE actions. Normally containers place these verbs on their Edit menu when an object is selected. The only verb defined so far by this control is the *Properties* verb, which will cause the control to display its property page(s).

Then there's an almost empty dispatch map, except for the *AboutBox* entry that was added by ControlWizard when you selected the About Box option. This is followed by the empty events map and a property page map. This second map contains an entry for each property page used by the control, including standard ones. The numeric parameter to *BEGIN_PROPPAGEIDS* is the number of pages in the map, and each entry contains the CLSID of the property page. *IMPLE-MENT_OLECREATE_EX* creates the object's class factory and initializes it with the CLSID and ProgID passed in. Likewise, *IMPLEMENT_OLETYPELIB* implements the functions declared by the *DECLARE* version of the macro in the header file. The next two lines of functional code declare the IIDs for the control's primary dispatch and events interfaces, and *_dwFirstOleMisc* is initialized with the control's OLEMISC status bits. Notice the flags *OLEMISC_CANTLINKINSIDE*, which stops the object from being used as a link source when it is embedded, and *OLEMISC_RE-COMPOSEONRESIZE*, which tells the container that the object would like the opportunity to re-create its rendition if its size is changed in the container. The other status bits are the standard ones I have already discussed. The initialization of *_dwFirstOleMisc* is followed by the last of the "big four" macros, *IMPLE-MENT_OLECTLTYPE*. This macro creates the member functions to retrieve the control's ProgID and misc status bits.

The *CFirstCtrl::CFirstCtrlFactory::UpdateRegistry* member function is one of the object factory methods implemented for you by the MFC library. It is used by code elsewhere to register or remove the control in the system registry.

This leaves me with only the implementation of the *CFirstCtrl* class itself. ControlWizard doesn't create too many member functions for your derived class. You can add more later, and you can also override any of the virtual functions in the base class. The constructor does nothing by default other than store the dispatch and events interface IDs in member variables and lock its internal type library cache. The destructor provided for you does less — that is, nothing.

Of greater interest is the next member function, *OnDraw*, which is called whenever the control receives a notification to draw itself. This function as created by ControlWizard does something that will in almost all cases of a real control be removed by the developer straightaway: it draws an ellipse! The reason for this is two-fold: to show something when the control is placed in a container and to mimic the Circ series of examples from the old Visual Basic Control Development Kit (VB CDK). I'll leave this exciting code in for now, but I can guarantee that you'll change it later. Note the parameters to this function: unlike a standard MFC application, it is passed the dimensions of the rectangle in which it can draw. An OLE control, as is true for other OLE objects, is expressly not allowed to write outside this area. Why? If the OLE control is being displayed in a container window rather than in one of its own, it would write over container information if it were to violate the bounds of the rectangle passed to it. Another significant point to bear in mind whenever you add drawing code to an OLE control is this: do <u>not</u> assume that the top left corner of the control's rectangle is at coordinate (0, 0); again, if it's in a container window, (0, 0) would represent the top left corner of the container, not of the control.

DoPropExchange comes next. This function is used to transfer persistent property values between the property member variables and the container-provided storage. At present, it calls only *ExchangeVersion*, which saves the control version so that a control's persistent state is stamped with its version number, and the base class *DoPropExchange*, which causes any standard properties used by the control that allow themselves to be saved to actually get saved. If you don't want this to happen, you can stop calling the base class version of the function and serialize any standard properties you want to save yourself.

FYI "Standard properties" are more often called "stock properties," but because that term hasn't been introduced yet, I won't use it!

OnResetState is called to reset the control's property values to their defaults. The default implementation provided by ControlWizard calls the base class version. Again, if you want to take other action, you can add it here. The last member function created by ControlWizard is the one that is called when the *AboutBox* method is invoked — also called *AboutBox*. The default implementation here creates an instance of *CDialog* using the supplied dialog template. It then calls *DoModal* on this object to display the about box. To create more sophisticated about boxes, such as those mega-popular ones that contain hidden gang-sheets, you'll need to replace this function with another.

The Property Page Class: *CFirstPropPage*

The only class left to examine is the property page class. As you saw in Chapter 3, a property page is a single page from a tabbed dialog that allows access to some of the control's properties. It's also an OLE object in its own right. A control can put whatever it likes on a property page, although typically there won't be much else other than property names and values, and it can use as many property pages as it chooses. ControlWizard creates one blank property page. It wraps this page in an MFC class derived from *COlePropertyPage*, and yours is called *CFirstPropPage*. Listing 4-15 (beginning on the next page) contains the FIRSTPPG.H header file, and Listing 4-16 contains the FIRSTPPG.CPP implementation file.

FIRSTPPG.H

```
// firstppg.h : Declaration of the CFirstPropPage property page
//    class.

/////////////////////////////////////////////////////////////////
// CFirstPropPage : See firstppg.cpp for implementation.

class CFirstPropPage : public COlePropertyPage
{
    DECLARE_DYNCREATE(CFirstPropPage)
    DECLARE_OLECREATE_EX(CFirstPropPage)

// Constructor
public:
    CFirstPropPage();

// Dialog Data
    //{{AFX_DATA(CFirstPropPage)
    enum { IDD = IDD_PROPPAGE_FIRST };
        // NOTE - ClassWizard will add data members here.
        //    DO NOT EDIT what you see in these blocks of generated
        //       code !
    //}}AFX_DATA

// Implementation
protected:
    // DDX/DDV support
    virtual void DoDataExchange(CDataExchange* pDX);

// Message maps
protected:
    //{{AFX_MSG(CFirstPropPage)
        // NOTE - ClassWizard will add and remove member functions
        //    here.
        //    DO NOT EDIT what you see in these blocks of generated
        //       code !
    //}}AFX_MSG
    DECLARE_MESSAGE_MAP()

};
```

Listing 4-15. *The FIRSTPPG.H header file.*

The FIRSTPPG.H header file contains nothing other than the property page class definition. The class is dynamically creatable and has a class factory, just like the control class, but it doesn't have a type library (it isn't automatable). It has a constructor and a data map, which is the area in which ClassWizard adds variables and their declarations whenever member variables are attached to dialog items. Yours is currently empty, except for an enumeration that identifies your property-page resource ID (*IDD_PROPPAGE_FIRST*). The only remaining member function is the *DoDataExchange* function, which is the standard MFC dialog data exchange/dialog data validation (DDX/DDV) routine for exchanging data between class member variables and dialog controls. The last item in the class declaration is the message map function declaration area for manipulation by ClassWizard; as you'd expect, this area is currently empty.

FIRSTPPG.CPP

```
// firstppg.cpp : Implementation of the CFirstPropPage property
//    page class.

#include "stdafx.h"
#include "first.h"
#include "firstppg.h"

#ifdef _DEBUG
#undef THIS_FILE
static char BASED_CODE THIS_FILE[] = __FILE__;
#endif


IMPLEMENT_DYNCREATE(CFirstPropPage, COlePropertyPage)


/////////////////////////////////////////////////////////////////
// Message map

BEGIN_MESSAGE_MAP(CFirstPropPage, COlePropertyPage)
    //{{AFX_MSG_MAP(CFirstPropPage)
    // NOTE - ClassWizard will add and remove message map entries
    //    DO NOT EDIT what you see in these blocks of generated
    //      code !
    //}}AFX_MSG_MAP
```

Listing 4-16. *The FIRSTPPG.CPP implementation file.* *(continued)*

(continued)

```
END_MESSAGE_MAP()


/////////////////////////////////////////////////////////////////////
// Initialize class factory and guid

IMPLEMENT_OLECREATE_EX(CFirstPropPage, "FIRST.FirstPropPage.1",
    0x14bc5f84, 0xdbd2, 0x11cd, 0x92, 0xb4, 0x8, 0x0, 0x2b,
    0x29, 0x1e, 0xed)


/////////////////////////////////////////////////////////////////////
// CFirstPropPage::CFirstPropPageFactory::UpdateRegistry -
// Adds or removes system registry entries for CFirstPropPage

BOOL CFirstPropPage::CFirstPropPageFactory::UpdateRegistry(
    BOOL bRegister)
{
    if (bRegister)
      return AfxOleRegisterPropertyPageClass(AfxGetInstanceHandle(),
          m_clsid, IDS_FIRST_PPG);
    else
      return AfxOleUnregisterClass(m_clsid, NULL);
}


/////////////////////////////////////////////////////////////////////
// CFirstPropPage::CFirstPropPage - Constructor

CFirstPropPage::CFirstPropPage() :
    COlePropertyPage(IDD, IDS_FIRST_PPG_CAPTION)
{
    //{{AFX_DATA_INIT(CFirstPropPage)
    // NOTE: ClassWizard will add member initialization here.
    //    DO NOT EDIT what you see in these blocks of generated
    //      code !
    //}}AFX_DATA_INIT
}


/////////////////////////////////////////////////////////////////////
// CFirstPropPage::DoDataExchange - Moves data between page and
//    properties
```

(continued)

```
void CFirstPropPage::DoDataExchange(CDataExchange* pDX)
{
    //{{AFX_DATA_MAP(CFirstPropPage)
    // NOTE: ClassWizard will add DDP, DDX, and DDV calls here.
    //     DO NOT EDIT what you see in these blocks of generated
    //       code !
    //}}AFX_DATA_MAP
    DDP_PostProcessing(pDX);
}
```

```
////////////////////////////////////////////////////////////////////
// CFirstPropPage message handlers
```

There's not a great deal to *CFirstPropPage*. As with the OLE control class, it has an empty message map and a call to the *IMPLEMENT_OLECREATE_EX* macro with its CLSID and ProgID. It also has a class factory object created for it as a nested class, and the *UpdateRegistry* member is used to add or remove details of this property page to the system registry.

Next is the class constructor, which in its default incarnation passes on the dialog ID and property-page caption to its base class constructor and then returns. You can add code to the constructor if there are things you want do before the page is displayed. The remaining member function is *DoDataExchange*, whose only default code is to call a DDX post-processing function, *DDP_PostProcessing*. Because member variables are added to this property page, this function will have code added to it automatically by ClassWizard as it adds routines to transfer information between the new variables and their corresponding dialog controls.

TESTING THE "FIRST" CONTROL WITH TEST CONTAINER

Now that you're at the position where you can build the control, let's do so. Building 16-bit controls is slightly more complicated than building 32-bit controls. This is because the compilation of the ODL file into a type library is performed by a utility called *MkTypLib*, which comes with the Microsoft Visual C++ compiler. *MkTypLib* can't be integrated into the build process with Visual C++ version 1.52, so you need to build the type library with a manual step before building the control itself. Initiate the manual step by selecting the newly added Make Type Library option from the Visual C++ Tools menu. When this has completed successfully, you can build the control by clicking the relevant build button on the Visual C++ toolbar. With 32-bit Visual C++ versions 2.0 and later, the build process is entirely integrated. You need only to press the build button — and the type library will be compiled immediately, before the OLE control DLL is built.

After you've built the First control, you can test it. Well, almost. Before you can test it, you need to register the control. The OLE CDK installation will have added two new options to the Visual C++ Tools menu: Register Control and Unregister Control. Both options call a utility provided with the OLE CDK, *RegSvr32* (or *RegSvr* in the 16-bit world), which calls either the *DllRegisterServer* or *DllUnregisterServer* functions in the selected control DLL. Invoke the Register Control option while FIRST.MAK is the open project; this will register the control's details so that you can test it. If you don't get a success message back, something is wrong. Given that you've done almost nothing by this point, any errors must be configuration or installation errors, or changes you've made to the source!

Recall that OLE controls are, by convention, held in DLL files with the extension OCX. The 32-bit compiler is capable of creating files with this extension directly, but 16-bit Visual C++ version 1.5x can only create DLLs if they're in files with the DLL extension. Therefore, when you distribute your 16-bit control, it's recommended that you rename the file. (Don't do it now, however, because you're merely testing the control.)

If you want to remove a control from the registry, it can be achieved by selecting the Unregister Control option on the Tools menu when the control's project is open, by choosing the File Register Controls option in Test Container, selecting the control from the list box and clicking Unregister, or by running *RegSvr32* directly. To register the control(s) in a DLL, use

```
regsvr32 control.ocx
```

where *control.ocx* is the real name of the DLL holding the control(s) you want to register. To unregister the controls, use

```
regsvr32 /u control.ocx
```

NOTE Removal of items from the registry comes in handy when you're playing around with OLE. The amount of information in the registry can quickly become overwhelming, so removal of information no longer pertinent is something you'll probably get into the habit of doing.

So how do you go about testing a control? When the OLE CDK was first released in September 1994, there was precisely one container in which OLE controls could be used, Microsoft Access version 2.0, and even that product didn't offer full functionality. Therefore, some method of control testing was required, which is why

Microsoft ships the Test Container application with the CDK. While Test Container has no programming language and, therefore, you can't write a script to test a control, it does provide access to the control's properties, methods, events, and property pages, as well as having a set of menu options to test how the control deals with certain conditions. It's a useful first-trial point.

FYI If you have a more sophisticated OLE Controls Test Container, such as Visual Basic version 4.0 or later or Visual FoxPro version 3.0 or later, you might prefer to test your controls in that environment. I tend to use both — Test Container first, as a quick test, and then more detailed testing in Visual Basic version 4.0. Test Container loads a good deal more quickly than does Visual Basic version 4.0, so that's one of my reasons for using Test Container first.

Using Test Container

Test Container can be run directly from the Microsoft Visual C++ Tools menu after the OLE CDK has been installed. I find it useful to add a toolbar button to the standard Visual C++ version 2.0 toolbar so that I can run it with one mouse click. Obviously, the program can also be run in the conventional ways — for example, by using Windows Explorer or the OLE Controls Program Manager group entry, or from File Manager.

After the program is running, insert an OLE control by clicking on the first toolbar button or by selecting the Insert OLE Control option from the Edit menu. In both cases, an Insert OLE Control dialog box appears, showing all the controls registered on your machine; choose First Control, which will be in the list after you've run the registration step above. Figure 4-4 shows the result of inserting the control.

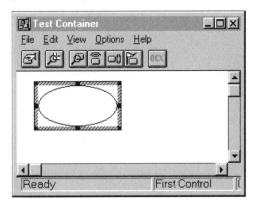

Figure 4-4.   *The First control embedded in Test Container.*

When a control is inserted into Test Container, it remains selected, so operations can be performed upon it. The first thing to do is to see the list of methods the control supports and to invoke one. If you choose the Invoke Methods option from the Test Container's Edit menu, the dialog box shown in Figure 4-5 appears.

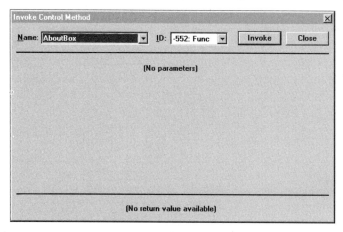

Figure 4-5.   *The Test Container's Invoke Control Method dialog box for the First control.*

The only method your control supports at this time is the *AboutBox* method, which causes the control's About dialog box to be displayed. Try it out by clicking the Invoke button. If you had other methods in your control, these would be listed in the Invoke Control Method dialog box and you could select one, pass it any parameters it requires, and invoke it. If it returns a value, that value will be displayed at the bottom of the dialog box.

Test Container learned about the control's methods by interrogating its type library. At the same time, it will have gotten details of its properties. Test Container then builds a simple property list for you, so you can get and set property values from within the container. This dialog box can be displayed by choosing Properties from the View menu when a control is selected. In your case, the dialog box will have no properties you can select.

You can also ask your control to display its user interface for property getting and setting — its property page. You do this by ensuring your control is selected and choosing the First Control Object menu item from the bottom of the Edit menu. This opens a further menu, on which Properties is the first entry. Selection of this item displays a blank property page, as shown in Figure 4-6.

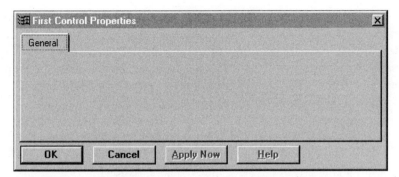

Figure 4-6. *The First control's (empty) property page display.*

If your control provided any events, you could see them being fired by opening Test Container's event log (on the View menu) or by choosing the relevant toolbar button. Likewise, if any of your properties were bound, you could see notifications from them in Test Container by opening the notification log (also on the View menu) or by choosing the relevant toolbar button.

The next thing of interest in Test Container is its ability to set up ambient properties. Test Container provides the same ambient properties to all control sites, and includes the Ambient Properties dialog box shown in Figure 4-7, chosen from the Edit menu, to display and set them. If your control had any functionality or any properties that might usefully inherit ambient property values, you could set the relevant ambients here, insert a new instance of your control, and see the effects as it took on some of the ambient property values. You'll see this happen as you progress over the next few chapters.

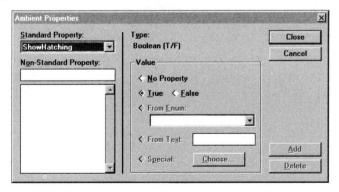

Figure 4-7. *Test Container's ambient properties dialog box.*

The final piece of functionality you might like to test here is the ability to move and resize your control, and how it reacts. Moving it is easy: simply move the mouse cursor to any edge of the control except where a sizing handle appears (a big black blob in Test Container — there's one at each corner and one in the middle of each border), and drag the control to a new position. This movement should not cause any action by the control at all; it won't be asked to redraw itself. If you resize the control on the other hand, it will be asked to redraw itself. Resize the control by grabbing a sizing handle and dragging to a new size. This will cause the control to redraw. Because you're using the default and exciting ellipse drawing code, the only effect you should see is the ellipse being redrawn to occupy the larger or smaller space.

A few of the other options offered by Test Container test various aspects of the control, including saving and loading the control's state to structured storage, saving and loading property sets, and checking various in-place active conditions. It's worth experimenting to see what some of these options do, although with the rather limited functionality offered by your control at present, you won't always notice any effect at all.

CLASSWIZARD CHANGES

ClassWizard is changed by the installation of the OLE CDK to provide OLE control-specific functionality. (Actually, only the 16-bit ClassWizard supplied with Visual C++ version 1.5x is changed; the one supplied with Visual C++ version 2.x already has full OLE control functionality.) In particular, the OLE Automation tab is enhanced, the OLE Events tab is enabled, and some small changes are made to the Member Variables tab.

The enhancements to the OLE Automation tab are the inclusion in the Add Property and Add Method dialogs of stock properties and methods, where "stock" means built-in and provided by the system. If you choose a stock property or method, you don't need to write any code for that property or method. (I'll look at which items are stock in the next few chapters.) The other enhancement to the OLE Automation tab is the enablement of the Data Binding button when a property is selected. This button allows a property to be assigned its data binding attributes.

The OLE Events tab allows you to define events your control can fire up to its container. Again, you can select stock events, or you can create custom events.

The change to the Member Variables tab is slight, but significant. Until you add some controls to the property page, you won't be able to see the changes. After a control is on the page, the addition of a member variable also allows that variable-and-control combination to be associated with one of the control's properties.

The Runtime DLL

Every OLE control developed with the OLE CDK makes extensive use of the MFC library, so they're bound to be big and slow, right? Wrong! The MFC library has never been big or slow. For the world to adopt OLE controls as quickly as it adopted VBXs, OLE controls could not be big and slow. Therefore, a lot of work has gone into both performance-tuning and code-size reduction. In my experience, there is little discernible difference in speed between a VBX and its equivalent OLE control. Judge this for yourselves as you create more and more complex examples throughout the rest of this book.

The size issue is addressed to a large extent by putting most of the implementation of *COleControl*, *COlePropertyPage*, and *COleControlModule*, as well as any other MFC support used by these classes, in a special runtime DLL. In addition to these classes, the runtime DLL also contains things such as the standard font and color objects.

The runtime DLL has both 16-bit and 32-bit versions, of course, and also comes in retail and debug builds. The 32-bit DLL also has ANSI and Unicode variants. The name of the retail DLL is *OC??.DLL*, where *??* is replaced by the version number of the MFC library with which the runtime is built. So, for the first release of the OLE CDK, the 16-bit DLL was called *OC25.DLL* and the 32-bit DLL was called *OC30.DLL*. The debug versions have a "D" appended to the name, as in *OC30D.DLL*. The Unicode version has a "U" appended, as in *OC30U.DLL* and *OC30UD.DLL*.

Whereas OLE is part of the system in 32-bit Windows, and is therefore shipped with the operating system, the OLE Controls runtime DLL isn't (yet). This means you've got to ensure that your installation program installs it, doing the normal version checks as you go to ensure that you don't overwrite a newer version!

It's important to realize that the OLE Controls runtime DLLs are not dependent on or replacements for the standard MFC runtime DLLs. The OLE Controls runtimes provide all the MFC functionality needed by OLE controls, while the standard MFC runtime DLLs provide MFC functionality for regular MFC programs and DLLs. There is also a runtime DLL for MFC ODBC support for OLE Controls: *OCD25.DLL* (for 16-bit operating systems) or *OCD30.DLL* (for 32-bit operating systems).

Finally, 16-bit OLE Controls need 16-bit OLE versions 2.02 or later, which is provided with Visual C++ versions 1.51 and later. OLE Controls cannot work with earlier versions of 16-bit OLE, so your installation program must check for which release of OLE is installed and then install the 2.02 DLLs over the top of the existing installation if necessary. One of the rules of this overwriting is that <u>all</u> the OLE DLLs must be distributed, not only the ones you use.

Part II

The Basics of OLE Controls

Chapter 5

Properties

Right, the excitement is rising, the pages of the book are beginning to shake, and voices are beginning to cry out, "Tell me more about properties!" Okay, perhaps I exaggerate somewhat. However, properties and the properties of properties, so to speak, is where you're at. You know how to build a rudimentary OLE control, and you know that ClassWizard can help us to add properties: so what properties do you add?

Cast your mind back to Chapter 3, where you learned about three types of property: ambient, extended, and control. "Ambient properties" are exposed by the client site in which the control is embedded, and they reflect values that the container wants to communicate to the control so that it can take on the characteristics of the form in which it lives. "Extended properties" are those properties which the container looks after on behalf of the control and which in most circumstances the control doesn't need or want to know about. "Control properties" are the ones you're really interested in here. A control property is one that the control itself implements. In Chapter 4, you read that the control property is further subdivided by the OLE CDK into stock properties (ones for which it supplies the implementation on your behalf) and custom properties (ones that you write).

Let's take a brief look at the ambient properties defined by the OLE Controls specification and an even briefer look at extended properties. Then you can write some properties of your own.

THE STANDARD AMBIENT PROPERTIES

If you take a look inside the OLECTL.H header file, you can find the set of ambient properties predefined in terms of symbolic names and the prescribed dispids. It doesn't tell you what they do, however, so I'll take a quick ramble through the list and describe the purpose of each one. The full list of standard ambient properties is shown in the following table, along with the dispid values:

STANDARD AMBIENT PROPERTIES

Name*	Symbol	Dispid
BackColor	DISPID_AMBIENT_BACKCOLOR	-701
DisplayName	DISPID_AMBIENT_DISPLAYNAME	-702
Font	DISPID_AMBIENT_FONT	-703
ForeColor	DISPID_AMBIENT_FORECOLOR	-704
LocaleID	DISPID_AMBIENT_LOCALEID	-705
MessageReflect	DISPID_AMBIENT_MESSAGEREFLECT	-706
ScaleUnits	DISPID_AMBIENT_SCALEUNITS	-707
TextAlign	DISPID_AMBIENT_TEXTALIGN	-708
UserMode	DISPID_AMBIENT_USERMODE	-709
UIDead	DISPID_AMBIENT_UIDEAD	-710
ShowGrabHandles	DISPID_AMBIENT_SHOWGRABHANDLES	-711
ShowHatching	DISPID_AMBIENT_SHOWHATCHING	-712
DisplayAsDefaultButton	DISPID_AMBIENT_DISPLAYASDEFAULT	-713
SupportsMnemonics	DISPID_AMBIENT_SUPPORTSMNEMONICS	-714
AutoClip	DISPID_AMBIENT_AUTOCLIP	-715

* These names are gathered from two sources: the OLE Controls specification and the Test Container application shipped with the OLE CDK.

As I said earlier, you should not use the dispid value directly because it might change; rather, you should rely on the symbolic name (for example, *DISPID_AMBIENT_FONT*). Also, do not rely on the name of the property because foreign languages will inevitably use different words than those used in English. The OLECTL.H header file can be found in the INCLUDE directory under the CDK directory created when the CDK is installed. The typical path is \MSVC20\CDK32\INCLUDE (or \MSVC\CDK16\INCLUDE for the 16-bit version).

A control container can add its own set of ambient properties to this list. If it does so, then clearly only those controls that know of the container-specific ambients can use them, meaning that a relationship is defined between a given container and a set of controls. This isn't necessarily a bad thing; it simply means that you can write controls that can take advantage of certain container features in some container(s) it knows about, but not in others.

Of the ambient properties that haven't been discussed before and that are not obvious (I assume that ones such as *BackColor* are obvious), the interesting ones are *LocaleID*, *MessageReflect*, *TextAlign*, *SupportsMnemonics*, and *AutoClip*:

- *LocaleID* lets the container tell the control in which locale (effectively, but not definitively, language) the control should consider itself to be running.

- *MessageReflect* tells a control that, if this property is *TRUE*, it will reflect Microsoft Windows messages back to the control. This is mostly useful to those OLE controls that are subclasses of standard Windows controls. This is because standard Windows controls typically send Windows messages to their parents when certain things happen. For example, a pushbutton sends a *WM_COMMAND* with a notification ID of *BN_CLICKED* to its parent when it is clicked. Like their VBX precursors, OLE controls have another model of parent notification — events — so most don't send messages to their parent. Just in case they do, the OLE CDK implements a special invisible window, called the "reflector window," which acts as the control's parent. This window is implemented by the *COleControl* class. The reflector window reflects the messages it receives back to the sending control, using custom message numbers (symbolic constants beginning with *OCM_*, defined in the OLECTL.H file). The control can then process these messages and deal with them in a more OLE control-centric manner, such as sending an event. If the container is prepared to deal with messages and reflect them back to the control — and most containers are not so prepared — it would set the *MessageReflect* ambient property to *TRUE*, causing *COleControl* not to use its reflector window.

- *TextAlign* tells the control how the client site would like the control to arrange the text it displays. If the value of the property is 0, the control should obey the "general" alignment principles: text aligned to the left, numbers to the right. A value of 1 means left alignment, 2 means center alignment, 3 means right alignment, and 4 means justification (fill the available space from the left margin to the right margin).

- *SupportsMnemonics* is used by a container to tell its controls that it supports the extended-keyboard interface and can accept mnemonic keypresses intended for controls. If this ambient property is not present at a given client site or has a value of *FALSE*, the control can assume that the container does not support this functionality and that as a consequence it should remove any visual hints as to its mnemonics (for example, the underline under the chosen letter).

- *AutoClip* indicates whether the container will automatically clip the control. If *TRUE*, the control can safely ignore the *lprcClipRect* parameter to *OleInPlaceObject::SetObjectRects*. If this ambient property isn't present, the control assumes a value of *FALSE*.

Ambient properties don't strictly <u>need</u> to be obeyed, but it's polite to do so when it makes sense. Some of the behavior that your control should adopt is carried out for you by the OLE CDK. For example, if your control implements the stock *Font* property, the initial value of the font will be determined from the client site's ambient *Font* property. If a given ambient property doesn't make sense for you, don't use it. As an example, consider a control that has a *BackColor* property; this control could, if it so chose, align itself with the client site's *BackColor* ambient property and therefore blend in with its surroundings. If the control expressly wants to stand out, however, selecting the same *BackColor* is not good.

Some Extended Properties

Extended properties are those that a user would certainly regard as being associated with the control but that are actually implemented by the container. For example, a control's size and position and its order in the tab sequence fall into the category of extended properties. These properties are associated with something called the "extended control," which is an object implemented by the container, generally by aggregating with the control. When the user gets or sets a property or invokes a method, the extended control gets access first. If the extended control recognizes the property or method, it performs whatever action the property or method requires; if the extended control doesn't recognize it, it will be passed on to the control itself. A control can get at the extended control's IDispatch interface and read extended properties itself.

A small number of standard extended properties are defined. It isn't a requirement that all containers implement all standard extended properties. A control should avoid naming properties or assigning dispids that are the same as those defined for standard extended properties. A container can implement further extended properties by overriding the behavior of certain properties defined by the control. The example given for this concept in the OLE CDK documentation is the *Enabled* property. The typical visual control will implement this property. A control, however, knows only whether it is enabled or disabled within itself. It might be enabled as far as it's concerned, but the form in which it is embedded might itself be disabled, so the control cannot actually be regarded as enabled. Consequently, a container that allowed such a scheme could also provide its own *Enabled* property for the extended control. This property would probably also call the control's implementation so that the control was made aware of the situation.

Extended properties must be given dispids in the range 0x80010000 to 0x8001FFFF. Some are predefined, although no constants are defined in

OLECTL.H for them. The following table lists the defined standard extended properties:

STANDARD EXTENDED PROPERTIES

Name	*Dispid*	*Description*
Name	0x80010000	The user-defined name for the object. (For example, when a control is inserted into a Visual Basic form, Visual Basic assigns a name (such as *Text1*) that is exposed as a property of the control and that can be changed.)
Visible	0x80010007	Indicates whether the control is visible within the container.
Parent	0x80010008	The automation interface of the form in which the control is embedded.
Cancel	0x80010037	Indicates whether the control is to act as the default Cancel button for the form that it's on.
Default	0x80010038	Set to *TRUE* for the control that is currently the default button on the form and to *FALSE* for all other controls.

NOTE OLE Controls at this point do not define any standard extended methods or events.

We've also discussed position and size properties as being extended properties; you can add the tab order and tag properties to this list. The "tag property" is one used by languages such as Microsoft Visual Basic to associate a user-supplied string of arbitrary data with a control. The difference between these extended properties and those in the table above is that OLE defines dispids that must be used for the extended properties listed in the table, while it doesn't define any for the others.

As this book is more concerned with the creation of OLE controls than with their use, extended properties will not be discussed in any great detail again.

CONTROL PROPERTIES

Control properties are by far the most interesting properties to talk about, primarily because it's you who implements them! Control properties can be named anything you choose, can take whatever parameters you want (so long as OLE Automation supports those types of the parameters), and can do whatever you choose.

Some control properties are likely to be implemented so frequently that the OLE CDK provides standard implementations of them. Further, these properties use standard names and dispids that are reserved and should not be overridden by any control properties, events, or methods you create. These standard properties are called "stock properties." The following table lists all the stock properties defined in the OLECTL.H file:

STOCK PROPERTIES DEFINED IN OLECTL.H

Name*	Dispid	Description
AutoSize	-500	If this property is *TRUE*, the control will resize itself on its form to enable it to display its entire contents.
BackColor**	-501	The color used to paint the background of the control.
BackStyle	-502	Determines whether the background of a control is opaque or transparent. When a control is transparent, anything underneath its background can be seen.
BorderColor	-503	Holds the control's border color value.
BorderStyle	-504	The value of this property determines what sort of border the control will have. This property can be used to completely remove the border from a control.
BorderWidth	-505	Determines the width of the control's border.
DrawMode	-507	If the control has methods that produce graphical output (such as a *Draw* method), this property can be used to determine how that drawing occurs. This relates to how the pen color and the background colors are merged.
DrawStyle	-508	The line style used in any drawing performed by a control's methods.
DrawWidth	-509	The width of the pen used in any drawing performed by a control's methods.
FillColor	-510	The color used to fill in shapes.
FillStyle	-511	The pattern used to fill in shapes.
Font	-512	The font used by the control for its text output.
ForeColor	-513	The color used by the control for text and drawing.
Enabled	-514	Determines whether the control is enabled.
hWnd	-515	The handle to the control's main window.
TabStop	-516	Determines whether the user can reach this control by tabbing to it.
Text	-517	The text in a control. (This is the same as the **Caption** property.)
Caption	-518	The caption assigned to a control. (This is the same as the **Text** property.)
BorderVisible	-519	Determines whether the control's border is visible.

* These names are gathered from two sources: the OLE Controls specification and the Test Container application shipped with the OLE CDK.

** The stock properties that are implemented by the OLE CDK that was released with Microsoft Visual C++ version 2.0 are marked in bold.

Just because a property is defined as a stock property does not mean that you support it implictly through invisible CDK code or that you must support it. It simply means that if you want to support such a property, you can ensure standard behavior and save yourself time and effort by using the built-in implementations. Any other property added to a control is a custom property, and you have to write any code to support it. One day you'll have wizards that can read minds and generate code directly, but in the meantime you get by as best you can by doing a little typing.

ADDING SOME STOCK PROPERTIES

You're now going to alter the First control from the previous chapter and add a few stock properties to it using ClassWizard. To add the properties, be sure the project file is open, and then invoke ClassWizard. Select the OLE Automation tab, check that the *CFirstCtrl* class is selected, and click the Add Property button. Select the appropriate property from the External Name combo box, and click OK. Repeat these last two steps until all the properties you need have been added: namely, *BackColor, Caption, Enabled, Font, ForeColor*, and *hWnd*.

After you've added the six stock properties, rebuild the project. (For 32-bit builds, it's simplest to use the ANSI build options, although you should feel free to use the Unicode build if you're running under Windows NT.) While that's going on, take a look at the changes ClassWizard has made to the project's ODL file.

If you examine the section where the new properties have been added, you'll notice these lines of code:

```
[id(DISPID_BACKCOLOR), bindable, requestedit] OLE_COLOR BackColor;
[id(DISPID_CAPTION), bindable, requestedit] BSTR Caption;
[id(DISPID_ENABLED), bindable, requestedit] boolean Enabled;
[id(DISPID_FONT), bindable] IFontDisp* Font;
[id(DISPID_FORECOLOR), bindable, requestedit] OLE_COLOR ForeColor;
[id(DISPID_HWND)] OLE_HANDLE hWnd;
```

Notice that five of the new properties are declared as *bindable*, meaning that the control is capable of notifying its container if changes are made to these properties. Also, four of the new properties are marked with *requestedit*, which means that the control will ask the container for permission to make a change to one of these properties before making the change. This allows a container to prevent the control from arbitrarily changing certain control attributes without the container knowing. I can't imagine there being very many containers that require this capability, but it would certainly make sense for elements of, say, a word processor, where the container (the word processor) might need to be in total control of the document's appearance.

The only other changes made to the First control's source files are the addition of a few macros to the control's dispatch map. As the properties added are all stock properties, the macros are not the generic ones discussed in the previous chapter. Instead, the ClassWizard uses a specific macro for each property, as shown here:

```
DISP_STOCKPROP_BACKCOLOR()
DISP_STOCKPROP_CAPTION()
DISP_STOCKPROP_ENABLED()
DISP_STOCKPROP_FONT()
DISP_STOCKPROP_FORECOLOR()
DISP_STOCKPROP_HWND()
```

By now, the control will have finished building. Just in case, register the control by choosing the Register Control option from the Tools menu. Why "just in case"? If you're like me, you walk around the registry from time to time, deleting entries that you think aren't important. You're then surprised when everything stops working. It was a great advance for people like me when Microsoft Corporation decided that OLE objects should register themselves on startup. This makes it just that little bit safer to delete entries from the registry!

Now for the fun part. You're going to need an appropriate container for this exercise, such as Visual Basic version 4.0. (Test Container will do, but you'll appreciate the flexibility of a programmable container later in this book.) If you're using Visual Basic version 4.0, register the control with Visual Basic using the Custom Controls option on the Tools menu. This will make it appear in the toolbox. As you've changed nothing so far, the toolbox bitmap presented by the control will be the standard one shown in Figure 5-1.

Figure 5-1. *The standard OLE control toolbox bitmap provided by ControlWizard.*

Continuing on the Visual Basic theme, insert an instance of the new control onto a form. Don't write any code — simply run the "program." What do you see? Well, nothing different from what you would have seen if you'd run the same program before you'd added the new stock properties. Okay, I guess so far it would have been reasonable to predict this behavior, for two reasons. Although you've added the properties to the control, you've done nothing with them. And the default drawing code provided by ControlWizard

```
pdc->FillRect(rcBounds, CBrush::FromHandle((HBRUSH)
    GetStockObject (WHITE_BRUSH)));
pdc->Ellipse(rcBounds);
```

fills the entire control background with white before drawing the ellipse.

If you examine the values of these properties at runtime, however, you'll notice that they do have sensible values. Where do these initial values come from? Are they defaults provided by the OLE Controls runtime? This is plausible, but in most cases it isn't the correct answer. To get closer to understanding what has occurred, alter some of the equivalent properties of the Visual Basic form in which you've embedded the control (the properties have the same names), delete the control, and insert it again. Now examine the control's properties; you'll notice that they've taken the same values as the ones used by the form. What has happened here is that Visual Basic uses form properties as the basis for each site's ambient properties, and the OLE control's stock properties read and assume the values of the relevant ambient property at startup. Clearly, this won't affect some stock properties, such as *Text*, *Caption*, and *hWnd*, as ambient values make no sense for such items.

If you now alter a control property by substituting a new value for its default ambient value and then resave the Visual Basic project, the saved value takes precedence. When the project is reloaded, the control (thankfully!) takes on the property values with which it was saved. You're going to look into property persistence in much greater detail in the next chapter, but in the meantime, take a look at the sort of form code file you get when you save the Visual Basic program. The relevant lines resulting from my setting the First control's properties are shown here:

```
Begin FirstLib.First First1
    Height          =    1335
    Left            =    240
    TabIndex        =    0
    Top             =    240
    Width           =    2895
    _version        =    65536
    _extentx        =    5106
    _extenty        =    2355
    _stockprops     =    79
    forecolor       =    16711680
    backcolor       =    16711935
    BeginProperty font {FB8F0823-0164-101B-84ED-
        08002B2EC713}
        name            =    "MS Sans Serif"
        charset         =    1
        weight          =    700
        size            =    9.75
        underline       =    0    'False
        italic          =    -1   'True
        strikethrough   =    0    'False
    EndProperty
End
```

The ones I've set are *ForeColor*, *BackColor*, and *Font*. Notice that while *ForeColor* and *BackColor* are saved in the normal Visual Basic way as decimal numbers representing the ratios of red, green, and blue in the color, the *Font* property is saved as an object in its own right, with its own set of properties. The only changes to the standard ambient font are that I've made it bold (weight = 700) and italic (italic = -1), and I've increased the point size (size = 9.75).

NOTE You might be interested in the two entries that are displayed at the top of the Visual Basic properties window when your control is selected. The first, *About*, causes your automatically added *AboutBox* method to be called. Try it, and you'll see exactly the same dialog box as that produced by Test Container. The second entry, *Custom*, invokes the control's property page(s). We've done no work so far on property pages, so selection of this entry will cause the control's currently blank property page to be displayed. This page is the default one created for us by ControlWizard.

Making the New Properties Work

To make the new properties take effect, you've got to write some new drawing code that reads the property values and uses them. Users of stock properties are provided with a number of helper functions by the OLE CDK to make the task easier.

For example, the stock font can be accessed with the *InternalGetFont* member function of the *COleControl* class, and the background color can be accessed through *GetBackColor*. Now, although *InternalGetFont* can be used to get hold of the font object, most of the time all you're going to want to do is to select the font into the control's device context (DC) during drawing. Consequently, the *COleControl* class provides another member function, *SelectStockFont*, which does this for you.

Here is the code for the new version of the control's *OnDraw* member function:

```
CFont *hfOld = SelectStockFont ( pdc );
CBrush cbBack ( TranslateColor ( GetBackColor ( ) ) );
pdc -> FillRect ( rcBounds, &cbBack );
pdc -> SetTextColor ( TranslateColor (
    GetForeColor ( ) ) );
pdc -> SetBkMode ( TRANSPARENT );
pdc -> DrawText ( InternalGetText ( ), -1, rcBounds,
    DT_SINGLELINE | DT_CENTER | DT_VCENTER );
pdc -> SelectObject ( hfOld );
```

You'll notice that it's not radically different from ordinary MFC drawing code except for the functions that provide access to the stock properties and the use of the bounding rectangle passed to *OnDraw*. This latter exception is an important point: although your control will often be displayed in its own window, it will on occasion, and depending on the container, be displayed in part of the containing form's window. Consequently, there's no guarantee that coordinate (0, 0) is actually in the drawing space of your control. If you were to draw at fixed coordinates like this, you might well find yourself writing into the containing form. By using the passed-in bounding rectangle as your guide, you can ensure that you create output only inside the client area of the control.

The code here first selects the stock font into the device context (DC), saving the previously selected font in *hfOld*. You've got to do this because one of the rules of device-context handling is that all (non-default) objects selected into a DC must be deselected before they can be destroyed. (It would be bad pratice, and a potential source of bugs, to leave the DC with your font still selected.) You then create a brush, *cbBack*, with which you're going to paint the background of the control. Therefore, set it to the control's *BackColor* property value by calling *GetBack-Color*. Notice that you don't pass the return value of *GetBackColor* directly to the *CBrush* constructor; instead, you first pass it through *TranslateColor*, which converts the *OLE_COLOR* value returned by *GetBackColor* to a *COLORREF* value expected by *CBrush::CBrush*. The routine then calls *FillRect* to draw the control's background, using the bounding rectangle as discussed. You then set the text color to the value of your *ForeColor* property, using *TranslateColor* to convert the return result of *GetForeColor* to the correct type. Another GDI call, *SetBkMode*, sets the mode in which text will be drawn on the control's background to *TRANSPARENT*, which means that the background is not altered before the text is drawn. If you left the background mode to the default value (*OPAQUE*), the area in which the text is to be drawn would first be erased to the current background color. This "current background color" is not the same as your *BackColor* property value — it's the current background color that's set in the device context. By default, this is white.

NOTE Bear in mind that there is no absolute guarantee that a device context passed to a drawing function actually has the defaults provided by Microsoft Windows, because some other drawing code might have used it before passing it on to your *OnDraw* and set up other values. In the case of a control, the drawing code is called (almost) directly by the MFC message map mechanism on receipt of a *WM_PAINT* message; therefore, it's extremely likely that the DC will have the standard default values, unless the control is not UI-active.

The next line calls *DrawText* to output the text, taking the text from the stock *Caption* property using *InternalGetText* and drawing the text in the center of the control's rectangle, using the *DT_VCENTER* and *DT_CENTER* flags to *DrawText* to accomplish this. (*DT_VCENTER* is ignored unless *DT_SINGLELINE* is also set, which is why you've passed this flag, too.) The last line of the function calls *SelectObject* to return the DC's selected font to the one you saved previously in *hfOld*. If you build the new control and reload it into the saved project, you'll notice that the control assumes the background color you set. If you also type some text into the *Caption* property from Visual Basic's properties window when the control is selected, you'll see the text you entered displayed in your chosen font and foreground color.

Accessing a Control's Properties Programmatically

Most OLE control containers will also provide some degree of language integration, allowing the control to be programmed in a language determined by the container. Visual Basic, for example, provides a dialect of the BASIC programming language. Exactly how a control is referenced and subsequently programmed depends entirely on the container. In general, however, containers will follow the principle adopted by Visual Basic: instances of embedded controls are given names, and properties and methods of that instance of the control can be accessed through some language-specific notation in the container. Visual Basic uses *object.property* or *object.method* as its mechanism, where *object* is the named instance of the control being programmed.

So, if you embed an instance of the First control in a new Visual Basic form, it will typically be given the name *First1*. You can then set properties at runtime, such as the *Caption* property:

```
First1.Caption = "I've been set programmatically."
```

If you attach this line of code to a new command button's *Click* event handler on the same form, you can change the control's caption from the one you set it to at design time to whatever you type between the quotes on the line above, simply by clicking the button at runtime.

ADDING CUSTOM PROPERTIES

Adding stock properties was pretty easy but is obviously of limited value. A control rarely becomes useful until you add your own properties. The technique for adding "custom properties" (another name for properties that you, the control writer, defines) is exactly the same as that used for stock properties, with the added step of having to write some code.

Before you add any new properties, you need to decide exactly what your control is going to do. As you increasingly program with OLE, you'll get to see more and more different SCODEs. During development, you'll need to look these up so that you can find out what your code is doing wrong. If you receive SCODEs at runtime in a program you've shipped, you'll want to know what the SCODEs mean so that you can take appropriate action and perhaps alert the user. So you're going to modify your control so that it accepts an SCODE value and returns, via its properties, that SCODE's meaningful text string, its severity (whether it's fatal or informational, for example), the facility in which it occurred (for example, RPC, Win32, or Interfaces), and the error code itself. To do this, you need to define your properties. The following table lists the custom properties you're going to define for the First control in this chapter. Although you will refine the First control over the next few chapters, you <u>will</u> have a working control at the end of this one.

Property	Type	Description
Code	*short*	The error code portion of an SCODE (the lower 16 bits). A read-only property.
ErrorName	*BSTR*	The name of the error as per its *#define*. A read-only property.
Facility	*BSTR*	The "facility" portion of the SCODE, converted to a meaningful string. A read-only property.
Message	*BSTR*	The meaningful message associated with the SCODE. A read-only property.
SCode	*SCODE*	The SCODE itself.
Severity	*BSTR*	The "severity" portion of the SCODE, converted to a meaningful string. A read-only property.

This table instantly raises a couple of questions. Firstly, what's a *BSTR*? Then, why are five of the new properties read-only?

A *BSTR* is the OLE-defined type for strings. A *BSTR* is actually the address of the first character in a string; as with standard C and C++ strings, the string is also (typically) zero-terminated. However, the word immediately prior to the start of the string holds the length of the string. Having the length of a string travel with the string makes it faster for the OLE API functions to copy and manipulate the strings. It also allows strings to contain embedded zero bytes. *BSTR*s are allocated and otherwise manipulated using a set of API functions provided as part of the OLE Automation library, including *SysAllocString* and *SysStringLen*. Automation controllers such as Visual Basic see *BSTR*-typed properties simply as strings, and the MFC library handles most of the allocation and de-allocation mechanics for us.

The five read-only properties that you're going to write are read-only because they should not be set directly. Because the control's purpose is to convert an existing SCODE to its component parts, it makes no sense to expose those component parts to change. Consequently, the values of these properties will be calculated each time a new SCODE is set, so that they can be retrieved by the control user, but they won't be alterable by the user.

So, let's do it. Load up the First control into Visual C++ and invoke ClassWizard. Select the OLE Automation tab; be sure that *CFirstCtrl* is selected as the class. Add the six properties as defined in the table above, bearing the following in mind:

- Each property uses the Get/Set Methods implementation scheme (which you select in the Add Property dialog box).

- For each property <u>other</u> <u>than</u> *SCode*, ensure that the property's Set Function name is blank so that ClassWizard generates no set property function, making the property read-only.

Although you've written no code, the skeleton code generated by ClassWizard will compile. Now is a good time to check this out, so build the project.

NOTE If you're using the 16-bit Visual C++ compiler, don't forget to rebuild the type library using the Make TypeLib command from the Tools menu before building the project itself. (This is a normal part of the build process in Visual C++ versions 2.0 and later.)

If you examine the code generated for the *Get* methods for any of the string properties, you'll notice that the methods each contain two executable lines. The first of these two lines declares a variable of type *CString* called *s*, and the second returns the result of the call to the *AllocSysString* method on that variable. Basically, MFC's *CString* class wraps the *BSTR* API's *AllocSysString* function to allow *CString* objects to be created as *BSTRs*.

Now let's try the newly built control out on Visual Basic. Load Visual Basic and add the First control to the project (if it isn't there already), using the Custom Controls option on the Tools menu. Now draw a copy of the control on the form and, while the control is still selected, move to the properties window. Go and set the *SCode* property to some arbitrary value.

Whadyamean *SCode*'s not there? *Code, ErrorName, Facility, Message,* and *Severity* are there, so it's interrogated the type library successfully. So why doesn't *SCode* appear in the property list? Well, let's try it another way. Add a command button to the form and add code to its click event. Set the *SCode* property of the First control to a value programmatically:

```
First1.SCode = &H8001FFFF
```

Run the program. Interestingly, it fails to compile, throwing up an error saying that you're trying to use a type that Visual Basic does not support. There's your clue: Visual Basic does not support variables of the *SCODE* type, which is the type you chose (logically enough) for your *SCode* property.

So what now? Clearly, if you want to make this control generally useful you've got to provide a way of setting the SCODE it's going to manipulate. You're going to do something which in general programming terms is definitely not recommended: you're going to rely on the fact that SCODEs are currently implemented as long integers (32 bits) and re-create the property as a *long*. To do this, you first need to delete the old property. Invoke ClassWizard once again, select the *SCode* property, and press the Delete button. A message box appears, telling you that you'll need to delete the implementations of *CFirstCtrl::GetSCode* and *CFirstCtrl::SetSCode* yourself: click OK. Now go to the code and, as it said, delete the existing code for the *GetSCode* and *SetSCode* methods. You don't need to alter the dispatch map, the class header file, or the project's ODL file, because ClassWizard has already made these alterations for you. The only reason it hasn't deleted the implementation itself is that you might make changes of this type considerably further into a project than you are now; if code were deleted from under your nose, you might not be too amused, so the Visual C++ designers decided that the tools would not delete any user code. Although in your case it's a (minor) inconvenience, it certainly becomes important when you delete a function with loads of code that you'll need to use in the new version of the function!

Now add the *SCode* property again, this time as one which is of type *long*. If you're feeling nervous, rebuild the project (remembering the type-library step in the 16-bit world), and try out the control again in Visual Basic. This time, not only should the *SCode* property appear in Visual Basic's property window, but you should be able to set it programmatically.

FYI If you're thinking that I must have thought long and hard to come up with an example program that just happened to demonstrate this error, fear not: I was caught out like this during the design of this control!

The format of an SCODE is defined in WINERROR.H, shipped with Microsoft Visual C++ version 2.0. (It's a Win32 header file, so if you're running 16-bit Windows, you'll need to go and copy it from the companion CD-ROM, from \MSVC20\INCLUDE.) The format is shown in Figure 5-2 on the next page.

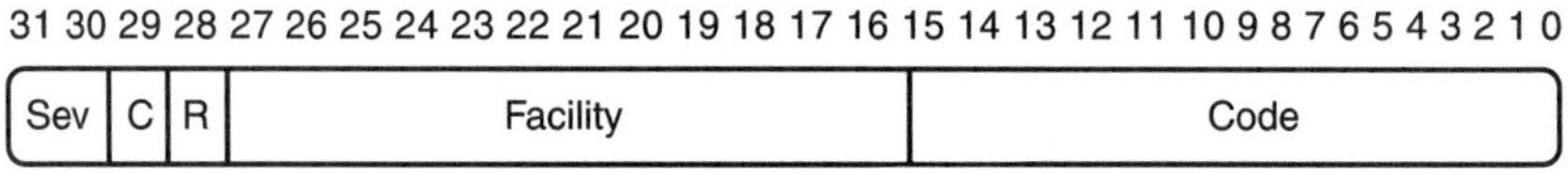

31 30 29 28 27 26 25 24 23 22 21 20 19 18 17 16 15 14 13 12 11 10 9 8 7 6 5 4 3 2 1 0

Sev	C	R	Facility	Code

Notes:

Sev - is the severity code

00 - Success
01 - Informational
10 - Warning
11 - Error

C - is the customer code flag

R - is a reserved bit

Facility - is the facility code

Code - is the facility's status code

Figure 5-2. *The layout of an SCODE.*

What we want to do with this control is to break up whatever value is currently held in the *SCode* property into the constituent parts <u>and</u> convert the SCODE as a whole into its message string. The *Facility* and *Severity* fields are more useful as strings than as numbers, so we'd also like to convert these fields into strings. So here's the sequence of steps that should be followed by users of the control when an SCODE interpretation is required:

1.   Set the control's *SCode* property to the chosen value.

2.   Retrieve the SCODE's message string by reading the control's *Caption* property. If this is the empty string (" "), the SCODE was not recognized.

3.   If the SCODE was recognized, the *Facility* property will hold the name of the facility that generated the SCODE, the *Code* property will hold the error code portion of the value, and the *Severity* property will hold a string representing the severity: "Successful," "Informational," "Warning," or "Error." Additionally, *ErrorName* will hold the symbolic name given to the SCODE, and *Message* will hold the message string. (In fact, the *Caption* property's text is made by combining these two properties.)

Here is how to set up the control's internal logic:

1.   At startup, set an internal flag to say "SCODE not valid."

2.   When the *SCode* property is set, look up SCODE.

3.   If found, clear the internal validity flag; otherwise, stop processing.

4. Store the message string of the SCODE in the *Message* property and its symbolic name in the *ErrorName* property. Combine these to form the *Caption* property.

5. When the *Code* property is requested, and if the SCODE is valid, return the low sixteen bits of *SCode* property.

6. When the *Facility* property is requested, and if SCODE is valid, extract the *Facility* portion of the *SCode* property value and load the appropriate string. Return this string.

7. When the *Severity* property is requested, and if SCODE is valid, extract the *Severity* portion of the *SCode* property value and load the appropriate string. Return this string.

To support this logic, you need to add some variables to the control class. Open up the FIRSTCTL.H header file, and add these lines to the bottom of the class definition:

```
private:
    long m_SCode;
    BOOL m_bIsValid;
    CString m_csSymbol;
    CString m_csMessage;
```

m_SCode is used to hold the SCODE passed in via the *SCode* property, and *m_bIsValid* is used to say whether the current value of *m_SCode* is recognized as a valid SCODE. *m_csSymbol* holds the SCODE's symbolic name, and *m_csMessage* holds the meaningful string. The first two are set to sensible start values in the class constructor; the *CString* variables are initialized to empty by the *CString* constructor. Add these lines to the *CFirstCtrl* constructor after the call to *InitializeIIDs*:

```
    m_SCode = 0L;
    m_bIsValid = FALSE;
```

The code for most of the property access methods manipulates the value held in the *SCode* property (that is, *m_SCode*) in a pretty straightforward manner. All the property access methods except *SetSCode* are shown in Listing 5-1.

Property Access Methods

```
long CFirstCtrl::GetSCode()
{
    // TODO: Add your property handler here
    return m_SCode;
```

Listing 5-1. *The code for all property access methods except* SetSCode. *(continued)*

(continued)

```
}

short CFirstCtrl::GetCode()
{
    // TODO: Add your property handler here
    if ( m_bIsValid )
    {
        return short ( m_SCode & 0XFFFFL );
    }
    else
    {
        return -1;
    }
}

BSTR CFirstCtrl::GetFacility()
{
    // TODO: Add your property handler here
    CString s;
    short nFacility = IDS_NOVALID_SCODE;
    if ( m_bIsValid )
    {
        nFacility = short ( ( m_SCode & 0x0FFF0000L ) >> 16L );
        switch ( nFacility )
        {
            case 0: case 1: case 2: case 3:
            case 4: case 7: case 8: case 10:
                break;
            default:
                nFacility = -1;
        }
        nFacility += IDS_FACILITY_NULL;
    }
    s.LoadString ( nFacility );
    return s.AllocSysString();
}

BSTR CFirstCtrl::GetSeverity()
{
    // TODO: Add your property handler here
    CString s;
    short nSeverity = IDS_NOVALID_SCODE;

    if ( m_bIsValid )
```

(continued)

```
    {
        nSeverity = short ( ( m_SCode & 0xC0000000L ) >> 30L ) +
            IDS_SEVERITY_SUCCESS;
    }
    s.LoadString ( nSeverity );
    return s.AllocSysString();
}

BSTR CFirstCtrl::GetMessage()
{
    // TODO: Add your property handler here
    return m_csMessage.AllocSysString();
}

BSTR CFirstCtrl::GetErrorName()
{
    // TODO: Add your property handler here
    return m_csSymbol.AllocSysString();
}
```

GetSCode does nothing more than return the current value of *m_SCode*. This property access method does not check for a valid SCODE before doing so. *GetCode* checks to see whether the SCODE is valid and then masks the high sixteen bits of the SCODE value, returning the low sixteen bits as its result.

NOTE The return value of -1 in case of an invalid SCODE here is not a definitive way of telling whether an SCODE is valid, because -1 is 0xFFFF in hex, which might well be a valid error code.

GetFacility is a little more interesting. First, you declare a *CString*, *s*, which will be used to hold the return value, and an integer, *nFacility*, which is used to hold the facility portion of the SCODE. The strings for each of the facility names are held in the control's string table section of its resources, along with a string returned when the SCODE is invalid. *nFacility* is initialized to the ID of the string that represents an invalid SCODE. The facility is isolated by "ANDing" the SCODE value with 0x0FFF0000, and then it's moved into the low sixteen bits to form a short integer by shifting it right sixteen times. The whole expression is then cast to a short integer and stored in *nFacility*. If the SCODE is valid, the ID of the first facility name string, *IDS_FACILITY_NULL*, is added to the *nFacility* value to form an index into the string table. Finally, the string is loaded from the string table using *CString::LoadString* and is returned as a *BSTR* through *CString::AllocSysString*. The string table indexing only works if each facility name string is given an ID equivalent to *IDS_FACILITY_NULL* plus the facility code (so facility Null, which is code 0, uses the string represented by *IDS_FACILITY_NULL*). If the facility is not recognized, the string at *IDS_FACIL-ITY_NULL* -1 is used.

The severity property *Get* method, *GetSeverity*, works in exactly the same way, although a switch isn't necessary because the severity field is 2 bits long and all values are valid. *GetMessage* and *GetErrorName* use the *CString::AllocSysString* member function to return their current values.

Now for the hard part. You need the *SCode* property *Set* method, *SetSCode*, to determine the validity of the SCODE passed to it and to set the control's *Message*, *ErrorName*, and *Caption* properties to the message string, the symbolic name, and the two combined, respectively. This chapter's version of the First control takes the easy way out and performs a linear (and therefore potentially <u>very</u> slow!) search through the machine-generated error code file, WINERROR.H. (This file is supplied with Microsoft Visual C++ versions 2.0 and later and is a standard part of the Win32 SDK.) Versions of the control in later chapters will gradually become more and more sensible in their approach. Listing 5-2 shows the *SetSCode* property method in its first incarnation.

Set SCode

```
void CFirstCtrl::SetSCode(long nNewValue)
{
    // TODO: Add your property handler here
    CString csFile;
    csFile.LoadString ( IDS_SCODE_FILE );
    CStdioFile cfCodes;

    m_csMessage.Empty ( );
    m_csSymbol.Empty ( );

    if ( cfCodes.Open ( csFile, CFile::modeRead |
        CFILE::typeText ) == 0 )
    {
        m_bIsValid = FALSE;
        return;
    }

    BOOL bOkay;
    CString csLine;
    while ( bOkay = GetNextDefineLine ( &cfCodes, csLine ) )
```

Listing 5-2. *The* SetSCode *property method and associated functions.*　　　*(continued)*

(continued)

```
    {
        if ( GetTheCode ( &csLine ) == nNewValue )
        {
            m_bIsValid = TRUE;
            break;
        }
    }
    if ( m_bIsValid )
    {
        csLine = m_csSymbol + _T ( ": " ) + m_csMessage;
    }
    else
    {
        csLine.LoadString ( IDS_NOVALID_SCODE );
    }
    m_SCode = nNewValue;
    SetText ( csLine );
    SetModifiedFlag();
    cfCodes.Close ( );      // Can throw an exception!!
}

BOOL CFirstCtrl::GetNextDefineLine ( CStdioFile *cfFile,
    CString& csLine )
{
    _TCHAR szBuf [ 256 ];
    CString csCompare;
    BOOL bFound = FALSE;
    LPTSTR lpszCnt;
    do
    {
        TRY
        {
            lpszCnt = cfFile -> ReadString ( szBuf, 255 );
        }
        CATCH ( CFileException, e )
        {
            break;
        }
        END_CATCH

        if ( lpszCnt == NULL )
        {
            break;
        }
```

(continued)

(continued)

```
        csCompare = szBuf;
        bFound = ( csCompare.Find (
            _T ( "// MessageText:" ) ) != -1 );
    }
    while ( bFound == FALSE );

    if ( bFound )
    {
     m_csMessage.Empty ( );
        TRY
        {
                // Discard blank comment line
            cfFile -> ReadString ( szBuf, 255 );
                // Get message line(s)
            m_csMessage.Empty ( )
            do
            {
                cfFile -> ReadString ( szBuf, 255 );
                if ( szBuf [ 3 ] )
                {
                    if ( ! m_csMessage.IsEmpty ( ) )
                    {
                        m_csMessage += _T ( " " );
                    }
                    szBuf [ _tcslen ( szBuf ) - 1 ] = TCHAR ( 0 );
                    m_csMessage += szBuf + 4;
                }
            }
            while ( szBuf [ 3 ] );

                // Get code line
            lpszCnt = cfFile -> ReadString ( szBuf, 255 );
        }
        CATCH ( CFileException, e )
        {
            m_csMessage.Empty ( );
            return FALSE;
        }
        END_CATCH

        if ( lpszCnt == NULL )
        {
            m_csMessage.Empty ( );
            return FALSE;
```

(continued)

(continued)

```
        }
        csLine = szBuf;
        return TRUE;
    }
    return FALSE;
}

long CFirstCtrl::GetTheCode ( CString *csLine )
{
        // Skip '#define
    int i = 7;

        // Skip white space
    while ( ( csLine -> GetLength ( ) > i ) &&
        ( _istspace ( csLine -> GetAt ( i ) ) ) )
    {
        ++i;
    }
    if ( csLine -> GetLength ( ) <= i )
    {
        return 0L;
    }

        // Collect symbol
    m_csSymbol.Empty ( );
    while ( ( csLine -> GetLength ( ) > i ) &&
        ! ( _istspace ( csLine -> GetAt ( i ) ) ) )
    {
        m_csSymbol += csLine -> GetAt ( i );
        ++i;
    }
    if ( csLine -> GetLength ( ) <= i )
    {
        m_csSymbol.Empty ( );
        return 0L;
    }

        // Skip white space
    while ( ( csLine -> GetLength ( ) > i ) &&
        ( _istspace ( csLine -> GetAt ( i ) ) ) )
    {
        ++i;
    }
    if ( csLine -> GetLength ( ) <= i )
```

(continued)

(continued)

```
    {
        m_csSymbol.Empty ( );
        return OL;
    }


    // Collect number
CString csNumber;
TRY
{
    csNumber = csLine -> Mid ( i );
}
CATCH ( CMemoryException, e )
{
    m_csSymbol.Empty ( );
    return OL;
}
END_CATCH
return _tcstoul ( csNumber, NULL, 0 );
}
```

You first set up the filename in a *CString* variable called *csFile*, initializing it to the (hard-coded!) name and path of the error file. Add this string to the resource file String Table, calling it *IDS_SCODE_FILE* and setting the text to C:\\MSVC20\\IN-CLUDE\\WINERROR.H (or to wherever else you have installed WINERROR.H). Two of the three string properties (*m_csMessage* and *m_csSymbol*) that will be set by a successful invocation of this function are then cleared.

You now create a variable of type *CStdioFile* called *cfCodes*. *CStdioFile* is an MFC library class that wraps file-handling API functions to allow easy access to text files. It also buffers them, making reads and writes generally faster. You want to use *CStdioFile* rather than the base *CFile* class because the error codes file is a text file, and the member functions provided by *CStdioFile* make it easier to read through text files line by line. The file is opened for read-only access in text mode; if an error occurs here, the function immediately stops processing and returns.

Assuming success, you enter a loop in which a function *GetNextDefineLine* is called to read the file and return each line that contains an error code. (You'll see how that works a little later.) After *GetNextDefineLine* finds such a line, it places it in *csLine*. Another function, *GetTheCode*, retrieves the error code represented by this line. If this value is the same as the SCODE value passed in, you break out of the loop. The loop is also broken if *GetNextDefineLine* returns *FALSE*, which it will do if it encounters an error, including reaching the end of the error file. If *GetSCode* finds the matching error code, *m_bIsValid* is set to *TRUE* and the caption string is created by combining *m_csSymbol* and *m_csMessage*; otherwise, the caption string is set to a standard string from the resource file. You can set this to a blank string, if you prefer.

The *GetSCode* method ends by setting the *m_SCode* variable and the caption property via *SetText*. It also tells the control that the control has been modified through the *SetModifiedFlag* function and closes the file. The *Close* function can throw an exception, but you choose to ignore it here for the moment (because an exception is highly unlikely on closing a read-only file).

GetNextDefineLine has the job of scanning through the file looking for lines that hold error codes. It relies on the fact that the WINERROR.H file has been created by a utility, Message Compiler (*MC*), which creates a specific format. (This program is supplied with Microsoft Visual C++ versions 2.1 and later and also with the Win32 SDK.) If that format changes, this control no longer works! The format is:

```
//
// MessageId: RPC_E_UNEXPECTED
//
// MessageText:
//
//  An internal error occurred.
//
#define RPC_E_UNEXPECTED                0x8001FFFFL
```

That is, one blank comment line, the message ID, another blank comment line, the string "MessageText," a further blank comment line, the line(s) of the message, another blank comment line, and the *#define* line itself. You find each of the lines containing "MessageID" using the *CStdioFile::ReadString* function, which reads a text file one line at a time, and *CString::Find*, which scans a string for a substring. *ReadString* can throw an exception, which you catch by exiting the read loop. Likewise, you exit the loop if *ReadString* returns *NULL*, indicating that the end of the file was reached. If the string is found, the loop is also broken, the difference being that the variable *bFound* is set to *TRUE*.

If the string is found, you collect the other lines of interest using multiple calls to *ReadString*. The message line is collected into *m_csMessage*, the complication here being that the message can be spread over many adjacent lines. The lines are joined by spaces and are terminated with a *NULL* character. Some things of interest . . . You use *TCHAR (0)* rather than *\0* for the terminator because *\0* is specifically a *char* constant, while in the Unicode world in which you might be operating, you need to use a value of zero, which fills the space of the entire last character in the array, rather than merely the first byte of the last character. Also, you use *_tcslen* rather than *strlen* to get the string length because *_tcslen* is a macro that expands differently depending on whether *_UNICODE* is defined. It will expand to *strlen* in an ANSI world and to the appropriate Unicode function otherwise. The horrible hack by which the message part of the line is added to *m_csMessage* using an offset of *4* relies on the fact that you know from the format that the message line starts four characters into the physical line — two comment characters followed by two spaces. You should really use a defined constant here. After the message string is collected, the loop ends by virtue of catching a blank comment line. The final action of the loop is to retrieve the *#define* line. If any of the *ReadString* calls throws an exception, the function clears the message string back to an empty string and returns; otherwise, the line is copied to the passed-in *CString* and returned.

NOTE The *CString* is passed as a reference into the function using *CString& csLine*, a technique with which you might or might not agree. Some purists say that because you modify the string, you should explictly pass a pointer to it. Change it if you don't like it.

GetTheCode pulls the symbolic name and the error code value from the line. It maintains a variable, *i*, which is used as a counter to iterate through the string. This is first set to *7* to skip the characters in "#define." Again, you should really use a symbolic constant rather than *7* here. *GetTheCode* then enters a loop to skip white space in the line, using the *_istspace* macro to identify characters as white space in a Unicode-safe way. The file format tells us that the next item in the string is the code's symbolic name, so it is collected into *m_csSymbol*. You then skip white space again, leaving only the error number. If you scan the file, you'll notice that some SCODEs are specified in hex and some in decimal, so you need a clever way of reading in the number. It just so happens that the *_tcstoul* function (Unicode-safe: maps to *strtoul* or *wcstoul* as appropriate) converts an ASCII string to an unsigned long, recognizing *0x* as starting a hex number, *0* for an octal and any other digit as meaning decimal, so use this function. By specifying zero as the function's last parameter, *tcstoul* automatically determines in what base the number is represented. The converted SCODE is the return value of the function.

You need to declare these two functions in the class header file, so add these two lines after the private variable declarations at the end of the header:

```
BOOL GetNextDefineLine ( CStdioFile *cfFile, CString& csLine );
long GetTheCode ( CString *csLine );
```

BUILDING AND TESTING THE CONTROL

So that's it: the control can now be built and tested. Be sure that WINERROR.H is in the path you specified. When you test the control, bear in mind that the *SCode* property is specified as a long integer. As such, it is signed, which means that values over 0x7FFFFFFF are technically negative numbers. This causes no problems in your control because you actually treat it always as unsigned. (To be absolutely accurate, there's no situation in your code where the distinction matters.) However, *SCode* causes problems for both Visual Basic and Test Container. To get around it (in Visual Basic), enter the number as a hexadecimal by prefixing it with *&H* so that Visual Basic will treat the number as unsigned or by converting the value to the appropriate negative number. Figure 5-3 shows the completed control embedded in Test Container with an SCODE value of 0.

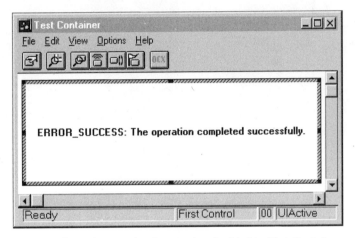

Figure 5-3. *The completed control embedded in Test Container.*

You've now built a control with both stock and custom properties, and you've gotten it to do something vaguely useful. However, it has a number of problems:

- It assumes a fixed format error file.

- It always does a sequential search through the file.

- It doesn't react that well to error conditions.

- It is entirely unable to decode SCODE values that aren't in WINERROR.H.

- The caption string is displayed as one line, causing long messages to be unreadable.

Each of these problems will be fixed in later chapters, as you learn more about what you can do with the OLE CDK.

Chapter 6

Property Persistence: Serialization

This chapter examines "property persistence," which means keeping property values around for longer than the duration of the program that manipulated them. If you create a program that uses an OLE control, and you set up the properties of that control to be just right for your application, it'll be a little disconcerting when you restart the program the next day and find that all the property values you entered have gone away. So how do you get them to stay? This chapter answers that question.

PREPARING FOR PERSISTENCE

If you embed the First control from Chapter 5 into a form in Microsoft Visual Basic version 4, set up some properties, and save the form, you'll get a textual representation of the form and its contents saved in the FRM file. This file includes the properties of each control on the form. It seems, however, that only a few of your control's properties are saved. For example, the section pertinent to the First control from a sample FRM file is shown here:

```
Begin FirstLib.First First1
    Height          =   1695
    Left            =   120
    TabIndex        =   0
    Top             =   120
    Width           =   4215
    _version        =   65536
    _extentx        =   7435
    _extenty        =   2990
    _stockprops     =   79
    caption         =   "Hello 32-bit VB4!"
    forecolor       =   255
    backcolor       =   16711680
    BeginProperty font {FB8F0823-0164-101B-84ED-08002B2EC713}
        name        =   "Algerian"
        charset     =   1
        weight      =   400
        size        =   20.25
        underline   =   0   'False
        italic      =   0   'False
        strikethrough =  0   'False
    EndProperty
End
```

The only entries you're going to recognize at this stage are *caption, forecolor, backcolor,* and *font.* Interestingly, these are all stock properties. There are no entries for your own properties, such as *SCode* or *Message.* Also, Visual Basic has decided to store the extended properties for the control, such as *Height* and *TabIndex,* alongside the stock properties. As you might imagine, the control itself neither creates nor reads the FRM file directly, and Visual Basic does not remember the values of each control's properties so that it can take responsibility for saving them. Instead, Visual Basic asks the control to save its properties as a property set to a stream or a storage via the control's *IDataObject* interface, and Visual Basic then creates the text format of the FRM file and saves it.

As you'll see later, all you need to do to have properties that can be saved and loaded by Visual Basic is to have them saved in the control's property set.

If you load the control into Test Container and choose the Save Property Set option from the File menu with the control selected, you'll notice a new file, TMP.DFL, has been created. The file will be placed in whichever directory Test Container regards as its current directory. (Which directory is somewhat difficult to predict, but it might be the directory containing the First control's binary image or the directory from which Test Container was run, usually C:\MSVC20\CDK32\BIN or C:\MSVC\CDK16\BIN.) This file is actually an OLE structured storage file, which can be examined with the *DocFile* viewer utility provided with the OLE SDK or Visual C++. The executable program is called DFVIEW.EXE. (On my machine, it's been installed to C:\MSVC\BIN as part of Visual C++ version 1.5x; there doesn't appear to be a 32-bit version.) Run the program and use it to examine the temporary file created by Test Container. Expand all streams within the storage so that you get to see the entire file. Your display should look something like that shown in Figure 6-1. Again, a cursory glance tells you that only stock properties are saved in this file.

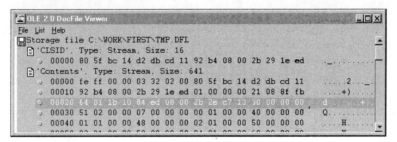

Figure 6-1. *A dump of the property set saved by Test Container for an instance of the First control.*

Given that a mechanism must exist to provide an arbitrary property with persistence, you need to determine which properties provided by your control should be made persistent. There's little point in saving dynamic properties that are recalculated each time they are retrieved. (This particularly applies to your *Code*, *Facility*, and *Severity* properties, which determine their values from the current *SCode* property value whenever their "get" functions are called.) But what about your other properties?

Is there any value in storing the *Message* and *ErrorName* properties? Your situation is particularly intriguing because the *Caption* property is built up from *Message* and *ErrorName;* however, because it is a stock property, it is saved for you. Couple this with the fact that you keep an internal state variable, *m_bIsValid*, to determine whether the current *SCode* value is valid, and a few problems come quickly to the fore:

■ If *SCode* is saved, then, when it is reloaded, how do you set the *m_b-IsValid* flag appropriately?

■ If you overcome the above problem, any saved values in all the other properties should be overwritten.

■ If you don't overcome the above problem but do save the other properties, their values are invalid because the *SCode* has not been recognized.

Let's take a look at some solutions to these problems. If you can get the control to tell you when its properties have been loaded, you can then call the *SetSCode* function to determine the validity of the restored value of *SCode* and set up all the other properties appropriately. Another solution, which is perhaps more interesting to explore, is not to save those properties that will later cause you problems. Whatever strategy you choose, you must first determine how to make properties persistent, and then you must work out which ones you'd like to be persistent.

MAKING YOUR PROPERTIES PERSISTENT

The OLE Control Developer's Kit (OLE CDK) wraps almost all OLE control functionality in the *COleControl* class, which you've been using fairly blindly so far. You're not going to get any further insights into the workings of this class just yet, but you will look at the support it provides for property persistence. When a container asks an OLE control to provide its persistent properties, the *COleControl::DoPropExchange* member function is called to serialize the control's properties. ControlWizard overrides this function on your behalf, so your class derived from *COleControl* contains its own version of *DoPropExchange*, which is called instead of the base class version. If you cast your mind back to Chapter 4, where the OLE CDK was first discussed, you'll remember that you examined the contents of this function as provided by ControlWizard, and it contains two lines of code,

```
ExchangeVersion(pPX, MAKELONG(_wVerMinor, _wVerMajor));
COleControl::DoPropExchange(pPX);
```

The first line of code saves the current control version number, and the second line invokes the base class implementation of the function, which calls *COleControl::ExchangeExtent* to serialize the control's extent (size) and calls *COleControl::ExchangeStockProps* to serialize the control's stock properties.

NOTE The *DoPropExchange* function can be used both to serialize properties (write them from the control to the requester) and to deserialize them (read them from a previously saved set).

For your own properties to be serialized, you need to add code to this function, which will be executed whenever the control's properties are being saved or restored. The OLE CDK provides a number of helper functions to make this a bit easier for you. The names of each of these helper functions begin with *PX_*, so they're known generically as PX functions. "PX" stands for "property exchange." The part of the name following the underscore is the type of variable with which the PX function deals. So, for example, *PX_Bool* is used to serialize a property of type BOOL. The first three parameters to each PX function are the same — a pointer to the

CPropExchange object passed into *DoPropExchange*, which is used to give the serialization context, such as whether the properties are being read or written; the name of the property being dealt with by this PX call; and a variable (or reference or pointer, depending on the type) to hold the value to be written or to receive the returned value. Most of the PX functions also accept a fourth parameter, which is the default value to be used if for some reason the serialization process fails. Some of the more complex PX functions, such as those used to serialize OLE interface pointers, have other parameters required by the type, such as an interface ID.

To provide serialization support for your *SCode* property, you'd use *PX_Long* as follows:

```
PX_Long ( pPX, _T ( "SCode" ), m_SCode );
```

You could also specify a default value for the property should serialization fail:

```
PX_Long ( pPX, _T ( "SCode" ), m_SCode, OL );
```

SCode is the only nonstock property exposed by your control at present that can be altered by the user, so it's logically the only one that needs to have persistence support. For the reasons discussed earlier, however, this might not be what you want. The *Caption* property, being a stock property, is saved unless you alter the default behavior of *DoPropExchange*. If you <u>do</u> take the step to save the *SCode* property as well, you need to ensure that the *m_bIsValid* flag is set accordingly. If you don't save *SCode*, you need to ensure that the *Caption* property is cleared; otherwise, it will be inconsistent with *SCode*. How do you do this?

Because you'll be providing persistence support for *SCode*, you also need to provide a way to initialize *m_bIsValid* and set up the dependent property values. A logical place to do this would be in *DoPropExchange*, immediately after the *SCode* value has been read. How do you know if the property is being serialized or deserialized? The *CPropExchange* class has a member function, *IsLoading*, which returns *TRUE* if the object of this class being addressed is currently in the "load the properties from the container" mode. Consequently, you need to modify the *DoPropExchange* method, as follows:

```
void CFirstCtrl::DoPropExchange(CPropExchange* pPX)
{
    ExchangeVersion(pPX, MAKELONG(_wVerMinor, _wVerMajor));
    COleControl::DoPropExchange(pPX);

    PX_Long ( pPX, _T ( "SCode" ), m_SCode, OL );
    if ( pPX -> IsLoading ( ) )
    {
        SetSCode ( m_SCode );
    }
}
```

Now your control will save and load its *SCode* property and, when loading it, will verify that the *SCode* value is valid, set internal variables, and set up the other properties accordingly. You could argue that you should alter the code so that it no longer saves the *Caption* property, but this is significantly more work than merely overwriting it each time, as you do here.

OTHER PX ROUTINES

In addition to the PX routines to handle the obvious types, the *PX_Blob* routine adds persistence support for properties of type BLOB. A "BLOB" is a "binary large object," which is a contrivance for "a bunch of binary data meaningful only to its creator"! The essential difference between *PX_Blob* and the other PX functions is that *PX_Blob* allocates memory for the object when the property value is being retrieved, whereas other PX routines save to a preallocated variable passed in by the caller. The allocation is performed using the C++ *new* operator, so it is the responsibility of the owner of the object to free the memory when it's no longer required by using the corresponding *delete* operator.

The *PX_Font* function also differs from other PX functions in that it takes an optional parameter that specifies the font object to be used to provide the default characteristics of the font if the property cannot be found when deserialized. This would typically be the client site's ambient font property, allowing a font to take on the same attributes as the ambient if not otherwise specified.

STOCK PROPERTY PERSISTENCE

Examination of the information saved for the First control on a Visual Basic form reveals entries that are as yet unexplained. In additon to the entries for your stock properties, for the control's extended properties and for your custom property, there are also entries for *_version*, *_extentx*, *_extenty*, and *_stockprops*. These are pieces of information saved by the control itself so that it can ensure correct restoration when the properties are reread. The *_version* value represents the control's version number. It is a long value: the high 16 bits represent the major version number, and the low 16 bits represent the minor version number. Unless you've changed the code, the value saved should be 65536, which in hex is 0x10000, representing a major version number of 1 and a minor version number of 0, or 1.0. The *_version* property is saved by the *COleControl::ExchangeVersion* member function during the call to *DoPropExchange*. By giving the control's properties a version number in this manner, it makes it easier to decide what action to take if a control reads in an earlier version's properties. An earlier version might not include all the properties of a later version or it might include properties no longer used. By checking the version number, your code in

DoPropExchange can initialize those properties not found in the earlier version to a sensible value. When *DoPropExchange* is called to retrieve property values, the call to *ExchangeVersion* results in the *CPropExchange* object's version number to be set to that retrieved. This can then be tested programmatically.

The two extent properties, *_extentx* and *_extenty*, are the saved dimensions of the control in *HIMETRIC* units. The OLE control uses these values to restore itself to the size it was when it was saved. The *ExchangeExtent* function, called by *COleControl::DoPropExchange*, saves and restores these values.

COleControl::ExchangeStockProps is called to provide persistence support for each of the stock properties for which persistence is required. A stock property such as *hWnd* is not given persistence because it makes no sense to save a value that is transient and is liable (almost certain, in fact) to change value between sessions. This function actually deals with all persistent stock properties, which makes it rather complex as there is no requirement for a control to use all stock properties. Therefore, in your case, where you use five persistent stock properties (*Caption*, *BackColor*, *ForeColor*, *Font*, and *Enabled*), how does the function know only to save or load those?

If you look back to page 192, you'll notice that one of the values saved in Visual Basic's FRM file for your control is the *_stockprops* entry. This entry represents the "stock property mask," which the OLE CDK uses to indicate which stock properties are used by a control. The mask is interpreted as a set of bits, and each bit represents a given stock property. (For example, 1 represents the *BackColor* property.) The mask bits currently defined can be found in CTLPROP.CPP in the \MSVC\CDK32\SRC directory. *STOCKPROP_BACKCOLOR* is defined as 0x00000001. Your stock property mask is 79, or 0x4F in hex. This equates to bits 0, 1, 2, 3, and 6, meaning *BackColor*, *Caption*, *Font*, *ForeColor*, and *Enabled* respectively. This value tells *ExchangeStockProps* to save or restore only those properties indicated.

If you don't want all the stock properties you use to be serialized, the easiest solution is to omit the call to the base class *DoPropExchange* and use the PX functions in your *DoPropExchange* for the stock properties that you do want to serialize.

As you can see, the OLE CDK makes it pretty easy to add persistence support to your controls. The only decisions you need to make are which properties you want to be persistent and what action needs to be taken when the values are restored. Then it's simply a question of doing the coding.

The next chapter examines the second large area of functionality essential to controls: methods.

Chapter 7

Methods

If you're used to creating or using Microsoft Visual Basic custom controls, commonly known as VBXs, this chapter introduces a subject that will be of interest. The VBX model did not allow the creation of "custom methods," in which a method is a way of asking an object to perform some given action. A classic method, for example, would ask a database object to save itself to the database or ask a button to respond to a mouse click. As VBXs are unable to support custom methods, a number of VBX authors used the concept of "action properties," which are properties exposed by the control that actually perform an action when their values are changed. Action properties are clearly a way for VBXs to simulate methods, but they have confused users who rightly expect properties to be attributes rather than precursors to actions.

OLE CONTROLS AND CUSTOM METHODS

The OLE Controls specification allows custom methods to be added to any control, and a method, like a property, can return any of the standard types supported by OLE Automation. Likewise, custom methods can also take parameters of any of these types, although the OLE CDK limits the number of parameters a method can take to 15. (Heaven forbid that we should ever need so many!) The provision of custom methods in OLE Controls means that control authors should shy away from using action properties, although if you're converting an existing VBX and want to maintain an identical interface, you might want to keep them. A useful technique used by some OLE controls that replace existing VBXs is to support the existing action properties for compatibility but also to provide a set of custom methods that new programs should use in preference to the old properties.

Methods are added to a control as easily as properties are if you're using the OLE CDK. ClassWizard provides for method addition through the OLE Automation tab, in the same way as is true for properties. Similarly, the OLE CDK provides two stock methods for which, if you need to support them in your control, you won't need to write any code. The stock methods are *DoClick* and *Refresh*. Both methods take no parameters and return no result. *DoClick* simulates the action of clicking the left mouse button on the control and is particularly useful for button-like controls. It causes the *COleControl* member function *OnClick* to be called and, if the control also supports the *Click* stock event (see also the next chapter), it will cause this event to be fired. *Refresh* calls *COleControl::Refresh*, which causes the control to be repainted. This method is useful if you want your users to be able to cause a control repaint at their discretion.

ADDING A CUSTOM METHOD TO YOUR CONTROL

The best way to demonstrate something is to do it, so you'll add a custom method to your First control, discussed in the previous two chapters. You'll also add the stock *Refresh* method, as a courtesy to those of your users who see value in being able to ask your control to redraw!

What will the new custom method do? One of the major deficiencies of the current implementation of First is that it always searches a file sequentially. Couple this with the fact that the name of the file is hard-coded into the application and that you can't add new SCODE definitions to the file, and it becomes clear that your control as it stands has some limitations that you'd rather do without.

Designing a Simple SCODE Database

In an ideal world, all SCODE definitions manipulated by this control would be in a database. You're going to create one now, but it isn't going to be a particularly sophisticated one because you're still going to treat it as a file. (You'll add true database support, via ODBC, in Chapter 10.)

Determining the "database" format is simple: you know that the legal set of facility and severity codes are predefined. Room is available for a great many more facility codes, making them potential candidates for a database too, but until you get to a more sophisticated control, it's considerably easier to stick with the fixed set. The only pieces of information you actually need to keep on an SCODE are its full 32-bit SCODE value, its symbolic name, and the message string associated with it. Of these, the SCODE itself forms a pretty good key, because you know it's unique; and the fact that it's numeric makes it particularly easy to search for. For now, you'll stick with sequential access to the file.

You still have a number of problems to consider:

■ The symbolic name and message string do not have fixed sizes. So, do you allocate maxima, to make file manipulation easy? or do you allow maximum flexibility?

■ Do you keep the entries sorted by SCODE, making searching easy at the expense of difficult insertion?

■ Do you use one file to hold all three data items per entry? or do you keep SCODEs in a separate file together with offsets into another file (or two files) holding the other data?

■ Do you add even more complication by allowing entries to be deleted?

■ How do you save yourself the grunt work of adding all the entries in WINERROR.H?

The first three problems are related: if you answer the first one properly, you can answer the others more easily. I'll keep your life as simple as possible by explicitly deciding not to support deletion (!), and you'll add a special bulk load method to take entries from an existing file and add them to your database.

A good approach would be to maintain a file that holds the SCODEs together with offsets into another file that holds the symbolic names and message strings. You'll aid efficiency (speed, in this case) by preloading the SCODE file into memory when the control starts up. This means that every instance of the First control on a system has its own copy of the SCODE file in memory. This shouldn't be too great a hit, because there can't be that many programs which need to use a control like this at the same time, and there can't be that many SCODEs in the world that memory becomes a premium, can there? Let's hope not. Of course, you're running in a 32-bit world now anyway (you're not?!?), so memory shortage is considerably less of a problem than it was in the good old 16-bit days.

So, here's the deal. . . .

Implementing the SCODE Database

A file called SCODES.IND, henceforth known as the "index file," contains an entry for each SCODE added to it. Each entry is eight bytes long. The first four bytes hold the SCODE itself, and the next four bytes hold the offset into another file, SCODES.MSG, where the data for this SCODE can be found. SCODES.MSG, the message file, also contains an entry for each SCODE added to the index file. The format here is a string holding the symbolic name followed by a zero terminator, a string holding the message, and another zero terminator. The index file will be sorted by SCODE.

Figure 7-1 shows the index and message file formats in graphical form.

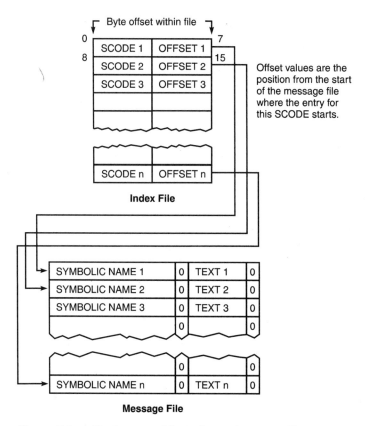

Figure 7-1. *The formats of the index and message files.*

You'll create a method, *Add*, which adds a new SCODE to the database. It will take three parameters: the SCODE, its symbolic name, and its message string. It will return *TRUE* if the addition succeeds, and it will return *FALSE* if it fails, for whatever reason. You'll have a second method, *BatchLoad*, which takes one parameter, the name of a file containing an arbitrary number of SCODE entries in the same format as WINERROR.H. It will return as a long integer the number of SCODEs loaded from the file and inserted into the database. In both cases, the index and message files will be saved after the entry is complete. "Complete" in the case of *BatchLoad* is reached when all SCODEs in the file have been added. You're not going to add the sophistication of transactions to these file manipulations, which would allow us to ensure that the index and message files are always in sync, because it would be overkill.

The first step is to add the three methods to the control. Load the relevant make file into Microsoft Visual C++ (FIRST32.MAK for Visual C++ 2.x or FIRST.MAK for Visual C++ 1.5x) and invoke ClassWizard, selecting the OLE Automation tab.

Ensure that *CFirstCtrl* is selected as the class name, and choose the Add Method button. Add the stock *Refresh* method. Then add the *Add* method, choosing *BOOL* as its return type and giving it three parameters:

- *SCode*, as a *long*

- *Symbol*, as an *LPCTSTR*

- *Message*, as an *LPCTSTR*

Finally, add the *BatchLoad* method, giving it a return type of *long* and providing it with one parameter, *FileName*, as an *LPCTSTR*. The control will continue to be compilable and runnable at this stage, but the new methods other than *Refresh* will have no effect.

For the new scheme to work, you need to follow these steps:

1. At control-creation time, open the index file (aka SCODES.IND), read it into memory, and close the file.

2. At control-destruction time, free up the resources used to hold the index file's memory image.

3. Change *SetSCode* to retrieve the information for an SCODE from the memory image and the message file (SCODES.MSG).

4. Write code for the *Add* and *BatchLoad* methods.

Sounds easy so far. To make life a little easier, you can begin by defining a data structure that will be used to hold the contents of the index file. First, you'll define in a FIRSTCTL.H a struct *CSCodeEntry* that will be used to hold each SCODE and offset:

```
struct CSCodeEntry
{
    long lSCode;
    unsigned long ulOffset;
};
```

FYI   Did you know that C++ treats *class* and *struct* almost as synonyms? The only difference is that, by default, members of a structure are public (to remain compatible with C structures), while those of a class are private.

The two elements of the structure you're defining are a long integer to hold the SCODE and an unsigned long integer to hold the offset of the SCODE's entry within the message file.

You'll then have an array of these *CSCodeEntry* structures, the size of which is obviously dynamic because you don't know at compile-time how many SCODEs are in the index file, and of course new ones can be added by the user at any time. Consequently, you're going to declare a private pointer in your *CFirstCtrl* class:

```
CSCodeEntry *m_lpseCodes;
```

This pointer will be initialized at control creation to hold as many entries as are found in the file. New SCODEs added using the *Add* method will be put into a linked list maintained by the control; those added through *BatchLoad* will go directly to the file and cause the file to be re-read at the completion of the load, re-allocating the array.

You also need to add a class to FIRSTCTL.H to manage the linked list of newly added entries:

```
class CSCodeEntryList
{
public:
    void SetNext ( CSCodeEntryList *selNew ) { m_pNext = selNew; }
    CSCodeEntryList *GetNext ( void ) const { return m_pNext; }
    CSCodeEntry *GetEntry ( void ) { return &m_seThis; }
private:
    CSCodeEntryList *m_pNext;
    CSCodeEntry m_seThis;
};
```

The *m_pNext* member variable holds a pointer to the next element in the list and *m_seThis* holds the SCODE entry for this list item. The *SetNext* member function sets *m_pNext* to point to the passed-in structure; this is usually used to add entries to the list, by setting the *m_pNext* member variable of the current end-of-list structure to point to the new end-of-list structure. *GetNext* is used to traverse the list; it returns a pointer to the next element in the list, and *GetEntry* returns a pointer to the *CSCodeEntry* object within the list item.

You also need two more private class member variables in the *CFirstCtrl* class: *m_lpseNewCodes* and *m_lpseListEnd*. The first points to the start of the list of newly added entries, and the second points to the end. You hold an end-of-list pointer simply to make it a little faster to add an entry to the end of the list.

Listing 7-1 shows the constructor and destructor code needed to read the index file into memory and to free up the memory when the control goes away. The constructor initializes each of the pointers to 0 and initializes another class member variable, *m_lSCodes*, which holds the number of SCODE entries found in the index file once it's been read. The function then calls *ReadIndexFile*, a new function which reads the index file into memory. This function will also be called after a call to the *BatchLoad* method, to reload the file into memory. The destructor frees up all memory for the index file and for the list of new entries via a separate function, *ClearList*. This makes it easier to reuse that piece of code later.

```
CFirstCtrl::CFirstCtrl()
{
    InitializeIIDs(&IID_DFirst, &IID_DFirstEvents);
    m_SCode = 0L;
    m_bIsValid = FALSE;
    m_lpseCodes = 0;
    m_lpseNewCodes = 0;
    m_lpseListEnd = 0;
    m_lSCodes = 0;

    ReadIndexFile ( );
}


CFirstCtrl::~CFirstCtrl()
{
    ClearList ( );
}

void CFirstCtrl::ClearList ( void )
{
    delete [] m_lpseCodes;
    CSCodeEntryList *pNext = m_lpseNewCodes;
    while ( pNext )
    {
        CSCodeEntryList *pTemp = pNext -> GetNext ( );
        delete pNext;
        pNext = pTemp;
    }
}
#define ENTRYSIZE     ( sizeof ( long ) + sizeof ( unsigned long ) )

void CFirstCtrl::ReadIndexFile ( void )
{
    CFile cfIndex;
    CString csIndex;

    csIndex.LoadString ( IDS_INDEXFILE );
    if ( cfIndex.Open ( csIndex, CFile::modeRead |
        CFile::shareDenyNone ) == TRUE )
    {
        TRY
```

Listing 7-1. *Control construction and destruction code, together*   *(continued)*
with the code to read the index file into memory.

(continued)

```
        {
            long lCode;
            unsigned long ulOffset;
            m_lSCodes = cfIndex.GetLength ( ) / ENTRYSIZE;
            m_lpseCodes = new CSCodeEntry [ m_lSCodes ];
            long lCurrent = 0L;
            UINT uRead1, uRead2;
            do
            {
                uRead1 = cfIndex.Read ( &lCode, sizeof ( lCode ) );
                uRead2 = cfIndex.Read ( &ulOffset,
                    sizeof ( ulOffset ) );
                if ( uRead1 == 0 && uRead2 == 0 )
                {
                    break;
                }
                if ( ( uRead1 == sizeof ( lCode ) ) &&
                    ( uRead2 == sizeof ( ulOffset ) ) )
                {
                    m_lpseCodes [ lCurrent ].lSCode = lCode;
                    m_lpseCodes [ lCurrent ].ulOffset = ulOffset;
                    ++lCurrent;
                }
                else
                {
                    AfxThrowFileException (
                        CFileException::endOfFile );
                }
            }
            while ( uRead1 );
            cfIndex.Close ( );
        }
        CATCH ( CException, e )
        {
            TRACE ( _T
                ( "Error reading index file or out of memory\n" ) );
            delete [] m_lpseCodes;
        }
        END_CATCH
    }
    else
    {
        TRACE ( _T ( "Index file not found - will be created\n" ) );
    }
}
```

ReadIndexFile uses a *CString, csIndex*, to load the name of the index file from the string table. (I've set my entry to C:\SCODES.IND, but obviously you can use any path and name you choose.) It then uses a *CFile* object, *cfIndex*, to open the file for read access. If this fails, all it does at present is throw an informative message out to the debug terminal. If the open succeeds, the main body of the function is executed. Notice that this is enclosed in one vast *TRY* block, so that all errors can be caught and dealt with uniformly. The function first determines the number of entries in the index file by dividing its length by the size of an entry. The entry size is held as a manifest constant (aka *#define*), defined as the size of a long integer (the SCODE) plus the length of an unsigned long integer (the file offset). In both current cases, this will be eight bytes in total. The number of entries is saved in *m_lSCodes. m_lpseCodes* is set to point to a dynamically allocated array of *m_lSCodes CSCodeEntry* structures. The MFC library's implementation of the *new* operator will throw a *CMemoryException* if it fails to allocate the memory.

The function then enters a loop in which it reads each SCODE and each offset into the relevant members of each array element. The loop is broken if the end of the file is reached or if any file exception occurs. Notice that if end of file is reached before it's expected (less than eight bytes are read for an entry), you use *AfxThrow-FileException* to throw an exception that you catch a few lines down.

All exceptions are caught in the *CATCH* block by specifying the MFC base exception class, *CException*, rather than each of the individual exception classes. You do this because you want to treat each exception the same way here — deleting the memory allocated for the array of entries. It is possible that this exception handler will be called before any memory has been allocated, in which case *m_lpseCodes* will have the value of 0 it was given during the control's constructor. Your code is simplified by taking advantage of the fact that C++ allows a null pointer to be passed to *delete*, which will ignore it and return.

Listing 7-2 (beginning on the next page) shows the code that you use to set a new value for the *SCode* property. The *SetSCode* function is now considerably simpler than the previous version. It first initializes the message and symbol strings and then calls a new function, *FindEntry*, to find the SCODE entry in the index file's memory image. If this succeeds, it sets up its second parameter to the offset in the message file in which the entry for this SCODE can be found. This offset is then used by the new *GetInfo* function to set the message and symbol string values to the entries in the message file. As with the previous version, you set the *Caption* property to a special error string if the SCODE cannot be found or if some error occurs.

FindEntry is also pretty simple. It first searches the array of entries read in from the index file and, if the SCODE is not found here, it searches the linked list of newly added entries. Obviously, there's room for improvement here: you could ensure that the index file (or at least its memory image) is sorted by SCODE, allowing you to search using a binary search rather than a linear search. This would improve performance a little but would complicate some other bits of code, such as the reading in of the file if it were not sorted or when new entries are written to it.

GetInfo is marginally more complicated. It opens the message file for read access and moves to the offset given. It then reads characters until a zero character is found and adds each character to the symbol string. Notice the complication of this code caused by Unicode: in the old days of ANSI-only characters, such code could be easier to write and easier to understand, at the expense of being completely unable to deal with messages in some languages. Having read the symbol, it then repeats the operation for the message, and closes the file.

SetSCode and Associated Routines

```
void CFirstCtrl::SetSCode(long nNewValue)
{
    CString csLine;

    m_csMessage.Empty ( );
    m_csSymbol.Empty ( );

    unsigned long ulOffset;
    if ( FindEntry ( nNewValue, &ulOffset ) )
    {
        m_bIsValid = TRUE;
        GetInfo ( ulOffset );
        csLine = m_csSymbol + _T ( ": " ) + m_csMessage;
    }
    else
    {
        csLine.LoadString ( IDS_NOVALID_SCODE );
    }
    m_SCode = nNewValue;
    SetText ( csLine );
    SetModifiedFlag();
}

BOOL CFirstCtrl::FindEntry ( long lCode, unsigned long *pulOffset )
{
    for ( long lEntry = 0L; lEntry < m_lSCodes; ++lEntry )
    {
        if ( m_lpseCodes [ lEntry ].lSCode == lCode )
```

Listing 7-2. *The code to set an SCODE's entry.*   *(continued)*

```
        {
            *pulOffset = m_lpseCodes [ lEntry ].ulOffset;
            return TRUE;
        }
    }
    CSCodeEntryList *lpEntry = m_lpseNewCodes;
    while ( lpEntry )
    {
        if ( lpEntry -> GetEntry ( ) -> lSCode == lCode )
        {
            *pulOffset = lpEntry -> GetEntry ( ) -> ulOffset;
            return TRUE;
        }
        lpEntry = lpEntry -> GetNext ( );
    }
    return FALSE;
}

void CFirstCtrl::GetInfo ( unsigned long ulOffset )
{
    CFile cfMsg;
    CString csMsg;
    TCHAR tcChar;

    csMsg.LoadString ( IDS_MESSAGEFILE );
    if ( cfMsg.Open ( csMsg, CFile::modeRead |
        CFile::shareDenyNone ) == TRUE )
    {
        TRY
        {
            cfMsg.Seek ( ulOffset, CFile::begin );
            UINT uRead;
            for ( ; ; )
            {
                uRead = cfMsg.Read ( &tcChar, sizeof ( tcChar ) );
                if ( uRead < sizeof ( tcChar ) )
                {
                    return;
                }
                if ( tcChar == 0 )
                {
                    break;
                }
                m_csSymbol += tcChar;
```

(continued)

(continued)

```
        }
        for ( ; ; )
        {
            uRead = cfMsg.Read ( &tcChar, sizeof ( tcChar ) );
            if ( uRead < sizeof ( tcChar ) )
            {
                return;
            }
            if ( tcChar == 0 )
            {
                break;
            }
            m_csMessage += tcChar;
        }
        cfMsg.Close ( );
    }
    CATCH ( CException, e )
    {
        TRACE ( _T ( "Error reading message file\n" ) );
    }
    END_CATCH
}
else
{
    TRACE ( _T ( "Message file not found\n" ) );
}
}
```

Now you can look at the code for the *Add* method itself, shown in Listing 7-3. This method first calls *FindEntry* to check whether the SCODE to be added already exists. If it does, the routine ends, indicating success. You only compare the SCODE values here, so you don't verify that the message and symbol are the same. You can easily add code to do this if you want. Assuming the code doesn't exist in the file, you add it onto the linked list of new entries. You first allocate a new *CSCodeEntryList* object, and then you initialize its contained *CSCodeEntry* object through the *GetEntry* method. The offset is initialized from the return value of *AddMessage*, described below. You then add the new item to the list by setting the next pointer of the list element currently at the end to point to this new element, and then set the end-of-list pointer, *m_lpseListEnd*, to the new entry. If this is the first entry in the list, you also set the start-of-list pointer, *m_lpseNew-Codes*, to point at this element.

Add and Associated Routines

```
BOOL CFirstCtrl::Add ( long SCode, LPCTSTR Symbol, LPCTSTR Message )
{
    unsigned long ulOffset;
    if ( FindEntry ( SCode, &ulOffset ) )
    {
        TRACE ( _T ( "SCODE already in database\n" ) );
        return TRUE;
    }

    CSCodeEntryList *pNew = 0;
    TRY
    {
        pNew = new CSCodeEntryList;
        pNew -> GetEntry ( ) -> lSCode = SCode;
        pNew -> GetEntry ( ) -> ulOffset =
            AddMessage ( Symbol, Message );
        WriteEntry ( pNew -> GetEntry ( ) );
        pNew -> SetNext ( OL );
        if ( m_lpseNewCodes )
        {
            m_lpseListEnd -> SetNext ( pNew );
            m_lpseListEnd = pNew;
        }
        else
        {
            m_lpseNewCodes = m_lpseListEnd = pNew;
        }
    }
    CATCH ( CException, e )
    {
        delete pNew;
        TRACE ( _T ( "Error adding SCODE\n" ) );
        return FALSE;
    }
    END_CATCH
    return TRUE;
}
    unsigned long CFirstCtrl::AddMessage ( LPCTSTR lpszSymbol,
        LPCTSTR lpszMessage )
{
    CFile cfMsg;
```

Listing 7-3. *The* Add *method and associated routines.*   *(continued)*

(continued)

```
    CString csMsg;
    unsigned long ulReturn = 0xFFFFFFFF;
    csMsg.LoadString ( IDS_MESSAGEFILE );
    if ( cfMsg.Open ( csMsg, CFile::modeWrite |
        CFile::shareExclusive ) == TRUE )
    {
        TRY
        {
            ulReturn = cfMsg.Seek ( 0L, CFile::end );
            cfMsg.Write ( lpszSymbol,
                _tcslen ( lpszSymbol ) + 1 );
            cfMsg.Write ( lpszMessage,
                _tcslen ( lpszMessage ) + 1 );
            cfMsg.Close ( );
        }
        CATCH ( CFileException, e )
        {
            TRACE ( _T ( "Error writing message file\n" ) );
            return 0xFFFFFFFF;
        }
        END_CATCH
    }
    else
    {
        TRACE ( _T
            ( "Failed to open message file for writing\n" ) );
    }
    return ulReturn;
}
void CFirstCtrl::WriteEntry ( CSCodeEntry *pNew )
{
    CFile cfIndex;
    CString csIndex;

    csIndex.LoadString ( IDS_INDEXFILE );
    if ( cfIndex.Open ( csIndex, CFile::modeWrite |
        CFile::shareExclusive ) == TRUE )
    {
        cfIndex.Seek ( 0L, CFile::end );
        cfIndex.Write ( &pNew -> lSCode,
            sizeof ( pNew -> lSCode ) );
        cfIndex.Write ( &pNew -> ulOffset,
            sizeof ( pNew -> ulOffset ) );
        cfIndex.Close ( );
    }
}
```

AddMessage has the job of adding the new symbol and message to the message file. It does this by opening the file for writing and "seeking" to the end of the file, so that new data added gets put at the end of the file. You then save this address (the current length of the file) for the return value and write the symbol, a zero terminator, the message, and another zero terminator to the message file. Notice the use of the *_tcslen* function, which will expand into the appropriate string length function depending on whether the control is being compiled for Unicode or ANSI. *WriteEntry* writes the SCODE and the message's offset into the message file to the index file. It opens the index file for writing, seeks to the end, and then writes out the two long integers held in the *CSCodeEntry* object passed in.

Finally, let's look at the *BatchLoad* method, shown in Listing 7-4. The algorithm used by this method is as follows:

- Open input file in text mode for read access

- Open index file for write access, seek to end

- Open message file for write access

- Until end-of-file on input:

    ❑   Get next SCODE, symbol and message from input file

    ❑   Check whether SCODE already exists in index file; if so, skip

    ❑   Seek to end of message file and take current position

    ❑   Write SCODE and offset into message file to the index file

    ❑   Write symbol and message into message file

- Loop

- Close all files

- Discard linked list of additions from *Add* method

- Discard memory holding index file image

- Reload image file into memory

BatchLoad and Associated Routines

```
long CFirstCtrl::BatchLoad ( LPCTSTR FileName )
{
    CFile cfIndex, cfMsg;
    CStdioFile cfInput;
    long lEntries = 0L;
```

Listing 7-4.   *The* Batchload *method and associated routines.*   *(continued)*

(continued)

```
if ( cfInput.Open ( FileName, CFile::typeText |
    CFile::modeRead ) == TRUE )
{
    CString csIndex;

    TRY
    {
        csIndex.LoadString ( IDS_INDEXFILE );
        if ( cfIndex.Open ( csIndex, CFile::modeWrite |
            CFile::shareExclusive ) == TRUE )
        {
            CString csMsg;

            csMsg.LoadString ( IDS_MESSAGEFILE );
            if ( cfMsg.Open ( csMsg, CFile::modeWrite |
                CFile::shareExclusive ) == TRUE )
            {
                lEntries = DoBatchLoad ( &cfInput,
                    &cfIndex, &cfMsg );
                cfMsg.Close ( );
            }
            else
            {
                TRACE ( _T
                    ( "Failed to open message file\n" ) );
            }
            cfIndex.Close ( );
        }
        else
        {
            TRACE ( _T
                ( "Failed to open index file\n" ) );
        }
        cfInput.Close ( );
    }
    CATCH ( CException, e )
    {
        TRACE ( _T ( "Error closing files\n" ) );
    }
    END_CATCH
}
else
{
    TRACE ( _T ( "Failed to open input file\n" ) );
```

(continued)

214

```
        }

    if ( lEntries )
    {
        ClearList ( );
        m_lpseCodes = 0;
        m_lpseNewCodes = 0;
        m_lpseListEnd = 0;
        m_lSCodes = 0;
        ReadIndexFile ( );
    }
    return lEntries;
}
long CFirstCtrl::DoBatchLoad ( CStdioFile *cfIn,
    CFile *cfIndex, CFile *cfMsg )
{
    long lEntries = 0L;

    TRY
    {
        cfIndex -> Seek ( .0L, CFile::end );

        CString csLine, csMsg, csSymbol;
        while ( GetNextDefineLine ( cfIn, &csLine, &csMsg ) )
        {
            long lCode = GetTheCode ( &csLine, &csSymbol );
            unsigned long ulOffset;
            if ( FindEntry ( lCode, &ulOffset ) )
            {
                TRACE1 ( _T
                    ( "SCODE %08X already in database - ignored\n" ),
                        lCode );
            }
            else
            {
                long lMsgPos = cfMsg -> Seek ( 0L, CFile::end );

                cfIndex -> Write ( &lCode, sizeof ( lCode ) );
                cfIndex -> Write ( &lMsgPos, sizeof ( lMsgPos ) );

                cfMsg -> Write ( ( LPCTSTR ) csSymbol,
                    csSymbol.GetLength ( ) + 1 );
                cfMsg -> Write ( ( LPCTSTR ) csMsg,
                    csMsg.GetLength ( ) + 1 );
```

(continued)

(continued)

```
            ++lEntries;
        }
      }
    }
    CATCH ( CException, e )
    {
        TRACE ( _T ( "Error writing SCODE to database\n" ) );
    }
    END_CATCH

    return lEntries;
}

BOOL CFirstCtrl::GetNextDefineLine ( CStdioFile *cfFile,
    CString *csLine, CString *csMessage )
{
    _TCHAR szBuf [ 256 ];
    CString csCompare;
    BOOL bFound = FALSE;
    LPTSTR lpszCnt;
    do
    {
        TRY
        {
            lpszCnt = cfFile -> ReadString ( szBuf, 255 );
        }
        CATCH ( CFileException, e )
        {
            break;
        }
        END_CATCH

        if ( lpszCnt == NULL )
        {
            break;
        }
        csCompare = szBuf;
        bFound = ( csCompare.Find ( _T
            ( "// MessageText:" ) ) != -1 );
    }
    while ( bFound == FALSE );

    if ( bFound )
```

(continued)

```
    {
        TRY
        {
                // Discard blank comment line
            cfFile -> ReadString ( szBuf, 255 );
                // Get message line(s)
            csMessage -> Empty ( );
            do
            {
                cfFile -> ReadString ( szBuf, 255 );
                if ( szBuf [ 3 ] )
                {
                    if ( ! csMessage -> IsEmpty ( ) )
                    {
                        *csMessage += _T ( " " );
                    }
                    szBuf [ _tcslen ( szBuf ) - 1 ] =
                        TCHAR ( 0 );
                    *csMessage += szBuf + 4;
                }
            }
            while ( szBuf [ 3 ] );

                // Get code line
            lpszCnt = cfFile -> ReadString ( szBuf, 255 );
        }
        CATCH ( CFileException, e )
        {
            csMessage -> Empty ( );
            return FALSE;
        }
        END_CATCH

        if ( lpszCnt == NULL )
        {
            csMessage -> Empty ( );
            return FALSE;
        }
            *csLine = szBuf;
        return TRUE;
    }
    return FALSE;
}

long CFirstCtrl::GetTheCode ( CString *csLine,CString *csSymbol )
```

(continued)

(continued)

```
{
        // Skip '#define'
    int i = 7;

        // Skip white space
    while ( ( csLine -> GetLength ( ) > i ) &&
        ( _istspace ( csLine -> GetAt ( i ) ) ) )
    {
        ++i;
    }
    if ( csLine -> GetLength ( ) <= i )
    {
        return 0L;
    }

        // Collect symbol
    csSymbol -> Empty ( );
    while ( ( csLine -> GetLength ( ) > i ) &&
        ! ( _istspace ( csLine -> GetAt ( i ) ) ) )
    {
        *csSymbol += csLine -> GetAt ( i );
        ++i;
    }
    if ( csLine -> GetLength ( ) <= i )
    {
        csSymbol -> Empty ( );
        return 0L;
    }

        // Skip white space
    while ( ( csLine -> GetLength ( ) > i ) &&
        ( _istspace ( csLine -> GetAt ( i ) ) ) )
    {
        ++i;
    }
    if ( csLine -> GetLength ( ) <= i )
    {
        csSymbol -> Empty ( );
        return 0L;
    }

        // Collect number
    CString csNumber;
```

(continued)

```
TRY
{
    csNumber = csLine -> Mid ( i );
}
CATCH ( CMemoryException, e )
{
    m_csSymbol.Empty ( );
    return 0L;
}
END_CATCH
return _tcstoul ( csNumber, NULL, 0 );
}
```

BatchLoad starts by initializing the count of entries added to zero and then opening the three files; the input file is opened using an object of the *CStdioFile* class rather than *CFile* directly because once again you want to take advantage of *CStdioFile*'s special text-handling capabilities. It then calls *DoBatchLoad*, which does the majority of the work and returns the number of entries it added to the database. Assuming all file-close operations succeed, the function ends by clearing out the image of the old index file, deleting any linked list entries created through the *Add* method and then reloading the index file using *ReadIndexFile*.

DoBatchLoad encloses the majority of its code in an all-encompassing *TRY...CATCH* block, as it performs a lot of file handling, some of which can throw exceptions. The first action inside the block is to seek to the end of the index file and then to enter a loop in which *DoBatchLoad* calls *GetNextDefineLine* until it reaches the end of the file or some other error. *GetNextDefineLine* is a variant of the one used in earlier chapters, the prime difference here being that the message *CString* object is now passed to the function as a parameter; the earlier version set the value of the class member variable, *m_csMessage*. When the function finds a set of lines that match its criteria for those which form an SCODE and its message string, it reads the message string and reads up to and including the line containing the symbolic name and integral value of the SCODE.

Another function borrowed in a slightly altered form from earlier chapters is *GetTheCode*, which is now passed the SCODE symbol name *CString* object as a parameter (rather than using the class member variable, *m_csSymbol*) to retrieve the SCODE symbol name. This function extracts the symbolic name from the string passed to it and also gets the SCODE's value. *DoBatchLoad* then uses *FindEntry* to determine whether the newly read-in SCODE matches one already in the database. If it does, the entry is skipped and the next line is read; otherwise, the function seeks to the end of the message file and writes out the SCODE and the current position in the message file to the index file. It then writes the symbolic name and message string to the message file and increments the count of entries successfully added.

The completed control from this chapter can be found on the companion CD-ROM under \OLECTRLS\CHAP07\FIRST. This directory also contains versions of SCODES.IND and SCODES.MSG created from the WINERROR.H file supplied with Visual C++ version 2.x using *BatchLoad*. This file is reported by *BatchLoad* as having 899 SCODEs defined inside it. I've also supplied EMPTY.IND and EMPTY.MSG, two files that you might want to use for testing purposes. These versions of the files contain only one SCODE — 0x00000000 — making them useful starting points for testing the *BatchLoad* method.

For a file to be recognized by *BatchLoad*, it must be in the same format as WINERROR.H: that is, it should appear as if it has been generated by the message compiler, *MC*. After you've loaded a set of SCODEs, you'll notice that this version of the control is considerably faster at looking up SCODEs than the earlier version.

WHAT ABOUT ERRORS AND EXCEPTIONS?

Throughout this code, I've taken a pretty lenient attitude towards errors and exceptions. This has also made some of the code less readable than it should be. In some cases, I've returned a value indicating that an error has occurred but without specifying what error, and in others I've simply ignored the error. I need to get more intelligent about this, but in order to do that you need to learn more about two additional aspects of controls: events and exceptions. These are covered in the next two chapters, and we'll use the knowledge gained to improve the robustness and friendliness of this control.

Chapter 8

Events

Events form the most exciting part of the OLE Controls specification, primarily because they're new and allow you to do things you couldn't have done previously. Now you have a model in which you can define an interface with which you can interact; this is the reverse of the normal situation, in which you define an interface with which others can interact.

As Chapter 3 showed, the mechanism provided by OLE Controls for the support of events is in fact a generic COM mechanism that can in theory be used by any COM object that wants to interact with another object's implementation of an interface. The theory is somewhat moot at present because current (as of mid-1995) implementations of OLE in both 16-bit and 32-bit guises don't provide marshaling support for the new interfaces (for example, *IConnectionPoint*), so they can only be used in-process. Marshaling support will be added to 32-bit OLE over time, but it is unlikely that there will ever be out-of-process support for these interfaces in 16-bit OLE.

I will again introduce the implementation of events in OLE controls and the OLE Control Developer's Kit (OLE CDK) by looking at the definition from the specification point of view and then examining what the OLE CDK provides. I will also, of course, add a couple of events to the control that has been developed over the past few chapters.

USES FOR EVENTS

Events are a powerful addition to a programmer's arsenal. Standard OLE Automation objects can only inform their containers that something has happened as the result of a call to one of the object's properties or methods — that is, as a synchronous response. OLE controls, on the other hand, are able to inform their containers at any time, asynchronously of any action by the container. I need to be specific about what I mean by "synchronous" and "asynchronous." I am talking here about the interface between the object and its container rather than any notion of asynchronous operation within the object itself. That is, a control can at any point notify its container of an event, but that does not mean that the notification is asynchronous within the control. After the control has called the function that ultimately notifies the container, it must wait until the notification has taken place before it can proceed.

What can events be used for? Literally any event that the creator of a control wants to tell the control's container about. Obvious candidates are erroneous situations such as network failures, notification that a currently viewed database record has been altered by some other agent, notification that a control has been clicked on or that some text within it has been altered, and so forth. The point is that while obvious candidates exist, events can be created by a control author to notify the container of literally any happening.

EVENT TYPES

The next chapter will cover events for exceptions and erroneous conditions. This chapter focuses on pure notifications. Events fall into four types:

- Request event
- Before event
- After event
- Do event

Request Event

A "Request event" is an event that a control fires when it wants to ask its container to allow it to do something. The last parameter to a Request event is a pointer to a variable, conventionally called *Cancel*, of type *CancelBoolean*, which is a standard type introduced by OLE Controls. The value of the variable pointed at by this parameter is set to *FALSE* by the control prior to the event being fired. If the container changes it to *TRUE*, it is asking the control not to perform the action signaled by the event. A Request event should be given a name that begins with "Request," so an event to request a database update might be called "RequestUpdate."

Before Event

A "Before event" is an event that a control fires before it takes a specific action, allowing the container or its user to take any actions required before the action is taken. For example, a "BeforeClose" event can be fired by a control immediately prior to shutting itself down; it is allowing the container to do whatever it needs to do before the shutdown. A Before event is not cancelable and should be named BeforeXxx, where Xxx is the action about to be performed by the control.

After Event

An "After event" is fired by a control when it wants to let the container or its user perform some action after an action has been taken. An After event is the classic notification. After events are the most common sort of event, so they don't require any special naming conventions, and they are not cancelable. A typical After event can be a mouse click event, in which a control is notifying its container than it has been clicked.

Do Event

A "Do event" is in some ways the OLE Controls analogue of a C++ virtual function — it allows a container or its user to override an action or to perform some behavior immediately before the default action is taken. If a Do event has a default action that it can take, it passes in as its last parameter a pointer to a Boolean variable, conventionally called *EnableDefault*, which is set to *TRUE* by the control prior to the event being fired. If the container sets this parameter to *FALSE*, it is asking the control not to perform its default action. Do events should typically be named *DoXxx*, where *Xxx* is the action to be performed.

Firing Events

An event is fired by a control by calling the *Invoke* method on the *IDispatch*-derived pointer it extracted from the container when the container connected to its connection point through *IConnectionPoint::Advise*. As connection points can support multi-casting, it is possible that there are numerous implementations of the event handler which need to be called: that is, the control fires the event to all sinks that have expressed an interest. The control does not need to look up any specifics of the call, as it defined the interface itself; therefore, it just packs up the parameters, if any, into *VARIANT*s and calls *Invoke*.

STANDARD EVENTS

The OLE Controls specification defines a set of standard events that controls can choose to fire. This doesn't mean that every control must be able to fire every one of these events; rather, it means simply that the semantics of certain common events have been defined. The standard events defined by OLE Controls are described in the table on the next page. In addition to the names (which are of course subject to localization) and dispids given, the parameters are also defined for these events.

STANDARD EVENTS (OLE CONTROLS SPECIFICATION)

Name	DispID	Description
Click	-600	This event typically is fired when a control is clicked on by the mouse. Some controls can be coded to fire it when their values change.
DblClick	-601	This event is fired when the user double-clicks the mouse on the control.
Error	-608	This event is fired by a control when the control wants to notify its container that an error has occurred. Normally, such notification would be synchronous in response to a property or method invocation. (This event allows the control to inform its container asynchronously, and it is discussed in greater detail in the next chapter.)
KeyDown	-602	This event is fired when a key is pressed while the control has focus.
KeyUp	-604	This event is fired when a key is released while the control has focus.
MouseDown	-605	This event is fired when the user clicks a mouse button over the control.
MouseMove	-606	This event is fired when the user moves the mouse over the control.
MouseUp	-607	This event is fired when the user releases a mouse button over the control.

Custom events (that is, ones that you write rather than those that are pre-defined) should use positive dispids so that they don't conflict with standard events, methods or properties.

Although the OLE Controls specification does not at this stage define any extended events, containers can choose to give a control extended events, just as they can provide extended properties and methods. Visual Basic version 4.0, for example, adds the following events to a control's standard list:

- DragDrop event

- DragOver event

- GotFocus event

- LostFocus event

As with other extended control attributes, these events are not implemented by the control.

EVENTS AND THE OLE CDK

The OLE Control Developer's Kit (OLE CDK) obviously supports the addition of events to OLE controls. As usual, the most apparent manifestation of this support is within ClassWizard. The OLE Events tab, which I deliberately didn't discuss in great detail in Chapter 5, is the key to all that support. After a class that includes an event map (analogous to a dispatch map, but for events) is selected, the OLE Events tab enables its Add Event button so that stock and custom events can be added. The OLE CDK implements the standard events listed in the table on page 224 as stock events; any other event is a custom event. A stock event is an OLE CDK implementation of the event as defined by the OLE Controls specification, so you can be sure that the implementation is correct. Figure 8-1 shows a stock event being added to a control project via the Add Event dialog box.

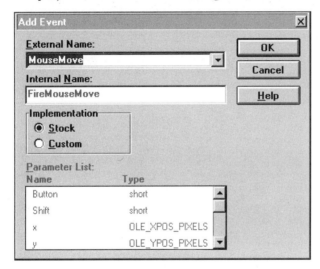

Figure 8-1. *The Add Event dialog box in Microsoft Visual C++ versions 2.0 and later can be used to add a stock event to a control project.*

Adding a Stock Event

When you add a stock event, such as Click, to a project, ClassWizard adds a macro invocation along the lines of

```
EVENT_STOCK_CLICK()
```

to the class's event map in the implementation file. (This macro is inserted when you add the standard Click event.) Now the function *FireClick* can be called anywhere within your code to fire the Click event up to the control's container. *FireClick* is a member function of the *COleControl* class and calls, via a helper function, the *Invoke* method of the *IDispatch* interface(s) attached to the control's events connection point. If nothing is connected to the connection point, no event gets fired.

Adding a Custom Event

When you add a custom event to a project through ClassWizard, it adds a *FireXxx* function to the class's event map in the header file, where *Xxx* represents the name of the event. (You actually have the option of customizing this function name, but why would you want to?) A typical entry would be

```
void FireInvalidSCode(long SCode)
    {FireEvent(eventidInvalidSCode,EVENT_PARAM(VTS_I4), SCode);}
```

for an event called InvalidSCode with one parameter, a long integer representing the SCODE. This entry basically defines a function, *FireInvalidSCode*, which takes one parameter and returns no result. No event invocations can return results. The *FireEvent* function is used by this and all other event invocations, including stock events, implemented by ClassWizard. It is a member function of *COleControl* and takes a variable number of parameters, as it is a generic function designed to handle all event invocations. All it does is call *FireEventV*, a further helper function which traverses the list of all connections to the control's events connection point and then uses *COleDispatchDriver*'s *InvokeHelperV* function to call *Invoke* on each one. *COleDispatchHelper* is a standard part of the MFC library, which is used to create and use the client side of OLE Automation objects in C++. That is, *COleDispatch-Driver* is used to invoke methods and properties on another object's *IDispatch* implementation. It's nice to see the MFC library using its own mechanisms to access an object's capabilities. The source for each of the *COleControl* event-handling functions can be found in CTLEVENT.CPP in the CDK sources.

Addition of custom events through ClassWizard also causes an entry to be added to the event map in the implementation file, along the lines of

```
EVENT_CUSTOM("InvalidSCode", FireInvalidSCode, VTS_I4)
```

which defines the event name, the function that fires it, and the parameter(s) it takes.

After an event firing function is defined in the event map, it can be called at any point within the control to cause the event to be fired up to its container. There is no guarantee, however, that a container is always ready to handle a control's events. For example, a container might have called *IOleControl::FreezeEvents* to tell the control that it should not fire events. In this case, the control's *OnFreezeEvents* function will have been called. *COleControl*'s implementation of this function does nothing, but you can choose to override this behavior so that you can store up all events that would be fired when the events are unfrozen, or so that you can set a flag to prevent you from firing events during the freeze. Another, more interesting case, is illustrated in the next section, when I add some custom events to the First control.

ADDING CUSTOM EVENTS TO THE "FIRST" CONTROL

Two failings of the current implementation of the First control developed over the past few chapters are as follows: it cannot create the index and message files if they don't already exist, and there is no way for it to notify you programmatically when an invalid SCODE has been used for the *SCode* property's value.

In the latter failing noted above, it is of course possible to set the property and then interrogate another to see whether it has a valid value, but this is counter-intuitive. You might agree that presents a classic case for an event, as it allows the control to notify its container that the last operation is erroneous. (As you'll see in the next chapter, there are actually better ways of doing this than the way I'm going to do it now, but that's not the point....)

To fix the two problems in First, then, I'm going to add two pieces of fairly basic functionality:

- Code to create the index and message files if they don't currently exist, and fire an event to the control's container when this has been done successfully.

- An event to let the container know when an invalid SCODE has been entered as the value of the *SCode* property. Its invalidity is determined by its absence from the current memory image of the index file.

At the same time, I can take the time to fix a bug in the current implementation of the First control, where it neglects to set the internal flag saying whether an SCODE is invalid during the *SetSCode* routine. To fix this, I add one line to *SetSCode* immediately after the two lines that empty the message and symbol strings:

```
m_bIsValid = FALSE;
```

This causes the SCODE to be treated as invalid until code later in the function determines that it is actually valid, when the flag is set to *TRUE*. (This line already exists!)

Following this, I add the two custom events: *InvalidSCode* and *FilesCreated*. The first takes one parameter, a long integer called *SCode*, while the second takes none. I add these events through ClassWizard, and verify that the event map in the header file looks like this:

```
// Event maps
    //{{AFX_EVENT(CFirstCtrl)
    void FireInvalidSCode(long SCode)
        {FireEvent(eventidInvalidSCode,EVENT_PARAM(VTS_I4),
        SCode);}
    void FireFilesCreated()
        {FireEvent(eventidFilesCreated,EVENT_PARAM(VTS_NONE));}
    //}}AFX_EVENT
    DECLARE_EVENT_MAP()
```

and that the event map in the implementation file looks like this:

```
BEGIN_EVENT_MAP(CFirstCtrl, COleControl)
    //{{AFX_EVENT_MAP(CFirstCtrl)
    EVENT_CUSTOM("InvalidSCode", FireInvalidSCode, VTS_I4)
    EVENT_CUSTOM("FilesCreated", FireFilesCreated, VTS_NONE)
    //}}AFX_EVENT_MAP
END_EVENT_MAP()
```

After these entries are complete, the event functions exist and can be called. If you look at the control's ODL file, you'll notice that the events interface description has been updated to include these two entries:

```
//  Event dispatch interface for CFirstCtrl

[ uuid(14BC5F82-DBD2-11CD-92B4-08002B291EED),
    helpstring("Event interface for First Control") ]
dispinterface _DFirstEvents
{
    properties:
        //  Event interface has no properties

    methods:
        // NOTE - ClassWizard will maintain event information
        //   here.
        //    Use extreme caution when editing this section.
        //{{AFX_ODL_EVENT(CFirstCtrl)
        [id(1)] void InvalidSCode(long SCode);
        [id(2)] void FilesCreated();
        //}}AFX_ODL_EVENT
};
```

This updating indicates that the control is going to be looking for an *IDispatch*-derived implementation called *_DFirstEvents*, which has two methods, the first with a dispid of 1 and the second with a dispid of 2, to be connected to its events connection point.

To fire an event when the *SCode* property is set to an illegal value, you need add only one line of code to *SetSCode*. This line calls the event firing function, *FireInvalidSCode*, and passes it the value of the illegal *SCode*, as follows:

```
FireInvalidSCode ( nNewValue );
```

This line should be inserted immediately after the

```
csLine.LoadString ( IDS_NOVALID_SCODE );
```

line in the *else* clause of the *if* statement in the function. Now, whenever the SCODE to which the *SCode* property is being set is not found in the index file (or if any other error occurs), the control will fire the *InvalidSCode* event up to its container. You might like to compile the new version of the control and try it out.

The second part, the creation of the index and message files, is of course a little more complex. There is only one logical place to create these files, which is when the first attempt to read them finds that they are not there. This actually happens very early on in the control's life, at the last statement in the *CFirstControl*'s constructor through the call to *ReadIndexFile*. Take a look at *ReadIndexFile*; its first operation of note is to attempt to open the index file for read access. Currently, this open attempt is embedded within an *if* statement, so if it fails you can take some action. The only action now taken is to output a string to the debug terminal and return, which isn't terribly useful. The function needs to be altered so that it can first check for the existence of these files (actually, it only checks for the index file) and then create them if they don't already exist.

The *CFile* class has a useful member function, *GetStatus*, for precisely this purpose. *GetStatus* has two flavors, one of which operates on an open *CFile* object and returns information about it. The other version is static and takes a filename; it then looks for a file of this name and returns information about it. It's the latter version I want to use, as I don't have an open *CFile* object at present. Because it's a static function, it does not need to act (actually, cannot act) on an instance of a *CFile*, so it can be called as if it were a standard global function — except that it needs to be qualified by the name of the class in which it is found. Consequently, the following lines check that the index file exists:

```
                // Does the index file exist?
        CFileStatus cfsDummy;
        if ( CFile::GetStatus ( csIndex, cfsDummy ) == 0 )
        {
                // No, so create it (and the message file).
```

```
        TRACE ( _T ( "Index file not found - being created\n" ) );
        if ( CreateFiles ( ) == FALSE )
        {
            return;
        }
    }
```

GetStatus returns *0* if it doesn't exist. If the index file does not exist, the lines call a new function, *CreateFiles*, which creates both the index file and message file. *GetStatus* takes a second parameter, a reference to a *CFileStatus* object, in which it places all the information it finds about the file. I'm only interested in the existence or nonexistence of the file, so I ignore the contents of this object. If *CreateFiles* fails, it returns *FALSE*. At this stage, there isn't a lot I can do about this, so I simply return. It's still possible for the open call to fail, but if it does it must be some error other than nonexistence of the file, so I've changed the trace message on the *else* clause to

```
TRACE ( _T ( "Cannot open the index file\n" ) );
```

CreateFiles itself looks like this:

```
BOOL CFirstCtrl::CreateFiles ( void )
{
    CFile cfFile;
    CString csFile;
    BOOL bRet = FALSE;

        // Index file first
    csFile.LoadString ( IDS_INDEXFILE );
    if ( cfFile.Open ( csFile, CFile::modeCreate |
        CFile::modeWrite | CFile::shareExclusive ) == 0 )
    {
        TRACE ( _T ( "Error creating index file\n" ) );
    }
    else
    {
        cfFile.Close ( );      // Instant close: we only
                               //   want creation.
    }

        // Then the message file
    csFile.LoadString ( IDS_MESSAGEFILE );
    if ( cfFile.Open ( csFile, CFile::modeCreate |
        CFile::modeWrite | CFile::shareExclusive ) == 0 )
    {
        TRACE ( _T ( "Error creating message file\n" ) );
    }
    else
```

```
      {
          cfFile.Close ( );
          bRet = TRUE;
          FireFilesCreated ( );
      }
      return bRet;
  }
```

This function is not rocket science. It uses *CFile*'s *modeCreate* flag to tell the *Open* member function to create the file, doing it first for the index file and then for the message file. In both cases, the file is closed immediately, as all I want to do at this stage is to create the file.

The act of creating a file and immediately closing it will obviously create zero-length files. This means that *ReadIndexFile* is now going to have to encounter empty index files from time to time. Looking back at the code, you'll see that it uses the file's length to determine how many entries are in the index file so that it can allocate memory for an array. Therein lies the problem: if the number of entries is zero, which it will be when the files are first created, this piece of code will attempt to allocate zero bytes. This is actually permissible with 32-bit Visual C++; it just writes a warning message to the debugger; however, 16-bit Visual C++ is far less friendly and fails an assertion, which stops the control from working at all (in debug build). This is unfortunate, because the C++ language certainly does not rule out *new* being called to allocate zero bytes. Changing the code to take account of this is trivial and also amounts to defensive programming — and therefore is generally a good thing.

The line that calculates the number of entries in the index file and assigns it to a member variable is the one to change. Whereas previously it said

```
m_lSCodes = cfIndex.GetLength ( ) / ENTRYSIZE;
```

it now says

```
if ( ( m_lSCodes = cfIndex.GetLength ( ) / ENTRYSIZE ) == 0 )
{
    TRACE ( _T ( "The index file is empty\n" ) );
    return;
}
```

which causes a message to be output to the debugger if the file is empty, but no further action is taken.

To try this out, build the control with these changes in and rename or remove the index and message files. Now start up Test Container and switch on the display of events by choosing Event Log from the View menu. Now insert an instance of the First control. Interestingly, nothing appears to happen, and the control displays its "invalid SCode" message. If you use File Manager or Windows

Explorer to check whether the index and message files were created, you'll find that they are indeed present. They are also empty (zero length), which is why the current *SCode* value is invalid and why, in fact, any SCODE you enter will be invalid. You can load the SCODE definitions into the control from WINERROR.H by choosing the Invoke Methods command on Test Container's Edit menu and choosing *BatchLoad*, and you'll need to reset the *SCode* property value to get it to rescan the file and display the correct message (a problem that is fixed at the end of the chapter). But why didn't the event fire?

This would in other circumstances be an ideal place at which to introduce control debugging techniques, but I want to focus specifically on events. (I'll cover debugging in Chapter 10.) What is happening here is that the control is effectively calling *FireFilesCreated* during the constructor of its *COleControl*-derived object, at which point very little interaction has occurred between the container and the control. In particular, the container has not yet connected to the control's events connection point, so there is no target at which to fire the event. So I had to invent a mechanism, described in the next paragraph, for causing the event to be sent as soon as possible.

Whenever something connects to a control's events connection point, it calls *IConnectionPoint::Advise*. This is sent on to the control's instance of the *COleControl* class by the OLE CDK to a member function called *OnEventAdvise*. This function will get called each time a connection is made. It also gets called each time a connection is broken, using a Boolean flag passed to it as a parameter to tell whether a connection is being made or broken. The base class function does nothing, but it is declared as virtual so that it can be overridden and implemented to perform whatever action is appropriate to the control.

Another *COleControl* virtual member function, *OnFreezeEvents*, is called whenever a control's *IOleControl::FreezeEvents* method is called. This function is also passed a Boolean parameter that tells it whether events are being frozen or released. In theory, the *FreezeEvents* method can get called a number of times, so the code behind it should treat calls to it with a *TRUE* value as incrementing a count and treat calls to it with a *FALSE* value as decrementing the count. By overriding the base class version of *OnFreezeEvents*, I can maintain a count that I can use to tell, at a glance, whether events are frozen.

The upshot of all this is that I can ensure that the *FilesCreated* event gets sent to all connections to the First control's events connection point by overriding both *OnFreezeEvents* and *OnEventAdvise*. So, on to the code.

First, some declarations in the *CFirstCtrl* class's header file: I add declarations for the two overridden virtual functions:

```
virtual void OnFreezeEvents ( BOOL bFreeze );
virtual void OnEventAdvise ( BOOL bAdvise );
```

Then I add these two member variable declarations:

```
BOOL m_bFilesCreated;
short m_nEventsFrozen;
```

The first will be used to indicate that the files have been created and therefore that the event should be fired; the second is the count of *IOleControl::FreezeEvents* calls with a *TRUE* parameter minus the number of calls to *IOleControl::FreezeEvents* with a *FALSE* parameter. (It's the outstanding frozen events calls; a value of zero indicates that events are not frozen.) I add code to *CFirstCtrl*'s constructor to set *m_bFilesCreated* to *FALSE* and *m_nEventsFrozen* to zero. Now I change the invocation of the event in *CreateFiles* to a setting of the flag:

```
m_bFilesCreated = TRUE;        // Cause the event to be fired later
```

Finally, I implement the two overridden virtual functions:

```
void CFirstCtrl::OnFreezeEvents ( BOOL bFreeze )
{
    m_nEventsFrozen += ( bFreeze ? 1 : -1 );
}


void CFirstCtrl::OnEventAdvise ( BOOL bAdvise )
{
    if ( bAdvise && m_bFilesCreated && ( m_nEventsFrozen == 0 ) )
    {
        FireFilesCreated ( );
    }
}
```

The implementation of *OnFreezeEvents* increments or decrements the class member variable, depending on the value of the Boolean parameter passed to it. You might want to alter it to ensure that it doesn't let the value go negative, which would happen if an erroneously written container were somehow to call it with a *FALSE* parameter before it called it with a *TRUE* parameter.

OnEventAdvise is similarly straightforward. If the parameter indicates that this invocation is due to an event connection (as opposed to a disconnection), and if the *FilesCreated* flag is set, and if events are currently not frozen, then the event is fired. This will cause all new connections to the control to receive the event and, because of the multi-casting nature of the events mechanism, it also means that all current connections to the control's events connection point will receive the event each time a new connection is made. This means that the "first" connection will receive the event as many times as there are connections to the control, while the "last" connection will receive it only once. I've put first and last in quotes because the implementation of the connection point will determine whether an iteration through the list of connections on a given point will return the list in the order in which the connections were made.

Having added this bit of finesse to the control, I felt the urge to alter the other event invocation so that it, too, respected the container's wish for events to be frozen. I did this by altering the one-line invocation of the event routine in *SetSCode* to this:

```
if ( m_nEventsFrozen == 0 )
{
    FireInvalidSCode ( nNewValue );
}
```

Now the invocation simply checks that events are not frozen before calling the *FireInvalidSCode* function.

This control still has a couple of problems. The first is that error-reporting remains atrocious, even though I've improved matters by making the control now fire an event if an attempt is made to set the *SCode* property to an illegal value. The second is that the *SCode*'s validity (and hence the values of its associated properties) is not revisited when the *Add* or *BatchLoad* method is called.

The first problem is the subject of the next chapter. The second I can fix now. Considering that both the *Add* and the *BatchLoad* methods could result in there being an entry in the index file for the current value of the *SCode* property where previously there wasn't, it makes sense to check. However, it only makes sense to check if the current *SCode* value is marked as invalid, and there's no point at all in refiring the *InvalidSCode* event if it remains invalid after one of these method calls.

I coded this by moving the generic code from *SetSCode* into a more reusable member function, called *CheckSCode*. This function returns *TRUE* if the *SCODE* is now valid and *FALSE* if not; it also sets the member variable *m_bIsValid* appropriately. In addition, it sets the related properties to the correct values, such as the symbol and message string. Here's the code:

```
BOOL CFirstCtrl::CheckSCode ( long nNewValue )
{
    CString csLine;
    BOOL bRet = FALSE;

    m_csMessage.Empty ( );
    m_csSymbol.Empty ( );

    unsigned long ulOffset;
    if ( FindEntry ( nNewValue, &ulOffset ) )
    {
        bRet = TRUE;
        GetInfo ( ulOffset );
        csLine = m_csSymbol + _T ( ": " ) + m_csMessage;
```

```
      }
      else
      {
          csLine.LoadString ( IDS_NOVALID_SCODE );
      }
      SetText ( csLine );
      return bRet;
  }
```

Don't forget to declare it in the header file! The only difference between the code taken from the old *SetSCode* function and the code in this one is that some trivial re-ordering has taken place. *SetSCode* itself changes to a rather simpler function:

```
void CFirstCtrl::SetSCode(long nNewValue)
{
    if ( CheckSCode ( nNewValue ) == FALSE )
    {
        if ( m_nEventsFrozen == 0 )
        {
            FireInvalidSCode ( nNewValue );
        }
    }
    m_SCode = nNewValue;
    SetModifiedFlag();
}
```

To get *Add* and *BatchLoad* to perform the check and update the control's caption if necessary, change them as follows; to *Add*, insert these lines:

```
if ( m_bIsValid == FALSE )
{
    CheckSCode ( m_SCode );
}
```

immediately before the

```
return TRUE;
```

statement at the end of the function. Add the same lines to *BatchLoad* inside the statements controlled by the

```
if ( lEntries )
```

statement immediately before the

```
return lEntries;
```

statement at the end of the function. Now, when you insert the control into Test Container and set the *SCode* property to an invalid value, you can add an entry using the *Add* method and see the control update itself, or you can batch load a whole set of values from a file and, again, if the file contains a value that matches the current *SCode* property value, the control will update itself to show the new text.

The version of the First control containing all the changes made in this chapter can be found on the companion CD-ROM under \OLECTRLS\CHAP08\FIRST.

Chapter 9

Errors and Exception-Handling

This chapter marks an important break from the earlier chapters of this book. Up to this point, I have been able to code sloppily and blame it on the fact that I hadn't yet talked about errors and exceptions. This chapter is all about errors and exceptions and how they affect OLE controls, so my excuse is no longer valid. As a consequence, programming becomes a little more difficult from now on, although the resulting code is easier to read and a lot more robust.

That's what good error-handling is all about — making a program more robust and better able to deal with situations it wouldn't normally expect to encounter. You might find it difficult to guarantee that your control is capable of dealing with everything that's thrown at it, but by using defensive programming techniques and taking advantage of the MFC library's exception-handling (or C++'s, depending on your compiler) as well as the reporting facilities offered to OLE Automation and OLE controls specifically by OLE, you'll be confident that most usual unusual situations, as it were, are covered!

First I'm going to talk about what exactly constitutes an exception. Then I'm going to look at how they might be caught in an OLE control and how they can be reported to the user in a meaningful way. Finally, I'm going to rewrite parts of the

"First" control, developed over the past few chapters, to enhance its robustness. A number of the techniques covered here will also apply to any kind of MFC-based application, and some pertain to standard OLE Automation servers as well as to controls.

WHAT IS AN EXCEPTION?

An "exception" as far as programs are concerned is best defined as an event whose occurrence is beyond your control — for example, a network connection going away or a file on a disk getting corrupted. (When a user enters bad information, such as a number that's out of range, this is not usually an exception. It's beyond your control, but you can take action to ensure that your program reacts appropriately.) Examples of the First control's exceptions might be lack of memory, problems with disk files, and invalid parameters. I'm going to change the First control so that it takes proper advantage of the MFC library and C++ exception-handling and it reports problems to the container application in as friendly a way as possible.

If the world were all 32-bit, I could use the proper C++ exception-handling constructs, *try* and *catch*. However, because every OLE control in this book needs to be usable in 16-bit Windows as well, I use the the MFC library's *TRY* and *CATCH* macros. When used with a 32-bit compiler with C++ exception-handling enabled (such as Microsoft Visual C++ version 2.x), the macros are pretty much the same as the C++ keywords, the only difference being that with the macros you don't need to delete the exception objects. Without compiler support, the macros make their best possible effort to simulate a C++ exception.

Exception-Handling in the MFC Library and in C++

Numerous MFC functions and class members are defined as being capable of throwing exceptions. A good example is the operator *new*, which, if you look it up in Books Online, tells you that it can throw a *CMemoryException*. This means that if an allocation fails, rather than returning zero to the caller, the *new* operator will create a *CMemoryException* object, initialize it to signify the nature of the problem, break the path of execution, and jump to the nearest *CATCH* block that traps either *CMemoryException* or its base class, *CException*. If C++ exception-handling is enabled, this jump will typically involve the proper destruction of any objects created between the point at which the exception is thrown and the point at which it is caught. I say "typically" because most C++ compilers allow you to switch exception-handling off on a function-by-function basis, which is fine unless one of those functions allocates objects. Even if the function doesn't throw exceptions or catch them itself, it will need proper "stack unwinding" (and therefore have exception-handling enabled) if a function it calls throws an exception that is not caught before it unwinds past the calling function. If you're using a compiler without C++ exception-handling capabilities (such as 16-bit Visual C++ version 1.5x), the macros do their best to clean up dynamically created objects, but they can't deal with all situations.

How do you catch exceptions? Let's suppose that your program allocates memory for an object using *new* and that you want to be able to deal with *new* failures. Then you might code something like:

```
TRY
{
    CMyObject *x = new CMyObject;
}
CATCH ( CException, e )
{
  AfxMessageBox ( "Help!" );
  return;
}
END_CATCH
```

This basically tells the compiler that any exceptions of type *CException* (or classes derived therefrom) thrown by the statements within the *TRY* block should be handled by the statements within the *CATCH* block. So, in this example, if the *new* operator fails, it will throw a *CMemoryException*. This is derived from *CException*, so it is caught by the *CATCH* block, which in this instance displays a message box.

If an exception is thrown that isn't caught by the nearest *CATCH*, it will move up the call chain until it is caught. If there are absolutely no handlers for the exception in the program, the MFC framework gets it and aborts the program. This means that exceptions can throw the path of execution back up a few functions in the call stack or even to the outermost function of the program.

Because *CATCH* blocks are sensitive to the kind of exceptions they catch, you can also decide to handle different types of exceptions differently. For example, a function that allocates memory, opens a file, and then reads from the file might choose to close the file if a file exception is thrown but not do so if a memory exception is thrown. You can even decide to handle some exceptions in the function in which they occur and handle others in higher-up functions. You can really get sophisticated (if you want to) by catching an exception locally, doing some local clean-up, and then rethrowing it using the *THROW* macro so that higher-up functions can see it or even by throwing a different exception in its place.

C++ exception-handling can throw and catch any type of object. The MFC library's exception-handling can deal only with *CException* objects and their derivatives. The MFC library defines a number of exception classes, including ones for memory, file-handling, database operations, OLE operations, OLE Automation operations, and Windows resource operations. Each of these classes is derived from *CException* and so can be caught by *CATCH* macros with specific exceptions or by a *CATCH* macro with a generic *CException* like the one above.

Because a given function might throw exceptions of different types, catch statements (MFC *CATCH* macros) can be chained together. So, if a function *MyFunc* could throw *CMemoryException*, *CFileException*, and *COleException* exception objects, they could be handled generically by a *CException CATCH* statement or given individual treatment as shown here:

```
TRY
{
   MyFunc();
}
CATCH ( CMemoryException, e )
{
   // Statements to handle memory exceptions
}
AND_CATCH ( CFileException, e )
{
   // Statements to handle file exceptions
}
AND_CATCH ( COleException, e )
{
   // Statements to handle OLE exceptions
}
END_CATCH
```

By the way, the second parameter to the *CATCH* and *AND_CATCH* macros is the name of the object as it will be referenced by the code within the block. This is always actually a pointer to the object, and its name is wholly arbitrary. I always use *e* because it's short. In C++ exception-handling, the syntax of the *catch* statement is slightly different from the syntax of the *CATCH* macro because it takes only one parameter, which is a pointer to the exception object.

It's also possible to derive your own exception objects from *CException*, which is useful if a class of exception is specific to your application or if you want to translate other exception types into another type so that you can handle disparate exception types as one type. I use derived exception objects in the version of the First control that appears in this chapter.

One last point: use of exception-handling means that you have to write code to deal with exceptions, logically enough, and this means that you'll be writing more code; also, more code is inserted by the compiler, so your programs will get bigger. The advantage is that the code is typically a great deal more robust and able to take what's thrown at it than is code that has been written without exception-handling. There is a speed penalty, too, because much of the compiler's extra code insertions are executed even when no exceptions are thrown. This is unavoidable, and that's why every major compiler vendor that supports exception-handling also allows you to turn it off!

Exception-Handling in OLE Controls

Ha! I bet you thought I'd forgotten I was writing a book about OLE controls. Well, all the stuff I just talked about is very useful for development of OLE controls. Combine it with the things I'm going to talk about now, and you get a very powerful model of robustness for both the developer and the user of OLE controls.

If you read Chapters 2 and 3, you might recall that OLE Automation servers can pass "exceptions" up to their controllers, including information such as the error code, the help file to go to for more information, and the error text. OLE controls of course rely on OLE Automation for much of their functionality, so it's no surprise that they also allow OLE Automation exceptions to be thrown to their containers. There is, however, an important difference between a conventional OLE Automation server and an OLE control. An automation server communicates with its controller only during a method call or property access — that is, at the behest of the controller; an OLE control, on the other hand, can also communicate with its container whenever it chooses to do so by firing an event. Because an event is not in response to a call from the container, different rules apply for exception-throwing. Basically, the following are true:

- If an exception needs to be thrown during a method invocation or property access, throw an exception using *ThrowError*.

- If an exception occurs at any other time, throw an exception using *FireError*.

ThrowError and *FireError* are member functions of the *COleControl* class and both take the same set of parameters: the SCODE relating to the exception, a string (or resource string ID), and a help context ID.

ThrowError translates to a variant of the standard MFC OLE Automation exception object, *COleDispatchException*. This variant, *COleDispatchExceptionEx*, ultimately causes the *IDispatch::Invoke* call that called this code to be notified of the exceptional condition so that it can pass the message onto user code or deal with it itself. The version of Test Container shipped with Microsoft Visual C++ 1.5x, for example, just beeps when it receives an exception from a control embedded within it. Most containers will adopt slightly more friendly methods of reporting problems than this!

FireError is more interesting. It causes the standard Error event to be fired. The Error event has a defined dispid, -608 (*DISPID_ERROREVENT*, defined in OLECTL.H) and a number of parameters:

- The error number, a short integer

- The error description, a pointer to a *BSTR*

- The error's SCODE

- The source, as a *BSTR*

- The help file, as a *BSTR*

- The help context ID, as a long integer

- A pointer to a Boolean variable, which if set to *TRUE* by the receiver of the event, causes the control <u>not</u> to display the error itself

The last parameter is a way to allow the control to display the error to the user if the container decides not to display it. I would imagine that most containers would prefer to display and/or deal with the error themselves; however, there might be situations or containers that want to delegate this task back to the control. By leaving the last parameter to the event as *FALSE*, a container can signal to the control that it should display the error. In controls developed with the OLE Control Developer's Kit (OLE CDK), this results in the *DisplayError* member function getting called, which by default displays a message box. This function is virtual, so its behavior can be overridden by the specific OLE control class.

The OLE CDK documentation warns against wanton use of the *FireError* method, recommending instead that a control should use other means (such as *HRESULTS*) to report errors to the container. Because this can't be done asynchronously (that is, without the container having first called the control), inevitably situations will arise in which the error event is the only means by which a control can communicate its predicament to its container. *FireError* is then the way in which this should be done.

The First control has few situations in which an error event must be fired, but it can happen. Most of the exceptions caught by First are in response to method calls or property access, so it can call *ThrowError* in these circumstances.

HANDLING EXCEPTIONS IN THE "FIRST" CONTROL

Right now, the First control is basically functional, but it has a number of stability and robustness problems. Further, most errors and exceptions are reported to the container in a manner that actually provides very little information about what went wrong. The version of First in this chapter changes that by adding extensive exception-handling support, both from the throwing exceptions point of view and from the catching and reporting them point of view. (There might be more that can be done to it even after these changes, but they're not obvious to me.) The source code of this version is on the companion CD-ROM in the \OLECTRLS\CHAP09\FIRST directory. Listings 9-1 through 9-4 contain the code changes (FIRSTCTRL.H and FIRSTCTRL.CPP are changed, FIRSTEX.H and FIRSTEX.CPP are a new file pair). There are also some additions to the resource string table that are not included in the text but that can be found in the version on the companion CD-ROM.

FIRSTCTL.H

```
// firstctl.h : Declaration of the CFirstCtrl OLE control class.

struct CSCodeEntry
{
    long lSCode;
    unsigned long ulOffset;
};

class CSCodeEntryList
{
public:
    void SetNext ( CSCodeEntryList *selNew ) { m_pNext = selNew; }
    CSCodeEntryList *GetNext ( void ) const { return m_pNext; }
    CSCodeEntry *GetEntry ( void ) { return &m_seThis; }
private:
    CSCodeEntryList *m_pNext;
    CSCodeEntry m_seThis;
};


/////////////////////////////////////////////////////////////////////
// CFirstCtrl : See firstctl.cpp for implementation.

class CFirstCtrl : public COleControl
{
    DECLARE_DYNCREATE(CFirstCtrl)

// Constructor
public:
    CFirstCtrl();

// Overrides
```

Listing 9-1. *FIRSTCTL.H with exception-handling support.* *(continued)*

(continued)

```cpp
    // Drawing function
    virtual void OnDraw(CDC* pdc,
        const CRect& rcBounds, const CRect& rcInvalid);

    // Persistence
    virtual void DoPropExchange(CPropExchange* pPX);

    // Reset control state
    virtual void OnResetState();

// Implementation
    virtual void OnFreezeEvents(BOOL bFreeze);
    virtual void OnEventAdvise(BOOL bAdvise);

protected:
    ~CFirstCtrl();

    DECLARE_OLECREATE_EX(CFirstCtrl)    // Class factory and guid
    DECLARE_OLETYPELIB(CFirstCtrl)      // GetTypeInfo
    DECLARE_PROPPAGEIDS(CFirstCtrl)     // Property page IDs
    DECLARE_OLECTLTYPE(CFirstCtrl)      // Type name and misc status

// Message maps
    //{{AFX_MSG(CFirstCtrl)
        // NOTE - ClassWizard will add and remove member functions
        //    here.
        //    DO NOT EDIT what you see in these blocks of generated
        //       code !
    //}}AFX_MSG
    DECLARE_MESSAGE_MAP()

// Dispatch maps
    //{{AFX_DISPATCH(CFirstCtrl)
    afx_msg long GetSCode();
    afx_msg void SetSCode(long nNewValue);
    afx_msg short GetCode();
    afx_msg BSTR GetFacility();
    afx_msg BSTR GetSeverity();
    afx_msg BSTR GetMessage();
    afx_msg BSTR GetErrorName();
    afx_msg BOOL Add(long SCode, LPCTSTR Symbol, LPCTSTR Message);
    afx_msg long BatchLoad(LPCTSTR FileName);
    //}}AFX_DISPATCH
    DECLARE_DISPATCH_MAP()
```

(continued)

```
    afx_msg void AboutBox();

// Event maps
    //{{AFX_EVENT(CFirstCtrl)
    void FireInvalidSCode(long SCode)
        {FireEvent(eventidInvalidSCode,EVENT_PARAM(VTS_I4), SCode);}
    void FireFilesCreated()
        {FireEvent(eventidFilesCreated,EVENT_PARAM(VTS_NONE));}
    //}}AFX_EVENT
    DECLARE_EVENT_MAP()

// Dispatch and event IDs
public:
    enum {
    //{{AFX_DISP_ID(CFirstCtrl)
    dispidSCode = 1L,
    dispidCode = 2L,
    dispidFacility = 3L,
    dispidSeverity = 4L,
    dispidMessage = 5L,
    dispidErrorName = 6L,
    dispidAdd = 7L,
    dispidBatchLoad = 8L,
    eventidInvalidSCode = 1L,
    eventidFilesCreated = 2L,
    //}}AFX_DISP_ID
    };

private:
    long m_SCode;
    BOOL m_bIsValid;
    CString m_csSymbol;
    CString m_csMessage;
    CSCodeEntry *m_lpseCodes;
    CSCodeEntryList *m_lpseNewCodes;
    CSCodeEntryList *m_lpseListEnd;
    long m_lSCodes;
    BOOL m_bFilesCreated;
    short m_nEventsFrozen;
    BOOL m_bInDispatch;
    CString m_csBadMessage;
    void ReadIndexFile ( void );
    BOOL FindEntry ( long lCode, unsigned long *pulOffset );
```

(continued)

Part II The Basics of OLE Controls

(continued)

```
        void GetInfo ( unsigned long ulOffset );
        unsigned long AddMessage ( LPCTSTR lpszSymbol, LPCTSTR
            lpszMessage );
        void WriteEntry ( CSCodeEntry *pNew );
        long DoBatchLoad ( CStdioFile *cfIn, CFile *cfIndex, CFile
            *cfMsg );
        BOOL GetNextDefineLine ( CStdioFile *cfFile, CString *csLine,
            CString *csMessage );
        long GetTheCode ( CString *csLine, CString *csSymbol );
        void ClearList ( void );
        BOOL CreateFiles ( void );
        BOOL CheckSCode ( long nNewValue );
        void DoError ( SCODE scode, UINT uDescription, UINT helpid );
        void ReallySetSCode (long nNewValue);
        SCODE GetFileExceptionString ( CFileException *cfEx, UINT& uStr
    ) const;

};
```

FIRSTCTL.CPP

```
// firstctl.cpp : Implementation of the CFirstCtrl OLE control class.

#include "stdafx.h"
#include "first.h"
#include "firstctl.h"
#include "firstppg.h"
#include "firstex.h"

#ifdef _DEBUG
#undef THIS_FILE
static char BASED_CODE THIS_FILE[] = __FILE__;
#endif


IMPLEMENT_DYNCREATE(CFirstCtrl, COleControl)


//////////////////////////////////////////////////////////////////////
// Message map
```

Listing 9-2. *FIRSTCTRL.CPP with exception-handling support.*   *(continued)*

```
BEGIN_MESSAGE_MAP(CFirstCtrl, COleControl)
    //{{AFX_MSG_MAP(CFirstCtrl)
    // NOTE - ClassWizard will add and remove message map entries.
    //    DO NOT EDIT what you see in these blocks of generated
    //       code !
    //}}AFX_MSG_MAP
    ON_OLEVERB(AFX_IDS_VERB_PROPERTIES, OnProperties)
END_MESSAGE_MAP()


/////////////////////////////////////////////////////////////////
// Dispatch map

BEGIN_DISPATCH_MAP(CFirstCtrl, COleControl)
    //{{AFX_DISPATCH_MAP(CFirstCtrl)
    DISP_PROPERTY_EX(CFirstCtrl, "SCode", GetSCode, SetSCode, VT_I4)
    DISP_PROPERTY_EX(CFirstCtrl, "Code", GetCode, SetNotSupported, VT_I2)
    DISP_PROPERTY_EX(CFirstCtrl, "Facility", GetFacility,
        SetNotSupported, VT_BSTR)
    DISP_PROPERTY_EX(CFirstCtrl, "Severity", GetSeverity,
        SetNotSupported, VT_BSTR)
    DISP_PROPERTY_EX(CFirstCtrl, "Message", GetMessage,
        SetNotSupported, VT_BSTR)
    DISP_PROPERTY_EX(CFirstCtrl, "ErrorName", GetErrorName,
        SetNotSupported, VT_BSTR)
    DISP_FUNCTION(CFirstCtrl, "Add", Add, VT_BOOL,
        VTS_I4 VTS_BSTR VTS_BSTR)
    DISP_FUNCTION(CFirstCtrl, "BatchLoad", BatchLoad, VT_I4, VTS_BSTR)
    DISP_STOCKFUNC_REFRESH()
    DISP_STOCKPROP_BACKCOLOR()
    DISP_STOCKPROP_CAPTION()
    DISP_STOCKPROP_ENABLED()
    DISP_STOCKPROP_FONT()
    DISP_STOCKPROP_FORECOLOR()
    DISP_STOCKPROP_HWND()
    //}}AFX_DISPATCH_MAP
    DISP_FUNCTION_ID(CFirstCtrl, "AboutBox", DISPID_ABOUTBOX,
        AboutBox, VT_EMPTY, VTS_NONE)
END_DISPATCH_MAP()


/////////////////////////////////////////////////////////////////
// Event map

BEGIN_EVENT_MAP(CFirstCtrl, COleControl)
```

(continued)

(continued)

```
    //{{AFX_EVENT_MAP(CFirstCtrl)
    EVENT_CUSTOM("InvalidSCode", FireInvalidSCode, VTS_I4)
    EVENT_CUSTOM("FilesCreated", FireFilesCreated, VTS_NONE)
    //}}AFX_EVENT_MAP
END_EVENT_MAP()


/////////////////////////////////////////////////////////////////
// Property pages

// TODO: Add more property pages as needed.  Remember to increase
//      the count!
BEGIN_PROPPAGEIDS(CFirstCtrl, 1)
    PROPPAGEID(CFirstPropPage::guid)
END_PROPPAGEIDS(CFirstCtrl)


/////////////////////////////////////////////////////////////////
// Initialize class factory and guid

IMPLEMENT_OLECREATE_EX(CFirstCtrl, "FIRST.FirstCtrl.1",
    0x14bc5f80, 0xdbd2, 0x11cd, 0x92, 0xb4, 0x8, 0x0, 0x2b, 0x29,
    0x1e, 0xed)


/////////////////////////////////////////////////////////////////
// Type library ID and version

IMPLEMENT_OLETYPELIB(CFirstCtrl, _tlid, _wVerMajor, _wVerMinor)


/////////////////////////////////////////////////////////////////
// Interface IDs

const IID BASED_CODE IID_DFirst =
    { 0x14bc5f81, 0xdbd2, 0x11cd, { 0x92, 0xb4, 0x8, 0x0, 0x2b,
    0x29, 0x1e, 0xed } };
const IID BASED_CODE IID_DFirstEvents =
    { 0x14bc5f82, 0xdbd2, 0x11cd, { 0x92, 0xb4, 0x8, 0x0, 0x2b,
    0x29, 0x1e, 0xed } };


/////////////////////////////////////////////////////////////////
// Control type information
```

(continued)

```
static const DWORD BASED_CODE _dwFirstOleMisc =
    OLEMISC_ACTIVATEWHENVISIBLE |
    OLEMISC_SETCLIENTSITEFIRST |
    OLEMISC_INSIDEOUT |
    OLEMISC_CANTLINKINSIDE |
    OLEMISC_RECOMPOSEONRESIZE;

IMPLEMENT_OLECTLTYPE(CFirstCtrl, IDS_FIRST, _dwFirstOleMisc)


/////////////////////////////////////////////////////////////////
// CFirstCtrl::CFirstCtrlFactory::UpdateRegistry -
// Adds or removes system registry entries for CFirstCtrl

BOOL CFirstCtrl::CFirstCtrlFactory::UpdateRegistry(BOOL bRegister)
{
    if (bRegister)
        return AfxOleRegisterControlClass(
            AfxGetInstanceHandle(),
            m_clsid,
            m_lpszProgID,
            IDS_FIRST,
            IDB_FIRST,
            FALSE,                          // Not insertable
            _dwFirstOleMisc,
            _tlid,
            _wVerMajor,
            _wVerMinor);
    else
        return AfxOleUnregisterClass(m_clsid, m_lpszProgID);
}


/////////////////////////////////////////////////////////////////
// CFirstCtrl::CFirstCtrl - Constructor

CFirstCtrl::CFirstCtrl()
{
    InitializeIIDs(&IID_DFirst, &IID_DFirstEvents);
    m_SCode = 0L;
    m_bIsValid = FALSE;
    m_lpseCodes = 0;
    m_lpseNewCodes = 0;
    m_lpseListEnd = 0;
    m_lSCodes = 0;
```

(continued)

249

(continued)

```
    m_bFilesCreated = FALSE;
    m_nEventsFrozen = 0;
    m_bInDispatch = FALSE;
    m_csBadMessage.LoadString(IDS_BADMESSAGE);

        // If reading the index file creates an exception,
        //   we're in big trouble.
        // Warn the user that the control is severely handicapped
        //   and continue.
    TRY
    {
        ReadIndexFile ( );
    }
    CATCH ( CException, e )
    {
        CString csExtra;
        UINT uStr = 0;
        if ( e -> IsKindOf(RUNTIME_CLASS(CFirstException)) )
        {
            ((CFirstException*)e) -> GetErrorString ( uStr );
        }
        else if ( e -> IsKindOf(RUNTIME_CLASS(CFileException)) )
        {
            GetFileExceptionString ( (CFileException*)e, uStr );
        }
        if ( uStr )
        {
            csExtra.LoadString ( uStr );
            m_csBadMessage += _T ( "\n\nActual error message:\n\n" );
            m_csBadMessage += csExtra;
        }
        AfxMessageBox ( m_csBadMessage, MB_OK );
        if ( uStr )
        {
            m_csBadMessage.Empty ( );
            m_csBadMessage.LoadString ( IDS_BADMESSAGE );
        }
    }
    END_CATCH
}


/////////////////////////////////////////////////////////////////////////
// CFirstCtrl::~CFirstCtrl - Destructor
```

(continued)

```
CFirstCtrl::~CFirstCtrl()
{
    ClearList ( );
}


/////////////////////////////////////////////////////////////////////
// CFirstCtrl::OnDraw - Drawing function

void CFirstCtrl::OnDraw(
            CDC* pdc, const CRect& rcBounds, const CRect& rcInvalid)
{
    CFont *hfOld = SelectStockFont ( pdc );
    CBrush cbBack ( TranslateColor ( GetBackColor ( ) ) );

    pdc -> FillRect ( rcBounds, &cbBack );
    pdc -> SetTextColor ( TranslateColor ( GetForeColor ( ) ) );
    pdc -> SetBkMode ( TRANSPARENT );
    pdc -> DrawText ( InternalGetText ( ), -1, rcBounds,
        DT_CENTER | DT_VCENTER | DT_SINGLELINE );
    pdc -> SelectObject ( hfOld );
}


/////////////////////////////////////////////////////////////////////
// CFirstCtrl::DoPropExchange - Persistence support

void CFirstCtrl::DoPropExchange(CPropExchange* pPX)
{
    ExchangeVersion(pPX, MAKELONG(_wVerMinor, _wVerMajor));
    COleControl::DoPropExchange(pPX);

    PX_Long ( pPX, _T ( "SCode" ), m_SCode, OL );
    if ( pPX -> IsLoading ( ) )
    {
        m_bInDispatch = FALSE;
        ReallySetSCode ( m_SCode );
    }
}


/////////////////////////////////////////////////////////////////////
// CFirstCtrl::OnResetState - Reset control to default state

void CFirstCtrl::OnResetState()
{
```

(continued)

(continued)

```
        COleControl::OnResetState();  // Resets defaults found in
                                      //    DoPropExchange

        // TODO: Reset any other control state here.
}


//////////////////////////////////////////////////////////////////////
// CFirstCtrl::AboutBox - Display an "About" box to the user

void CFirstCtrl::AboutBox()
{
        CDialog dlgAbout(IDD_ABOUTBOX_FIRST);
        dlgAbout.DoModal();
}


//////////////////////////////////////////////////////////////////////
// CFirstCtrl message handlers

long CFirstCtrl::GetSCode()
{
        return m_SCode;
}

void CFirstCtrl::SetSCode( long nNewValue )
{
        m_bInDispatch = TRUE;
        ReallySetSCode ( nNewValue );
        m_bInDispatch = FALSE;
}

void CFirstCtrl::ReallySetSCode (long nNewValue)
{
        if ( CheckSCode ( nNewValue ) == FALSE )
        {
            if ( m_nEventsFrozen == 0 )
            {
                FireInvalidSCode ( nNewValue );
            }
        }
        m_SCode = nNewValue;
        SetModifiedFlag();
```

(continued)

```
}

short CFirstCtrl::GetCode()
{
    if ( m_bIsValid )
    {
        return short ( m_SCode & 0xFFFFL );
    }
    else
    {
        return -1;
    }
}

BSTR CFirstCtrl::GetFacility()
{
    CString s;
    short nFacility = IDS_NOVALID_SCODE;
    if ( m_bIsValid )
    {
        nFacility = short ( ( m_SCode & 0x0FFF0000L ) >> 16L );
        switch ( nFacility )
        {
            case 0: case 1: case 2: case 3:
            case 4: case 7: case 8: case 10:
                break;
            default:
                nFacility = -1;
        }
        nFacility += IDS_FACILITY_NULL;
    }
    s.LoadString ( nFacility );
    return s.AllocSysString();
}

BSTR CFirstCtrl::GetSeverity()
{
    CString s;
    short nSeverity = IDS_NOVALID_SCODE;

    if ( m_bIsValid )
    {
        nSeverity = short ( ( m_SCode & 0xC0000000L ) >> 30L ) +
            IDS_SEVERITY_SUCCESS;
    }
```

(continued)

253

(continued)

```
        s.LoadString ( nSeverity );
        return s.AllocSysString();
    }


    BSTR CFirstCtrl::GetMessage()
    {
        return m_csMessage.AllocSysString();
    }


    BSTR CFirstCtrl::GetErrorName()
    {
        return m_csSymbol.AllocSysString();
    }


    // Handles exceptions now
    BOOL CFirstCtrl::Add ( long SCode, LPCTSTR Symbol, LPCTSTR Message )
    {
        unsigned long ulOffset;
        if ( FindEntry ( SCode, &ulOffset ) )
        {
            TRACE ( _T ( "Add: SCODE %ln already in database\n" ),
                SCode );
            return TRUE;
        }

        CSCodeEntryList *pNew = 0;
        m_bInDispatch = TRUE;
        TRY
        {
            // Can't cope with NULL or empty strings.
            if ( Symbol == 0 || Message == 0 || *Symbol == 0 ||
                *Message == 0 )
            {
                THROW ( new CFirstException ( CFirstException::bad
                    Parameters ) );
            }

            pNew = new CSCodeEntryList;
            pNew -> GetEntry ( ) -> lSCode = SCode;
            pNew -> GetEntry ( ) -> ulOffset =
                AddMessage ( Symbol, Message );
            WriteEntry ( pNew -> GetEntry ( ) );
            pNew -> SetNext ( 0L );
            if ( m_lpseNewCodes )
```

(continued)

```
            {
                m_lpseListEnd -> SetNext ( pNew );
                m_lpseListEnd = pNew;
            }
            else
            {
                m_lpseNewCodes = m_lpseListEnd = pNew;
            }
    }
    CATCH ( CException, e )     // Generic catch
    {
        delete pNew;
        SCODE sc;
        UINT uStr;
        if ( e -> IsKindOf(RUNTIME_CLASS(CFirstException)) )
        {
            sc = ((CFirstException*)e) -> GetErrorString ( uStr );
        }
        else if ( e -> IsKindOf(RUNTIME_CLASS(CFileException)) )
        {
            sc = GetFileExceptionString ( (CFileException*)e, uStr );
        }
        else if ( e -> IsKindOf(RUNTIME_CLASS(CMemoryException)) )
        {
            sc = CTL_E_OUTOFMEMORY;
            uStr = IDS_MEMORYERROR;
        }
        else
        {
            sc = CTL_E_ILLEGALFUNCTIONCALL;
            uStr = IDS_UNEXPECTEDEXCEPTION;
        }
        DoError ( sc, uStr, 0 );
        m_bInDispatch = FALSE;
        return FALSE;
    }
    END_CATCH

    if ( m_bIsValid == FALSE )
    {
        CheckSCode ( m_SCode );
    }
    m_bInDispatch = FALSE;
    return TRUE;
}
```

(continued)

(continued)

```
long CFirstCtrl::BatchLoad ( LPCTSTR FileName )
{
    CFile cfIndex, cfMsg;
    CStdioFile cfInput;
    long lEntries = 0L;

    m_bInDispatch = TRUE;

    TRY
    {
        // Don't allow filename to be NULL or empty.
        if ( FileName == 0 )
        {
            THROW ( new CFirstException
                ( CFirstException::badParameters ) );
        }

        if ( cfInput.Open ( FileName, CFile::typeText |
            CFile::modeRead ) == TRUE )
        {
            CString csIndex;

            csIndex.LoadString ( IDS_INDEXFILE );
            if ( cfIndex.Open ( csIndex, CFile::modeWrite |
                CFile::shareExclusive ) == TRUE )
            {
                CString csMsg;

                csMsg.LoadString ( IDS_MESSAGEFILE );
                if ( cfMsg.Open ( csMsg, CFile::modeWrite |
                    CFile::shareExclusive ) == TRUE )
                {
                    lEntries = DoBatchLoad ( &cfInput,
                        &cfIndex, &cfMsg );
                    cfMsg.Close ( );
                }
                else
                {
                    TRACE ( _T (
                        "Failed to open message file for writing \n"
                            ) );
                    cfIndex.Close ( );
                    cfInput.Close ( );
                    THROW ( new CFirstException
```

(continued)

```
                        ( CFirstException::noWriteMsg ) );

            }
            cfIndex.Close ( );
        }
        else
        {
            TRACE ( _T (
                "Failed to open index file for writing \n" ) );
            cfInput.Close ( );
            THROW ( new CFirstException
                ( CFirstException::noWriteIdx ) );
        }
        cfInput.Close ( );
    }
    else
    {
        TRACE ( _T ( "Failed to open input file %s \n" ),
            FileName );
        THROW ( new CFirstException
            ( CFirstException::noInputFile ) );
    }

    if ( lEntries )
    {
        ClearList ( );
        m_lpseListEnd = 0;

        ReadIndexFile ( );
        if ( m_bIsValid == FALSE )
        {
            CheckSCode ( m_SCode );
        }
    }
}
CATCH ( CFirstException, e )
{
    UINT uStr;
    SCODE sc = e -> GetErrorString ( uStr );
    DoError ( sc, uStr, 0 );
}
AND_CATCH ( CFileException, e )
{
    UINT uStr;
    SCODE sc = GetFileExceptionString ( e, uStr );
    DoError ( sc, uStr, 0 );
```

(continued)

(continued)

```
    }
    AND_CATCH ( CMemoryException, e )
    {
        DoError ( CTL_E_OUTOFMEMORY, IDS_MEMORYERROR, 0 );
    }
    END_CATCH

    m_bInDispatch = FALSE;
    return lEntries;
}

#define ENTRYSIZE ( sizeof ( long ) + sizeof ( unsigned long ) )
// Can throw CFirstException, CFileException, and CMemoryException.
void CFirstCtrl::ReadIndexFile ( void )
{
    CFile cfIndex;
    CString csIndex;

    csIndex.LoadString ( IDS_INDEXFILE );

        // Does the index file exist?
    CFileStatus cfsDummy;
    if ( CFile::GetStatus ( csIndex, cfsDummy ) == 0 )
    {
            // No, so create it (and the message file)...
        TRACE ( _T ( "Index file not found - being created\n" ) );
        if ( CreateFiles ( ) == FALSE )
        {
                // ...and throw an exception if that failed.
            THROW ( new CFirstException
                ( CFirstException::noCreateFile ) );
        }
    }

        // Open the index file for read.
    if ( cfIndex.Open ( csIndex, CFile::modeRead |
        CFile::shareDenyNone ) == TRUE )
    {
        TRY
        {
            long lCode;
            unsigned long ulOffset;
            if ( ( m_lSCodes = cfIndex.GetLength ( ) / ENTRYSIZE )
                == 0 )
```

(continued)

```
        {
            TRACE ( _T ( "The index file is empty\n" ) );
            cfIndex.Close ( );
            return;
        }
        m_lpseCodes = new CSCodeEntry [ m_lSCodes ];
        long lCurrent = 0L;
        UINT uRead1, uRead2;
        do
        {
            uRead1 = cfIndex.Read ( &lCode, sizeof ( lCode ) );
            uRead2 = cfIndex.Read ( &ulOffset,
            sizeof ( ulOffset ) );
            if ( uRead1 == 0 &&
                 uRead2 == 0 )
            {
                break;
            }
            if ( ( uRead1 == sizeof ( lCode ) ) &&
               ( uRead2 == sizeof ( ulOffset ) ) )
            {
                m_lpseCodes [ lCurrent ].lSCode = lCode;
                m_lpseCodes [ lCurrent ].ulOffset = ulOffset;
                ++lCurrent;
            }
            else
            {
                AfxThrowFileException
                ( CFileException::endOfFile );
            }
        }
        while ( uRead1 );
        cfIndex.Close ( );
    }
    CATCH ( CException, e )
    {
        // Do local clear-up and then re-throw.
        delete [] m_lpseCodes;
        m_lpseCodes = 0;
        m_lSCodes = 0;          // Remember to do this!
                                //   Otherwise, leads to an access
                                //      violation.
        cfIndex.Close ( );
        THROW_LAST();
    }
```

(continued)

(continued)

```
        END_CATCH
    }

    else
    {
        THROW ( new CFirstException
            ( CFirstException::noIndexFile ) );
    }
}


// Throws no exceptions.
BOOL CFirstCtrl::FindEntry ( long lCode, unsigned long *pulOffset )
{
        // Scan the in-memory copy of the file for SCODE.
    for ( long lEntry = 0L; lEntry < m_lSCodes; ++lEntry )
    {
        if ( m_lpseCodes [ lEntry ].lSCode == lCode )
        {
            *pulOffset = m_lpseCodes [ lEntry ].ulOffset;
            return TRUE;
        }
    }

        // Not found, so scan the list of newly added ones.
    CSCodeEntryList *lpEntry = m_lpseNewCodes;
    while ( lpEntry )
    {
        if ( lpEntry -> GetEntry ( ) -> lSCode == lCode )
        {
            *pulOffset = lpEntry -> GetEntry ( ) -> ulOffset;
            return TRUE;
        }
        lpEntry = lpEntry -> GetNext ( );
    }
    return FALSE;
}


// Can throw CFirstException, CFileException, and CMemoryException.
void CFirstCtrl::GetInfo ( unsigned long ulOffset )
{
    CFile cfMsg;
    CString csMsg;
    TCHAR tcChar;

    csMsg.LoadString ( IDS_MESSAGEFILE );
```

(continued)

```
if ( cfMsg.Open ( csMsg, CFile::modeRead |
    CFile::shareDenyNone ) == TRUE )

{
    cfMsg.Seek ( ulOffset, CFile::begin );
    UINT uRead;

            // Read the symbol name string from the file.
    for ( ; ; )
    {
        uRead = cfMsg.Read ( &tcChar, sizeof ( tcChar ) );
        if ( uRead < sizeof ( tcChar ) )
        {
            cfMsg.Close ( );
            TRACE ( _T (
                "Error reading symbol name from message file\n" ) );
            THROW ( new CFirstException
                ( CFirstException::invalidFile ) );
        }
        if ( tcChar == 0 )
        {
            break;
        }
        m_csSymbol += tcChar;
    }

            // Read the message string from the file.
    for ( ; ; )
    {
        uRead = cfMsg.Read ( &tcChar, sizeof ( tcChar ) );
        if ( uRead < sizeof ( tcChar ) )
        {
            cfMsg.Close ( );
            TRACE ( _T (
                "Error reading message string from file\n" ) );
            THROW ( new CFirstException
                ( CFirstException::invalidFile ) );
        }
        if ( tcChar == 0 )
        {
            break;
        }
        m_csMessage += tcChar;
    }
    cfMsg.Close ( );
```

(continued)

261

(continued)

```
    }
    else
    {

        TRACE ( _T ( "Message file not found\n" ) );
        THROW ( new CFirstException
            ( CFirstException::noMessageFile ) );
    }
}

// Can throw CFirstException, CFileException, and CMemoryException.
unsigned long CFirstCtrl::AddMessage ( LPCTSTR lpszSymbol,
    LPCTSTR lpszMessage )
{
    CFile cfMsg;
    CString csMsg;
    unsigned long ulReturn = 0xFFFFFFFF;

    csMsg.LoadString ( IDS_MESSAGEFILE );
    if ( cfMsg.Open ( csMsg, CFile::modeWrite |
        CFile::shareExclusive ) == TRUE )
    {
        ulReturn = cfMsg.Seek ( 0L, CFile::end );
        cfMsg.Write ( lpszSymbol,
            ( _tcslen ( lpszSymbol ) + 1 ) * sizeof ( TCHAR ) );
        cfMsg.Write ( lpszMessage,
            ( _tcslen ( lpszMessage ) + 1 ) * sizeof ( TCHAR ) );
        cfMsg.Close ( );
    }
    else
    {
        TRACE ( _T ( "Failed to open message file for writing\n" ) );
        THROW ( new CFirstException ( CFirstException::noWriteMsg ) );
    }
    return ulReturn;
}

// Can throw CFirstException, CFileException, and CMemoryException.
void CFirstCtrl::WriteEntry ( CSCodeEntry *pNew )
{
    CFile cfIndex;
    CString csIndex;

    csIndex.LoadString ( IDS_INDEXFILE );
```

(continued)

```
    if ( cfIndex.Open ( csIndex, CFile::modeWrite |
        CFile::shareExclusive ) == TRUE )
    {
        cfIndex.Seek ( 0L, CFile::end );

        cfIndex.Write ( &pNew -> lSCode, sizeof ( pNew -> lSCode ) );
        cfIndex.Write ( &pNew -> ulOffset,
        sizeof ( pNew -> ulOffset ) );
        cfIndex.Close ( );
    }
    else
    {
        TRACE ( _T ( "Unable to open index file for writing\n" ) );
        THROW ( new CFirstException (
            CFirstException::noWriteIdx )
            );
    }
}


// Does no trapping itself, so it can throw anything thrown by
//   functions it calls.
// These include CFirstException, CFileException, and
//   CMemoryException.
long CFirstCtrl::DoBatchLoad ( CStdioFile *cfIn, CFile *cfIndex,
    CFile *cfMsg )
{
    long lEntries = 0L;

    cfIndex -> Seek ( 0L, CFile::end );

    CString csLine, csMsg, csSymbol;
    while ( GetNextDefineLine ( cfIn, &csLine, &csMsg ) )
    {
        long lCode = GetTheCode ( &csLine, &csSymbol );
        unsigned long ulOffset;
        if ( FindEntry ( lCode, &ulOffset ) )
        {
            TRACE1 ( _T ( "SCODE %08X already in database -
                ignored\n" ), lCode );
        }
        else
        {
            long lMsgPos = cfMsg -> Seek ( 0L, CFile::end );

            cfIndex -> Write ( &lCode, sizeof ( lCode ) );
```

(continued)

263

(continued)

```
            cfIndex -> Write ( &lMsgPos, sizeof ( lMsgPos ) );

            cfMsg -> Write ( ( LPCTSTR ) csSymbol,
                ( csSymbol.GetLength ( ) + 1 ) * sizeof ( TCHAR ) );
            cfMsg -> Write ( ( LPCTSTR ) csMsg, (
                csMsg.GetLength ( ) + 1 ) * sizeof ( TCHAR ) );

            ++lEntries;
        }
    }
    return lEntries;
}
// Again, passes any exceptions up to its caller (it can pass at
//    least CFirstException, CFileException, and CMemoryException).
BOOL CFirstCtrl::GetNextDefineLine ( CStdioFile *cfFile, CString
    *csLine,  CString *csMessage )
{
    _TCHAR szBuf [ 256 ];
    CString csCompare;
    BOOL bFound = FALSE;
    LPTSTR lpszCnt;

    do
    {
        lpszCnt = cfFile -> ReadString ( szBuf, 255 );
        if ( lpszCnt == NULL )
        {
            break;
        }
        csCompare = szBuf;
        bFound = ( csCompare.Find ( _T ( "// MessageText:" ) )
            != -1 );
    }
    while ( bFound == FALSE );

    if ( bFound )
    {
            // Discard blank comment line.
        cfFile -> ReadString ( szBuf, 255 );
            // Get message line(s).
        csMessage -> Empty ( );
        do
        {
```

(continued)

```
        cfFile -> ReadString ( szBuf, 255 );
        if ( szBuf [ 3 ] )
        {
                // If this isn't the first line, add a space.
            if ( ! csMessage -> IsEmpty ( ) )
            {
                *csMessage += _T ( " " );
            }
            szBuf [ _tcslen ( szBuf ) - 1 ] = TCHAR ( 0 );
            *csMessage += szBuf + 4;
        }
    }
    while ( szBuf [ 3 ] );

        // Get the code line.
    lpszCnt = cfFile -> ReadString ( szBuf, 255 );

        // If the code line is blank, the file's in the wrong
        //   format.
    if ( lpszCnt == NULL )
    {
        TRACE ( _T (
            "The file given to BatchLoad is in the wrong
            format\n" ) );
        THROW ( new CFirstException
            ( CFirstException::badCodesFile ) );
    }
    *csLine = szBuf;
    return TRUE;
    }
    return FALSE;
}


long CFirstCtrl::GetTheCode ( CString *csLine, CString *csSymbol )
{
        // If #define doesn't occur or is not at the start of the
        //   line, the file wasn't created with MC.
    if ( csLine -> Find ( _T ( "#define" ) ) )
    {
        TRACE ( _T (
            "#define line doesn't start with exactly '#define'\n" ) );
        THROW ( new CFirstException (
            CFirstException::badCodesFile ) );
    }
```

(continued)

(continued)

```
        // Skip '#define'.
    int i = 7;

        // Skip white space.
    while ( ( csLine -> GetLength ( ) > i ) &&
        ( _istspace ( csLine -> GetAt ( i ) ) ) )
    {

        ++i;
    }
    if ( csLine -> GetLength ( ) <= i )
    {
        TRACE ( _T ( "#define line is only '#define'\n" ) );
        THROW ( new CFirstException (
            CFirstException::badCodesFile ) );
    }

        // Collect the symbol.
    csSymbol -> Empty ( );
    while ( ( csLine -> GetLength ( ) > i ) &&
        ! ( _istspace ( csLine -> GetAt ( i ) ) ) )
    {
        *csSymbol += csLine -> GetAt ( i );
        ++i;
    }
    if ( csLine -> GetLength ( ) <= i )
    {
        TRACE ( _T ( "#define line is only '#define SYMBOL'\n" ) );
        THROW ( new CFirstException (
            CFirstException::badCodesFile ) );
    }

        // Skip white space.
    while ( ( csLine -> GetLength ( ) > i ) &&
        ( _istspace ( csLine -> GetAt ( i ) ) ) )
    {
        ++i;
    }
    if ( csLine -> GetLength ( ) <= i )
    {
        TRACE ( _T ( "#define line is only '#define SYMBOL'\n" ) );
        THROW ( new CFirstException (
            CFirstException::badCodesFile ) );
```

(continued)

```
    }

        // Collect the number.
    CString csNumber;
    csNumber = csLine -> Mid ( i );
        // We can't easily report errors that happen here.
    return _tcstoul ( csNumber, NULL, 0 );
}

void CFirstCtrl::ClearList ( void )
{
    delete [] m_lpseCodes;
    m_lpseCodes = 0;
    m_lSCodes = 0;
    CSCodeEntryList *pNext = m_lpseNewCodes;
    while ( pNext )
    {
        CSCodeEntryList *pTemp = pNext -> GetNext ( );
        delete pNext;
        pNext = pTemp;
    }
    m_lpseNewCodes = 0;
}

// Throws no exceptions.
BOOL CFirstCtrl::CreateFiles ( void )
{
    CFile cfFile;
    CString csFile;
    BOOL bRet = FALSE;

    TRY
    {
            // Create the index file first.
        csFile.LoadString ( IDS_INDEXFILE );
        if ( cfFile.Open ( csFile, CFile::modeCreate |
            CFile::modeWrite | CFile::shareExclusive ) == 0 )

        {
            TRACE ( _T ( "Error creating index file\n" ) );
        }
        else
        {
            cfFile.Close ( ); // Instant close - we only want
                              //    creation.
```

(continued)

(continued)

```
        }

            // Then create the message file.
        csFile.LoadString ( IDS_MESSAGEFILE );
        if ( cfFile.Open ( csFile, CFile::modeCreate |
            CFile::modeWrite | CFile::shareExclusive ) == 0 )
        {
            TRACE ( _T ( "Error creating message file\n" ) );

        }
        else
        {
            cfFile.Close ( );
            bRet = TRUE;
            m_bFilesCreated = TRUE;      // Cause our event to be
                                         //   fired later.

        }
    }
    CATCH ( CException, e )
    {
            // Return FALSE for all exceptions.
        return FALSE;
    }
    END_CATCH

    return bRet;
}

void CFirstCtrl::OnFreezeEvents ( BOOL bFreeze )
{
    m_nEventsFrozen += ( bFreeze ? 1 : -1 );
}

void CFirstCtrl::OnEventAdvise ( BOOL bAdvise )
{
    if ( bAdvise && m_bFilesCreated && ( m_nEventsFrozen == 0 ) )
    {
        FireFilesCreated ( );
    }
}

// Throws no exceptions.
BOOL CFirstCtrl::CheckSCode ( long nNewValue )
```

(continued)

```
    {
        CString csLine;

        m_csMessage.Empty ( );          // Prepare string properties.
        m_csSymbol.Empty ( );
        m_bIsValid = FALSE;             // Assume invalid unless proven
                                        //   otherwise.

        unsigned long ulOffset;
        TRY
        {
            if ( FindEntry ( nNewValue, &ulOffset ) )    // Valid?
            {
                m_bIsValid = TRUE;
                GetInfo ( ulOffset );
                csLine = m_csSymbol + _T ( ": " ) + m_csMessage;    //
                Build the caption.
            }
            else
            {
                csLine.LoadString ( IDS_NOVALID_SCODE );
            }
            SetText ( csLine );
        }
        CATCH ( CFirstException, e )
        {
            UINT uStr;
            SCODE sc = e -> GetErrorString ( uStr );
            DoError ( sc, uStr, 0 );
        }
        AND_CATCH ( CFileException, e )
        {
            UINT uStr;
            SCODE sc = GetFileExceptionString(e, uStr);
            DoError ( sc, uStr, 0 );
        }
        AND_CATCH ( CMemoryException, e )
        {
            DoError ( CTL_E_OUTOFMEMORY, IDS_MEMORYERROR, 0 );
        }
        END_CATCH
        return m_bIsValid;
    }

// If any exceptions are thrown here, we'll probably abort!
```

(continued)

(continued)

```
void CFirstCtrl::DoError ( SCODE scode, UINT uDescription,
    UINT helpid )
{
    CString csDescription;
    csDescription.LoadString ( uDescription );

    if ( m_bInDispatch )
    {
        m_bInDispatch = FALSE;      // Reset it now.
        ThrowError ( scode, csDescription, helpid );
    }
    else
    {
        if ( m_nEventsFrozen == 0 )
        {
            FireError ( scode, csDescription, helpid );
        }
    }
}

SCODE CFirstCtrl::GetFileExceptionString ( CFileException *cfEx,
    UINT& uStr ) const
{
    SCODE sc = S_OK;
    uStr = IDS_FILEEXCEPTIONBASE + cfEx -> m_cause;
    switch ( cfEx -> m_cause )
    {
        case CFileException::generic:
            sc = CTL_E_ILLEGALFUNCTIONCALL;
            break;

        case CFileException::fileNotFound:
            sc = CTL_E_FILENOTFOUND;
            break;

        case CFileException::badPath:
            sc = CTL_E_PATHFILEACCESSERROR;
            break;

        case CFileException::tooManyOpenFiles:
            sc = CTL_E_TOOMANYFILES;
            break;

        case CFileException::invalidFile:
```

(continued)

```
            sc = CTL_E_BADFILENAMEORNUMBER;
            break;

        case CFileException::directoryFull:
        case CFileException::diskFull:
            sc = CTL_E_DISKFULL;
            break;

        case CFileException::badSeek:
        case CFileException::hardIO:
            sc = CTL_E_DEVICEIOERROR;
            break;

        case CFileException::accessDenied:
        case CFileException::removeCurrentDir:
        case CFileException::sharingViolation:
        case CFileException::lockViolation:
            sc = CTL_E_PERMISSIONDENIED;
            break;

        case CFileException::endOfFile:
            sc = CTL_E_BADRECORDLENGTH;
            break;

        default:
            sc = CTL_E_ILLEGALFUNCTIONCALL;
            uStr = IDS_UNKNOWNEXCEPTIONCAUSE;
            break;
    }
    return sc;
}
```

FIRSTEX.H

```
class CFirstException : public CException
{
    DECLARE_DYNAMIC ( CFirstException )

public:
    enum {
        none = 0,
```

Listing 9-3 *FIRSTEX.H, the First control's exception class header file.*   *(continued)*

(continued)

```
        noMessageFile,
        invalidFile,
        noWriteMsg,
        noWriteIdx,
        noIndexFile,
        noCreateFile,
        noInputFile,
        badCodesFile,
        badParameters
    };
// Constructor
    CFirstException ( int cause = CFirstException::none )
    { m_cause = cause; }

// Attributes
    int m_cause;

// Operations
    SCODE GetErrorString ( UINT& uStr ) const;

// Implementation
    virtual ~CFirstException()
    { }
};
```

FIRSTEX.CPP

```
#include "stdafx.h"
#include "first.h"
#include "firstex.h"

IMPLEMENT_DYNAMIC ( CFirstException, CException )

SCODE CFirstException::GetErrorString ( UINT& uStr ) const
{
    SCODE sc = S_OK;
    uStr = IDS_FIRSTEXCEPTIONBASE + m_cause;
    switch ( m_cause )
    {
        case noMessageFile:
        case noIndexFile:
        case noInputFile:
```

Listing 9-4. *FIRSTEX.CPP, the First control's exception class implemen-*   *(continued)*
                      tation file.

```
            sc = CTL_E_FILENOTFOUND;
            break;

    case invalidFile:
    case badCodesFile:
            sc = CTL_E_INVALIDFILEFORMAT;
            break;

    case noWriteMsg:
    case noWriteIdx:
            sc = CTL_E_PATHFILEACCESSERROR;
            break;

    case noCreateFile:
            sc = CTL_E_PERMISSIONDENIED;
            break;

    case badParameters:
            sc = CTL_E_INVALIDUSEOFNULL;
            break;

    default:
            sc = CTL_E_ILLEGALFUNCTIONCALL;
            uStr = IDS_UNKNOWNEXCEPTIONCAUSE;
    }
    return sc;
}
```

Looking at Listing 9-1 first, the FIRSTCTRL.H header file, the only changes you'll notice here are the addition of two member variables,

```
    BOOL m_bInDispatch;
    CString m_csBadMessage;
```

and the addition of three member functions:

```
    void DoError ( SCODE scode, UINT uDescription, UINT helpid );
    void ReallySetSCode (long nNewValue);
    SCODE GetFileExceptionString ( CFileException *cfEx,
        UINT& uStr ) const;
```

The *m_bInDispatch* variable is used to tell whether an exception that is to be reported to the container occurred during a call from the container (in which case *ThrowError* will be used) or whether it happened asynchronously (in which case, *FireError* is used). The *m_csBadMessage* variable is used to hold a message that the control displays to the user at startup if the control's message and index files cannot be opened or created. The *DoError* function is used to report an exception to the container, using either *ThrowError* or *FireError*, depending on the value of *m_bInDispatch. ReallySetSCode* contains the code from the old *SetSCode* function because *ReallySetSCode* can be called both by the container (from within *SetSCode* during a property access) and by the control (during property persistence); exceptions that it wants to report can therefore occur both synchronously and asynchronously. *GetFileExceptionString* is a simple lookup function that converts the cause code in a *CFileException* object to a meaningful string.

Moving to the implementation file for *FirstCtrl*, you'll notice a new *#include* statement for FIRSTEX.H. This is the header file in which the *CFirstException* class is declared. This exception class is derived from *CException*, and it forms the basis for some specific exception-handling later in the code. I'll get to the description of that exception class after I've been through all the changes to *FirstCtrl*.

The next change is in the *CFirstCtrl* constructor:

```
m_bInDispatch = FALSE;
m_csBadMessage.LoadString(IDS_BADMESSAGE);

    // If reading the index file creates an exception,
    //   we're in big trouble.
    // Warn the user that the control is severely handicapped
    //   and continue.
TRY
{
    ReadIndexFile ( );
}
CATCH ( CException, e )
{
    CString csExtra;
    UINT uStr = 0;
    if ( e -> IsKindOf(RUNTIME_CLASS(CFirstException)) )
    {
        ((CFirstException*)e) -> GetErrorString ( uStr );
    }
    else if ( e -> IsKindOf(RUNTIME_CLASS(CFileException)) )
    {
    GetFileExceptionString( (CFileException*)e, uStr );
    }
    if ( uStr )
    {
        csExtra.LoadString ( uStr );
        m_csBadMessage += _T ( "\n\nActual error message:\n\n" );
        m_csBadMessage += csExtra;
    }
    AfxMessageBox(m_csBadMessage,MB_OK);
    if ( uStr )
    {
```

```
            m_csBadMessage.Empty ( );
            m_csBadMessage.LoadString ( IDS_BADMESSAGE );
            }
        }
    END_CATCH
```

Here, I set up the two new member variables to their default values and then *ReadIndexFile* is called. Now, however, this function can throw an exception, so I enclose it within a *TRY* block and catch a generic *CException*. If *ReadIndexFile* fails, the control is in big trouble because it can't find or create its index and/or message files. Therefore, the control is not very useful in this condition. Rather than cause the control to destroy itself, I elected to have it display a warning message to the user and then continue. I do this by displaying a message box containing *m_csBadMessage* no matter what type of exception is thrown — that's why the handler is for generic *CExceptions*. The default string loaded into *m_csBadMessage* is "This control was unable to read its index and/or message files. While you may continue to use it, it will have severely limited functionality." Notice the use of *IsKindOf* and *RUN-TIME_CLASS* to determine whether the exception thrown is a *CFirstException* or *CFileException*; if it is either of these exceptions, I extract the cause of the exception and convert it to a text string (using a *CFirstException* member function, *GetErrorString*, or, if it's a *CFileException,* one of the new additions to *CFirstCtrl*, *GetFileExceptionString*). The text string is added to the message box. In this case, I don't fire an error event: it's in the control's constructor, so there won't be anything to catch the event anyway.

This is only one way to handle exceptions of different types. The strategy I adopted was to have the same handling for any exception type but with the addition of some minor processing if the exception was one of a couple of specific types. I could equally have had three *CATCH* clauses, one for each exception type, and each would have done much the same thing. I actually do that a little lower down in the code because I want to demonstrate each of the different exception-handling possibilities.

There's a small change to *DoPropExchange:* I used to call *SetSCode* directly, but now, because *DoPropExchange* is called without being invoked through an automation method, I need to change it so that if an exception occurs, it fires an event rather than trying to throw an OLE Automation exception. Therefore, I set the *m_bInDispatch* flag to *FALSE* and call a new function, *ReallySetSCode*. Likewise, *SetSCode* itself changes to three lines: set *m_bInDispatch* to *TRUE* (because this function is invoked only as the result of property manipulation through OLE), call *ReallySetSCode,* and then reset *m_bInDispatch*. *ReallySetSCode* then contains all the code that *SetSCode* used to contain. It doesn't trap exceptions because *CheckSCode* doesn't throw any, but exceptions can still occur because *CheckSCode* traps ones from functions that it calls. In this case, the exceptions are trapped lower down and execution never returns to *ReallySetSCode*.

None of the "get" property functions has changed because they don't do anything likely to throw exceptions (except that they allocate memory if they're returning a string, but I'm taking the chance that this is unlikely to fail). The methods, on the other hand, have extensive changes. Taking *Add* first, after it's checked to see whether the SCODE being added is already in the database (using *FindEntry*, which doesn't throw exceptions), it sets *m_bInDispatch* to *TRUE* and enters a *TRY* block. The first statement within this block checks to see whether the string parameters passed to *Add* are valid; if they're not, it throws a *CFirstException* using the *THROW* macro. Notice that the *CFirstException* constructor takes a parameter that ends up being the exception "cause" — that is, it is held within the exception object so that *CATCH* code can determine what went wrong. In this case, I'm setting it to a class enumeration constant called *badParameters*.

The *CATCH* clause in *Add* is generic, just like the one in the constructor. Again, the reason I've chosen to do it this way is that there is a lot of generic code. Once again, I extract the error string from the exception, but this time I call *DoError*, a function that will call *ThrowError* or *FireError* (depending on the value of *m_bInDispatch*). In this case it calls *ThrowError*. Notice that I get the SCODE from the exception through the same function that returns the meaningful string.

There's some bogus code in this exception handler, which is there for demonstration purposes. After *ThrowError* has been called in response to an automation method, the path of execution has left the control. Therefore, the statements following *DoError* in this exception handler (resetting *m_bInDispatch* and returning *FALSE*) will never get called!

BatchLoad also has a *TRY* block enclosing most of its code. It checks its string parameter to ensure that it is valid and then tries to open the message file, the index file, and the given input file. A failure in any of these attempts causes a *CFirstException* to be thrown, the "cause" value being set according to which file could not be opened. This time, though, the function catches each exception class individually, calling *DoError* with the appropriate information. Decide for yourself which of these strategies you prefer.

On to *ReadIndexFile*. The *CATCH* block here is generic because what I'm doing is local clean-up, before throwing the exception onto the next handler (that is, the one in the function that called *ReadIndexFile* or the one that called that, and so forth) with *THROW_LAST*. One bug that came up here and which I've fixed: in the previous version of First, if anything went wrong while the index file was being read, I freed up the memory allocated in *m_lpseCodes* and set it to zero, but I neglected to set the count of SCODEs read, *m_lSCodes*, to zero, so there were occasions when it was possible to cause an access violation (GPF in 16-bit Windows!)

because one variable was saying that there were SCODEs in the array, but the array itself was not allocated. Hence, the addition of the line

```
m_lSCodes = 0;
```

to the *CATCH* block. If *ReadIndexFile* is unable to open the index file, it throws a *CFirstException*.

Each of the other functions follows the same pattern, throwing exceptions up when things go wrong and expecting them to be caught by higher-level code. Take a look at *DoBatchLoad*, for instance. At first glance, it has absolutely no exception-handling. However, although it doesn't throw or catch any exceptions itself, it calls functions that do throw exceptions. Consequently, any exception thrown by a lower-down function goes through *DoBatchLoad* before being caught by its caller, *BatchLoad*.

Another bug: *AddMessage* and *DoBatchLoad* both contained a bug in earlier versions of First that would only come to light if you worked exclusively in Unicode. When either of these functions writes out a string to the message file, it uses expressions such as

```
cfMsg -> Write ( ( LPTCSTR ) csSymbol, csSymbol.GetLength() + 1 );
```
or
```
cfMsg.Write ( lpszSymbol, _tcslen ( lpszSymbol ) + 1 );
```

which would actually cause only a portion of each string to be written, because these functions return the length of the string in characters, not in bytes. This is an especially annoying bug when you consider the second line, where I've explicitly thought about Unicode by using *_tcslen*. I just didn't think hard enough! To get these lines to work properly, I've changed them to

```
cfMsg -> Write ( ( LPTCSTR ) csSymbol,
    ( csSymbol.GetLength() + 1 ) * sizeof ( TCHAR ) );
```
and
```
cfMsg.Write ( lpszSymbol,
    ( _tcslen ( lpszSymbol ) + 1 ) * sizeof ( TCHAR ) ;
```

The next interesting function is *GetTheCode*, which I've changed so that it's more robust. Now, rather than simply assuming that the SCODE file is in the correct format, it checks, and it throws an exception if it determines that the file is in error. The only place I can't easily throw an exception when I want to is at the end of the function, where it calls *_tcstoul* to convert the string to a number. This function will tell you if it fails by returning zero, which is of course a valid number. The function also takes a parameter that is set to point at the first invalid character found; conversion stops at that point. So a valid number such as *123L* will fail at the *L*, as you'd expect, and return *123*, as you'd expect. An invalid number, on the other hand, such as *123X4*, will return *123* and set the pointer to the *X*. So, working out what is actually a failure and what is actually success is not entirely straightforward. I took the lazy way out and decided not to check. You might want to alter this behavior!

CreateFiles has been changed to catch all exceptions and convert them into return values of *FALSE*, so any problem simply causes the function to report that it didn't work.

DoError is pretty basic. It loads the error description string from the string table, works out whether to fire an event or throw an automation error, and does it (that is, fires or throws). Events are fired only if the container has not frozen them.

GetFileExceptionString converts a *CFileException m_cause* value into an appropriate SCODE and a meaningful error string. Note that my implementation is flawed because it relies on each of the *CFileException m_cause* values being adjacent in value and starting at zero. C++ enumerations, which is what *m_cause* turns out to be, follow this rule by default but can be overridden. It just so happens that the current implementation of *CFileException* follows my assumption!

This takes me to the *CFirstException* class. I've implemented this in its own file, FIRSTEX.CPP, so that it's clear. The header file declares the class as being derived from *CException*, as all MFC exceptions must be, and as being capable of being dynamically created, as all MFC exceptions must be. An enumeration then lists all the causes this exception class supports, followed by the constructor, which does nothing more than initialize the *m_cause* member variable. The destructor also does very little. The only "real" function in this class is *GetErrorString*, which converts the current value of *m_cause* to a string ID and an SCODE. That function is defined in FIRSTEX.CPP, and it's a simple look-up to match *m_cause* values to SCODEs. Each of the SCODEs I've used are predefined ones; it is possible to add your own SCODEs using the *CUSTOM_CTL_SCODE* macro, but you should do this only if you really have to. Again, the string IDs are created by adding the *m_cause* value to a constant, which happens to be the first error message for this exception in the string table. Every other message follows this one in sequential order.

As you can see, *CFirstException* is very straightforward, and that's really the general rule about exception-handling. You need to use it, it isn't difficult, and its rewards are great. You'll find that you can simulate a number of error conditions with this version of First, and it should be able to cope gracefully with all of them. I strongly encourage you to use exceptions in your code and to deal with caught exceptions wisely. The points to remember are that you're using this functionality to enhance the robustness of your control and you're ensuring that the control user gets as much information as possible about the error.

FYI If you compile this program with a compiler that doesn't support proper C++ exception-handling, such as Microsoft Visual C++ version 1.5x, you might notice that the control reports a number of memory leaks when it is destroyed. These leaks only occur if exceptions are thrown, so what's happening? Well, the answer lies in *CString*. *CString* objects allocate memory from the heap (using the *new* operator) for the strings contained within them, and this memory is freed when the *CString*'s destructor is called. Without proper C++ exception-handling, destructors aren't always called, so this memory is never freed. The way to avoid these memory leaks is to explicitly free the memory by calling *CString::Empty* whenever an exception is thrown. So, if you're writing 16-bit OLE controls and you're writing code such as this:

```
CString csMsg;
csMsg.LoadString ( IDS_INDEX_FILE );
if ( DoSomething ( ) == FALSE )
{
    THROW ( new CAnException );
}
```

you need to alter this code in the non-C++ exception-handling world like so:

```
CString csMsg;
csMsg.LoadString ( IDS_INDEX_FILE );
if ( DoSomething ( ) == FALSE )
{
    csMsg.Empty ( );
    THROW ( new CAnException );
}
```

I haven't done this in the First control, as you'll have figured out by the memory leaks. It's left as an exercise for the reader!

Chapter 10

A Consolidation

Over the past few chapters, I've taken you through the steps involved in designing and refining a fully functional OLE control. I've used each chapter to introduce a new concept, such as properties, events, or exceptions. So, now that you know it all, you can get to work designing and writing your own controls, right? Well, yes, you can — but there's still a lot more to learn. All along I've said that there are problems with the First control that I don't really want to live with, and I haven't really demonstrated yet how one should go about debugging a control. Therefore, I've decided to take time out in this middle chapter to refine and consolidate (rather than to introduce sparkling new concepts). Consequently, in this chapter I examine additional control design issues, debugging, the use of ODBC to access data, control versioning issues, and control help files.

At the end of this chapter, you'll have an almost-definitive version of the First control. The only thing missing from it will be a set of property pages. They get added in the next chapter. From that point on, I'll leave the First control behind and concentrate on a new control. Maybe I'll call it the Second control.

CONTROL DESIGN ISSUES

When you design an OLE control, what do you need to consider that is different from what you would need to consider if you were designing a conventional application? Reusability, of course, because an OLE control is explicitly a component, so one design criterion must be reusability. You could, in some cases, argue that you don't care about reuse and the componentware aspects of a particular control because you're developing it for a specific purpose. For example, you might be making it a control because you want to take advantage of some feature that OLE controls offer (events?) or you might want to write most of the code in Microsoft Visual Basic but this little bit needs to be done in C++. Certainly these circumstances arise, but I think that they're not typical of most control writer's needs, so I concentrate (and will continue to concentrate) on component-oriented controls.

Visual Controls and Composite Controls

Do controls need to be visual? Certainly not, although once again it's arguable that an invisible OLE control is really not required to be a control and could be implemented as an OLE Automation server with event support. You'll see this happen in the next few years as tools such as C++ compilers provide the facilities to add events to standard automation servers without having also to have the extra overhead of an in-place editing server; you'll also see OLE containers capable of accepting events from objects other than controls. Which leads me to the conclusion that most "real" OLE controls <u>will</u> be visual.

Does an OLE control need to be composed of only one "control" object (list box, edit box, and so forth)? No. Imagine a piece of functionality encapsulated in an OLE control such that the user interface for that functionality is provided by the control itself. A good example might be the customer object I referred to very briefly in Chapter 1. This object is designed to provide the entire programming interface to an insurance company's customer database as well as an implementation of the entire user interface through which it can be manipulated. Such a user interface would necessarily involve a large number of individual user interface elements within the same control, and this is a perfectly valid use for an OLE control. What's also interesting is that the user interface offered by this control could be "replaced" by one provided by the container. The container would still use the same programming interface to the control, but it would ask the control not to display its user interface. Why? If you write software which can be used by a large number of companies in the same business (such as life insurance), you'll often find that they all want the same basic functionality but they all want the user interface to work in different ways. Some will want to take your wonderful, highly-engineered user interface. Others will have company standards that they want to maintain. (Sometimes it's valuable to argue strongly against this, as some user interface guidelines enforced by companies I've come across have had the effect of making software <u>harder</u> to use, not easier.) Others yet will want to hand off the software component to a third party, which it then commissions to develop the system.

So, if an OLE control is typically visible, it needs to be fast, right? Well, most user interface elements are so fast in comparison to human reactions that the only things we typically notice are drawing speed and visual feedback speed. "Drawing speed" relates to how quickly your control draws itself. It always surprises me just how good the human brain is at noticing differences. It isn't too good with absolutes ("this control draws too slowly"), but it is very good at the deltas ("this control draws much more slowly than that one"). Which means that if your control is the one that draws more slowly, it'll stand out. "Visual feedback speed" is related to the amount of time it takes a control to change itself visually to acknowledge a user action such as a click. If, for example, a button takes half a second to draw itself in the "down" state, it's probably okay; if it takes a second or longer, it becomes noticeable.

The point is that most visual cues are in fact perception-based rather than reality-based. So, if your control appears to be fast, it is fast! This is why progress indicators (you know, "56% done" and so on) are so popular: they make a program appear to be quicker than ones without such an indicator. Imagine an installation program that just sat there copying files without giving you any clue as to what was going on: it might be as fast as the one with a progress indicator, but it'll seem a lot slower. Even compiler vendors have learned this trick; some will deliberately slow down their compiler with text output just so that they can display the number of lines compiled. The impact is dramatic, and people perceive such a product as fast. Therefore, a control should be able to make most graphical updates pretty quickly. Complicated ones, such as graph controls, might immediately update some basic elements (the chart frame, for example, or the legend) and then draw the rest later, using idle-time processing or some such mechanism.

The Control's Object Model

One of the most important aspects of a control's design actually applies to any OLE Automation object and, ultimately, any object-based system design. That is, what properties and methods should the object expose? What events should it fire? And is there an underlying hierarchy to be modeled? A customer object, for example, might include information about the customer's address. If so, is this information held as just another part of the customer's data? Or is it held as an object in its own right, so that it has the inherent intelligence to verify itself, to save itself to the database, and even to check that its postal code/zip code makes sense in the designated country?

How do you make this choice? You need to consider two things:

- Are addresses used elsewhere within the system?

- Is it a requirement that an address have intelligence?

If the answer to either question is "yes," you might as well write the address object. If the answer to both is "yes," you have a pretty compelling reason for doing so. Then you've got to look at the implementation details and think about how to expose this object. Do you make it a control or automation server in its own right? For an address, this is probably overkill and would be too slow. Therefore, you might choose to implement the address object inside the customer object so that the customer control has a property, *Address*, which returns a pointer to the address object's progammability interface (that is, *IDispatch*-derived). This allows users of your control to write Visual Basic code such as this:

```
If TheCustomer.Address.IsValidZip = False Then
    MsgBox ("The zip code is invalid - please re-enter")
End If
```

When you implement the address object inside your control, you'd first use ClassWizard to add the *Address* property to the OLE-control derived class, and you'd ensure that it has a type of *LPDISPATCH*. You'd then use ClassWizard again to add a new class to the project, derived from *CCmdTarget* and with OLE Automation enabled. Typically, you wouldn't make this class OLE-creatable (that is, directly creatable from client applications such as Visual Basic) because you want to enforce the object hierarchy. You'd then add the address object's properties and methods to this new class and implement them. If you did decide to make the class OLE-creatable, you'd have to be very careful: OLE controls implemented by the CDK are <u>not</u> the same as standard OLE automation in-process servers, and they need to be initialized properly. Creating <u>any</u> object in an OLE control using a mechanism that doesn't cause that control's initialization code to be executed is asking for trouble, so you should <u>not</u> expect to be able to do something like this:

```
Dim TheCustomer As Customer
Set TheCustomer = CreateObject("Customer.Control.1")
...etc.
```

Why? Because the creation via *CreateInstance* implied here is not guaranteed to initialize the control properly, and usually won't. In simple controls, it might work, but it's not behavior you should rely upon.

There is likely to be a data structure or two that your control wants to be able to pass back and forth between instances of itself and its container. As OLE Automation limits the types you can pass, what's the best strategy for this? There are many:

■ Create separate properties for each element in the structure. This is easy to do, but it can be mightily inefficient if a lot of elements are present.

■ Pack all the structure elements into a lump of memory and pass it over as a *BSTR*. This is extremely hacky and is difficult to read and prone to error, particularly if anything between your control and its container tries to be intelligent about the string and convert it from, say, Unicode to ANSI. Definitely <u>not</u> recommended!

■ Convert all structure elements to text and then pack the text into a *BSTR*. This is also still hacky and is prone to error — and now even slower! Do <u>not</u> do this.

■ Pass the data via *IDataObject*. Now, that might work. Of course, containers need to know how to deal with this.

■ Write everything to a file and pass the filename across. Hmm, let's assume you're not even going to begin to consider this one!

■ Write everything to shared memory and pass across the name of the shared memory. But this is just a way of doing what *IDataObject* does for you.

I'm sure that there are other ways you can do this, too.

The trade-off here is ease of programming and ease of use (separate properties) versus efficiency and container compatibility (*IDataObject*).

Subclassed Controls

One class of OLE control that needs careful consideration is one that mimics the behavior of a standard Windows control and that enhances it in some way, such as an edit box that will only accept dates or currency values or whatever. In most cases, the best answer is to use the existing functionality where possible, by making the OLE control a subclass of the Windows control. ControlWizard makes this easy by having an option especially for this, but there are some problems (such as bugs) in some of the standard controls (such as combo boxes), which means that they don't draw properly in the inactive state. In this case, you'll need to write code specifically to draw them. In most cases, this is easier than reimplementing the control yourself.

ODBC IN OLE CONTROLS

One of the things I really want to be able to do with the First control is to make its code lookup scheme more intelligent. The best way of doing this (to my mind, at least) is to use a database to hold all the codes, their symbolic names, and the messages associated with them. That database can then be accessed through ODBC to find a given SCODE, to add a new SCODE, and even to delete an obsolete SCODE from the database. (This last piece of functionality I don't provide, but it's easy to add.) I used a class derived from the MFC *CRecordset* class to implement this, and in most aspects the code for the control got simpler. Listings 10-1 and 10-2 show the new class derived from *CRecordset*, which provides database access. Listings 10-3 and 10-4 show the new main control file and its header. (The source code in this chapter can be found on the companion CD-ROM in the \OLECTRLS\CHAP10\FIRST directory.)

NOTE ODBC does not support Unicode, so if you've been building Unicode variants of the First control up to now, they will no longer build successfully. Therefore, this version of the First control can exist only as an ANSI control on Win32 platforms until such time as ODBC supports Unicode or another data access mechanism is provided that does support Unicode.

The database itself is a Microsoft Access database (so you have to install the Microsoft Access ODBC driver to use it), which I've provided as SCODES.MDB. I've set up the database to contain a table with three columns: the SCODE as a *long*, the symbol as a text field with a maximum length of 255 characters, and the message as a memo field (which is much like a text field except that its maximum length can exceed 255 characters) with a maximum length of 1023 characters. Set up the data source name to be "SCODES." The *CDbSet* class was created by ClassWizard, and then I made a few tweaks to it. To get ClassWizard to generate the class, I clicked the Add Class button and typed in *CDbSet* as the class name. Then I chose *CRecordset* as its base class. This will cause ClassWizard to show a list of available ODBC data sources: choose the SCODES one you added earlier. Now a list of tables is visible in the data source; there should be only one, again called SCODES. I chose this one. ClassWizard now creates the class with three member variables, to hold the three columns.

After the class is created, I need to make a couple of minor alterations to it to get it to work in the way required by this control. The first thing I do is edit the *RFX_Text* calls in *DoFieldExchange* to set the length of the fields. This simply involves the addition of a fourth parameter to each call. The first, the symbol field, is up to 255 characters long, so I add a parameter of *256*. The second, the message, can be up to 1023 characters long, so I add a parameter of *1024*. Why do I need to do this? When a recordset binds its member variables to the data source, it passes the address of each of the variables through to ODBC. The two text fields here are implemented as *CStrings*. Now, when a *CString* is assigned a longer string than it currently holds, it will typically allocate another buffer to hold the new string. This new buffer is almost 100 percent certain not to be at the same address, so ODBC is now binding to an invalid address, which will cause it to fail in all sorts of horrible and unpredictable ways. The debug version of the MFC library catches this with an *ASSERT* (which is actually how I knew I had a problem!). It turns out that *RFX* functions have a fourth parameter for precisely this reason.

NOTE The fourth parameter for the symbol field is not strictly necessary, as it is set to this length anyway by default. I'm merely being consistent and giving you the opportunity to type in more code.

The only other change to the recordset class is to add a parameter. This parameter is a value that is passed to ODBC during a query; it allows me to specify the record I want to retrieve. Because I know that I want to retrieve only one record at a time, using a parameter in this manner is a whole lot more efficient than retrieving the entire set of records and moving through them until I find the right record. Let the database do the work — that's what it's for!

I define this parameter in the header file in the public section:

```
long m_SCodeParam;
```

It needs to be public so that it can be accessed outside of the recordset. It is then referenced in *DoFieldExchange* immediately after the wizard-generated code:

```
pFX->SetFieldType(CFieldExchange::param);
RFX_Long(pFX, "SCODE", m_SCodeParam);
```

This tells the recordset that the variable is a parameter and that it's attached to the SCODE field. Finally, for this class, I need to bump up the number of parameters in the class by incrementing the *m_nParams* member variable in the constructor. This variable is used internally by the class to tell it how many parameters it has. As you'll see when I discuss the use of the *CDbSet* class, this parameter is set to the SCODE value that I want to find in the database, and it's then treated by the database as part of the SQL statement I give it.

DBSET.H

```
// dbset.h : header file
//


/////////////////////////////////////////////////////////////////////
// CDbSet recordset

class CDbSet : public CRecordset
{
public:
    CDbSet(CDatabase* pDatabase = NULL);
    DECLARE_DYNAMIC(CDbSet)

// Field/Param Data
    //{{AFX_FIELD(CDbSet, CRecordset)
    long    m_SCODE;
    CString m_Symbol;
    CString m_Message;
    //}}AFX_FIELD
```

Listing 10-1.   *DBSET.H, the recordset class header file.*   *(continued)*

(continued)

```
    long m_SCodeParam;

// Overrides
    // ClassWizard generated virtual function overrides
    //{{AFX_VIRTUAL(CDbSet)
    public:
    virtual CString GetDefaultConnect();    // Default connection
        string
    virtual CString GetDefaultSQL();    // Default SQL for Recordset
    virtual void DoFieldExchange(CFieldExchange* pFX);  // RFX
        support
    //}}AFX_VIRTUAL

// Implementation
#ifdef _DEBUG
    virtual void AssertValid() const;
    virtual void Dump(CDumpContext& dc) const;
#endif
};
```

DBSET.CPP

```
// dbset.cpp : implementation file
//

#include "stdafx.h"
#include "first.h"
#include "dbset.h"

#ifdef _DEBUG
#undef THIS_FILE
static char BASED_CODE THIS_FILE[] = __FILE__;
#endif


/////////////////////////////////////////////////////////////////////
// CDbSet

IMPLEMENT_DYNAMIC(CDbSet, CRecordset)

CDbSet::CDbSet(CDatabase* pdb)
    : CRecordset(pdb)
{
    //{{AFX_FIELD_INIT(CDbSet)
```

Listing 10-2. *DBSET.CPP, the recordset class implementation file.* *(continued)*

```
        m_SCODE = 0;
        m_Symbol = _T("");
        m_Message = _T("");
        m_nFields = 3;
        //}}AFX_FIELD_INIT
        ++m_nParams;      // We have one parameter.
}

CString CDbSet::GetDefaultConnect()
{
        return _T("ODBC;DSN=SCODES;");
}

CString CDbSet::GetDefaultSQL()
{
        return _T("SCODES");
}

void CDbSet::DoFieldExchange(CFieldExchange* pFX)
{
        //{{AFX_FIELD_MAP(CDbSet)
        pFX->SetFieldType(CFieldExchange::outputColumn);
        RFX_Long(pFX, "SCODE", m_SCODE);
        RFX_Text(pFX, "Symbol", m_Symbol, 256);
        RFX_Text(pFX, "Message", m_Message, 1024);
        //}}AFX_FIELD_MAP
        pFX->SetFieldType(CFieldExchange::param);
        RFX_Long(pFX, "SCODE", m_SCodeParam);
}


//////////////////////////////////////////////////////////////////////
// CDbSet diagnostics

#ifdef _DEBUG
void CDbSet::AssertValid() const
{
        CRecordset::AssertValid();
}

void CDbSet::Dump(CDumpContext& dc) const
{
        CRecordset::Dump(dc);
}
#endif //_DEBUG
```

FIRSTCTL.H

```
// firstctl.h : Declaration of the CFirstCtrl OLE control class.

struct CSCodeEntry
{
    long lSCode;
    unsigned long ulOffset;
};

class CSCodeEntryList
{
public:
    void SetNext ( CSCodeEntryList *selNew ) { m_pNext = selNew; }
    CSCodeEntryList *GetNext ( void ) const { return m_pNext; }
    CSCodeEntry *GetEntry ( void ) { return &m_seThis; }
private:
    CSCodeEntryList *m_pNext;
    CSCodeEntry m_seThis;
};


/////////////////////////////////////////////////////////////////////
// CFirstCtrl : See firstctl.cpp for implementation.

class CFirstCtrl : public COleControl
{
    DECLARE_DYNCREATE(CFirstCtrl)

// Constructor
public:
    CFirstCtrl();

// Overrides

    // Drawing function
    virtual void OnDraw(CDC* pdc, const CRect& rcBounds,
        const CRect& rcInvalid);
    // Persistence
    virtual void DoPropExchange(CPropExchange* pPX);

    // Reset control state
    virtual void OnResetState();

// Implementation
```

Listing 10-3. *FIRSTCTL.H, the control's main header file.* *(continued)*

```
        virtual void OnFreezeEvents(BOOL bFreeze);

protected:
    ~CFirstCtrl();

    DECLARE_OLECREATE_EX(CFirstCtrl)      // Class factory and guid
    DECLARE_OLETYPELIB(CFirstCtrl)        // GetTypeInfo
    DECLARE_PROPPAGEIDS(CFirstCtrl)       // Property page IDs
    DECLARE_OLECTLTYPE(CFirstCtrl)        // Type name and misc status

// Message maps
    //{{AFX_MSG(CFirstCtrl)
        // NOTE - ClassWizard will add and remove member functions
        //    here.
        //     DO NOT EDIT what you see in these blocks of generated
        //       code !
    //}}AFX_MSG
    DECLARE_MESSAGE_MAP()

// Dispatch maps
    //{{AFX_DISPATCH(CFirstCtrl)
    afx_msg long GetSCode();
    afx_msg void SetSCode(long nNewValue);
    afx_msg short GetCode();
    afx_msg BSTR GetFacility();
    afx_msg BSTR GetSeverity();
    afx_msg BSTR GetMessage();
    afx_msg BSTR GetErrorName();
    afx_msg BOOL Add(long SCode, LPCTSTR Symbol, LPCTSTR Message);
    afx_msg long BatchLoad(LPCTSTR FileName);
    afx_msg void Reset();
    //}}AFX_DISPATCH
    DECLARE_DISPATCH_MAP()

    afx_msg void AboutBox();

// Event maps
    //{{AFX_EVENT(CFirstCtrl)
    void FireInvalidSCode(long SCode)
        {FireEvent(eventidInvalidSCode,EVENT_PARAM(VTS_I4), SCode);}
    //}}AFX_EVENT
    DECLARE_EVENT_MAP()
// Dispatch and event IDs
```

(continued)

291

(continued)

```
public:
    enum {
    //{{AFX_DISP_ID(CFirstCtrl)
    dispidSCode = 1L,
    dispidCode = 2L,
    dispidFacility = 3L,
    dispidSeverity = 4L,
    dispidMessage = 5L,
    dispidErrorName = 6L,
    dispidAdd = 7L,
    dispidBatchLoad = 8L,
    dispidReset = 9L,
    eventidInvalidSCode = 1L,
    //}}}AFX_DISP_ID
    };

private:
    long m_SCode;
    BOOL m_bIsValid;
    CString m_csSymbol;
    CString m_csMessage;
    short m_nEventsFrozen;
    BOOL m_bInDispatch;
    CString m_csBadMessage;
    CDbSet *m_rsTable;

    BOOL FindEntry ( long lCode );
    void GetInfo ( void );
    long DoBatchLoad ( CStdioFile *cfIn );
    BOOL GetNextDefineLine ( CStdioFile *cfFile,
        CString *csLine, CString *  csMessage );
    long GetTheCode ( CString *csLine, CString *csSymbol );
    BOOL CheckSCode ( long nNewValue );
    void DoError ( SCODE scode, UINT uDescription, UINT helpid );
    void DoError ( SCODE scode, CString& strDescription,
        UINT helpid );
    void ReallySetSCode (long nNewValue);
    SCODE GetFileExceptionString ( CFileException *cfEx,
        UINT& uStr ) const;
        void CheckDatabase ( void );
    };
```

FIRSTCTL.CPP

```
// firstctl.cpp : Implementation of the CFirstCtrl OLE control class.

#include "stdafx.h"
#include "first.h"
#include "dbset.h"
#include "firstctl.h"
#include "firstppg.h"
#include "firstex.h"

#ifdef _DEBUG
#undef THIS_FILE
static char BASED_CODE THIS_FILE[] = __FI__;
#endif

IMPLEMENT_DYNCREATE(CFirstCtrl, COleControl)


/////////////////////////////////////////////////////////////////////
// Message map

BEGIN_MESSAGE_MAP(CFirstCtrl, COleControl)
    //{{AFX_MSG_MAP(CFirstCtrl)
    // NOTE - ClassWizard will add and remove message map entries
    //    DO NOT EDIT what you see in these blocks of generated
    //        code !
    //}}AFX_MSG_MAP
    ON_OLEVERB(AFX_IDS_VERB_PROPERTIES, OnProperties)
END_MESSAGE_MAP()


/////////////////////////////////////////////////////////////////////
// Dispatch map

BEGIN_DISPATCH_MAP(CFirstCtrl, COleControl)
    //{{AFX_DISPATCH_MAP(CFirstCtrl)
    DISP_PROPERTY_EX(CFirstCtrl, "SCode", GetSCode, SetSCode, VT_I4)
    DISP_PROPERTY_EX(CFirstCtrl, "Code", GetCode, SetNotSupported, VT_I2)
    DISP_PROPERTY_EX(CFirstCtrl, "Facility", GetFacility,
        SetNotSupported, VT_BSTR)
    DISP_PROPERTY_EX(CFirstCtrl, "Severity", GetSeverity,
        SetNotSupported, VT_BSTR)
    DISP_PROPERTY_EX(CFirstCtrl, "Message", GetMessage,
        SetNotSupported, VT_BSTR)
```

Listing 10-4. *FIRSTCTL.CPP, the control's implementation file.* *(continued)*

(continued)

```
    DISP_PROPERTY_EX(CFirstCtrl, "ErrorName", GetErrorName,
        SetNotSupported, VT_BSTR)
    DISP_FUNCTION(CFirstCtrl, "Add", Add, VT_BOOL, VTS_I4 VTS_BSTR
        VTS_BSTR)
    DISP_FUNCTION(CFirstCtrl, "BatchLoad", BatchLoad, VT_I4,
        VTS_BSTR)
    DISP_FUNCTION(CFirstCtrl, "Reset", Reset, VT_EMPTY, VTS_NONE)
    DISP_STOCKFUNC_REFRESH()
    DISP_STOCKPROP_BACKCOLOR()
    DISP_STOCKPROP_CAPTION()
    DISP_STOCKPROP_ENABLED()
    DISP_STOCKPROP_FONT()
    DISP_STOCKPROP_FORECOLOR()
    DISP_STOCKPROP_HWND()
    //}}AFX_DISPATCH_MAP
    DISP_FUNCTION_ID(CFirstCtrl, "AboutBox", DISPID_ABOUTBOX,
        AboutBox, VT_EMPTY, VTS_NONE)
END_DISPATCH_MAP()


///////////////////////////////////////////////////////////////////
// Event map

BEGIN_EVENT_MAP(CFirstCtrl, COleControl)
    //{{AFX_EVENT_MAP(CFirstCtrl)
    EVENT_CUSTOM("InvalidSCode", FireInvalidSCode, VTS_I4)
    //}}AFX_EVENT_MAP
END_EVENT_MAP()


///////////////////////////////////////////////////////////////////
// Property pages

// TODO: Add more property pages as needed.  Remember to increase
//    the count!
BEGIN_PROPPAGEIDS(CFirstCtrl, 1)
    PROPPAGEID(CFirstPropPage::guid)
END_PROPPAGEIDS(CFirstCtrl)


///////////////////////////////////////////////////////////////////
// Initialize class factory and guid

IMPLEMENT_OLECREATE_EX(CFirstCtrl, "FIRST.FirstCtrl.1",
```

(continued)

```
        0x14bc5f80, 0xdbd2, 0x11cd, 0x92, 0xb4, 0x8, 0x0, 0x2b, 0x29,
            0x1e, 0xed)


/////////////////////////////////////////////////////////////////////
// Type library ID and version

IMPLEMENT_OLETYPELIB(CFirstCtrl, _tlid, _wVerMajor, _wVerMinor)


/////////////////////////////////////////////////////////////////////
// Interface IDs

const IID BASED_CODE IID_DFirst =
        { 0x14bc5f81, 0xdbd2, 0x11cd, { 0x92, 0xb4, 0x8, 0x0, 0x2b,
        0x29, 0x1e, 0xed } };
const IID BASED_CODE IID_DFirstEvents =
        { 0x14bc5f82, 0xdbd2, 0x11cd, { 0x92, 0xb4, 0x8, 0x0, 0x2b,
        0x29, 0x1e, 0xed } };


/////////////////////////////////////////////////////////////////////
// Control type information

static const DWORD BASED_CODE _dwFirstOleMisc =
    OLEMISC_ACTIVATEWHENVISIBLE |
    OLEMISC_SETCLIENTSITEFIRST |
    OLEMISC_INSIDEOUT |
    OLEMISC_CANTLINKINSIDE |
    OLEMISC_RECOMPOSEONRESIZE;
IMPLEMENT_OLECTLTYPE(CFirstCtrl, IDS_FIRST, _dwFirstOleMisc)


/////////////////////////////////////////////////////////////////////
// CFirstCtrl::CFirstCtrlFactory::UpdateRegistry -
// Adds or removes system registry entries for CFirstCtrl

BOOL CFirstCtrl::CFirstCtrlFactory::UpdateRegistry(BOOL bRegister)
{
    if (bRegister)
        return AfxOleRegisterControlClass(
            AfxGetInstanceHandle(),
            m_clsid,
            m_lpszProgID,
            IDS_FIRST,
            IDB_FIRST,
```

(continued)

295

(continued)

```
            FALSE,                          // Not insertable
            _dwFirstOleMisc,
            _tlid,
            _wVerMajor,
            _wVerMinor);
    else
        return AfxOleUnregisterClass(m_clsid, m_lpszProgID);
}


/////////////////////////////////////////////////////////////////////
// CFirstCtrl::CFirstCtrl - Constructor

CFirstCtrl::CFirstCtrl()
{
    InitializeIIDs(&IID_DFirst, &IID_DFirstEvents);
    m_SCode = 0L;
    m_bIsValid = FALSE;
    m_nEventsFrozen = 0;
    m_bInDispatch = FALSE;
    m_rsTable = 0;
    m_csBadMessage.LoadString(IDS_BADMESSAGE);

    TRY
    {
        CString csSql;
        csSql.LoadString(IDS_SQL);
        m_rsTable = new CDbSet ( );

        m_rsTable -> m_SCodeParam = 0L;
        if ( m_rsTable -> Open ( CRecordset::snapshot, csSql ) ==
            FALSE )
        {
            THROW ( new CFirstException (
                CFirstException::noDatabase ) );
        }
    }
    CATCH ( CException, e )
    {
        CString csExtra;
        UINT uStr = 0;
        if ( e -> IsKindOf(RUNTIME_CLASS(CFirstException)) )
        {
```

(continued)

```
            ((CFirstException*)e) -> GetErrorString ( uStr );
        }
        else if ( e -> IsKindOf(RUNTIME_CLASS(CFileException)) )
        {
            GetFileExceptionString ( (CFileException*)e, uStr );
        }
        else if ( e -> IsKindOf(RUNTIME_CLASS(CDBException)) )
        {
            csExtra = ((CDBException*)e) -> m_strStateNativeOrigin;
        }

        // Load an error message string if there is one.
        if ( uStr )
        {
            csExtra.LoadString ( uStr );
        }

        // If there's a message, add it to the message box.
        if ( !csExtra.IsEmpty() )
        {
            m_csBadMessage += _T ( "\n\nActual error message:\n\n" );
            m_csBadMessage += csExtra;
        }
        AfxMessageBox ( m_csBadMessage, MB_OK );

        // Reset the error message string.
        m_csBadMessage.LoadString ( IDS_BADMESSAGE );
    }
    END_CATCH
}


/////////////////////////////////////////////////////////////////////
// CFirstCtrl::~CFirstCtrl - Destructor

CFirstCtrl::~CFirstCtrl()
{
    if ( m_rsTable )
    {
        if ( m_rsTable -> IsOpen() )
        {
            m_rsTable -> Close();
        }
```

(continued)

(continued)

```
        delete m_rsTable;
    }
}


/////////////////////////////////////////////////////////////////////
// CFirstCtrl::OnDraw - Drawing function

void CFirstCtrl::OnDraw(
            CDC* pdc, const CRect& rcBounds, const CRect& rcInvalid)
{
    CFont *hfOld = SelectStockFont ( pdc );
    CBrush cbBack ( TranslateColor ( GetBackColor ( ) ) );

    pdc -> FillRect ( rcBounds, &cbBack );
    pdc -> SetTextColor ( TranslateColor ( GetForeColor ( ) ) );
    pdc -> SetBkMode ( TRANSPARENT );
    pdc -> DrawText ( InternalGetText ( ), -1, rcBounds, DT_CENTER |
        DT_VCENTER | DT_SINGLELINE );
    pdc -> SelectObject ( hfOld );

}


/////////////////////////////////////////////////////////////////////
// CFirstCtrl::DoPropExchange - Persistence support

void CFirstCtrl::DoPropExchange(CPropExchange* pPX)
{
    ExchangeVersion(pPX, MAKELONG(_wVerMinor, _wVerMajor));
    COleControl::DoPropExchange(pPX);

    PX_Long ( pPX, _T ( "SCode" ), m_SCode, OL );
    if ( pPX -> IsLoading() )
    {
        ReallySetSCode ( m_SCode );
    }
}


/////////////////////////////////////////////////////////////////////
// CFirstCtrl::OnResetState - Reset control to default state

void CFirstCtrl::OnResetState()
```

(continued)

```
{
    COleControl::OnResetState();   // Resets the defaults found in
                                   //   DoPropExchange.
}


/////////////////////////////////////////////////////////////////
// CFirstCtrl::AboutBox - Display an "About" box to the user

void CFirstCtrl::AboutBox()
{
    CDialog dlgAbout(IDD_ABOUTBOX_FIRST);
    dlgAbout.DoModal();
}


/////////////////////////////////////////////////////////////////
// CFirstCtrl message handlers

long CFirstCtrl::GetSCode()
{
    return m_SCode;
}

void CFirstCtrl::SetSCode(long nNewValue)
{
    m_bInDispatch = TRUE;
    ReallySetSCode ( nNewValue );
    m_bInDispatch = FALSE;
}

void CFirstCtrl::ReallySetSCode ( long nNewValue )
{
    if ( CheckSCode ( nNewValue ) == FALSE )
    {
        if ( m_nEventsFrozen == 0 )
        {
            FireInvalidSCode ( nNewValue );
        }
    }
    m_SCode = nNewValue;
    SetModifiedFlag();
}

short CFirstCtrl::GetCode()
{
```

(continued)

(continued)

```
        if ( m_bIsValid )
        {
            return short ( m_SCode & 0xFFFFL );
        }
        else
        {
            return -1;
        }
    }

    BSTR CFirstCtrl::GetFacility()
    {
        CString s;
        short nFacility = IDS_NOVALID_SCODE;
        if ( m_bIsValid )
        {
            nFacility = short ( ( m_SCode & 0x0FFF0000L ) >> 16L );
            switch ( nFacility )
            {
                case 0: case 1: case 2: case 3:
                case 4: case 7: case 8: case 10:
                    break;
                default:
                    nFacility = -1;
            }
            nFacility += IDS_FACILITY_NULL;
        }
        s.LoadString ( nFacility );
        return s.AllocSysString();
    }

    BSTR CFirstCtrl::GetSeverity()
    {
        CString s;
        short nSeverity = IDS_NOVALID_SCODE;

        if ( m_bIsValid )
        {
            nSeverity = short ( ( m_SCode & 0xC0000000L ) >> 30L ) +
                IDS_SEVERITY_SUCCESS;
        }
        s.LoadString ( nSeverity );
        return s.AllocSysString();
    }
```

(continued)

```
}

BSTR CFirstCtrl::GetMessage()
{
    return m_csMessage.AllocSysString();
}

BSTR CFirstCtrl::GetErrorName()
{
    return m_csSymbol.AllocSysString();
}
BOOL CFirstCtrl::Add ( long SCode, LPCTSTR Symbol, LPCTSTR Message )
{
    m_bInDispatch = TRUE;
    TRY
    {
            // FindEntry checks status of database and throws
            //    exceptions if bad.
        if ( FindEntry ( SCode ) )
        {
            TRACE ( _T ( "Add: SCODE %08X already in database\n" ),
                SCode );
            return TRUE;
        }

            // Can't cope with NULL or empty strings.
        if ( Symbol == 0 || Message == 0 || *Symbol == 0 ||
            *Message == 0 )
        {
            THROW ( new CFirstException (
                CFirstException::badParameters ) );
        }

        if ( m_rsTable -> CanAppend() == FALSE )
        {
            TRACE ( _T ( "Database is read-only\n" ) );
            return FALSE;
        }

        m_rsTable -> AddNew();
        m_rsTable -> m_SCODE = SCode;
        m_rsTable -> m_Symbol = Symbol;
        m_rsTable -> m_Message = Message;
        m_rsTable -> Update();
```

(continued)

(continued)

```
    }
    CATCH ( CException, e )          // Generic catch
    {
        SCODE sc;
        UINT uStr;
        if ( e -> IsKindOf(RUNTIME_CLASS(CFirstException)) )
        {
            sc = ((CFirstException*)e) -> GetErrorString ( uStr );
        }
        else if ( e -> IsKindOf(RUNTIME_CLASS(CFileException)) )
        {
            sc = GetFileExceptionString ( (CFileException*)e, uStr );
        }
        else if ( e -> IsKindOf(RUNTIME_CLASS(CDBException)) )
        {
            DoError ( FIRSTCTL_E_ODBCERROR,
                ((CDBException*)e) -> m_strStateNativeOrigin, 0 );
        }
        else if ( e -> IsKindOf(RUNTIME_CLASS(CMemoryException)) )
        {
            sc = CTL_E_OUTOFMEMORY;
            uStr = IDS_MEMORYERROR;
        }
        else
        {
            sc = CTL_E_ILLEGALFUNCTIONCALL;
            uStr = IDS_UNEXPECTEDEXCEPTION;
        }
        DoError ( sc, uStr, 0 );
    }
    END_CATCH

    if ( m_bIsValid == FALSE )
    {
        CheckSCode ( m_SCode );
    }
    m_bInDispatch = FALSE;
    return TRUE;
}

long CFirstCtrl::BatchLoad ( LPCTSTR FileName )
{
    CStdioFile cfInput;
```

(continued)

```
long lEntries = OL;

m_bInDispatch = TRUE;

TRY
{
    CheckDatabase();
    if ( m_rsTable -> CanAppend() == FALSE )
    {
        TRACE ( _T ( "Database is read-only\n" ) );
        return FALSE;
    }

        // Don't allow filename to be NULL or empty.
    if ( FileName == 0 || *FileName == 0 )
    {
        THROW ( new CFirstException (
            CFirstException::badParameters ) );
    }

    if ( cfInput.Open ( FileName,
        CFile::typeText | CFile::modeRead ) == TRUE )
    {
        lEntries = DoBatchLoad ( &cfInput );
        cfInput.Close();
    }
    else
    {
        TRACE ( _T ( "Failed to open input file %s\n" ),
            FileName );
        THROW ( new CFirstException (
            CFirstException::noInputFile ) );
    }

    if ( lEntries )
    {
        if ( m_bIsValid == FALSE )
        {
            CheckSCode ( m_SCode );
        }
    }
}
CATCH ( CFirstException, e )
{
```

(continued)

(continued)

```
            UINT uStr;
            SCODE sc = e -> GetErrorString ( uStr );
            DoError ( sc, uStr, 0 );
        }
        AND_CATCH ( CFileException, e )
        {
            UINT uStr;
            SCODE sc = GetFileExceptionString ( e, uStr );
            DoError ( sc, uStr, 0 );
        }
        AND_CATCH ( CMemoryException, e )
        {
            DoError ( CTL_E_OUTOFMEMORY, IDS_MEMORYERROR, 0 );
        }
        AND_CATCH ( CDBException, e )
        {
            DoError ( FIRSTCTL_E_ODBCERROR,
                e -> m_strStateNativeOrigin, 0 );
        }
        END_CATCH

    m_bInDispatch = FALSE;
    return lEntries;
}

// Throws CFirstException, CDBException, CFileException,
//   and CMemoryException.
BOOL CFirstCtrl::FindEntry ( long lCode )
{
    CheckDatabase();

    m_rsTable -> m_SCodeParam = lCode;
    if ( m_rsTable -> Requery() == FALSE )
    {
        THROW ( new CFirstException (
            CFirstException::queryFailed ) );
    }
    return !m_rsTable -> IsBOF();
}

// Can throw CFirstException, CMemoryException, CDBException,
//   and CFileException.
void CFirstCtrl::GetInfo()
{
```

(continued)

```
        CheckDatabase();
        m_csSymbol = m_rsTable -> m_Symbol;
        m_csMessage = m_rsTable -> m_Message;
}


// Does no trapping itself, so can throw anything thrown by
//    functions it calls.
// These include CFirstException, CFileException, and CMemoryException.
long CFirstCtrl::DoBatchLoad ( CStdioFile *cfIn )
{
    long lEntries = 0L;

    CString csLine, csMsg, csSymbol;
    while ( GetNextDefineLine ( cfIn, &csLine, &csMsg ) )
    {
        long lCode = GetTheCode ( &csLine, &csSymbol );
        if ( FindEntry ( lCode ) )
        {
            TRACE1 ( _T (
                "SCODE %08X already in database - ignored\n" ),
                lCode );
        }
        else
        {
            m_rsTable -> AddNew();
            m_rsTable -> m_SCODE = lCode;
            m_rsTable -> m_Symbol = csSymbol;
            m_rsTable -> m_Message = csMsg;
            m_rsTable -> Update();
            ++lEntries;
        }
    }
    return lEntries;
}


// Again, passes any exceptions up to its caller. (It can pass at
//    least CFirstException, CFileException, and CMemoryException.)
BOOL CFirstCtrl::GetNextDefineLine ( CStdioFile *cfFile,
    CString *csLine, CString *csMessage )
{
    _TCHAR szBuf [ 256 ];
    CString csCompare;
    BOOL bFound = FALSE;
    LPTSTR lpszCnt;

    do
```

(continued)

(continued)

```
{
    lpszCnt = cfFile -> ReadString ( szBuf, 255 );
    if ( lpszCnt == NULL )
    {
        break;
    }
    csCompare = szBuf;
    bFound = ( csCompare.Find ( _T ( "// MessageText:" ) )
        != -1 );
}
while ( bFound == FALSE );
if ( bFound )
{
        // Discard the blank comment line.
    cfFile -> ReadString ( szBuf, 255 );
        // Get the message line(s).
    csMessage -> Empty ( );
    do
    {
        cfFile -> ReadString ( szBuf, 255 );
        if ( szBuf [ 3 ] )
        {
                // If this isn't the first line, add a space.
            if ( ! csMessage -> IsEmpty() )
            {
                *csMessage += _T ( " " );
            }
            szBuf [ _tcslen ( szBuf ) - 1 ] = TCHAR ( 0 );
            *csMessage += szBuf + 4;
        }
    }
    while ( szBuf [ 3 ] );

        // Get the code line.
    lpszCnt = cfFile -> ReadString ( szBuf, 255 );

        // If the code line is blank, the file's in the wrong
        //    format.
    if ( lpszCnt == NULL )
    {
        TRACE ( _T (
        "The file given to BatchLoad is in the wrong format\n"
        ) );
```

(continued)

```
            THROW ( new CFirstException (
                CFirstException::badCodesFile ) );
        }
        *csLine = szBuf;
        return TRUE;
    }
    return FALSE;
}


long CFirstCtrl::GetTheCode ( CString *csLine, CString *csSymbol )
{
        // If #define doesn't occur or is not at the start of the
        //   line, the file wasn't created with MC.
    if ( csLine -> Find ( _T ( "#define" ) ) )
    {
        TRACE ( _T (
            "#define line doesn't start with exactly '#define'\n" )
            );
        THROW ( new CFirstException (
            CFirstException::badCodesFile ) );
    }
        // Skip '#define'.
    int i = 7;

        // Skip white space.
    while ( ( csLine -> GetLength ( ) > i ) &&
        ( _istspace ( csLine -> GetAt ( i ) ) ) )
    {
        ++i;
    }
    if ( csLine -> GetLength ( ) <= i )
    {
        TRACE ( _T ( "#define line is only '#define'\n" ) );
        THROW ( new CFirstException (
            CFirstException::badCodesFile ) );
    }

        // Collect symbol.
    csSymbol -> Empty ( );
    while ( ( csLine -> GetLength ( ) > i ) &&
        ! ( _istspace ( csLine -> GetAt ( i ) ) ) )
    {
        *csSymbol += csLine -> GetAt ( i );
        ++i;
    }
```

(continued)

(continued)

```
    if ( csLine -> GetLength ( ) <= i )
    {
        TRACE ( _T ( "#define line is only '#define SYMBOL'\n" ) );
        THROW ( new CFirstException (
            CFirstException::badCodesFile ) );
    }

        // Skip white space.
    while ( ( csLine -> GetLength ( ) > i ) &&
        ( _istspace ( csLine -> GetAt ( i ) ) ) )
    {
        ++i;
    }
    if ( csLine -> GetLength ( ) <= i )
    {
        TRACE ( _T ( "#define line is only '#define SYMBOL'\n" ) );
        THROW ( new CFirstException (
            CFirstException::badCodesFile ) );
    }

        // Collect number.
    CString csNumber;
    csNumber = csLine -> Mid ( i );
        // We can't easily report errors that happen here.
    return _tcstoul ( csNumber, NULL, 0 );
}

void CFirstCtrl::OnFreezeEvents ( BOOL bFreeze )
{
    m_nEventsFrozen += ( bFreeze ? 1 : -1 );
}

// Throws no exceptions
BOOL CFirstCtrl::CheckSCode ( long nNewValue )
{
    CString csLine;

    m_csMessage.Empty();        // Prepare string properties.
    m_csSymbol.Empty();
    m_bIsValid = FALSE;         // Assume invalid unless
                                //    proven otherwise.

    TRY
```

(continued)

```
    {
        if ( FindEntry ( nNewValue ) )     // Valid?
        {
            m_bIsValid = TRUE;
            GetInfo();
            csLine = m_csSymbol + _T ( ": " ) +
                m_csMessage;    // Build caption.
        }
        else
        {
            csLine.LoadString ( IDS_NOVALID_SCODE );
        }
        SetText ( csLine );
    }
    CATCH ( CFirstException, e )
    {
        UINT uStr;
        SCODE sc = e -> GetErrorString ( uStr );
        DoError ( sc, uStr, 0 );
    }
    AND_CATCH ( CFileException, e )
    {
        UINT uStr;
        SCODE sc = GetFileExceptionString ( e, uStr );
        DoError ( sc, uStr, 0 );
    }
    AND_CATCH ( CDBException, e )
    {
        DoError ( FIRSTCTL_E_ODBCERROR, e -> m_strStateNativeOrigin,
            0 );
    }
    AND_CATCH ( CMemoryException, e )
    {
        DoError ( CTL_E_OUTOFMEMORY, IDS_MEMORYERROR, 0 );
    }
    END_CATCH
    return m_bIsValid;
}

// If any exceptions are thrown here, we'll probably abort!
void CFirstCtrl::DoError ( SCODE scode, UINT uDescription,
    UINT helpid )
{
```

(continued)

(continued)

```
    CString csDescription;
    csDescription.LoadString ( uDescription );
    DoError ( scode, csDescription, helpid );
}

void CFirstCtrl::DoError ( SCODE scode, CString& strDescription,
    UINT helpid )
{
    if ( m_bInDispatch )
    {
        m_bInDispatch = FALSE;            // Reset it now.
        ThrowError ( scode, strDescription, helpid );
    }
    else
    {
        if ( m_nEventsFrozen == 0 )
        {
            FireError ( scode, strDescription, helpid );
        }
    }
}

SCODE CFirstCtrl::GetFileExceptionString ( CFileException *cfEx,
    UINT& uStr ) const
{
    SCODE sc = S_OK;
    uStr = IDS_FILEEXCEPTIONBASE + cfEx -> m_cause;
    switch ( cfEx -> m_cause )
    {
        case CFileException::generic:
            sc = CTL_E_ILLEGALFUNCTIONCALL;
            break;

        case CFileException::fileNotFound:
            sc = CTL_E_FILENOTFOUND;
            break;

        case CFileException::badPath:
            sc = CTL_E_PATHFILEACCESSERROR;
            break;

        case CFileException::tooManyOpenFiles:
            sc = CTL_E_TOOMANYFILES;
```

(continued)

```
            break;

        case CFileException::invalidFile:
            sc = CTL_E_BADFILENAMEORNUMBER;
            break;

        case CFileException::directoryFull:
        case CFileException::diskFull:
            sc = CTL_E_DISKFULL;
            break;

        case CFileException::badSeek:
        case CFileException::hardIO:
            sc = CTL_E_DEVICEIOERROR;
            break;

        case CFileException::accessDenied:
        case CFileException::removeCurrentDir:
        case CFileException::sharingViolation:
        case CFileException::lockViolation:
            sc = CTL_E_PERMISSIONDENIED;
            break;

        case CFileException::endOfFile:
            sc = CTL_E_BADRECORDLENGTH;
            break;

        default:
            sc = CTL_E_ILLEGALFUNCTIONCALL;
            uStr = IDS_UNKNOWNEXCEPTIONCAUSE;
            break;
    }
    return sc;
}

void CFirstCtrl::Reset()
{
    m_bInDispatch = TRUE;
    OnResetState();
    m_bInDispatch = FALSE;
}

void CFirstCtrl::CheckDatabase()
{
```

(continued)

```
if ( m_rsTable == 0 )
{
    THROW ( new CFirstException ( CFirstException::noRecordSet )
        );
}
if ( ! m_rsTable -> IsOpen() )
{
    THROW ( new CFirstException ( CFirstException::dbClosed ) );
}
}
```

Looking at the changes I've made to the control implementation file, you'll notice that in general it's become a whole lot simpler. The first change is in the control constructor. Here, many of the variables that were initialized in the old file-based version are no longer required, so I've deleted all references to them and removed them from the class definition. I do have a new variable, though, *m_rsTable*, which is a pointer to a *CDbSet* object. This will contain a pointer to the one recordset object the control uses. This object is created a few lines down, inside the *TRY* block. The first thing I do is use *new* to create the object, and then I set the parameter variable inside it to zero. Before the recordset can be used, it needs to be opened, so I called its *Open* member function with two parameters. The first parameter to *Open* tells the database what sort of open this should be. This first parameter, *CRecordset::snapshot*, is a view of the database taken at the time the snapshot is created; it does not reflect other people's edits. As there will be no one else using this database at the same time, that's fine. If you want to, you can change this first parameter to *CRecordset::dynaset*, which will reflect other people's edits. The second parameter to *Open* is the SQL statement that I want to be used as the query through which the recordset fills itself with records. The SQL statement, SELECT * FROM SCODES WHERE SCODE=?, is stored in the resource file. If you don't speak SQL, this means "get all columns from all records in the SCODES table where the value of the SCODE column is ?" The "?" isn't valid SQL and is replaced by the value of the first (and, in this case, only) parameter in the recordset. So, with the value of zero for the parameter, the statement becomes "SELECT * FROM SCODES WHERE SCODE=0." I've made the SCODE column the primary key in the database; this means that there can only be one record (row) matching each discrete value of SCODE. Therefore, only one row is ever returned.

If the *Open* call fails, I throw an exception. This and any other exceptions are caught in the *CATCH* block, which is much the same as the previous version except that it now deals with *CDBException* errors (the MFC exception class that deals specifically with database problems) and has been optimized somewhat over the last version. Notice that I use the *m_strStateNativeOrigin* member variable of the

CDBException for the error's meaningful string. This is a string provided by ODBC to the MFC library, and it isn't necessarily user friendly!

The control's destructor checks whether the recordset variable has been allocated, and deletes it if it has. Before this deletion, it also checks to see whether it is open — and closes it if it is.

DoPropExchange changes very slightly, by the removal of the assignment of *FALSE* to *m_bInDispatch*, for reasons that are explained in "Resetting the Control," beginning on page 314.

Nothing else is changed until you get to *Add*. Here, the *Add* method calls *FindEntry* as before, and returns if the SCODE being added is already in the database. It also checks the parameters it is passed as before. After that, things are different. It first checks to see whether the recordset object will accept "appends" (that is, new rows); if not, it returns. Notice that I access the *m_rsTable* variable without seemingly determining whether the object it points to is valid. This is in fact performed by *FindEntry*, which I explain shortly.

If the recordset object is able to accept appended data, I call its *AddNew* method, which prepares it to accept a new record's worth of data. Now I set up the values for each of the three fields in the record using the values passed to *Add*, and then I call *Update*. This causes the data to be written to the database, which is much easier than seeking through two files and writing offsets and the like!

At the end, if the new entry has been added successfully and the current SCODE value is marked as invalid, I call *CheckSCode* to see whether the new entry happens to match the current SCODE.

BatchLoad has also changed in similar ways. It calls a new member function, *CheckDatabase*, which checks whether *m_rsTable* is valid and whether the object it points to is currently open. If either of these is not true, it throws a *CFirstException* exception. If *CheckDatabase* returns, *BatchLoad* checks that the database can be appended to and tries to open the input file for read access as a text file. If this succeeds, it calls *DoBatchLoad* as before. As does *Add*, *BatchLoad* calls *CheckSCode* at the end if it successfully adds at least one record to the database and the current SCODE value is invalid.

FindEntry is now very simple and can throw exceptions. It checks *m_rsTable* using *CheckDatabase* and then sets the recordset parameter to the value of the SCODE it's trying to verify. It then calls the recordset's *Requery* method, which exercises the SQL statement against the database and returns all records that match. In this case, either zero records or one record is returned. The *IsBOF* member function checks to see whether the recordset is at the "beginning of file" after the requery; if it is, no records were returned, so the SCODE is not in the database. Otherwise, the recordset now holds the only matching record as its current record, and the values can be retrieved through the bound variables.

This is precisely what *GetInfo* does, retrieving the symbol and message values into class member variables inside the control class. It checks the database first through *CheckDatabase*, an action that isn't strictly necessary because the only code paths to *GetInfo* have already ensured that the database is valid. (I regard this, however, as good defensive programming style. It's your choice.) As a result of this, it can throw a variety of exceptions.

DoBatchLoad is vastly simpler than its earlier incarnation, the *GetNextDefineLine* loop now simply using an *AddNew*/set fields/*Update* sequence to write the values from the input file to the database. *GetNextDefineLine* and *GetTheCode* have not changed, as they both act on the input file, not the database. *OnFreezeEvents* has also not changed, while *OnEventAdvise* has gone altogether because there is no need to fire the FilesCreated event. I've therefore also taken the step of removing this event (using ClassWizard) from the control's event map.

CheckSCode changes slightly to handle *CDBExceptions*. Its reliance on higher-level functions such as *FindEntry* insulates it from the change in the control's data storage/retrieval mechanism (from a hacked-up file-based system to a real database via ODBC). The new *CheckDatabase* member function throws an exception if the *m_rsTable* variable holds zero (which means that the allocation failed in the constructor) and also if the pointer is valid but points to a recordset object that is not open. An open failure would most likely indicate that the data source is not installed properly in ODBC or that the database file cannot be found.

Oh, one difficult-to-see but vital change: as the control now uses ODBC classes, it must include the relevant header file, AFXDB.H, which I've thrown into STDAFX.H so that it becomes part of the precompiled header.

NOTE I've added a new set of cause values to *CFirstException*, which you'll see in FIRSTEX.H and FIRSTEX.CPP for this chapter. However, although many of the old values are no longer used, I've left them in the file. I've also left the message strings for these exception causes in the control's resource file. You don't actually need to, but you might like to make the control smaller by removing these strings.

Resetting the Control

Notice also in Listing 10-4 that I've added a new method, *Reset*, and that it calls *OnResetState*. I've also surrounded that call with assignments of *TRUE* and *FALSE* to *m_bInDispatch*. The control's version of *OnResetState* does nothing more than call the base class's version, which merely calls *DoPropExchange* to reset all the property values to the defaults (either from the storage from which the control was created or, if there is none, to each property's default value). This also explains the removal of the assignment to *m_bInDispatch* from *DoPropExchange*. In earlier versions, this function would only get called outside a property or method invocation, meaning that any exceptions it encountered would have to be reflected as events. Now it can be called as a result of a method, *Reset*, so it needed to change.

WARNING   Resetting the control is an important action that can occur at various times. You need to be very careful to reset any class member variables, globals, and so forth during this call so that the control will be in a defined and stable state. Failure to do so could cause the control to crash later if one variable is out of sync with another.

CONTROL DEBUGGING

How do you debug an OLE control? EXE-based OLE servers are notoriously difficult to debug in the 16-bit world, although a lot has been done to the 32-bit debugger to make this a more straightforward process on Windows NT and Windows 95 for 32-bit servers. Luckily, OLE controls are (almost always) implemented as in-process servers, which means that they're DLLs and share the same process space as the controller containing them. This makes debugging much easier.

The first step is to specify the executable that will be run for debug sessions. In most cases, this will be Test Container, as it allows you to try out most of the features of your control and catch any errors early. So, to specify Test Container as the executable, choose Debug from the Options menu and enter the full path to it in the Debug dialog box in Visual C++ version 1.5x, or choose Settings from the Project menu in Project...Settings...Debug in Visual C++ version 2.x. The full path includes the extension, so be sure you enter exactly that — for example, C:\MSVC20\CDK32\BIN\TSTCON32.EXE. After you've done this, clicking the Go button on the toolbar (or choosing Go on the debug menu) will execute Test Container. All versions of Visual C++ will complain that Test Container contains no debugging information and will ask whether you want to continue? The answer is "yes"! To see messages produced from *TRACE* output, you also need to ensure that trace output is on — which you accomplish by running the MFC Trace Options program in the Visual C++ program group. You actually need to do this <u>before</u> you click Go. This will cause any *TRACE* output generated to go to the Output window.

To actually debug your control, you now need to insert it into the copy of Test Container that the debugger has invoked for you. You can set breakpoints in the control before or after it's loaded into Test Container, so if you want to debug the constructor, you'll most likely want to set breakpoints in it before you load. If you're debugging a method, on the other hand, you might want to set it after it's been loaded.

Now, whenever you do something with your control that causes it to hit one of the breakpoints you've set, or you hit an error that causes the debugger to stop execution (such as a failed *ASSERT*), your code will stop executing and the debugger will display the current line. At this point you can examine local variables, look at memory, change variables, and do any of the other things you're likely to do during a debugging session.

Occasionally, you'll step into a CDK or MFC source file; when this occurs, you might be asked (particularly by the 16-bit compiler, which is less intelligent about these things) for the path in which the source file can be found.

CONTROL VERSIONING

Let's imagine you've developed a control — say, the First control. At present, it has very few persistent properties, only one that is really its own, the *SCode* property value. Suppose that you sell lots of copies of this control (vivid imagination required).

Now, time passes and you realize that you could make a heap more money and make your control more useful by doing x, y, and z. It doesn't matter what those x, y, and z things are (although if you ever find out, please tell me) — all that matters is that this new version of the control has an extra property, *NewProp*.

So, you ship out this new version of the control to all your users and you expect it to work plug-compatibly with the earlier release: that is, users can simply replace the old control file with the new one, and every program written against the old control still works. One question that ought to come to mind about now is: just how does the new control manage to read (and possibly write) property values saved by the old control version and yet still manage to set its new property to an appropriate value?

The key is in *DoPropExchange*. If you examine the First control, you'll notice that I call *ExchangeVersion* inside of *DoPropExchange* and then validate the restored value of the *SCode* property if this invocation of *DoPropExchange* is in response to a "load properties" request. The same logic applies to version-checking. Basically, *ExchangeVersion* saves away (or restores) the control's version number in the properties image. When it restores the version number, the restored version number is of course relating to the saved properties rather than to the control that happens to be running. Therefore, a version 2.0 control can detect that it is loading version 1.0 properties and set up any new-to-version 2.0 properties to default values. When saving properties, you get to choose whether to save version 1.0 properties or version 2.0 properties. Whichever version you decide to save, you need to ensure that you tell *ExchangeVersion* to save the correct version number (again, the one that pertains to the saved properties, not necessarily the same as the version number of the control currently running). When a control is created with ControlWizard, two global variables are created and initialized to hold the major and minor version numbers. These should be altered if the control version changes and then used as reference values during *DoPropExchange*.

So, to change a hypothetical version 2.0 of the First control's *DoPropExchange* function so that it correctly handles version 1.0 properties, you need to do the following:

```
void CFirstCtrl::DoPropExchange(CPropExchange* pPX)
{
    ExchangeVersion(pPX, MAKELONG(_wVerMinor, _wVerMajor));
    COleControl::DoPropExchange(pPX);

    PX_Long ( pPX, _T ( "SCode" ), m_SCode, 0L );
    if ( pPX -> IsLoading ( ) )
    {
        ReallySetSCode ( m_SCode );
    }
        // Version 2.0 or greater?
    if ( pPX -> GetVersion() >= MAKELONG( 0, 2))
    {
        PX_Long ( pPX, _T ( "NewProp" ), 1234L );
    }
}
```

This checks the version number of the loaded property values and loads the new property, *NewProp*, if that version is 2.0 or greater.

It is also possible to drop properties between versions, so, for example, a version 3.0 of the control would no longer store the *NewProp* property. Although Microsoft recommends that controls do <u>not</u> drop properties between versions (rather, it recommends that you save and load them anyway, ignoring the values in versions of the control that no longer use them), this is "just software" and therefore anything can be done.

USING HELP FILES IN CONTROLS

Although the last topic of this chapter won't take up a lot of space, it is something that you should consider as an important ease-of-use and/or sales helper for your controls: the provision of help. Help can be used in a control in a number of situations; an obvious one is the provision of a help topic and Help file name when an error occurs. If your control is at all complex to use, however, it would be nice if you ensured that the user of the control could get user-oriented help (as opposed to programmer-oriented help) on its operation. This might mean general help topics, in addition to help topics relating to specific dialog box items, or to properties, methods, and events provided by the control.

Use of help in a control is pretty straightforward. When you choose Context Sensitive Help in ControlWizard, nothing very revolutionary is added to your control. The only manifestations you will see are a new HLP subdirectory containing a very basic Help file in RTF (rich text format, the prescribed "source code" for Help files), an HPJ file, and a MAKEHELP batch file. The HPJ file is a help compiler project file, which directs the operation of the Windows help compiler (HC31.EXE). MAKE-HELP.BAT is a batch file, which converts resource IDs used by your control into an include file for the help compiler (using MAKEHM.EXE, a help-maintenance tool supplied with Visual C++) and then runs the help compiler. You need to add hooks in suitable locations to actually cause help to be invoked.

NOTE Windows 95 and Windows NT versions 3.51 and later use a more modern, more functional version of help than does Windows 3.1, with a new Windows-based help compiler, HCW.EXE. However, everything created with HC31 is compatible with this new help system, even though it can't take advantage of some of the new features. If you want to use new help features, you'll need to convert the help system provided by ControlWizard to one that uses HCW.

An obvious hook to add is the one to react to the pressing of the F1 key. To add such a hook, use ClassWizard to add a handler to your main control window (the one derived from *COleControl*) for *WM_KEYDOWN*, if you don't already have one. Also add a similar handler to any other window class you have in your control that you want to recognize F1. The body of the handler should examine the keycode and, if it is F1 that is pressed, it should call *CWinApp::WinHelp*. A typical example is:

```
void CConvolveCtrl::OnKeyDown(UINT nChar, UINT nRepCnt, UINT nFlags)
{
    if ( nChar == VK_F1 )
    {
        AfxGetApp() -> WinHelp ( 0L, HELP_CONTENTS );
    }
    else
    {
        COleControl::OnKeyDown(nChar, nRepCnt, nFlags);
    }
}
```

AfxGetApp returns a pointer to the control's *CWinApp*-derived object, and this example calls its *WinHelp* member function to display the help file's contents page. You can get a whole lot more complex than this if you choose, setting up context-sensitive help so that a press of Shift-F1 puts the control in a special mode that causes it to display help about a specific screen item when that item is clicked on. If you want to see an example of the code required to do that, create a standard AppWizard application with context-sensitive help.

The filename of the control's help file is stored in the application object's *m_pszHelpFilePath* member variable, and by default it is set to the same name and location as the control itself, but the extension is changed to HLP.

FYI Help can also be provided for property pages. Property pages, however, are the subject of the next chapter, so I'd be jumping the gun somewhat if I told you how to set up help for property pages before I'd told you how to use property pages! Therefore, the next chapter also contains a small section on help in property pages.

Chapter 11

Property Pages

You're over halfway through the book, and you might be wondering why I still haven't given you any real hints on how to get your controls to present their own user interface for property access. Although property pages are critically important to integrating your control with the rest of a system, and also to its ease of use, I don't see them as fundamentally difficult beasts or as things that need to be developed as the main body of a control develops. I almost always add my property pages at the end of a project. Is this bad practice? Perhaps, but consider this before deciding....

Every control you've created with the CDK has a property page, unless you've deliberately removed it. If you load up any control you've created thus far into Test Container and invoke the Properties OLE verb, you'll see the default property page that ControlWizard creates for every control. It's a completely blank property sheet, titled "General" in a standard tabbed dialog.

NOTE   You can invoke the Properties OLE verb in many ways. The easiest way is to move the mouse over the border of the control until it becomes only a four-way pointer and then right-click. A context menu will appear with one item: Properties. Choose it.

Now's the time to start doing things with that page so that it becomes a proper part of your control.

WHAT ARE PROPERTY PAGES?

The simple answer to this question is that a "property page" is a user interface defined by an OLE control for directly manipulating the control's properties without requiring any intervention from the control's container.

Here's a more complicated answer, which hints at why property pages are important. Every OLE control is useful only inside a container. Any container that is aware of OLE controls is almost certain to provide a way to access each control's property values and set them. In most containers, this capability is provided at design-time. Some containers might also allow a similar facility at runtime (via programmatic access). The mechanism each container provides for this property access is likely to be reasonably container-specific, as there are no guidelines set down. It's very unclear that guidelines would help; because containers are going to be different, they're going to provide different user-interface paradigms — and it rarely makes sense to constrain people's creativity by telling them that something must be done a certain way. That assumes, of course, that any person or organization has the power to dictate such things. (I doubt if any has or wants to.)

Some controls, however, will require their properties to be viewable and settable at runtime without the need for programmatic access. Also, controls will over time begin appearing as operating system elements, integrated with system components in such a way that they need to provide a user-interface for property access. The move to a new user-interface mechanism with Windows 95 and with later versions of Windows NT has already brought about what is pretty much a standard for an object's property pages, regardless of the type of that object. In the new environments, every object is supposed to have a set of property pages that the user can display and manipulate by right-clicking the mouse. The property-page mechanism has therefore become a recognized attribute of OLE controls. No dictate states that your control must have a set of property pages, but if yours doesn't, it will be one of the few without them. The CDK makes it so easy to add property pages to your control that you don't need to expend that much effort in getting your control to supply its set of property pages.

"Property pages" as defined by the current user-interface paradigm, are sets of related dialogs that appear as a number of "pages" in a tabbed dialog box. Figure 11-1 shows a typical set of property pages — in fact, it shows the set of property pages you're going to implement for the First control as you progress through this chapter. (The source code in this chapter can be found on the companion CD-ROM in the \OLECTRLS\CHAP11\FIRST directory.)

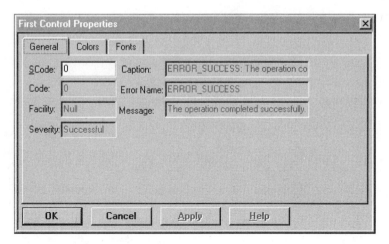

Figure 11-1. *The First control's property pages.*

Property pages are more than merely a set of dialog box pages. Each one is an OLE object in its own right and supports interfaces for its creation and for setting the focus to a specific control on a specific page, for example. The "system" (currently, this means the OLE Controls runtime DLLs, but one day it's likely that this really will mean the operating system) implements some standard property pages such as those for color, font, and picture objects.

The Windows 95 user-interface style guidelines contain a set of recommended sizes (two, at present) for property pages, and the CDK will, in debug builds, issue a warning message box if a request is made to display a property page that is not one of these standard sizes. The message is intended to be informative rather than dictatorial, as there will be instances when a specific control really needs to have a property page of nonstandard size.

When you create a control using the CDK's ControlWizard, it creates a default, blank property page for you. You can add controls to this page, add new pages, and tie the controls on each page to specific properties exposed by the control. You can even use the MFC library's standard DDX and DDV routines to transfer data between the pages and member variables and to validate that the entered values fall within specific ranges (See Appendix A for more details on MFC mechanisms such as DDX and DDV.) The CDK's property-page functionality is wrapped in a class, *COlePropertyPage*, from which ControlWizard and ClassWizard derive specific classes to wrap your control's property pages.

HOW TO USE PROPERTY PAGES

Property pages are, on the face of it, rather easy to implement and use. You seldom need more intelligence in a property page than you'd have in a standard dialog box. To demonstrate the techniques required, I'm going to take the First control example from the previous chapter and modify its property page to show the value of the *SCode* property and allow it to be altered.

The first step in adding a field to a property page is deciding exactly what sort of control the property page should use to represent the property. Sometimes it's obvious: a check box for a Boolean property value or an edit box for the caption. Sometimes it's not so easy to decide: should you display a color-based property as a hexadecimal number or as a signed decimal number or as a set of colored pushbuttons? (This is why stock implementations of color property pages exist!)

For the *SCode*, the most logical representation is as an edit box, but the contents must be numeric. The DDX routine for long integers does that for you, translating between the value typed and the long integer value you want to store. If you happen to want range checking (which you don't in this case), you can use the MFC library's DDV routines to do that. Here's the entire process for adding the *SCode* property to the property page:

1. Using the resource editor (or AppStudio, if you're doing a 16-bit version), edit the dialog resource called *IDD_PROPPAGE_FIRST* by adding to it a label (static text) with *&SCode:* as the text. (The *&* signifies the mnemonic character in dialog boxes, so it is removed at display-time and causes the *S* in *SCode* to be underlined.)

2. By the side of this label, add an edit box.

3. Invoke ClassWizard by pressing Ctrl+W. Switch to the Member Variables tab and ensure that *CFirstPropPage* is the selected class.

4. You should see an entry in the list box for a control with an ID of *IDC_EDIT1*. This is the newly entered edit box. Click the Add Variable button.

5. Enter a name for the variable, such as *m_SCode*.

6. Be sure that the Category drop-down list box says *Value*, and then choose *long* as the variable's type.

7. Type in *SCode* as the OLE Property Name.

8. Close the Add Member Variable dialog box and the ClassWizard dialog box by clicking the OK button in each.

9. Build the control.

Not a lot of programming effort there! Steps 3 and 4 can be combined into one by holding down the Control key while double-clicking on the edit box in the dialog editor, which takes you straight to ClassWizard's Add Member Variable dialog box for the class and dialog item in question. Now, if you run the control in Test Container and invoke the property page (for example, by moving the cursor to the control's edge until the cursor changes to a four-way pointer <u>without</u> an arrow, right-clicking, and selecting Properties from the shortcut menu), you should see something similar to the property page shown in Figure 11-2.

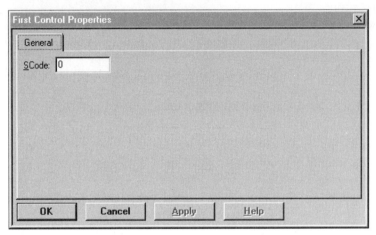

Figure 11-2. *The first incarnation of the First control's property page.*

You can enter new *SCode* values and click OK to dismiss the property page, and the control will update itself to reflect the new *SCode* value.

NOTE Because the property page uses the control's standard mechanism (OLE Automation) to update the property, setting the property to an invalid *SCode* value will still cause the *InvalidSCode* event to be fired. Property pages don't have magic access to the control — they use the same mechanisms as any other tool would. This is why stock property pages can be added to arbitrary controls.

You will see another button on the property page — the Apply button. This button is grayed out (that is, it's unavailable) until at least one property value is changed on a page. After the Apply button is enabled, clicking it allows you to set the control's properties to the currently set values in the property page(s) — but without dismissing the Properties dialog box.

DESIGNING EFFECTIVE PROPERTY PAGES

This section of the chapter is where irony takes over: I'm going to advise you on user interface-design. As you can tell from my efforts so far, this advice is probably best taken with a large pinch of salt. Of course, a number of basic concepts and general principles apply to user-interface design, and you can learn about these from any textbook on graphical user interface (GUI) design or human-computer interface (HCI) techniques. All I'm looking at here here is what works and what doesn't work for a control's property pages.

First and foremost in my mind is the "dialog from hell" — the set of property pages displayed by a control that has so many pages that the user is overwhelmed and doesn't know where to look to set a particular property. There are controls on the market now that in my opinion exhibit this problem (and one of those is a Microsoft-created control).

So the the solution here is to adhere to the golden rule of user-interface design (and much else in life, it seems): <u>keep</u> it <u>simple</u>. Really, an adage as hackneyed as this remains so fundamentally important because it reflects a user's needs when interacting with a computer.

Do you need to display all the control's properties on the property sheet? This is a question that only you, as the control's designer, can really answer. Some of the properties exposed by your control might be sufficiently obscure for you to discount them immediately. Another interesting possibility occurs when you can combine property values held by the control into one composite display value. This doesn't happen too often, but it did apply in the case of the life-insurance control I have mentioned from time to time. This control can choose to expose three properties pertaining to a customer's name: first name, middle name, and surname. The control's property page, however, can be designed to display the name as one string, by concatenating the three properties. Again, this sort of thing should be evaluated on a case-by-case basis, typically evaluating ease of use versus program- mer complexity. I'm told that in conflicts like these, ease of use should always win. I'm a little more pragmatic: make compromises that work and you'll get useful and usable controls — <u>and</u> they'll be maintainable in the future! You also need to bear in mind who the typical audience for an OLE control's property page might be. Your control, for example, might be used only by programmers, or it might be used only by those familiar with investment banking, or whatever. Therefore, the property page(s) should address the main intended audience rather than some generic user.

Property pages should be one of two defined standard sizes: 250-by-62 or 250-by-110 dialog units. The debug version of the CDK displays a warning in a message box the first time a control's property page is displayed that doesn't conform to these sizes — but takes no other action. In release mode, no message box is displayed. That there are standard sizes does not mean that you are physically constrained to using these sizes, but if you don't, your property page will look different from other property pages displayed by controls as well as different from the standard built-in property pages for color, fonts, and pictures. It's best to try to conform to these sizes if at all possible.

If you use the MFC library's DDV routines to validate the contents of fields within a property page, the routines are invoked only when the OK or Apply button is clicked. Users often find it much more useful to be told of validation errors as they enter data; this can usually be done successfully by checking a field's contents when the focus passes to another field.

If you have implied connections between fields, such as some property values only making sense within the context of others, make this obvious to the user by taking appropriate visual action with the other fields. This might include setting up a new set of allowable values for given fields when another is changed, or graying out a field, and so forth.

Most of these guidelines are little more than applying common sense and are always focused on making the property-page user's life easier. If something doesn't seem right to you when you use a property page, it will almost certainly seem wrong to someone else, so change it.

Displaying Read-Only Properties

The First control has a large set of properties that are read-only — that is, they cannot be set directly by the programmer or user but they are set as a consequence of the value of the *SCode* property. Is there any reason why these properties shouldn't be displayed in the property page too? If, like me, you'd find it useful to see all the property values at once, then there's a good case to add them. It's easy to do, of course. Go through the same steps as you did for adding the *SCode* property in the first place, with the extra step of marking each edit box as read-only and as disabled. This can be done by double-clicking on the edit box, which invokes the Edit Properties dialog box. The *Disabled* flag is set in the General tab of the Edit Properties dialog box, and the *Read-Only* flag is set in the Styles tab. When you add member variables to the dialog to act as holders for the value, you'll need to break with intuition for a while and ensure that you use only types supported by OLE Automation. This means, for example, that the *Code* property should be set as an *int* rather than as the *UINT* it really is. (In an ideal world, type coercion would occur and you would be able to use the real type. If you try this, however, you'll find that an exception is thrown when you display the page.)

By setting the dialog control to read-only in this way, the property will be displayed in the property page but cannot be altered. Therefore, in this case the property-page user interface becomes a means of displaying a relatively large number of values in one fell swoop. Figure 11-3 shows the property page as I designed it. (The implication here is that you might like to redesign it.)

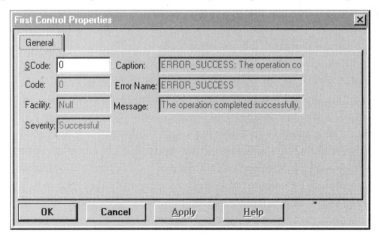

Figure 11-3.   *The First control's property page with read-only properties added.*

Adding Extra Property Pages

If your control has a number of properties, it might make sense to use more than one property page to display them. This certainly makes sense in the case of property types covered by the stock property pages (colors, fonts, and pictures, discussed in detail in the next section, "Adding Stock Property Pages"), and it also makes sense if you have too many controls to fit on one page. In all cases, though, you should aim to keep the number of pages to a minimum, keep the pages themselves uncluttered, and keep related properties on the same page. (Managing to meet all three guidelines can be quite a challenge!)

To add a new page, you need to add a new dialog and then create a new class to wrap that dialog. Here are the steps:

1. Using the dialog editor, create a new dialog and name it. Name it something like *IDD_PROPPGE2_FIRST*.

2. Delete the OK and Cancel buttons (so kindly placed on the dialog) by selecting each control and pressing the Delete key.

3. Open the Dialog Properties dialog box by right-clicking the property page and choosing Properties from the shortcut menu. Set the page's properties on the Styles tab as follows: Child, no border, and no other options selected. (All check boxes displayed in this tab should be clear or grayed out, especially Titlebar and Visible.)

4. Set the size of the dialog as appropriate; if you want to use a standard property-page size, be sure it conforms to one of the two allowed sizes.

5. Invoke ClassWizard by pressing Ctrl+W.

6. You'll see the MFC ClassWizard Add Class dialog box. Select a class name (for example, *CMyPage2*), and ensure that its class type is *COleProperty-Page*.

7. Click Create Class in the Add Class dialog box, and then click OK in the MFC ClassWizard dialog box.

8. Locate the invocation of the *BEGIN_PROPPAGEIDS* macro in the control's main implementation file (for example, FIRSTCTL.CPP for the First control).

9. Increment the last parameter to this macro. (So, if you have two pages now, change the *1* to *2*)

10. Add an entry for the new page below the existing entry (or entries) but before the invocation of *END_PROPPAGEIDS*. Name it something like *PROPPAGEID(CMyPage2::guid)*.

11. Add controls and DDX/DDV routines to this page as appropriate, using ClassWizard.

12. Write some code if you need to for handling special situations.

13. Include the new class's header file in your control implementation file.

14. Create a caption for the property page by creating a new resource string containing the caption (for example, *Page Two* or something equally inventive) and an ID (such as *IDS_PROPPGE2_FIRST_CAPTION*). Go to the property page's constructor and change it so that it passes this caption ID on to its base class constructor, by replacing the *0* parameter to *COlePropertyPage* with the ID you assigned the string. (ControlWizard placed a "to do" comment above the property-page constructor; for real completeness, you should remove this after you've added the string!)

15. Create a name for the new property page as you'd like to see it appear in the registry: for example, the default property page will have been assigned a name like *First Property Page* by ControlWizard; you might want this new page to be named something like *First's Second Property Page*. Add a new string to the resource file, using the text you've chosen and an ID like *IDS_PROPPGE2_FIRST*. (It really doesn't matter what the ID is named, but there's a sort-of convention used by the CDK). Be sure that this string ID is passed to *AfxOleRegisterPropertyPageClass* by

replacing the *0* last parameter in the call to this function inside the property page's class factory's *UpdateRegistry* member function (in the new property-page's source file) with the ID you've chosen. This class factory function will be near the head of the file and will be named something like *CMyPage2::CMyPage2Factory::UpdateRegistry*. (Again, ControlWizard placed a "to do" comment there which should be removed after you've performed the action.)

16. Rebuild the project.

Presto! You now have a new property page.

I don't know if there's a limit to the number of pages you can have, but you ought to bear in mind that there should be a limit as far as the poor user is concerned — so only add a new page when you need to.

Adding Stock Property Pages

The system currently provides three stock property pages — pages that are already implemented and that can be added to your control. The page types provided are for colors, fonts, and pictures. The pages are "intelligent" in that they interrogate your control to learn which properties have the requisite types, and then they allow you to view and set the attributes of those properties. For example, the color property page, when added to the First control, will determine that its *BackColor* and *ForeColor* properties are both of type *OLE_COLOR* and so will allow both of these to be viewed and set.

To add a stock property page to your control, identify the block of code that declares your property pages inside your control's main module. In First, you can find this code in FIRSTCTL.CPP. The block of code looks like this:

```
/////////////////////////////////////////////////////////////////////
// Property pages

// TODO: Add more property pages as needed. Remember to increase
//    the count!
BEGIN_PROPPAGEIDS(CFirstCtrl, 1)
    PROPPAGEID(CFirstPropPage::guid)
END_PROPPAGEIDS(CFirstCtrl)
```

Stock pages can then be added by following these steps:

1. Increment the page count in the invocation of the BEGIN_PROPPAGEIDS macro.

2. Add an entry for the relevant stock property page. The color page, for example, is added by entering the line

```
PROPPAGEID(CLSID_CColorPropPage)
```

immediately after the PROPPAGEID line for the first property page. (The font page uses *CLSID_CFontPropPage*, and the picture property page uses *CLSID_CPicturePropPage*.)

3. Rebuild your control.

One limitation with the current implementation of the stock property pages is that their behavior cannot be altered. For example, if you want to make the font property page display only fixed-pitch fonts, you'll have to write your own font property page. Writing customized stock property pages code is further complicated by the fact that Microsoft does not supply the source code to the stock property pages, so you'll also have to invent the code from scratch.

Stock property pages will automatically read the control's type library and assume responsibility for any property of the appropriate type. So, if you add the color page to the First control, you'll notice that it handles both the *ForeColor* and *BackColor* properties. It does this by putting all the conforming properties into a drop-down list box from which you can select the desired property and view and then edit it.

Adding Help to Property Pages

Adding help to a property page is pretty easy. All you do is call the *COleProperty-Page::SetHelpInfo* member function in your class derived from *COlePropertyPage*. *SetHelpInfo* takes three parameters: the first is a string that will appear in a status bar or as a tooltip if the property frame in which the page is displayed supports it; the second parameter is the name of the property page's Help file; and the third is the help context ID of the topic within the Help file that relates to the property page. Calling this function (and ensuring that the Help file and help topic exist!) causes the Help button on the property page to become enabled; clicking it invokes *WinHelp* with the file and topic selected.

As with any dialog box, it sometimes makes sense to provide context-sensitive help for each control. You'll have to manually write the handlers for this yourself, treating the property page as a standard dialog, trapping F1, and causing the relevant *WinHelp* call to be made.

So far, none of the controls in this book to date have used Help files, but of course they should. It is always acceptable to provide help, and it is often not acceptable not to!

Chapter 12

A Closer Look at the *COleControl* and *COlePropertyPage* Classes

This chapter looks at the two major new classes implemented by the OLE CDK, *COleControl* and *COlePropertyPage*, in a little more depth than I have so far. Up to this point, I've been using the classes and their member functions without giving them too much thought or discussion. Now it's time to review the classes, seeing what member functions they have and what opportunities there are for calling them. I certainly don't want this chapter to end up reading like a reference listing or a copy of the OLE CDK documentation: so if you want reference information, please go to the reference documentation.

BE AWARE In many places throughout this chapter, I discuss implementation specifics and perhaps even show source code from the classes being discussed. Please bear in mind that the details are true only for the version of the CDK with which this book was written, version 1.1 (shipped with Visual C++ version 2.1). It is entirely possible that the mechanics of a particular function will change in later versions of the CDK and/or the MFC library. The code is shown, however, because it demonstrates quite clearly how some complex parts of the OLE control classes have been implemented. The only real caution in all this is that it is a very bad idea to rely on these implementation details!

COLECONTROL

COleControl is, as you know, the class from which all OLE controls created by the OLE CDK are derived. It itself is derived from the MFC library's generic window class, *CWnd*. *CWnd* is a very large class with numerous member functions, and many of these are themselves useful in OLE controls. *COleControl* adds a whole new set of member functions: some of these member functions are designed to be used in place of similar *CWnd* member functions. Why? Because an OLE control's behavior is, in some respects, different from that of a generic window. Others are of course new methods of use only to OLE controls, such as methods to fire events, to read ambient properties, and to interact with the control's container and its control site.

Automation and Properties, Events, and Methods

One of the groups of member functions provided by *COleControl* allows you to interrogate the value of any of a given set of common ambient properties. Each member of this set is named *Ambient???*, where *???* is the name of the ambient property being requested. Each interrogates the control site for the property, returning the provided value if it is supported. If the container doesn't support that ambient property (and also if it doesn't support any ambient properties), each member function returns an appropriate default value. There is also a generic "get ambient property" member function, *GetAmbientProperty*, which can be used to get the values of other ambient properties as well as the values of any nonstandard (that is, container-specific) ambient properties. This function differs from the others in that it doesn't attempt to make up a default value because it can't know beforehand which ambient property you're asking for.

If the container changes the value of one or more ambient properties at a control site, it calls the control through the *IOleControl::OnAmbientPropertyChange* method, passing the dispid of the changed ambient property, or *DISPID_UNKNOWN* (–1) if more than one ambient has changed at the same time. *COleControl* reflects this up to the control author through the virtual function *OnAmbientPropertyChange*. If you want to detect ambient-property changes and perhaps change the way you draw your control, you should override this function in your *COleControl-*derived class.

Another situation relevant to ambient properties occurs when a control is first created. If the control has set the *OLEMISC_SETCLIENTSITEFIRST* bit, it is asking its container to set the client site for the control prior to any persistent state being loaded. A container that does this will therefore also need to make the site's ambient properties available to the control at this time. If you need to know whether a control can rely on ambients at load-time, call *COleControl::WillAmbientsBeValidDuringLoad*. This will return *TRUE* if the container set the control's site early enough, meaning that ambients can be used, and *FALSE* if not. Obviously, if the function returns *FALSE*, you might need to read your persistent state and then later go back and change some property values depending on the values of the site's ambient properties.

Another group of functions is used to fire events. All stock events have associated member functions; so, for example, the Click event has a corresponding *FireClick* member function, which when called causes the control to fire the Click event. In current implementations, all event-firing member functions ultimately call the *FireEvent* member function, which is the generic "fire an event" function and is analogous to *GetAmbientProperty*. It takes as parameters the dispid of the event being fired and then any number of parameters as defined by the event being fired. It ends up calling the *IDispatch::Invoke* implementation provided as the event sink by the control's container. Generally speaking, you won't call this function directly. Instead, you'll use ClassWizard to generate the event type for you, and it'll also generate for you a new member function that calls *FireEvent* on your behalf. This is obviously the recommended way of creating and firing events, as the ClassWizard-created functions are type-safe, while *FireEvent* is not.

The *FireEvent* member function uses the MFC library's *COleDispatchDriver* class to act as an automation controller, by getting the dispatch interface for each connection to the event source connection point on the control and by calling its *Invoke* method. The event-firing code is shown in Listing 12-1 on the next page.

```
void COleControl::FireEventV(DISPID dispid, BYTE FAR* pbParams,
    va_list argList)
{
    COleDispatchDriver driver;

    const CPtrArray* pConnections = m_xEventConnPt.GetConnections();
    ASSERT(pConnections != NULL);

    int i;
    int cConnections = pConnections->GetSize();
    LPDISPATCH pDispatch;

    for (i = 0; i < cConnections; i++)
    {
        pDispatch = (LPDISPATCH)(pConnections->GetAt(i));
        ASSERT(pDispatch != NULL);
        driver.AttachDispatch(pDispatch, FALSE);
        TRY
            driver.InvokeHelperV(dispid, DISPATCH_METHOD, VT_EMPTY,
                NULL, pbParams, argList);
        END_TRY
        driver.DetachDispatch();
    }
}
```

Listing 12-1. *An excerpt from* COleControl's *event-firing code (from the OLE CDK version 1.1).*

Here, the *FireEventV* function is passed the event's dispid and the list of parameters to it, which have been converted to a standard *va_list* type by *FireEvent* itself, which then calls this one. (See the *Microsoft Visual C++ Run-Time Library Reference* if you need more information on variable parameter lists and *va_list* and other types.) *FireEventV* creates an instance of the MFC OLE Automation client class, *COleDispatchDriver*, on the stack. It then interrogates the connection-point wrapper class for the events interface for the connections currently attached to it, which returns a *CPtrList* pointer. If there are no current connections, an assertion is thrown in debug builds. It then walks through the list of connections, getting the *IDispatch*-based pointer to each.

Remember that a connection point stores the relevant OLE interface pointer for each attachment; as the events connection point recognizes only connections for the event interface (derived from *IDispatch*), these pointers can be cast into *IDispatch* pointers safely. The function then attaches each dispatch pointer in turn to the *COleDispatchDriver* object using its *AttachDispatch* member function, and it calls through this pointer to *Invoke* via the helper function, *InvokeHelperV*. This helper simply packs the parameters into variants and calls *IDispatch::Invoke*. If this call throws an exception, it is caught but ignored. The function then disconnects the current connection's dispatch interface and carries on through the list.

TYPE-SAFE?

One of the advantages of a language such as C++ is that it allows you to write "type-safe" access functions. What does this mean? Imagine that you have a function that can take a number of parameters of different types, such as the standard *printf* library function. There's no way that the compiler can check that the parameters you're passing to *printf* are correct because *printf* is defined as taking a variable list of parameters of varying types. The compiler can only check that the first parameter, the format string, is of the right type, because this parameter <u>is</u> defined accurately. The *printf* function can therefore be described as not type-safe.

A type-safe version of *printf* would in fact be a family of functions, each of which is defined to take a certain set of parameters. For example, a version of *printf* designed only to print out integer numbers could be defined as:

```
int IntPrintf ( const char *pszFormat, int nNumber )
{
    return printf ( pszFormat, int nNumber );
}
```

This sort of type-safe function doesn't even require C++. Likewise, the *COleControl::FireEvent* member function, the generic event-firing function described in this chapter, is not type-safe but can be wrapped in new functions to make it so. The advantage? The compiler, when it processes your source code, can check that you're calling the function correctly and passing parameters of the right type (or ones that can be coerced by the compiler into the right types).

C++ takes type safety a stage further through templates — a sort of compile-time macro, but more so. A "template" is a mechanism for defining a set of classes or functions that can be created for a number of types. The coder instantiates a particular variety of this class or function and specifies the type to be used. The compiler then creates a new class based on the combination of the template class and the specified type. Examples of template classes are the MFC library's *CArray* and *CList* classes.

Inside *COleControl* are a whole series of member functions to handle stock properties and methods. For example, the *GetText* member function gets the current value of the stock *Text* or *Caption* property (which are the same — setting one sets the other), and *SetText* sets the property. There is also an *InternalGetText* member function, which is designed to be used whenever the *Text* or *Caption* property value is to be retrieved by the control's own code. The difference is that *GetText* calls *InternalGetText* and then copies the string returned to a *BSTR* and returns that.

All stock properties are marked as bound properties that also have the *RequestEdit* attribute, which means that whenever an attempt is made to alter the value of a stock property, the control will first ask the container for permission by calling *COleControl::BoundPropertyRequestEdit*. If the container says "yes" (or ignores the notification, which would happen if it knew nothing about data binding), the property is changed, and the control notifies the container using *COleControl::BoundPropertyChanged*.

NOTE I examine data binding in more detail in Chapter 14, but hopefully it's clear that already the simple "bind property to database column" idea has been expanded to mean "tie property state to container, if the container wants the tie."

When a stock property is changed, the framework also calls a member function inside your control as a notification. Unless you specifically override such a function, the base class implementation is used. This typically does no more than call *InvalidateControl* to make the control redraw itself and hopefully take note of the new property value. An example is *OnTextChanged*, which is called whenever the *Text* or *Caption* stock property is altered. If you don't override *OnTextChanged* in your derived class, the *COleControl* version is called, which causes the control to redraw itself. In most cases, the default behavior is what you want; however, there will be occasions when you'll want to do more when a stock property is changed. *COleControl* gives you that option.

From time to time, and typically at a control's initialization, the container will not be in a position to deal with events. This does not mean that events sent to it will cause it to crash — only a <u>very</u> badly behaved container would do this! — but it does mean that events won't be handled. A container notifies a control that events are being ignored by calling *IOleControl::FreezeEvents* with a parameter of *TRUE*; likewise, it notifies the control that it will honor events by calling this interface member function with a value of *FALSE*. This is reflected up to the control programmer through the virtual function *COleControl::OnFreezeEvents*. By overriding this member function, you can decide to throw away events during a freeze, store them up until the container unfreezes events, or perhaps simply store those that are important enough to need to be fired later.

Marginally related to this is the *COleControl::OnEventAdvise* member function, which is called whenever something successfully connects to the control's events connection point. If nothing has yet connected to the connection point, there is no point in firing an event. Likewise, you might have an event that is so important that you have to ensure that every connection sees it. You can do this by overriding *OnEventAdvise* and being sure that you fire the event each time this function is called (if events are not frozen at that time, of course). You might recall that I used both *OnFreezeEvents* and *OnEventAdvise* in an early version of the First control so that it could notify any clients if it could not find or open its index and message files.

If you support stock events such as KeyDown for keyboard handling, you might need to override the *OnKeyDownEvent* function, which is called by the framework after the event has been fired. You'd use this function (and/or one of its siblings, if you also use other stock keyboard events) if you wanted to handle the keypress internally as well as fire the event.

Error-Handling and Automation Exceptions

In Chapter 9, I discussed errors and exception-handling. OLE controls can fire error events when errors occur outside of any automation invocation, and they can throw standard OLE Automation exceptions during method calls and property access. *COleControl* provides a few member functions to aid you in this. When you're creating properties that are designed to be read-only, you'll typically do so by deleting the name of the set function inside ClassWizard. Doing so causes ClassWizard to put a call to *COleControl::SetNotSupported* into the set function's place in the property-creation macro. This member function simply throws an OLE Automation exception using *ThrowError*. There's also an analogous function for the write-only property case, called *GetNotSupported*. One further case along the same lines is when a control asks its container if it's okay to change a bound property — using *BoundPropertyRequestEdit*. If the container says "yes," the control proceeds and does what it wants to do; otherwise, it needs to throw an exception back to its caller, which it does by calling *SetNotPermitted*. You can imagine situations in which a control might want to use the same mechanism in other cases — namely, refusing to allow properties to be changed at a specific instant because some other condition is wrong. However, if you have controls that need to do this, do <u>not</u> use *SetNotPermitted* to report the error to the user, because this function throws an exception code that is meant to be specific to bound edit failures. It will only serve to confuse if an error code meant for one condition gets used for another similar, but different, situation. Therefore, you'll need to create your own SCODE for this condition.

ThrowError itself I discussed in detail in Chapter 9. Two versions of the function are provided, one that takes a string as the description parameter and one that takes a resource ID for this parameter. The only difference between the two is that the latter loads the string from the resource file. In most cases, you're going to want to use this latter version. The exception would be when an error description needs to be built up at runtime (for example, ODBC errors). However, the advantages of keeping static text in resource files should be compelling enough to convince you to use them where possible. What are the reasons? Oh well, first, they only get loaded into memory when they're needed, and second, they're much easier to localize that way.

If you look at the code for *ThrowError*, you'll find that it's remarkably straightforward. In essence, all it does is throw an exception of type *COleDispatchExceptionEx*. This exception class is directly derived from the standard MFC exception class *COleDispatchException*, its only difference being that the SCODE field of the OLE Automation exception is filled in rather than the *m_wCode* field. The OLE Automation specification defines those two fields as mutually exclusive: if one is filled in, the other is not.

When an OLE control throws an error by firing the Error event, the container receiving the event will obviously get the chance to handle it. In addition, the last parameter to the event itself is a pointer to a Boolean variable that is set to *FALSE* by the control before the event is fired. If the container leaves it as *FALSE*, the control will call *COleControl::DisplayError* (or your override, if you've created one) on return from the container's event handler. The default implementation of this function displays a message box with the error description string. If, for example, you want more sophisticated reporting or error logging, all you need to do is to override this function in your derived class.

Property Persistence Member Functions

The *COleControl* class provides a set of functions to aid the saving and loading of a control's properties to persistent storage. Some of these functions are typically used invisibly, such as *ExchangeExtent* and *ExchangeStockProps*, which are called by the standard version of *DoPropExchange* created for you by ControlWizard. *DoPropExchange* reads and writes properties to permanent storage (actually, to wherever the container tells it to write), and it calls *ExchangeExtent* to save or restore the control's current size and *ExchangeStockProps* to save and restore any stock properties used by the control. The latter function uses a "mask" (a set of bits) to tell it which stock properties are used by the control. The mask is also saved and read from permanent storage.

FYI If you write a control that uses stock properties but you don't want to save any or all of the properties you use, then the best way of changing *ExchangeStockProps'* behavior is to write your own version. Far better to do this than to play around with the stock properties mask, which is of course implementation-specific and liable to change.

Another function usually called automatically for you is *ExchangeVersion*. This function saves and retrieves the version number of the properties, which is usually the same as the version number of the control. However, if a new control is reading in an old version of the control's data, it can use the version number retrieved by *ExchangeVersion* to determine which new properties it needs to synthesize values for and which old no-longer-used properties it should ignore.

When a property is changed, either within the control itself as a consequence of some happening or as a result of user interaction through programmatic means or through the control's property pages, the control should modify its internal state to reflect the fact that it has changed by calling *SetModifiedFlag*. This will then cause the *IsModified* member function to return *TRUE*, indicating that the control is "dirty" and should be given the opportunity to save its new state if the container so requires.

Two other member functions in *COleControl* are of relevance to persistent properties. The first, *WillAmbientsBeValidDuringLoad*, can be called by the control at initialization time to determine if it is able to read ambient properties from the container during its load sequence. If a control is marked with *OLEMISC_SET-CLIENTSITEFIRST*, it is asking for this ability — and the container should honor it by calling *IOleObject::SetClientSite* before asking the control to load its persistent properties. When the container sets the control's site, the *OnSetClientSite* member function will be called, so you can override this if you want to do anything special at this point.

The second function that is of relevance to persistent properties, *IsConvertingVBX*, is one you're likely to see less and less of as time progresses. This function returns *TRUE* if the control determines that it is loading property data saved by an older, VBX version of this control. A "VBX" is a Visual Basic custom control, similar in nature to OLE controls but more restricted in what they can do. The number of containers that support VBXs is very limited. Visual Basic version 4.0 supplies OLE-control versions of all its toolbox controls rather than the VBX versions supplied with earlier versions of Visual Basic, and one of the features it provides is the ability to upgrade automatically any VBX used by a program into its OLE control equivalents. It does this by replacing references to the VBX with references to an equivalent OLE control and then converting saved properties from the VBX into ones compatible with the OLE control. The main difference lies in the *Font* property, which is now a sub-object of the OLE control with its own set of attributes. These attributes are saved in the Visual Basic form file (FRM) as a distinct part of the containing form. VBXs, on the other hand, save fonts as sets of individual properties, such as *FontSize*, *FontName*, and *FontItalic*.

OLE-Related Member Functions

In addition to the large set of member functions inside *COleControl* for OLE Automation support for properties, events, methods, and ambient properties, the class also contains a diverse set of functions for other OLE-related purposes. *SetControlSize*, for example, sets the control's size internally and then calls *IOleObject::SetExtent* to set the control's physical size within the container. *GetControlSize*, on the other hand, is optimized, and doesn't make the OLE interface call because the size was already cached internally by *SetControlSize*. *SetRectInContainer* is similar except that it also allows the control to move within the container. There is a matching "get" function, *GetRectInContainer*, which retrieves the control's size and position relative to the container.

A control should call the *ControlInfoChanged* member function if it alters any of the mnemonics it recognizes; this results in a call to the container, telling it to call *IOleControl::GetControlInfo* to retrieve the new information. This in turn causes the *OnGetControlInfo* function to be called inside *COleControl*. If a container supports extended controls, the control can call the *GetExtendedControl* member function to retrieve the automation interface for the extended control. It is extremely unwise to rely on there being an extended control because not all containers support them — and there is certainly no need to support them abitrarily.

If you want to ensure that your control doesn't become deactivated during a particular circumstance, such as firing an event, it should call the *LockInPlaceActive* member function with a parameter of *TRUE*, which informs the container that now is a really bad time to deactivate this control. A balancing call to *LockInPlaceActive* with a parameter of *FALSE* must be made at some point, and a control should not impose this restriction on its container for lengthy periods of time. A related set of functions are *PreModalDialog* and *PostModalDialog*. Your control should wrap any modal dialog invocations between these two function calls, to notify the container that the control is going modal and therefore asking the container to do the same. If these calls aren't made, a container can still act as if no modal dialog was being displayed. At best, this is bizarre behavior; at worst, it can cause all sorts of random problems if, for example, the user of the container does something drastic such as deleting the control!

When a container wants to UI-activate a control, it does so either by invoking the control's primary verb (*OLEIVERB_PRIMARY*) or its *OLEIVERB_UIACTIVATE* verb. A control can UI-activate itself by calling its *OnEdit* member function. If you want to write a control with custom OLE verbs, you can add new entries to the message map using *ON_OLEVERB*; these entries are automatically enumerated by the control when the container asks it to enumerate its verbs. You can override the standard verb-enumeration scheme by overriding the *COleControl::OnEnumVerbs* member function. (I'm hard-pressed to think of a place where you'd want to do this.)

When a control is asked to draw itself, its *OnDraw* function will be called. If the container in which the control is embedded does not activate the control (for example, some containers such as Microsoft Access 2.0 do this in design mode), then the container might ask the control to draw itself into a Windows metafile; this causes the *OnDrawMetafile* member function to be called. The default action of *OnDrawMetafile* is to call *OnDraw*; the default action of *OnDraw* as created by ControlWizard is to draw an ellipse! You obviously need to change this to draw your control's contents appropriately. If your *OnDraw* implementation does things that aren't supported in metafiles, you'll need to be sure that your override of *OnDrawMetafile* does the appropriate thing and takes actions that are compatible with metafiles.

One situation in which metafile drawing is important is when you're creating a control that is a subclass of a standard Windows control, such as a combo box. Some of these controls unfortunately have bugs (at least in Windows version 3.x) that cause them to draw themselves incorrectly in metafiles. Under these circumstances, you'll need to write your own code to draw these controls. If you want to cause your control to update its appearance at any time, you can do the equivalent of sending yourself a *WM_PAINT* message by calling *InvalidateControl*. This function takes an optional parameter specifying which part of the control's rectangle is invalid. Use this value in intelligent painting code to make your display-updating more efficient. Although this function seems very similar to the standard Windows API function, *InvalidateRect* (or its *CWnd* analogue), don't try to use the Windows API variant. Why? Because a control that is not active has no window, and yet it is still capable of output through a container-supplied metafile or to the container's window (the more usual case). You'll only get a request to redraw the metafile from the container if you use *InvalidateControl*, because *InvalidateControl* will detect this situation and call the container via *IAdviseSink::OnViewChange*. This won't happen with the standard *InvalidateRect*.

Sometimes a control needs to act as if it had just been initialized, such as when a failure occurs during property loads. The *OnResetState* member function is provided for this purpose, and ControlWizard provides a default override in your control class, which calls only the base class variant. In turn, this function calls *DoPropExchange* to read the properties. If you need to do other initialization during a reset, you should do it here. CDK Books Online gives a list of the points at which this function can be called by the framework.

COLEPROPERTYPAGE

The OLE CDK's wrapper class for property pages, *COlePropertyPage*, is derived from the MFC library's standard dialog class, *CDialog*. This makes it a *CWnd*, too, as *CDialog* is itself derived from *CWnd*. Consequently, it shares many member functions with *COleControl* and, like it, also has a large set of new functions for its specific purpose. A generalized property page is far simpler in concept, and far more specific in purpose, than a generalized OLE control, so it follows that *COlePropertyPage* is a good deal simpler than *COleControl*.

When you create a control using ControlWizard, it creates an empty property-page dialog for you, and it also derives a class from *COlePropertyPage*. Having a *COlePropertyPage* object without an associated Windows dialog resource makes no sense. As with standard *CDialogs*, this class has a member function, *OnInitDialog*, which is called when the dialog box associated with the page is just about to be displayed. If you want any special behavior at initialization, you'll need to override this function and add your special behavior to it. Although a *COlePropertyPage* object is typically given the resource ID of the dialog with which it is to work at construction-time, it is possible to create a page dynamically and then pass the in-memory dialog resource to the property-page object by calling its *SetDialogResource* member function. This might be useful if you need to create the page dynamically at runtime.

The other parameter passed to *COlePropertyPage* objects at construction time is the ID of the string representing the page's caption. It, too, can be set dynamically by calling *SetPageName*, which takes an actual string rather than a string ID. This is very useful if you want to build up the string at runtime, which you might want to do if you want the caption to reflect a particular runtime state.

Property pages, being user interfaces, are perfect places in which to provide help. To make this easier, the *COlePropertyPage* class has a *SetHelpInfo* function, which takes a string to be used as a caption in a status bar or as ToolTip text, the name of the help file containing help for this page, and the help context ID within that help file. The first parameter is particularly interesting because it allows a container providing the property-page frame (the dialog into which all the property pages go) to get meaningful text from the property page itself and then display this meaningful text somewhere when the user selects or moves the mouse over the relevant page. Another function, *OnHelp*, is called when the user asks for help in the property page (for example, by clicking the Help button). Usually there is no need to override this function, but you can do so if you want to provide custom help.

Containers get all information about a property page, including the help text referred to in the paragraph above, by calling the page's *IPropertyPage* or *IPropertyPage2* interface. Likewise, the container tells the property page about itself by calling *IPropertyPage::SetPageSite*. This gives the property page an OLE interface through which it can communicate with its frame when it needs to. When the frame calls this interface method, the *COlePropertyPage* class reflects it up to the member function *OnSetPageSite*. In the unlikely event that you need to alter the default behavior, do so here. After this function has been called, the property page can retrieve a pointer to its site by calling *GetPageSite*, which returns a pointer to the site's *IPropertyPageSite* interface. The *IPropertyPage2* interface is identical to the *IPropertyPage* interface except for one additional method that allows a container to set the focus to a specific control on a page. Calls to this additional method are reflected up to the programmer by *COlePropertyPage* through the *OnEditProperty* member function.

NOTE If you want to observe the interface semantics properly, you should override this function to cause it to set focus to the control representing the property whose dispid is passed in as a parameter. By default, the framework does nothing.

In the normal case, a property page is invoked to act on one instance of a control at a time. It is perfectly possible, however, to select a number of controls of the same type (in a Visual Basic form, for example) and then invoke the property page on them all. Any changed properties would be set in all selected instances. The property page maintains a list of objects for which it has been invoked, and these are stored as an array of *IDispatch* pointers. The *COlePropertyPage* member function *GetObjectArray* can be used to retrieve them. Don't call *Release* on any of these pointers if you do retrieve them, unless you have called *AddRef* first.

When a property value is changed by a user through a property-page control, the page can set itself as modified by calling *SetModifiedFlag*. The value of this flag can be retrieved (just as in the *COleControl* case) by calling the *IsModified* function. The property page attempts to keep track of changes made by the user by keeping a flag for each control on the page to say whether it has been changed. This flag can be read with *GetControlStatus* and can be explictly set one way or the other with *SetControlStatus*. Any controls marked as being dirty (that is, changed) when the property page is closed or when the user clicks the Apply button will cause their corresponding properties in the control(s) to get updated. The Apply button normally gets enabled whenever a control within the property page is marked as dirty; if you have some controls that you don't want to affect the Apply button, call *IgnoreApply* for each of them. The property-page class then stops keeping track of those controls and won't enable the Apply button if they're changed.

Part III

Advanced Concepts in OLE Controls

Chapter 13

Custom Font-Based Properties (and Pictures, Too)

Let's get out of the theory and back into the practice again. In the previous twelve chapters, I've stepped through various iterations of a control that uses a stock property, the *Font* property. If you use this property value as the font to be used for any text output your control makes, then obviously you can change the font, cause the control to be invalidated, and redraw the text in the new font. But what if you want to use more than one font in the same control? How do you do that? You certainly can't have two versions of the same stock property with different values, so you need to find another way. The use of multiple fonts is further complicated by the facts that they're complex by nature (for example, lots of attributes with interrelated effects) and they're implemented as OLE objects in their own right by OLE controls.

The last point is in fact the key to the solution, too. Font objects implement an *IDispatch*-derived interface, *IFontDispatch*, as well as an *IFont* interface. They also use connection points to notify whatever uses them that they have been changed in some way — say, the name of the font used or the size. Therefore, the first thing to do is to implement a new font-based property. The First control is rather old hat now, and adding further modifications to it will make it more difficult to understand. So I'm going to create a new control that, in addition to showing the use of multiple font-based properties, also demonstrates a few other peculiarities of OLE controls. This new control is called "Children."

CAUTION For the purposes of the early part of this chapter, please don't try to embed this control in any container other than Test Container. If you do, you'll steal my thunder. (There, that's got you intrigued—no better way of ensuring that you <u>do</u> try it elsewhere!)

FYI All the techniques described in this chapter also apply pretty much unchanged to custom picture properties. In most cases, all you need to do is to replace the word "font" with "picture."

THE "CHILDREN" CONTROL

The basic idea behind the Children control is that it is an OLE control with two child windows: an edit box and a pushbutton. The edit box is used to enter some arbitrary text, and the pushbutton causes that text to be validated against some set of rules contained within the control. To make it more interesting, the validation can be pre-processed and post-processed by the calling program, through the auspices of two events. The edit box has its own font, which can be set and changed manually through the control's property pages or programmatically through the *EditFont* property. So it's an example of a control that is really two controls, both of which are children of the main OLE control window. The OLE control window's sole purpose is to be the parent of the two controls. Figure 13-1 shows the Children control embedded in Test Container.

To create the control, I used ControlWizard to create a new control project, naming it "Children." I left all options at their default values. (If you like, you can choose to turn on context-sensitive help, allowing you to add help at a later stage.) After the project was created, I added the *EditFont* property as a property with get/set methods and a type of *LPFONTDISP*. I added two events, one called *BeforeValidation* and one called *Validated*, neither of which takes a parameter. The first is a "before" event, and the second is an "after" event. These are the events that allow the calling program to pre-process and post-process the validation. Finally, I added three stock properties: *BackColor*, *Font*, and *ForeColor*.

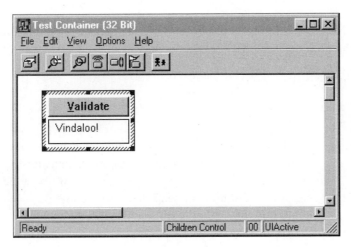

Figure 13-1. *The Children control embedded in Test Container.*

Now I add the code to create the two child controls and to implement the custom *EditFont* property. The two child controls will be wrapped in the appropriate MFC classes, *CEdit* and *CButton*. To the control header file, I add the following line to the "overrides" section:

```
virtual void OnFontChanged(void);
```

This overrides the base class stock-font change notification function. Then I add these member variables and function into the "implementation" section:

```
CButton m_btnValidate;
CEdit m_editEntry;
CRect m_rBtn;
CRect m_rEdit;
CFontHolder m_fontEdit;
void ChangeEditFont();
```

The first two are the member variables that will be used to wrap the controls; the two *CRect* objects hold the size and position of each control, and the *CFontHolder* object will be used to wrap the custom *EditFont* property. *ChangeEditFont* is a function that is called whenever the *EditFont* property is changed; its purpose is to tell the edit control to redraw itself with the new font.

After the closing comment line

```
//}}AFX_MSG
```

I add a function in the message map section:

```
afx_msg void OnValidate();
```

This function will be used to handle *BN_CLICKED* messages from the button. Now I use the Message Maps tab in ClassWizard to add a *WM_CREATE* handler to the *COleControl*-derived class. Finally, at the very end of the file, outside the class definition, I define two constants:

```
#define  IDC_VALIDATE        1
#define  IDC_ENTRY           2
```

These will be used as the child window IDs for the two controls.

In the control's implementation file, I add the message map entry for *BN_CLICKED*. As it is being added manually (because ClassWizard doesn't know about the button), I add it outside the special ClassWizard comments. So, after the line

```
ON_OLEVERB(AFX_IDS_VERB_PROPERTIES, OnProperties)
```

I add this line:

```
ON_BN_CLICKED(IDC_VALIDATE, OnValidate)
```

This tells the framework to call *OnValidate* whenever the button with ID *IDC_VALIDATE* sends a *BN_CLICKED* notification to the control window.

Now I add the two stock property pages for colors and fonts in the normal way, by amending the entry for the default property page as follows:

```
BEGIN_PROPPAGEIDS(CChildrenCtrl, 3)
    PROPPAGEID(CChildrenPropPage::guid)
    PROPPAGEID(CLSID_CColorPropPage)
    PROPPAGEID(CLSID_CFontPropPage)
END_PROPPAGEIDS(CChildrenCtrl)
```

The new custom font property needs to be initialized with a default font, so I create a static variable for this purpose:

```
static const FONTDESC _fontdescEdit =
    { sizeof(FONTDESC), "Arial", FONTSIZE( 10 ), FW_NORMAL,
    ANSI_CHARSET, FALSE, FALSE, FALSE };
```

This will set up the font initially to be 10-point Arial, with normal weight and no special effects. (If you want a different default, change this.)

The constructor for the control class sets up the size and position of each control in the *CRect* member variables (the controls don't exist yet, so no action is taken), and then it calls *SetInitialSize* to tell the container what size this control would like to be. Not all containers honor this, but Test Container does. The parameters given to *SetInitialSize* amount to the total width of each control (they're both the same width) plus 6 pixels, and the total height of the two controls, together with the space between them and the margin at top and bottom.

```
CChildrenCtrl::CChildrenCtrl() : m_fontEdit ( &m_xFontNotification )
{
    InitializeIIDs(&IID_DChildren, &IID_DChildrenEvents);
    m_rBtn = CRect ( 3, 3, 103, 27 );
    m_rEdit = CRect ( 3, 30, 103, 60 );
    SetInitialSize ( m_rBtn.right+m_rBtn.left,
        m_rEdit.bottom+m_rBtn.top);
}
```

Notice also that the constructor passes a value to the *CFontHolder* object's constructor, *&m_xFontNotification.* (This is described in more detail on page 356.)

Now I change *OnDraw* so that, rather than drawing an ellipse, it draws only a rectangle in the background color, effectively erasing the window:

```
void CChildrenCtrl::OnDraw(CDC* pdc, const CRect& rcBounds,
    const CRect&  rcInvalid)
{
    CBrush cbBack ( TranslateColor ( GetBackColor ( ) ) );
    pdc -> FillRect ( rcBounds, &cbBack );
}
```

The standard *DoPropExchange* function must also be altered, to save and load the new *EditFont* property. As an aside, during property loading, the function also calls *ChangeEditFont*, a function described on page 355, which sends a message to the edit control telling it to change to the given font. The code for *DoPropExchange* is

```
void CChildrenCtrl::DoPropExchange(CPropExchange* pPX)
{
    ExchangeVersion(pPX, MAKELONG(_wVerMinor, _wVerMajor));
    COleControl::DoPropExchange(pPX);
    PX_Font ( pPX, _T( "EditFont" ), m_fontEdit, &_fontdescEdit );
    if ( pPX -> IsLoading() )
    {
        ChangeEditFont();
    }
}
```

Notice that the value is loaded into or saved from the *CFontHolder* member variable, and the default value is obtained from the static structure I initialized earlier if no stored property value is found.

When the OLE control's window is created, it must create the child button and edit controls. This is done inside the control's handler for the *WM_CREATE* message, which is sent just as the window is being created but before it is displayed. The create handler looks like this:

```
int CChildrenCtrl::OnCreate(LPCREATESTRUCT lpCreateStruct)
{
    if (COleControl::OnCreate(lpCreateStruct) == -1)
        return -1;
    if ( m_btnValidate.Create ( _T( "&Validate" ), BS_PUSHBUTTON |
        WS_VISIBLE, m_rBtn, this, IDC_VALIDATE ) == FALSE )
    {
        MessageBox ( _T( "Could not create button" ) );
        return -1;
    }
    if ( m_editEntry.Create ( ES_AUTOHSCROLL | WS_BORDER
        WS_VISIBLE, m_rEdit, this, IDC_ENTRY ) == FALSE )
    {
        MessageBox ( _T( "Could not create edit box" ) );
        return -1;
    }
    return 0;
}
```

This function first calls the base class implementation of the create handler, to initialize the window correctly, and then it attempts to create the button. The button is given a caption of "Validate" and *IDC_VALIDATE* as its ID. It's also told to be visible and to be a pushbutton style. If the creation fails, a message box is displayed. The edit control is created in the same manner, except that it is given the *WS_BORDER* style so that you can actually see where the edit box has been created.

To handle the button press, the *OnValidate* function will be called, as I've added a message map entry for *ON_BN_CLICKED* with the control ID of the button, *IDC_VALIDATE*:

```
void CChildrenCtrl::OnValidate()
{
    FireBeforeValidation();
    MessageBox ( "Button Pressed" );
    FireValidated();
}
```

This function does very little. Here, it fires the "before" event, displays a message box, and then fires the "after" event. (In the next incarnation of this control in this chapter, I'll be putting some slightly more useful code in there.)

The "get" and "set" functions for the custom *EditFont* property are pretty basic:

```
LPFONTDISP CChildrenCtrl::GetEditFont()
{
    return m_fontEdit.GetFontDispatch();
}

void CChildrenCtrl::SetEditFont(LPFONTDISP newValue)
{
    m_fontEdit.InitializeFont ( &_fontdescEdit, newValue );
    ChangeEditFont();
    SetModifiedFlag();
}
```

The get function simply calls a member function of the *CFontHolder* class to return the font dispatch interface for the contained font object. The set function sets up the contained font based on the font object passed in as a parameter to the set function, and then it tells the edit control to change itself to use the new font. It also marks the control as "dirty" by calling *SetModifiedFlag*.

When the stock font property is changed, the *COleControl::OnFontChanged* function is called. By default, this causes the control to redraw itself, letting it get hold of the new font for any textual output it performs. I override this function here, making it set the edit control's font to the current value of the *EditFont* property (<u>not</u> to the stock font property!) and then calling the base class implementation:

```
void CChildrenCtrl::OnFontChanged()
{
    ChangeEditFont();
    COleControl::OnFontChanged();
}
```

Interesting. So, I'm changing the edit control's font whenever the stock font property changes, even though I'm not using the stock font property for the edit control. How does this work, and why do I do it? I'll explain in the next section, "Using the Stock Font Property Notification." First, let's look at the final function in the control, *ChangeEditFont*:

```
void CChildrenCtrl::ChangeEditFont()
{
    if ( m_editEntry.GetSafeHwnd() )
    {
        m_editEntry.SendMessage ( WM_SETFONT,
            ( WPARAM )m_fontEdit.GetFontHandle(), TRUE );
    }
}
```

This function uses the *CWnd* member *GetSafeHwnd* to get the window handle of the edit control. If the control does not exist, this function returns *NULL*, in which case no further action is taken. If the window does exist, it is sent the *WM_SETFONT* message with the HFONT handle of the font object contained within the *CFontHolder* object. This causes the edit control to redraw itself with the new font. Figure 13-2 shows the edit control with the same font as its default but with the weight set to bold.

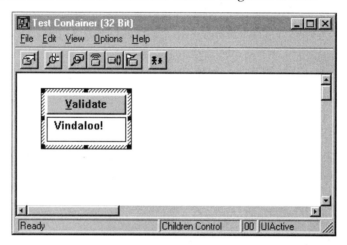

Figure 13-2.   *The Children control with the EditFont property set to a bold font.*

Using the Stock Font Property Notification

Why did I write the *OnFontChanged* function so that it told the edit control to update itself with the current setting of the <u>custom</u> *EditFont* property whenever the value of the <u>stock</u> *Font* property changed? Certainly, that particular operation is redundant. In simple cases such as this, however, it is often satisfactory to reuse the stock font notification mechanism for other, custom, font properties. It's easily done. All you need to do is to pass along the address of the implementation of the *IPropertyNotifySink* interface used for stock font notifications to the *CFontHolder* object's constructor. This is what I did by passing *&m_xFontNotification* to the constructor during the *CChildrenCtrl* constructor. The *CFontHolder* object will then connect this interface pointer to the font object's connection point for property change notifications. Therefore, changes to either the stock *Font* property or to any font property that shares this *IPropertyNotifySink* implementation will cause *OnFontChanged* to be called. There's no easy way to determine which font object was changed, so that's why I always update the edit control. (The only hard way I can think of is to do something you really wouldn't want to do—keep a cached clone of each font object inside the control and compare these against the real font objects to see what has changed during *OnFontChanged*. Yeuch!)

NOTE This version of the Children control can be found on the companion CD-ROM in the \OLECTRLS\CHAP13\CHILDREN1 directory.

This technique is clearly pretty simple, but it's also pretty limiting and prone to inefficiency. To improve on this technique, I need to implement my own notification interface and connect this to the font object. This isn't dramatically difficult using the MFC library's interface map macros.

Implementing Another Font Notification Interface

To create a new font notification interface, all I need to do is implement another *IPropertyNotifySink* interface and ensure that it's called when the *EditFont* property is changed. First, I declare the interface using the MFC library's interface map macros inside the implementation section of the class definition inside the header file. I've called the class implementing the new interface *EditFontNotify*.

```
BEGIN_INTERFACE_PART(EditFontNotify, IPropertyNotifySink)
INIT_INTERFACE_PART(CChildrenCtrl, EditFontNotify)
    STDMETHOD(OnRequestEdit)(DISPID);
    STDMETHOD(OnChanged)(DISPID);
END_INTERFACE_PART(EditFontNotify)
```

In addition to the three *IUnknown* methods, this interface has two methods, both of which take a *DISPID* parameter and return an HRESULT. I'm not going to do anything with *OnRequestEdit* except return success, which means that all requests for edits will be honored. *OnChanged*, however, will have a tiny piece of code to update the edit control's font.

```
STDMETHODIMP_(ULONG) CChildrenCtrl::XEditFontNotify::AddRef()
{
    METHOD_MANAGE_STATE ( CChildrenCtrl, EditFontNotify )
    return 1;
}

STDMETHODIMP_ ( ULONG ) CChildrenCtrl::XEditFontNotify::Release()
{
    METHOD_MANAGE_STATE ( CChildrenCtrl, EditFontNotify )
    return 0;
}

STDMETHODIMP CChildrenCtrl::XEditFontNotify::QueryInterface (
    REFIID iid, LPVOID FAR* ppvObj )
{
    METHOD_MANAGE_STATE ( CChildrenCtrl, EditFontNotify )
    if ( IsEqualIID ( iid, IID_IUnknown ) ||
```

```
        IsEqualIID ( iid, IID_IPropertyNotifySink ) )
    {
        *ppvObj= this;
        AddRef();
        return NOERROR;
    }
    return ResultFromScode ( E_NOINTERFACE );
}

STDMETHODIMP CChildrenCtrl::XEditFontNotify::OnChanged ( DISPID )
{
    METHOD_MANAGE_STATE ( CChildrenCtrl, EditFontNotify )
    pThis -> ChangeEditFont();
    return NOERROR;
}

STDMETHODIMP CChildrenCtrl::XEditFontNotify::OnRequestEdit ( DISPID )
{
    return NOERROR;
}
```

The first thing you'll notice about all these routines is that they all invoke the *METHOD_MANAGE_STATE* macro, which switches MFC's context to the one appropriate for the control DLL. This is important, as it ensures that any module-specific settings, such as locale ID, aren't lost by being overwritten by the container. One interesting aspect of this is the *new* handler, the function that is called whenever the C++ operator *new* fails. As you know, the MFC library expects *new* to throw an exception when it fails; other, non-MFC-based, programs might expect it to return *NULL*, as the older C++ implementations are defined to do. By setting the *new* handler to point at a function you provide, you get the chance to change its behavior. However, if the container of an OLE control sets the *new* handler to return *NULL*, the control will never see out-of-memory exceptions like it expects to, but will instead get *NULL* pointers. Because this behavior is unexpected, all sorts of errors could crop up. Likewise, if a container expected *new* to return *NULL* on failure but an OLE control changed it to throw exceptions, the container will die with unexpected exceptions. In Microsoft Visual C++ version 2.0, and in the accompanying CDK, the *new* handler is <u>not</u> saved on a per-module basis, so this problem could in theory occur.

There's nothing spectacular in this implementation of *IPropertyNotifySink*; *OnRequestEdit* says "yes" every time, and *OnChanged* simply calls *ChangeEditFont*. Pretty simple. Now, if you compile and run this version of the control in Test Container, it will all work as expected, except that the edit control will not have its font initially set correctly. Why? If you were to walk through the code, you'd find that the properties are read, and therefore the font initialized, before the edit control has been created, so it is obviously not possible to send it a message telling it to change its font. One extra call to *ChangeEditFont*, immediately after the creation of the edit control, will solve the problem. As window creation is effectively atomic, I can be sure that on return from a *CWnd::Create* call, the window will actually exist. *CEdit::Create* has the same advantage. Therefore, I changed the *OnCreate* handler for the OLE control window to look like this:

```
int CChildrenCtrl::OnCreate(LPCREATESTRUCT lpCreateStruct)
{
    if (COleControl::OnCreate(lpCreateStruct) == -1)
        return -1;
    if ( m_btnValidate.Create ( _T( "&Validate" ), BS_PUSHBUTTON |
        WS_VISIBLE, m_rBtn, this, IDC_VALIDATE ) == FALSE )
    {
        MessageBox ( _T( "Could not create button" ) );
        return -1;
    }
    if ( m_editEntry.Create ( ES_AUTOHSCROLL
        WS_VISIBLE, m_rEdit, this, IDC_ENTRY ) == FALSE )
    {
        MessageBox ( _T( "Could not create edit box" ) );
        return -1;
    }
    ChangeEditFont();
    return 0;
}
```

This will then ensure that the edit control is given the correct font in which to display its text at startup.

Implementing a Validation Function

To make this control a little more useful, it needs some validation functionality. Then, whenever the button is pressed, the text in the edit box can be validated. The rule I'm going to use is very simple: the string will fail validation if it contains a space.

The first thing to do is to provide programmatic access to the contents of the edit box. I do this by adding a new property, *EditText*, to the control; giving it get/set methods; and ensuring that it returns a string (a *BSTR*). I also make the property the control's default property so that the value of the text in the box is equivalent to the value of the control itself. This allows you to write Visual Basic code such as

```
Children1 = "Assigning to Children1.EditText"
```

rather than having to write the slightly more verbose

```
Children1.EditText = "Assigning to Children1.EditText"
```

I implement the two functions with this code:

```
BSTR CChildrenCtrl::GetEditText()
{
    if ( m_editEntry.GetSafeHwnd() )
    {
        CString s;
        m_editEntry.GetWindowText ( s );
        return s.AllocSysString();
    }
    else
    {
        ThrowError ( CTL_E_ILLEGALFUNCTIONCALL, IDS_NOEDITCTRL );
        return NULL;
    }
}

void CChildrenCtrl::SetEditText(LPCTSTR lpszNewValue)
{
    if ( m_editEntry.GetSafeHwnd() )
    {
        m_editEntry.SetWindowText ( lpszNewValue );
        SetModifiedFlag();
    }
    else
    {
        ThrowError ( CTL_E_ILLEGALFUNCTIONCALL, IDS_NOEDITCTRL );
    }
}
```

Again, nothing startlingly new for you here. The get function checks that the edit box exists and throws an OLE Automation exception if it doesn't. This requires the addition of a new string to the control's string table, called *IDS_NOEDITCTRL*. The text I use for this is "This operation can only be performed when a valid edit control is present. Please activate the control and try again." If the control does exist, the function retrieves its value using *GetWindowText* and then returns that value as a *BSTR*. The set function also validates the control before proceeding, and it throws exactly the same error on failure. If the control does exist, though, it sets its text using *SetWindowText* and then marks the control as dirty by calling *SetModifiedFlag*.

To perform the validation itself, I modify the *OnValidate* handler, which is called whenever the button is pressed. I modify this to retrieve the text from the edit box into a *CString*. (Notice that I call *CEdit::GetWindowText* rather than go through the *EditText* property, as this is far more efficient when I'm inside the control's code.) I then call *CString::Find* to determine whether the string contains one or more spaces. If it does, *Find* will return the offset into the string of the first occurrence, otherwise it returns -1. I therefore check explicitly for -1 (failure), which in this case means that the string is actually valid. The final thing I did was to change the Validated event to take a parameter, a Boolean value saying whether the string was validated. To do this, I deleted the current event using the OLE Events tab inside ClassWizard, and then I added a new one with the same name but with the new parameter. (I called my parameter *Success*; be sure it is a Boolean variable.) Then I ensured that the result of the validation is passed to the Validated event when it is fired.

```
void CChildrenCtrl::OnValidate()
{
    FireBeforeValidation();
    CString s;
    m_editEntry.GetWindowText ( s );
    BOOL bRet = s.Find ( _T( " " ) ) == -1;
    FireValidated ( bRet );
}
```

Obviously, in a real-world situation, the validation function is likely to be a great deal more complex than this. One thing of interest here: in all other references to the edit control, I've first checked that it exists by calling *CEdit::GetSafeHwnd*. Why didn't I do this in *OnValidate*? Well, I'm making the assumption that as the button control exists (it must, to send this notification), the edit control must exist as well. (This isn't a particularly dangerous assumption.) If you're worried about situations like these in your own code, you always have the opportunity to perform the tests or to do exception-handling or whatever so that you can handle the situation gracefully without crashing your control or your container.

I also did one other thing to complete this version of the control; I created a field for the *EditText* property on the control's property page so that I could change it easily. This version of the Children control can be found on the companion CD-ROM in the \OLECTRLS\CHAP13\CHILDREN2 directory.

Control Drawing Problems

At the start of this chapter, I requested that you not try to embed this control into any container other than Test Container. (How well did you keep to this?) The reason is that other containers, such as Microsoft Visual Basic, cause the Children control to draw in a way that perhaps you wouldn't expect. To demonstrate this effect in Test Container, run Test Container and insert an instance of the Children control. Now choose Save Property Set from the File menu, which saves the control's persistent properties to a docfile. Now choose Load Property Set from the same menu, which reloads the property set from the file and creates a new control with those values. This new control will appear as a blank rectangle, as shown in Figure 13-3 on the next page. Why?

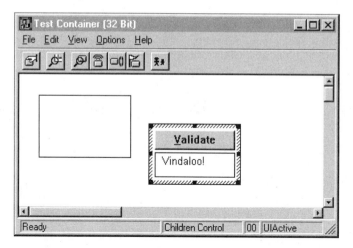

Figure 13-3. *A new Children control (a blank rectangle) created from a saved property set.*

If you have Visual Basic, you'll get a better clue. Visual Basic causes the Children control to appear as a blank rectangle during design mode, so you won't be able to see anything on it. Furthermore, if you invoke the control's property page inside Visual Basic in design mode, you'll get a couple of Internal Application Error message boxes first. If you then type some text into the property page and press the OK or Apply button, you'll get a message box displaying the text you set for the automation exception *GetEditText* and *SetEditText* throw. You're basically being told that the edit box doesn't exist and therefore can't be given attributes. So why doesn't it exist, if the control has thrown no other sort of exception up to the container?

When a control is created inactive, most containers don't give the control a window but instead allow it to draw within a confined space within the container's window. Because no window creation occurs, the *OnCreate* handler is not called, so no child controls are created. Also, if controls were created, which window would be their parent?

I'm not going to answer the two preceding questions yet, even though they will affect many OLE controls that you'll create. The reason? I cover this subject, together with general Windows subclassing issues, in Chapter 17, "Converting a VBX and Subclassing Windows Controls."

Chapter 14

An Introduction to Data Binding

One of the features of Microsoft Visual Basic custom controls (VBXs) used by a number of programmers is the ability to bind a property within the VBX to a column within a database. After a property is so bound, it is initialized with data from the column and, when data in the column changes, the data in the property changes too. Likewise, changes made to the property are reflected in the database.

DATA-BINDING MECHANICS OF OLE CONTROLS

OLE controls provide a functionality similar to that of VBXs. A control can mark one or more of its properties as *Bindable*, meaning that they have the capacity to be bound and will notify the container when they're changed. If a property is also marked as *DisplayBind*, then containers can show users that the property is bindable. Often, an OLE control will want to ask the container if a particular bound field can be edited. A control will do this by marking the property with the *RequestEdit* attribute and then calling the container for permission whenever a user attempts to modify the property. Finally, if there is one property that most accurately represents the control, such as the *Caption* property of an edit control, then that property can be marked as *DefaultBind*, which tells the container of its special status. All these attributes are marked in the control's type library by using the requisite keywords in the ODL file. For example, a property that is bindable, requests permission to be changed, can be displayed to the user, and is the default bindable property would be marked thus:

```
[id(1), bindable, requestedit, displaybind, defaultbind] short
    DataBoundProp;
```

This defines a property called *DataBoundProp*, which has a dispid of 1 and which is a short integer.

A bound property notifies its container of changes, and requests permission to change, through a connection point the control provides. This connection point is for *IPropertyNotifySink*, the same interface used for font notifications (as shown in the previous chapter). *IPropertyNotifySink* has two methods over and above the *IUnknown* ones: *OnChanged* and *OnRequestEdit*. Both methods take one parameter, the dispid of the property affected. When a container that also supports data binding embeds such a control, it will implement *IPropertyNotifySink* and connect its implementation to the control's property notification event sink. Then, whenever a bound property changes, it will call through this connection point to the *OnChanged* method on the interface at the container. Likewise, when a bound property that is also a request-edit property wants to know if it can be changed by a user, it calls through the connection point to the *OnRequestEdit* method on the interface at the container.

That is the extent of data-binding support as provided by the OLE Controls specification at present. The programmer's responsibility at the control end of things is to ensure that the *IPropertyNotifySink* methods are called at the appropriate points and that *OnRequestEdit*'s result is honored if it is called. The container is therefore responsible for the bulk of the data-binding support. So that's the end of this chapter....

Well, not quite. There's still a lot to be discussed. I'll go through the mechanics of creating a control with a bound property, showing it calling through the connection point in Test Container. You can also try connecting it to a real data source in Visual Basic version 4.0.

Now, there's an interesting point: OLE controls leave all data-binding logistics up to the container, but containers such as Visual Basic act as little more than a conduit through to another type of control, the "data source control." How do you create one of those? Sadly, the story right now is that you don't. The specification for data source controls, which is meant to be specific to Visual Basic's form of data binding, had not been released by Microsoft Corporation to the general public at the time of publication of this book (Fall 1995). It might be later on, but until it is, you'll have to satisfy yourself with more work at the container end.

Work is also progressing at Microsoft on a technology called "OLE Database," which is a specification for (and an implementation of) a set of interfaces for, among other things, data sources. This specification will provide for far more advanced and sophisticated data-binding mechanisms than OLE controls now support and will, for example, allow a data-bound OLE control to talk to disparate data sources including traditional relational and indexed sequential access method (ISAM) databases, word processor files, spreadsheets, and even file systems.

CREATING A CONTROL WITH A DATA-BOUND PROPERTY

Demonstrating data-bound properties with Test Container is not difficult, and it's quite enlightening. First, create a control project with ControlWizard and call it "Bound." Stick with all the default options, and create the control. (You might want to build it at this point to speed up operations later.) Add a property called *DataBound-Property*, of type string (*BSTR*) with get and set methods as its implementation. While in the OLE Automation tab of ClassWizard, and with the *DataBoundProperty* selected, click the Data Binding button; this will cause the Data Binding dialog box to appear. Turn on all the check boxes in this dialog box: allow data binding in the first place; then let the data-boundness of this control be displayed to the user, let the property be the default bindable property on the control, and tell it to request permission to change. Now implement the property by creating a member variable of type *CString*, *m_strDBProp*. Put this in the "protected" section of the header file. Change the *DataBoundProperty* get and set methods to look like this:

```
BSTR CBoundCtrl::GetDataBoundProperty()
{
    return m_strDBProp.AllocSysString();
}

void CBoundCtrl::SetDataBoundProperty(LPCTSTR lpszNewValue)
{
    if ( BoundPropertyRequestEdit ( dispidDataBoundProperty ) )
    {
        m_strDBProp = lpszNewValue;
        SetModifiedFlag();
        BoundPropertyChanged ( dispidDataBoundProperty );
    }
    else
    {
        SetNotPermitted();
    }
}
```

The "get" function simply allocates a *BSTR* from the *CString* member variable and returns it. The "set" function has a lot more work to do. It first asks the container for permission to change, by calling *BoundPropertyRequestEdit*, which ultimately calls through the connection point to the container's implementation of *IPropertyNotifySink::OnRequestEdit*. If this returns *TRUE*, the edit can proceed. If this returns *FALSE*, the control reports a "set not permitted" exception to the user by calling *SetNotPermitted*. This amounts to a call to *ThrowError*, with an SCODE parameter of *CTL_E_SETNOTPERMITTED*.

FYI Notice the parameter to *BoundPropertyRequestEdit,* which is the dispid of the property. When properties and methods are added to a control through ClassWizard, it automatically maintains a table of dispids in an enumeration inside the control. You can use the members of the enumeration, such as *dispidDataBoundProperty* in this case, whenever you need the dispid of a property or method. The advantage of this is that the name never changes, whereas the dispid value itself might change. By using the name, you remove yourself from any problems that might occur if you use a hard-coded value that changes subsequently.

Now, back to the code. If the edit is allowed, the set function copies the new value for the property to the *CString* member variable, marks the control as "dirty" by calling *SetModifiedFlag*, and then notifies the container of the change by calling *BoundPropertyChanged*.

Because it's useful to be able to see the value of the property, change *OnDraw* so that it clears the control rectangle and then outputs the value of *m_strDBProp* as text:

```
void CBoundCtrl::OnDraw(CDC* pdc,
    const CRect& rcBounds, const CRect& rcInvalid)
{
    pdc->FillRect(rcBounds,
        CBrush::FromHandle((HBRUSH)GetStockObject(WHITE_BRUSH)));
    pdc->TextOut(rcBounds.left+3, rcBounds.top+3, m_strDBProp);
}
```

FYI By the way, notice that I haven't used absolute coordinates here for the text output, but I have done the proper thing and offset them by the top left corner of the bounding rectangle. This is because the control might not be painting to its own window but might be painting to part of its client window (as discussed briefly at the end of the previous chapter). You cannot therefore assume that the control's top left corner is itself at (0, 0). If you do make this assumption, it's very easy to have an erroneous control that writes all over its container's window. Not very friendly!

The final change I made to the source code was to add a property-page field to the control for the *DataBoundProperty* property, so the page looks like the one shown in Figure 14-1.

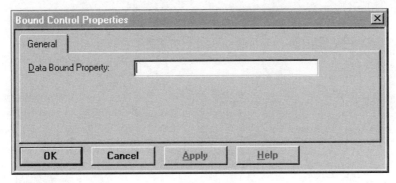

Figure 14-1.   *The property page of the Bound control.*

If you don't recall how to do this, follow these steps:

1. Open the project's resources.

2. Open the *IDD_PROPPAGE_BOUND* dialog resource.

3. Add a static text label, such as "&Data Bound Property." (The leading ampersand precedes the character that will be underlined and that will act as a mnemonic.) Be sure that the static text control is large enough to hold all the text.)

4. Add an edit box by the side of the label.

5. Hold down the Ctrl key and double-click on the edit box. This brings up the Add Member Variable dialog box from ClassWizard's Member Variables tab.

6. Type in a name for the variable (for example, *m_strDBProp*), and be sure the category is *Value* and the type is *CString*.

7. Type in the name of the property (*DataBoundProperty*) with which this member variable is to be associated.

8. Click OK, and rebuild the project.

That's it! You can find the completed project on the companion CD-ROM in the \OLECTRLS\CHAP14\BOUND directory.

Testing the Control with Test Container

To really understand how data binding works, nothing beats seeing it in action. Register the Bound control, and invoke Test Container. Embed the control in Test

Container, and then ask Test Container to display its notification log (either by selecting Notification Log on the View menu or by pressing the last of the toolbar buttons). Figure 14-2 shows Test Container's Bound control and the Notification Log.

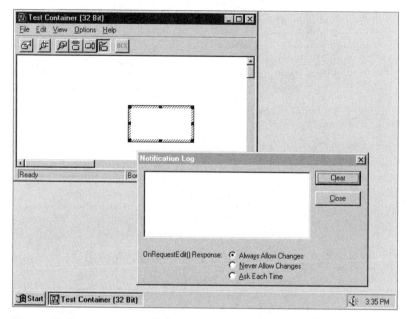

Figure 14-2. *The Bound control in Test Container, with the Notification Log.*

The Notification Log is a dialog box in which Test Container displays all calls from controls to *OnRequestEdit* and *OnChanged*, together with the return value of each call. By default, Test Container will say "yes" to all requests for edits, so each change to a bound property will result in the log showing two calls — one for *OnRequestEdit* and one for *OnChanged*. Try it: embed an instance of the Bound control in Test Container and, with the Notification Log still displayed, change *DataBoundProperty* through the control's property page. A successful change will produce output like this:

```
00_BoundControl: 'DataBoundProperty'; OK to change? (YES)
00_BoundControl: 'DataBoundProperty' changed
```

If you then change the Test Container to fail all edit requests (there's a set of radio buttons in Test Container's Notification Log dialog box to let you do this), you'll first see the exception reported, as shown in Figure 14-3, and then you'll see the following output in the log:

```
00_BoundControl: 'DataBoundProperty'; OK to change? (NO)
```

There's only one line of output this time because the edit was refused, so no change notification can be sent. You can even set Test Container to ask you to accept or refuse edit requests each time an edit request is made, so you can try success and failure randomly as you choose.

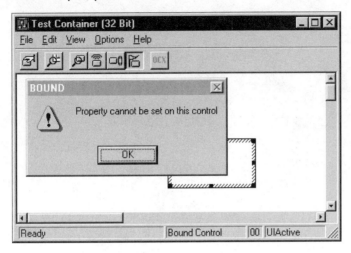

Figure 14-3.   *The Bound control in Test Container, with the container saying "no" to an edit.*

CHANGE NOTIFICATION

As you can see from the small amount of code I've used in this chapter, the basics of data binding are easy to understand and easy to implement. You've probably also noticed that so far data binding from the control's point of view is more akin to change notification than to anything specific to do with databases. In fact, various containers do use this notification process for another purpose. Imagine a container that displays a modeless properties browser for controls embedded within it, such as the Properties window in design-time Visual Basic. What happens then, when a user action <u>to the control</u> (as opposed to through the container) changes a property value? For example, someone could invoke a control's property page and use it to change the values of any number of properties. This would make the container's properties browsing window out of date with respect to the control's view of its property values (which also happens to be the correct view, of course!). So, some containers, including Visual Basic version 4.0 and Visual FoxPro version 3.0, rely on the *OnChanged* notifications to keep their property browsers in sync with the control.

Chapter 15

Licensing

You're in software development for the love of it, right? You don't really want to get paid for what you do, so why would you care about something so horribly legal-sounding as licensing? Surprisingly (or perhaps not), most of the people who develop software <u>do</u> like to make something from it, particularly those who write the killer component that everyone wants. (If only!)

This chapter shows that adding licensing to a control is not particularly difficult, and the OLE CDK provides a basic scheme that is sufficient for most purposes. Altering the scheme is also pretty straightforward, either to make it more sophisticated in terms of the verification algorithms used or to provide multiple levels of licensing.

THE LICENSING PROBLEM

If you're an OLE control writer, you have an interesting problem: if you let someone ship your control with their application, as it's part of their application, what's to stop those receiving it from using that control in another application? And then shipping it on....

NOTE The first premise is this: no matter how sophisticated your licensing scheme, it can <u>always</u> be broken by someone with enough determination. Therefore, a licensing scheme should not attempt to enforce, but it should be difficult enough to make the people breaking the scheme aware that they are breaking the terms of the license.

First, you need to determine whether licensing is something you care about for your control. If you don't, you don't need to take any action. If you do, you need to consider the various licensing situations to determine which ones are important for you. The first licensing requirement is for people who use your control in a design-time environment to build applications. Such people should be able to do so only if they have an appropriate license to do so on their machine. Without such a license, your control cannot be used in design-time environments. When people create an application that uses your control, you might decide to let them and anyone else run the application without any further licensing, or you might choose to require even end users to have a license. It's unlikely, however, that you'll want these end users of an application that happens to use your control also to be able to create new applications with it unless they also are licensed appropriately.

The OLE Controls specification provides a mechanism for license-checking that is pretty flexible. The OLE CDK provides a default implementation that is fairly basic but essentially equivalent to the old Visual Basic VBX license-checking scheme. The point is that the scheme can be adapted to make it offer more features, such as differing levels of functionality offered by a control depending on the level of license found, as well as being adaptable to more secure licensing schemes. I want to look first at what the OLE Controls specification and the CDK offer without any effort, and then I want to see what can be done to adapt this to specific scenarios.

OLE CONTROLS LICENSING — THE BASICS

All OLE controls licensing is provided through the new variant of the class factory, *IClassFactory2*. This is a new interface, defined and implemented first for OLE controls, so containers that aren't specifically OLE-control-aware won't know about it. If your control uses *IClassFactory2* to provide licensing, then a container that uses the original *IClassFactory* interface won't be able to make use of your control at all in certain situations. Likewise, there are certain OLE API functions in existence today that containers will typically use to create instances of OLE objects, including controls. These API functions, such as *CoCreateInstance* and *OleCreate*, use *IClass-Factory* rather than *IClassFactory2* and therefore cannot be used to create licensed OLE controls in these same situations. Microsoft Corporation is working on new variants of these API functions for release with future operating systems, so they will use *IClassFactory2* if it exists on a control. In the meantime, container writers will have to write their own code to create instances of licensed objects. (If you want to know where *IClassFactory* fails to succeed with licensed controls, please wait a few paragraphs, until I discuss the four places in which licensing becomes important.)

IClassFactory2 is derived from *IClassFactory* and contains a few more methods. The *GetLicInfo* method retrieves information from a control about its current licensed state: can it provide a license key for embedding into applications using this control? is it licensed for use on the current machine or by the current user? The *RequestLicKey* method asks the control for a runtime copy of the license key, if it supports this. The *CreateInstanceLic* method is analogous to *CreateInstance* except that it also takes a license key as a parameter.

These three methods provide the basis for all control-licensing requirements. The control can be created only if a license key is in possession of the creating application, and, if the control supports it, a copy of the key can be retrieved by the creating application so that it can embed this in the end-user application to allow the end user to run the application. (Without this, the end-user application cannot run because it would be unable to create an instance of the licensed control unless the user happened to have a valid license for that control.)

In all cases, *IClassFactory2* treats a license key as a *BSTR*. This doesn't mean that the license key is limited to being represented as a string, as a *BSTR* can in fact contain any arbitrary data, including *NULL* bytes.

Let's look at the moments in a control's life when these methods might be called. There are four times when licensing becomes an issue:

- When the control is being written

- When the control is placed in a container in design mode

- When the container creates a runtime version of the program containing the control (for example, Visual Basic's Make EXE File command)

- When the runtime version of the progam is executed

Clearly, none of the *IClassFactory2* methods are called when you're still writing the control! The point here, though, is that at the time you create a control, you'll invent the licensing key(s) your control is going to recognize and save the key(s) in the control's source code, ready to be checked against passed-in keys. If your licensing scheme is file-based (that is, the key is held in a file, which is the default behavior of the CDK-generated licensing scheme), you'll also need to save this key in a file that is distributed along with the control.

When the control is placed on a container's form in design mode, the container will call the control's *IClassFactory2::CreateInstanceLic* method with a *NULL* value for the license key parameter. This will cause the control to verify that the current machine or user is licensed to use this control in design mode. Again, the default mechanics for this involve checking the key held in the license file against the key held in the control itself.

If the keys match, the control can be created, so from that point on the method behaves like a standard *IClassFactory::CreateInstance* call. If they don't match, the control will typically display some meaningful message box to the user and then return an appropriate error. This is one instance in which a container that uses

IClassFactory to create a control instance can continue to do so, as the license key is not passed from container to control. All that is important is that the *IClassFactory::CreateInstance* implementation should check for a valid license.

When the container creates a runtime version of the program containing the control, it will call *IClassFactory2::GetLicInfo* to determine whether the control can return a runtime copy of the license key. If it can, the container will call *IClassFactory2::RequestLicKey* to get a copy of this key to be stored in the created application. Why? When the runtime version of the program is executed, different requirements are in effect because the general intention is to allow the program to run on any user's machine, regardless of whether they are licensed to use the control. On a machine where the machine or the user is not licenced, there will be no license file. Therefore, the executable passes the key to the control by including it as the last parameter to *IClassFactory2::CreateInstanceLic*. This time, because the key is not *NULL*, the control won't attempt to determine whether the machine or user are licensed but will instead compare this passed-in key to the copy it has embedded within itself. If they match, the control gets created; if they don't, it doesn't. Obviously, if the keys don't match in this scenario, something has gone wrong.

Here is where containers that persist in using *IClassFactory* rather than *IClassFactory2* will fail. As *IClassFactory* has no means by which a key can be passed from the container to the control, the container also has no means by which it can create an instance of the control like this. Therefore, an executable program created by a container that uses *IClassFactory* can be executed successfully only on a computer that is licensed to use the control or by a user who is so licensed.

LICENSING PROVIDED BY THE OLE CDK

The OLE CDK provides a pretty basic implementation of the scheme discussed in the previous section. When you choose to have a licensed control in ControlWizard, it creates a text file with the extension LIC. This file holds the license key, which is generated to be

```
Copyright (C) 1995 <Your registered name>
```

Your registered name is replaced by whatever name you used to register the OLE CDK when you installed it. This same key is also saved to a static string in the control's source file, and a few extra functions are added to provide the license-checking.

It's worth looking at this stuff in a little more detail, and a good way to do that is to create a small control project with licensing support turned on.

CREATING A LICENSED CONTROL

As usual, the place to start is with ControlWizard. Invoke it, and create a project called "License." Leave all options as default, except that this time you want to turn on licensing support. Do so by checking the License Validation check box in the Project Options dialog box, and then create the project.

If you now go through all the source files looking for differences, the first place you're going to find one is in the ODL file, where one extra attribute has been added to the control's coclass. Not surprisingly, this attribute is called *licensed*. The next change you'll notice is that the header file for the control, LICENCTL.H, contains a rather different class factory declaration from the norm. Whereas other controls have used the *DECLARE_OLECREATE_EX* macro to declare a class factory object, this one uses

```
BEGIN_OLEFACTORY(CLicenceCtrl)          // Class factory and guid
    virtual BOOL VerifyUserLicense();
    virtual BOOL GetLicenseKey(DWORD, BSTR FAR*);
END_OLEFACTORY(CLicenceCtrl)
```

These macros create a C++ object that wraps the *IClassFactory2* interface; the base class for this object is *COleObjectFactoryEx*, which is itself derived from the standard MFC class factory object, *COleObjectFactory*. The macros also declare two member functions of this class, *VerifyUserLicense* and *GetLicenseKey*, because they're going to be overridden in the implementation file. Apart from that, the macros are functionally equivalent to a single *DECLARE_OLECREATE_EX* invocation.

The control implementation file itself, LICENCTL.CPP, contains all its licensing additions in one contiguous block, as shown in Listing 15-1.

```
/////////////////////////////////////////////////////////////////////////
// Licensing strings

static const TCHAR BASED_CODE _szLicFileName[] = _T("LICENSE.LIC");

static const TCHAR BASED_CODE _szLicString[] =
    _T("Copyright (c) 1995 Microsoft");


/////////////////////////////////////////////////////////////////////////
// CLicenseCtrl::CLicenseCtrlFactory::VerifyUserLicense -
// Checks for existence of a user license

BOOL CLicenseCtrl::CLicenseCtrlFactory::VerifyUserLicense()
```

Listing 15-1. *The code to deal with licensing that is generated by*   *(continued)*
              ControlWizard.

(continued)

```
{
    return AfxVerifyLicFile(AfxGetInstanceHandle(), _szLicFileName,
        _szLicString);
}


/////////////////////////////////////////////////////////////////////////
// CLicenseCtrl::CLicenseCtrlFactory::GetLicenseKey -
// Returns a runtime licensing key

BOOL CLicenseCtrl::CLicenseCtrlFactory::GetLicenseKey(
    DWORD dwReserved, BSTR FAR* pbstrKey)
{
    if (pbstrKey == NULL)
        return FALSE;

    *pbstrKey = SysAllocString(_szLicString);
    return (*pbstrKey != NULL);
}
```

The first thing you see is a definition of a static variable to hold the name of the file containing the license key; yours is "LICENSE.LIC." (ControlWizard always names the file with the same name as the project, and with an LIC extension.) No path is specified here because the CDK code that looks for the file always looks for it only in the same directory as the control itself.

Another variable definition is for the license string — in this case, "Copyright (c) 1995 Microsoft." (In your control, unless you happen also to work for Microsoft, you'll see something different.) This is the key against which all others are compared.

The next thing in the file is the override of the *VerifyUserLicense* function. The default version here calls a CDK global function called *AfxVerifyLicFile*, which opens up the file given to it and verifies that its first line is the same as the string passed to it. *VerifyUserLicense* is one of the functions that you'll want to change if you want to change the CDK's licensing behavior.

The final piece of licensing code that ControlWizard creates for you is the override of the *GetLicenseKey* member function. Again, the default implementation is extremely simple: it creates a *BSTR* from the license string and returns that.

You can find the source code for this control in the \OLECTRLS\CHAP15\LICENSE directory on the companion CD-ROM. If you build this control and run it in Test Container, you'll be able to verify that the control is successfully created only if the license file that ControlWizard created for you is in the same directory as the control. Also, if you change the text in the first line of the LIC file, the license verification will fail, meaning that once again the control won't be created successfully.

You might also want to try to embed this control in more sophisticated containers, such as Visual Basic, to see how they react. The behavior will be the same as Test Container's, except that with Visual Basic you also get to test the other scenarios by creating an application that "uses" this control (as it has no functionality, "use" is not particularly accurate) and by choosing the Make EXE File command from the File menu. You can then run that executable, move the LIC file around, change the text in it, and find that it makes no difference because the control is now verifying the license by comparing its internal copy with that provided by the Visual Basic application during the call to *IClassFactory2::CreateInstanceLic*.

Adapting the Licensing Scheme

Admittedly, the scheme used by the OLE CDK by default for control licensing is basic. Its purpose isn't to be the world's best licensing scheme; rather, it's simply designed to cover the basic need and, more importantly, show that by customizing a few functions, control licensing can really be as sophisticated as you'd like it to be. For example, you can make your licensing scheme look up entries in the registry rather than use a file. (It might even be possible to get really clever and attach it to NT's security model. I don't know how to do this — I'm just suggesting that it might be possible.)

To give a simple example of license customization, I'm going to stick with the file-based idea, and still stay with string-based license keys — but I'm going to up the ante very slightly by making the control check the string in a slightly different way. I'm going to make it check that the first line of the file is just eight characters long and that the first five characters are different from the one stored in the key. The last three must be the same, and will be "OLE". When the container asks this version of the control for the license key, it will get the same key as is stored in the control, except that the first few characters will be randomly changed to ensure that the algorithm still works.

The first function to override is the object factory's *GetLicenseKey* member. If you scan the CDK source code, you'll find that this is called in just a few places. The first is during the default implementation of *VerifyLicenseKey* in the object factory. You're going to override this function, too, so its use here is not important right now. The second is during the implementation of *IClassFactory2::GetLicInfo*, in which it is used to determine whether the license key can be obtained at runtime. You'll notice that the actual value of the key is not used here and the *BSTR* allocated for it is returned back to the system immediately. The final use is in the implementation of *IClassFactory2::RequestLicKey*, where the allocated *BSTR* is returned to the caller (the container) as the embeddable license key. Your override needs to do little more than the default override created by ControlWizard, except that it must also change the first five characters, as per the licensing "algorithm" above. I'm going to take the easy way out here and change the characters in a fixed way each time this function is called, so each caller actually receives the same license key (but different from the original in the first five characters).

First, you need to change the static license key held by the control, in the ControlWizard-generated variable _szLicString. Change it to the following text:

```
ILOVEOLE
```

Then change the *GetLicenseKey* member as shown in Listing 15-2.

```
BOOL CLicenseCtrl::CLicenseCtrlFactory::GetLicenseKey(
    DWORD dwReserved, BSTR FAR* pbstrKey)
{
    if (pbstrKey == NULL)
        return FALSE;
    CString strLicense = _T( "PATCH" );
    strLicense += _szLicString + 5;
    *pbstrKey = strLicense.AllocSysString();
    return (*pbstrKey != NULL);
}
```

Listing 15-2. *The modified* GetLicenseKey *member function, altered to use a slightly different verification scheme.*

This code in Listing 15-2 is pretty basic. It creates a new *CString* object with a five-character string, PATCH, as its initial value. It then tacks onto the end of this the remaining characters from the license string following its fifth character (that is, *OLE*). It then uses the *CString* member function *AllocSysString* (why couldn't it be called *SysAllocString*, just like the API function it wraps?!?) to convert the string into a *BSTR*.

If you modify this function only and recompile, the only thing you'll notice initially is that you won't be able to embed the control in a container until you modify the license file to contain the same string as that now held in the control, *ILOVEOLE*. After you've done that, all operations will succeed until you create and run an executable application using this control. What will happen is that the container will call your new implementation to get the license key, but the comparison mechanics are still the same as they ever were, so the comparison will fail because the strings are now different. Therefore, when you try to run the application, it will fail to embed the control.

The next function to change is the *VerifyUserLicense* member of the object factory. Again, all you need to do here is to alter the default override prepared for you by ControlWizard. This function is called only once by the framework, by the

IsLicenseValid function. To ensure that the control is currently licensed, however, that function is called in numerous places, such as in *CreateInstance* and *CreateInstanceLic*.

The default code calls an MFC global function, *AfxVerifyLicFile*, which compares the license string it is passed in with the requisite number of characters from the start of the file. This is what you need to change, so the new function (borrowing heavily from the implementation of *AfxVerifyLicFile*), looks like that shown in Listing 15-3.

```
BOOL CLicenseCtrl::CLicenseCtrlFactory::VerifyUserLicense()
{
    // Assume the worst...
    BOOL bVerified = FALSE;

    // Look for license file in same directory as this DLL.
    TCHAR szPathName [ _MAX_PATH ];
    ::GetModuleFileName ( AfxGetInstanceHandle(), szPathName,
        _MAX_PATH );
    LPTSTR pszFileName = _tcsrchr( szPathName, '\\' ) + 1;
    _tcscpy( pszFileName, _szLicFileName );

    unsigned int nLen = _tcslen( _szLicString );
    LPTSTR pszBuf = new TCHAR [ nLen + 3 ];

    TRY
    {
        // Open file, read content and compare.

        CStdioFile file ( szPathName, CFile::modeRead |
            CFile::typeText );
        file.ReadString ( pszBuf, nLen + 2 );
        if ( pszBuf [ nLen ] == '\n' )
        {
            pszBuf [ nLen ] = '\0';
        }
            // Strings are the same length?
        if ( _tcslen( pszBuf ) == nLen )
        {
                // Are first five characters different?
            if ( _tcsncmp( pszBuf, _szLicString, 5 ) != 0 )
            {
                    // And the last three the same?
                if ( _tcscmp( pszBuf + 5, _szLicString + 5 ) == 0 )
                {
```

Listing 15-3. *The modified* VerifyUserLicense *function, using the new comparison scheme.* (continued)

(continued)

```
                bVerified = TRUE;
            }
        }
    }
}
END_TRY

delete [] pszBuf;
return bVerified;
}
```

This function now looks more complicated than before, but that's mainly because everything you see here now was previously held in the innocuous-looking call to *AfxVerifyLicFile*. Let's look at what the code is doing. The first thing it does is to attempt to open the license file, using the same path as the one in which the control DLL resides but changing the filename to be that of the license file. If this succeeds, it reads in a string of text. This read ends either when a new line is encountered or the end of file is reached or the number of characters read gets to the specified maximum. If the string ended with a new line (perfectly valid for it to do so, of course), the newline character put into the receiving buffer is removed again. Notice that I only replace it if it occurs at the position it would be in if the string read in was the same length as the license key held in the control file. There's no point in changing it under any other circumstance, because a new line at any other point indicates that the string read in is longer or shorter than the stored license key string. The next line catches this, where its length is explicitly compared against the license key length. If the lengths are the same, the comparison continues to ensure that the first five characters of the string are different. If this also succeeds, the final test is performed: are the strings identical from the sixth character onwards? If they are, the local variable intended for the return value is set to *TRUE*; in all other cases it remains at *FALSE*. Then, when the function ends, it returns success or failure as appropriate.

If you compile the control with this change and try it again in Test Container, it will now fail because the string in the license file is identical to that in the control. Change one or more of the first five characters in the license file to get it to work.

This control will still fail if it's used to create an executable application, because the OLE CDK implementation of *IClassFactory2::CreateInstanceLic* uses a different function for license verification: a member function of the *COleObjectFactoryEx* class, named *VerifyLicenseKey*. This function is used to compare the license key passed into the *CreateInstanceLic* method against the one stored in the control itself. You'll need to override this function, too, if you want the last case to work properly. Add the *VerifyLicenseKey* declaration to the factory object in LICENCTL.H (just after the declaration for *GetLicenseKey*), and then add the source code for the function to LICENCTL.CPP. Listing 15-4 shows how to do the latter.

```
BOOL CLicenseCtrl::CLicenseCtrlFactory::VerifyLicenseKey ( BSTR
    bstrKey )
{
    BOOL bVerified = FALSE;
        // Strings are the same length?
    if ( _tcslen( bstrKey ) == _tcslen( _szLicString ) )
    {
            // Are first five characters different?
        if ( _tcsncmp( bstrKey, _szLicString, 5 ) != 0 )
        {
                // And the last three the same?
            if ( _tcscmp( bstrKey + 5, _szLicString + 5 ) == 0 )
            {
                bVerified = TRUE;
            }
        }
    }
    return bVerified;
}
```

Listing 15-4. *The override of* VerifyLicenseKey, *the member function used during* IClassFactory2::CreateInstanceLic *to verify the passed-in license key.*

Most of the mechanics of *VerifyLicenseKey* are similar to those in the previous function, as the algorithm for comparison remains the same. The only real difference is that there's no need to open the licensing file.

NOTE I'm assuming textual license keys in this code by treating the *BSTR* passed in as a normal string. If you want binary keys, you'll need to modify the way in which each of these three modified functions works, being explicit about the binary nature of your keys.

You can find the source code for this modified version of the control in the \OLECTRLS\CHAP15\LICENSE WITH MODIFIED SCHEME directory on the companion CD-ROM.

MULTI-LEVEL LICENSING

The last thing to look at in this chapter is the way in which the licensing scheme can be adapted in another way — this time to provide different levels of functionality and/or different user interfaces to users, depending on what level of license they have. To get the basics of such a scheme working, the modifications required to the standard licensing scheme provided by the CDK are remarkably similar to the example in the previous section. The same three functions need modification, and this time I'll also show you a way to add a means for the control to expose its current level of licensing to the outside world.

To accomplish all this, I'm going to create a version of the License control that has two levels of license: Level 1, the basic level, is akin to the idea of a "standard edition" product; Level 2, which adds more functionality, equates to a "professional edition."

The control has a property, *LicenseLevel*, which is Boolean and is set to *FALSE* when the control is licensed at the standard-edition level and set to *TRUE* when licensed at the professionial-edition level. It displays a single line of text, "Standard" or "Professional," depending on its license level, and the About box is altered to show the same string when it is displayed. Finally, the control's property page has a check box on it labeled Professional Features Enabled, which will be checked when the *LicenseLevel* property is *TRUE* and unchecked when it is *FALSE*.

As a small twist, the control has reduced functionality in standard mode: the *LicenseLevel* property becomes read-only and cannot be altered. Not a significant drop in functionality, I agree, but it does demonstrate the possibilities.

Changing the "License" Control for Multi-Level Licensing

So, the first steps required are to change the licensing scheme itself. This one's going to work by looking for one of these two strings:

```
Copyright (c) 1995 Microsoft Corporation (Standard Edition)
```

or

```
Copyright (c) 1995 Microsoft Corporation (Professional Edition)
```

The first string sets the license level to standard, the second string to professional. If the license key matches neither of these strings, then (just as in the original License control) the control considers itself unlicensed and can't be created.

Replace the one license string variable with two, thus:

```
static const TCHAR BASED_CODE _szLicStringStdEdition[] =
    _T("Copyright (c) 1995 Microsoft Corporation (Standard Edition)");

static const TCHAR BASED_CODE _szLicStringProEdition[] =
    _T("Copyright (c) 1995 Microsoft Corporation (Professional Edition)");
```

and change the three licensing functions so they are like the ones shown in Listing 15-5.

```
//////////////////////////////////////////////////////////////////
// CLicenseCtrl::CLicenseCtrlFactory::VerifyUserLicense -
// Checks for existence of a user license

BOOL CLicenseCtrl::CLicenseCtrlFactory::VerifyUserLicense()
{
    BOOL bLicensed = FALSE;

    if ( AfxVerifyLicFile ( AfxGetInstanceHandle(), _szLicFileName,
        _szLicStringStdEdition ) )
    {
        bLicensed = TRUE;
        m_bProEdition = FALSE;
    }
    else if ( AfxVerifyLicFile ( AfxGetInstanceHandle(),
        _szLicFileName, _szLicStringProEdition ) )
    {
        bLicensed = TRUE;
        m_bProEdition = TRUE;
    }
    return bLicensed;
}


//////////////////////////////////////////////////////////////////
// CLicenseCtrl::CLicenseCtrlFactory::GetLicenseKey -
// Returns a runtime licensing key

BOOL CLicenseCtrl::CLicenseCtrlFactory::GetLicenseKey(DWORD
    dwReserved, BSTR FAR* pbstrKey)
{
    if (pbstrKey == NULL)
        return FALSE;
    if ( m_bProEdition )
    {
        *pbstrKey = SysAllocString ( _szLicStringProEdition );
    }
    else
    {
        *pbstrKey = SysAllocString ( _szLicStringStdEdition );
    }
    return (*pbstrKey != NULL);
}
BOOL CLicenseCtrl::CLicenseCtrlFactory::VerifyLicenseKey ( BSTR
```

Listing 15-5. *The three licensing functions, modified for a simple multi-*   *(continued)*
level license scheme.

(continued)

```
    bstrKey )
{
    BOOL bLicensed = FALSE;

    if ( bstrKey != NULL )
    {
        UINT cch = SysStringLen ( bstrKey );
        if ( memcmp ( _szLicStringProEdition, bstrKey, cch ) == 0 )
        {
            bLicensed = TRUE;
            m_bProEdition = TRUE;
        }
        else if ( memcmp ( _szLicStringStdEdition, bstrKey, cch )
            == 0 )
        {
            bLicensed = TRUE;
            m_bProEdition = FALSE;
        }
    }
    return bLicensed;
}
```

As you can see by looking through the code, the only difference between this variant of the scheme and the original is that the code now checks against each string possibility and sets a member variable (of the OLE factory) as appropriate. By the way, you need to declare this member variable inside your factory object, so modify the declaration in the header file to look like this:

```
BEGIN_OLEFACTORY(CLicenseCtrl)          // Class factory and guid
    virtual BOOL VerifyUserLicense();
    virtual BOOL GetLicenseKey(DWORD, BSTR FAR*);
    virtual BOOL VerifyLicenseKey ( BSTR );          // Runtime
    BOOL m_bProEdition;
END_OLEFACTORY(CLicenceCtrl)
```

which declares a Boolean member variable called *m_bProEdition*.

Change the *OnDraw* member function of the control so that it displays the relevant license level as its output text by replacing the default call to the *Ellipse* function with the following code, which looks at the factory's member variable and draws the appropriate string:

```
pdc -> TextOut ( rcBounds.left + 3, rcBounds.top + 3,
    factory.m_bProEdition ? "Professional" : "Standard" );
```

As you can see, the *COleControl* class has a member variable called *factory*, which is declared for it by the class factory macros (for example, *DECLARE_OLE-CREATE_EX* or *BEGIN_OLEFACTORY*) and which holds the factory object.

The next thing is to make the About box more functional. First use the dialog editor to add a static text box saying "Current License Held." Add another static text box directly to the right of this, with no caption initially. Be sure that it is big enough to hold the text "Professional" and call it *IDC_LICLEVEL*. Now add a wrapper class and a member variable for the About box by invoking ClassWizard. It will notice that there is currently no wrapper class for the About box dialog, so it will ask if you want to create one based on *CDialog*. Say "yes," and name it *CAbout*. Add a member variable to it called *m_strLevel*, attached to the *IDC_LICLEVEL* static text box. Don't worry about length validation.

Now change the *AboutBox* method handler to look like this:

```
void CLicenseCtrl::AboutBox()
{
    CAbout dlgAbout ( this );
    dlgAbout.m_strLevel = factory.m_bProEdition ?
        "Professional" : "Standard";
    dlgAbout.DoModal();
}
```

This is very similar to the original version except that it's now invoking an instance of the *CAbout* class, rather than a generic *CDialog* as before. That's why the constructor parameter has changed from the resource ID of the dialog template to a pointer to the parent window. By setting the *CAbout* class's *m_strLevel* variable to a given string, the actual *IDC_LICLEVEL* text box will get the same value to display during the default *CAbout::InitDialog*. You'll also need to add an *#include* for ABOUT.H to the LICENCTL.CPP file.

The next change is to add the *LicenseLevel* property to the control. Do so using ClassWizard, and ensure that it has type *BOOL* and uses get and set methods. The code for these methods is shown in Listing 15-6.

```
BOOL CLicenseCtrl::GetLicenseLevel()
{
    return factory.m_bProEdition;
}

void CLicenseCtrl::SetLicenseLevel(BOOL bNewValue)
{
    if ( factory.m_bProEdition )
```

Listing 15-6. *The implementation of the* LicenseLevel *property.*   *(continued)*

(continued)

```
    {
        factory.m_bProEdition = FALSE;
        SetModifiedFlag();
        InvalidateControl();
    }
    else
    {
        SetNotSupported();
    }
}
```

The set function is the only one of interest. It checks the current license level and, if it is professional level, switches it to standard, tells the control that it is now "dirty," and tells it to repaint itself. If, on the other hand, the license level is already standard mode, the property refuses to let itself be changed and throws an exception up to the caller using the standard *SetNotSupported* function.

The only outstanding change is to add the new property to the control's property page, using a check box. Attach a member variable to this check box inside the property page class, and ensure that it is attached to the *LicenseLevel* property. You can find the source code for the final version of the License control in the \OLECTRLS\CHAP15\LICENSE WITH MULTIPLE LEVELS directory on the companion CD-ROM.

Chapter 16

ISimpleFrameSite (or Who's in Control?)

Sometimes one control needs to be the visual "host" of other controls. Obvious examples are group boxes and three-dimensional frames. Now, because there is no means within a control to specify that it is the parent or child of another control, all OLE controls within a given container are, at best, siblings. So what happens when a group box containing three radio buttons is moved? And what happens when the group box is clicked on, or, even more interestingly, when a radio button is clicked on? If all the controls are active, at least the hit-testing will work, and it is easy for the container to move the contained controls in concert with the group box, and each control will be able to draw itself properly. Some containers, however, such as Visual Basic version 4.0, don't activate all controls in design-time. Therefore, without further support, contained controls won't be drawn properly, hit-testing will fail, and the contained controls won't move along with the group box.

Unless the group box control declares itself capable of supporting the *ISimpleFrameSite* interface, it will behave exactly like any other independent window would. The behavior you'd want in these situations, though, might be that the radio buttons move with the group box, and you might want the clicks on it to be translated to clicks on the radio buttons. It would seem reasonable for you also to expect the radio buttons to be able to draw themselves. Visual Basic in design mode activates only those controls marked as "simple frame" controls. For the desired behavior to occur, the container itself needs to support the other end of the simple-frame protocol.

THE *ISIMPLEFRAMESITE* INTERFACE

If you're writing controls using the OLE CDK (which of course you are), all you need to know about *ISimpleFrameSite* is that if you want its support, you must call *EnableSimpleFrame* early on in your control's life, such as during its construction. You really ought to set one of the miscellaneous status bits on the control, too, called *OLEMISC_SIMPLEFRAME*.

NOTE   If you're creating the control from scratch, there's a ControlWizard option that does precisely these things for you. If you'd like to know some of the details of what the simple-frame protocol does and how it does it, read the rest of this extremely short chapter. Otherwise, skip now to Chapter 17, happy in the knowledge that if you ever need this support, it's just a function call away.

A control that needs to use the facilities offered by the simple-frame protocol will do a few things:

- It will set the *OLEMISC_SIMPLEFRAME* bit.

- It will get a pointer to the container's implementation of *ISimpleFrameSite*.

- If this pointer is not *NULL*, it will call through it to the methods on the interface at appropriate moments.

If the third point seems a little vague, that's because I have yet to describe the interface's methods or appropriate moments to call them. The interface has two methods in addition to the standard *IUnknown* ones, named *PreMessageFilter* and *PostMessageFilter*. The names of these methods alone provide excellent clues as to where they should be called. *PreMessageFilter* should be called when a message is received, to give the container a chance to deal with it first; and *PostMessageFilter* is called after the control has processed a message, to allow it to take any action based on the handling.

If you take a look at the CDK source code, you'll notice that, if simple-frame support is enabled, these two methods are called in the *COleControl::WindowProc* member, which dispatches messages through the message map. Both methods take the handle of the control window, the message, its *WPARAM* and *LPARAM* values, and a pointer to a location to store the result as parameters. To keep messages in sync inside the container, *PreMessageFilter* also passes the address of a variable that will hold a "magic cookie," which is then passed as the last parameter to *PostMessageFilter*, allowing the container to match the two calls. The magic-cookie value is assigned by the container during the call to *PreMessageFilter*.

From the control perspective, that's all there is to simple-frame support. Bear in mind, however, that not all containers support a simple frame. The support required of a container, even though it's manifested through only two interface methods, is considerably more complex than this. A container with simple-frame support (such as design-time Visual Basic version 4.0) will ensure that controls inside simple-frame controls will see keyboard and mouse events that are really meant for them but that are hidden by the overlaying simple frame control. It will also ensure that the controls are drawn properly, by intercepting *WM_PAINT* messages for the containing control and ensuring that the contained controls also get asked to render themselves — and of course it will also ensure that movement of the containing control also causes the contained controls to move.

When Visual Basic version 4.0 is in runtime mode, simple-frame support becomes a lot less important, as each control then has a real, active window of its own, and Visual Basic also physically reparents the contained controls to be children of the containing control. (This is *HWND* parenting; from the OLE perspective, they remain and must remain siblings so that the real container gets the events.) This reparenting, together with the creation of windows for the controls, ensures that hit-testing works and also ensures that movement of the parent window (the containing control) causes its children (the contained controls) to move as well. Finally, as the contained controls are now real child windows of the containing control, they'll render themselves properly in response to *WM_PAINT* messages. So it all "just works"!

Is simple-frame support important? Without it, containers that don't activate all controls in design-time will not interact correctly with those controls. With it, you're at least able to tell the container that your control is a containing control and would therefore be really happy if the container could honor your control's wishes. Some containers will simply refuse to listen, of course, and some don't need to care too much because they always activate all their controls. Even with these latter containers, however, some things won't work unless the containers also dynamically reparent the contained controls with the *HWND* of the containing control.

Chapter 17

Converting a VBX and Subclassing Windows Controls

Early in this book, I contended that Visual Basic custom controls, or VBXs, were the true start of the component software revolution. I also stated that VBXs were limited in that they could not be ported easily to 32-bit platforms or to non-Intel architectures, and that Microsoft had chosen OLE controls as the new model. For porting to work really well, there must be a mechanism to convert between current VBXs and new OLE controls. This manifests itself in two ways. First, there needs to be a way in which control developers can take an existing VBX and convert it to an OLE control. Second, there needs to be a way in which VBX containers can adapt to the new model.

If I take the second aspect first, the good news is that Visual Basic version 4.0 can read in existing Visual Basic projects and convert any VBXs used in that project that it knows about and convert them to OLE controls. The bad news is that at present very few other VBX hosts can do this. For example, Visual C++ cannot convert a 16-bit form containing VBXs to a similar form using OLE controls, although obviously it can "convert" a 16-bit form to a 32-bit equivalent. So, in all likelihood you'll have some work to do.

The first part is more significant to control writers, and is also the most difficult part. Converting a VBX to an OLE control is by no means an automatic process, and this chapter examines the process and the related issues.

Many controls are variations on existing themes, using built-in Windows controls to provide the majority of functionality and then altering the behavior in some way to make it a custom control. The same technique, known as "control subclassing," can be used with OLE controls, and the second half of this chapter looks at the mechanism and the pitfalls associated with it.

FYI Why lump VBX migration and subclassing in the same chapter? Because numerous VBXs are actually subclassed Windows controls, so if you're interested in one you're likely to be interested in the other.

VBX CONVERSION

An ideal tool for converting a VBX to an OLE control would be able to look at the VBX module and reverse-engineer it to provide an OLE control with identical functionality. Such a tool does exist—the only problem is that it's you, the control author! The OLE CDK does provide a tool that does some of the grunt work for you, but it can't convert the actual working code of your control to the OLE control model, for two reasons:

- It's potentially illegal, as it allows you to take any existing VBX, regardless of who wrote it, and create your own personal OLE control version.

- It's difficult!

I'll take a look at the things that are done for you, and then I'll concentrate on those things that are not done, and how you might go about doing them. A host of detail could have been covered in this chapter, but I restrained myself. Why? Because if you've read through the majority of this book and are happy building OLE controls, most of the conversion aspects I don't cover have solutions that will seem pretty obvious to you.

What ControlWizard Does

When you create a control project with ControlWizard, one of the options available to you is to take an existing VBX and create a skeleton OLE control from it. This OLE control will have the same properties and events as the original VBX, but it will have no functionality inside those properties and methods. A VBX has no concept of custom methods, so no conversion is possible between a VBX's methods and those of the newly created OLE control.

What you'll be left with at the end of the process is a set of source files for an OLE control, similar in most ways to a standard OLE control project except that the ODL file will have entries for each of the properties and events inherited from the VBX; in addition, the control source file and header file will have the appropriate macros, functions, and variables to actually implement all the properties and methods. As an example of the output, Listing 17-1 contains the ODL file generated by running the conversion process on the standard Visual Basic OLE container control, MSOLE2.VBX. Listings 17-2 (beginning on page 396) and 17-3 (beginning on page 401) contain the generated header and source files for the control itself. Notice that the conversion was carried out to a new control project called VBX1 — hence the names of the files and objects in these listings.

VBX1.ODL

```
// vbx1.odl : type library source for OLE Custom Control project.

// This file will be processed by the Make Type Library (mktyplib)
//    tool to produce the type library (vbx1.tlb) that will become a
//    resource in vbx1.ocx.

#include <olectl.h>

[ uuid(14A99103-A8BF-11CE-99BF-00AA0047D4FD), version(1.0),
  helpstring("Vbx1 OLE Custom Control module"), control ]
library Vbx1Lib
{
    importlib(STDOLE_TLB);
    importlib(STDTYPE_TLB);

    //  Primary dispatch interface for CVbx1Ctrl

    [ uuid(14A99101-A8BF-11CE-99BF-00AA0047D4FD),
      helpstring("Dispatch interface for Vbx1 Control"), hidden ]
    dispinterface _DVbx1
    {
        properties:
            // NOTE - ClassWizard will maintain property information
            //   here.
            //    Use extreme caution when editing this section.
            //{{AFX_ODL_PROP(CVbx1Ctrl)
            [id(1)] BSTR Class;
            [id(2)] short OLEType;
            [id(3)] BSTR SourceDoc;
```

Listing 17-1. *The ODL file output by ControlWizard as a result of converting MSOLE2.VBX.* (continued)

(continued)

```
        [id(4)] BSTR SourceItem;
        [id(5)] short UpdateOptions;
        [id(6)] BSTR HostName;
        [id(7)] short SizeMode;
        [id(8)] short AutoActivate;
        [id(9)] boolean AutoVerbMenu;
        [id(10)] boolean AppIsRunning;
        [id(11)] IPictureDisp* Picture;
        [id(12)] IDispatch* Object;
        [id(13)] long Data;
        [id(14)] BSTR DataText;
        [id(15)] BSTR Format;
        [id(17)] short ObjectAcceptFormatsCount;
        [id(19)] short ObjectGetFormatsCount;
        [id(20)] short OLETypeAllowed;
        [id(21)] boolean PasteOK;
        [id(24)] short ObjectVerbsCount;
        [id(25)] short Verb;
        [id(26)] short FileNumber;
        [id(27)] short Action;
        [id(28)] short MiscFlags;
        [id(29)] long OleObjectBlob;
        [id(30)] long cxTHk;
        [id(31)] long cyTHk;
        [id(32)] boolean fFFHk;
        [id(33)] short DisplayType;
        [id(34)] long LpOleObject;
        [id(DISPID_BACKCOLOR),bindable,requestedit] OLE_COLOR
            BackColor;
        [id(DISPID_BORDERSTYLE),bindable,requestedit] short
            BorderStyle;
        [id(DISPID_ENABLED),bindable,requestedit] boolean
            Enabled;
        [id(DISPID_HWND)] short hWnd;

        //}}AFX_ODL_PROP

    methods:
        // NOTE - ClassWizard will maintain method information
        //   here.
        //    Use extreme caution when editing this section.
        //{{AFX_ODL_METHOD(CVbx1Ctrl)

        [id(16), propget] BSTR ObjectAcceptFormats(short index);
```

(continued)

```
[id(16), propput] void ObjectAcceptFormats(short index,
    BSTR strObjectAcceptFormats);
[id(18), propget] BSTR ObjectGetFormats(short index);
[id(18), propput] void ObjectGetFormats(short index,
    BSTR strObjectGetFormats);
[id(22), propget] BSTR ObjectVerbs(short index);
[id(22), propput] void ObjectVerbs(short index, BSTR
    strObjectVerbs);
[id(23), propget] long ObjectVerbFlags(short index);
[id(23), propput] void ObjectVerbFlags(short index,
    long lObjectVerbFlags);

//}}AFX_ODL_METHOD

[id(DISPID_ABOUTBOX)] void AboutBox();
};


// Event dispatch interface for CVbx1Ctrl

[ uuid(14A99102-A8BF-11CE-99BF-00AA0047D4FD),
  helpstring("Event interface for Vbx1 Control") ]
dispinterface _DVbx1Events
{
    properties:
        // Event interface has no properties

    methods:
        // NOTE - ClassWizard will maintain event information
        //    here.
        //     Use extreme caution when editing this section.
        //{{AFX_ODL_EVENT(CVbx1Ctrl)
        [id(1)] void Resize(float* HeightNew, float* WidthNew);
        [id(2)] void Updated(short* Code);
        [id(DISPID_CLICK)] void Click();
        [id(DISPID_DBLCLICK)] void DblClick();
        [id(DISPID_KEYDOWN)] void KeyDown(short* KeyCode,
            short Shift);
        [id(DISPID_KEYPRESS)] void KeyPress(short* KeyAscii);
        [id(DISPID_KEYUP)] void KeyUp(short* KeyCode, short
            Shift);
        [id(DISPID_MOUSEDOWN)] void MouseDown(short Button,
            short Shift, OLE_XPOS_PIXELS X, OLE_YPOS_PIXELS Y);
        [id(DISPID_MOUSEMOVE)] void MouseMove(short Button,
            short Shift, OLE_XPOS_PIXELS X, OLE_YPOS_PIXELS Y);
```

(continued)

(continued)

```
            [id(DISPID_MOUSEUP)] void MouseUp(short Button, short
                Shift, OLE_XPOS_PIXELS X, OLE_YPOS_PIXELS Y);

            //}}AFX_ODL_EVENT
    };

    //  Class information for CVbx1Ctrl

    [ uuid(14A99100-A8BF-11CE-99BF-00AA0047D4FD),
      helpstring("Vbx1 Control"), control ]
    coclass Vbx1
    {
        [default] dispinterface _DVbx1;
        [default, source] dispinterface _DVbx1Events;
    };


    //{{AFX_APPEND_ODL}}
};
```

VBX1CTL.H

```
// vbx1ctl.h : Declaration of the CVbx1Ctrl OLE control class.

/////////////////////////////////////////////////////////////////
// CVbx1Ctrl : See vbx1ctl.cpp for implementation.

class CVbx1Ctrl : public COleControl
{
    DECLARE_DYNCREATE(CVbx1Ctrl)

// Constructor
public:
    CVbx1Ctrl();

// Overrides

    // Drawing function
    virtual void OnDraw(
            CDC* pdc, const CRect& rcBounds, const CRect&
            rcInvalid);
```

Listing 17-2. *The header file output by ControlWizard as a result of* *(continued)*
converting MSOLE2.VBX.

```
    // Persistence
    virtual void DoPropExchange(CPropExchange* pPX);

    // Reset control state
    virtual void OnResetState();

// Implementation
protected:
    ~CVbx1Ctrl();

    DECLARE_OLECREATE_EX(CVbx1Ctrl)      // Class factory and guid
    DECLARE_OLETYPELIB(CVbx1Ctrl)        // GetTypeInfo
    DECLARE_PROPPAGEIDS(CVbx1Ctrl)       // Property page IDs
    DECLARE_OLECTLTYPE(CVbx1Ctrl)        // Type name and misc status

    // VBX port support
    BOOL PreCreateWindow(CREATESTRUCT& cs);

    // Storage for Get/Set properties
    CString m_strClass;
    CString m_strSourceDoc;
    CString m_strSourceItem;
    short m_enumUpdateOptions;
    CString m_strHostName;
    short m_enumSizeMode;
    CPictureHolder m_cPicPicture;
    CString m_strFormat;
    short m_iFileNumber;
    long m_cxcxTHk;
    long m_cycyTHk;
    BOOL m_bfFFHk;
    short m_enumDisplayType;


// Message maps
    //{{AFX_MSG(CVbx1Ctrl)
        // NOTE - ClassWizard will add and remove member functions
        //   here.
        //    DO NOT EDIT what you see in these blocks of generated
        //      code !
    //}}AFX_MSG
    DECLARE_MESSAGE_MAP()

// Dispatch maps
    //{{AFX_DISPATCH(CVbx1Ctrl)
```

(continued)

397

(continued)

```
        // NOTE - ClassWizard will add and remove member functions
        //   here.
        //     DO NOT EDIT what you see in these blocks of generated
        //       code !
    afx_msg BSTR GetClass();
    afx_msg void SetClass(LPCTSTR);
    afx_msg short GetOLEType();
    afx_msg void SetOLEType(short);
    afx_msg BSTR GetSourceDoc();
    afx_msg void SetSourceDoc(LPCTSTR);
    afx_msg BSTR GetSourceItem();
    afx_msg void SetSourceItem(LPCTSTR);
    afx_msg short GetUpdateOptions();
    afx_msg void SetUpdateOptions(short);
    afx_msg BSTR GetHostName();
    afx_msg void SetHostName(LPCTSTR);
    afx_msg short GetSizeMode();
    afx_msg void SetSizeMode(short);
    short m_enumAutoActivate;
    BOOL m_bAutoVerbMenu;
    afx_msg BOOL GetAppIsRunning();
    afx_msg void SetAppIsRunning(BOOL);
    afx_msg LPPICTUREDISP GetPicture();
    afx_msg void SetPicture(LPPICTUREDISP);
    afx_msg LPDISPATCH GetObject();
    afx_msg void SetObject(LPDISPATCH);
    afx_msg long GetData();
    afx_msg void SetData(long);
    afx_msg BSTR GetDataText();
    afx_msg void SetDataText(LPCTSTR);
    afx_msg BSTR GetFormat();
    afx_msg void SetFormat(LPCTSTR);
    afx_msg BSTR GetObjectAcceptFormats(short index);
    afx_msg void SetObjectAcceptFormats(short index, LPCTSTR);
    afx_msg short GetObjectAcceptFormatsCount();
    afx_msg void SetObjectAcceptFormatsCount(short);
    afx_msg BSTR GetObjectGetFormats(short index);
    afx_msg void SetObjectGetFormats(short index, LPCTSTR);
    afx_msg short GetObjectGetFormatsCount();
    afx_msg void SetObjectGetFormatsCount(short);
    short m_enumOLETypeAllowed;
    afx_msg BOOL GetPasteOK();
    afx_msg void SetPasteOK(BOOL);
```

(continued)

```
    afx_msg BSTR GetObjectVerbs(short index);
    afx_msg void SetObjectVerbs(short index, LPCTSTR);
    afx_msg long GetObjectVerbFlags(short index);
    afx_msg void SetObjectVerbFlags(short index, long);
    afx_msg short GetObjectVerbsCount();
    afx_msg void SetObjectVerbsCount(short);
    short m_iVerb;
    afx_msg short GetFileNumber();
    afx_msg void SetFileNumber(short);
    afx_msg short GetAction();
    afx_msg void SetAction(short);
    short m_iMiscFlags;
    afx_msg long GetOleObjectBlob();
    afx_msg void SetOleObjectBlob(long);
    afx_msg long GetcxTHk();
    afx_msg void SetcxTHk(long);
    afx_msg long GetcyTHk();
    afx_msg void SetcyTHk(long);
    afx_msg BOOL GetfFFHk();
    afx_msg void SetfFFHk(BOOL);
    afx_msg short GetDisplayType();
    afx_msg void SetDisplayType(short);
    afx_msg long GetLpOleObject();
    afx_msg void SetLpOleObject(long);

    //}}AFX_DISPATCH
    DECLARE_DISPATCH_MAP()

    afx_msg void AboutBox();

// Event maps
    //{{AFX_EVENT(CVbx1Ctrl)
        // NOTE - ClassWizard will add and remove member functions
        //    here.
        //     DO NOT EDIT what you see in these blocks of generated
        //        code !
    void FireResize(float FAR* HeightNew, float FAR* WidthNew)
        { FireEvent(eventidResize, EVENT_PARAM( VTS_PR4 VTS_PR4),
        HeightNew, WidthNew); }
    void FireUpdated(short FAR* Code)
        { FireEvent(eventidUpdated, EVENT_PARAM( VTS_PI2), Code); }

    //}}AFX_EVENT
```

(continued)

(continued)

```
    DECLARE_EVENT_MAP()

// Dispatch and event IDs
public:
    enum {
    //{{AFX_DISP_ID(CVbx1Ctrl)
        // NOTE: ClassWizard will add and remove enumeration
        //    elements here.
        //     DO NOT EDIT what you see in these blocks of generated
        //      code !
    dispidClass = 1L,
    dispidOLEType = 2L,
    dispidSourceDoc = 3L,
    dispidSourceItem = 4L,
    dispidUpdateOptions = 5L,
    dispidHostName = 6L,
    dispidSizeMode = 7L,
    dispidAutoActivate = 8L,
    dispidAutoVerbMenu = 9L,
    dispidAppIsRunning = 10L,
    dispidPicture = 11L,
    dispidObject = 12L,
    dispidData = 13L,
    dispidDataText = 14L,
    dispidFormat = 15L,
    dispidObjectAcceptFormats = 16L,
    dispidObjectAcceptFormatsCount = 17L,
    dispidObjectGetFormats = 18L,
    dispidObjectGetFormatsCount = 19L,
    dispidOLETypeAllowed = 20L,
    dispidPasteOK = 21L,
    dispidObjectVerbs = 22L,
    dispidObjectVerbFlags = 23L,
    dispidObjectVerbsCount = 24L,
    dispidVerb = 25L,
    dispidFileNumber = 26L,
    dispidAction = 27L,
    dispidMiscFlags = 28L,
    dispidOleObjectBlob = 29L,
    dispidCxTHk = 30L,
    dispidCyTHk = 31L,
    dispidFFFHk = 32L,
    dispidDisplayType = 33L,
    dispidLpOleObject = 34L,
```

(continued)

```
    eventidResize = 1L,
    eventidUpdated = 2L,

    //}}AFX_DISP_ID
    };
};
```

VBX1CTL.CPP

```
// vbx1ctl.cpp : Implementation of the CVbx1Ctrl OLE control class.

#include "stdafx.h"
#include "vbx1.h"
#include "vbx1ctl.h"
#include "vbx1ppg.h"


#ifdef _DEBUG
#undef THIS_FILE
static char BASED_CODE THIS_FILE[] = __FILE__;
#endif


IMPLEMENT_DYNCREATE(CVbx1Ctrl, COleControl)


/////////////////////////////////////////////////////////////////////
// Message map

BEGIN_MESSAGE_MAP(CVbx1Ctrl, COleControl)
    //{{AFX_MSG_MAP(CVbx1Ctrl)
    // NOTE - ClassWizard will add and remove message map entries
    //     DO NOT EDIT what you see in these blocks of generated
    //        code !
    //}}AFX_MSG_MAP
    ON_OLEVERB(AFX_IDS_VERB_PROPERTIES, OnProperties)
END_MESSAGE_MAP()


/////////////////////////////////////////////////////////////////////
// Dispatch map

BEGIN_DISPATCH_MAP(CVbx1Ctrl, COleControl)
    //{{AFX_DISPATCH_MAP(CVbx1Ctrl)
```

Listing 17-3. *The source file output by ControlWizard as a result of* (continued)
converting MSOLE2.VBX.

(continued)

```
// NOTE - ClassWizard will add and remove dispatch map entries
//     DO NOT EDIT what you see in these blocks of generated
//     code !
DISP_PROPERTY_EX(CVbx1Ctrl, "Class", GetClass, SetClass, VT_BSTR)
DISP_PROPERTY_EX(CVbx1Ctrl, "OLEType", GetOLEType, SetOLEType,
    VT_I2)
DISP_PROPERTY_EX(CVbx1Ctrl, "SourceDoc", GetSourceDoc,
    SetSourceDoc, VT_BSTR)
DISP_PROPERTY_EX(CVbx1Ctrl, "SourceItem", GetSourceItem,
    SetSourceItem, VT_BSTR)
DISP_PROPERTY_EX(CVbx1Ctrl, "UpdateOptions", GetUpdateOptions,
    SetUpdateOptions, VT_I2)
DISP_PROPERTY_EX(CVbx1Ctrl, "HostName", GetHostName,
    SetHostName, VT_BSTR)
DISP_PROPERTY_EX(CVbx1Ctrl, "SizeMode", GetSizeMode,
    SetSizeMode, VT_I2)
DISP_PROPERTY(CVbx1Ctrl, "AutoActivate", m_enumAutoActivate,
    VT_I2)
DISP_PROPERTY(CVbx1Ctrl, "AutoVerbMenu", m_bAutoVerbMenu,
    VT_BOOL)
DISP_PROPERTY_EX(CVbx1Ctrl, "AppIsRunning", GetAppIsRunning,
    SetAppIsRunning, VT_BOOL)
DISP_PROPERTY_EX(CVbx1Ctrl, "Picture", GetPicture, SetPicture,
    VT_PICTURE)
DISP_PROPERTY_EX(CVbx1Ctrl, "Object", GetObject, SetObject,
    VT_DISPATCH)
DISP_PROPERTY_EX(CVbx1Ctrl, "Data", GetData, SetData, VT_I4)
DISP_PROPERTY_EX(CVbx1Ctrl, "DataText", GetDataText,
    SetDataText, VT_BSTR)
DISP_PROPERTY_EX(CVbx1Ctrl, "Format", GetFormat, SetFormat,
    VT_BSTR)
DISP_PROPERTY_PARAM(CVbx1Ctrl, "ObjectAcceptFormats",
    GetObjectAcceptFormats, SetObjectAcceptFormats, VT_BSTR,
    VTS_I2)
DISP_PROPERTY_EX(CVbx1Ctrl, "ObjectAcceptFormatsCount",
    GetObjectAcceptFormatsCount, SetObjectAcceptFormatsCount,
    VT_I2)
DISP_PROPERTY_PARAM(CVbx1Ctrl, "ObjectGetFormats",
    GetObjectGetFormats, SetObjectGetFormats, VT_BSTR, VTS_I2)
DISP_PROPERTY_EX(CVbx1Ctrl, "ObjectGetFormatsCount",
    GetObjectGetFormatsCount, SetObjectGetFormatsCount, VT_I2)
DISP_PROPERTY(CVbx1Ctrl, "OLETypeAllowed", m_enumOLETypeAllowed,
    VT_I2)
DISP_PROPERTY_EX(CVbx1Ctrl, "PasteOK", GetPasteOK, SetPasteOK,
```

(continued)

```
            VT_BOOL)
    DISP_PROPERTY_PARAM(CVbx1Ctrl, "ObjectVerbs", GetObjectVerbs,
        SetObjectVerbs, VT_BSTR, VTS_I2)
    DISP_PROPERTY_PARAM(CVbx1Ctrl, "ObjectVerbFlags",
        GetObjectVerbFlags, SetObjectVerbFlags, VT_I4, VTS_I2)
    DISP_PROPERTY_EX(CVbx1Ctrl, "ObjectVerbsCount",
        GetObjectVerbsCount, SetObjectVerbsCount, VT_I2)
    DISP_PROPERTY(CVbx1Ctrl, "Verb", m_iVerb, VT_I2)
    DISP_PROPERTY_EX(CVbx1Ctrl, "FileNumber", GetFileNumber,
        SetFileNumber, VT_I2)
    DISP_PROPERTY_EX(CVbx1Ctrl, "Action", GetAction, SetAction,
        VT_I2)
    DISP_PROPERTY(CVbx1Ctrl, "MiscFlags", m_iMiscFlags, VT_I2)
    DISP_PROPERTY_EX(CVbx1Ctrl, "OleObjectBlob", GetOleObjectBlob,
        SetOleObjectBlob, VT_I4)
    DISP_PROPERTY_EX(CVbx1Ctrl, "cxTHk", GetcxTHk, SetcxTHk, VT_I4)
    DISP_PROPERTY_EX(CVbx1Ctrl, "cyTHk", GetcyTHk, SetcyTHk, VT_I4)
    DISP_PROPERTY_EX(CVbx1Ctrl, "fFFHk", GetfFFHk, SetfFFHk, VT_BOOL)
    DISP_PROPERTY_EX(CVbx1Ctrl, "DisplayType", GetDisplayType,
        SetDisplayType, VT_I2)
    DISP_PROPERTY_EX(CVbx1Ctrl, "LpOleObject", GetLpOleObject,
        SetLpOleObject, VT_I4)
    DISP_STOCKPROP_BACKCOLOR()
    DISP_STOCKPROP_BORDERSTYLE()
    DISP_STOCKPROP_ENABLED()
    DISP_STOCKPROP_HWND()
    DISP_DEFVALUE(CVbx1Ctrl, "Action")

    //}}AFX_DISPATCH_MAP
    DISP_FUNCTION_ID(CVbx1Ctrl, "AboutBox", DISPID_ABOUTBOX,
        AboutBox, VT_EMPTY, VTS_NONE)
END_DISPATCH_MAP()


/////////////////////////////////////////////////////////////////
// Event map

BEGIN_EVENT_MAP(CVbx1Ctrl, COleControl)
    //{{AFX_EVENT_MAP(CVbx1Ctrl)
    // NOTE - ClassWizard will add and remove event map entries
    //     DO NOT EDIT what you see in these blocks of generated
    //        code !
    EVENT_CUSTOM("Resize", FireResize,  VTS_PR4 VTS_PR4)
    EVENT_CUSTOM("Updated", FireUpdated,  VTS_PI2)
    EVENT_STOCK_CLICK()
```

(continued)

(continued)

```
    EVENT_STOCK_DBLCLICK()
    EVENT_STOCK_KEYDOWN()
    EVENT_STOCK_KEYPRESS()
    EVENT_STOCK_KEYUP()
    EVENT_STOCK_MOUSEDOWN()
    EVENT_STOCK_MOUSEMOVE()
    EVENT_STOCK_MOUSEUP()

    //}}AFX_EVENT_MAP
END_EVENT_MAP()


/////////////////////////////////////////////////////////////////////
// Property pages

// TODO: Add more property pages as needed.  Remember to increase
//    the count!
BEGIN_PROPPAGEIDS(CVbx1Ctrl, 1)
    PROPPAGEID(CVbx1PropPage::guid)
END_PROPPAGEIDS(CVbx1Ctrl)


/////////////////////////////////////////////////////////////////////
// Initialize class factory and guid

IMPLEMENT_OLECREATE_EX(CVbx1Ctrl, "VBX1.Vbx1Ctrl.1",
    0x14a99100, 0xa8bf, 0x11ce, 0x99, 0xbf, 0x0, 0xaa, 0x0, 0x47,
    0xd4, 0xfd)


/////////////////////////////////////////////////////////////////////
// Type library ID and version

IMPLEMENT_OLETYPELIB(CVbx1Ctrl, _tlid, _wVerMajor, _wVerMinor)


/////////////////////////////////////////////////////////////////////
// Interface IDs

const IID BASED_CODE IID_DVbx1 =
        { 0x14a99101, 0xa8bf, 0x11ce, { 0x99, 0xbf, 0x0, 0xaa, 0x0,
        0x47, 0xd4, 0xfd } };
const IID BASED_CODE IID_DVbx1Events =
```

(continued)

```
            { 0x14a99102, 0xa8bf, 0x11ce, { 0x99, 0xbf, 0x0, 0xaa, 0x0,
            0x47, 0xd4, 0xfd } };


//////////////////////////////////////////////////////////////////////
// Control type information

static const DWORD BASED_CODE _dwVbx1OleMisc =
    OLEMISC_ACTIVATEWHENVISIBLE |
    OLEMISC_SETCLIENTSITEFIRST |
    OLEMISC_INSIDEOUT |
    OLEMISC_CANTLINKINSIDE |
    OLEMISC_RECOMPOSEONRESIZE;

IMPLEMENT_OLECTLTYPE(CVbx1Ctrl, IDS_VBX1, _dwVbx1OleMisc)


//////////////////////////////////////////////////////////////////////
// CVbx1Ctrl::CVbx1CtrlFactory::UpdateRegistry -
// Adds or removes system registry entries for CVbx1Ctrl

BOOL CVbx1Ctrl::CVbx1CtrlFactory::UpdateRegistry(BOOL bRegister)
{
    if (bRegister)
        return AfxOleRegisterControlClass(
            AfxGetInstanceHandle(),
            m_clsid,
            m_lpszProgID,
            IDS_VBX1,
            IDB_VBX1,
            FALSE,                          //  Not insertable
            _dwVbx1OleMisc,
            _tlid,
            _wVerMajor,
            _wVerMinor);
    else
        return AfxOleUnregisterClass(m_clsid, m_lpszProgID);
}


//////////////////////////////////////////////////////////////////////
// CVbx1Ctrl::CVbx1Ctrl - Constructor

CVbx1Ctrl::CVbx1Ctrl()
{
```

(continued)

(continued)

```
    InitializeIIDs(&IID_DVbx1, &IID_DVbx1Events);

    // TODO: Initialize your control's instance data here.
}


/////////////////////////////////////////////////////////////////////
// CVbx1Ctrl::~CVbx1Ctrl - Destructor

CVbx1Ctrl::~CVbx1Ctrl()
{
    // TODO: Cleanup your control's instance data here.
}


/////////////////////////////////////////////////////////////////////
// CVbx1Ctrl::OnDraw - Drawing function

void CVbx1Ctrl::OnDraw(
            CDC* pdc, const CRect& rcBounds, const CRect& rcInvalid)
{
    // TODO: Replace the following code with your own drawing code.
    pdc->FillRect(rcBounds,
        CBrush::FromHandle((HBRUSH)GetStockObject
        (WHITE_BRUSH)));
    pdc->Ellipse(rcBounds);
}


/////////////////////////////////////////////////////////////////////
// CVbx1Ctrl::DoPropExchange - Persistence support

void CVbx1Ctrl::DoPropExchange(CPropExchange* pPX)
{
    ExchangeVersion(pPX, MAKELONG(_wVerMinor, _wVerMajor));
    COleControl::DoPropExchange(pPX);

    // TODO: Call PX_ functions for each persistent custom property.

    PX_String(pPX, _T("Class"), m_strClass);
    PX_String(pPX, _T("SourceDoc"), m_strSourceDoc);
    PX_String(pPX, _T("SourceItem"), m_strSourceItem);
    PX_Short(pPX, _T("UpdateOptions"), m_enumUpdateOptions);
```

(continued)

```
    PX_String(pPX, _T("HostName"), m_strHostName);
    PX_Short(pPX, _T("SizeMode"), m_enumSizeMode);
    PX_Short(pPX, _T("AutoActivate"), m_enumAutoActivate);
    PX_Bool(pPX, _T("AutoVerbMenu"), m_bAutoVerbMenu);
    PX_Short(pPX, _T("OLETypeAllowed"), m_enumOLETypeAllowed);
    PX_Short(pPX, _T("Verb"), m_iVerb);
    PX_Short(pPX, _T("MiscFlags"), m_iMiscFlags);
    PX_Bool(pPX, _T("fFFHk"), m_bfFFHk);
    PX_Short(pPX, _T("DisplayType"), m_enumDisplayType);

}


/////////////////////////////////////////////////////////////////////
// CVbx1Ctrl::OnResetState - Reset control to default state

void CVbx1Ctrl::OnResetState()
{
    COleControl::OnResetState();  // Resets defaults found in
                                  //    DoPropExchange

    // TODO: Reset any other control state here.
    m_strClass = "";
    m_strSourceDoc = "";
    m_strSourceItem = "";
    m_enumUpdateOptions = 0;
    m_strHostName = "";
    m_enumSizeMode = 0;
    m_enumAutoActivate = 0;
    m_bAutoVerbMenu = FALSE;
    m_cPicPicture.CreateEmpty();
    m_strFormat = "";
    m_enumOLETypeAllowed = 0;
    m_iVerb = 0;
    m_iFileNumber = 0;
    m_iMiscFlags = 0;
    m_cxcxTHk = 0;
    m_cycyTHk = 0;
    m_bfFFHk = FALSE;
    m_enumDisplayType = 0;

}


/////////////////////////////////////////////////////////////////////
// CVbx1Ctrl::AboutBox - Display an "About" box to the user
```

(continued)

(continued)

```
void CVbx1Ctrl::AboutBox()
{
    CDialog dlgAbout(IDD_ABOUTBOX_VBX1);
    dlgAbout.DoModal();
}


/////////////////////////////////////////////////////////////////////
// CVbx1Ctrl::PreCreateWindow

BOOL CVbx1Ctrl::PreCreateWindow(CREATESTRUCT& cs)
{
    // TODO: Modify windows style flags as necessary
    cs.style |= WS_BORDER;
    return COleControl::PreCreateWindow(cs);
}


/////////////////////////////////////////////////////////////////////
// Member functions ported from VBX control

BSTR CVbx1Ctrl::GetClass()
{
    return SysAllocString(m_strClass);
}

void CVbx1Ctrl::SetClass(LPCTSTR pszClass)
{
    m_strClass = pszClass;
}

short CVbx1Ctrl::GetOLEType()
{
    // TODO: For PF_fNoShow - Return error if (AmbientUserMode
    //    == FALSE)
    // TODO: Return property value
    return 0;
}

void CVbx1Ctrl::SetOLEType(short enumOLEType)
{
    // TODO: For PF_fNoRuntimeW - Return error if (AmbientUserMode
    //    == TRUE)
```

(continued)

```
    // TODO: Set property value
    // TODO: For DT_ENUM properties - check the value for legal range
}

BSTR CVbx1Ctrl::GetSourceDoc()
{
    return SysAllocString(m_strSourceDoc);
}

void CVbx1Ctrl::SetSourceDoc(LPCTSTR pszSourceDoc)
{
    m_strSourceDoc = pszSourceDoc;
}

BSTR CVbx1Ctrl::GetSourceItem()
{
    return SysAllocString(m_strSourceItem);
}

void CVbx1Ctrl::SetSourceItem(LPCTSTR pszSourceItem)
{
    m_strSourceItem = pszSourceItem;
}

short CVbx1Ctrl::GetUpdateOptions()
{
    return m_enumUpdateOptions;
}

void CVbx1Ctrl::SetUpdateOptions(short enumUpdateOptions)
{
    // TODO: For DT_ENUM properties - check the value for legal range
    m_enumUpdateOptions = enumUpdateOptions;
}

BSTR CVbx1Ctrl::GetHostName()
{
    return SysAllocString(m_strHostName);
}

void CVbx1Ctrl::SetHostName(LPCTSTR pszHostName)
{
    m_strHostName = pszHostName;
}
```

(continued)

(continued)

```
short CVbx1Ctrl::GetSizeMode()
{
    return m_enumSizeMode;
}


void CVbx1Ctrl::SetSizeMode(short enumSizeMode)
{
    // TODO: For DT_ENUM properties - check the value for legal range
    m_enumSizeMode = enumSizeMode;
}


BOOL CVbx1Ctrl::GetAppIsRunning()
{
    // TODO: For PF_fNoShow - Return error if (AmbientUserMode
    //    == FALSE)
    // TODO: Return property value
    return FALSE;
}


void CVbx1Ctrl::SetAppIsRunning(BOOL bAppIsRunning)
{
    // TODO: For PF_fNoRuntimeW - Return error if (AmbientUserMode
    //    == TRUE)
    // TODO: Set property value
}


LPPICTUREDISP CVbx1Ctrl::GetPicture()
{
    // TODO: For PF_fNoShow - Return error if (AmbientUserMode
    //    == FALSE)
    return m_cPicPicture.GetPictureDispatch();
}


void CVbx1Ctrl::SetPicture(LPPICTUREDISP pPicPicture)
{
    // TODO: For PF_fNoRuntimeW - Return error if (AmbientUserMode
    //    == TRUE)
    m_cPicPicture.SetPictureDispatch(pPicPicture);
}


LPDISPATCH CVbx1Ctrl::GetObject()
{
    // TODO: For PF_fNoShow - Return error if (AmbientUserMode
    //    == FALSE)
```

(continued)

```
    // TODO: Return property value
    return NULL;
}

void CVbx1Ctrl::SetObject(LPDISPATCH pDispObject)
{
    // TODO: For PF_fNoRuntimeW - Return error if (AmbientUserMode
    //   == TRUE)
    // TODO: Set property value
}

long CVbx1Ctrl::GetData()
{
    // TODO: For PF_fNoShow - Return error if (AmbientUserMode
    //   == FALSE)
    // TODO: Return property value
    return 0;
}

void CVbx1Ctrl::SetData(long lData)
{
    // TODO: Set property value
}

BSTR CVbx1Ctrl::GetDataText()
{
    // TODO: For PF_fNoShow - Return error if (AmbientUserMode
    //   == FALSE)
    // TODO: Return property value
    return NULL;
}

void CVbx1Ctrl::SetDataText(LPCTSTR pszDataText)
{
    // TODO: Set property value
}

BSTR CVbx1Ctrl::GetFormat()
{
    // TODO: For PF_fNoShow - Return error if (AmbientUserMode
    //   == FALSE)
    return SysAllocString(m_strFormat);
}

void CVbx1Ctrl::SetFormat(LPCTSTR pszFormat)
```

(continued)

(continued)

```
{
    m_strFormat = pszFormat;
}

BSTR CVbx1Ctrl::GetObjectAcceptFormats(short index)
{
    // TODO: For PF_fNoShow - Return error if (AmbientUserMode
    //    == FALSE)
    // TODO: Return property value
    return NULL;
}

void CVbx1Ctrl::SetObjectAcceptFormats(short index,
    LPCTSTR pszObjectAcceptFormats)
{
    // TODO: For PF_fNoRuntimeW - Return error if (AmbientUserMode
    //    == TRUE)
    // TODO: Set property value
}

short CVbx1Ctrl::GetObjectAcceptFormatsCount()
{
    // TODO: For PF_fNoShow - Return error if (AmbientUserMode
    //    == FALSE)
    // TODO: Return property value
    return 0;
}

void CVbx1Ctrl::SetObjectAcceptFormatsCount(
    short iObjectAcceptFormatsCount)
{
    // TODO: For PF_fNoRuntimeW - Return error if (AmbientUserMode
    //    == TRUE)
    // TODO: Set property value
}

BSTR CVbx1Ctrl::GetObjectGetFormats(short index)
{
    // TODO: For PF_fNoShow - Return error if (AmbientUserMode
    //    == FALSE)
    // TODO: Return property value
    return NULL;
}
```

(continued)

```
void CVbx1Ctrl::SetObjectGetFormats(short index,
    LPCTSTR pszObjectGetFormats)
{
    // TODO: For PF_fNoRuntimeW - Return error if (AmbientUserMode
    //   == TRUE)
    // TODO: Set property value
}

short CVbx1Ctrl::GetObjectGetFormatsCount()
{
    // TODO: For PF_fNoShow - Return error if (AmbientUserMode
    //   == FALSE)
    // TODO: Return property value
    return 0;
}

void CVbx1Ctrl::SetObjectGetFormatsCount(
    short iObjectGetFormatsCount)
{
    // TODO: For PF_fNoRuntimeW - Return error if (AmbientUserMode
    //   == TRUE)
    // TODO: Set property value
}

BOOL CVbx1Ctrl::GetPasteOK()
{
    // TODO: For PF_fNoShow - Return error if (AmbientUserMode
    //   == FALSE)
    // TODO: Return property value
    return FALSE;
}

void CVbx1Ctrl::SetPasteOK(BOOL bPasteOK)
{
    // TODO: For PF_fNoRuntimeW - Return error if (AmbientUserMode
    //   == TRUE)
    // TODO: Set property value
}

BSTR CVbx1Ctrl::GetObjectVerbs(short index)
{
    // TODO: For PF_fNoShow - Return error if (AmbientUserMode
    //   == FALSE)
    // TODO: Return property value
    return NULL;
```

(continued)

413

(continued)

```
}

void CVbx1Ctrl::SetObjectVerbs(short index, LPCTSTR pszObjectVerbs)
{
    // TODO: For PF_fNoRuntimeW - Return error if (AmbientUserMode
    //    == TRUE)
    // TODO: Set property value
}

long CVbx1Ctrl::GetObjectVerbFlags(short index)
{
    // TODO: For PF_fNoShow - Return error if (AmbientUserMode
    //    == FALSE)
    // TODO: Return property value
    return 0;
}

void CVbx1Ctrl::SetObjectVerbFlags(short index, long
    lObjectVerbFlags)
{
    // TODO: For PF_fNoRuntimeW - Return error if (AmbientUserMode
    //    == TRUE)
    // TODO: Set property value
}

short CVbx1Ctrl::GetObjectVerbsCount()
{
    // TODO: For PF_fNoShow - Return error if (AmbientUserMode
    //    == FALSE)
    // TODO: Return property value
    return 0;
}

void CVbx1Ctrl::SetObjectVerbsCount(short iObjectVerbsCount)
{
    // TODO: For PF_fNoRuntimeW - Return error if (AmbientUserMode
    //    == TRUE)
    // TODO: Set property value
}

short CVbx1Ctrl::GetFileNumber()
{
    // TODO: For PF_fNoShow - Return error if (AmbientUserMode
    //    == FALSE)
```

(continued)

```
        return m_iFileNumber;
}

void CVbx1Ctrl::SetFileNumber(short iFileNumber)
{
        m_iFileNumber = iFileNumber:
}

short CVbx1Ctrl::GetAction()
{
        // TODO: For PF_fNoRuntimeR/PF_fNoShow - Return error
        // TODO: Return property value
        return 0;
}

void CVbx1Ctrl::SetAction(short iAction)
{
        // TODO: Set property value
}

long CVbx1Ctrl::GetOleObjectBlob()
{
        // TODO: For PF_fNoRuntimeR/PF_fNoShow - Return error
        // TODO: Return property value
        return 0;
}

void CVbx1Ctrl::SetOleObjectBlob(long lOleObjectBlob)
{
        // TODO: For PF_fNoRuntimeW - Return error if (AmbientUserMode
        //   == TRUE)
        // TODO: Set property value
}

long CVbx1Ctrl::GetcxTHk()
{
        // TODO: For PF_fNoShow - Return error if (AmbientUserMode
        //   == FALSE)
        return m_cxcxTHk;
}

void CVbx1Ctrl::SetcxTHk(long cxcxTHk)
{
        m_cxcxTHk = cxcxTHk;
}
```

(continued)

(continued)

```
long CVbx1Ctrl::GetcyTHk()
{
    // TODO: For PF_fNoShow - Return error if (AmbientUserMode
    //    == FALSE)
    return m_cycyTHk;
}

void CVbx1Ctrl::SetcyTHk(long cycyTHk)
{
    m_cycyTHk = cycyTHk;
}

BOOL CVbx1Ctrl::GetfFFHk()
{
    // TODO: For PF_fNoShow - Return error if (AmbientUserMode
    //    == FALSE)
    return m_bfFFHk;
}

void CVbx1Ctrl::SetfFFHk(BOOL bfFFHk)
{
    m_bfFFHk = bfFFHk;
}

short CVbx1Ctrl::GetDisplayType()
{
    return m_enumDisplayType;
}

void CVbx1Ctrl::SetDisplayType(short enumDisplayType)
{
    // TODO: For DT_ENUM properties - check the value for legal range
    m_enumDisplayType = enumDisplayType;
}

long CVbx1Ctrl::GetLpOleObject()
{
    // TODO: For PF_fNoShow - Return error if (AmbientUserMode
    //    == FALSE)
    // TODO: Return property value
    return 0;
}

void CVbx1Ctrl::SetLpOleObject(long lLpOleObject)
```

(continued)

```
{
    // TODO: For PF_fNoRuntimeW - Return error if (AmbientUserMode
    //    == TRUE)
    // TODO: Set property value
}
```

```
///////////////////////////////////////////////////////////////////////
// CVbx1Ctrl message handlers
```

Scanning through this source code, you'll notice a few things. In particular, notice how ControlWizard has inserted comments at appropriate points that tell you how you should react to certain VBX situations in an OLE control context. For example, the *SetLpOleObject* function at the end of Listing 17-3 contains a comment that says that the VBX flag *PF_fNoRuntimeW* is set for this property (which means that the property cannot set at runtime, only at design-time). The OLE control equivalent is to check the value of the *UserMode* ambient property; if this property is *TRUE* (you're in runtime mode), you should return an error if this function is called. An appropriate error in this case might be to call *SetNotSupported*, which will throw an OLE Automation exception.

You'll also notice that any stock events and properties have been converted, so there's no work to do with them. Also, *DoPropExchange* will have been populated by the conversion process to make persistent all the properties that were persistent in the VBX.

Converting a VBX

Here are the steps for converting a VBX to an OLE control:

1. Ensure that your VBX meets the requirements for conversion — that is, that it exports a function called *VBGetModelInfo*.

2. Create a new OLE control project using ControlWizard.

3. In the Control Options dialog box (shown in Figure 17-1 on the next page), select the Use VBX Control As Template option, and choose the appropriate VBX by clicking the Select VBX Control button.

4. In the Use VBX Control As Template dialog box, select the VBX by clicking the Browse button or by typing in the full pathname.

5. If your chosen VBX file contains more than one control, choose the appropriate one from the Control Name drop-down list.

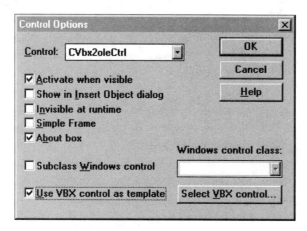

Figure 17-1. *ControlWizard's Control Options dialog box.*

6. Select any other options required by your control (for example, the control might be a subclassed Windows control).

7. Click the relevant number of OK buttons, and let the wizard generate the code for you.

8. Now you can edit the source files to provide the functionality of the VBX.

Let's look at the first step in a bit more detail. VBXs have a mechanism for letting Visual Basic know what functionality they have, by giving Visual Basic a pointer to a *MODELINFO* structure. Visual Basic gets this pointer by calling *VBGetModelInfo*, which is passed a parameter that specifies which version of Visual Basic is requesting this information. (Controls can have different versions of the structure for different versions of Visual Basic, if they have added support for new Visual Basic features in later versions of the control.) The *MODELINFO* structure contains a pointer to a *NULL*-terminated array of *MODEL* structures.

The *MODEL* structure itself contains a wealth of information, most of which is not important to us as OLE control writers. (For example, there is a field in the structure that points to the control's window procedure.) However, other information in there is definitely relevant, such as the name of the control class, a list of properties, a list of events, and a set of flags. There's also a set of window style bits, which would normally be passed to the Windows *CreateWindow* API function. In the converted version, you'll notice that an override of *PreCreateWindow* has been provided, and the extra style bits from the VBX have been OR'd into the standard ones here. *WS_BORDER* is added by default to all converted VBXs.

Some of the *MODEL* flags that are interpreted by the ControlWizard VBX converter or that need special action from you are listed in Table 17-1.

VBX *MODEL* Flags

Flag	Value	Notes
MODEL_fArrows	1	You must send arrow key messages (and other extended key messages, such as Home and PgDn) to your control by using *SendMessage* in your override of *PreTranslateMessage* for your control class. For a subclassed control, you actually use *CallWindowProc* rather than *SendMessage*.
MODEL_fChildrenOk	8	ControlWizard uses this flag to enable simple frame support.
MODEL_fDesInteract	64	This flag allows interaction with your control at design-time. If your container does not UI-activate a control in design mode (Visual Basic, for example), you'll need to add a mechanism to do this, such as an Edit OLE verb.
MODEL_fFocusOk	2	This flag indicates that the control can legally receive focus. If your control is actually a label (or something similar), which means that it shouldn't receive focus, you'll need to add the *OLEMISC_ACTSLIKELABEL* flag to your control.
MODEL_fGraphical	256	This flag indicates that your VBX is a window-less control. This is not currently supported in the OLE Controls model, so you'll need to think of another way of working. Typically, this flag is set in a VBX to improve its performance.
MODEL_fInitMsg	16	This flag causes a VBX to receive a *VBM_INITIALIZE* message. It has no equivalent in the OLE Controls world, so you'll need to ensure that your control initializes itself correctly in its constructor (and in its *OnResetState* member function, if required).
MODEL_fInvisAtRun	128	This flag, which causes the control to be invisible at runtime, is converted by Control-Wizard to *OLEMISC_INVISIBLEATRUNTIME*. However, VBXs in such a state typically get

Table 17-1. *Some of the VBX MODEL flags interpreted by ControlWizard or requiring action from you. (The number to the right of each flag is the actual flag value from VBAPI.H.)*   *(continued)*

419

VBX *MODEL* Flags *(continued)*

Flag	Value	Notes
		drawn using their toolbox bitmap at design-time, whereas OLE controls do not. You'll need to add code to your OLE control to perform this drawing if you want to emulate the behavior.
MODEL_fLoadMsg	32	This flag causes creation messages and loading messages to be sent to the VBX. It has no equivalent in the OLE Controls world, so you'll need to alter your control's behavior.
MODEL_fMnemonic	4	Again, OLE controls have no direct equivalent of this flag or its corresponding *VBM_ISMNE-MONIC* message. See the section in Chapter 3 on control mnemonic-handling.

The name of the control class is taken from the name of the *CoClass* in the type library. If you want to change this, simply edit the *CoClass* line in the control's ODL file to match that in the *npszClassName* field of the *MODEL* structure. The class name of your OLE control needs to be the same as the VBX's because this allows Visual Basic and other tools to port your VBX-using forms to their OLE control equivalents.

If your control is a subclass of a Windows standard control, the *npszParentClassName* field of the *MODEL* structure will be used as the name of the OLE control's parent class, and code will be added to *PreCreateWindow*. The *nDefProp* field of *MODEL* is the index of the control's default property, and *nValueProp* is the control's "value" property. In the OLE Controls world, these are the same. The ControlWizard VBX converter automatically reads *nValueProp* and adds an appropriate *DISP_DEFVALUE* macro for that property. OLE controls have no concept of the VBX default event, so *nDefEvent* is ignored.

The Programmer-Defined Structure

VBX controls reserve an amount of data per instance of each control; this is commonly referred to as the "programmer-defined structure." It holds variables for property storage as well as extra data storage as required by the internal implementation of the VBX. During the conversion process, some member variables will have been allocated by the converter to hold property values. For example, some of the properties will have been implemented by the converter as member variable properties. Therefore, a member variable is created for each of these. The conversion of the OLE container control, for example, created variables such as

```
short m_iMiscFlags;
```

In addition, the converter will have created member variables to hold some of the properties accessed via get/set method pairs. An example is

```
CString m_strClass;
```

Typically, each of these would have corresponding entries in the original VBX's instance data. When porting a VBX, you'll need to copy your original programmer-defined structure, but remove (comment out) any fields previously used for property storage that are now implemented elsewhere in the class. Be sure that you declare your structure appropriately and then include a protected or private instance of it as a member variable of your class. Whereas the instance data is initialized to 0 by Visual Basic when a control is loaded, this isn't done automatically for you in your ported control. You'll need to alter the control constructor and *OnResetState* to include code to zero out the remaining fields of the structure. You could clear each field individually or use a C runtime function such as *_memset* to clear out the whole thing in one go.

Message-Handling

The next stage in VBX porting is ensure that any Windows messages that the original VBX handled are also dealt with by the new OLE control. Some messages, such as *WM_PAINT*, are handled automatically by the OLE control code. Others, you'll need to add, using ClassWizard to create new message-handler functions. Bear in mind that in some circumstances, such as in Visual Basic's design mode, the OLE control will not have a window and so it will not receive messages; therefore, any initialization you do during *WM_CREATE* and so forth needs to be moved. Handlers for some messages cannot be added through ClassWizard and will have to be typed in by hand.

If your control is a subclass, you might have handled Visual Basic notification messages, all of the form *VBN_Xxx*. These are replaced with "reflected" messages in OLE controls, of the form *OCM_Xxx*.

By the way, sometimes the ClassWizard-generated skeleton for a message handler function might mislead you by putting a call to the base class version of the function in the "wrong" place. ClassWizard is generating code for a generic Windows application and knows nothing of VBX controls. Whereas in a VBX you passed a message on to the default handler using *VBDefControlProc*, you now pass it on by calling the base class version of the handler, and sometimes you will want to do this at a slightly different location in the code than that created by ClassWizard. For example, ClassWizard's default *WM_SIZE* handler (*OnSize*) calls the base class version first and expects you to insert your code afterwards. If your VBX handler code for *WM_SIZE* calls the *VBDefControlProc* after your custom code, you'll need to ignore what ClassWizard is trying to tell you and instead be sure you do things the same way you did in the VBX.

VBM-Handling

Visual Basic sent special messages to VBXs, called VBM messages. Of course, OLE controls do not get sent these messages, and Visual Basic has changed the way it communicates to controls with the OLE Controls model.

Typically, a VBX will handle many different VBM messages. Some of these messages are used to get at property values, and of course they're replaced by OLE Automation calls. Other message handlers might need to be replaced by new mechanisms or deleted altogether. For example, Visual Basic would send a *VBM_CHECKPROPERTY* message to a VBX control when it wanted to determine whether a particular property value was actually valid, without setting the property. The OLE Controls model has no equivalent of property checking other than by attempting to set the property and seeing what happens! In other cases, OLE provides similar functionality to the VBM message and its handler.

The data-binding model used in Visual Basic comes in two flavors: the basic one, which OLE controls can easily implement, and a variety of complex ones, which are proprietary to Visual Basic. In Visual Basic version 3.0, these advanced flavors were handled through the *VBM_DATA_GET* message, which has a flag specifying what action is to be performed. None of that can be emulated without extensive knowledge of the new data-binding model in Visual Basic version 4.0 — which of course ties your control down to being specific to Visual Basic version 4.0.

Toolbox Bitmaps

This is a minor point, but one that might make you need to call in your graphics designers again! Visual Basic toolbox bitmap images stored in a VBX are a different size from those in an OLE control. The OLE control images are significantly smaller, which means that you'll need to revisit your icons when porting over your VBX.

Some Issues Concerning Properties and Methods

Most properties and events exposed by a VBX control are automatically ported over to the newly created OLE control project successfully. However, some points need consideration.

Although VBXs do not support custom methods, they do support some standard methods. The ControlWizard converter will successfully port one of these, *Refresh*, to the new OLE control. Other standard methods will need to be implemented with ClassWizard and the code moved by hand. Finally, some of the standard methods used by VBXs are in fact extended methods in the OLE Controls model — that is, they're implemented by the container of the control rather than the control itself. These methods obviously can't be ported over to the new OLE control.

If your control used the standard *Align* property, this is assumed to be implemented as an extended property by the control converter. However, you'll need to add the *OLEMISC_ALIGNABLE* flag to your control to get the container to add *Align* to its extended control. The *BorderStyle* property is automatically ported to its OLE control stock implementation for you, but it does not include an enumeration of the legal values for the property in the control's type library: you'll need to add it yourself. Also, for VBXs that have the *PROPINFO_STD_BORDER-STYLEON* flag set, you'll need to set the border style to 1 (fixed single) at the appropriate points.

VBXs initialize the *Caption* and *Text* properties with the name of the control; OLE controls don't do this, so you'll need to add code to do so if you want to emulate the behavior.

MousePointer and *MouseIcon* properties are not implemented at all: you'll need to write your own copies of these properties if you want to use them in your ported OLE control.

The way that font properties are handled in OLE controls is completely different from how they were handled in VBXs. Whereas VBXs had a set of properties for font attributes (such as *FontBold* and *FontName*), OLE controls have a single *Font* property that is itself an object and that has a number of properties. The control converter, if it finds one or more of these properties, will first create a new *Font* property and will then include *FontXxx* properties analogous to those of the VBX. These analog properties will be written to use the new font object referred to by the *Font* property.

Property arrays in OLE controls are actually easier to implement than they were in VBXs. You no longer need to worry about a *DATASTRUCT* structure, and you can use an additional index parameter to the property to refer to the appropriate element of the array.

Finally, some VBXs have so-called "enum" properties, which can have one of a set of values. These will get ported as properties of type *short* by the converter, and you'll need to add a *typedef* for the enumeration to the type library <u>and</u> change the property type to get them to work properly.

Visual Basic API Functions and New Private Interfaces

Numerous VBXs make calls to Visual Basic itself, using a set of functions available to VBXs and declared in the VBAPI.H header file. During the porting exercise, many of these API functions can be replaced by other means (Visual Basic's string-handling, for example) which you can now do more easily with normal C strings or, even better, with MFC's *CString* class. In those instances where you need to take or return strings to Visual Basic, use OLE's *BSTR* type). Pictures, fonts, and colors have their own special MFC objects to wrap the underlying OLE objects that you'll use, and arrays are handled by OLE Automation's *SAFEARRAY* type. However, some functionality provided by these API functions can't easily be moved to the OLE Controls model. For example, there's an API function for formatting date and currency strings, and a whole set for dynamic data exchange (DDE). So, Visual Basic's solution has been to provide a new set of private (OLE) interfaces for OLE control use, with names such as *IVBFormat*, *IVBDDE*, and *IVBFiles*. Please, if there's any other way in which you can get this functionality, do <u>not</u> use these new interfaces. Why? Because they're not in anything but Visual Basic at present, although they might also appear in containers that support Visual Basic for Applications (VBA). These interfaces will remain private to Visual Basic (and perhaps to VBA), limiting any control that uses them to working only with those containers. If you decide that you do need to use them, see if it's possible for your control to work (with perhaps less functionality) without them. Then, when you call *QueryInterface* on your client site to get a pointer to the interface(s) in question, you can either use the interface if the *QueryInterface* succeeds or use another mechanism if it doesn't. Whatever you do, I implore you to check the return value from *QueryInterface* to be sure that the interface really does exist. You might be surprised to learn that there are controls around that just assume they're working in Visual Basic and call through the returned interface pointer without first checking whether it's *NULL*.

DDE might be regarded as one of these cases, as it's something that you can support if you find yourself in a container that supports IVBDDE (the Visual Basic interface for DDE support) but that you don't support otherwise. There are alternatives to DDE, including OLE's more powerful *IDataObject* interface.

Some Bugs and Limitations

While I was writing this chapter, I came across a couple of bugs in the conversion process that you might also run across. The first is known by Microsoft and is referenced in the OLE CDK documentation. If you attempt to port a VBX that does not correctly export its *MODELINFO* structure, ControlWizard can crash and cause Visual C++ to fail. Quite why this should be so, I don't claim to understand. Nevertheless, be sure that you follow the guidelines for porting very closely so that this doesn't happen!

The second bug is one that I've yet to track down. When I first tried porting a VBX, I chose the common control VBX. The ported code then contained various properties without names, causing me to have a project that wouldn't compile, due to the number of functions called simply "Get" and "Set". I don't know if this is a problem with the converter or with the control.

Staying on this subject, VBX properties might have names with illegal C++ characters in them, such as parentheses. The converter will innocently convert these names verbatim, meaning that you'll need to edit the code produced by hand to get it to compile properly. The exception is the *(About)* property, which the converter correctly translates into the *AboutBox* method.

Also, the ControlWizard VBX converter has some known limitations that are unlikely to affect most control writers. Only up to 256 properties can be converted; others are ignored. Likewise, only up to 256 events can be translated. Finally, the converter can only handle as many as 15 parameters to each event; all parameters to an event after the fifteenth are ignored by the converter.

NOTE Some time near the publication date of this book (Fall 1995), it's likely that Microsoft will include guidelines for porting VBXs to OLE controls on the Microsoft Developer Network (MSDN) and other media. Some of the information in this chapter was taken from preliminary editions of that work. For additional advice and guidance, and a lot more detail, please check the MSDN.

Subclassing a Windows Control

So you want to create an edit control that is smarter than the average edit control, huh? So how do you do it? Well, the answer is, as you will have guessed from the section title, by subclassing the standard Windows edit control and writing special code to do the things that you want to do. ControlWizard provides support for this through the Subclass Windows Control option in the Control Options dialog box. If you check this box, the combo box to the side of it is enabled, and from that you can choose any of the standard built-in Windows control classes. If you continue to create the control project, you'll arrive at a control that looks and works exactly like an edit box, until you add special functionality to do all the things you have planned for it.

If you look at the code that ControlWizard generates, you'll see that it's pretty much identical to a standard OLE control, except for a few additions and one change. The additions are manifested as three new member functions. They are declared in the header file, as shown here:

```
// Subclassed control support
BOOL PreCreateWindow(CREATESTRUCT& cs);
WNDPROC* GetSuperWndProcAddr(void);
LRESULT OnOcmCommand(WPARAM wParam, LPARAM lParam);
```

And they appear in the main control source file, as shown in Listing 17-4 on the next page.

```
///////////////////////////////////////////////////////////////
// CSubclassCtrl::PreCreateWindow - Modify parameters for
//    CreateWindowEx

BOOL CSubclassCtrl::PreCreateWindow(CREATESTRUCT& cs)
{
    cs.lpszClass = _T("EDIT");
    return COleControl::PreCreateWindow(cs);
}



///////////////////////////////////////////////////////////////
// CSubclassCtrl::GetSuperWndProcAddr - Provide storage for
//    window proc

WNDPROC* CSubclassCtrl::GetSuperWndProcAddr(void)
{
    static WNDPROC NEAR pfnSuper;
    return &pfnSuper;
}



///////////////////////////////////////////////////////////////
// CSubclassCtrl::OnOcmCommand - Handle command messages

LRESULT CSubclassCtrl::OnOcmCommand(WPARAM wParam, LPARAM lParam)
{
#ifdef _WIN32
    WORD wNotifyCode = HIWORD(wParam);
#else
    WORD wNotifyCode = HIWORD(lParam);
#endif

    // TODO: Switch on wNotifyCode here.

    return 0;
}
```

Listing 17-4. *The additional member functions created by ControlWizard in an OLE control that subclasses the standard Edit control.*

Let's take a look at the code in Listing 17-4. First, there's *PreCreateWindow*, which fills in the name of the window class. By putting a name in here, it prevents the MFC library from putting its own class name in, so a window of the specified class is created rather than a generic MFC window. In this case, the class name is "Edit," making it create an instance of the standard Windows Edit control.

GetSuperWndProcAddr contains a static variable whose address is returned whenever the function is called. This will be filled in with the address of the window procedure for the Edit class and is then used subsequently to return that address whenever the program requires to speak directly to the Edit window class.

OnOcmCommand is a generic command handler for OCM messages — messages reflected back to the control by the hidden window created by the CDK. This makes the control class able to react to messages that its superclass would normally send to the parent window procedure. Message reflection like this is used to allow the control to talk to its parent in an OLE-centric way (for example, through events) rather than through Windows messages. If the control happens to be inserted into a container that is itself capable of reflecting Windows messages back to the control (that is, if the ambient property *MessageReflect* on the control site is *TRUE*), then the CDK won't create the hidden window, making operations that much more efficient. Microsoft recommends that all containers implement message reflection. (Reflecting messages is relatively low-cost to the containers, and it gives the control a performance boost.)

You'll notice that this function does not yet contain any code; you need to add a switch statement to work out which OCM message was sent and then take appropriate action. Typically, this would involve firing an event to the control's container.

The handler provided by ClassWizard handles *OCM_COMMAND* only; this would be used by controls that send notifications to their parent, such as *BN_CLICKED* from a button when it's been clicked. However, the control can also receive other reflected messages, such as *OCM_MEASUREITEM*, *OCM_COMPAREITEM*, and *OCM_DRAWITEM* if the control is a list box. If your control will receive messages like this that you want to reflect up the container as events, you'll need to add handlers for them. ClassWizard doesn't provide automatic support for these OCM messages, so you'll need to add the message map entries and the handlers yourself, by hand.

The modified function call in a subclassed control is *OnDraw*. You'll notice here that, rather than drawing the by-now customary ellipse, this version of *OnDraw* simply calls the *DoSuperclassPaint* member function of *COleControl*, which causes the edit control to draw itself into the given device context:

```
/////////////////////////////////////////////////////////////////
// CSubclassCtrl::OnDraw - Drawing function

void CSubclassCtrl::OnDraw(
            CDC* pdc, const CRect& rcBounds, const CRect& rcInvalid)
{
    DoSuperclassPaint(pdc, rcBounds);
}
```

This causes the control to be drawn even when it is inactive, as long as the control class chosen can react successfully to *WM_PAINT* messages with a device context handle in its *wParam* parameter. The only built-in controls that work reliably are the Pushbutton control and the Vertical and Horizontal scrollbar controls. You'll have to implement code to draw the other controls yourself. Also, some standard controls aren't very good at drawing themselves into metafiles, so unless you write specific drawing code, they're not going to be very good at being printed.

So that's all there is to subclassing. Well, almost. Some other considerations are also important.

If you want to pass on extra window-style flags to the class being subclassed, OR them into the *cs.style* and *cs.dwExStyle* members of the *CREATESTRUCT* structure passed to *PreCreateWindow*. For example, if you want the edit box to convert all letters typed into it into lowercase, you could specify the *ES_LOWERCASE* style bit here.

Making the "Children" Control Work Properly

If you cast your mind back to Chapter 13, "Custom Font-Based Properties (and Pictures, Too)," you'll remember the Children control, which contains a button and an edit box. You may also remember that the version I left you with there does not work properly in containers that don't activate the control immediately, such as Visual Basic's design mode. (See Figure 17-2.) I said at the end of that chapter that I'd defer getting a working version until this chapter because it's relevant to control subclassing. Well, you're at that part of the book now, so I'd better go off and write some code to get the thing working.

What does the Children control borrow from subclassing? Simply the fact that it needs to use the same tricks employed by subclassed controls to get its child controls to draw themselves when they're inactive.

You might remember that the Children version I left you with (version 2) allows you to get and set its child control-related properties when those children existed (that is, when the control itself has a window), but that it threw OLE Automation exceptions if you attempted to access one of these properties when it has no window of its own. The solution to this bit, at least, is easy. The revised version now creates a hidden window to act as the parent for the child controls if the control is found not to have a window; when the control gets a window, it re-parents the children so that they now use the control window as their parent. With this version, all the properties can always be accessed, and the child windows become visible whenever the control gets a window. You could therefore leave this version as it stands quite happily, with the following two provisos:

- If the control window is destroyed, the text inside the edit control is lost, because the edit control is destroyed as part of the control window destruction before being re-created with a new parent.

- The child windows will not be displayed when the control is without a window (for example, in Visual Basic's design mode).

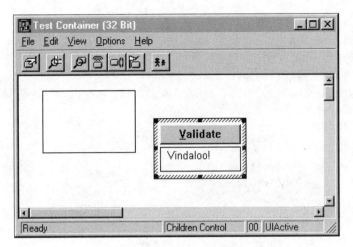

Figure 17.2. *An earlier version of the Children control, which doesn't draw itself correctly unless it is immediately activated by its container.*

Both of these problems are worth solving, so the version of the control in this chapter goes as far as it can. As a side-effect, it draws metafiles (reasonably) well, now, too. The changed files are the control class's header and implementation files, shown in Listings 17-5, below, and 17-6, beginning on page 432. (There's also an extra string in the string table and a corresponding entry in RESOURCE.H, but I'll cover these in the text.) You can find the source code for this control on the companion CD-ROM in the \OLECTRLS\CHAP17\CHILDREN3 directory.

CHILDCTL.H

```
// childctl.h : Declaration of the CChildrenCtrl OLE control class.

/////////////////////////////////////////////////////////////////
// CChildrenCtrl : See childctl.cpp for implementation.

class CChildrenCtrl : public COleControl
{
    DECLARE_DYNCREATE(CChildrenCtrl)

// Constructor
public:
    CChildrenCtrl();

// Overrides

    // Drawing function
```

Listing 17-5. *The header file for the final version of the Children control.*

(continued)

```
    virtual void OnDraw(
                CDC* pdc, const CRect& rcBounds,
                const CRect& rcInvalid);
    virtual void OnDrawMetafile(CDC *pDC, const CRect& rcBounds);

    // Persistence
    virtual void DoPropExchange(CPropExchange* pPX);

    // Reset control state
    virtual void OnResetState();

// Implementation
protected:
    ~CChildrenCtrl();

    DECLARE_OLECREATE_EX(CChildrenCtrl)      // Class factory and guid
    DECLARE_OLETYPELIB(CChildrenCtrl)        // GetTypeInfo
    DECLARE_PROPPAGEIDS(CChildrenCtrl)       // Property page IDs
    DECLARE_OLECTLTYPE(CChildrenCtrl)        // Type name and misc
                                             //   status

    CButton m_btnValidate;
    CEdit m_editEntry;
    CWnd m_HiddenWnd;
    CRect m_rBtn;
    CRect m_rEdit;
    CFontHolder m_fontEdit;
    CString m_strEditText;
    void ChangeEditFont();
    int CreateChildren ( CWnd *pThis );
    void DrawButton ( CDC* pdc, const CRect& rcBounds );
    void DrawEditbox ( CDC* pdc, const CRect& rcBounds );
    CWnd *CreateHiddenWindow();

    BEGIN_INTERFACE_PART(EditFontNotify, IPropertyNotifySink)
    INIT_INTERFACE_PART(CChildrenCtrl, EditFontNotify)
        STDMETHOD(OnRequestEdit)(DISPID);
        STDMETHOD(OnChanged)(DISPID);
    END_INTERFACE_PART(EditFontNotify)

    // Message maps
    //{{AFX_MSG(CChildrenCtrl)

    afx_msg int OnCreate(LPCREATESTRUCT lpCreateStruct);
    //}}AFX_MSG
```

(continued)

```
    afx_msg void OnValidate();
    DECLARE_MESSAGE_MAP()

// Dispatch maps
    //{{AFX_DISPATCH(CChildrenCtrl)
    afx_msg LPFONTDISP GetEditFont();
    afx_msg void SetEditFont(LPFONTDISP newValue);
    afx_msg BSTR GetEditText();
    afx_msg void SetEditText(LPCTSTR lpszNewValue);
    //}}AFX_DISPATCH
    DECLARE_DISPATCH_MAP()

    afx_msg void AboutBox();

// Event maps
    //{{AFX_EVENT(CChildrenCtrl)
    void FireBeforeValidation()
        {FireEvent(eventidBeforeValidation,EVENT_PARAM(VTS_NONE));}
    void FireValidated(BOOL Success)
        {FireEvent(eventidValidated,EVENT_PARAM(VTS_BOOL), Success);}
    //}}AFX_EVENT
    DECLARE_EVENT_MAP()

// Dispatch and event IDs
public:
    enum {
    //{{AFX_DISP_ID(CChildrenCtrl)
    dispidEditFont = 1L,
    dispidEditText = 2L,
    eventidBeforeValidation = 1L,
    eventidValidated = 2L,
    //}}AFX_DISP_ID
    };
};

#define IDC_VALIDATE        1
#define IDC_ENTRY           2
```

The changes in the header file are what you'd expect — more variable and function declarations. Each of the function additions will be explained as I walk through the code changes. The member variables are as follows:

■ *m_HiddenWnd* is a *CWnd* that holds the hidden window used to parent the child controls when there is no control window.

■ *m_strEditText* is a *CString* used to hold the edit control's text at various times, in particular when the control is created from storage.

CHILDCTL.CPP

```cpp
// childctl.cpp : Implementation of the CChildrenCtrl OLE control
//    class.

#include "stdafx.h"
#include "children.h"
#include "childctl.h"
#include "childppg.h"


#ifdef _DEBUG
#undef THIS_FILE
static char BASED_CODE THIS_FILE[] = __FILE__;
#endif


IMPLEMENT_DYNCREATE(CChildrenCtrl, COleControl)


/////////////////////////////////////////////////////////////////
// Message map

BEGIN_MESSAGE_MAP(CChildrenCtrl, COleControl)
    //{{AFX_MSG_MAP(CChildrenCtrl)
    ON_WM_CREATE()
    //}}AFX_MSG_MAP
    ON_OLEVERB(AFX_IDS_VERB_PROPERTIES, OnProperties)
    ON_BN_CLICKED(IDC_VALIDATE,OnValidate)
END_MESSAGE_MAP()


/////////////////////////////////////////////////////////////////
// Dispatch map

BEGIN_DISPATCH_MAP(CChildrenCtrl, COleControl)
    //{{AFX_DISPATCH_MAP(CChildrenCtrl)
    DISP_PROPERTY_EX(CChildrenCtrl, "EditFont", GetEditFont,
        SetEditFont, VT_FONT)
    DISP_PROPERTY_EX(CChildrenCtrl, "EditText", GetEditText,
        SetEditText, VT_BSTR)
    DISP_DEFVALUE(CChildrenCtrl, "EditText")
    DISP_STOCKPROP_BACKCOLOR()
    DISP_STOCKPROP_FONT()
    DISP_STOCKPROP_FORECOLOR()
```

Listing 17-6. *The implementation file for the final version of the Children*   *(continued)*
control.

```
    //}}AFX_DISPATCH_MAP
    DISP_FUNCTION_ID(CChildrenCtrl, "AboutBox", DISPID_ABOUTBOX,
        AboutBox, VT_EMPTY, VTS_NONE)
END_DISPATCH_MAP()


///////////////////////////////////////////////////////////////////
// Event map

BEGIN_EVENT_MAP(CChildrenCtrl, COleControl)
    //{{AFX_EVENT_MAP(CChildrenCtrl)
    EVENT_CUSTOM("BeforeValidation", FireBeforeValidation, VTS_NONE)
    EVENT_CUSTOM("Validated", FireValidated, VTS_BOOL)
    //}}AFX_EVENT_MAP
END_EVENT_MAP()


///////////////////////////////////////////////////////////////////
// Property pages

// TODO: Add more property pages as needed.  Remember to increase
//   the count!

BEGIN_PROPPAGEIDS(CChildrenCtrl, 3)
    PROPPAGEID(CChildrenPropPage::guid)
    PROPPAGEID(CLSID_CColorPropPage)
    PROPPAGEID(CLSID_CFontPropPage)
END_PROPPAGEIDS(CChildrenCtrl)


static const FONTDESC _fontdescEdit =
    { sizeof(FONTDESC), "Arial", FONTSIZE( 10 ), FW_NORMAL,
    ANSI_CHARSET, FALSE, FALSE, FALSE };


///////////////////////////////////////////////////////////////////
// Initialize class factory and guid

IMPLEMENT_OLECREATE_EX(CChildrenCtrl, "CHILDREN.ChildrenCtrl.1",
    0x987c13c0, 0x840e, 0x11ce, 0x99, 0xbf, 0x0, 0xaa, 0x0, 0x47,
    0xd4, 0xfd)


///////////////////////////////////////////////////////////////////
// Type library ID and version
```

(continued)

(continued)

```
IMPLEMENT_OLETYPELIB(CChildrenCtrl, _tlid, _wVerMajor, _wVerMinor)


/////////////////////////////////////////////////////////////////
// Interface IDs

const IID BASED_CODE IID_DChildren =
        { 0x987c13c1, 0x840e, 0x11ce, { 0x99, 0xbf, 0x0, 0xaa, 0x0,
        0x47, 0xd4, 0xfd } };
const IID BASED_CODE IID_DChildrenEvents =
        { 0x987c13c2, 0x840e, 0x11ce, { 0x99, 0xbf, 0x0, 0xaa, 0x0,
        0x47, 0xd4, 0xfd } };


/////////////////////////////////////////////////////////////////
// Control type information

static const DWORD BASED_CODE _dwChildrenOleMisc =
    OLEMISC_ACTIVATEWHENVISIBLE |
    OLEMISC_SETCLIENTSITEFIRST |
    OLEMISC_INSIDEOUT |
    OLEMISC_CANTLINKINSIDE |
    OLEMISC_RECOMPOSEONRESIZE;

IMPLEMENT_OLECTLTYPE(CChildrenCtrl, IDS_CHILDREN, _dwChildrenOleMisc)


/////////////////////////////////////////////////////////////////
// CChildrenCtrl::CChildrenCtrlFactory::UpdateRegistry -
// Adds or removes system registry entries for CChildrenCtrl

BOOL CChildrenCtrl::CChildrenCtrlFactory::UpdateRegistry(
    BOOL bRegister)
{
    if (bRegister)
        return AfxOleRegisterControlClass(
            AfxGetInstanceHandle(),
            m_clsid,
            m_lpszProgID,
            IDS_CHILDREN,
            IDB_CHILDREN,
            FALSE,                          //  Not insertable
            _dwChildrenOleMisc,
```

(continued)

```
            _tlid,
            _wVerMajor,
            _wVerMinor);
    else
        return AfxOleUnregisterClass(m_clsid, m_lpszProgID);
}


/////////////////////////////////////////////////////////////////////
// CChildrenCtrl::CChildrenCtrl - Constructor

CChildrenCtrl::CChildrenCtrl() : m_fontEdit ( &m_xEditFontNotify )
{
    InitializeIIDs ( &IID_DChildren, &IID_DChildrenEvents );
    m_rBtn = CRect ( 3, 3, 103, 27 );
    m_rEdit = CRect ( 3, 30, 103, 60 );
    SetInitialSize ( m_rBtn.right+m_rBtn.left,
        m_rEdit.bottom+m_rBtn.top );
}


/////////////////////////////////////////////////////////////////////
// CChildrenCtrl::~CChildrenCtrl - Destructor

CChildrenCtrl::~CChildrenCtrl()
{
    if ( m_HiddenWnd.GetSafeHwnd() )
    {
        m_HiddenWnd.DestroyWindow();
    }
}


/////////////////////////////////////////////////////////////////////
// CChildrenCtrl::OnDraw - Drawing function

void CChildrenCtrl::OnDraw(
            CDC* pdc, const CRect& rcBounds, const CRect& rcInvalid)
{
    CBrush cbBack ( TranslateColor ( GetBackColor() ) );
    pdc -> FillRect ( rcBounds, &cbBack );

        // If we have no window, we might need to create the child
        //   controls and a hidden parent window.
```

(continued)

(continued)

```
   if ( GetSafeHwnd() == 0 )
   {
       if ( m_editEntry.GetSafeHwnd() == NULL &&
            m_btnValidate.GetSafeHwnd() == NULL )
       {
             // Yep, we'll have to.
           if ( CreateChildren ( 0 ) == -1 )
           {
               return;
           }
       }
       // Child controls exist and are parented to a hidden
       //   window. Get them to draw themselves into this
       //   DC - not so easy, so we draw them ourselves.
       DrawButton ( pdc,rcBounds );
       DrawEditbox ( pdc,rcBounds );
   }
}


/////////////////////////////////////////////////////////////////
// CChildrenCtrl::DoPropExchange - Persistence support

void CChildrenCtrl::DoPropExchange(CPropExchange* pPX)
{
    ExchangeVersion(pPX, MAKELONG(_wVerMinor, _wVerMajor));
    COleControl::DoPropExchange(pPX);
    PX_Font ( pPX, _T( "EditFont" ), m_fontEdit, &_fontdescEdit );
    if ( pPX -> IsLoading() )
    {
        ChangeEditFont();
        PX_String ( pPX, _T( "EditText" ), m_strEditText );
        if ( m_editEntry.GetSafeHwnd() )
        {
            m_editEntry.SetWindowText ( m_strEditText );
        }
    }
    else
    {
        if ( m_editEntry.GetSafeHwnd() )
        {
```

(continued)

```
            m_editEntry.GetWindowText ( m_strEditText );
        }
        PX_String ( pPX, _T( "EditText" ), m_strEditText );
    }
}


/////////////////////////////////////////////////////////////////////
// CChildrenCtrl::OnResetState - Reset control to default state

void CChildrenCtrl::OnResetState()
{
    COleControl::OnResetState();   // Resets defaults found in
                                   //    DoPropExchange

    // TODO: Reset any other control state here.
}


/////////////////////////////////////////////////////////////////////
// CChildrenCtrl::AboutBox - Display an "About" box to the user

void CChildrenCtrl::AboutBox()
{
    CDialog dlgAbout(IDD_ABOUTBOX_CHILDREN);
    dlgAbout.DoModal();
}


/////////////////////////////////////////////////////////////////////
// CChildrenCtrl message handlers

int CChildrenCtrl::OnCreate(LPCREATESTRUCT lpCreateStruct)
{
    if (COleControl::OnCreate(lpCreateStruct) == -1)
        return -1;

    return CreateChildren ( this );
}

void CChildrenCtrl::OnValidate()
{
    FireBeforeValidation();
    m_editEntry.GetWindowText( m_strEditText );
    BOOL bRet = m_strEditText.Find ( _T( " " ) ) == -1;
```

(continued)

437

(continued)

```
    FireValidated ( bRet );
}

LPFONTDISP CChildrenCtrl::GetEditFont()
{
    return m_fontEdit.GetFontDispatch();
}

void CChildrenCtrl::SetEditFont(LPFONTDISP newValue)
{
    m_fontEdit.InitializeFont ( &_fontdescEdit, newValue );
    ChangeEditFont();
    SetModifiedFlag();
}

void CChildrenCtrl::ChangeEditFont()
{
    if ( m_editEntry.GetSafeHwnd() )
    {
        m_editEntry.SendMessage ( WM_SETFONT,
            (WPARAM) m_fontEdit.GetFontHandle(), TRUE );
    }
}

STDMETHODIMP_ (ULONG) CChildrenCtrl::XEditFontNotify::AddRef()
{
    METHOD_MANAGE_STATE ( CChildrenCtrl, EditFontNotify )
    return 1;
}

STDMETHODIMP_ (ULONG) CChildrenCtrl::XEditFontNotify::Release()
{
    METHOD_MANAGE_STATE ( CChildrenCtrl, EditFontNotify )
    return 0;
}

STDMETHODIMP CChildrenCtrl::XEditFontNotify::QueryInterface(
    REFIID iid, LPVOID FAR* ppvObj )
{
    METHOD_MANAGE_STATE ( CChildrenCtrl, EditFontNotify )
    if ( IsEqualIID ( iid, IID_IUnknown ) ||
        IsEqualIID ( iid, IID_IPropertyNotifySink ) )
    {
        *ppvObj= this;
```

(continued)

```
        AddRef();
        return NOERROR;
    }
    return ResultFromScode ( E_NOINTERFACE );
}


STDMETHODIMP CChildrenCtrl::XEditFontNotify::OnChanged( DISPID )
{
    METHOD_MANAGE_STATE ( CChildrenCtrl, EditFontNotify )
    pThis -> ChangeEditFont();
    return NOERROR;
}


STDMETHODIMP CChildrenCtrl::XEditFontNotify::OnRequestEdit( DISPID )
{
    return NOERROR;
}


BSTR CChildrenCtrl::GetEditText()
{
    if ( m_editEntry.GetSafeHwnd() )
    {
        m_editEntry.GetWindowText ( m_strEditText );
        return m_strEditText.AllocSysString();
    }
    else
    {
        ThrowError ( CTL_E_ILLEGALFUNCTIONCALL, IDS_NOEDITCTRL );
        return NULL;
    }
}


void CChildrenCtrl::SetEditText( LPCTSTR lpszNewValue )
{
    if ( m_editEntry.GetSafeHwnd() )
    {
        m_editEntry.SetWindowText ( lpszNewValue );
        SetModifiedFlag();
        InvalidateControl();
    }
    else
    {
        ThrowError ( CTL_E_ILLEGALFUNCTIONCALL, IDS_NOEDITCTRL );
    }
}
```

(continued)

(continued)

```cpp
void CChildrenCtrl::OnDrawMetafile( CDC  pDC, const CRect& rcBounds )
{
    COleControl::OnDrawMetafile ( pDC, rcBounds );
    DrawButton ( pDC, rcBounds );
    DrawEditbox ( pDC, rcBounds );
}

int CChildrenCtrl::CreateChildren ( CWnd  pThis )
{
        // If passed-in parent is NULL, use the hidden window as
        //   parent.
    if ( pThis == 0 )
    {
        pThis = CreateHiddenWindow();
        if ( pThis == 0 )
        {
            return -1;
        }
    }
        // If children exist, just re-parent.
    if ( m_btnValidate.GetSafeHwnd() )
    {
        m_btnValidate.SetParent ( pThis );
    }
    else
    {
        CString s;
        s.LoadString(IDS_BUTTONCAPTION);
        if ( m_btnValidate.Create ( s, BS_PUSHBUTTON | WS_VISIBLE,
            m_rBtn, pThis, IDC_VALIDATE ) == FALSE )
        {
            MessageBox ( _T( "Could not create button" ) );
            return -1;
        }
    }

    if ( m_editEntry.GetSafeHwnd() )
    {
        m_editEntry.SetParent ( pThis );
    }
    else
    {
        if ( m_editEntry.Create ( ES_AUTOHSCROLL | WS_BORDER |
            WS_VISIBLE, m_rEdit, pThis, IDC_ENTRY ) == FALSE )
```

(continued)

```
        {
            MessageBox ( _T( "Could not create edit box" ) );
            return -1;
        }
        m_editEntry.SetWindowText ( m_strEditText );
    }
    ChangeEditFont();
    return 0;
}

void CChildrenCtrl::DrawButton( CDC* pdc, const CRect& rcBounds )
{
    CPen pBlack ( PS_SOLID, 1, COLORREF(RGB(0,0,0)) );
        // black pen
    CPen pDark ( PS_SOLID, 1, ::GetSysColor ( COLOR_BTNSHADOW ) );
    CPen pLite ( PS_SOLID, 1, ::GetSysColor ( COLOR_BTNHIGHLIGHT ) );

    CPen *pOld = pdc -> SelectObject ( &pBlack );

    CRect rBox = m_rBtn;
    rBox += CPoint ( rcBounds.left, rcBounds.top );

    CString s;
    s.LoadString ( IDS_BUTTONCAPTION );

    CBrush bFace ( ::GetSysColor ( COLOR_BTNFACE ) );
    pdc -> FillRect ( rBox, &bFace );
    pdc -> MoveTo ( rBox.left, rBox.bottom );
    pdc -> LineTo ( rBox.right - 1, rBox.bottom );
    pdc -> LineTo ( rBox.right - 1, rBox.top - 2 );
    pdc -> SelectObject ( &pDark );
    pdc -> MoveTo ( rBox.left + 1, rBox.bottom - 1 );
    pdc -> LineTo ( rBox.right - 2, rBox.bottom - 1 );
    pdc -> LineTo ( rBox.right - 2, rBox.top - 1 );
    pdc -> SelectObject ( &pLite );
    pdc -> MoveTo ( rBox.left, rBox.bottom -1 );
    pdc -> LineTo ( rBox.left, rBox.top - 1 );
    pdc -> LineTo ( rBox.right - 1, rBox.top - 1 );

    rBox.InflateRect ( -1, -1 );
    int nMode = pdc -> SetBkMode ( TRANSPARENT );
    pdc -> DrawText ( s, -1, rBox, DT_CENTER | DT_VCENTER |
        DT_SINGLELINE  );

    pdc -> SelectObject ( pOld );
```

(continued)

(continued)

```
      pdc -> SetBkMode ( nMode );
}

void CChildrenCtrl::DrawEditbox ( CDC* pdc, const CRect& rcBounds )
{
    CPen pBlack ( PS_SOLID, 1, COLORREF(RGB(0,0,0)) );
        // black pen
    CBrush bWhite ( COLORREF(RGB(255,255,255)) );     // white brush

    CPen *pOld = pdc -> SelectObject ( &pBlack );
    CBrush *bOld = pdc -> SelectObject ( &bWhite );

    CRect rBox = m_rEdit;
    rBox += CPoint ( rcBounds.left, rcBounds.top );

    CString s;
    m_editEntry.GetWindowText ( s );

    pdc -> Rectangle ( &rBox );
    rBox.InflateRect ( -1, -1 );
    CFont *fOld = pdc->SelectObject ( CFont::FromHandle (
        m_fontEdit.GetFontHandle() ) );
    pdc -> DrawText ( s, -1, rBox,
        DT_LEFT | DT_VCENTER | DT_NOPREFIX | DT_SINGLELINE );

    pdc -> SelectObject ( pOld );
    pdc -> SelectObject ( bOld );
    pdc -> SelectObject ( fOld );
}

CWnd *CChildrenCtrl::CreateHiddenWindow()
{
    if ( m_HiddenWnd.GetSafeHwnd() == 0 )
    {
        m_HiddenWnd.CreateEx ( 0, AfxRegisterWndClass ( 0 ),
            "", 0, 0, 0, 0, 0, 0, 0 );
    }
    return &m_HiddenWnd;
}
```

The first change is to the destructor, which I now use to kill off the hidden window if it exists. *OnDraw* is a whole lot more complicated; if the control doesn't have a window, I check to see whether the two child windows exist yet. If they don't, I call *CreateChildren* to create them with a parameter of 0. As you'll see when I get to that function, a parameter of 0 tells it to use the hidden window as the parent.

After the children exist, I call two functions, *DrawButton* and *DrawEditbox*, to actually draw the child windows correctly. (I'll get to those functions soon.)

DoPropExchange is also different. I want to be able to store away the edit text and retrieve it later, but there's no guarantee that the edit box exists when *DoPropExchange* is called. (For example, when it is first called, the edit box does not exist.) Therefore, if the function is called to load properties, I load the string value into the class member variable *m_srtEditText*. If the edit box does exist, I copy this string to the edit box. If the function is called to save properties, I first extract the string from the edit box, if it exists, and then I write it out. This way, I ensure that the property value can be maintained even if the edit box does not yet exist.

OnCreate, the handler for *WM_CREATE*, creates the child windows if they don't exist by calling *CreateChildren* with a parameter of *this*, which causes the children to be created with the control window as their parent. *OnValidate* has been marginally changed to use the new class member variable *m_strEditText* as the (temporary) storage for the edit box's textual value, as has *GetEditText*, the *EditText* property get function. I've changed *OnDrawMetafile* so that it now also calls *DrawButton* and *DrawEditbox* to draw the controls into the metafile. It nearly works, but I must admit that I find metafiles a bit of a black art, so I've left to you the task of making it work properly!

CreateChildren first checks whether the passed-in parameter is 0. If it is, this call is a request to create the children with the hidden window as their parent. It calls *CreateHiddenWindow* to create the hidden window (or to return a pointer to it if it already exists). Should this fail, the control will have a problem working at this point. If the children already exist, which will be the case if the control was once inactive (so that the controls were created with the hidden window as parent) and is now active (so this call is as a result of the control window receiving *WM_CREATE*), they are simply re-parented to the passed-in parameter. When the control becomes active, this causes the child controls to be parented to it, so that they will draw themselves correctly. If the child controls don't exist when this function is called, it creates them. Notice the change in button creation: the button caption is now retrieved from the control's string table, as it's used again by the *DrawButton* code. Also, after the edit control is created, its text is set to the current value of *m_strEditText*, which will typically hold the value retrieved from permanent storage during *DoPropExchange*.

DrawButton itself shows the bad side of subclassing and similar techniques. As I said earlier, some Windows controls can react to having a device context handle sent to them in the *wParam* parameter of a *WM_PAINT* message, rendering themselves onto this device context. Others can't, and in that case you need to do the drawing yourself. That's what I've done here, although buttons can draw themselves into a passed DC. My drawing code is fairly naive, and is wrong in a couple of places. However, the drawn button looks identical to the one drawn by Windows 95, so I'm happy. The errors are that it doesn't explicitly set the font with which the caption is drawn, and it doesn't set the text color to *COLOR_BTNTEXT*. These changes are easy to make if you regard them as important. Other than that, *DrawButton* creates a few appropriately colored pens, and then it fills in the majority of the button surface with the approved button color (*COLOR_BTNFACE*) and draws some lines to provide the three-dimensional effect. It then outputs the caption text (*IDS_BUTTONCAPTION*, a newly added string resource) using *DrawText*, which handily converts the & in the caption name to the mnemonic underscore expected on a button.

DrawEditbox is simpler because there's no three-dimensional stuff to worry about. The only interesting things here are the retrieval of the text from the actual edit box control (you know, the one that won't draw itself!); the setting of the *DT_NOPREFIX* flag on *DrawText* so that, unlike the button case, & characters are <u>not</u> converted to underscores; and the bad use of absolute RGB values for black and white pens and brushes, when perfectly good stock ones exist that I could use courtesy of *::GetStockObject*. Another change you can make if you want.

The final function is *CreateHiddenWindow*. If the hidden window already exists, this function simply returns a pointer to it. If it doesn't exist, it's created through a call to *CWnd::CreateEx*. I have to use *CreateEx* because this window has no parent, making it either a popup or overlapped window. *CWnd::Create* cannot be used for these sorts of creations. I let *AfxRegisterWndClass* create a magical window class name for me (I don't care what it is), and all the parameters to *CreateEx* are 0 or as close to that as I can get! The lack of a *WS_VISIBLE* flag means that the window is created invisible, with dimensions of 0-by-0 pixels.

After you've built this control, you can verify that it now draws itself correctly when not active by inserting a Children control into Test Container (when it will of course be created active, so none of the drawing code is tested yet), typing some random text into the edit control, perhaps setting the edit control's font to something unusual, and then choosing the Save Property Set option from the File menu. This will save all the persistent parts of the current control into a file called TMP.DFL. To load the stuff, and as a by-product create an initially <u>inactive</u> control, choose the Load Property Set option from the File menu. You'll notice that an identical control is created and drawn, with the correct edit control text and font. Magical! (Both controls are shown in Figure 17-3.) Of course, this is all a lot harder for more complex controls to draw than the two I've chosen.

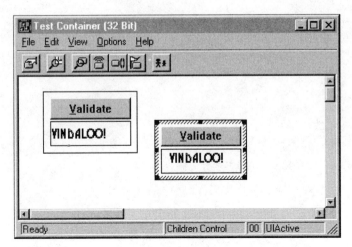

Figure 17-3. *A UI-active Children control, and an initially inactive Children control that is (very nearly) correctly drawn.*

Chapter 18

16-Bit-to-32-Bit and Cross-Platform Issues

Microsoft Corporation, in common with most other large software companies, wants to move the world to 32-bit computing. This move allows it to take advantage of features that 32-bit operating systems can offer more easily and cleanly than can (Intel-based) 16-bit systems. With the wide availability now of 32-bit operating systems and also of the programming languages and applications that together make an operating system successful, the motivation to move has never been higher. Nevertheless, the sheer size of the Windows version 3.x installed base forces you to the conclusion that it's going to take some time to get everyone across the 32-bit bridge. I often make comparisons between this migration and the use of unleaded petrol (gas). Initially, very few cars used unleaded petrol and it was more expensive than regular, leaded petrol. When enough people were motivated by the benefits of unleaded petrol to lobby car manufacturers, petrol companies, and even the government, it led to the eventual widespread use of unleaded petrol. Although the current climate suggests that it's unlikely that the government will legislate on the mandatory use of 32-bit operating systems by 1999, developers are mostly convinced that the move to 32 bits is also just as inevitable. And as more end users become enlightened, they'll likely come to the same conclusion.

This book participates in that lobbying, by assuming that the default platform is a 32-bit version of Windows. All the programs and controls in this book were built and tested as 32-bit versions first, running on Windows 95 and Windows NT 3.51, and sometimes tested using the 32-bit version of Visual Basic version 4.0. Nevertheless, proper heed is paid to the large number of developers remaining with 16 bits. Every program and control has also been built and tested using 16-bit Visual C++ and has been run on Windows 95 and Windows NT 3.51 as 16-bit applications.

It is undeniable, however, that the better OLE control story happens in 32-bit land. Although this book was written prior to its release, Visual C++ version 4.0 and its accompanying release of the MFC library, also version 4.0, supports both OLE control creation and OLE control containment, but only in a 32-bit environment. Likewise, you'll see more support added to 32-bit OLE for control-like things in the future, and some technologies such as OLE Database and OLE Transactions will never have 16-bit implementations. Even connection points, the most exciting thing that controls added to the Component Object Model (COM), will only be usable across-process in 32-bit environments.

So, what do you do if you want to develop 16-bit controls? All the techniques in this book apply: I've made sure that nothing is specific to 32 bits. Some issues, however, will come back to haunt you if you don't deal with them now. I'm going to take the unusual step of looking at 16-bit-to-32-bit portability from the opposite point of view — that is, taking 32-bit components as the starting point, and figuring out some of the problems that become apparent as you move them down to 16 bits. I hope this approach works for you.

CROSS-PLATFORM ISSUES

This chapter includes the words "cross-platform" in its title because OLE controls do not need to be specific to Windows platforms or, indeed, to Intel platforms. Obviously, versions of Visual C++ that target RISC versions of Windows NT (such as the PowerPC, DEC Alpha, and MIPS R4400 computers) will include versions of the OLE CDK for that platform, so in theory any 32-bit control project can be taken fom this book and, with some make file changes, be rebuilt for Windows NT on the chosen RISC platform. I have not tried this with any of the controls.

Then there's the Macintosh. Visual C++ version 2.0 also has a Mac variant, which still compiles, links, and debugs on an Intel-based PC but that generates 680x0 code for Apple Macintosh computers and allows you to develop MFC-based applications that will run on the Macintosh with little change from their Win32 counterparts. This is all done through a special mapping layer called WLM (Windows Libraries for Macintosh), which provides a lot of the Win32 API on the Macintosh. The version of WLM shipped with the cross-platform edition of Visual C++ version 2.0 does not include support for OLE, so OLE controls cannot be built for Macintosh environments with this development system.

Visual C++ version 4.0, however, also has a cross-platform edition for the Macintosh, and this time it targets both 68000 and PowerMac variants, with compilers for each included in the box. The PowerMac variant includes a host of OLE support, including automation and visual editing. Unfortunately, significant work remains to be done before we'll see the technology evolve to the point where OLE controls can be created and used on this platform.

A few software vendors have licensed from Microsoft the source code to Windows (which includes OLE in its 32-bit variant) and to the MFC library, so they are able to port it to other platforms. Already, in 1995, you can buy development systems that allow you to recreate your MFC and Win32 applications on various Unix platforms, and most of these vendors are also working on getting OLE implemented on Unix. When this happens, and as long as they also support in-process servers, it's probable that one could build and use OLE controls for use on Unix systems, using the same source code, with perhaps a little change, as you have for the Windows versions of the same controls.

None of this is here at the time of the writing of this book (mid 1995), so there are no cross-platform issues that explicitly need to be addressed now. Always bear in mind, however, that you might want to port your code to another platform at some future time. Therefore, be aware of issues such as unsupported features (threads often being a fine example) and byte-ordering and alignment requirements (some RISC processors require things to be aligned on 8-byte boundaries lest performance be atrocious because processor exceptions occur to handle the nonstandard offsets).

32-BIT-TO-16-BIT PORTING ISSUES

Now it's time to look at some of the issues involved in moving a 32-bit OLE control project down to 16-bit, assuming for the most part the use of Microsoft development tools. Much of the same stuff applies to other vendors' toolsets.

Alignment

Alignment is not something you need to get heavily wound up about, because it rarely causes things to stop working. It can, however, cause significant performance problems. Alignment refers to the way in which data (and code, but I'll ignore that) is accessed and stored. A general rule of thumb is that a processor always accesses data more quickly if the address of that data is aligned on a boundary of the same size as the processor's data bus. So, an 8-bit processor such as the venerable Z80 could happily read data anywhere in its huge 64-KB address space. 16-bit processors such as the 8086 and 80286 were far more efficient when data was aligned on 16-bit (that is, 2-byte) boundaries. Intel processors from the 80386 on prefer 32-bit boundaries.

Most of the time, you don't need to care about this stuff if you're writing in C++, although each compiler offers the facility to pack data members in classes and structures along given boundaries. A common trick in 16-bit Windows programs of old (that is, when the world still ran in real mode, back in the days before Windows version 3.x) was to pack everything on 1-byte boundaries, so that the data structure was as small as possible. Memory was the premium resource then, far more so than it is now. Progams performed better, and allowed other programs to perform better (if at all!), if they occupied as small a chunk of memory as possible. Don't do this!

These days, the performance hit of a misaligned data access is something you're far more likely to get upset about than the use of another three measly bytes by your program. Visual C++ by default aligns to a 64-bit (8-byte) boundary, and there's really no reason to change it. The only time you'd need to is when you need to map a C++ structure onto a given memory layout, such as protocol headers in network packets. If you have an OLE control doing this sort of stuff, you're probably far too advanced to be reading this book! Seriously, though, in these cases, you can pack the structure concerned on a 1-byte boundary, but keep packing elsewhere at the default value. You do this in Microsoft C++ by surrounding the structure with reasonably arcane *#pragma pack* statements.

Unicode, ANSI, and MBCS

I introduced Unicode very early on in this book, back in Chapter 3, but you weren't constrained to read that chapter so you might have missed it. Unicode is a 16-bit character set system. ANSI characters, those of which most of us are used to, are of course 8 bits wide. MBCS (multi-byte character set) characters make life more difficult by being of variable length.

The 32-bit version of OLE, regardless of which Windows platform it's implemented on, uses Unicode for all strings. Windows NT uses Unicode internally for all strings, but implements all string-taking or returning API functions in two flavors, one of which takes Unicode strings and the other of which takes ANSI strings and converts on the way. The Unicode variants will always, by definition, be faster on Windows NT than the ANSI variants. Windows 95 supports only MBCS/ANSI, although it does implement a few of the Unicode API functions from Windows NT to make it easier to get programs working on both platforms and to translate between Unicode and ANSI or MBCS. Now, Windows 95's flavor of OLE is 32-bit and therefore speaks Unicode only. An OLE program that wants to be most efficient on Windows 95 should therefore try to talk to OLE in Unicode; otherwise, automatic ANSI-Unicode translation will be performed for it.

The MFC library also has two flavors — one for Unicode and one for ANSI and MBCS. You can only use the Unicode flavor on Windows NT systems, whereas programs developed with the ANSI variant will run on all Win32 platforms. Windows NT uses wrappers to convert between ANSI and Unicode, so an ANSI control is going to be less efficient on Windows NT than a Unicode version would be. However, because Windows 95's implementation of OLE is also 32-bit and therefore also Unicode-based, it too must translate. I guess the ideal solution is to get to the point where all flavors of Windows are Unicode-enabled, at which point you can stop worrying about ANSI and just program always to Unicode APIs. That day, I suspect, is still some ways off.

And 16 bits? Well, the 16-bit version of Windows has always been a great deal poorer in its handling of international issues than the 32-bit flavors of Windows, so it follows that 16-bit Windows, 16-bit OLE, and 16-bit MFC support only ANSI and MBCS characters. However, Visual C++ versions 1.51 and later provide the same macros as 32-bit Visual C++, so you can write Unicode-safe code such as

```
_T ( "This is a string" )
```

and 16-bit Visual C++ will understand it. My advice is to code always to be Unicode-aware, even of it seems unlikely that you'll use it. It's considerably easier to enable Unicode support by throwing a compiler switch than it is to go through all your code, checking all your variable declarations, all your functions and classes, and then wrapping every string in the requisite macro. It isn't that much work to do it up-front as you code.

Natural 16-Bit Differences

Some changes you'll notice are a natural result of the move back to 16 bits. For example, a native integer on 16-bit systems is only 16 bits wide, compared to 32 bits wide on 32-bit systems. Likewise, 32-bit operations, such as those involving long integers, are slower on 16-bit systems because more machine instructions are required to perform them than on 32-bit systems. A long integer on 32-bit systems is the same size as a long integer on 16-bit systems, but a long integer is no longer than a plain integer on 32-bit systems. If you really need 32 bits, use the right type. If you only need 16 bits, use a short integer. This is rarely, if ever, more efficient on 32-bit systems (but it is no less efficient), but it is certainly faster on 16-bit systems.

Take particular care when you are serializing data to a file or some other storage medium. If you've saved integers on a 32-bit system to a file, reading them in as integers on a 16-bit system will fail. You also need to take into account actual variable size when you're performing bit operations such as masking and shifting.

Both the MFC library and the Windows header files define a set of types that can be used when you want to use a specific size.

Message and API Changes

When Microsoft moved the Windows API to 32 bits, it naturally made every effort to ensure backward compatibility. However, because of concerns such as integer size, some things simply couldn't be kept the same. Take, for example, the Windows message structure, which has a *wParam* field and an *lParam* field. On 32-bit systems, these fields are 32 bits wide. On 16-bit systems, *wParam* is only 16 bits wide. 16-bit Windows took advantage of the fact that *lParam* was long enough to hold two 16-bit values and in some messages, such as *WM_COMMAND*, passed three values in *wParam* and *lParam*, whereas on 32-bit systems only two will fit. Consequently, there have been some changes to messages that you'll need to deal with if you handle messages directly. If you use MFC's message maps to handle messages, MFC handles all this stuff for you.

The graphics coordinate system on Windows NT is 32 bits wide, while on Windows 95 and on 16-bit Windows it is only 16 bits wide. This means that coordinate ranges in Windows NT can be significantly larger than on other Windows systems.

There have been a number of API revisions, too, because again Windows was relying on 32 bits being able to convey two pieces of information whereas now it can handle only one. Some new API functions were added to the system to replace such limited 16-bit ones, and macros for these API functions were created for 16-bit Windows programs so that you can use the same API functions without noticing the difference. Again, the MFC library hides most of this, but if you need to call native Windows API functions, try to use the real 32-bit versions rather than the older, 16-bit versions that have limitations and restrictions under Win32. An example of this is the *MoveTo* API function, which has now been replaced by the *MoveToEx* API function.

Also, remember that a large number of the API functions you'd naturally use on a 32-bit system don't exist on 16-bit Windows; these include the file and heap functions, security functions, and some of the advanced graphics functions.

Windows Differences

Windows itself has changed dramatically in going from its 16-bit version to its 32-bit version. Apart from the obvious significant user-interface changes introduced in Windows 95 and likely to appear on Windows NT before the end of 1995, there's a host of new functionality that you should be using but that you can't use on 16-bit Windows. A trivial example is the registry, which is a far cleaner interface than the plethora of INI files and the registration database on Windows version 3.x.

User-interface changes are important. Your controls should try to look like the rest of the system, so they should use the 3D beveled effect for items such as buttons, and they should take advantage of the new common controls introduced in Windows 95 and in Windows NT version 3.51 (not to mention in Win32s version 1.30).

Your controls should also try to integrate with the system as closely as possible, using Windows 95 property pages, integrating with the shell where it makes sense, and so forth. They should use long filenames and generally do all the things Microsoft recommends to be good Windows 95 citizens. They might even use features of 32-bit Windows that can't be found on 16-bit Windows. Most of the items described above fall into this category, and so does the use of threads. (Threads are such an important aspect of 32-bit life that a section is devoted to them, beginning on the next page.)

Other parts of Windows are different in the 16-bit flavor, too. For example, Windows 95 and Windows NT include the concept of asynchronous input message queues, which means that one application not reading its input queue (for example, as the result of a hang) will <u>not</u> stop other applications from proceeding. This is not the case in 16-bit Windows, where a misbehaving application can quite easily stall all other Windows applications. This is important for you, too, if your control spends a lot of time doing something without checking the message queue. While this behavior will go unpunished on Win32 systems (barring Win32s), problems will be very noticeable on Win16.

Another difference is the semantics of mouse capture. Whereas a captured mouse in Win32 is purely application-wide, it's system-wide on 16-bit Windows. The upshot of this is that mouse capture might work slightly differently from what you'd expect when you run your control in a 16-bit environment.

Tool Differences

If you're using Microsoft tools, you'll inevitably notice some differences between the 16-bit flavor and the 32-bit ones. Generally, the 32-bit variants will be invested in more significantly by Microsoft, so you'll see new features appearing there that might never make it into an equivalent 16-bit version. As an example, the 32-bit version of Visual C++ supports real C++ exceptions and templates, while the 16-bit compiler does not and never will. Moreover, the make system in 32-bit land is better and can deal with the *MkTypLib* utility successfully, as well as filename extensions such as

OCX. The 16-bit make system, on the other hand, requires you to invoke *MkTypLib* manually as a separate step, and it can cope only with EXE and DLL extensions.

Other subtle differences occur here and there, such as enhancements to the MFC library that appear only in version 3.x or later and are therefore 32-bit specific. Even things such as the debugger are more powerful and easier to use in the 32-bit product. Microsoft's story is also not too different from other compiler vendors, who are also now beginning to focus very much on 32-bit development at the expense of their 16-bit systems.

Threads

One obvious portability problem is the use of threads. The 16-bit version of Windows does not support multiple threads, and is not pre-emptively multi-tasked (with respect to other running 16-bit Windows programs). Win32, on the other hand, does support threads. So, should you use them? Threads are a very lightweight way to achieve background processing, so they most certainly are useful in the right context. Think back to the First control developed over the first few chapters of this book; the final version uses ODBC to access a database of SCODEs. You might also recall that the control has a method called *BatchLoad*, which loads a set of SCODE records from a file into the database. This can be quite a lengthy operation and can take some time, so it might be logical to do it on a thread. Processing would then be along the lines of:

1. On invocation of the *BatchLoad* method, check parameters.

2. Spawn a thread to process the invocation.

3. Return immediately, with success.

4. The spawned thread then opens the file, processes it, and updates the database, throwing any errors through *FireError* (as it's no longer in the context of an automation invocation).

5. At the end of processing, a new BatchLoadSucceeded event or similar is fired, and the thread then kills itself.

But this scheme has two problems (at least!). The first problem is that you are relying on OLE (and the control runtime) to be thread-safe. This problem probably isn't too vast, as 32-bit OLE can be used on separate threads in the same process. As long as you don't try to share objects between threads, the control runtime should be okay, too.

The second problem is more serious. In normal, single-threaded circumstances, communication between a control and its container takes place entirely within the context of the one thread. Therefore, when a control fires an event, the container receives the event in the same thread. Now add a new thread to this scheme, with the new thread firing events. All of a sudden, the container has to respond to events on one thread, while doing whatever it was doing before on its original thread. The control has therefore made the assumption that the container is thread-safe. In a lot of cases, this simply isn't the case — and it's a very unsafe assumption.

Bottom line, then: threads are excellent devices for certain tasks, and if you intend to use multiple threads in an OLE control, keep all interaction between control and container on the one, initial thread. For example, rather than getting the newly created thread to fire an event, get it instead to post a message to the initial thread so that the initial thread can fire the event.

NOTE   If you target Win32s, this is a variant of the Win32 API that does not offer thread support.

16-BIT-TO-32-BIT OLE INTEROPERABILITY

You might remember that in Chapter 2, when I introduced some of the basic concepts behind OLE, I talked briefly about the ability of an OLE object to work across bit boundaries as well as to process boundaries. That is, a 16-bit OLE container can make use of 32-bit OLE servers. Well, that's true — but there is a caveat of importance to controls.

16-bit-to-32-bit interoperability always works if both container and server are implemented as out-of-process objects (that is, as executables). When the server is a DLL, an in-process server, things are rather more limited. There are circumstances in which a 16-bit executable can make use of a 32-bit in-process server, except that for some reason not entirely clear to me, the *IDispatch* interface is not supported in this way. Hence, 16-bit containers cannot make use of 32-bit OLE controls. 32-bit executables cannot make use of 16-bit in-process servers at all, so 32-bit containers cannot use 16-bit OLE controls. The upshot of this is that a container can only use controls that have the same "bitness" as it does.

Chapter 19

Microsoft Guidelines for OLE Controls and OLE Control Containers

Throughout this book I've been showing you how to write OLE controls, but I haven't commented on what containers these controls will and won't work in. You might remember the book's first chapter, "Componentware," in which I said that OLE controls were one further step along the road to true plug-and-play component software. This is a true statement, qualified by the facts that a number of controls will be written to be specific to a given container, such as Microsoft Visual Basic, and that some containers will have a greater level of support for controls than others.

To make it easier for users and developers to know which controls will work where, Microsoft Corporation has set some guidelines that it will obey in both its containers and controls and that it hopes other control and container vendors will adopt. These guidelines first set forth a minimum set of features that a control or container must support, followed by a set of "function groups," or elements of functionality, that it doesn't make sense to force all controls or containers to support.

When I say that a control or container must support the minimum set, there is of course no mandate that sets this forth. Instead, the intention is that industry momentum will build up behind these guidelines so that no control or container vendor will be willing to ignore it. Nothing compels vendors to support the guidelines, but vendors that don't will find it much harder to sell their wares than vendors that do.

The document itself is available on most major online forums, on the Microsoft Developer Network (MSDN), and with development tools such as Microsoft Visual C++. The document is broken into two sections, one for controls and one for control containers. The minimum bar ensures that a control that conforms to the guidelines will work in any container that also complies. Likewise, a container that complies is guaranteed to support all compliant controls.

NOTE   This chapter was prepared immediately before the guidelines were published to the outside world for general comment; therefore, minor changes might have been made in it that are not reflected here. Also, Microsoft Corporation anticipates that the guidelines will be a living document, with revisions occurring perhaps annually, to reflect new features, de facto standards, user-interface guidelines, and other amendments. Be sure to check online sources or MSDN for later versions of the document on which this chapter was based and amend what I say here accordingly.

One of the just-mentioned concepts in the guidelines is that of a "function group." This is a functional area that does not need to be supported by all controls or by all control containers. If a particular function group is supported by a control, it might also be required to be supported by containers in which that control is embedded. For example, controls that rely on the support of *ISimpleFrameSite* might not work in containers that don't provide *ISimpleFrameSite* support. To aid the users of such controls and containers, each feature group has an OLE "informal type" associated with it. (See the sidebar "OLE Informal Types," on the facing page.) A well-behaved container will then display in its "insert control" dialog only those controls that it can support.

If a control finds itself being asked to work in a container that doesn't support all that it wants, the guidelines say that it should "degrade gracefully." This means that rather than crashing when it finds that a particular interface or API doesn't exist, the control should attempt to work without it and perhaps warn the user of deficiencies if it makes sense to do so. Likewise, a container that finds a control being embedded within it that doesn't support an interface or an expected API should allow the control to be embedded. If these scenarios simply don't work for a given control/container combination, the appropriate element (control or container) should fail the embedding and explain why.

So, the general rule is that any interface required must be obtained through a call to *QueryInterface* (except in those rare cases where an interface is returned through some other means), and, most importantly, the return result from the *QueryInterface* call must be checked to ensure that the returned pointer is valid. If it is not, the control or container must take appropriate action, rather than calling through the pointer anyway. This will cause controls and containers to degrade gracefully rather than crashing.

OLE INFORMAL TYPES

An "informal type" in OLE is an indication that a particular object is of a type that holds no particular relevance to OLE itself but that might be of interest to consumers of that object. For example, many objects are marked as "insertable," which means only that they can be embedded into an OLE server. Such attributes of objects are typically found as registry keys under the object's CLSID registry entry.

The problem with such registry entries is that nothing makes them unique to a given purpose other than convention. Suppose someone else were to define the "insertable" key to mean something different. How would you as an object consumer know how to differentiate between OLE's understanding of "insertable" and the other definition? What meaning does "insertable" have for someone who does not speak English?

To get around this potential problem, the OLE group at Microsoft Corporation has introduced the concept of an informal type. An "informal type" is entirely analogous to the "insertable" key except that GUIDs are used, rather than natural language words or phrases, to notify the consumer of an object that the object is of a specific type.

So, in the future, you might see objects that previously marked themselves as insertable now being marked with a specific GUID, which means that they are insertable in the manner defined by the creator of the informal type (in this case, OLE).

The guidelines for OLE controls and control containers use informal types to mark function groups implemented by a control; if a control has a registry key under its CLSID entry for the GUID associated with function group 1, for example, then that control implements function group 1 as defined by the guidelines.

The rest of this chapter sets out the guidelines and explains what it takes to make your control or container compliant. It also, in some senses, justifies the decisions made by the authors of the guidelines (of which I am one).

CONTROLS

The premise here is that a control is useful only if it can be used in a given container. The guidelines first set out the minimum set of interfaces, APIs, and features expected of a control. If a control matches up to that set, it is guaranteed to work in all containers that implement the container side of these guidelines. A control that falls below this set is not verified to work in arbitrary containers, and the vendor's advice should be sought as to which containers the control works with.

The Guidelines

The guidelines for controls are best viewed as the minimum set of interfaces, APIs, and features that a control supports. The elements of the guidelines can be relied on to be present, but that is all that can be assumed about the control. It might implement more advanced features, or it might not. If a control implements advanced features covered by a function group, that control will have the appropriate informal type defined for its CLSID.

Table 19-1 shows the set of interfaces a control can support, and it specifies those that a control is expected to support to meet the guidelines.

OLE AND COM INTERFACES*

Interface	Support Mandatory?	Notes
IOleObject	Yes	
IOleInPlaceObject	Yes	
IOleInPlaceActiveObject	No	Must be supported by controls with UI.
IOleControl	No	Must be supported by controls with mnemonics and/or which use ambient properties.
IDataObject	Yes	Needed by controls with property sets; must always be available with *CF_METAFILE* format.
IOleCache	No	
IOleCache2	No	

Table 19-1. *The interfaces a control can support and indications of whether they are required by the standard.* (continued)

OLE AND COM INTERFACES* *(continued)*

Interface	Support Mandatory?	Notes
IOleCacheControl	No	
IViewObject2	Yes	
IRunnableObject	No	
IExternalConnection	No	Must be supported if a control has external links to itself other than from its immediate container.
IDispatch	No	Only needed by controls with methods and/or properties (and therefore by most controls). Dual interface support is strongly recommended.**
IConnectionPointContainer	No	Must be supported by controls with events or property notifications.
IConnectionPoint	No	As per *IConnectionPointContainer*.
IProvideClassInfo	Yes	
ISpecifyPropertyPages	No	Must be supported by controls with property pages.
IPersistStream	No	See "Storage" section.
IPersistStreamInit	No	See "Storage" section.
IPersistStorage	Yes	See "Storage" section.
IClassFactory	Yes	
IClassFactory2	No	Must be supported by controls that want licensing support.
IPerPropertyBrowsing	No	
IPropertyNotifySink (be a source for)	No	Must be supported by controls that provide property change notifications.
IPersistPropertyBag	No	Strongly recommended.‡

Note:
*Any interface listed here <u>can</u> be supported by an OLE control and often will be. Only those marked specifically as mandatory <u>must</u> be.
**Dual interface support is strongly recommended but optional.
‡Support for *IPersistPropertyBag* is strongly recommended but optional, and would be used only as an optimization on the control side for containers that implement a "save as text" mechanism using this interface.

Interface Method Support

It is possible to implement an OLE or COM interface without implementing all the semantics of each of the interface's methods (that is, you just return *E_NOTIMPL* or *S_OK* as appropriate). OLE controls, however, are required to implement some of these "optional" methods. Table 19-2 shows which methods in a confined set of interfaces can return *E_NOTIMPL*. Any method of any interface marked as mandatory in Table 19-1 that is not shown in this table must be considered mandatory.

OPTIONAL INTERFACE METHODS

Interface::Method	Notes
IOleControl::GetControlInfo	Must be supported by controls with mnemonics.
IOleControl::OnMnemonic	Must be supported by controls with mnemonics.
IOleControl::OnAmbientProperty-Change	Must be supported by controls that use ambient properties.
IOleControl::FreezeEvents	
IOleObject::DoVerb	Must be supported by controls with property pages for *OLEIVERB_PROPERTIES* and *OLEIVERB_PRIMARY*. Controls must support *OLEIVERB_INPLACEACTIVATE* if they can become active, and if they can become UI-active, *OLEIVERB_UIACTIVATE* as well.
IOleInPlaceObject::ContextSensitiveHelp	
IOleInPlaceObject::ReactivateAndUndo	
IOleInPlaceActiveObject::ContextSensitiveHelp	
IOleObject::SetMoniker	
IOleObject::GetMoniker	
IOleObject::InitFromData	
IOleObject::GetClipboardData	
IOleObject::SetExtent	Optional for aspects other than *DVASPECT_CONTENT*.
IOleObject::GetExtent	Optional for aspects other than *DVASPECT_CONTENT*.
IOleObject::SetColorScheme	
IViewObject::Freeze	
IViewObject::Unfreeze	

Table 19-2. *Interface methods that controls do not need to implement.* (continued)

Interface::Method	Notes
IPersistStreamInit::GetSizeMax	If a control supports *IPersistStream* and can support this method meaningfully, it should do so. "Meaningfully" means rather than returning an arbitrarily large value to cover all possibilities, it should return an accurate value. This is very difficult for controls with string properties to achieve.

Properties

There is no guideline to say that a control <u>must</u> have properties. Of course, a control without any properties at all is rarely interesting! If a control wants to support a stock property, it should follow the defined semantics for that stock property.

Methods (through OLE Automation)

Whether a control supports any methods is entirely up to the control implementor. There are no methods that <u>must</u> be supported. Again, a control that does not implement any methods at all might not be very useful. If a control wants to support a stock method, it should follow the defined semantics for that stock method.

Events

Whether a control fires any events or not is entirely up to the control implementor. There are no events that <u>must</u> be fired. If a control wants to fire a stock event, it should follow the defined semantics for that stock event.

Ambient Properties

An OLE control must take note of the following ambient properties if they exist at the control site into which they're embedded:

- *LocaleID* (if Locale is significant to the control — for example, for text output)
- *UserMode* (if the control behaves differently in user mode and run mode)
- *UIDead* (if the control reacts to UI events, then it should honor this ambient)
- *ShowHatching*
- *ShowGrabHandles*
- *DisplayAsDefault* (only if the control is marked *OLEMISC_ACTSLIKE-BUTTON*)

Registry Information

To be compliant, an OLE control must support self-registration. In addition to the standard registry entries for embeddable objects and automation servers that must be supported, there are three registry keys that can apply to OLE controls that are <u>not</u> mandatory:

■ ToolBoxBitmap32

■ Insertable

■ Control

If a control supports any of the function groups defined in the guidelines, it must also include registry entries for the appropriate informal types.

Property Pages

A control does not need to support property pages or per-property browsing. Both of these features, however, aid a user's interaction with the control and therefore it is recommended that controls do support them.

Function Groups

As of this writing (mid 1995), the guidelines define two function groups for controls:

■ *ISimpleFrameSite* support required from the container

■ Simple data binding supported by at least one property on this control (requires an implementation of *IPropertyNotifySink* on the container)

These groups are examined in greater detail in the next sections.

ISimpleFrameSite Support

If a control "implements" function group 1, it's asking for the *ISimpleFrameSite* protocol to be supported by the container in which it is embedded. This means that the control expects to be used as a visual container for other controls and will not work properly (if at all) if it is embedded in a container that does not support *ISimpleFrameSite*.

Containers that always activate every control in a window effectively provide most of the support for this anyway. If the container also provides programmatic support for reparenting controls (which most won't unless the programming language used is low-level enough, such as C++), then all the semantics of *ISimpleFrameSite* can be supported even if the interface itself is not. Containers that don't always activate each control (such as Visual Basic version 4.0's design-time) will need to implement this interface if they intend to host function group 1 controls.

If a control is marked as function group 1 and is successfully inserted into a container that doesn't implement the protocol, the control should at least be aware that its container is not *ISimpleFrameSite*-compliant, and if necessary it should warn the user.

Some controls simply cannot work without container-side support for *ISimpleFrameSite*. If your control falls into this category, then it should stop itself from being inserted if it detects that the *ISimpleFrameSite* interface is not present on the container.

Simple Data Binding

Any control that implements data binding for any of its properties should support the so-called "simple" data-binding model provided by the OLE Controls specification. This means that it should call a container's implementation of *IPropertyNotify-Sink::OnChanged* whenever a bound property is changed and, if the property is also marked as *requestedit*, it should call *IPropertyNotifySink::OnRequestEdit* prior to any actual change to the property's value. Clearly, if this method is supported, the control must also take note of the return value.

CONTROL CONTAINERS

It is generally accepted wisdom that, as was the case with VBXs, there will be significantly fewer OLE control containers on the market than OLE controls. This is what the component market is all about. Various vendors, however, will provide a substantial number of containers. Within a few months of the publication date of this book (Fall 1995), Microsoft Corporation itself will release four applications that can be used as general OLE control containers:

- Visual C++ version 4.0

- Visual Basic version 4.0

- Visual FoxPro version 3.0

- Access version 7.0

Each of these containers, except FoxPro, meets the guidelines for OLE control containers discussed below. FoxPro addresses the areas in which it doesn't meet the guidelines in the next release.

Any container that doesn't implement the basic necessities for OLE controls will make it more difficult for users to pick and choose OLE controls from their local store. If, on the other hand, containers do meet the guidelines, users have a guarantee that controls they buy that are marked as compliant will work in those containers. Of course, there is one proviso: if a particular control also implements or uses a certain function group, and that function group isn't implemented by a container, then that control won't work (or at least won't provide its full functionality, depending on the function group in question) in that container.

A compliant container should list only those controls it can support inside any dialog boxes it creates to allow users to pick controls for insertion (although this isn't yet a requirement of the guidelines). A container would typically do this by reading each control's informal type information from the registry. By showing only those controls it can support, a container makes it substantially more difficult for a user to make erroneous use of a control that the container doesn't support.

The Guidelines

A compliant OLE control container must be an OLE in-place active container capable of supporting the following:

- Embedded objects from in-process servers

- Inside-out activation

- *OLEMISC_ACTIVATEWHENVISIBLE*

- Visual editing of embedded objects

Explicit support for local servers is not required because OLE controls cannot presently be implemented in local servers. It is likely a container will support this anyway in the course of normal in-place container implementation.

In addition, a compliant OLE control container has a number of other interfaces it must support, and a few that it can optionally support. These are shown in Table 19-3.

OLE AND COM INTERFACES*

Interface	*Support Mandatory?*	*Notes*
IOleClientSite	Yes	
IAdviseSink	Yes	Except where it is not needed, such as where controls are always active.
IOleInPlaceSite	Yes	
IOleControlSite	Yes	
IOleInPlaceFrame	Yes	
IOleContainer	Yes	Implemented on the "document" or "form" object (or an appropriate analog) that holds the container sites. This permits a

Table 19-3. *The interfaces an OLE control container can implement and*   *(continued)*
            indications of whether they are mandatory for the standard.

OLE AND COM INTERFACES* *(continued)*

		control to navigate to other controls in the same document or form.
IDispatch for ambient properties	Yes	Certain ambient properties must be supported by all OLE control containers.
ISimpleFrameSite	No	*ISimpleFrameSite* and nested simple frames are optional.
IDispatch for events	Yes	
IPropertyNotifySink	No	Property notification sinks are optional.
Extended control	No	

*Any interface listed here <u>can</u> be supported by an OLE control container and often will be. Only those marked specifically as mandatory <u>must</u> be.

An OLE control container must also support OLE Automation exceptions. If it supports calling through dual interfaces, it must support capture of automation exceptions through *IErrorInfo*. Dual interface support for the following is optional for containers but is strongly recommended:

- calling control methods and properties

- responding to events fired by controls

- returning ambient property values

Note that, currently, controls created with the Microsoft OLE CDK do not support dual interfaces themselves. By providing support in your container now, you'll be enhancing performance in the future.

It is possible to implement an OLE interface without implementing all the semantics of each of the interface's methods — that is, you simply return *E_NOTIMPL* or *S_OK* as appropriate. Compliant OLE control containers, however, are required to implement some of these "optional" methods. Table 19-4 shows which methods in a confined set of interfaces can return *E_NOTIMPL*. Any method of any interface marked as mandatory in Table 19-3 that is not shown in this table must be considered mandatory.

Optional Interface Methods

Interface::Method	*Notes*
IOleClientSite::SaveObject	
IOleClientSite::GetMoniker	
IOleClientSite::RequestNewObjectLayout	
IOleInPlaceSite::ContextSensitiveHelp	

Table 19-4.   *Optional methods on OLE interfaces implemented by OLE control containers.* *(continued)*

Optional Interface Methods *(continued)*

Interface::Method	Notes
IOleControlSite::GetExtendedControl	Necessary only for containers with extended controls. A control should be written to deal with this call failing!
IOleControlSite::ShowPropertyFrame	A control that wishes to display property pages must make this call.
IDispatch::GetTypeInfoCount	This is the *IDispatch* for ambient properties.
IDispatch::GetTypeInfo	This is the *IDispatch* for ambient properties.
IDispatch::GetIDsOfNames	This is the *IDispatch* for ambient properties.
Event sink*::GetTypeInfoCount*	The control knows its own type information, so it has no need to call this.
Event sink*::GetTypeInfo*	The control knows its own type information, so it has no need to call this.
Event sink*::GetIDsOfNames*	The control knows its own type information, so it has no need to call this.
IOleInPlaceFrame::ContextSensitiveHelp	
IOleInPlaceFrame::GetBorder	Necessary if the control has toolbar UI (which is optional).
IOleInPlaceFrame::RequestBorderSpace	Necessary if the control has toolbar UI (which is optional).
IOleInPlaceFrame::SetBorderSpace	Necessary if the control has toolbar UI (which is optional).
IOleInPlaceFrame::InsertMenus	Necessary if the control has menu UI (which is optional).
IOleInPlaceFrame::SetMenu	Necessary if the control has menu UI (which is optional).
IOleInPlaceFrame::RemoveMenus	Necessary if the control has menu UI (which is optional).
IOleInPlaceFrame::SetStatusText	
IOleInPlaceFrame::EnableModeless	
IOleContainer::ParseDisplayName	
IOleContainer::LockContainer	
IOleContainer::EnumObjects	Must be implemented, but is not guaranteed to return all objects in the container because there's no guarantee that all objects are OLE controls; some may be regular Windows controls.

Miscellaneous Status Bits Support

OLE controls use a set of *OLEMISC* status bits that must be recognized by and handled correctly by an OLE control container as shown in Table 19-5. Some of these status bits are newly introduced with OLE Controls.

OLEMISC STATUS BITS

Status Bit	Support Mandatory?
OLEMISC_ACTIVATEWHENVISIBLE	Yes
OLEMISC_INSIDEOUT	Yes
OLEMISC_INVISIBLEATRUNTIME	Yes
OLEMISC_ALWAYSRUN	Yes
OLEMISC_ACTSLIKEBUTTON	Yes
OLEMISC_ACTSLIKELABEL	Yes
OLEMISC_NOUIACTIVATE	Yes
OLEMISC_ALIGNABLE	No
OLEMISC_SIMPLEFRAME	No
OLEMISC_SETCLIENTSITEFIRST	Yes
OLEMISC_IMEMODE	No

Table 19-5. *The OLEMISC status bits used by OLE controls.*

Keyboard Handling

A container must support these types of "handling":

- Default button handling
- Mnemonic handling
- Tab handling including tab order

Optionally, containers can allow users to designate buttonlike OLE controls as the Cancel button. The only effect of this is that the container treats the pressing of the Escape key as being equivalent to the so-designated control being clicked on.

Ambient Properties

A compliant OLE control container must support ambient properties; the following is the minimum set allowed:

- *LocaleID*
- *UserMode* (where there is a difference in the container)

- *SupportsMnemonics* (which must always be *TRUE*, as per above)
- *DisplayAsDefault* (for those containers where a default button makes sense)

Extended Properties, Events, and Methods

A container does not need to support the idea of an extended control, but if it does, it must as a minimum support the following set of extended properties:

- *Visible*
- *Parent*
- *Default*
- *Cancel*

There are no mandatory extended events or methods.

Message Reflection

It is strongly recommended that an OLE control container support message reflection. This will result in more efficient operation for subclassed controls. If message reflection is supported, the *MessageReflect* ambient property must be supported and have a value of *TRUE*.

Automatic Clipping

It is strongly recommended that an OLE control container support automatic clipping of its controls. This will result in more efficient operation for nearly all controls. If automatic clipping is supported, the *AutoClip* ambient property must be supported and have a value of *TRUE*.

Data Binding

Neither a control nor a control container needs to support data binding. If a control does support data binding, it should use the simple mechanism defined in the OLE Controls specification. It can, in addition, use other means.

If a container supports data binding, it must at a minimum support the simple mechanism defined in the OLE Controls specification. It can, in addition, use other means, such as the Data Access Objects (DAO).

Function Groups

Rather than require a control container to support all possible control functionality, which is clearly pointless for containers in which such support is meaningless, containers can choose to support one or more function groups. If a container supports a function group, then when it is asked to display a list of controls it can successfully embed, it should check each control's registry entry for the GUID(s) of the function group(s) it supports. This way, it can display those that it knows will work.

The function groups that a control container can support are of course the same as those that controls can support.

ISimpleFrameSite Support

A control container that wants to allow a control to act as a frame for other controls to be embedded within must implement the *ISimpleFrameSite* interface. Actually, this isn't quite true, because it's perfectly possible for a container that always activates all controls in a form to provide all *ISimpleFrameSite*-type support without actually providing the interface itself. Doing so, however, makes it difficult for a control to verify that it will behave properly, because when it calls *QueryInterface* on the client site to get a pointer to its *ISimpleFrameSite* interface, the call will fail. Therefore, the control will believe that *ISimpleFrameSite* support is not present. The recommendation, therefore, is that containers that support the protocol should support the interface, too.

Data Binding

Any container that has a concept of data binding must support the simple data-binding mechanism defined by the OLE Controls specification. This means that it must implement *IPropertyNotifySink* and connect it to the relevant connection point on a bound control. All containers that provide this support must implement the *OnChanged* method on *IPropertyNotifySink*. Support for *OnRequestEdit* is optional; if you don't support it, always return *S_OK* to indicate that the property value can be changed.

STORAGE MECHANISMS

All OLE controls must support *IPersistStorage*, and any container can rely on this mechanism being present. Then, the control also has the option to support stream persistence using either *IPersistStream* or *IPersistStreamInit*. These interfaces must be regarded as mutually exclusive, and the latter is strongly recommended as a preference.

When a container determines which storage mechanisms a control supports, it must choose between *IPersistStorage* and *IPersistStream/IPersistStreamInit* — and stay with that choice for the lifetime of that control.

A container does not need to support a "save as text" mechanism.

OVERLOAD OF *IPROPERTYNOTIFYSINK*

Many containers implement modeless property browsing windows, which means that it is possible for a control's view of its properties to get out of sync with its container's view (the control is always right, of course) if the properties are altered through the control's property pages. To rectify this, some containers have chosen to overload the original intention of the *IPropertyNotifySink* interface (data binding) and use it also to be notified that a control property has changed.

A control does not need to support this, as it represents a fair overhead for each property set operation. A control should not use the *OnRequestEdit* method of this interface for anything but data binding, and it is free to use *OnChanged* for either or both purposes.

CONTAINER PRIVATE INTERFACES

Some controls are written specifically for a given container, and rely on private interfaces supplied with that container. Clearly, these controls cannot work in other containers unless they can live without the support of these interfaces. If a control cannot survive without these supporting interfaces, it should destroy itself gracefully when it finds that they do not exist. If the control can survive, it should take appropriate action (such as warn the user of reduced functionality) but should continue to work.

GENERAL GUIDELINES

One area of growth for the current version of the guidelines is in the provision of development guidelines for such things as ways in which you might want to implement a feature or user interface. While this work will be done, it is unlikely ever to become dogmatic. At the same time, work will be done on the actual OLE Controls specification (not the guidelines) to update it in some of the same areas. Two of those areas — event handling and multiple threads — are briefly examined in the remainder of this chapter.

Whether these issues are ever covered in the guidelines remains to be seen, as the document will eventually become driven by the ISV community itself. I urge you always to check for the latest version of the guidelines document.

Event-Handling Protocol

What should a control do when events have been frozen by the container (through *IOleControl::FreezeEvents*)? A number of choices are available:

- Fire all events regardless.

- Discard all events that would otherwise be fired.

- Queue up all events so that they're fired when the container unfreezes events.

- Queue up significant events so that they're fired when the container unfreezes events.

What is the appropriate action? First, you need not be worried about the consequences of firing events to containers in this state. All the "frozen" state means is that the container cannot react to an event right now; a container would be in error if it were to crash or otherwise react badly in this state. Simply put, a container that freezes events must remain prepared to receive any events fired without error, but it can choose to ignore the events altogether.

Therefore, you can safely adopt the first option — continue firing events without caring — so long as your control can cope with having its events ignored. The first option also requires the least coding, as you won't need to change anything at all. The second option is also pretty easy to implement and at least makes you write code inside your control that is aware that events are being ignored or not seen. However, the first two options aren't wise if you need to ensure that the container sees some of your events.

You might want to go to the extreme of the third option, where you keep a record of all the events your control wanted to fire during the events freeze, and then you cause them all to be fired in succession when the container finally gets around to unfreezing its events. Queuing events in concept is straightforward, but it will get considerably more difficult if those events are time-based or require a response before the course of action can be determined. Also, if you're firing something like mouse movement events, there are potentially a large number of them in a short space of time: do you <u>really</u> want to fire <u>all</u> those mouse move events? or can you safely discard a whole chunk?

If you determine that you can discard some events and queue up others for firing later, then the fourth option is probably the best solution. I conclude from this that the second option is great if you don't care about a container's reactions to your events (which would seem to be true of most controls) and that the fourth option is the best compromise if you need to ensure that certain events get through.

Let's face it: handling an events freeze is so much a control writer's design decision that there can never be more than a guideline for this. All four options are entirely valid, and there might well be others that I haven't thought about (unlikely, I know!).

Multiple Threads in a Control

The Win32 API supports multiple threads of execution in a program in all incarnations except Win32s, the subset implemented for Windows 3.1 users. If you want to know more about threads, see the sidebar "Quickly — What's a Thread?" on the facing page. 32-bit OLE as implemented in versions of Windows up to Windows NT version 3.5 only allowed one thread to make OLE calls, and that needed to be the thread that called *OleInitialize* (or *CoInitialize*). The OLE implemented in Windows 95 and Windows NT version 3.51 also allows you to take advantage of multiple threads, using something known as the "apartment" model. This model sets out some rules in which OLE can be used across multiple threads. In future versions of Microsoft's Win32 operating systems, OLE will run in a "free-threaded" model in which these rules are removed.

The apartment model rules basically say that each OLE interaction must be on its own thread, keeping things to their own apartments. Multiple threads in a program can call *OleInitialize* and then interact with OLE API functions and OLE objects. Therefore, a control can itself create threads and use those threads for any purpose. Also, so long as those threads call *OleInitialize*, they can then interact with the control's container through OLE — but this is <u>very</u> dangerous!

Why is this dangerous? The main thing to consider is that an in-process server, such as an OLE control, really <u>is</u> in-process, which means that threads it creates are threads in the container's process space. Therefore, a call up from the control to the container on a thread other than the one on which the control was created will cause the container code to be invoked on the same thread. All well and good so long as the container has been designed to itself be thread-safe. This is a consideration that often passes by control designers: if you use multiple threads in a control to communicate with a container, the container by implication uses multiple threads, too. If it wasn't designed to handle multiple threads, it's almost guaranteed <u>not</u> to work in this situation.

Most containers are not written to be thread-safe, so here is a general rule to keep in mind: don't use multiple threads to talk to your container (say, to fire events); if you want a thread you've created to communicate with your container, use a standard Win32 API function such as *PostThreadMessage* to post a standard Windows message to the main thread asking it to perform the action for you.

You can break this rule in some instances — for example, if you're writing a special control and know that your control is only going to get embedded within a thread-safe container.

QUICKLY — WHAT'S A THREAD?

Depending on who you ask, the definition of a thread can seem pretty simple or very complex. I'll try to keep it simple: a "thread" is a unit of execution through a program (process) that can have many simultaneous paths of execution. In 16-bit Windows programs, in MS-DOS programs, and in many existing 32-bit Windows programs, all execution is performed on one thread.

A multi-threaded program is one that creates threads to perform additional tasks at the same time. So, for example, a database server program can create a thread to deal with every user connection to it; a word processor can create a thread to spell-check in the background and a C++ compiler may create a thread to compile each individual file given on its command line.

Threads are preemptively multi-tasked with respect to each other, so any program that uses multiple threads needs to be written to ensure that any access to data shared between threads is synchronized. This means making sure that one thread isn't reading from a location while another is writing to it.

Threads are pretty "lightweight" in that they are cheap to create compared to processes. Therefore, whereas complex tasks might have been addressed by a network of separate processes in the past, multi-threading allows for greater efficiency, so the same problems can be more effectively solved now with the use of multiple threads in a single application.

Finally, one note of interest to those users of high-end equipment: if you have a multi-processor machine, Windows NT will allocate threads between processors. This means that a two-processor machine will literally run two threads at a time, a four-processor machine will run four threads, and so forth. So if you've got a big box with lots of processors, take proper advantage of it with Windows NT. Note that Windows 95 and most other operating systems won't take advantage of multiple processors.

Part IV

Appendixes

Visual C++ and MFC: Writing OLE Objects

This book is all about writing OLE controls, and in theory you can do this with any C/C++ compiler package for Microsoft Windows, or indeed with any other language capable of creating COM and OLE interface implementations. The use of a control development kit, however, greatly eases the task, and, not surprisingly, this book assumes you're using the Microsoft OLE Control Developer's Kit (OLE CDK). The OLE CDK is heavily geared toward Microsoft Visual C++ developers for a number of reasons, the important ones for us being that it uses the Visual C++ ClassWizard and that it makes extensive use of the Microsoft Foundation Class Library (the MFC library, for short). Of course, many other compiler vendors license the MFC library from Microsoft Corporation and therefore are also excellent candidates for OLE CDK developments.

So what exactly is this MFC thing? This appendix looks into that, and also examines some of the standard Visual C++ tools and working practices. You certainly don't need to have read this appendix to be in a position to use and create OLE controls.

NOTE As with Chapters 2 and 3 of this book, this appendix is optional reading that provides a refresher for those already familiar with the subject and a backgrounder for those who are not yet up to speed with the technology.

THE MFC LIBRARY

Books and magazines will tell you that the MFC library is the class library for Microsoft Windows development. A "class library" is a set of standard classes and routines for use in C++ programs, whose main reason for existing is to allow programmers to use someone else's code in their development efforts. This makes development easier because it reduces the amount of work programmers have to do. The MFC library takes this further: it's designed to make Windows programming in C++ easier. While it is perfectly possible to write Windows programs in C++ without a class library, there are very few reasons for doing so. Windows class libraries, such as MFC, typically provide an application framework around which you build your application. An "application framework" is code that provides the basic shell of a Windows application. Apart from the shell, there are also sets of classes to manipulate a program's data, to view and alter a program's data, to manipulate various programming entities such as strings, arrays, and lists, and of course one hell of a lot of OLE support.

Although the OLE Automation example in Chapter 2 was fairly straightforward, I'll demonstrate that the MFC library can make its creation even easier. I didn't write any OLE objects capable of being visually edited or any containers in which visual editing can take place, but the descriptions of the interfaces involved made it pretty clear that automation is much the simpler end of OLE programming! With the MFC library, this is no longer true. Most of OLE is now easy. It is possible to create an application capable of having objects embedded within it and capable of providing objects that can be embedded elsewhere with absolutely no code written by you. True, you'd need to write some code to make the application at all useful, but the fact remains that the basic mechanics of OLE and all the other aspects of Windows programming that so daunt us all are done for you by the MFC library.

MFC's Portability

The MFC library also makes it rather easier to port code. A 16-bit MFC program can be recompiled for 32 bits with little or no change and can also be ported to the Apple Macintosh without too much effort. Further, other vendors have licensed the MFC library and provided it on platforms (such as various flavors of Unix) that Microsoft doesn't support.

Even more interestingly, various vendors of Intel 80x86 compilers have licensed the MFC library, meaning that you can use their build tools, debuggers, code generators, and so forth in addition to or instead of Microsoft's compilers. Therefore, much the same code base can be used for an application that can be made to run on Windows 3.x, Windows 95, Windows NT (all platforms), Apple Macintosh, and Unix. That's a pretty powerful story.

MFC's Evolution

The MFC library first saw the public light of day in 1992 as version 1.0, when Microsoft Corporation released C/C++ version 7.0. Version 1.0 was little more than a set of C++ classes that wrapped the Windows API (application programming interface). Version 2.0 of the MFC library, released with Microsoft Visual C++ version 1.0 in early 1993, abstracted a lot further and provided the implementation of a concept known to Smalltalk programmers as "model, view, controller," where the "model" represents data, the "view" is the visualization of that data, and the "controller" is the application's logic (which controls the operation of the program). In MFC terms, these are "document, view, and application" — but don't be fooled by this "document" word. It does <u>not</u> mean that you're limited to writing MFC programs that handle documents. A document object is simply the representation of the application's data, and it can be any sort of data. It's also important to understand that the provision of this architecture does not mean that you need to use it in all cases — but if you do, you get extra benefits.

Version 2.5 of the MFC library was released with Visual C++ version 1.5 in late 1993. It added a wide set of OLE classes and C++ wrappers for the ODBC (open database connectivity) API. With version 2.5 of MFC, it was possible to write OLE objects, OLE containers, and OLE database applications using many fewer lines of code than before. Version 3.0 of the MFC library was released with Visual C++ version 2.0 in September 1994. Version 3.0 of MFC added 32-bit OLE and ODBC support, multi-threading support, collection classes using real C++ templates (Visual C++ 2.0 was the first Microsoft C++ compiler to support C++ templates), property sheets and property pages, dockable toolbars with tooltips, and a few other bits and pieces. Version 3.1 of MFC was released with Visual C++ version 2.1 in January 1995 and included a few enhancements to version 3.0 such as sockets support, basic MAPI support, and "wrappers" for the new Windows 95 common controls. Sockets and property pages were also added to 16-bit MFC version 2.52, shipped on the Visual C++ 2.1 CD-ROM. Version 4.0 of the MFC library is due to ship very close to the publication of this book; it includes wrappers for Windows 95 user interface features and the ability to create OLE control containers.

The MFC library is therefore on its fifth or sixth release, depending on when you read this book, so it's a very stable set of classes that have been tested thoroughly in real-life applications. It's also become the standard class library for Windows development.

MFC's Structure

Let's take a moment now to examine the structure of the MFC library. Everything starts off from the *CObject* class, which is the object from which almost all other MFC objects are derived. *CObject* doesn't do much except provide four basic services to the other classes:

- Serialization — the ability to save an object to permanent storage and retrieve it later.

- Runtime class information — the class name of a particular object and its position in the object hierarchy, available at runtime. Note that Visual C++ versions 4.0 and later support the native C++ "RTTI" (runtime type information) constructs, which provides for all classes to have this functionality. The MFC library might be altered (in a later release) to take advantage of a compiler's RTTI support.

- Diagnostic output — for debugging.

- Compatibility — with the MFC collection classes.

The MFC library contains six major sets of classes:

- General-purpose classes (such as strings, files, exceptions, date/time, and rectangles)

- Visual object classes (such as windows, device contexts, GDI, and dialogs)

- Application architecture classes (such as application, documents, and views)

- Collection classes (such as lists and arrays)

- OLE classes

- Database classes, accessing the underlying data through ODBC and, from MFC version 4.0 onwards, through DAO (Data Access Objects, Microsoft's OLE interface to its Jet database engine)

Be aware that membership in these sets is not exclusive; a class can live in more than one of them. For example, the *CCmdTarget* class appears in all the sets except the general-purpose classes and collection classes.

COMMAND TARGETS AND MESSAGE MAPS

A number of classes in the MFC hierarchies are derived directly or indirectly from *CCmdTarget*. *CCmdTarget* itself is directly derived from *CObject*. *CCmdTarget* implements the MFC notion of a "command target," an object capable of receiving and dealing with commands. A "command" means menu commands, toolbar button presses, and the like. Command targets that represent actual Microsoft Windows windows can also receive regular Windows messages, and non-window command targets can have these messages routed to them.

CCmdTarget provides this functionality through a data structure called a "message map," which ties a given message to a specific class member function. For example, the Windows *WM_CLOSE* message can be routed to a class's *OnClose* member function. The *WM_COMMAND* message, which is sent whenever a menu option is selected, is not generally handled by a single member function. Rather, the map contains a set of entries for values expected in the *wParam* parameter of the *WM_COMMAND* message. In the case of a menu option, this would be the menu option's ID.

A class's message map does not need to contain an entry for every message the application might receive. Often, a large number of messages will be defaulted so that the MFC library and Windows handle them themselves. Normally, more than one command target class is in a given program, as I'll show, so the message map mechanism needs a way of deciding which class gets which message. Also, messages that are not handled by any of your classes need to go somewhere and be handled.

The message map contains a pointer to its parent class's map, so a message not present in the map of one class can next be examined by its parent, and then by that class's parent, and so on up the class tree. Any unhandled messages are shipped off to Windows' *DefWindowsProc* to be handled in a way determined by Windows' defaults. *WM_COMMAND* messages, on the other hand, are treated specially. After a class tree has decided that it doesn't handle a given command, the command is routed to another class tree to see if that one can handle it. As an example, a command message received by a frame window is first passed by the frame window object to a currently open document window (that is, view) object. If that object — or any object in its hierarchy — doesn't handle the command, it is passed on to the object that looks after the document's data. The chain ultimately ends at the application object's tree, and it is discarded if that tree fails to deal with it. A class can determine its routing behavior by overriding the *CCmdTarget* class's implementation of *OnCmdMsg*.

Why would a class tree want a command to be routed? Although C programmers familiar with the Windows SDK will be used to gigantic *switch* statements to handle messages on a per-window basis, the MFC library abstracts this somewhat and allows the most logical object to handle a command: for example, the File Open command is logically handled by the application, the File Save command by the document being saved, and a Select Font command by the view on the data.

If you're a seasoned C++ programmer, you might well be asking yourself why ordinary C++ virtual functions aren't used for message-handling functions. Such a scheme would certainly work and, indeed, some other class libraries use this technique. The problem lies in the way in which C++ compilers typically implement virtual functions. In Chapter 2, where I introduced OLE, I discussed the virtue of C++ compilers creating a vtable (virtual function table) to hold a list of pointers to the virtual functions of a given class. As these vtables meet the needs of an OLE interface especially well, it's a good mechanism for interface implementation. However, when you have a hierarchy of classes in which messages are handled by virtual functions, each consecutive derivation gets a vtable with all the entries of its parent together with entries for any virtual function it adds. Clearly, even with a hierarchy only a few classes deep, the proliferation and size of the vtables becomes a problem. Having said all that, the vtable mechanism will be slightly faster than the message map mechanism, as the map needs to be searched for a matching entry. Message maps are implemented in such a way that they cache command-to-function matches, making routing of a cached command that much faster after it's been handled once. Overall, the difference in speed is imperceptible, so the MFC library's designers chose the smaller message map solution. The size of a program, or rather the amount of memory it uses as it runs, is often a significant determining factor in the program's performance: generally, smaller is faster.

Message maps are declared and defined for a class using MFC-provided macros. The *BEGIN_MESSAGE_MAP* macro opens a message map definition. It has two parameters: the name of the class for which this map is being defined and the class from which that class is derived. This latter parameter allows automatic searching through a class hierarchy. The message map is closed with the *END_MESSAGE_MAP* macro. Between these two macro statements are the map entries themselves. For any Windows message other than *WM_COMMAND*, there is a corresponding *ON_WM_???* macro that causes the message to be handled by a member function with a name predefined by the MFC library. For example, *WM_CLOSE* is represented by *ON_WM_CLOSE* and is handled by the *OnClose* member function. Most command messages are handled by *ON_COMMAND* macro entries. This macro takes the ID of the command as its first parameter and the name of the handler function as its second. Some command messages are actually notifications from controls and other child windows, and specific macros handle these. Again, the second parameter identifies the handling function. Macros are also provided for registered messages and user-defined messages.

In addition to these definitions, the class must include a declaration of the message map structure and the prototypes of each of the handler functions. The map itself is declared using the *DECLARE_MESSAGE_MAP* macro.

In the old days of version 1.0 of the MFC library, the only way of creating and maintaining message maps was by typing them in and editing them by hand. While that remains perfectly possible, Visual C++ and other C++ compilers that ship with the MFC library come with tools to do it automatically and safely.

In addition to being the source of the message map, command target classes are also potentially programmable through OLE Automation. I examine this in greater detail later in this appendix; for now, it's interesting to note that the message map concept is reused for OLE Automation properties and methods, through something called a "dispatch map."

CWINAPP — THE APPLICATION CLASS

In the good old days of C programming — a long, long time ago — every program started execution at a function named *main*. Since the introduction of Microsoft Windows, programs have started with *WinMain* (and DLLs with *LibMain*). Now that there are class libraries such as MFC, you no longer need to bother with the startup code, so you never need to write *WinMain* code again. The MFC library provides the *WinMain/LibMain* entry point as necessary, and all you need to do is to provide an application object. An "application object" is an instance of a class derived from MFC's *CWinApp* class, and its purpose in life is to manage the execution of the application. It contains startup and termination code, it manages application-wide data (such as registration settings), and it executes the "message pump" (the part of a Windows program that takes messages from Windows and dispatches them to the appropriate window procedures).

In the MFC library versions prior to 3.0, *CWinApp* is derived directly from *CCmdTarget*. In versions 3.0 and later, it's derived from *CWinThread*, which is MFC's way of wrapping operating system threads; *CWinApp* simply represents the first thread. MFC versions 3.0 and later are also "thread-safe," which means that they've been coded to deal with the situation in which one thread in a program gets pre-emptively switched out by another thread in the same process. Any global memory owned by the application needs to be guarded in these situations to ensure that one thread doesn't change a variable's value while another is reading it.

CWinApp is not useful in your application until you derive from it, so all MFC programs have one class derived from *CWinApp*. *AutoProg*, introduced in Chapter 3, calls its derived application class *CAutoProg*. After you've established your own class, you can override the startup and termination member functions as well as take advantage of many other facilities offered by *CWinApp*. Only one *CWinApp* object can exist in a given program, and this instance must be created before the program per se runs. Consequently, the *CWinApp*-derived object in a program is generally declared as a "global object," which means that it is constructed before the main code in the program is called.

The member functions *InitInstance* and *ExitInstance* are key ones to override. *InitInstance* is called when the program has just started (but after global objects have been created), and it's generally used to create the program's main window, initialize OLE, allocate application memory, and perform any other initialization required. *ExitInstance* is called just as a program is terminating, and it's used to undo most of what was done by *InitInstance*. Even if the program is compiled as a DLL, these member functions will nevertheless get called at the appropriate times. That's one of the useful features of MFC: the application code you write for a DLL or an EXE implementation of something doesn't necessarily need to be aware of which version it ends up being. (Of course, there might be instances when you need to write code that will recognize which version it is.)

CWinApp also has a member function called *InitApplication*, which is called when an application first starts, as is *InitInstance*. The differences are that it is called just before *InitInstance* and that it is called only if this is the first instance of the given program currently running. This is geared entirely towards 16-bit Windows, under which a program can detect whether it is already running and take advantage of that fact by sharing the same code among all instances of the application. Now, with Win32 providing applications with separate address spaces, the concept doesn't really hold. There is no way that two, running 32-bit applications can share things implicitly like this, even if they're the same application, so 32-bit programs <u>always</u> call *InitApplication*. This makes *InitApplication* superfluous, so typically there's very little or no code in *InitApplication* (often, it's not even overridden in the derived class), and all initialization code appears in *InitInstance*.

CWinApp-derived classes also contain various document-centric member functions, such as *AddDocTemplate*, *OpenDocumentFile*, *OnFileNew*, and *OnFileOpen*. *AddDocTemplate* and *OpenDocumentFile* relate to the document–view architecture, which is discussed later, beginning on page 490. *OnFileNew* is called when the File New command is issued, and it creates a new, empty document in the application. Again, the document–view architecture is called into play here. *OnFileOpen* is called in response to the File Open command and attempts to open a given document file. *CWinApp* also provides support for printer setup and Help menu items.

OnIdle allows the programmer to write code (such as code for background tasks) that is executed during Windows idle time. "Idle time" is when the system has nothing to do, as there are no messages pending for any application. In 16-bit

Windows, a great deal of time is actually idle time, so you can do quite a bit of processing here, but you need to ensure that you do it in short stages so that you don't slow down the rest of the system or otherwise affect its responsiveness. In Win32, although idle time still exists and you can still override this member function, it is generally more efficient to create a new thread to perform background tasks of any significant size.

FYI The MFC library uses the idle-time mechanism internally for such things as maintaining status bar text and enabling or disabling toolbar items. It actually calls member functions in *CCmdTarget*-derived classes to deal with these user interface issues.

PreTranslateMessage is called by the framework when a Windows message for the application is received but prior to it being dispatched to the relevant handler. It allows for preprocessing of messages and is particularly useful in DLLs when messages are passed to the DLL's message pump via its *CWinApp*-derived *PreTranslateMessage* member.

CWinApp contains a number of data members (variables) that hold useful information such as the application's Help file name, the handle to the application's main window, the command line, and the registry key used to hold information about this application. *CWinApp* also hides many other pieces of functionality, although a great deal of them you can take for granted.

CWND AND ITS DERIVATIVES

It's not surprising that the MFC library also contains a generic window class — given that it has a generic application class. *CWnd* is the class from which all other window classes are derived, and it handles the basics of window functionality — such as receiving and dispatching messages, setting the focus and mouse capture, moving the window and changing its attributes, preparing for output to the window, scrolling, drag and drop, treating the window as a dialog, and attaching and querying menus.

CWnd objects do not directly equate to Microsoft Windows windows — they can't, as Windows owns the window while the MFC library owns the object. Therefore, a *CWnd* object must be connected to a window shortly after creation. The typical sequence of events is creation of the *CWnd* object and then creation of the underlying Windows window using the *Create* member function. It is also possible to attach an already existing window to a *CWnd* object using the *Attach* member function. The MFC library contains its own window procedure, which is used for all non-dialog *CWnd* objects. This is tied closely to the message map mechanism discussed above. Any message received is dealt with by the owning

CWnd-derived object and passed down through the chain of parent message maps until a handler is found or *DefWindowProc* is called.

CWnd contains a huge number of member functions to deal with messages. Of course, the member function in a given class is called only if the object of that class has a message map entry for that message. All message handler member functions can be overridden to create custom handlers. Most *CWnd* manipulation actually takes place in message handlers, just as it does in the window procedure in a standard Windows SDK C-language program.

Many derivations of *CWnd* exist in the MFC framework. *CDialog*, for example, is the standard MFC dialog class and is directly derived from *CWnd*. The classes in which you shall be writing the vast majority of your OLE control code are also derived from *CWnd*. There are also classes for frame windows, document windows, all manner of control windows (such as buttons and list boxes), property-page windows, and, most importantly of all, view windows. I'll get to those a little later.

Output Mechanisms

One of the common uses of a window is to display output — pretty fundamental if you're writing a visual application! The Windows mechanism for doing this is to send a window a *WM_PAINT* message whenever any part of that window becomes "invalid," or potentially no longer current. The majority of these messages are actually initiated by the application itself, as the way to signal itself to update its display in some way. Because output to a device is generally a pretty time-consuming operation, Windows treats *WM_PAINT* specially. If there are other messages in a queue, these get to the application before *WM_PAINT*s. Also, if more than one *WM_PAINT* message is pending on a window, they are coalesced into one and their invalid areas are combined. The net effect of this is to make outputting as efficient (as in quick) as possible.

When an application receives a paint message, it calls the Windows *BeginPaint* function to prepare the ground. The main work of this function is to return a handle to a device context (DC) through which the output will go. A "device context" is a Windows data structure that identifies various bits of information about a device to which output is about to proceed. The information stored includes the current colors to be used and the mode (transparent or opaque) in which text will be output. Any output through this device context reflects these stored values. Generally, the values are stored only for the duration of a paint, as the device context is re-used for another device as soon as the application calls *EndPaint*, the balance function to *BeginPaint*. It is possible to define a window class as having its own device context, which will be used exclusively by windows of that class. However, 16-bit Windows allowed only a maximum of five device contexts, so this capability was rarely used; Win32 removes this restriction, but the practice remains.

When a program wants to output some information to a device and it has a handle to the relevant device context, it can call the appropriate output function directly, such as *TextOut* or *Rectangle*. These functions use the current state of the device context to determine how to output. For example, the *TextOut* function will generally output black text on a white background using the system font to a screen device context unless changes have been made to the context beforehand.

NOTE Never assume that device-context values are what you think they are. If, for example, you want to output in black on white, set these colors before outputting the text.

A program changes the values held in a device context by selecting objects into the context and storing the old value so that it can be restored before *EndPaint* is called. (A device context must be left in the state in which it was found, at least as far as selected objects go.) Objects are selected through the *SelectObject* function, which takes a handle to a GDI object such as a pen, brush, font, or region. The "graphics device interface," or GDI, is the drawing engine in Microsoft Windows.

In addition to dealing with paint messages, an application can also get a device context for a window and output directly.

The MFC library wraps all of this functionality into a number of classes: device contexts are handled by the *CDC* class and a number of its derivatives, and GDI objects are handled by *CGdiObject* and thence by derivations such as *CPen*, *CBrush*, *CFont*, and *CRgn*. One derivative of *CDC*, *CPaintDC*, is the one used in MFC programs when a window's *OnPaint* handler member function is called (which occurs when a *WM_PAINT* message is received by a class that has such a handler declared in its message map). The only differences between a *CDC* and a *CPaintDC* are that *BeginPaint* is called as part of *CPaintDC*'s construction (and the device context returned therein is attached to this *CPaintDC* object) and that *EndPaint* will be called as part of its destruction.

So, to output a string to a window using default device context attributes, *OnPaint* code such as this could be used:

```
COurWnd::OnPaint ( void )
{
    CPaintDC dc ( this );
    CString csOut = "Hello, world!";
    dc.TextOut ( 4, 4, csOut );
}
```

There isn't much to explain here: the creation of the *CPaintDC* object also causes *BeginPaint* to be called. The *TextOut* member function of the device context is then called with the text starting at coordinate (4, 4) in the window and using the

MFC string object *csOut* as the text to display. The *CPaintDC* is implicitly destroyed at the end of the function, causing the *EndPaint* function to be called, which in turn validates the previously invalid area of the window.

The MFC library's handling of device contexts and GDI objects is not significantly more intelligent than the native Microsoft Windows mechanism. There are some improvements in further derived classes, such as views, but the underlying mechanism in general dictates the wrapping.

DOCUMENTS AND VIEWS

During the introduction to this appendix, I described the MFC library as a framework. So far, I've introduced some classes that seem to do little more than wrap existing Microsoft Windows functionality. So where's the beef? Well, some of the classes I've talked about provide quite a bit of extra functionality, which saves writing huge chunks of code each time you sit down to write a program. To get the real benefit of a framework such as MFC, however, you do need to invest some time to understand its philosophy and architecture. The MFC library uses the concepts of documents and views as the heart of its offering.

You saw that the *CWinApp* class models the control part of an application, taking the grunge work out of setting up the basic functionality needed in any reasonable executable or DLL. It also has links into the document and view architecture (hereinafter, the document–view architecture) through member functions such as *OpenDocumentFile* and *OnFileNew*. The basic premise of the document–view architecture is that programs manipulate data internally and also allow it to be viewed and potentially altered by user interaction. The class that manages the data is known as the "document class," and the class that allows view and modification is known as the "view class." Don't be fooled, as many people have been, by this word "document." As I said near the beginning of this appendix, it's purely a metaphor that means "application data." Yes, in some cases it will represent what you would recognize as a document. In other applications, however, it might be a database or a real-time data feed or any other abstraction of data you can imagine. A "view," on the other hand, is a view: it allows the user to examine the data in whatever way(s) the view chooses to display it. Most programs also allow the user to alter the data and to save it back to its source or elsewhere. A document can have many views open on it at the same time, if the application containing the document is capable of supporting this.

Another point about the document–view architecture: it is <u>not</u> prescriptive! You don't have to use it in all programs, and you don't stop yourself from using the MFC library if you don't use it. Bear in mind that MFC version 1.0 didn't support documents and views — yet all MFC programs can be recompiled directly in later versions, barring some minor OLE version 1.0 stuff that was changed for later versions of OLE. Also, of course, the *AutoProg* example from Chapter 3 uses the MFC library (albeit minimally), but it has no concept of documents and views.

So why use documents and views? Most of all, the abstraction of data and viewer in this manner makes programming fundamentally easier because it's a logical way in which to regard data and its manipulation. As you begin to write applications that do use documents and views, you find yourself beginning to think in these terms. Just as objects are great for programmers because they more nearly model how we think, so documents and views fit the majority of applications well. The MFC library also bundles a good deal of functionality into the default document and view classes that is fairly difficult to use outside of them. Finally, OLE Documents maps nicely into this model, and some features such as embedding and visual editing are much easier to implement if you do use documents and views.

Document Templates

Document templates are the link between an application and the documents it supports. A "document template" is an instance of a class that ties a document type to an application. Document templates represent a given document type. If you were writing your own version of Microsoft Excel, for example, you could have document types representing worksheets, charts, and macros. You'd therefore also have three document template classes.

Document templates come in two flavors: single document templates, which allow one document of that type to be open at a time, and multiple document templates, which allow many documents of that type to be open. A single document interface (SDI) application, allows only one document to be open at a time and uses single document templates and a multiple document interface (MDI) application (such as Excel or Word) uses multiple document templates.

A document template connects three key classes together: the document class, the view class associated with that document, and the frame window. A document template stores enough information to allow it to create objects of these three classes dynamically. It also contains the name of the document type it represents, the file extension used for this document type, and, if the application is an OLE server, the ID of the menu that will be merged with the container's menu when items of this type are embedded. The base class for document templates is *CDocTemplate*. This is an "abstract base class," which means that instances of it cannot be created; you must first derive from it. The MFC library derives two classes, *CSingleDocTemplate* and *CMultiDocTemplate*, which support SDI and MDI respectively. It is also possible to derive directly from *CDocTemplate* if you want to create a user-interface mechanism that is neither SDI or MDI.

Document template objects are usually created during an application's *InitInstance* function. This allows the application to create new documents and/or open files early on in its life.

This is the type of call usually made to *CWinApp::AddDocTemplate* during a program's initialization:

```
AddDocTemplate(new CMultiDocTemplate(IDR_HEXEDITYPE,
    RUNTIME_CLASS(CHexedit2Doc),
    RUNTIME_CLASS(CMDIChildWnd),
    RUNTIME_CLASS(CHexedit2View)));
```

This creates an object of class *CMultiDocTemplate* with a resource ID (*IDR_HEXEDITYPE*) that allows it to load the document resources (for example, icon) and the runtime class information of the document class (*CHexedit2Doc*), the view class (*CHexedit2View*), and the frame window class (*CMDIChildWnd*, the MFC library's MDI child wrapper). Now, when the user issues a command to create a new document of this type, the document-template object can create each of the objects it needs. If this application supported more than one document type, which both SDI and MDI applications can do, there would be additional calls to *AddDocTemplate* for each additional document type.

Document templates are pretty much hidden away by the framework; however, their job as glue between applications and documents is fundamental. When a File New command is issued and the application supports many document types, the framework presents a dialog box listing all the document types. The user then selects one from this list. As with all parts of the MFC library, this behavior, and the dialog associated with it, is entirely customizable using normal C++ inheritance.

Documents

Document classes are data-manipulation classes, so they don't have any user interface. Also, the ones that come with the MFC library are pretty much file-oriented, in that they support file opening, loading, and saving. It's a fairly straightforward process to create your own document class that doesn't rely on files or to disable the file-handling capabilities of the standard document class.

The document class provided by the MFC library is *CDocument*. This contains member functions to add and remove views; to handle document creation, opening, saving, and closing; and to get information about the data contained within it (such as whether it has changed). You need only to derive from this class to create your own document class.

A document object is also a command target, so it is capable of receiving and reacting to commands for which it has entries in its message map. The commands handled by a document would normally be ones that relate to the data as a whole rather than to a particular view on the data. File-handling commands are a typical example. As I'll show later, any command target class is capable of supporting OLE Automation — and, by default, Microsoft Visual C++'s code generation tool, AppWizard, sets up the application's document class to be the application's external interface for OLE Automation.

If a document has more than one view displaying its data and that data is changed (potentially by one of the views), all connected views can be told of the change through a call to *UpdateAllViews*.

Views

A view object is basically a window: therefore, all view classes are derived from *CWnd*. The basic *CView* class is the one derived from for your own view class. In some instances, other specializations of this class are useful, so the MFC library also provides the following: *CEditView*, which is rather like a multi-line edit control; *CScrollView*, which is a *CView* with automatic scrolling support; and *CFormView*, which is a view derived from *CScrollView* that takes a dialog template (a description of a dialog box) and displays the dialog box as a modeless form window. *CRecordView* is derived from *CFormView* and is used to display database records directly from a database object. The MFC library also provides support for multiple views in the same logical window, using splitter windows.

Given that a view is a window, writing code for a view is not conceptually that different from writing standard Windows SDK window procedure code. Most of it is about dealing with messages such as mouse moves and clicks, keyboard input, and menu commands. Normally, a view is used to deal with view-centric menu commands such as font changes and other display options.

SOME OTHER CLASSES

There's more to the MFC library than windows, applications, documents, and views. A whole host of general-purpose classes (as well as specializations of some of the other classes) provide specific functionality.

Utility Classes and Exceptions

The *CString* class, for example, represents a string. Unlike C/C++ strings defined as arrays of *chars*, these strings have some intelligence. For example, *CString* objects have methods to perform actions such as loading a string from the application's resources, comparing strings, assigning strings, and splitting strings into substrings and then formatting them. A string class such as *CString* is without a doubt one of the most useful classes a C++ class library can provide and one that you'll see littered around the examples in this book and elsewhere. The MFC library's *CString* class is also double-byte character sets (DBCS) aware and Unicode aware.

The MFC library also implements a set of "collection classes," which are classes that can be used to hold instances of other classes. Examples of collection implementations include arrays, lists, and maps. The MFC library provides a range of classes for each type of collection. Arrays are handled through classes such as

CByteArray, *CObArray*, and *CStringArray*. *CObArray* holds arrays of any item derived from *CObject*, and *CStringArray* holds *CStrings*. MFC versions 1.0 through 2.5 were written for C++ compilers that didn't support templates. With MFC version 3.0, which saw the light of day with Visual C++ version 2.0, C++ template support was added, so the class *CArray* is a template class that can be used to make type-safe arrays. If you intend to create arrays to hold your own type of objects, then *CArray* is a good place to start. Prior to version 2.0, the MFC library came with a tool that simulated templates to some extent. Real templates are a great deal easier!

Lists are handled through the *CxxxList* set of classes, where *xxx* is the type of element held in the list. Again, *CList* is the templated version of this class, which can be used to create your own list classes. "Maps," also known as "dictionaries," store collections of objects and allow them to be accessed through a unique key.

> **NOTE** The advantage that a map has over an array or a list is that you can find an element more quickly because you don't need to scan through the entire array or list until you find what you want.

The *CMap* class is the templated version of MFC's map class, and the *CMapxxxToyyy* classes are the old forms. Here, *xxx* refers to the type used as the key, and *yyy* refers to the type stored in the collection. It is likely that the collection classes provided by the MFC library will become more and more functional and represent a larger number of types in the future.

The MFC library also wraps files, through classes such as *CFile*, *CStdioFile*, and *CMemFile*. As with a large number of MFC classes, the file classes report certain types of error through exceptions. Although MFC existed for Microsoft C++ compilers before they supported true C++ exception-handling, MFC supported a pseudo-exception mechanism through macros. When a call throws an exception (which, in the case of files, can happen during reads, writes, opens, closes, and so forth), the calling code can catch it inside a *TRY...CATCH* block. A thrown exception actually creates an object of a given class, and the *CATCH* clauses trap each exception type expected:

```
TRY
{
    CMyClass *cmcThis = new CMyClass;
    cmcThis -> DoSomething ( param1, param2 );
```

```
}
CATCH ( CMemException, e )
{
    HandleMemoryShortage();
}
END_CATCH
```

If either the creation of the new *CMyClass* object or the call to its *DoSomething* method causes a memory exception, the code in the *CATCH* clause is executed. If other exceptions are thrown, there is no code to deal with them here, so the default MFC handler catches them and aborts the program. If a series of statements protected by a *TRY* statement can throw more than one exception type, and if you want to deal with each type, there need to be *AND_CATCH (exception_class, var)* clauses after the first *CATCH* block. The second parameter to *CATCH* and *AND_CATCH* is the name of the object of the specific type that is created by the exception. (It can be any name you choose.) The object can then be manipulated inside the *CATCH* block, perhaps to find out more information on what caused the exception, through this variable.

These exception-handling mechanisms have some problems. First, they don't conform fully to the syntax of C++. Second, if they're being used in MFC implementations for C++ compilers that don't handle true C++ exceptions (that is, MFC versions prior to 3.0), then "stack unwinding" (removal of objects created prior to the exception being thrown that would ordinarily have been destroyed) is not performed. Nevertheless, these problems are minor and less important now that the majority of C++ compilers on the PC support C++ exceptions. The problems are far outweighed by the benefits that sensible exception-handling brings to a program's robustness and clarity.

If you have existing code that uses the MFC exception-handling macros, it will still compile and execute as before. Versions 3.0 and later of MFC (that is, 32-bit implementations) use the C++ exception-handling mechanisms within the macros and also do the cleanup things that the macros have always done. The 16-bit macros don't use C++ exception handling. If you are writing new code that is intended only for 32-bit platforms, you should be using normal C++ exceptions rather than the macros.

Why use exceptions? Traditionally, functions that fail return error codes, and the callers of the functions react to this code. In most situations, this is great and should remain as it is. In certain circumstances, however, it's very difficult to recover from the failure cleanly, and so a jump to some outer function is required. Regardless of the problem, C++-style exception-handling can make programs more robust and more structured and can aid readability.

Want another good reason for using exceptions? Consider this code:

```
void func1 ( void )
{
    TRY
    {
        func2();
    }
    CATCH ( CSomeException, e )
}

void func2 ( void )
{
    CAnObject x;
    func3();
}

void func3 ( void )
{
    THROW ( CSomeException );
}
```

Here, *func1* calls *func2*, which allocates an object on the stack of type *CAnObject*. This function then calls *func3*, which throws an exception that will be caught by *func1*'s exception handler. This means that the path of execution jumps straight from *func3* to *func1*, bypassing *func2* and therefore denying it the option of calling *CAnObject*'s destructor. If *CAnObject* did anything that needs to be undone, the undoing simply will not happen. If the compiler supports C++ exception-handling, though, the stack unwinding mechanism ensures that destructors of all objects created this way are called before the code in *func1*'s exception handler is called.

WARNING Most C++ compilers, including Microsoft Visual C++, allow exception-handling to be enabled on a per-module basis. Thus, it is possible to disable exception-handling for the module containing *func2*, which would erroneously stop it from having *CAnObject* destroyed properly when *func3* throws an exception. So beware!

One of the most useful (and under-appreciated) classes provided by the MFC library is *CRuntimeClass*. All classes derived from *CObject* include an instance of this class, which allows you to determine the class type at runtime as well as the parent of this class. *CRuntimeClass* also provides information to allow instances of a class to be created at runtime without compile-time knowledge of the class type to be created. The MFC library supplies some macros to implement these features, most notably *IMPLEMENT_DYNAMIC*, *IMPLEMENT_DYNCREATE*, and *IMPLEMENT_SERIAL*. Most of the classes created by the MFC framework and the Visual C++ tools support dynamic creation, and it's easy to add the same support to your own classes. This functionality is used by classes (such as document templates) that need to create document, view, and frame window objects based on the document type.

Windows NT and Windows 95, as well as all subsequent implementations of the Win32 API barring Win32s, support multi-threading. A thread represents the unit of schedulability, which means that threads are the entities dealt with by the preemptive scheduler, rather than processes or tasks. A given program has one thread of execution at startup, but it can create and destroy additional threads throughout its executing life as it sees fit. A thread represents a path of execution through a program, so "multi-threading" implies that a program can have more than one path of execution. Threads are often used to implement background tasks, such as printing, or to provide a sort of parallel processing, where more than one operation is performed by a program at the same time. If the machine on which a multi-threaded program is executing has more than one processor and if a multi-processor-aware Win32 operating system (such as Windows NT), is running, then it's perfectly possible for separate threads in the same program to run <u>literally</u> at the same time, one per processor.

MFC versions 3.0 and later support threads in two ways. First, they are "thread-safe," which means that they are aware that a program might contain multiple threads of execution and therefore they ensure that any internal data structures are protected from simultaneous access. Second, they provide a class, *CWinThread*, which allows threads to be easily created and used in MFC programs.

MFC documentation describes the class library as being thread-safe at a class level but not at an object level. This means that it is permissable to have more than one thread create and use objects of a given class, but it is not permissible to share one object of a given class between threads. This is because the code required to implement such thread safety would make the class library bigger and slower.

If you want more than one thread to access a given object — and there are certainly places where you would — you can do it. All you need to do is to synchronize access to the object so that only one thread at a time can get access. The Win32 API provides all sorts of mechanisms, such as critical sections and mutexes, that a programmer can use for synchronization. A "critical section" object marks code that can be executed by one thread at a time only, and a "mutex" (mutual exclusion) object acts like a gate on a data item, with only one thread at a time capable of using the gate. When a thread wants to access a data item controlled by a mutex, it asks for ownership of the mutex. If it's already owned by a thread, the "calling" thread will wait until it's free. The owning thread can then go and do whatever it needs to on that data item until it relinquishes the mutex, unblocking the other thread.

When a program starts, it has one thread of execution. This is modeled by the *CWinApp* object in an MFC application. This *CWinApp* thread can create more threads at will. The MFC library differentiates between user interface threads and worker threads. To the operating system, there is no distinction; however, the MFC library needs to differentiate so that it can ensure correct operation. A user interface thread is created by deriving from the *CWinThread* class and using the *AfxBegin-Thread* function. The *CWinThread*-derived object will have a message pump and can create visual objects as it chooses. A worker thread requires no derivation from *CWinThread*; the call to *AfxBeginThread* for a worker thread simply creates an object of the base class (that is, *CWinThread*). Worker threads can use any MFC functionality except that which relates to user interfaces.

Controls and Dialogs

The MFC library provides extensive support for dialog boxes and dialog controls (but not for OLE controls in versions of MFC prior to 4.0). The *CDialog* class, used to implement modal and modeless dialogs, is derived directly from *CWnd*, as are the majority of control classes. As far as the MFC library is concerned, there's no major difference between a dialog box and a normal window, so everything's accomplished through message maps and other standard *CWnd* mechanisms. *CDialog* does include some extra functionality, such as the ability to create a dialog box from a dialog template (sort of useful!) as well as handlers for dialog initialization and OK and Cancel button presses.

The CWnd class contains functionality that is intended mainly for dialog boxes but that will in fact work for any window containing controls. This functionality is the ability to read and write information from controls on a dialog box into member variables of the class used to manage the dialog box. In addition to transferring data, the framework can also validate the content to ensure that it is of the correct type. Further, it is possible to write your own validation routines, which hook into this mechanism and make it pretty easy to design specialized dialogs with custom validation.

These two bits of functionality are called DDX (dialog data exchange) and DDV (dialog data validation). *CWnd* has a member function called *DoDataExchange,* which can be overridden. This function contains a set of calls to DDX and DDV routines for each control from which data is to be transferred. DDV calls exist only if the data is to be validated. Most of the time, the set of calls in the *DoDataExchange* member function are provided and maintained by the ClassWizard tool inside Visual C++, but if your needs are more complex than it can support, it is possible to add your own calls. If all you want is simple data transfer and perhaps a bit of validation such as maximum string length, minimum and maximum values for integer values, and so forth, then you don't need to write any DDX or DDV routines or alter the *DoDataExchange* function manually. If you need to exchange data types that aren't provided, or if you want to perform special validation, you'll have to write a bit of code.

Property Pages and Property Sheets

MFC version 3.0 introduced another much-sought-after feature in the MFC world: the tabbed dialog box. Tabbed dialog boxes, like the one in Figure A-1, became popular when applications such as Microsoft Word and Microsoft Excel began to use them. Suddenly, everyone wanted to have them! The property pages of OLE Controls as implemented by the OLE CDK also use tabbed dialog boxes. MFC version 3.0 makes them rather easy to implement.

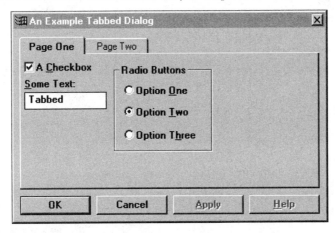

Figure A-1. *A simple property sheet (tabbed dialog box).*

The *Tabs* program, parts of which are listed below, creates the simple two-page tabbed dialog box shown in Figure A-1. The entire program can be found in the \APPA\TABS directory on the companion CD-ROM. The source files of note are TABS.H (see Listing A-1 on the next page) and TABS.CPP (see Listing A-2), which define and implement the application's *CWinApp*-derived class and create the tabbed dialog box; PAGE1.H (see Listing A-3 on page 501) and PAGE1.CPP (see Listing A-4 on page 502), which define and implement the first page of the dialog box; and PAGE2.H and PAGE2.CPP, which define and implement the second page. So that we can look at the DDX/DDV features in greater detail,

I've also added some to the program. The clever thing is that no part of the Page1 or Page2 source files were typed by hand.

TABS.H

```
#include "resource.h"

class CTabApp : public CWinApp
{
public:
    BOOL InitInstance ( void );
};
```

Listing A-1. *The TABS.H header file.*

TABS.CPP

```
#include <stdafx.h>

#include "tabs.h"
#include "page1.h"
#include "page2.h"

CTabApp theApp;

BOOL CTabApp::InitInstance ( void )
{
    CPropertySheet cpsTab ( "An Example Tabbed Dialog" );
    CPage1 cp1;
    CPage2 cp2;

    cpsTab.AddPage ( &cp1 );
    cpsTab.AddPage ( &cp2 );

        // Initialize page one values.
    cp1.m_bCheck = TRUE;
    cp1.m_csText = "Tabbed";
    cp1.m_iButton = 2;

        // Initialize page two values.
    cp2.m_csChoice = "Line 2";
    if ( cpsTab.DoModal() == IDOK )
    {
        CString csOut = "Text is '";
        csOut += cp1.m_csText;
```

Listing A-2. *The TABS.CPP implementation file.*

(continued)

(continued)

```
        csOut += "'; Selection is '";
        csOut += cp2.m_csChoice;
        csOut += "'";

        AfxMessageBox ( csOut );
    }
    return TRUE;
}
```

PAGE1.H

```
// page1.h : header file
//

/////////////////////////////////////////////////////////////////////////
// CPage1 dialog

class CPage1 : public CPropertyPage
{
    DECLARE_DYNCREATE(CPage1)

// Construction
public:
    CPage1();
    ~CPage1();

// Dialog data
    //{{AFX_DATA(CPage1)
    enum { IDD = IDD_PAGE1 };
    BOOL m_bCheck;
    CString m_csText;
    int m_iButton;

    //}}AFX_DATA

// Overrides
    //ClassWizard generated virtual function overrides
    //{{AFX_VIRTUAL(CPage1)
    protected:
    virtual void DoDataExchange(CDataExchange* pDX);
        //DDX/DDV support
    //}}AFX_VIRTUAL

// Implementation
protected:
```

Listing A-3. *The PAGE1.H header file.* *(continued)*

(continued)

```
    //ClassWizard generated message map functions
    //{{AFX_MSG(CPage1)
        //NOTE: the ClassWizard will add member functions here
    //}}AFX_MSG
    DECLARE_MESSAGE_MAP()
};
```

PAGE1.CPP

```cpp
// page1.cpp : implementation file
//
#include "stdafx.h"
#include "tabs.h"
#include "page1.h"

#ifdef _DEBUG
#undef THIS_FILE
static char BASED_CODE THIS_FILE[] = __FILE__;
#endif

/////////////////////////////////////////////////////////////////////
// CPage1 property page
IMPLEMENT_DYNCREATE(CPage1, CPropertyPage)

CPage1::CPage1() : CPropertyPage(CPage1::IDD)
{
    //{{AFX_DATA_INIT(CPage1)
    m_bCheck = FALSE;
    m_csText = _T("");
    m_iButton = -1;
    //}}AFX_DATA_INIT
}

CPage1::~CPage1()
{
}

void CPage1::DoDataExchange(CDataExchange* pDX)
{
    CPropertyPage::DoDataExchange(pDX);
    //{{AFX_DATA_MAP(CPage1)
    DDX_Check(pDX, IDC_CHECK1, m_bCheck);
    DDX_Text(pDX, IDC_EDIT1, m_csText);
```

Listing A-4. *The* PAGE1.CPP *implementation file.*

(continued)

(continued)

```
    DDV_MaxChars(pDX, m_csText, 8);
    DDX_Radio(pDX, IDC_RADIO1, m_iButton);
    //}}AFX_DATA_MAP
}

BEGIN_MESSAGE_MAP(CPage1, CPropertyPage)
    //{{AFX_MSG_MAP(CPage1)
        //NOTE: the ClassWizard will add message map macros here
    //}}AFX_MSG_MAP
END_MESSAGE_MAP()
```

TABS.H and TABS.CPP represent the main application. Thanks to the MFC library, there isn't much to them. I declare a class, *CTabApp*, derived from *CWinApp*, and override the standard *InitInstance* member function. This function creates an object of class *CPropertySheet*, *cpsTab*. *CPropertySheet* is the MFC class that manages the display of the pages of a tabbed dialog box. Unless you want to do some special processing, you generally don't need to derive from it. Pages are added to the property-sheet object using its *AddPage* method, which takes the address of an object derived from *CPropertyPage*. This program contains two, *CPage1* and *CPage2*, and I create an object of each class, called *cp1* and *cp2*. The constructor of each property-page object sets to default values the member variables that will be used later to transfer information to and from the dialog controls. I could edit the constructor code and set my required values there, but instead I've chosen to set the values after construction. *m_bCheck* represents the check box on the dialog box, so it's a Boolean value. If the variable's value is *FALSE*, the box will appear unchecked; if it's *TRUE*, the box will be checked. *m_csText* represents the text in the edit box, and *m_iButton* represents the set of radio buttons in the group box. This variable has as many valid values as there are radio buttons. As there are three buttons in my page, valid values are 0, 1, and 2. A value of 0 causes the first radio button to be selected, 1 the second, and so forth. Any other value causes none of the buttons to be selected. *m_csChoice* is the string that will be passed to the combo box as its selection in page two.

Property sheets are handled pretty much like other dialog boxes are handled by the MFC library, so invocation of the *DoModal* member function causes the property sheet to display itself and one of the pages (the first usually, but any other can be set as the default). *DoModal* causes the sheet to be "modal," which means that the application containing it can accept no input until the sheet has been removed. Modeless property sheets (and dialogs) can be created using the class's *Create* member function. *DoModal* returns whatever the dialog passes as its result to *CDialog::EndDialog*. My code calls this implicitly whenever the OK or Cancel button is pressed, passing the ID of the button. Consequently, a return value of *IDOK*, the value of the OK button, means that the property sheet was dismissed through the use of the OK button. In this case, I read the values out of the text box on page 1 and out of the combo box on page 2, and then I display a message box showing the values.

Looking at the header code for page 1, you'll see that the class *CPage1* is derived directly from *CPropertyPage* (which, incidentally, is derived from *CDialog*) and that it contains the public variables I set in the *InitInstance* function. (I'll explain the weird comments surrounding these and other parts of the code later.) The class also overrides the *DoDataExchange* member function and contains a message map. The PAGE1.CPP file contains the implementation of the class. Notice how the constructor sets the variables to default values.

The *DoDataExchange* member function is called by the framework to transfer data between the controls on the page and the class's member variables. The pointer to a *CDataExchange* object passed in contains context information, telling the function to copy data from the controls to the variables or from the variables to the controls. This function consists, in my simple case, of nothing more than a set of calls to transfer functions (*DDX_ routines*), with one validation routine (*DDV_Max-Chars*) to check that the length of the string passed to or from the control does not exceed eight characters.

At the very end of the file, I have an empty message map. Page 2's implementation is pretty much identical except that it contains a combo box rather than the set of controls on page 1. As you can see, there isn't much to a property page implementation. When you consider that all the code for the two property pages themselves were created automatically by tools provided with Visual C++, it's clear that the productivity benefits of a framework such as MFC bear fruit.

GLOBAL FUNCTIONS AND MACROS

Despite being a C++ class library, MFC still needs a set of global functions that can be used in various parts of a program to perform non-class specific actions. For example, *AfxMessageBox* was used in *CTabApp::InitInstance* in the *Tabs* program to display a message box. The MFC library provides macros and global functions to implement some of the basic *CObject* facilities, such as runtime class information, dynamic creation, serialization, and debugging support. A set of macros exists for exception-handling, which can be used both by compilers that support native C++ exception-handling and by those that don't. There's also the set of macros that declare and implement message maps, and a set of functions for application management. For example, *AfxRegisterWndClass* can be used to create new window classes that implement special features but that can still take advantage of the *CWnd* class facilities and message maps.

The DDX and DDV routines provided by the MFC library are not class-specific, and there are similar ones for database exchange, discussed in the "ODBC" section beginning on page 513. OLE also requires a set of global functions and macros to assist in the implementation of some of its facilities in MFC. Finally, there is a set of functions to assist in the creation of customized collection classes.

OLE SUPPORT

When Microsoft Visual C++ version 1.5 was released in December 1993, it included MFC version 2.5. This version of the MFC library included extensive COM and OLE support, and its release helped bring OLE application development into the mainstream. MFC's OLE implementation supplies automation, visual editing, drag and drop, structured storage, and automatic registration. It's easy to create containers with the MFC library, as well as object servers and even applications that are both containers and object servers. Used in conjunction with the wizards supplied with Visual C++, addition of OLE support to an application can involve no more than a few lines of code. As an example, later in this appendix I rewrite the *AutoProg* sample from Chapter 3, using full MFC support.

I'm most interested in MFC's automation implementation in this book, and it's salutary to see how MFC's designers have reused the concept of a message map to support automation, through the dispatch map.

Dispatch Maps

As I showed in Chapter 2, OLE Automation implementations use tables of function pointers to allow an external program to access an object's properties and methods. The MFC library models this through a dispatch map and also adds a few conveniences. First, MFC allows the object designer to differentiate between the way a property is accessed: it can be treated purely as a public variable, allowing indiscriminate gets and sets. It can act like a public variable with a notification function, so any sets to that variable cause the notification function to be called <u>after</u> the set. The case that most closely maps to what I've shown before (in Chapter 3) is the provision of individual functions for getting and setting the property. The MFC library also allows you to specify parameters to the property, which is useful if you're exposing an array of elements through a property.

Dispatch maps are created just like message maps — with a set of macros. *DECLARE_DISPATCH_MAP* is used in the class declaration to declare the presence of a dispatch map. *BEGIN_DISPATCH_MAP* is used in the class implementation to open the map, taking two parameters: the first is the name of the class for which this map is being created, and the second is the name of the class from which this one is derived. The map is closed with *END_DISPATCH_MAP*.

Inside the map, a set of macros declare properties and methods. *DISP_PROP-ERTY* declares a property that acts as if it were a global variable. The parameters to this macro are the name of the class, the external name of the property, the name of the variable acting as the property, and the type of the property (for example, *VT_I2* is a two-byte integer). *DISP_PROPERTY_NOTIFY* is almost identical except that it takes a further parameter — the name of the function that will be called by the framework after the property value has been changed through automation. *DISP_PROPERTY_EX* is the version of the macro that creates get and set functions for a property; the parameters to this are the name of the class, the external name of the property, the name of the get function, the name of the set function, and the property type. It's possible to create a read-only property with this macro by setting the set function's name to *SetNotSupported*, a function provided by the MFC framework. It's also possible, although considerably less useful, to create write-only properties in an analogous way.

DISP_PROPERTY_PARAM is also similar to *DISP_PROPERTY_EX*, except that it takes an additional parameter: a space-separated list of the types of each of the parameters taken by the property. So, to declare a property that is an array of short integers, the type of the property itself would be *VT_I2*, and the type of the parameter, if you chose to provide numeric indices, would be *VTS_I2*. Note that *VT_I2* and *VTS_I2* refer to the same type, but one is used for parameters and the other is used for properties and methods. It's perfectly possible to have properties that take strings as parameters, so you could implement an array that is indexed by string values. This is particularly useful if the property represents, for example, the set of open files managed by the object.

As an example,

```
DISP_PROPERTY_PARAM ( CMyClass, "Property", GetProperty,
    SetProperty, VT_I2, VTS_I4 VTS_BSTR )
```

declares a property for the class *CMyClass* called *Property*. It is handled by two functions, *GetProperty* and *SetProperty*, and its type is short integer. It takes two parameters, the first of which is a long integer (*VTS_I4*) and the second of which is a string (*VTS_BSTR*).

NOTE *BSTR* is OLE's string type.

Properties with get and set functions are able to validate access to the property and therefore are useful where a property should only accept a set of legal values. If the value being assigned is out of this range or is otherwise in error, the property set function will typically throw an OLE Automation exception, which can be caught by the controlling application and dealt with accordingly. The get function can be used to validate that the property currently has a meaningful value, and it can throw an exception if it hasn't. Likewise, it can be used to validate that the reader of the property is authorized to read it. I prefer to use the get/set paradigm rather than the member-variable concept because it just feels safer and has a more object-oriented feel. (Perhaps I'm just an OO fanatic!)

OLE Automation passes all parameters to and from objects in variables of a type known as *VARIANT*. A "*VARIANT*" is basically a union that can hold one of a large number of types at a time. It's very easy, therefore, to create automation methods or properties that accept parameters of more than one type. For example, it might be useful to have a property that represents the set of open files that can be indexed either by file name or by file number. By declaring the property as taking a *VARIANT* parameter and checking in the property-handling functions for the type actually held within the variant, either can be used.

OLE Automation allows parameters that are themselves pointer types to be passed to properties and methods so that the parameter is passed by reference rather than by value. Consequently, it allows methods and properties to alter the values of parameters passed to it. OLE Automation controllers need to be written with this knowledge; otherwise, by-reference parameters don't work properly. For example, Visual Basic version 3.0 did not allow parameters to be passed by reference, so properties and methods could not change parameters passed to them from Visual Basic version 3.0. Later versions of Visual Basic and Visual Basic for Applications Edition fixed this problem.

Indexed arrays are very similar in concept to OLE collections implemented with *IEnumVARIANT*, the difference being that collections can be iterated over in such a way that the number of elements in the collection does not need to be known. This is because the *IEnumVARIANT* interface's *Next* method returns "failure" when the end of the array is reached, and the high-level language construct used to iterate over a collection is typically written to handle this (for example, Visual Basic's *For Each* loop construct). Parameterized properties, on the other hand, will typically throw an OLE Automation exception if an array index that is out of range is passed in.

One further property macro of interest is *DISP_DEFVALUE*, which defines the property that is to act as the default property of the object. For example,

```
Text1.Text = "A string value"
```

could be made equivalent to

```
Text1 = "A string value"
```

where the assignment to the default property (*Text*) is implicit. Only one property per dispatch interface can be declared as the default. The macro takes as parameters the name of the class for which the default is being defined and the external name of the property being so defined.

Methods are declared in similar ways to properties; however, there are fewer choices because methods always equate directly to functions. *DISP_FUNCTION* declares a standard method and takes the class name, the external method name, the name of the internal function that provides the method's functionality, the type of the return value, and a space-separated list of parameter types taken by the method.

Assignment of Dispids

Okay, so you now know how to declare entries for properties and methods in a class's dispatch map. The outstanding problems are how the dispids for these methods and properties are determined, and whether you can have any influence over that choice. The MFC library's implementation defines a standard through which dispids are allocated, and therefore they can be predicted with ease. Also, by moving entries around in the dispatch map, customizations can be made. However, if you need to allocate a specific dispid to a property or method, which you'd need to if you wanted to implement a "standard" property or method (that is, one for which the dispid is already defined elsewhere), you'll have to adopt a slightly different technique.

As an example of a standard OLE Automation method, consider the way in which collections are implemented. When a controller wants to iterate over a collection, it calls the dispatch interface's _NewEnum_ property, which returns a pointer to the object's *IEnumVARIANT* interface. _NewEnum_ is defined as having a dispid of -4 (*DISPID_NEWENUM*), so to be implemented in MFC code, you need a way of allocating it this dispid explicitly.

The MFC library provides a set of macros that do all the things the macros described above do but that also take an extra parameter. This parameter is always the third parameter to each macro, and it is the dispid you want given to the specified property or method. These dispid macros have the same names as the earlier examples, but all end in _ID_. Taking the example I used above and altering it to allocate a specific dispid, will create exactly the same parameterized property, the only difference now being that it will have a dispid of *123*:

```
DISP_PROPERTY_PARAM_ID ( CMyClass, "Property", 123,
    GetProperty, SetProperty, VT_I2, VTS_I4 VTS_BSTR )
```

NOTE The following applies to all dispatch map entries except *DISP_-DEFVALUE*: just as with message map entries, all member variables and member functions referred to by the macros must be declared in the class's header file. (As I'll demonstrate later, if you use the tools that come with Microsoft Visual C++ to create these macro entries, the appropriate declarations are also created.)

When dispatch map entries are created or altered, it is also important to remember to edit the ODL file for the application at the same time; this ensures that they both reflect the same dispatch interface details. Toward the end of this appendix, I discuss some of the tools that come with Visual C++ to create and maintain applications; as I show there, these tools also automatically manipulate the ODL file on your behalf.

OLE Documents

The MFC library versions 2.5 and later support OLE Documents pretty much completely, in that containers can be created that support visual editing, servers that supply visually-editable objects can be created, and drag and drop is supported. There is also limited support for structured storage. The next few sections take a brief look at how these things are done, but bear in mind that this is very much a simplification. If you really want to know the gory details, I refer you to the MFC documentation and source code.

Embedding and Linking

From the container standpoint, the ability to include objects from other applications is supported through the view class and the document class, which needs to be derived from either *COleDocument* or *COleLinkingDoc* if you want linking ability as well as embedding. The document sees embeddable items as *COleClientItem* objects.

Whenever a new object is embedded or linked in a document, a new *COleClientItem*-derived object is created. *COleClientItem* implements, among other things, the client site for the embedded or linked object.

From the server point of view, applications that support embeddable objects use a document class derived from *COleServerDoc* rather than use *CDocument* directly. Then the application needs to create an item derived from *COleServerItem*, which has the same base class as *COleClientItem* (*CDocItem*). This "server item" represents the embedded or linked object. In the case of an embedding, it represents the entire document object; in the case of a linked object, a link can refer to only part of a document or to all of it.

Visual Editing Support

The MFC library makes it easy to go that extra step from embeddable and linkable objects to visual editing-capable objects and containers. The expectation is that you'll take that step, so what's discussed for linking and embedding happens to implement a lot of the visual editing code too.

Some additional things need to be done, such as the creation of menu and toolbar resources for use in visual editing situations. (These resources are merged with the container's menus when the object is UI-activated.) Likewise, a window class derived from *COleIPFrameWnd* needs to be created to support the window that will be created in the container when the object is brought UI active.

If you're implementing a container that wants to support the visual editing of its embedded objects, you need to call *CDocTemplate::SetContainerInfo* early on in the application's life. This tells the framework what menu and accelerator resources the container wants to use for itself when it UI-activates an embedded item.

The container's view class also needs to maintain a list of pointers to embedded and linked items (as it would even without visual editing) and must override certain drawing and focus member functions so that it properly handles visual editing.

Drag and Drop

OLE Drag and Drop is used to transfer or copy items between applications in a user-oriented paradigm. If the item being dragged is an OLE server item, you simply call the *DoDragDrop* member function of that item's *COleServerItem* class. If you're a container and the item being dragged from you is an OLE object, you can call its *DoDragDrop* member function in your *COleClientItem* class. If you're anything other than a container, or if the object is not a data object, then create a *COleDataSource* object (a wrapper for *IDataObject*) representing the item to be dragged and call its *DoDragDrop* member function. Couldn't be easier!

If you want to accept dropped items, making your application a drop target, you need to create an object of class *COleDropTarget* and register it with the system by calling its *Register* member function during your window's creation (for example, during *OnCreate*). You then need to write some code to define how the icon being dragged appears as it's dragged over your window, as well as a function to deal with what happens when the user actually lets go of the item over your window and drops it.

One complication regards the user being able to scroll through your document during a drag-and-drop operation. You'll need to write code to perform the scrolling when it's required.

Structured Storage

Support for OLE structured storage in the MFC library is minimal. Basically, a container can be asked to use compound files rather than flat files when saving data files by calling the *EnableCompoundFile* member of *COleDocument*. There's also a derivation of *CFile*, *COleStreamFile*, which wraps the *IStream* interface.

Creating Other COM Interfaces — Interface Maps

The MFC library goes beyond merely providing easy access to the sexier features of OLE: it also allows code to be written to support any arbitrary COM interface. Again, the message map concept is reused, this time as the "interface map." Interface maps are used to add interface declarations and implementations to a class derived from

CCmdTarget. The MFC library actually implements the interfaces through nested classes, just as I did in the early chapters of this book in my COM interface implementations.

Interface maps provide a standard implementation of *IUnknown* in the *CCmdTarget* class and provide a data-driven implementation of *QueryInterface* (that is, it walks the interface maps to find which interfaces are supported). As you'll soon see, interface maps also make it easy to use aggregation, both as a user of an object that is to be aggregated and as the provider of an object that can be aggregated. Finally, a low-level hook, *CCmdTarget::GetInterfaceHook,* is provided to allow implementations to get at calls to *QueryInterface* and to perform special action. (For example, this could be useful in some of the versioning scenarios examined in Chapter 3, allowing an object's *QueryInterface* to say that it supports a given interface when in fact it supports a slightly later version.)

To use an interface map in a class derived from *CCmdTarget*, declare the map in the class header using *DECLARE_INTERFACE_MAP*. Then, for each interface you want to support, put the declaration of the interface, minus the standard *IUnknown* methods, between *BEGIN_INTERFACE_PART* and *END_INTERFACE_PART* macros. *BEGIN_INTERFACE_PART* takes a parameter that tells the MFC library the name of the nested class to create. It takes this name and prepends an *X*. The second parameter to the macro is the name of the interface being declared, from which the nested class will be derived.

This is matched in the class implementation file with the map itself. Here, the map is enclosed between *BEGIN_INTERFACE_MAP* and *END_INTERFACE_MAP* macros, and each entry consists of an *INTERFACE_PART* macro that takes three parameters. The first parameter is the name of the class to which this interface is being added, the second is the IID of the interface, and the third is the name of the nested class used in the corresponding *BEGIN_INTERFACE_PART* macro, minus the (still implicit!) *X*. The MFC library creates a member variable in the outer class of the type specified (for example, *XClassName*) with the name *m_xClassName* and declares the class as being a friend of the outer class. This allows the nested class to access private members of its outer class.

As an example, I'll consider the declaration and implementation of an MFC version of the *IClassFactory* interface, chosen because it's nice and simple — it only has two methods. First, I need a class to contain the interface, derived from *CCmdTarget*. I'll call this *CCOMClass*. I then need to declare the interface map and declare an entry for *IClassFactory*. Bear in mind that if you wanted to support more interfaces, you simply add more *BEGIN_INTERFACE_PART* and *END_INTERFACE_PART* pairs.

```
class CCOMClass : public CCmdTarget
{
protected:
    DECLARE_INTERFACE_MAP()
    BEGIN_INTERFACE_PART ( ClassFactory, IClassFactory )
```

```
        STDMETHOD ( CreateInstance ) ( LPUNKNOWN pUnkOuter,
            REFIID riid, LPVOID FAR *ppvObj );
        STDMETHOD ( LockServer ) (BOOL fLock );
    END_INTERFACE_PART ( ClassFactory )
};
```

This actually expands to create a nested class called *XClassFactory* and a member variable in *CCOMClass* of type *XClassFactory* called *m_xClassFactory*. It also declares *XClassFactory* to be a friend class of *CCOMClass*. In normal circumstances, it's quite likely that there would be more to the *CCOMClass* class than only the interface map — and you can put there any code you like.

The next thing is to add the interface map code to the class implementation file:

```
BEGIN_INTERFACE_MAP ( CCOMClass, CCmdTarget )
    INTERFACE_PART ( CCOMClass, IID_IClassFactory, ClassFactory )
END_INTERFACE_MAP ( )
```

The only task remaining now is actually to implement the functions. Although the macros declare the *IUnknown* methods for you, they don't implement them. Thankfully, it isn't difficult. A typical *QueryInterface* implementation, for example, becomes:

```
STDMETHODIMP CCOMClass::XClassFactory::QueryInterface
    ( REFIID riid, LPVOID FAR *ppv )
{
    METHOD_PROLOGUE(CCOMClass, ClassFactory)
    return (HRESULT)pThis->ExternalQueryInterface(riid, ppv);
}
```

The *METHOD_PROLOGUE* macro returns a pointer to the object's containing *CCmdTarget*-derived class in *pThis*. The two *IClassFactory* methods need to be implemented in the same way.

The interface map is clearly a very easy way to remove the grunge work in the creation of COM interfaces. It doesn't remove the task of implementing the interface, but its simplicity probably encourages the creation of more interfaces.

Another situation in which interface maps are useful is in the creation of an interface to support an automation server's named dispatch interface in addition to the generic *IDispatch*. If you cast your mind back to Chapter 3, you'll recall that I showed extracts from a type-library source file which defined an application's dispatch interface as *_DHexocx*, which had its own class ID (CLSID). By default, an automation-enabled MFC application supports *IDispatch* and will return a pointer to an object's *IDispatch* interface when asked to via *QueryInterface*. This supports Visual Basic statements such as

```
Dim x As Object
Set x = CreateObject ("Hexedt32.Gateway")
```

because these statements cause Visual Basic to ask for *IDispatch*. Modern versions of Visual Basic, including Visual Basic for Applications, allow you to define type-safe variables that equate to a specific dispatch interface and that therefore use the type library at compile-time for type-checking and name-checking. Visual Basic code such as

```
Dim x As IGateway
Set x = CreateObject("Hexedt32.Gateway")
```

invokes this type safety by asking the object for its *IGateway* interface. Unless you take specific action, MFC applications created with Visual C++ versions 2.x or earlier will fail this call. All you need to do to get it to support the call is to create an interface map entry for the specific dispatch interface in question and point it at the regular *IDispatch* implementation (by making the third parameter to the *INTER-FACE_PART* macro *Dispatch*).

Aggregation Support

MFC also supports aggregation, both for the creation of objects that can be aggregated and for the creation of an object from aggregates.

To aggregate an object, create a pointer to the requisite object interface during the call to your override of *CCmdTarget::OnCreateAggregates*, and reference this pointer in an *INTERFACE_AGGREGATE* macro in your class's interface map. The *IUnknown* pointer to pass to the aggregated object's *IClassFactory::CreateInstance* method can be obtained by calling *CCmdTarget::GetControllingUnknown*.

To make your object aggregatable, all you've got to do is to call *CCmdTarget::EnableAggregation* and ensure that whenever you manipulate reference counts in your implementation, you do so by calling the functions provided by *CCmdTarget*, *ExternalAddRef*, and *ExternalRelease*. This ensures that the reference count call is passed to the correct interface.

ODBC

In addition to the OLE support it added to the MFC library version 2.5, Microsoft Corporation also added extensive ODBC support. ODBC stands for "open database connectivity," and it is the standard API for database access. The basic theme of ODBC is that it presents a common API for database access to applications, and a set of ODBC drivers map these calls onto the calls supported by a given database. For example, the SQL Server ODBC driver will map all ODBC calls onto native SQL Server calls. The clear advantage of ODBC is that it allows applications to be written to work with a number of disparate databases, even ones that aren't known about at the time the application is written and ones that don't necessarily follow the standard relational model. At the time of this writing, about 55 databases from a variety of vendors are supported by ODBC drivers. Microsoft ships some of its drivers with Visual C++, including a set of 32-bit ODBC drivers with Visual C++ version 2.1.

With the release of Windows NT 3.5 in September 1994, ODBC became available for 32-bit Windows as well, and MFC version 3.0 provides C++ access to it.

So what does the MFC library do for ODBC? Consistent with the MFC philosophy, the database access classes are designed around the theme of making ODBC easier to program. Consequently, its designers chose the Visual Basic–Microsoft Access model as the way to map database functionality to classes. The *CRecordSet* class, for example, closely resembles a dynaset or recordset in one of these products.

CRecordSet is the fundamental class. It represents the set of records that satisfy a given SQL *SELECT* statement and can be stepped through in sequence (both forward and reverse). Records can also be added, updated, and deleted from a *CRecordSet* object. The record set can be dynamic, in that it gets changed as the database underlying it changes: this is dynaset functionality. It can also be static, representing a snapshot of the database.

Record sets are given a connection to a database through a *CDatabase* object, which encapsulates the way in which ODBC initiates and terminates conversations with databases (specifically, with the database driver). To view the records in a set, one would normally attach an object of a class derived from *CRecordView* to the *CRecordSet* object. *CRecordView* is derived from *CFormView*, and is the easiest way to represent a database form. The view uses DDX routines to transfer data between the form's visual elements and the record set's data fields. The record set then can use an analog of DDX known as RFX (record field exchange) to transfer data between its data variables and the database.

The ODBC classes, as is the case with the OLE visual editing classes, are geared towards use by applications that use the document–view architecture. Nevertheless, it is possible to create database applications using the MFC library's database support, which don't make use of the architecture.

The first release of the OLE CDK did not allow the MFC database classes to be used in OLE controls. The second release, version 1.1, which is provided with Visual C++ version 2.1, added support for the *CDatabase* and *CRecordSet* classes; thus, OLE controls can now access databases through ODBC in the same way as do other MFC programs.

TOOLS FOR USING MFC WITH VISUAL C++

Microsoft Visual C++ comes with a variety of tools to make the task of programming with the MFC library easier: specifically, AppWizard and ClassWizard. In addition, there are other bits and pieces throughout the toolset geared toward MFC programming.

AppWizard

Using AppWizard is the easy way to create the shell of a new application. It is used once only per project, at the very start. It almost always creates applications that utilize the document–view architecture. The exception is when you select a dialog box as the application's front end, rather than SDI or MDI — an option that exists only in the 32-bit AppWizard supplied with Visual C++ versions 2.0 and later.

AppWizard presents a series of options, such as whether you want to be an OLE container, and then creates code based on those options. (See Figure A-2.) The output of AppWizard is always executable once compiled, although you need to bear in mind that its purpose is to create a shell; therefore, not all the functionality does something useful at this stage. For example, Print Preview will work but it can only show you an empty page; OLE server support works so your application can be embedded within another application, but there's nothing in the window that shows the embedding because you've written no drawing code yet.

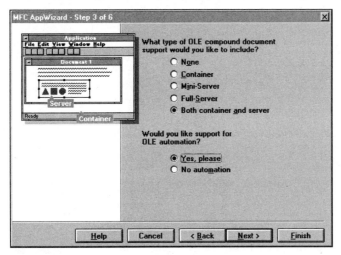

Figure A-2. *The OLE options presented by Visual C++ version 2.0's MFC AppWizard.*

AppWizard does do some particularly powerful things. If you select full ODBC support in your application, it will prompt you to select an ODBC data source. Having done this, it will then present you with a list of the tables in that data source and ask you to select one. When you've done that, it creates a *CRecordSet*-derived object that contains data elements corresponding to the columns in the selected table. It also creates the appropriate *CDatabase*-derived class.

If you choose OLE server support, a CLSID is generated for you and your view is instantly embeddable within containers. You can also choose to have container support, which means that your application can embed other applications' objects. Click both check boxes and you get an application that is capable of both. There's also an OLE Automation selection, which adds the shell of a dispatch map to the created application's document class, allowing the ClassWizard to add properties and methods.

AppWizard allows you to choose whether the application uses the MFC library statically linked to it or whether it uses the DLL implementation of the MFC library. The latter option produces smaller executables, which are slightly slower to load. You also need to ensure that you distribute the appropriate DLL(s) with your application. In general, this is the better option, as a number of executables can share the same MFC implementation. It's also the default choice with the AppWizard that ships with Visual C++ version 2.0.

You can also choose whether the generated application has a dockable toolbar, a status bar, print preview functionality, split views, and context-sensitive help and whether it uses three-dimensional controls (the only choice possible for Windows 95 and user-interface-equivalent versions of Windows NT). The Advanced options allow you to select the OLE name used by applications, the file extension used by this application, and the formats of the main frame window and the MDI child windows, if any. Finally, you even get to choose whether AppWizard-generated code is to include comments and whether or not the make file generated by the wizard is compatible with the Visual C++ integrated development environment. I'm hard-pressed to think of a good reason why this last option shouldn't always be answered "yes, please."

Visual C++ version 2.1 added AppWizard options for Windows Sockets and MAPI (messaging API) support. The latter adds a Send command to the application's File menu and allows a document to be e-mailed through any MAPI-enabled messaging system.

I said that AppWizard is a once-only-per-project tool. Well, this isn't strictly true. Currently, it cannot go back and alter the code it generated; however, you can add options later by creating a new application with the options you want and copying over the relevant source files and extra lines.

One final point about AppWizard: it's a convenience, not a dictator. If you don't like the code it generates, you can always type in your own.

ClassWizard

ClassWizard is the king of tools in Visual C++. Even if you choose not to use the other tools, this is one which you'd be wise to try. In its first incarnation, in Visual C++ version 1.0, its purpose was twofold: to tie messages and visual elements to code (that is, to manipulate message maps) and to add member variables to window and dialog classes for dialog data exchange. With the release of Visual C++ version 1.5, ClassWizard was enhanced to support OLE Automation and ODBC. Subsequent versions build on this framework, so the one supplied with the OLE CDK supports OLE Events as well.

As ClassWizard adds and removes entries from maps of various kinds, it uses special delimiter comments in the source code to note where to make its changes. You will have seen some of these already. As an example, an empty message map that ClassWizard can edit looks like this:

```
BEGIN_MESSAGE_MAP(CAutopro3Doc, CDocument)
    //{{AFX_MSG_MAP(CAutopro3Doc)
        // NOTE - the ClassWizard will add and remove mapping macros
        //    here.
        //    DO NOT EDIT what you see in these blocks of generated
        //       code!
    //}}AFX_MSG_MAP
END_MESSAGE_MAP()
```

and an empty dispatch map looks like this:

```
BEGIN_DISPATCH_MAP(CAutopro3Doc, CDocument)
    //{{AFX_DISPATCH_MAP(CAutopro3Doc)
    //}}AFX_DISPATCH_MAP
END_DISPATCH_MAP()
```

You'll see similar comments in header files and ODL files. All ClassWizard's delimiters follow the same pattern. Changing anything between the comment delimiters by hand is hazardous as it might stop ClassWizard from being able to parse the code. Changing the delimiter lines themselves <u>will</u> stop ClassWizard from reading the code!

Message Maps in ClassWizard

ClassWizard's message map functionality allows you to select a class whose map is to be manipulated and then to add and remove things from this map. The Message Maps tab of the MFC ClassWizard dialog box presents a list of messages that the class can receive, together with a set of command IDs for menu options defined in the program and generic ones added by the framework. To add a member function to a message map, select the class name in the Object Ids list box, find the Windows message ID in the Messages list box that you want the class to handle, and then double-click it. To add a handler for a menu command, select the command in the Object Ids list box and then double-click COMMAND in the Messages list box. ClassWizard will suggest a function name, which you can alter if you want; it then adds the map entry, declares the function in the class header, and writes a skeleton function in the class implementation file.

The extra functionality added to this section in Visual C++ version 2.0 is the ability to select virtual functions to override. The virtual function names appear in the Messages list box and are added to the message map by double-clicking them.

Member Variables Manipulation Through ClassWizard

The Member Variables tab of the MFC ClassWizard dialog box is used to add member variables to dialog boxes, windows, and record sets. Whenever variables are being added to classes based on a window, the dialog box lists all control IDs within the window to which member variables can be bound. Remember that this binding is purely an association between a control on a dialog box and a variable in your code: it is <u>not</u> the same as data binding. By selecting one of these IDs and clicking the Add Variable button, a dialog box appears in which you can specify the name and type of the variable. If the type you've chosen supports a DDV validation routine, the ClassWizard tab allows validation entries to be added, such as the maximum length of a string variable or the maximum and minimum values of an integral variable.

Controls can have two types of variables bound to them: one to hold the value, which participates in DDX and DDV, and one to wrap the control (that is, an object of the class specific to the control, such as *CListBox* for a list box). The control variable is added much less often than the value variable, but it is useful in those situations in which the control is to have customized functionality, such as an owner-draw list box. (MFC'ers prefer to call these "self-draw list boxes," as MFC reflects the messages back to the control object so that it draws the actual control.)

If the class selected in the tab is a recordset class, the tab shows the database columns that can be bound. Addition of variables to this class type cause them to participate in RFX, so values are transferred from these variables to and from the database. Generally, AppWizard will have bound all columns when it created the application, although ClassWizard can be used if the database definition changes or if you're adding a new recordset class.

ClassWizard and OLE Automation

Figure A-3 shows the OLE Automation tab in Visual C++ version 2.0's MFC ClassWizard dialog box. This tab allows the addition and removal of automation properties and methods as well as the creation of C++ classes that have the same set of properties and methods as automation objects defined in a type library. (You can open and read a type library by clicking the "Read Type Library" button.) This latter functionality is used when you're creating C++ applications that <u>use</u> automation objects; however, the more normal case will be when you're creating applications that <u>expose</u> automation objects.

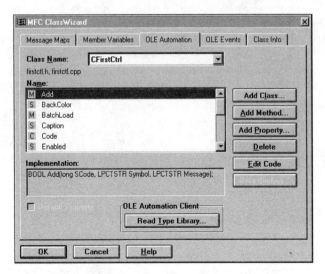

Figure A-3. *The OLE Automation tab from Visual C++*
version 2.0's MFC ClassWizard dialog box.

OLE Automation properties and methods can be added to any *CCmdTarget*-derived class, but ClassWizard will only add them if the class already has a dispatch map defined and if that map contains the appropriate set of ClassWizard delimiter comments. If the project has an ODL file and that file also has the appropriate set of delimiters, ClassWizard will maintain the ODL file as properties and methods are added and removed.

When you add a method, ClassWizard displays a dialog box into which the method name can be entered, together with the name of the function by which it will be implemented. You also specify the return type from a drop-down list of available types, together with any parameters and their types. (Again, the list of supported types is pre-defined, by OLE Automation.)

Property addition is very similar, except that you get to specify how the property is implemented. It can be a member variable with or without a notification function, in which case you get to specify the name of the variable and the name of the notification function, if any. It can also be implemented as a get/set function pair, when you get to specify the names of the functions. If either function name is left out, that aspect of the property is disabled, so removing the name of the set property function causes the property to be read-only.

The ClassWizard's OLE Events Tab

See Chapter 4 for a discussion of this tab.

Setting Class Information with ClassWizard

The Class Info tab allows you to examine the characteristics of a class and to change certain of its aspects. Aspects that can be changed include the filter that ClassWizard is to use in its Message Maps tab: selecting a window type causes Windows messages to appear in the tab. Depending on the type of window class chosen, more or fewer of the messages available appear in the Messages list box in the Message Maps tab for this class.

Other aspects that can be changed are the foreign class and foreign variable attached to a class. This is most useful in *CRecordView*-derived classes, in which an attached *CRecordSet*-derived class is considered to be the "foreign class" and the member variable holding an object of that class is the "foreign variable."

ClassWizard's Add Class Dialog Box

Whenever you want to create a new class from one of the MFC library's base classes or whenever the system determines that you need to do this (for example, if you create a new dialog), the Add Class dialog box is used. (See Figure A-4.) This allows you to specify the name of the class to be created and the files in which it will reside, together with the base class type. If the base class is *CCmdTarget* or one derived from it, the class can also support OLE Automation. In this case, it can also be OLE creatable, which means that an external program can create an object of this type. To put it yet another way, an OLE creatable class is one that has a class factory.

The Add Class dialog box can also be used to import a class from another MFC application.

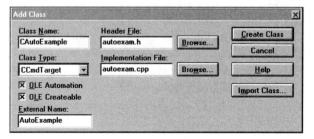

Figure A-4. *The Add Class dialog box from ClassWizard, with an OLE Automation class being prepared.*

Resource Editing

Microsoft Visual C++ includes an integrated resource editor with knowledge of the way in which MFC resource scripts are built. As an example of this, try creating a new dialog box in the resource editor and then invoke ClassWizard. It will notice that the dialog currently has no mapping C++ class and will prompt you to create one. This is how the two property-page classes in the *Tabs* example were created — absolutely no coding by hand!

The same applies to other resources that are typically wrapped by C++ classes. ClassWizard and the resource editor work together in other ways too; ClassWizard can, for example, detect that you are editing a menu resource and present you with the appropriate list of command IDs in the MFC ClassWizard dialog box.

Finally, addition of string table resources to menu items as prompt strings makes them used automatically by the framework to display a line of menu-related help in the status bar when the mouse moves over the menu option. This same string is used for any corresponding toolbar buttons as well as for tooltips if you have them selected. The tooltip is actually formed from the text in the string table resource following a newline (\n) character.

Visual C++ versions 1.5x and earlier don't have an integrated resource editor, but one is shipped with the compiler as a separate application and is called *App Studio*. It has almost identical functionality to the integrated one, with the exceptions: it supports up to 16-color bitmaps rather than 256-color ones; it's missing a few tools (for example, the text on bitmap tool); and it doesn't directly support version information editing.

A current limitation of all 32-bit versions of Visual C++ and its toolset is that the resource editors cannot edit resources held in 32-bit executables. This is likely to change in a later version.

AUTOPRO3

Now is the time to put all this together and create the MFC version of the *AutoProg* example. This new version will have exactly the same OLE Automation functionality as the original. However, because you're going to be using AppWizard to generate the code for you, the application will have a great deal more functionality than the original *AutoProg*. The MFC'd *AutoProg* will be able to display a toolbar and a status bar and will have MDI support and any of the other features provided by AppWizard that you decide to include. I've taken this approach because I want to show how easy automation support can be. The irony is that you could use MFC's OLE support to create a version of *AutoProg* that does just as much as the original *AutoProg* and no more, but it would be more work than the one you're creating now because you couldn't use AppWizard! If you want to do this, the basic approach would be to create a *CWinApp*-derived class similar to the original *CAutoProg* and ensure it calls *AfxOleInit*. Then use ClassWizard to create a new class derived from *CCmdTarget* that supports OLE Automation and is OLE-creatable. Add a variable to hold the salary to this class. Finally, add the property and two methods through ClassWizard, and copy the code from the original. You're done!

Alternatively, follow these rather more simple steps (assuming you're using the Visual C++ 2.0 version of AppWizard):

1. Using AppWizard, create a new application called *AutoPro3* as an MFC executable.

2. Click the Multiple Documents option for MDI support, and then click Next.

3. Click the None option for no database support, and then click Next.

4. Click the "Yes, please" option for OLE Automation support, and then click Next.

5. Select only the Dockable Toolbar, Initial Status Bar, and Use 3D Controls options, and then click Next.

6. Click the Visual C++ Make file and Use MFC in a Shared DLL options.

7. Click Finish, and then click OK to create the application.

8. Invoke ClassWizard, choose the OLE Automation tab, and select *CAutoPro3Doc* as the class name.

9. Click Add Property and add a property called *Salary* with return type *long*, and change the member variable name to *m_lSalary*. Delete the notification function name.

10. Click Add Method and add a method *Payraise* of type *long* that takes one *long* parameter called *Increment*.

11. Click Add Method and add a method *Store* with return type *void* that takes no parameters.

12. Open AUTOPRO3.ODL; notice the automatic maintenance of the ODL file.

13. Copy the code for the two methods from the original *AutoPro2* source.

14. Initialize the member variable *m_lSalary* to a sensible value in the constructor of the document class.

15. Compile, build, and run the application to register it.

16. The end!

Let's look at some of the code generated. (All the source code can be found on the companion CD-ROM in the \OLECTRLS\APPA\AUTOPRO3 directory.)

In AUTOPRO3.CPP, you'll see a CLSID declaration (although the numbers in your generated CLSID will be different):

```
static const CLSID BASED_CODE clsid =
    { 0x265e40e0, 0xd71f, 0x11cd, { 0x92, 0xb4, 0x8, 0x0, 0x2b,
    0x29, 0x1e, 0xed } };
```

The *BASED_CODE* macro causes the compiler to put this data into the code segment — because it is read-only, because it is static, and because the 16-bit Windows data segment is relatively precious as it's limited to 64 Kb.

This line from *InitInstance* connects a class factory to the document class:

```
m_server.ConnectTemplate(clsid, pDocTemplate, TRUE);
```

and this line registers the class factory object as running:

```
COleTemplateServer::RegisterAll();
```

These next two lines ensure that the registry is up to date with respect to this application whenever it is run:

```
m_server.UpdateRegistry(OAT_DISPATCH_OBJECT);
COleObjectFactory::UpdateRegistryAll();
```

The document class is contained in AUTOPDOC.CPP. The dispatch map created by ClassWizard contains the following entries:

```
BEGIN_DISPATCH_MAP(CAutopro3Doc, CDocument)
    //{{AFX_DISPATCH_MAP(CAutopro3Doc)
    DISP_PROPERTY(CAutopro3Doc, "Salary", m_lSalary, VT_I4)
    DISP_FUNCTION(CAutopro3Doc, "Payraise", Payraise, VT_I4, VTS_I4)
    DISP_FUNCTION(CAutopro3Doc, "Store", Store, VT_EMPTY, VTS_NONE)
    //}}AFX_DISPATCH_MAP
END_DISPATCH_MAP()
```

The constructor contains a call to *EnableAutomation* followed by a call to *AfxOleLockApp*. This is matched by a call to *AfxOleUnlockApp* in the destructor. *AfxOleLockApp* is used by the framework to prevent the application from being closed down if any objects are currently active.

The end of the document class implementation file contains the code for the two automation methods you added, *Payraise* and *Store*. That's it! You do also have an ODL file, which is built by the make file into a type library. The ODL file's contents are shown in Listing A-5.

AUTOPRO3.ODL

```
// autopro3.odl : type library source for autopro3.exe

// This file will be processed by the Make Type Library (mktyplib)
//   tool to produce the type library (autopro3.tlb).

[ uuid(265E40E1-D71F-11CD-92B4-08002B291EED), version(1.0) ]
```

Listing A-5. *The ODL file generated and maintained by the Microsoft Visual C++ wizards for* AutoPro3. *(continued)*

523

(continued)

```
library autopro3
{
    importlib("stdole32.tlb");

    //  Primary dispatch interface for CAutopro3Doc

    [ uuid(265E40E2-D71F-11CD-92B4-08002B291EED) ]
    dispinterface IAutopr
    {
        properties:
            // NOTE - ClassWizard will maintain property information
            //    here.
            //     Use extreme caution when editing this section.
            //{{AFX_ODL_PROP(CAutopro3Doc)
            [id(1)] long Salary;
            //}}AFX_ODL_PROP

        methods:
            // NOTE - ClassWizard will maintain method information
            //    here.
            //     Use extreme caution when editing this section.
            //{{AFX_ODL_METHOD(CAutopro3Doc)
            [id(2)] long Payraise(long Increment);
            [id(3)] void Store();
            //}}AFX_ODL_METHOD

    };

    //  Class information for CAutopro3Doc
    [ uuid(265E40E0-D71F-11CD-92B4-08002B291EED) ]
    coclass CAutopro3Doc
    {
        [default] dispinterface IAutopr;
    };

    //{{AFX_APPEND_ODL}}
};
```

Having seen all the things that the MFC library and the accompanying tools can do for you, it should be no surprise to you that the OLE Controls team at Microsoft Corporation decided to leverage the MFC library for use in the OLE CDK.

Visual C++ 4.0 and MFC 4.0

When I started writing this book, Microsoft Corporation had not yet released Visual C++ version 2.0, and therefore the OLE CDK was not available to the public. Also, at that time I didn't work for the Visual C++ group but was stuck in a remote outpost (often fetchingly called "England"), with e-mail as the only real means of communication. (I'm now stuck in Redmond, Washington, with e-mail as the only real means of communication....) I also planned to write this book in a lot less time than it actually took (now, where have you heard that before?), so I was pretty confident that it would be published before any major update to Visual C++ version 2.0.

I was wrong.

As this book reaches its press date, the next major release of Visual C++, version 4.0, is also nearing completion. (Version 3.0 was skipped to get the product version number in line with the MFC version number.) Consequently, it's quite likely that you'll be reading this book and using that new version of Visual C++ or perhaps an even later version. You might therefore be somewhat bemused by some of the things you read here, because Microsoft has improved and built upon the version 2.x product. Some of the things I write about in this book are now untrue or irrelevant, if you use Visual C++ version 4.0 or later.

This appendix takes a very brief look at the new features added to the product from the OLE Controls specification standpoint, and it also points out some of the procedures that have changed.

THE OLE CDK

The OLE Control Developer's Kit (OLE CDK) is no more. Microsoft's MFC group decided to incorporate all the control classes into the rest of the MFC library, so you can now build OLE controls in the same way that you create other MFC components. The advantages of this change are that a control can now use all parts of the MFC library, MFC DLLs (AFXDLLs as opposed to USRDLLs) can now be called by arbitrary programs (previously, their clients had to be MFC programs), and, as you'll see later in this appendix, OLE controls can now contain OLE controls. Also, of course, if a container is written with MFC, it will share the MFC DLLs with any controls it loads, reducing memory overhead and generally making things operate faster. Before this, the container would use the MFC DLLs, while the OLE controls would have to use their own special version, in OC30.DLL. OC30.DLL isn't too much smaller than MFC itself, so this combination was not particularly efficient.

MFC 4.0

The version of the Microsoft Foundation Class Library (the MFC library) shipped with Visual C++ version 4.0 is MFC version 4.0. In addition to the inclusion of the old OLE CDK classes, it has significant new functionality:

- OLE control containment
- DAO support
- Enhanced Windows 95 support, including common controls and common dialogs

The next few sections examine each of these items and their relevance to OLE controls.

OLE Control Containment

Perhaps the biggest feature in MFC version 4.0, which is supported by the Visual C++ Integrated Development Environment (IDE) and the wizards, is that you can now actually begin to use those OLE controls you've developed in real C++ programs.

The *CWnd* class has been enhanced to allow it to represent an OLE control in addition to representing a normal Windows window. So the *CWnd::Create* function has a new control-specific analogue, *CreateControl*, which takes a CLSID rather than a class name and creates an instance of the named control inside the *CWnd* object. As *COleControl* is also derived from *CWnd*, it follows that it is now possible to have an OLE control that contains another OLE control (because *COleControl*, being derived from *CWnd*, is as capable of holding OLE controls as any other *CWnd*-derived class). *CDialog*, being derived from *CWnd* itself, can also host OLE controls, so you can now create dialog boxes that use OLE controls.

The designers of MFC version 4.0 wanted to make OLE controls as easy to use in forms and dialogs as are normal Windows controls, and they've come pretty close. For example, controls can now be added from the dialog editor's toolbox to a *CFormView*-derived object or to a *CDialog*-derived object, just as if they were standard controls. Further, the inserted control is automatically wrapped by ClassWizard in an appropriate proxy class that contains type-safe member function wrappers for the properties and methods of the control, so you can access the control's properties and methods programmatically. Likewise, ClassWizard now supports the control's events, by showing them in the Message Maps tab as messages to which code can be attached. Even notifications, such as those from simple data-bound controls, can be connected to container-side code, although there's no direct wizard support for this.

So, how does the implementation work? A call needs to be made early on in the life of your application (typically, inside *InitInstance* along with all the other initialization code), which enables the OLE Controls hosting code inside the *CWnd* class. This function is *AfxEnableControlContainer*, which simply sets a static member variable for the *CWnd* class to point at an object that manages the OLE control containment. Without this call, the static member variable is *NULL*, which means that any attempt to use an OLE control fails (gracefully, of course). Also, each *CWnd*-derived object contains a pointer to a control site object, which is *NULL* if there are no OLE controls contained by this *CWnd* derivation. Why did the MFC team choose to do it this way? Primarily because the *CWnd* class is used in a whole lot of programs for a whole lot of windows, so it makes little sense to increase the size of each and every *CWnd* object in a program just so that they are enabled for OLE controls. Instead, each object takes on the overhead only when one or more OLE controls are actually embedded within it.

Any *CWnd*-derived object that then wants to host OLE controls can do so, and if that object also contains an event sink map, it can catch a control's events. The event sink map is analogous to MFC's message map, and it allows a control-containing class to treat control events as messages. The control events actually appear in ClassWizard as entries in the Message Maps tab, the reason being that most programmers will view an event fired by a control as similar in nature to a message sent by a control. The same map technique applies to other notifications from a control, such as data binding, although ClassWizard does not in this version show those "events" to the programmer. As with button notification messages, such as *BN_CLICKED*, this is something you'll need to add manually.

The steps for using a control in a dialog box (or form view) within a program are as follows:

1. Ensure that the control appears in Component Gallery. If it doesn't, register the control.

2. Choose Insert Component to invoke Component Gallery, choose the control you want from the list it shows, and then click the Insert button.

3. A dialog box appears in which Component Gallery is suggesting to you the name of a class and the names of the files that make up that class. This class is the wrapper class, which acts like a proxy object and provides access to the control's properties and methods. This class will automatically be included in your project, although you'll need to include its header in any file that uses it.

4. After you've allowed the class to be created, close Component Gallery.

5. If the dialog box in which this control is to embedded doesn't yet exist, create it — and then invoke ClassWizard to create the class to wrap the dialog box.

6. Open the dialog box in which the control is to appear.

7. You'll see the toolbox icon for the control that you've inserted into the project appear at the bottom of the toolbox.

8. Select the control from the toolbox, and place it wherever it needs to be on your dialog box; resize the control as necessary.

9. Invoke ClassWizard and select the Message Maps tab; now choose the class that wraps the dialog box and select the control you've just inserted from the list labeled Object IDs. If your chosen control has any events, you'll see them listed in the box labeled Messages. You can add a handler for any event in that list in the usual ClassWizard ways; the most convenient way is to double-click on the event for which you want to write a handler.

10. If you want to set any of the control's properties at design-time, you can do so by ensuring that the control is selected within the dialog editor and invoking its property pages by right-clicking on it and choosing the appropriate option from the context menu.

11. If you want to access the control's properties and methods, you can do so easily by invoking ClassWizard as per step 9, but this time choose the Member Variables tab. Choose the control you want to access and add a member variable. You'll notice that ClassWizard has already determined the defaults you want, in that it has selected a control object of the type that Component Gallery has created for you when you inserted the

component into the project. All you need to do now is to complete the name; ClassWizard provides you with *m_*.

12. Be sure that all necessary include files are included, and then rebuild the project. Now, when you invoke the program and select the dialog box, your OLE control will appear with whatever properties you set through the property pages. If you've set up handlers for any events, you'll find that these handlers will be called when you get the control to fire the relevant event (thankfully!).

Adding controls to a *CFormView*-derived class is a similar process. Using OLE controls in dialog boxes and forms adds a bit of "form persistence" to your project, because the property values of each OLE control are stored away with the dialog template (so long as the control itself makes those properties persistent, of course).

In addition to the design-time addition of OLE controls to a project, you can also create them at any time dynamically using a new *CWnd* member function, called *CreateControl*. This function takes parameters similar to the normal *CWnd::Create* function for standard Windows controls, and also takes a CLSID representing the control to be created. Don't expect magic here: if you insert an OLE control of which you knew nothing until it was selected by a user at runtime, you won't have any automatic access to that control's events, and you'll get no wrapper class for its properties and methods. You'll need to parse the control's type library yourself and wire up your own event handlers. Event sink maps are dependent on compile-time information. The upshot of this is that you can't use MFC's OLE control container support to write your own version of Visual Basic; its goal is to make the use of OLE controls in forms and dialogs easy.

DAO Support

The Jet engine used by Microsoft Access and Microsoft Visual Basic has traditionally had to be accessed through Open Database Connectivity (ODBC) by Visual C++ programs. This is fine; however, the engine has a richer set of functions than can be easily exposed through ODBC. Therefore, the Jet engine now has its own application programming interface (API), except that it is implemented as a set of OLE Automation objects, with properties and methods, through which the engine and databases attached to it can be manipulated. This API is called DAO (Data Access Objects).

The MFC library version 4.0 wraps DAO in the same way as it wraps ODBC, with similar record set classes. You can use these in OLE controls just as you can use the ODBC classes. When would you choose to use one over the other? If you want to talk to a wide variety of databases efficiently or if you don't know which database vendor your user will choose when your application is deployed, then ODBC remains your best choice. Some of the 32-bit ODBC drivers, such as the

Microsoft SQL Server driver, offer outstanding performance. There will be instances, though, when you only want to talk to Access-style data, and in many of these instances DAO will be easier, more powerful, and often faster. The richness of the database support offered though DAO means that you can do more with the data access objects than you can with ODBC. You so do, however, at the risk of making your code substantially harder to port to other databases.

The MFC library does not wrap all DAO objects, and even where it does wrap, its intent is to make the DAO API behave similarly to MFC's wrapping of the ODBC API. On those occasions when you want to do DAO-specific things, MFC provides this capability by providing access to the native *IDispatch* interface pointers to the wrapped DAO objects. DAO actually implements all its OLE Automation interfaces as dual interfaces, so if you want even more speed, you can write your own code to call through the vtable side of the dual interface.

DAO also includes its own C++ class library, which uses the MFC library and is complementary to it. It is designed to make it very much easier for programmers familiar with data access in Visual Basic and Access to move to C++. Its classes don't resemble the MFC classes at all; their appearance and programming model more closely resemble BASIC than C++.

Which do you choose to use? It depends on your needs and abilities. The MFC classes make database access easy for C++ and MFC programmers, and they integrate very well with the rest of the MFC architecture. The DAO C++ classes are targeted fairly and squarely at BASIC programmers; they do things differently from both the MFC database classes themselves and from the MFC philosophy.

Enhanced Windows 95 Support

Visual C++ version 4.0 was released at around the same time as Windows 95, and it is being positioned as the ideal Windows 95 C++ development system. The MFC library aids and abets this intent by having significantly improved its Windows 95 support over its earlier incarnations. This can be seen in many places, and the key places are in the wrapping of Windows 95 common controls, such as the progress bar (for percent-completed displays), and the wrapping of the Windows 95 common dialog boxes. Remember that these controls and dialog boxes are also present on Windows NT versions 3.51 and later and Win32s version 1.30.

While Visual Basic provides OLE control wrappers for these common controls, which can be used in Visual C++ if you so desire, Visual C++ does not include them in its box because there's no reason to when the MFC library wraps the native controls. OLE controls are slower than their native counterparts, so, unless worthwhile value is being added, there's no virtue in using an OLE control version of a wrapped control.

The controls that Windows 95 provides range from the fairly basic, such as the already mentioned progress bars, to tracker bars and animated dialog boxes, to fairly complex beasts such as the tree view and list view controls and the rich text edit control. The rich text edit control provides significant word processor-like functionality, and it's wrapped by the MFC library in two ways — as a control in its own right and as a control that forms a view, akin to the rather more basic *CEditView*.

MFC version 4.0 also contains changes to some of its native implementations of user interface features (such as status bars, tool bars, and property pages); they now use the underlying Windows 95 versions instead.

Finally, a lot of work has been carried out to ensure that Visual C++ version 4.0 can do all the things on Windows 95 that it can do on Windows NT. You can build on both platforms, debug on both, and so forth, and you can also run the cross-platform editions (Mac 68000 and PowerMac) just as happily on Windows 95 as on NT.

THE BUILD PROCESS

Visual C++ version 4.0 includes a significantly enhanced build engine, which allows projects to contain a number of other projects, so you can finally build multi-file projects in one go. For example, if you're creating a project that builds three DLLs and an EXE, you can now do this as one project file rather than having to have four separate ones, as you do on Visual C++ version 2.x.

You can also add custom build steps to internal make files, whereas previously you'd have needed to use an external make file to run any non–Visual C++ components, such as the macro assembler.

Another change is the incorporation of the ControlWizard into the heart of Visual C++. You can now write "custom App Wizards," which are basically application shell generators that follow <u>your</u> rules. ControlWizard is itself one of these custom AppWizards, so it appears in the drop-down list when you choose to create a new project.

One set of features certain to please most of us is the set that is focused on build throughput. Microsoft has spent a lot of time and effort ensuring that the build process, after you're past the first compilation, is as fast as possible. Okay, it's true that as a Microsoft employee working in the Visual C++ group, I'm bound to say this, but consider these features nevertheless:

- Incremental compilation — Only functions that have changed are recompiled, using information stored in a project database.

- Incremental linking — Although Visual C++ version 2.x also has incremental linking, the algorithms used in Visual C++ version 4.0 to determine whether it can link incrementally have been substantially improved, so it will perform the significantly faster incremental link rather than a full link in many more cases.

■   Minimal rebuild (or what you might call "intelligent" rebuild) — As long as you use ClassWizard to maintain a project (and you do, don't you?!?), the IDE is able to keep track of the changes you make and can determine whether files that have changed have actually changed in a material way that really requires recompilation. In those cases where a header file is added or where changes are made to a dependent file (but have no impact elsewhere), no recompilation is necessary. The minimal rebuild system throws out an informative message and continues, looking at the next file in the project.

Taken together, the impact of these build system improvements typically makes the edit-compile-debug cycle much shorter and therefore much faster.

THE COMPONENT GALLERY AND OTHER IDE ENHANCEMENTS FOR CONTROLS

Visual C++ version 4.0's IDE (Integrated Development Environment — the place where you write code, compile it, and debug it) contains a wealth of new features, some of which are targeted specifically at OLE controls or which help the creation or use of OLE controls in some material way.

Figure B-1 shows the IDE of Visual C++ version 4.0 in all its glory.

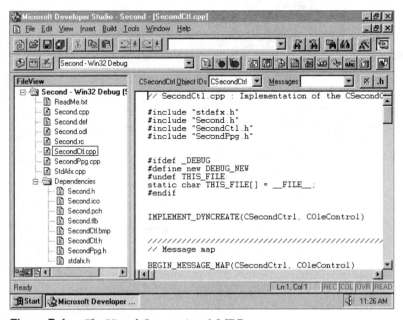

Figure B-1.   *The Visual C++ version 4.0 IDE.*

AppWizard

The first of these improved IDE features is AppWizard, which does all the things its earlier incarnations did and also allows "custom AppWizards" to be generated. A custom AppWizard is one that you write and that creates a skeleton application (or control) along specifications you define. Thus, you can have your own custom steps and can generate whatever code you like. As an example, if you work for a company that has specific user-interface requirements, you can build a custom AppWizard that generates the basic shell of these applications for you. If you're building a lot of OLE controls, you might decide to augment the default code produced for you by ControlWizard with company-specific methods, about boxes, or whatever. You might even be building a family of controls that follow a similar pattern; if so, it might be worth writing your own custom AppWizard to do this.

FYI The version of ControlWizard that ships with VC++ version 4.0 is actually a custom AppWizard. Like any other custom AppWizard, it appears in the drop-down list of application types when you choose File New Project Workspace.

Figure B-2 shows the AppWizard being used to generate a custom AppWizard.

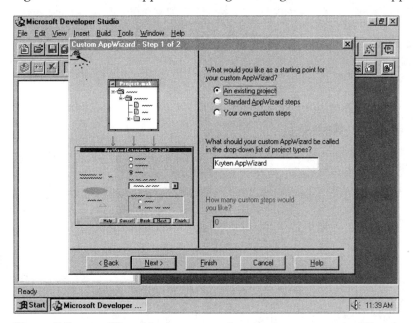

Figure B-2. *AppWizard in the process of generating a custom AppWizard.*

Importing Visual Basic Forms

Most Windows programmers have used, or do use, more than one tool at a time. Sometimes, these tools compete with each other, like two vendors' C++ compilers. At other times, they're complementary, like Visual C++ and Visual Basic. Because there are many schools of thought, you'll always find disagreement between programmers. My general rule is: be pragmatic rather than dogmatic, and achieve the task at hand with as little complication as possible. So, for example, on occasion I've used Visual Basic to create an application's user interface. User-interface code is rarely performance-critical, because it usually takes a great deal longer for a user to react to a user-interface prompt than it does for the code that handles that prompt to execute. Therefore, on the surface, there's no reason to convert a user interface written in Visual Basic to one written in C++.

Consider, for a moment, those developers who use Visual Basic purely as a user-interface programming environment or who want to achieve a higher degree of flexibility than Visual Basic will allow. You could even think of cases where people don't want the overhead of having Visual Basic's runtime DLL in memory at the same time as MFC's. Consequently, there are times when it is important to be able to convert a Visual Basic program into a C++ program fairly easily. Visual C++ version 4.0 does not offer any kind of Visual Basic-to-MFC language translation facilities (although there are third parties who do), but it does offer a facility to read in Visual Basic form definitions and convert them to MFC-compatible resource files. This feature allows you to take an existing Visual Basic form and convert it to a Visual C++ dialog box or form view. Any old-style Visual Basic custom controls (VBXs) will <u>not</u> be automatically converted to the corresponding OLE controls by this process. My advice in this instance would be for you first to get Visual Basic version 4.0 to convert the VBXs and then to convert the form into a resource file with Visual C++.

Component Gallery

Visual C++ version 4.0 introduces a new way of adding functionality to your program — via Component Gallery, which holds three types of "component" and allows them to be applied to your source code. The types are:

- An OLE control
- A C++ class
- A Component Gallery object

The first type, an OLE control, is used to hold all the OLE controls registered on your system so that each control can be added to a project at any time by selecting and inserting it. This causes the selected control to appear on the resource editor's toolbox and also generates a C++ wrapper class that allows you to access its properties and methods. The second type, a C++ class, is the mechanism used to hold any generic, reusable class and to add it to other programs. One classic example of this would be a class that implements a splash screen, such as that displayed when a major Microsoft application (such as Word or Visual C++ or Visual Basic) is first executed.

The third type is the most interesting and potentially the most powerful. By writing an object that exposes a set of specific OLE interfaces and that uses another set, an object can be added to the gallery that can be inserted "with intelligence" into an application. For example, an object can be created that adds an AppWizard option to a program after the fact — that is, after the program has been generated with AppWizard. You can go as far as you like with this concept: the interfaces exposed by Component Gallery allow you to alter a project in any way you choose, including adding and removing source files, changing source code, adding project options, and so forth. In many ways, this aspect of Component Gallery most closely resembles the Visual Basic version 4.0 add-in feature. Think of this as the ability to add a feature or set of features to a project, with rules about the addition expressed and executed by the feature being inserted.

Figure B-3 shows the Component Gallery OLE Controls pane.

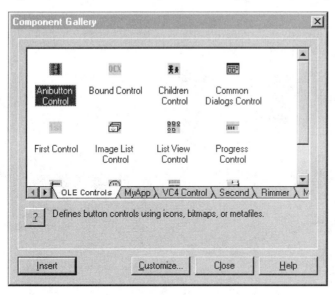

Figure B-3.   *The OLE Controls pane of Component Gallery.*

Resource Editor

On the face of it, the Visual C++ version 4.0 resource editor doesn't look vastly different from its earlier incarnations. There are, however, a number of new features that together make it much easier to create good-looking dialog boxes.

Of course, the editor is also now OLE control–aware and allows you to insert OLE controls (from Component Gallery) into your project's dialog boxes and forms. You can also set each control's properties, and they're saved with the dialog box or form definition. You can invoke each control's property pages and manipulate them directly; they're actually displayed inside the resource editor's properties modeless dialog box, so this is an example of a container providing its own implementation of the property frame.

Other features include the ability to set margins on a dialog box so that controls can be aligned more easily and placed in sensible default locations. Also, a ruler is present on each side of the dialog editor, so placements can be more precise. Finally, you can create resources that can then be used as template resources by other projects, so you can create a set of standard dialog boxes for your company's applications and reuse them very easily.

ClassWizard

ClassWizard has been extended to take advantage of OLE controls, in that a control's events now appear as messages in the Message Maps tab. In addition, the Visual C++ IDE takes the essence of ClassWizard and adds it as a "wizard bar" to any window containing any source file for which ClassWizard information exists. Figure B-4 shows the wizard bar.

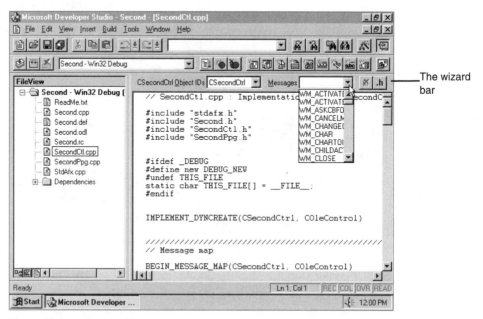

Figure B-4.   *The Visual C++ version 4.0 IDE showing a source file with the wizard bar displayed.*

The wizard bar allows a class's member functions to be found easily, and it also allows you to quickly go to any message handler or event handler. If you attempt to go to a message handler or event handler that hasn't yet been created, the IDE will ask you whether you want to add the relevant handler. As with Visual Basic, the wizard bar shows you which handlers are currently implemented for a particular class by showing them in bold in the drop-down list. Those in ordinary text do not yet exist but can be added.

Class View

One of the nicest features of Visual C++ version 4.0 is the ability to examine the class hierarchy of your application at any point and to jump to any class or any member of any class simply by selecting it in a tree view control. This so-called "class view" has the additional advantage of being populated by a technology known within Microsoft as the "no-compile browser" because the IDE works in the background to parse your source code and to keep this class view up to date (whether or not you've compiled your code). As it is precompilation, it can show only definitions and is unable to take you to references. For this, you still need the full browsing capabilities.

Figure B-5 shows the class view for a typical default AppWizard application, with one class expanded to show its members.

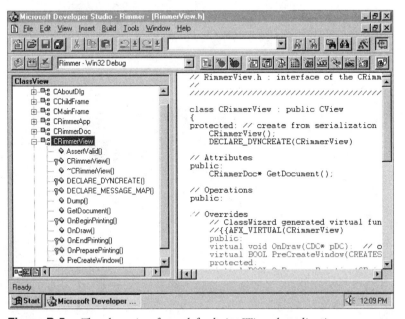

Figure B-5. *The class view for a default AppWizard application.*

CONCLUSION

All in all, Visual C++ version 4.0, together with MFC version 4.0, represents a great leap forward for OLE controls. For once, you can actually use them in C++ programs as easily as (actually, more easily than!) you can create them. For me, it's a great liberation because it allows me to experiment with all this technology in ways that were not feasible previously.

It's difficult to predict what features will come in later versions of Visual C++ that will be relevant to OLE controls. The controls themselves are destined to get smaller and faster, and this might mean updates to the current OLE Controls specification. As long as there is a wrapping facility for controls, which is what the MFC library provides, you don't really need to care about this stuff. My belief is that you should be able to write controls fairly easily that can be used by a wealth of different containers, including ones of your own design. The MFC library's goal is certainly to continue to cover as much of the Windows API as possible and still make C++ programming as easy as it can. The OLE Controls specification helps this goal by providing binary reusable components that can provide off-the-shelf functionality in ways that individual C++ classes cannot.

Index

OLE Structured Storage technology,
 continued
  MFC support for, 510
  Microsoft guidelines for, 471–72
  OLE controls and, 42
  persistence and, 40–41 (*see also*
   persistence; property persistence)
  serialization, 40–41
  transactions and, 41–42
OLE technology, 17–53
  COM (Component Object Model),
   18–20
  containment and, 32–34 (*see also*
   containment)
  getting first interface pointer, 28–32
   (*see also IDispatch* interface)
  IDataObject interface, 50–51
  IMoniker interface, 51–52
  interfaces and, 50–52 (*see also*
   interfaces)
  IRunningObjectTable interface, 52
  IUnknown interface and, 21–27 (*see
   also IUnknown* interface)
  MFC support for, 505–13
  navigating this book and, 15, 53, 82,
   114
  OLE Automation, 34–40 (*see also* OLE
   Automation technology)
  OLE Controls (*see* OLE Controls
   technology)
  OLE Documents, 42–50 (*see also* OLE
   Documents technology)
  OLE Structured Storage, 40–42 (*see
   also* OLE Structured Storage
   technology)
  reference-counting, 23–24
  references to interface IDs, 24–26
  remoting and marshaling, 27
  result handles and status codes, 27–28
   (*see also* SCODEs)
OOA. *See* object-oriented analysis

OOP. *See* object-oriented programming
Open Database Connectivity. *See* ODBC
operating system issues. *See also*
   Microsoft Windows
  16-bit-to-32-bit OLE interoperability,
   455
  32-bit-to-16-bit porting issues
   (*see* porting issues)
  character sets, 56–57, 136, 450–51
  cross-platform issues, 448–49
  MFC portability, 480–81
  SCODEs, 28
  system requirements, xxii, 13–14
  VBX controls, xix, 11
output mechanisms, MFC, 488–90
outside-in activation, 45
overloading *IPropertyNotifySink,* 472
overriding methods, 5

P
PARAMDATA structure, 71–72
parameters
  C++ functions, 71
  named, 36–37
  ODBC symbol fields, 286
  OLE Automation structures, 71–74
  property, 35
  QueryInterface, 23
pascal calling convention, 72
performance issues. *See also* design
   issues
  dual interfaces, 38
  exception-handling, 241
  runtime DLLs, 159
  visible controls, 282–83
  Windows controls vs. OLE controls,
   xxiv
per-property browsing, 107
persistence, 101–3. *See also* OLE
   Structured Storage technology;
   property persistence

S

ADAM DENNING is currently a program manager in the Visual C++ group at Microsoft Corporation, responsible for the Microsoft Foundation Class (MFC) Library and the C runtimes. He's also involved in the present and future of OLE controls, being the prime author of the OLE Controls guidelines. He arrived at Microsoft about halfway through the Visual C++ 4.0 project (back when it was still called Visual C++ 3.0) and was also involved in the Visual C++ 2.2 subscription release. Prior to moving to Redmond, Washington, Adam worked as a senior consultant for Microsoft Consulting Services (MCS) in the United Kingdom, where he led a group that designed business solutions involving client/server systems using OLE and written in C++ (with MFC) and Visual Basic.

Author Adam Denning with his daughters Phoebe (sitting) and Asphodel (standing.) His wife, Melissa, was five hours from giving birth and could not attend the photo shoot. In the next edition, the photo will include Melissa and daughter #3, Xanthe.

Adam has done presentations at various conferences around the world, including the MFC Conference, Tech Ed, VBITS, Solution Developers' Foundation Course, DevTech, and the Windows 95 technical seminar series. He has also written numerous articles for the UK technical press, including more than 200 articles for magazines such as *.EXE*, *Program Now*, and *Which Micro*. He once wrote about 100 words for the *Times* (London), the pinnacle of visibility if not of credibility. He's the author of two other books, one on C programming techniques for PC users called *C at a Glance* and one on 68000 assembly language programming for the Sinclair QL called *Advanced Assembly Language Programming for the Sinclair QL*. He foolishly imagines that this experience can be converted into an ability to write the next *Four Weddings and a Funeral*.

Adam has never been formally educated. Well, okay, he went to Chelsea College in London briefly, where he was supposedly studying electronics. Instead, he got involved in a truly no-hope band (but then, he was a no-hope bass player) and left college to get a job working as a booking clerk (someone who sells train tickets) at London's Victoria Station so that he could finance the band. The train job outlasted the band, thankfully. After a couple of years getting bored, Adam started to program in his spare time and got some contract work. He also managed to convince a few magazines that he could write, and began a few years of freelance technical journalism, interspersed with real programming contracts in languages as arcane as 6502 and Z80 assembler, BCPL, and C. The programming gradually overtook the journalism until eventually he took a job at a small compiler and utilities company, Hisoft. It wasn't until a year or so later, when he was made redundant at Hisoft, that his career really took off, with a variety of respectable technical jobs. He got into Windows programming and C++ at the same time, in 1989, and joined Microsoft in early 1992.

The manuscript for this book was prepared and submitted to Microsoft Press in electronic form. Text files were prepared using Microsoft Word 6.0 for Windows. Pages were composed by Editorial Services of New England, Inc., using Ventura Publisher for Windows, with text in Garamond and display type in Helvetica Black. Composed pages were delivered to the printer as electronic prepress files.

Cover Graphic Designer

Rebecca Geisler

Cover Illustrator

Glenn Mitsui

Interior Graphic Designer

Kim Eggleston

Interior Graphic Artist

Michael Victor

Principal Compositor

Editorial Services of New England, Inc.

Principal Proofreader/Copy Editor

Editorial Services of New England, Inc.

Indexer

Shane-Armstrong Information Systems

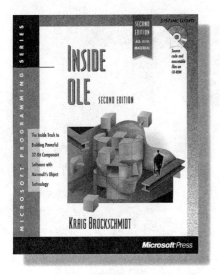

ISBN 1-55615-843-2, 1232 pages, $49.95 ($67.95 Canada)

OLE is a unified and extensible environment of object-based services with the overall purpose of enabling rich integration between components. As Microsoft's object technology, it represents major innovations in object-based programming, making it possible to create applications and software components with unprecedented capabilities. But with this power come additional complexity and new programming paradigms.

INSIDE OLE provides both a clear tutorial and a strong set of example programs, giving you the tools to incorporate OLE into your own development projects. Written by a member of the Microsoft® OLE team, this book truly gives you the insider's perspective on the power of OLE for creating the next generation of innovative software.

INSIDE OLE provides detailed coverage and reference material on:

- **OLE and object fundamentals:** Objects and interfaces, connectable objects, custom components and the Component Object Model, and Local/Remote Transparency

- **Storage and naming technologies:** Structured storage and compound files, persistent objects, and naming and binding

- **Data transfer, viewing, and caching:** Uniform Data Transfer, viewable objects, data caching, OLE Clipboard, and OLE Drag and Drop

- **OLE Automation and OLE Properties:** Automation controllers; property pages, changes, and persistence

- **OLE Documents:** OLE Documents and embedding containers, OLE Documents and local embedding servers, in-process object handlers and servers, linking containers, and in-place activation (visual editing) for containers and objects

- **OLE Controls and the future of OLE:** OLE Controls, future enhancements, and component software

VALUABLE INFORMATION INCLUDED ON CD!

CD includes 75 source code examples (more than 100,000 lines of code) that demonstrate how to create components and how to integrate OLE features into applications.

System Requirements

32-Bit Platforms: Windows® 95 or Windows NT™ 3.51 and Visual C++™ 2.0 or later (Win32® SDK required for some samples). 16-Bit Platforms: Windows 3.1 or later and Visual C++ 1.51 or later (some samples are 32-bit only and will not work with 16-bit Windows).

If you're interested in fully exploring and understanding OLE and component software, there's no better source than INSIDE OLE.

Microsoft® Press

This book is destined to be read by software designers, developers, marketers, technical managers, and industry insiders for many years to come.

ISBN 1-55615-823-8
208 pages, $24.95 ($33.95 Canada)

Jim McCarthy has distilled a veteran's hard-won know-how into 54 memorable, pragmatic maxims—short essays on defining, building, shipping, and marketing software successfully, whether commercially or in-house. With a grown-up wit that's by turns homespun and sophisticated, McCarthy tells you how to maintain your cool (**"Don't Flip the Bozo Bit"**), organize a crack team (**"Get Their Heads into the Game"**), analyze the customer and the competition (**"Alone? A Market Without a Competitor Ain't"**), handle uncertainty and schedule slips (**"When You Slip, Don't Fall"**), make commitments with integrity (**"Be Like the Doctors"**), and stabilize the product so that you can ship it (**"Don't Shake the Jell-O®"**). McCarthy shows you how to develop a marketing message and how to launch your product too, and in the appendix, he tells you how to hire smart people and keep them happy and productive.

Along the way, McCarthy meditates on software aesthetics and familiar software development phenomena—the "death march to Egghead," burn-out, internecine quarrels, being lost in software, the software dream and successive awakenings, the self-critical customer. McCarthy's preoccupation with the dynamics of the process infected his brother, artist Patrick McCarthy, with a sense of the "rich, deep, psychocultural extravaganza" that is software development, and themes both humorous and dark emerge in the handsome illustrations for the book.

You'll find **DYNAMICS OF SOFTWARE DEVELOPMENT** as engrossing and exciting as software development itself. This book is destined to be read by software designers, developers, marketers, technical managers, and industry insiders for many years to come.

More Ways to Smooth Software Development with the *Programming Practices Series* from Microsoft Press

Code Complete
Steve McConnell
ISBN 1-55615-484-4
880 pages
$35.00 ($44.95 Canada)

Debugging the Development Process
Steve Maguire
ISBN 1-55615-650-2
216 pages
$24.95 ($32.95 Canada)

Writing Solid Code
Steve Maguire
ISBN 1-55615-551-4
288 pages
$24.95 ($32.95 Canada)

Microsoft Press® books are available wherever quality books are sold and through CompuServe's Electronic Mall—GO MSP.
Call **1-800-MSPRESS** for more information or to place a credit card order.* Please refer to **BBK** when placing your order. Prices subject to change.
*In Canada, contact Macmillan Canada, Attn: Microsoft Press Dept., 164 Commander Blvd., Agincourt, Ontario, Canada M1S 3C7, or call 1-800-667-1115.
Outside the U.S. and Canada, write to International Coordinator, Microsoft Press, One Microsoft Way, Redmond, WA 98052-6399 or fax +(206) 936-7329.

Microsoft Press

IMPORTANT—READ CAREFULLY BEFORE OPENING SOFTWARE PACKET(S). By opening the sealed packet(s) containing the software, you indicate your acceptance of the following Microsoft License Agreement.

MICROSOFT LICENSE AGREEMENT

(Book Companion Disks)

This is a legal agreement between you (either an individual or an entity) and Microsoft Corporation. By opening the sealed software packet(s) you are agreeing to be bound by the terms of this agreement. If you do not agree to the terms of this agreement, promptly return the unopened software packet(s) and any accompanying written materials to the place you obtained them for a full refund.

MICROSOFT SOFTWARE LICENSE

1. GRANT OF LICENSE. Microsoft grants to you the right to use one copy of the Microsoft software program included with this book (the "SOFTWARE") on a single terminal connected to a single computer. The SOFTWARE is in "use" on a computer when it is loaded into the temporary memory (i.e., RAM) or installed into the permanent memory (e.g., hard disk, CD-ROM, or other storage device) of that computer. You may not network the SOFTWARE or otherwise use it on more than one computer or computer terminal at the same time.

2. COPYRIGHT. The SOFTWARE is owned by Microsoft or its suppliers and is protected by United States copyright laws and international treaty provisions. Therefore, you must treat the SOFTWARE like any other copyrighted material (e.g., a book or musical recording) except that you may either (a) make one copy of the SOFTWARE solely for backup or archival purposes, or (b) transfer the SOFTWARE to a single hard disk provided you keep the original solely for backup or archival purposes. You may not copy the written materials accompanying the SOFTWARE.

3. OTHER RESTRICTIONS. You may not rent or lease the SOFTWARE, but you may transfer the SOFTWARE and accompanying written materials on a permanent basis provided you retain no copies and the recipient agrees to the terms of this Agreement. You may not reverse engineer, decompile, or disassemble the SOFTWARE. If the SOFTWARE is an update or has been updated, any transfer must include the most recent update and all prior versions.

4. DUAL MEDIA SOFTWARE. If the SOFTWARE package contains both 3.5" and 5.25" disks, then you may use only the disks appropriate for your single-user computer. You may not use the other disks on another computer or loan, rent, lease, or transfer them to another user except as part of the permanent transfer (as provided above) of all SOFTWARE and written materials.

5. SAMPLE CODE. If the SOFTWARE includes Sample Code, then Microsoft grants you a royalty-free right to reproduce and distribute the sample code of the SOFTWARE provided that you: (a) distribute the sample code only in conjunction with and as a part of your software product; (b) do not use Microsoft's or its authors' names, logos, or trademarks to market your software product; (c) include the copyright notice that appears on the SOFTWARE on your product label and as a part of the sign-on message for your software product; and (d) agree to indemnify, hold harmless, and defend Microsoft and its authors from and against any claims or lawsuits, including attorneys' fees, that arise or result from the use or distribution of your software product.

DISCLAIMER OF WARRANTY

The SOFTWARE (including instructions for its use) is provided "AS IS" WITHOUT WARRANTY OF ANY KIND. MICROSOFT FURTHER DISCLAIMS ALL IMPLIED WARRANTIES INCLUDING WITHOUT LIMITATION ANY IMPLIED WARRANTIES OF MERCHANTABILITY OR OF FITNESS FOR A PARTICULAR PURPOSE. THE ENTIRE RISK ARISING OUT OF THE USE OR PERFORMANCE OF THE SOFTWARE AND DOCUMENTATION REMAINS WITH YOU.

IN NO EVENT SHALL MICROSOFT, ITS AUTHORS, OR ANYONE ELSE INVOLVED IN THE CREATION, PRODUCTION, OR DELIVERY OF THE SOFTWARE BE LIABLE FOR ANY DAMAGES WHATSOEVER (INCLUDING, WITHOUT LIMITATION, DAMAGES FOR LOSS OF BUSINESS PROFITS, BUSINESS INTERRUPTION, LOSS OF BUSINESS INFORMATION, OR OTHER PECUNIARY LOSS) ARISING OUT OF THE USE OF OR INABILITY TO USE THE SOFTWARE OR DOCUMENTATION, EVEN IF MICROSOFT HAS BEEN ADVISED OF THE POSSIBILITY OF SUCH DAMAGES. BECAUSE SOME STATES/COUNTRIES DO NOT ALLOW THE EXCLUSION OR LIMITATION OF LIABILITY FOR CONSEQUENTIAL OR INCIDENTAL DAMAGES, THE ABOVE LIMITATION MAY NOT APPLY TO YOU.

U.S. GOVERNMENT RESTRICTED RIGHTS

The SOFTWARE and documentation are provided with RESTRICTED RIGHTS. Use, duplication, or disclosure by the Government is subject to restrictions as set forth in subparagraph (c)(1)(ii) of The Rights in Technical Data and Computer Software clause at DFARS 252.227-7013 or subparagraphs (c)(1) and (2) of the Commercial Computer Software — Restricted Rights 48 CFR 52.227-19, as applicable. Manufacturer is Microsoft Corporation, One Microsoft Way, Redmond, WA 98052-6399.

If you acquired this product in the United States, this Agreement is governed by the laws of the State of Washington.

Should you have any questions concerning this Agreement, or if you desire to contact Microsoft Press for any reason, please write: Microsoft Press, One Microsoft Way, Redmond, WA 98052-6399.

097-000-680

Register Today!

Return this
OLE Controls Inside Out
registration card for:

✔ a Microsoft Press® catalog

✔ special offers on Microsoft Press books

U.S. and Canada addresses only. Fill in information below and mail postage-free. Please mail only the bottom half of this page.

1-55615-824-6A   *OLE Controls Inside Out*   *Owner Registration Card*

_____

NAME

_____

INSTITUTION OR COMPANY NAME

_____

ADDRESS

_____

_____

CITY   STATE   ZIP

Microsoft Press

Quality Computer Books

**For a free catalog of
Microsoft Press® products, call
1-800-MSPRESS**